Acknowledgments

Original FastTrac Program Authors

Richard H. Buskirk, Ph.D.
R. Mack Davis
Courtney Price, Ph.D.

Project Consultant

Kathryn Nadlman

Editorial Team

Ewing Marion Kauffman Foundation
   Judith Cone
   Stefanie Weaver
Doug Allen, Executive Director of Information Services,
   Johnson County Community College
David J. André, Attorney & Counselor at Law
J. Diane Awbrey, Ph.D.
Andreanna Kounas, Pallas Information Services
Todd M. Pitman, CPA, TMPitman LLC
Andrea F. Sellers, Stinson Mag & Fizzel PC
Jodie Trana, Advant•Edge Business Services

Graphic Design Team

Leslee Anne Terpay, Terpay Knowledge Resources
Amy Flammang-Carter

Reviewers

Mary Beth Izard, Professor of Entrepreneurship and Management,
   Johnson County Community College
Ronald F. Johnson, Adjunct Professor, University of New Mexico
Edward M. Moldt, Chairman of the Board,
   John Pappajohn Entrepreneurial Center, University of Iowa
Terry Noel, Ph.D., Assistant Professor of Marketing and Entrepreneurship,
   Rudd Fellow of Entrepreneurship, Wichita State University
Normand Paquin, Ph.D., Associate Director,
   Office for Strategic Business Initiatives, University of Illinois at Urbana-Champaign

Ewing Marion Kauffman

The Ewing Marion Kauffman Foundation is the only foundation in the country truly dedicated to the advancement of entrepreneurship at all levels. The Kauffman Foundation was established by the late Ewing Marion Kauffman, a genuine entrepreneurial leader and philanthropist.

There is more to Ewing Kauffman's beneficence than his fortune. He had an instinct for the future. He understood how to bring organizations to life to be productive and vital. Above all, he had a zest for life and a social awareness that was grounded in his belief in people. The Kauffman Foundation develops and advances innovative ideas that set the groundwork for institutional change by supporting bright people and giving them the wherewithal and freedom to recognize opportunity, take risks, and develop their abilities.

From modest beginnings, Kauffman grew Marion Laboratories into a billion dollar pharmaceutical giant and established the Kansas City Royals, bringing major league baseball back to Kansas City. His business succeeding beyond his wildest dreams, Kauffman turned his vigor, intellect, and wealth to a new style of philanthropy. He lost patience with charity work that never seemed to attack the core problem it sought to remedy. He wanted to dig deep and get at the roots of issues rather than talk about addressing the symptoms. Undaunted by the size of the challenge or the lack of resources, Kauffman encouraged his staff to become immersed in research, consult with the best minds, and devise bold approaches to address complex social problems. He told friends he was having more fun giving money away than he had earning it. He told associates he expected his foundation to be uncommon.

An epitome of American entrepreneurship, Kauffman saw such enterprise as one of the most effective ways to unleash human potential and stir the economy to life. Today the Kauffman Foundation is devoted to advancing entrepreneurship as one of the fundamental aspects of life in the United States. Focusing on research, education, technical assistance, and policy, we work to increase the number and success rate of individuals engaged in the process of starting or growing their own business or idea. Programs are designed to share the principles, techniques, and leadership tactics to make starting and growing a business a more common choice for Americans of all walks of life.

To that end, the Kauffman Foundation's FastTrac programs are part of a wide range of learning resources developed by and with hundreds of successful entrepreneurs who have shared their knowledge, insights, and stories so that others might learn from them. It is hoped that all entrepreneurs will find them useful as they work to write their own entrepreneurial success stories.

For more information on FastTrac, the nation's leading, award-winning business training program for entrepreneurs, go to www.fasttrac.org or call (800) 669-1740. To order FastTrac materials, including *Planning and Growing a Business Venture: Venture Planning Field Guide*, *Venture Planning Workbook*, and *The Business Mentor* CD-ROM, call the FastTrac fulfillment center at (877) 450-9800. For more information about the Kauffman Foundation and entrepreneurship, go to www.entreworld.org, www.kauffman.org, or call (800) 489-4900.

Planning & Growing a Business Venture

VENTURE PLANNING

FIELD GUIDE

2004 EDITION

FAST TRAC

TAKE CHARGE OF YOUR BUSINESS™

A program of the Kauffman Foundation of Kansas City

WITHDRAWN

KAUFFMAN
Foundation

TAKE CHARGE OF YOUR BUSINESS™

Visit our Web sites at:
www.fasttrac.org
www.entreworld.org
www.kauffman.org

Table of Contents

Introduction: The Planning Process

Americans are living in a new economy—powered by technology, fueled by globalization, and driven by entrepreneurial spirit. Entrepreneurship is indeed a mainstream phenomenon; opportunities have never been greater.

Entrepreneurial success, however, is far from guaranteed. Some businesses seem to succeed in spite of themselves, especially when customer demand for their products or services is great. In this situation, many start-up and operating mistakes are simply forgiven by the marketplace. But don't be misled by inspiring stories of successful start-ups in the media. Some estimate that about 70 percent close after two to five years of operation.

Sound business planning is critical for launching, operating, and growing successful ventures. Too many entrepreneurs, however, carry critical planning records in their heads and never transfer these ideas to paper. Entrepreneurs often struggle with producing a usable outline for these plans and may find them tedious and boring. In reality, these types of plans save precious time, prevent mistakes, and in many instances, save businesses.

Even at the corporate level, feasibility and business plans are rarely written on new projects. Understanding the process of writing good feasibility and business plans is a valuable asset and would be an impressive skill to include on a resume.

Business planning should continue after a venture is launched to track performance against planned projections as a matter of course. The management team can then adjust directions as needed and keep a venture running smoothly as it learns from its mistakes and successes.

Critical Planning Documents

Each of the essential business planning documents for business ventures—feasibility plan, business plan, strategic plan, and operational plan—is briefly discussed below.

The first step: The feasibility plan

Typically, the first planning document required of new ventures is the feasibility plan. This plan seeks to determine if an idea has market potential—whether it is a business opportunity. There is an old saying: "Nothing matters until you sell something." The feasibility plan consists of researching a business idea—its workability, marketability, and profitability—and assessing the entrepreneur's and management team's capabilities. The process of writing a feasibility plan helps guard against starting an unworkable venture idea that does not fit the proposed market, is too costly, takes too many resources, has too many risks, cannot compete with other companies, and is simply not worth the time and effort.

The big kahuna: The business plan

A business plan is a written document that articulates the business concept, opportunities, the entry, the entrepreneur's role, the management team, the potential market, financial requirements, and growth strategies. It also identifies potential risks, problems, and trade-offs. It's an excellent way to help evaluate the opportunity and guide the start-up. It forces an entrepreneur to consider every facet of a proposed business idea and places approval and funding decisions on paper where they can be evaluated and considered by everyone involved. Sitting down and developing the business plan, section by section, forces the entrepreneur to think critically, evaluate, and plan. Writing a business plan causes the entrepreneur to rethink many aspects of the venture because some fatal flaws in the venture will become apparent. The entrepreneur can examine the consequences of different strategies and determine the human and financial requirements for launching and building a venture. A business plan can be a powerful tool for convincing investors to consider the business.

Other planning documents

The Business Mentor CD-ROM, which accompanies this text, deals with just two planning documents, the feasibility and business plans. There are two other plans that need to be written after a business is started: the strategic plan and the operational plan.

A strategic plan is a long-range plan covering two to five years. This plan includes objectives, action plans, needed resources, and costs. It takes into account the organization's external environment as well as the venture itself and helps develop competitive strategies that stimulate growth and profitability. A strategic plan identifies what market opportunities exist at this stage in the business and what resources are needed to offer the right products and services to customers. It outlines what internal changes are necessary to reallocate resources, realign a venture's market opportunities, refocus its research and development on high-potential products and services, or redefine its image.

The operational plan contains a series of action steps to coordinate the efforts of running and growing a venture to achieve its goals and objectives. It is a benchmark with which to measure the performance of the venture and its management team. It is a detailed monthly plan of activities needed for each person on the management team.

Why Write Planning Documents

Written goals help entrepreneurs work smarter, rather than just harder. The process of analysis and goal-setting enables them to better understand and clarify risks, thereby devising ways to manage and reduce those risks. Goal-setting keeps the venture in a future-oriented mode, always anticipating new trends and directions. It also develops strategies for testing the validity of projections in business planning documents.

The process of writing business planning documents is an indispensable learning experience. It focuses thinking. It forces one to take an objective, critical, and unemotional view of a venture. In addition, the process creates the following benefits:

- Highlights strengths of the business
- Identifies current and potential problems by pointing out weak spots and vulnerabilities
- Eliminates blind spots
- Identifies major flaws in strategic directions
- Communicates the venture idea to others

Savvy Entrepreneurs Plan Their Odysseys

The back-of-the-napkin approach to business planning has a storied place in the mythology of entrepreneurship. The journey starts something like this: Over dinner, two promising entrepreneurs start talking about ideas for launching a company and sketch out their business plan on the nearest napkin. The next day, they show their back-of-the-napkin plan to a venture capitalist who immediately writes a check for what they need, and the two are off on their entrepreneurial odyssey.

Too bad it really isn't like that! Bankers, private investors, and venture capitalists, even family and friends, want some assurance that a concept is feasible and expect to see a detailed, written business plan. Entrepreneurs, on the other hand, just want to get started. Given their unflagging optimism and their ready-fire-aim tendency for getting things done, most entrepreneurs have little desire to take time and effort to put things down on paper when they could be out there selling their products and making money. I know that running one's own business is the fun part of being an entrepreneur; writing about it usually is not.

So why should an entrepreneur determine the feasibility of a concept and then write an effective business plan? Because this process can significantly increase his or her chance of success! Preliminary research at the Ewing Marion Kauffman Foundation has shown that firms having a written business plan have 50 percent greater sales growth and 12 percent higher gross profit margins than firms without written plans.

Savvy entrepreneurs realize that to wind up where they want to go on their own epic entrepreneurial journeys, they need a good map by which to travel. To get where you want to go, rely on a compelling business plan rather than the sketch on the back of a napkin.

— Raymond W. Smilor, Author of *Daring Visionaries: How Entrepreneurs Build Companies, Inspire Allegiance and Create Wealth*

- Provides the necessary information needed by others to evaluate an idea
- Uncovers hidden opportunities
- Serves as an operating tool to help manage the business and achieve projections
- Identifies additional ways for the business to develop and grow
- Clarifies the venture's financial requirements
- Can be used to obtain financing
- Measures and monitors performance of the business and its managers

The discipline of writing business planning documents is a learned process that will be used by the entrepreneur many times. The best news about developing and writing business planning documents is that once a person has been through the process, additional plans take half the time to write. One will discover valuable planning skills that are critical to venture success.

Value of Planning

Business planning documents can be used as a blueprint to follow when operating the business. They force entrepreneurs to consider many of the essential aspects that are otherwise overlooked. They force managers to take goals more seriously. They help expose flaws and develop plans for contingencies. They outline a plan of action in the present and during the next several years of growth and expansion. Therefore, carefully written planning documents lay out the operational and strategic plans for the upcoming years.

Goals in the business plan can also be used to help set the venture team members' operational goals for their respective departments. A manager can obtain greater commitment and a higher level of motivation when department performance is tied to achieving the goals outlined in the business plan. In turn, the entrepreneur can use these goals to evaluate team members' performance. Founders find the business plan to be even more beneficial after start-up phases of the business. It can be especially helpful in product pricing, competitive strategy, and financial planning.

Business plans are living documents that will change as the entrepreneur receives new information about the venture's performance or external environment. In many industries, business plans may need to be revisited and reevaluated every few weeks, not years, in many sectors of the economy. An entrepreneur who does not anticipate and plan for rapid change may well be doomed. But a wise planner who revisits his or her plans often may be better equipped to respond quickly to market fluctuations.

Interactive Resources

Two interactive resources are designed for use with *Planning and Growing a Business Venture: Venture Planning Field Guide*. *The Business Mentor* CD-ROM and the *Venture Planning Workbook* walk students through the steps of planning a new business venture or growing an existing business. The CD-ROM also contains sample plans, advice from real entrepreneurs, and links to web sites. To order these resources call the FastTrac fulfillment center at (877) 450-9800. For more information, contact FastTrac (www.fasttrac.org) at (800) 689-1740.

Entrepreneur's Personal and Business Criteria

Learning Objectives

In this chapter, students will learn to

- Recognize the entrepreneur's personal strategies that will help decide which new venture he or she wants to start.
- Transition personal criteria into a focus on specific business strategies.

Planning is a process to develop a sound business concept and provide details in each and every section of the feasibility and business plans. Entrepreneurs cannot write plans without having made numerous strategic decisions.

The very first decision an entrepreneur makes about how to start a business or exploit some business opportunity is a strategic decision. For example, an entrepreneur might begin a new venture from scratch, buy an existing business, sell the business concept to another company, or encourage some other firm to license the concept. The way entrepreneurs decide to capitalize upon their concepts is well worth serious and thoughtful consideration. It is important to recognize the strategic alternatives available.

There are many books on business planning that develop models of various complexities. Most of them concentrate on market and product strategies; that is, in what business shall entrepreneurs engage? What target markets should they pick to penetrate? This text avoids that product-market-only approach and focuses instead on the larger issues that involve distribution, finance, and the vital force of the entrepreneur's own persona as well as product and market. Fundamental personal and business strategies that are critical to success are stressed. It is important, for example, to deliberately consider a long list of issues that will ultimately affect the entrepreneur's life and that of the business.

By starting with personal strategies, entrepreneurs will be able to determine, at least initially, why they are thinking of forming new ventures or buying existing ones. A fledgling firm will reflect the personal values of its leader, and these values eventually form the culture of the company. For instance, if the entrepreneur hates debt, his or her business will not likely use borrowed funds with which to expand, even though it might be the approach to take from an economic viewpoint. A business in its early stages is an extension of the numerous values of its founder; the values may change over time as leadership expands and changes.

The following discussion of personal criteria will transition into a focus on specific business strategies. A set of personal and business criteria questions appears on pp. 18-24. By sincerely and thoughtfully answering these questions, entrepreneurs will be able to determine their personal requirements, and then can decide what kinds of business strategies they should be pursuing in operating existing businesses or in evaluating new business concepts.

Personal Criteria

There are several criteria to consider on a personal level when making plans to start a new business.

Job security

Is the purpose of this enterprise to provide the entrepreneur and family with a good living? To what extent is the enterprise simply a personal money machine? Is the goal of the business to provide a job or to build a larger enterprise?

There are many examples of owners whose basic goal for being in business is to make a comfortable and stable living for themselves, while being in total control of their businesses. They don't want outside investors or others having power over them. This security factor affects every decision being made. These types of owners are not interested in expanding into multiple operations, for instance, even though that might be done quite easily with the talents that are available within the company.

Such owners make certain that they always have total control of the company's stock. To ensure that they have job security, they take few risks. This conservative business strategy works exceedingly well for many owners.

What role will the business play in life? What does the entrepreneur want from it? The key is to match personal desires with those of the business and then make decisions in line with personal criteria.

Not everyone will make a good entrepreneur. As a student writes a feasibility plan on a concept, he or she might make the decision that the entrepreneurial lifestyle does not provide the required job security or does not fit with his or her personal risk or risk tolerance level. This discovery is another valuable outcome of planning. It is better to find out that entrepreneurship isn't right for the person at that time than after a business has been started.

One entrepreneur said the only reason he started his own business was because no one would hire him. Another entrepreneur wanted to start a business to provide job opportunities for her husband and their three children. She started a restaurant and the entire family worked in the restaurant. It was extremely popular and all the customers enjoyed the family atmosphere and watching the children grow up. Each child started out busing tables, then became a waiter, and finally either a chef, maître d', or bartender. The entrepreneur and her husband have retired and now spend six months of every year in Hawaii while the children operate the business.

Money

How much money is expected from the business venture? What does that amount of money mean? What is enough? Many people are driven by money motives. Entrepreneurs must ask: What is a fair and comfortable living, and how will that change five and 10 years from now? Can this business opportunity produce the income desired?

In just two years, Pete Estler turned a simple idea into an e-mail marketing firm MatchLogic. He sold it in 1998 for $90 million to Excite@Home. Before that, Estler turned another basement computer project, dbIntellect, into $50 million in just three years. He sold that database company to Electronic Data Corp. for stock.

Estler has started a new company iBelay.com, which will be a $100 million venture capital fund, a data center, and an incubator for dot-com start-up ventures. In two months after start-up in late 1999, he has made investments in six dot-com new ventures and received another 200 e-mails from entrepreneurs who want to meet him.

Estler says, "The biggest thrill is taking two people and an idea and making them worth $100 million."

Of course, some entrepreneurs put making money lower on their lists of priorities and place creating highly successful ventures first. They believe the money will follow.

The managers of a medium-sized consulting firm list making money fifth on their priorities. Unsurpassed customer service and employee satisfaction are among their primary goals. They consider everyone who works there a professional. No time clocks here! They turned their management chart upside down; the management serves its employees. They hire self-actualized employees and deliberately foster innovation by their employees. The results are increasing profits year after year, outpacing their industry averages.

If creating wealth is not a primary goal, the entrepreneur might be motivated by building a company that pursues an altruistic goal. Maybe it is more meaningful to market a new cure for an illness or provide a novel service. There are many different types of rewards for entrepreneurs in successful businesses, and each should give considerable thought to what is most important.

Some people find that starting a nonprofit business to help others is a rewarding experience. Making a profit or building a business to sell is not what drives this kind of entrepreneur. Actualizing the mission of the nonprofit can be very important.

An entrepreneur started G52, a service firm that plans to provide technical services, management mentoring, office space, networking, legal counsel, and marketing strategy to 12 to 20 Internet companies in exchange for 5 to 20 percent ownership stakes. She said "What is fun is growing new businesses and helping entrepreneurs get started and be first in a market niche because that is how a web site becomes successful. If I can make money helping entrepreneurs start their companies, that would be a by-product from the thrill of helping others."

Lifestyle

How important is it to maintain a present lifestyle or seek a different one? Can one only be comfortable with an existing lifestyle? It is often called a lifestyle business when an entrepreneur wants to start and maintain a business at a certain comfortable level rather than grow a business.

A young graduate bought a profitable tavern right out of college. She earned healthy profits, but late nights at the tavern left her little time to spend with her family. As a result, she felt she had to sell the business to maintain her family life.

Many entrepreneurs develop personal and professional troubles if they sacrifice or change their own set of morals or values. Self should not be compromised. It is important to determine what type of lifestyle is desired and then to pursue a business venture that can provide it.

Consider the case of an entrepreneur who started a fishing rod business because he was an avid fishing enthusiast and wanted a lifestyle that matched his hobby. He loved the endless, and potentially tax-deductible, freedoms that this business allowed him. Friends envied this entrepreneur when he stated, "I'm off to test the new model of fishing rod in British Columbia. I love doing market research for my business."

Power

Is attaining power important? Some people are more comfortable running an operation than taking directions from others. Some crave power, while others find it distasteful.

A power player usually has some strategic game plan for obtaining power. Howard Hughes wanted an abundance of power. He would buy businesses just to obtain a power position in an industry. Ted Turner wanted power in the television industry. He tried to buy it through the acquisition of Columbia Broadcasting System (CBS) but was rebuffed. Turner did become a media mogul by pioneering the concept of TV superstation broadcasting to cable systems nationwide by satellite. The merger of his Turner Broadcasting Station with Time Warner created the largest entertainment company in the world.

Many people become bankers for the power it gives them in the community. The owners of radio, newspaper, and television companies often are power driven. William Randolph Hearst is often cited as an example. He inspired the film *Citizen Kane*, a classic study of the blind pursuit of power. A visit to Hearst Castle shows what absolute power can buy.

If power is important to the entrepreneur, he or she should pursue business opportunities that fulfill those needs. Beware—the quest for power is often driven by ego, which many entrepreneurs say is their most negative trait. Ego can drive entrepreneurs to stop listening to their advisers and employees and start thinking they are always right.

Age

Where is the entrepreneur in life? How many years has he or she to look forward to? Young entrepreneurs can undertake ventures in ways that an older person might not. Those who must move fast because of aging or plans to retire soon may need to look for an injection of outside capital to speed up the growth rate.

Look at the example of a 47-year-old man who took over the presidency of ZDC, Inc., a high-tech firm. It was his third business venture, and he made a personal decision that he would give the company no more than two years before his stock in the company would be turned into cash. He wanted to be out of the venture by age 49. Consequently, his every decision was aligned with that personal objective. For instance, the growth plan was targeted to be great enough for him to have an initial public offering, to sell the company for cash, or to merge with a public company at the end of this two-year period. ZDC merged with Synergetics International within 24 months. This business strategy was accomplished as planned.

As a contrast, another person at age 67 wanted to exit her commercial mortgage company. The employees, to whom she would like to sell the company, do not want to risk a small down payment on a very favorable leveraged buyout (LBO). It appears that she is stuck for the time being, frustrated in her desire to relax more and reap the rewards of years of hard work. She should have planned more carefully, selling the company when she was younger.

When he was a 23-year-old student at the University of Southern California, Jim Breen started a business that sold ice cream from a vending cart. He obtained permission to sell the ice cream at special events, giving a percentage of the revenue to the sponsor of the event. He enjoyed this business because it provided enough money to cover his living expenses and gave him time to pursue his hobby of surfing. Later he had the opportunity of supplying all the concession stands for air shows that were sponsored by the U.S. Air Force. He now has a large company that provides this service for all air shows in the United States and Canada.

Health

Good health is required to withstand the stresses of starting a new venture. Spending long hours each day building the business can be a detriment to health. Entrepreneurs must weigh the mental and physical requirements of the business against their current physical conditions.

Consider the situation in which a business consultant was suddenly struck by a heart attack. His business strategies were quickly altered to accommodate this new circumstance. He then chose to no longer accept more than $40,000 a year in consulting contracts. His new strategy was to earn only this amount, since his medical condition required that he work just a few days per month. Health considerations dictated this new strategy.

Health issues and a disabling condition created a unique business opportunity for another founder who was frustrated at the discomfort caused by regular-fitting clothes. This person was wheelchair bound, and thus required specially designed and sewn clothes, in which Velcro was used instead of zippers and buttons. Seeing an opportunity, she soon formed a joint venture with a major wheelchair manufacturer and founded a firm in a niche market that specializes in meeting the clothing needs of wheelchair users.

Sandy Gooch became violently ill and was diagnosed as having a chemical imbalance in her system. With the help of her father, a chemist, she undertook finding the culprit chemical, which was apparently in the food she ate. When she discovered that the cause of her problem was food additives, she started a very successful and growing natural health food store chain on the West Coast, turning her life-threatening experience into one that is helping thousands.

Location

Where is the desired location to live and work? Why do many people work really hard all of their lives so that they can retire to Hawaii or Arizona or Florida? It is possible to live in any of these vacation wonderlands by locating there and starting a new venture. Why wait?

A ski buff, for example, wanted to move to Vail, Colorado, so she found an opportunity she could develop into a business that would give her that location and lifestyle. She began her search by sitting alongside the incoming road and watching the traffic that entered the town coming from Denver. She noticed one audio/visual equipment truck coming in and out of town twice a week. She decided to follow it and found that it made deliveries to the hotels in Vail. An opportunity flashed into her head. No hotel in town owned its own audio/visual equipment for use by its lodgers and conventioneers. She decided to visit the local hotels to determine if they would be interested in renting audio/visual equipment from her locally. They were thrilled with the prospect of renting the equipment right in town. Today, this entrepreneur has a very profitable business, plus the opportunity to ski every day during the ski season.

Location choices are often dictated by health considerations. For example, Dean Funk ran a successful newspaper operation in Santa Monica, California. He wanted to retire in Bishop, Idaho, to fish and to get out of the smog, which aggravated his asthma. He sold his firm to Copley Papers and bought a small paper company in Bishop. He says the move is adding years to his life. How many people say they would like to get out of the big city and move to a place like Idaho?

An eye doctor who decided to start an eye clinic that would provide complete eye care did not have a specific location in mind. She made a list of what she wanted a town to have: climate, population, outdoor recreational activities, educational facilities. She then took a trip across the United States looking for the location that fit her personal criteria. Reno, Nevada, had all the qualities she wanted, so she located there and started her clinic.

Investment

Will the entrepreneur invest any money in the venture? An early decision must be made about the extent to which a person is willing to expose him or herself to financial risk. There are entrepreneurs who strategically refuse to invest in their own ventures. Instead, they insist on using their brains and somebody else's money—which is not an easy thing to pull off.

Remember that each type of business requires some cash investment. Even the smallest of companies will need business cards, phone services, a computer, and similar basic items. Internet companies being started with the idea of going public quickly will require large investments and multiple rounds of financing. Investment will limit the type of business venture a person can pursue by its accompanying cash requirements.

The advantage of investing his or her own money is that the entrepreneur will start out owning 100 percent of the company. Also, if the business requires money in the later stages, the potential investors know that the entrepreneur has invested money in the concept.

There are many business concepts that do not require a large capital investment. Most of these are in the service sector such as consulting practices, professional organizer, home tutoring, house cleaning, pet sitting, and others. Entrepreneurs starting these types of businesses use the entry strategy of customer in hand (discussed in Chapter 5: Entrepreneurial Entry Strategies) to launch their new ventures.

Two women founded Yakalo Solutions to provide application services for real estate brokers looking to launch their own web sites. Yakalo's back-room software allows brokers to launch their sites, update listings, and manage the intricacies of complicated web programming tools such as hypertext markup language (HTML).

One of the partners spent three years building, operating, and updating web sites for brokers in their area. She reasoned the brokers could save money and time if they could update their sites on their own. Not having a great deal of money, she developed the first version software with the help of her husband at night and on weekends. After the software was tested and all the bugs were eliminated, she and a friend started Yakalo.

The next step was to get accepted by a technology incubator that supports fledgling high-tech firms by providing them inexpensive office space, guidance, and connections to financing sources. The company had revenue the first year and reached cash break-even the first part of its second year. The investment in the company has been small and now investors are interested in financing its growth.

Attitudes

Basic attitudes and values directly affect business strategy. Often the only reason behind a company's actions is that the entrepreneur simply wants it that way. Some of the areas in which basic attitudes of the founder affect business are discussed below: use of debt, unions, employees, values and beliefs, and government.

Use of debt. Many people do not function well in highly leveraged situations. Debt places stress upon them that adversely affects their decisions. If someone is uncomfortable using debt, then he or she should try to avoid it and start the company with cash or customers in hand.

As corporations downsize, reorganize, and lay off people, many displaced employees leave their companies with significant severance pay or funds from their retirement plans. They use these funds and sometimes acquire a bank loan to start or purchase a business. Often, they use all of their savings plus go into debt to start their entrepreneurial careers. If they should fail and lose all their assets, it could be a financial disaster. Individuals not comfortable with debt should avoid this type of financing option with a new venture because they will never be happy with becoming entrepreneurs and spending sleepless nights constantly worrying about losing their investments and all of their assets.

Unions. Many entrepreneurs detest unions, so they operate their businesses in ways to avoid them.

The founders of Texas Instruments adamantly rejected any thoughts of unionization to the extent that they passed up many sound business deals that might have resulted in union inroads into the company. The firm was offered—at a most attractive price—a deal to buy the Benrus Watch Co. by the bankers who were holding the Benrus debt. Texas Instruments needed the watchcase production of Benrus for its watches. But it passed up the deal because Benrus was unionized and located in New England, a union stronghold. One reason this company remains in Texas is that unions have made comparatively few inroads there.

Similarly, the Coors Brewery in Golden, Colorado, reflects the values of Adolph Coors and the Coors family. Its attitudes toward unions cost the company dearly in market share when the unions led a boycott against Coors products.

Employees. Some entrepreneurs do not want to hire anyone. Some are uncomfortable supervising other people and do not want the hassle that goes along with being an employer. Managing employees can be a challenging task. Thus, they prefer to subcontract everything. In today's entrepreneurial world, a person can have a large business and not have any direct employees. However, an entrepreneur still has to manage subcontractors to have them perform for a company. If managing people is a problem, then the entrepreneur needs to make sure the concept requires very few people; perhaps he or she should consider consulting, becoming a manufacturers' rep, or starting a service business alone.

If a business concept requires a staff of many employees and the entrepreneur is not comfortable in managing people, then the first person hired should be a person who is good at managing people.

Values and beliefs. Some firms strongly reflect the moral and religious values of their founders. The firm may follow the dictates and values of its founder's church.

A founder of a shopping center, for example, followed the beliefs of his church in its attitudes toward the use of alcohol. He prohibited the sale of any alcoholic beverages in the center, thus preventing many restaurants from leasing there. It hurt business, but his moral views about alcohol took higher priority in his value system.

The concept that a person pursues must fit his or her own personal criteria.

In another situation, a young woman was a minority owner in a business that designed web sites for the Internet. The owners had an offer from a potential customer in Japan to design pornographic materials to put on the Internet. The Japanese prospect offered an attractive price to design marketing materials for a series of these products. The majority partner wanted to accept the offer and said he would do all the design work involved on this project. The minority partner could continue to work with their regular customers, and with the increase of sales from Japan, both partners would make a lot of money. Because of her religious beliefs, the minority partner could not tolerate accepting the Japanese project and the partnership broke up.

Many people have strong prejudices against other regions and other cultures. There are Southerners who will refuse to do business with Northerners and vice versa. It is important to consider what types of people the customers will be and what their prejudices are.

An owner of a fuel station and convenience store had a manager who knew how to buy cigarettes and sell them at a price lower than the competition. The convenience store was selling about $60,000 annually in tobacco products. The manager introduced the new cigarette pricing policy and during the first year, the convenience store sold $700,000 worth of tobacco products. The owner does not smoke and feels that smoking is harmful to the health of his customers. What should he do? Should he continue selling cigarettes? His manager wanted to make one section of the convenience store into a cigarette store, increasing the volume and potential sales of tobacco products to $1 million. The owner struggled with his decision. However, the opportunity of selling $1 million in the cigarette store was too tempting and the owner let the manager have his way.

Government. Some entrepreneurs so detest governmental regulations and interference in business that they avoid contact with the government as much as possible. They won't bid on government contracts. They avoid regulation by staying out of highly regulated businesses.

Family Issues

Regardless of the type of business a person starts, critical family issues must be considered. It is important that entrepreneurs recognize these issues, evaluate their impact on the proposed venture, and discuss them with family members before launching new ventures. Family issues fall into two categories: balancing commitments and hiring family members.

Family members should fully understand and accept the inherent risks in starting a new venture.

Balancing commitments

Unless both the goals of the family and the business are met, the venture is likely to be a disaster. Family approval of starting and operating a new venture is critical. First, the entrepreneur should consider how starting and operating a business will affect the amount of time spent with family members. Changes in family life are inevitable, and the demands of a new venture are enormous.

Entrepreneurs tend to be preoccupied with their businesses day and night. The commitment of almost all leisure time and energies is usually inescapable when starting a new venture. Consequently, founders are obsessed with making it a success, sometimes at the expense of the family, and this obsession can lead to the downfall of the business and the family.

It is difficult to balance family responsibilities with owner responsibilities. Vacations may have to be postponed, weekend outings vanish, school visits are missed, social invitations must be declined, and meals get cold. Entrepreneurs must consider how they will balance the demands of business with the demands of family. Priorities for nonbusiness activities must be set and then met. Time needs to be scheduled for activities unrelated to the business. On the positive side, increased absence from the family as a business owner will decline over time.

Secondly, the entrepreneur must explain to family members how the entrepreneurial opportunity being considered will benefit them. He or she needs to explain the goals set for the business.

Family members should read feasibility plans or business plans and ask questions about the proposed venture. The downside and the risks involved should be discussed. It is important to obtain their commitment to support entrepreneurial efforts to launch and manage a new venture.

Entrepreneur and family should discuss the amount of money required to start the venture, with an explanation of how much money will be invested and how additional capital will be raised. The amount of money spent on family needs and entertainment may need to be cut. Reduced family cash flow is often necessary. All these factors put an added strain on the family. The entrepreneur should determine if his or her family is comfortable with the financial resources required, the amount of collateral that must be pledged, and potential financial sacrifices necessary from family members.

Smooth family relationships up front are an essential ingredient to successful ventures. Stress and conflicts within the family will affect the entrepreneur's ability to launch a new venture and manage it successfully. An unsupportive family will ultimately undermine the business and subconsciously work against it.

Hiring family members

Many mid-career entrepreneurs start family-owned businesses for a good reason—they have a spouse and three kids. Family members can go to work for the business immediately and could become partners or eventually owners. This is an example of the traditional family-farming idea that a large family will provide cheap, diligent labor. But entrepreneurs should not assume that family members will solve staffing problems or that they will make good employees.

The entrepreneur should assess whether family members have the talents and skills needed to operate the business. Differences in personalities, experience, work habits, talents, and spousal relationships must be considered. Many entrepreneurs make the fatal mistake of assuming family members will work for them without seriously considering whether the work matches the person's desires, experiences, and skills. Founders often treat their ventures like a family picnic. They act like parents instead of like staff managers. This behavior causes numerous problems. It is hard to hire highly qualified and motivated employees. Hiring a relative can be a double threat. It is difficult to wear two hats: one as a boss and one as a parent.

There are inherent conflicts and personality clashes when family members are involved in the business. Emotions and hidden agendas often interfere with business decisions. Family members have different views of business and styles of management. Likewise, in-laws often become silent partners (and sometimes not so silent partners) or consultants and interfere with making rational and sound business decisions.

Hiring family members can turn out to be a satisfying team effort or a disaster.

Sometimes family members just don't make good employees. They lack essential skills or experience needed in the business. They may be thrust into a position of power but are incompetent and undermine the morale of nonfamily employees. Other times, they just don't have the desire to work as hard as other staff members. Family fights and power struggles are not only demoralizing, but the results can be disastrous for the business. Other workers can take sides with family members, which will increase tensions and lead to employee turnover. They may try to manipulate the business based on their knowledge of the family's internal problems or struggles. It may be nearly impossible to fire a family member who is a menace to the business. Careful consideration of these issues is critical before deciding to launch a new venture staffed with family members.

On the other hand, many entrepreneurs have turned their businesses into exciting adventures and rewarding experiences for their families. The rewards of entrepreneurship are great, including a sense of social contribution, professional satisfaction, and esteem of peers. The key is going in with eyes open. Family businesses make up a large segment of all U.S. businesses.

Risk Issues

A certain amount of risk is involved in any entrepreneurial venture, but entrepreneurship is not as risky as many people think. Sometimes the real risk is associated with exchanging a comfortable situation for the unknown. That is why some potential entrepreneurs "retire on the job." The willingness to take a risk means that a person is willing to go beyond what is familiar and safe.

Entrepreneurs take both personal and financial risk to get what they want. A good question to ask is what would be the worst thing that could happen if the new venture were unsuccessful? What is the downside? The entrepreneur could always get another job if the business folds. All the risks associated with starting a new business need to be considered. There are always financial risks in starting a new business, such as losing savings, house equity, and possibly income.

Astute entrepreneurs take calculated risks and reduce the risk factor by thoroughly researching their business concepts, industries, and markets. The more entrepreneurs learn about the marketplace, customers, suppliers, money sources, and the like, the more courage they have and the better decisions they make. In addition, if people have worked 10 or 20 years for another organization, they have accumulated valuable experience that can be applied to the new venture.

"Knowledge is the antidote to fear."
— Ralph Waldo Emerson

One way to reduce risk is to start small—perhaps at home—and test the business concept. Experiment with the marketplace on a small scale and obtain customer feedback; ask potential customers to buy the product or service. But entrepreneurs shouldn't ask friends if they think the venture idea will work. Instead, they should ask customers to give them letters of intent to purchase. This forces potential customers to seriously think about whether they would really buy a product or service. If the entrepreneur is unable to obtain a letter of intent, then maybe the business concept is not such a good one.

Another way to minimize risk is to carefully plan a business by writing feasibility and business plans. Proper business planning can reduce risk. Writing feasibility and business plans is critical to determine whether a business idea is sound. A completed plan helps determine whether a venture has a market, can make a profit, and can provide what an entrepreneur needs. With proper planning, entrepreneurs will reduce the risk by replacing guesses and suppositions with facts and research.

Failure is another component of risk. Entrepreneurs learn from failure. They become stronger, wiser, and more determined by seeking criticism and continual feedback. Temporary setbacks or failures build character, stamina, and business skills. Entrepreneurs don't consider themselves weak because they have had a misstep. Failure means finding out what does not work, deciding how to eliminate it, and discovering what will work. Entrepreneurs learn to fail quickly and cheaply. Failing on paper is the cheapest way possible, which is why feasibility and business planning is so important.

Potential risks, money requirements, or time required need not deter people from achieving what is important. If they have the drive, leadership ability, and desire to be their own bosses, they're well on the way to becoming entrepreneurs. A good beginning is to research the industry, test the markets, and write a feasibility or business plan. The chances of starting and operating a successful venture will be significantly increased.

> Those who never risk anything may never attain what they really want.

Starting a business is fun. It is a lot more fun and rewarding to solve problems in one's own business than to solve problems in someone else's business. There's no denying that it takes hard work and long hours in the beginning. With sound business planning and defined operating strategies, entrepreneurs can reduce both the personal and financial risks inherent in starting new ventures.

Business Criteria

> Looking at both the business and personal criteria will create trade-offs, stretch thinking, and allow prioritizing the issues that are within control.

Business strategy is often discussed in the context of big business and thus becomes overly simplistic, theoretical, and market oriented. Much has been written about portfolio management, product development, market segmentation, positioning, and the like. Large companies tend to have departments and personnel who specialize in these exact areas of strategic planning. For small businesses, it is most important to focus on more fundamental aspects of business strategy.

The preceding section dealt with personal aspects of starting a new venture. Each of the following subheads includes questions designed to help people think about the business aspects of their entrepreneurial dreams. The following are some issues to consider.

Size and growth

How big should the business be, and how fast should it grow? Many entrepreneurs do not want to establish a large organization. Instead, they build a smaller-sized business in which they are more comfortable.

Some entrepreneurs want to be big and grow quickly. A word of warning: One of the most frequent causes of failure for otherwise sound and successful enterprises is unwise growth strategies. Boston Chicken, once one of the fastest growing fast-food chains, found itself in huge financial trouble due in large part to its rapid expansion. America Online grew so quickly that it was unable to handle the large demand, resulting in customers becoming angry about getting busy signals and signing up with other service providers.

Other firms try to grow faster than their management base warrants; they run out of skilled personnel as well as capital. Still others try to grow when neither the market nor the economics of the situation supports a growth strategy. Growth strategy is a complex dilemma worthy of much thought and deliberation. It is important to chart growth strategy, evaluate it, and frequently adjust it to be in tune with the marketplace.

For example, two students who graduated from the Entrepreneur Program at the University of Southern California (USC) developed a concept of writing and publishing a fraternity and sorority yearbook. In the process, they developed some proprietary software to design the yearbook and lay out the pages. Their plan was to first test it at USC and then expand by getting sales representatives on other campuses across the United States to produce the fraternity and sorority yearbooks for a commission based on how many yearbooks were sold.

The fraternity and sorority yearbook was successful at USC and earned about $20,000 in profit for the founders. When the two students expanded to other campuses, problems began to surface. Their sales representatives would not meet deadlines. They would quit in the middle of the school year. They would not be truthful about actual sales. The two owners were miserable with growing the business and dealing with many unanticipated problems from a distance. Finally, one of them decided that they should just publish the yearbook at USC and then turn it into a lifestyle business. They both had other jobs and worked on the yearbook on weekends. They still continue to publish and sell it and earn about $20,000 profit per year, which provides extra cash.

LaserCycle, a remanufacturer of toner cartridges for laser printers, laser fax machines, and copy machines, was started in 1992 by Rick Krska. Krska was constantly trying new business ideas, but he never hit it big, until LaserCycle. He dipped into his personal savings account for $20,000 to start the business, and during the first year of start-up, he invested an additional $10,000. The business supported itself for the first three years. By 1995, sales reached $2.2 million; in 2001, sales approached $15 million. There are more than 7,000 companies in the world that do what LaserCycle does, but LaserCycle is in the top 10. Krska had a sound plan for managing growth.

Mack & Moore, Inc., is a successful children's clothing design and wholesale company created by Gerri Mack as a result of her desire to design original, high-quality clothing for children. Since the first year of operation, Mack & Moore grew from $175,000 in sales to nearly $2 million in 1996 sales. The company's products are sold primarily in upscale department and specialty stores and catalogs. In a highly competitive apparel market, Mack & Moore has been able to differentiate itself from the competition and create a profitable market niche for the company and product line.

The company has focused on designing high end, children's fleece outerwear. With the success of the products have come requests for Mack & Moore to produce other products. And to stay competitive and profitable, company officers believe that some product diversification is required. Mack & Moore has, therefore, expanded its line into children's outerwear products made from wool. It is also planning an Ali Mack line that includes children's stories and accessories to complement the clothing line. "The new Ali Mack look would have a story that goes beyond just our clothing. So, when someone thinks Ali Mack, she may also have a book, a doll, a diary, stationery, furniture, sheets, and pillowcases."

Mack & Moore has been successful, in part, because of its commitment to doing all things in a quality manner and expanding at a rate that is sensible for the company.

Sources of money

"Debt or equity?" That is the question. The entrepreneur's life will be greatly affected the instant other people's money is used. If the entrepreneur uses only personal money, there is a wide latitude in how the business can be operated but growth will be limited. Once money is taken from other people, those people will dictate and control many aspects of the business.

A menswear chain followed a strategic plan of using retained earnings to support growth. The owner/manager would not open a new store until sufficient profits had been earned and kept in the company to finance one-half of the investment needed for the new outlet; the other half would be borrowed from the bank. The strategy was successful. However, it took the menswear chain 20 years to build six stores.

A more aggressive strategy was offered to this entrepreneur and his associates by a major shoe manufacturer. Overtures were made to buy the menswear chain and to launch a five-store expansion the next year using the shoe manufacturer's funds. The proposal was rejected. It did not fit into the company's strategic plan.

The earlier example of the high-tech firm, ZDC, Inc., indicated a different kind of strategy. For ZDC, Inc., the goal was to obtain outside funds to attain rapid growth. Within two years, the company undertook a private placement for $500,000, a venture-capital round for $250,000, and a merger with a public company that yielded about $600,000. While this strategic plan cost a great deal in equity in the company, it was accepted by the owners, because it was part of the firm's strategic plan.

Position in system

Where does the expertise of the entrepreneur meet the external realities of the business system? Many founders try to play to their strong suits and buy the services of others, thus avoiding their own weaknesses.

Some firms want to market and not manufacture. Ralph Lauren, owner of the Polo clothing firm, for example, does not want to manufacture any goods. Instead, he licenses the Polo name to others to make and market products. Other firms want to manufacture, not market.

RELA, a software-engineering concern, chose to develop only custom software programs for other companies. It would develop the software for part cash and part stock in its customers' companies. Since many of these companies would later go public or be sold to public companies, this could make large sums of money for RELA. This formula worked well for the company.

Jeff Bezos of Amazon.com felt his expertise was in creating efficient online e-commerce systems. So Amazon has no Amazon products, but simply is an online order processing and shipping entity.

Many different types of alternatives for positioning are available. They must be analyzed to fit how founders perceive their strengths and weaknesses, as well as how they view the various opportunities and threats in the varied external environments.

Ownership

Who will own the enterprise: the founder, the employees, the public, the investors, or the customers?

Many plywood manufacturers are organized as worker-owned cooperatives. A purchase of a $20,000 share of stock entitles the investor to a job with the company.

Staar Surgical, which manufactures products for eye surgery, focused its stock-selling effort on ophthalmologists, its target customers. Thus, its customers own much of the company.

On the other hand, some entrepreneurs strongly feel that they want to own the whole show. They want no partners in their business ventures.

If the entrepreneur wants to sell to the public, this must be part of the strategic plan because the firm must behave in certain well-defined ways if it is to go public. These restricted behaviors are often mandated by the various governmental agencies. Thus, an owner who wants no government intervention in his or her company now invites it when seeking a public offering. These paradoxes must be resolved over time.

If an entrepreneur really wants to control his or her own destiny, it is wise to develop a business concept where he or she can own the majority of a venture. Being a minority owner or owning 50 percent of a business can be a risky position. In these cases, the minority owner does not have control of the venture or many of the business decisions. A majority owner can control all of the business decisions such as hiring, firing, compensation, bonuses, and decisions about marketing, finance, and expansion. The only way for minority owners to protect themselves is to have strong corporate bylaws. Another way to protect minority interests is to have a good employment contract addressing such areas as salaries, vacation time, health benefits, and severance pay.

Control

Many entrepreneurs feel strongly that they must be totally in control, from raw material through delivery to customers.

The more an entrepreneur wishes to be in control, the more money it will take to do so.

Weyerhauser of Tacoma, Washington, from its inception, controlled all aspects of its wood-products system. The founding patriarch's strategy was to control the wood supply—that is, own the forests. "If you control the wood supply, you'll control the industry." Those words were frequently voiced in the corporate hallways and boardroom. This strategy became part of the corporate culture. From the woods, the company wants to control as much of its distribution system as possible, down to selling the finished goods to the buyers.

Some forest-products companies own the retail lumberyards through which they sell. Others want to own as little as possible; they buy their logs on the open market and then sell their finished lumber on the commodity market.

Certainly, the entrepreneur must identify supplies and resources that are critical to the firm's existence and operation. Steps must be taken to ensure that the flow of vital resources is as planned. For example, *The Times Mirror*

Press owns stands of pulp timber both as a control issue and as a hedge in a world market. During the paper shortages and seller-imposed quotas that followed the first OPEC oil bump, many printers were pleased that they had several suppliers. Control requires additional financial resources.

Marcia Israel, founder of Judy's, a 100-store chain of women's-wear stores in California, wanted to assume more control over her production processes. She hired a manufacturing firm in Hong Kong to make most of what she sold, thus controlling the quality and the look, as well as the costs.

Legal strategy

The entrepreneur's legal plans can be both complex and comprehensive. The law permeates all aspects of business operations. A business owner may decide as a matter of policy that he or she does not wish to own the productive assets; they may be leased instead. These trade-offs have varied and interesting tax consequences. Some owners may wish to avoid as much liability as possible by having other firms make their goods, especially if there is much liability connected with the goods.

Some firms, as a matter of strategy, try to monopolize their markets by frightening away potential competitors with lawsuits. They harass little firms with legal actions. Some entrepreneurs refuse to do business in certain states simply because of their legal climate. Many companies refuse to do business in foreign countries for reasons of legal strategy or to avoid problems with the protection of their intellectual-property rights.

If the founder has an exit strategy to sell the company sometime in the future, then he or she should form some legal strategies that will allow this to be done with ease. Planning today will avoid legal roadblocks in the future.

A common problem, for example, occurs when the company grants distribution rights for its goods to firms with contracts that cannot be easily cancelled. Later, when management considers merging with a larger company, distribution contracts can block the merger. Often the acquiring company does not want to be saddled with other distributors since it already has its own distribution system.

Any time the entrepreneur wants to play in the public market either as a merger partner or an initial public offering (IPO), legal strategies are critical. Much thought should be given to legal structures, bylaws, stock ownership, rights, and contracts.

One of the major legal problems a company faces is when there are multiple owners. Shareholders should consider a buy/sell agreement. Put simply, a buy/sell agreement addresses what happens if one of the shareholders dies, becomes disabled, or wants to get out of the business. An experienced business attorney can assist in developing a strong buy/sell agreement to be signed by all equity partners. It generally should be executed immediately after a new shareholder joins the company.

Compensation

How will the company pay its people? Will payment be money solely or also a piece of the rock? How about an employee stock ownership plan (ESOP)? Will the owner use these methods in the future as an exit strategy? Will the company use bonuses, profit sharing, options, stock grants, and so forth?

Several Silicon Valley firms used the strategy that the initial management team would work for less-than-market wages but receive generous stock options. Then they could make their fortunes from the public sale of the stock, not from company revenue flows. Shipping clerks became millionaires.

Many business concepts do not have the possibility of providing a large exit for the entrepreneur and management team. Therefore, the entrepreneur cannot motivate employees by giving them stock. The alternative is to pay good salaries and employee benefits and provide good working conditions.

Compensation methods should become a part of the strategic plan.

A high-tech manufacturing company that made computers had many hourly employees who received low- to mid-level salaries working on the assembly line. It was hard to give any substantial wage increases to staff because higher labor costs made the product too expensive. The owner was always coming up with different ways to make employees happy without continually giving wage hikes. One of his most successful incentives was changing to a four-day work-week, which gave employees a three-day weekend. These employees were very happy and treated it as a luxury, since a four-day workweek was a benefit their friends didn't have. Paying small cash bonuses, awarding prizes, or other types of recognition to employees exceeding performance expectations are other ways to reward staff for excellent performance.

Tax strategy

New tax laws cause a considerable flurry of activity in corporate boardrooms as managers scurry to alter their strategies to fit the new environment. Keeping on top of tax law changes is critical. The sign of a successful company is that it does not avoid taxes but pays them fairly as taxes represent profit generation.

Entrepreneurs need to always be aware of any tax law change, because it can greatly affect business stability and profitability.

In most businesses, the most important tax decision made is the type of legal entity that owners choose for their ventures. It is recommended that entrepreneurs seek advice from their accountants and lawyers on such matters. Also, they are advised to talk to other entrepreneurs in the same industry and ask them to share the pros and cons of the different legal entities.

Many businesses struggle when the government and the IRS change tax laws affecting small businesses. For example, there used to be investment tax credits for people who purchased solar energy products. When the government changed its tax laws, many solar energy companies had to close.

Conclusion

Entrepreneurs should appreciate how every personal and external factor that surrounds the business concept affects strategies and that a feasibility or business plan is not a static parameter. Instead, it is a dynamic plan constantly being subjected to the realities of the environment to which it applies. It should be reviewed and revised often.

Exercise 1a: Personal Criteria Questions

After reading about personal criteria, answer the following questions. This exercise will help you choose the type of business opportunity that best fits your personal desires.

1. Explain how the business will provide sufficient money to meet your minimum needs. Evaluate you financial needs and project what the business concept can pay you in salary, benefits, and profits.

2. Explain how the proposed business will provide sufficient job security to meet your needs. Must you secure an outside job to have a reasonably satisfactory life? Family considerations also enter here. Will you have enough time to give to the new business?

3. How long do you intend to work in the business? How much of your time will the business demand? Will you work at it full-time or part-time or be an investor? Consider your first year as well as years five and ten.

4. Will you be happy working in this environment? Consider whether your new working environment will be indoors, outdoors, noisy, dirty, odoriferous.

5. What type of people do you work best with? What kind of people will you be working with in the proposed business, for example, blue collar, white collar, doctors, engineers?

6. Is status and prestige important to you? Will your business provide these by helping you meet important people in certain fields?

7. How much travel will be required? Consider your feelings about international travel, car travel, air travel, weekend travel, and nights away from home.

8. How much political/community involvement will the business require? (Networking in the community is a great asset for entrepreneurs. Not only does it help them meet new customers, but it also helps their communities become better places in which to live.)

9. How much energy is required to get the venture launched and developed? Explain. Consider such things as physical demands and mental stress.

10. Explain why your age is an asset or liability in the business. For example, younger people tend to have more energy and older people tend to have more experience.

11. How many years of productivity are needed to build the business? Some concepts have a long start-up time before profit is realized—biotech and product development, for example. Such concepts often need to educate the marketplace that the product/service is needed.

12. Explain why you can or cannot afford a failure. Consider potential loss of income, erosion of savings, age vs. time for recovery of losses, and ego.

13. What does your spouse/family think about the venture? Will they support you during the start-up stage both mentally and during time spent away from home?

14. Have you the education/credentials needed for the business? Do you need certain qualifications, such as a real estate license?

15. Where do you want to live? Consider size of city, weather, lifestyle, and so on. Will the business allow you to live in such a place?

16. What are you bringing to the venture? Do you have the necessary expertise, money, and experience? Consider whether you need outside talent for your management team.

17. In the end, what kind of exit do you want from the business? Can you take it to the public market, sell it for cash, or merge it with another company?

18. Will your business likely be unionized? If so, what issues does this raise?

19. Explain why you will be an effective manager of employees. Will the venture require employees, or can the work be subcontracted? Remember that subcontractors can be manufacturers of your product, sales agents, consultants, and the like.

20. How will the business fit into your moral and religious beliefs?

21. How well can you work with governmental authorities? Consider that you may be subject to regulation by city, county, state, and federal agencies.

Exercise 1b: Business Criteria Questions

After reading about business criteria, answer the following questions. These answers, along with those from the personal criteria section, will help you further narrow down the right business opportunity on which to write your feasibility or business plan.

1. What size do you want your company to be in terms of annual sales and number of employees at the end of years one, two, and three?

2. What source of money will be used to start the business—personal money, debt, outside equity?

3. What position will the company occupy in the total business system in which it will operate; for example, service firm, manufacturer, distributor, or retailer.

4. Who will own the enterprise? For example, the entrepreneur, the employees, the public, the investors, or a combination of these.

5. What legal rights will the business retain? What rights will be given up? Consider licenses, distribution rights, patents, and the like.

6. What legal structure will be used, and what are the benefits of this structure? Consider such structures as C corporation, S corporation, limited liability company, sole proprietorship, or partnership.

7. Does the business have any tax sheltering that you do not have at this time? Consider car expenses, entertainment, travel, and the like.

8. What risks should be transferred to insurance underwriters, and which should you bear yourself? Consider such areas as property insurance, product liability, and major medical.

9. How will the key employees be motivated? Consider such ways as salary, performance bouses, stock ownership, or benefit packages.

Entrepreneurial Characteristics

CHAPTER 2

Learning Objectives

In this chapter, students will learn to
- Identify desirable characteristics of a successful entrepreneur.
- Identify undesirable traits for an entrepreneur.
- Self-assess for entrepreneurial characteristics.

By observing both successful and unsuccessful entrepreneurs, a wide range of personalities will be discovered. Still, studies provide some useful clues about the behavior that is most likely to lead to business success. Conversely, those who have failed in business teach what to avoid.

There is merit in studying the traits of entrepreneurs for two reasons. First, after seeing what it takes to be successful in the entrepreneurial world, one may conclude that he or she should look elsewhere for fame and fortune. Second, an entrepreneur who decides that he or she has the "right stuff" can develop those traits that seem to be most important. Contrary to the belief of some people that one's personality is a fixed set of behavioral tendencies, there is evidence suggesting that people can change their behavioral patterns if they want to do so badly enough. There is choice: we can believe that we must play the game of life with the cards dealt at birth, or we can believe that we not only call the game we want to play but can also draw new cards until we win.

Characteristics of Successful Entrepreneurs

Many successful entrepreneurs do not have all of these entrepreneurial characteristics, but have employees that possess the characteristics that the entrepreneur doesn't have. People could have all the entrepreneurial characteristics and decide not to be entrepreneurs but be employees of an entrepreneurial company. Not everyone wants to be the boss.

Desire

Unquestionably, a successful entrepreneur must fervently want to be one. If someone doesn't want success passionately, he or she probably won't do the things it takes to be successful. Desire is the foundation that supports most of the other characteristics that follow. Successful entrepreneurs almost universally report that they definitely wanted to be their own bosses. Many of them report that they cannot work for other people. They rebel at authority. They don't take orders easily. They just want "to do their own thing."

A group of physicians, for example, seeking to escape their problems with malpractice insurance considered a new venture to manufacture medical equipment that looked quite promising, according to the business plan that had been prepared by a large accounting firm. The group met for a kickoff meeting. The money was in place. The management team, experienced in the industry, was in place. Still, the venture never got off the ground. Why? The doctors did not want to be in that business. They all walked out of the room at the end of four hours, firmly convinced they should fold the enterprise. They had no business going into the venture without the true dedication and desire needed for the venture's success.

Initiative/aggressiveness

In the entrepreneurial world, nothing happens unless it is made to happen. Entrepreneurs start everything. If they don't, their world will just sit there, running up bills. Entrepreneurs must have the initiative to begin operations. It is not by mere coincidence that our favorite retort to the person who relates some wonderful idea is, "Do it!" Don't talk about it, do it. The world is full of talkers, while doers are scarce. Often encountered are some successful entrepreneurs whose main claim to fame is simply that they took action, plunged into business, and worried about it later. Truly, initiative has to be one of the key characteristics of successful people.

Of course, many unsuccessful people also have shown initiative; they have gone into business but did not do well. They did show initiative, but that was not enough. Initiative is a daily, even an hourly, matter. There are all sorts of things that require action. Entrepreneurs must do something about those things. They must initiate action. Many unsuccessful business people procrastinate about taking action on critical matters. "It will wait. No need to hurry." Many things won't wait, and there is often a need to hurry. Customers don't favor firms that don't come after their business. A founder of a publishing firm said, "Everything I have, I owe to being 10 minutes early."

Perhaps the single most important show of initiative an entrepreneur makes each day is the simple act of rolling out of bed in the morning. Successful ones hit the deck early and running, looking forward to the challenges ahead. They "take care of business," all business, and know that no one else will do it for them.

Energy

Energy levels obviously vary tremendously among people. Sometimes it is a matter of health; healthy people definitely have more energy than those who suffer from some malady. Here is not the place to extol the virtues of living a healthful life, but be advised that health is a vital factor in entrepreneurial success. Sometimes energy seems to be more a matter of temperament. Some people are just "laid back." They don't care to exert themselves any more than necessary. Such people should think twice about entrepreneurial endeavors. High energy levels are most common among successful entrepreneurs. They just can't sit still for a minute. They must always be doing something. Often just having one business going is not enough; they will have several going at the same time. When a business becomes boring, they sell it to go look for some new action.

Low support needs

When people work for the typical large corporation, they are surrounded with others ready to support their activities. They have secretaries, researchers, accountants, and all sorts of staff to assist them with whatever missions they have been charged with. Entrepreneurs, particularly beginning ones, have little support.

One new entrepreneur, when asked what skills were required to start a business, replied, "You'd better know how to type, do bookkeeping, sell, answer phones—just about everything." Unfortunately, some people just cannot operate on their own. They have been pampered too long in large organizations. One of the commonly observed weaknesses in people who leave the corporate world for entrepreneurial endeavors is that they just don't know how to operate in their new environments. They don't understand that few entrepreneurial enterprises can afford much in the way of staff support. In trying to impose their habitual way of managing upon the entrepreneurial organization, they can do considerable damage.

Thriving on ambiguity

Structure and certainty are seldom found in the entrepreneurial world. An entrepreneur must exist and prosper in an environment that is confusing and has few answers. There are so many alternatives from which to choose and few people know which to select and which to shun. Ambiguity destroys many people. They just cannot work in unstructured environments that continually bombard them with so many confusing clues about what to do. People who cannot accept the ambiguous world as it is and thrive in it should stay out of owning businesses.

Bear in mind that the true entrepreneurs love ambiguous situations, for they present great opportunities for exploitation. While others are frozen by the confusion, entrepreneurs plunge into the maelstrom with confidence that somehow they will find ways to cope with whatever problems they encounter.

Perseverance

Call it perseverance, mental toughness, determination, or whatever, successful entrepreneurs are determined to win, to be successful. They don't quit easily, even when it would probably be the wisest thing to do. Numerous platitudes, such as "Quitters don't win and winners don't quit" and "Show me a quitter and I'll show you a loser," reflect the general observation that success is likely to elude people who give up too quickly on their ventures.

This creates a problem: when should good judgment prevail over determination with a failing endeavor? The problem is really not so difficult if one puts goals into proper perspective. While one's determination to be successful may remain unchanged, the route taken may be altered as roadblocks appear. The entrepreneur's basic determination to achieve some fundamental goals is not attached to any particular means for reaching them.

But even in the matter of goals, some qualifications are necessary. What about people who aim for goals they are incapable of realizing? Let the market make the judgment. The business world is full of successful people who never in their wildest dreams foresaw the eventual success they enjoy. As Leo Burnett, the famous advertising agent, once said, "Reach for the stars. You may not get them, but you won't come up with a handful of mud, either."

Determination is one of the key factors that leads to a winning attitude. Entrepreneurs must make up their minds that they will not be beaten. Entrepreneurs report, time and again, that the only thing that forced them to make a success of their businesses, when things looked hopeless, was that they just could not allow themselves to become losers. It was totally unacceptable. Success was the only acceptable result.

Responsibility

Winners realize that if they are to be successful, they are the only ones who can make success happen. No one else is going to do it for them. Until people accept full and total responsibility for their futures, they won't have much future.

Successful entrepreneurs are so used to taking full responsibility for their lives and everything around them that they think little about it. It comes naturally.

They forget about the hordes of people in large organizations who spend most of their days avoiding responsibility, who don't even want to be responsible for their own lives. They want the company or the government to be responsible for them. "Take care of me!"

Such attitudes quickly lead to the poorhouse for people in their own businesses. Entrepreneurs must take care of their own businesses. Nobody else will!

Problem solving

Running a business is an ongoing puzzle, a long series of problems that must be solved. If people don't like solving problems, particularly ones that they may know little about, then an entrepreneurial career might be difficult for them. Business owners often spend most of their time troubleshooting, trying to locate the problems that are plaguing their businesses and then doing something about them.

Some people thrive on problem solving. They enjoy it. Problems don't bother them. Others seem to be worn down by the constant strain of conflict and frictions that result from an ongoing series of problems. People who are not able to face problems and solve them in stride, without allowing the problems to affect them personally, will be unhappy in entrepreneurship.

Persuasiveness

Successful entrepreneurs are usually persuasive people. They must be. They must persuade other people to do all sorts of things for them, such as lend them money, work hard for them, buy from them, and sell to them on favorable terms. Persuasion is their main tool. An entrepreneur must be able to persuade people to do what he or she wants them to do. If a person is not adept at the art, then he

"Nothing in the world can take the place of persistence. Talent will not; nothing is more common than unsuccessful men with talent. Genius will not; unrewarded genius is almost a proverb. Education will not; the world is full of educated derelicts. Persistence and determination alone are omnipotent. The slogan 'Press On' has solved and always will solve the problems of the human race."
— Calvin Coolidge

or she should make certain to have someone on the team who is. Selling skills are necessary in the organization, or else it will be lost.

Note that negotiating skills are just one application of persuasion. Certainly, entrepreneurs must be able negotiators to be successful in business. They cannot make bad deals and survive for long. The key to negotiation is persuasion. Entrepreneurs must persuade the other party to make the deals they want, the deals they need. They must sell their thoughts to the other person. People who feel that they haven't the necessary skills can cheer up. They can learn those skills, if they really want to.

Self-discipline

There are many things that must be done in business that people don't want to do. Some things are just not the type of work they enjoy, while some things are quite enjoyable. A businessperson may play golf with a customer on a beautiful day when she'd be better off working with a large account at the office. Entrepreneurs must be able to force themselves to do what must be done. If a person can't control him or herself, who can? And what can the person control?

Belief in value of money

It is difficult to be successful in business if owners pay too much for the things they buy and fail to get enough for the things they sell. Entrepreneurs must know value: the value of money and the value of things. Many successes are based on buying right. If business owners buy low enough, a profit is ensured.

Many start-up ventures fail when the entrepreneur spends far too much money on things that have little bearing on success, such as fancy cars, posh offices, large facilities, and high living. Successful entrepreneurs, in their early years, are usually careful with their money. They work hard for it and appreciate it. Normally, when someone is squandering money in business, undoubtedly it is someone else's money.

Self-confidence

Obviously, if people aren't confident of their abilities, they aren't likely to go into their own business. It takes a great deal of self-confidence to break away from the pack and go it alone. So it is not surprising to find that most successful entrepreneurs reek of self-confidence, almost to a fault. It can also lead to disaster. They can be so confident of their abilities that they come to believe they can be successful doing almost anything. Few people are that talented.

The problem arises that most people initially lack self-confidence. They can be scared to death of failure. The unknown, the future, is somewhat fearful to most rational people. However, the big difference between entrepreneurs and others is that entrepreneurs are able to control their fears and go ahead with the venture. They believe in themselves and have confidence that somehow they will solve whatever problems arise. They don't become paralyzed by fear.

Ego development

Closely akin to the previous trait of self-confidence, ego development relates to what successful entrepreneurs think of themselves. They like themselves very much. They are proud of what they have done. They often have well-developed egos, and that can be a problem. Some entrepreneurs become difficult to work for.

Others come to think that they are always right. While a healthy ego is a good thing, too much of a good thing can be detrimental. A little humility maintains the balance.

Market awareness

Entrepreneurs are aware of what is going on in the market. They are attuned to it. They take their directions from the market. The marketing chapters of this handbook address this critical business aspect.

Some people claim that perhaps an entrepreneur's most significant discriminating characteristic is his or her sensitivity to market opportunities. It is true that many people can be surrounded with tremendous market opportunities yet fail to perceive their existence. One mark of entrepreneurs is that at every turn they see an opportunity.

Undesirable Traits

There are some character traits that are especially unfortunate if shown by entrepreneurs. These undesirable traits can pose serious problems for the entrepreneur.

Greed

Undesirable Traits
Greed
Dishonesty
Paranoia
Poor people judgment
Impatience
Lack of business knowledge
Disdain for controls

Entrepreneurial greed can take several forms. Some people are so greedy that they will not share success with their employees, the ones who helped them become successful. By refusing to pay their employees what they are worth, they lose them, or worse. Stories abound of entrepreneurs whose key people left to form competitive enterprises when the boss refused to share the wealth.

Another form of greed manifests itself in people who are so eager for profit that they won't provide the potential customers with sufficient value.

Perhaps product quality has been sacrificed for a few cents more margin. Perhaps the level of follow-up service has been lowered to save a few dollars. Perhaps the employees are somehow shorted. Whatever the case, the greedy entrepreneur often fails to give the customer sufficient value for the money and thus doesn't do much business.

And then there are those people who are so greedy that they are never content with the success they have. While these people may successfully widen the scope of their activities, more often than not, such greed pushes them into all sorts of endeavors in which failure awaits. It seems that there is a line somewhere between a healthy regard for money and what it will buy and liking money too much. Greed seems to be associated with short-run actions that sacrifice long-run success.

Dishonesty

The importance of credibility to entrepreneurial success cannot be stressed enough. In the American business system, all sorts of wonderful things can happen to an entrepreneur that other people trust and believe in. If people don't, the entrepreneur will have a difficult time. The annals of business are crowded with examples of successful people whose careers were ruined by one act of dishonesty. The cynic might hasten to add ". . . that was discovered." However, it has been observed that dishonesty has a way of becoming habitual and thus eventually discovered. The banker "borrows" some money from an inactive account and gets it back undetected. No one ever knew. So the next time the banker needs money, what is likely to happen? Each time it gets easier, perhaps greed creeps in, and he takes more. Sooner or later, the banker will be discovered.

Credibility of the entrepreneur is his or her most valuable asset.

One person who sold goods to the PXs on military bases found out one day that he could easily bill them for products he did not deliver. He got away with it for several years and made a lot of money doing so. Now he is spending some years as a guest of the government. He was sure to get caught sooner or later.

Paranoia

Repeatedly, would-be entrepreneurs say something like, "I need your advice. I have a product that is a real winner. But I can't tell you anything about it because it can be stolen too easily . . . " This kind of person really can't talk to anyone for fear the idea will be stolen. The only reply can be, "Good-bye. I can't help you if I don't know what you are talking about."

A variation of this occurs with people who have a batch of legal papers for an advisor to sign before they disclose their concepts. They are always shocked when the documents are returned unsigned and the advisor says, "Why should I sign anything like this? I didn't ask you to come here." The entrepreneurs usually mumble something about their lawyers saying it was the way to do it. The lawyers would be right if the entrepreneur was dealing with someone who was motivated to sign the agreement. In that case, an agreement is a valid way to protect the entrepreneurs' concepts when dealing with others who want to learn of those concepts.

However, some people are so fearful of being cheated that they cannot deal with others. Their attitudes are so antagonistic that they get little cooperation. And entrepreneurs need cooperation, lots of it. There is a psychological theory that people tend to project into the behavior of others their own behavior patterns. Thus, people who suspect the motives of everyone with whom they deal may be reflecting their own standards of conduct.

It is true, however, that there are situations in which a person would be a fool to disclose his or her materials without some sort of signed legal agreement.

Poor people judgment

It is difficult to be successful in business without help. We use other people— associates, employees, investors, suppliers, and customers. Yet, many failures have resulted from misjudging other people. Perhaps they were not as talented as first thought. Perhaps they did not have the talents required for the job. Perhaps they were dishonest. Perhaps they were lazy. Whatever, people often just do not live up to one's expectations. If a person has somehow associated with the wrong people, he or she will have some sleepless nights. Rare is the person who cannot recall some painful experiences dealing with unfortunate selections of associates.

On the other hand, an ability to pick the right people is a very valuable skill. Work on it! Try to ignore characteristics in people that are irrelevant to the tasks they are supposed to do. Focus on the person's accomplishments in life, not on appearances. Try to ignore words and evaluate deeds. Above all, prize integrity. Regardless of a person's skills, if integrity is lacking, little good will come from the association.

Impatience

It often simply takes time, a great deal of time, to develop a new enterprise. Some things simply cannot be rushed. It may take a year to perfect a product, and that delay may absolutely drive an entrepreneur up the wall. People have often been heard to say, "Well, I'll give it a year, and, if it's not successful, I'll go back to my old job." The best advice is, "Stay put. You'll simply waste your time and money, as well as others', with that attitude."

On the other hand, this is not to say that the entrepreneur should not do everything possible to expedite the development of a new enterprise. It's easy to allow patience to become a synonym for laziness. Patience should never be used as a cop-out to advance the venture. The successful entrepreneur pushes, pushes, pushes, and pushes some more. The thought that must be understood here is that despite all the pushing, it still takes time for the results to manifest themselves. Just because the entrepreneur is working hard and pushing does not mean results will automatically land at his or her feet. He or she may work hard on a large account for six months before seeing results from the efforts.

Moreover, impatience often causes one to take actions that later prove unfortunate. In impatience to get an order from a customer, an entrepreneur may grant a price concession that he or she cannot live with. Impatience may cause the entrepreneur to hire the wrong people. Impatient to get the plant open, the entrepreneur may sign a disastrous lease. The wise entrepreneur simply cannot allow eagerness to overrule good business judgment.

Patience can be learned. Once entrepreneurs accept that certain things or people take longer than expected, they will reduce anxiety and increase sleep at night. And, too, they will learn the merits of the old saying, "Anything worthwhile is worth waiting for."

Lack of business knowledge

A great many entrepreneurial disasters can be traced solely to the lack of business knowledge. The entrepreneur simply did not know enough about the business venture to be successful. There is a tremendous body of knowledge to be acquired in any endeavor. If entrepreneurs don't know how to grant credit wisely, they're likely to lose their enterprises quickly to bad debts. Disaster is surely right around the corner for people who do not know how to establish needed control systems.

Disdain for controls

Studies of business failures clearly indicate that one of the biggest causes of bankruptcy is the lack of control systems in the business. The entrepreneur simply did not know how to control costs, control inventories, control cash, and control people. Often, the accounting systems are nonexistent.

The root of the problem is that the so-called entrepreneurial personality hates control systems. Many entrepreneurs hate to be controlled. They want their freedom. They want to do as they please. That sounds like fun and a delightful existence, but it doesn't work in the business world. Good businesses are controlled economic activities. Business owners must have control over their costs and their money and the things they own. If they do not understand control systems and the need for controls, they'll have some unfortunate experiences in the entrepreneurial world.

Conclusion

Much can be learned by studying the characteristics of successful entrepreneurs. But the real basis for future success lies within the individual. It does not lie with personal characteristics being predictive of his or her future success as an entrepreneur nor with the business techniques that this course provides.

Exercise 2a: Self-Assessment for Entrepreneurial Competencies

Evaluate the strength of your entrepreneurial competencies by circling the number that best represents how well each of the characteristics below applies to you. Use a scale from 1 to 10, in which 1 indicates your competency is weak and 10 indicates your competency is strong.

	Weak Strong		Weak Strong
Desire	1 - 2 - 3 - 4 - 5- 6 - 7 - 8 - 9 - 10	Belief in value of money	1 - 2 - 3 - 4 - 5 - 6 - 7 - 8 - 9 - 10
Initiative/aggressiveness	1 - 2 - 3 - 4 - 5- 6 - 7 - 8 - 9 - 10	Self-confidence	1 - 2 - 3 - 4 - 5- 6 - 7 - 8 - 9 - 10
Energy	1 - 2 - 3 - 4 - 5- 6 - 7 - 8 - 9 - 10	Balanced ego development	1 - 2 - 3 - 4 - 5- 6 - 7 - 8 - 9 - 10
Low support needs	1 - 2 - 3 - 4 - 5- 6 - 7 - 8 - 9 - 10	Market awareness	1 - 2 - 3 - 4 - 5- 6 - 7 - 8 - 9 - 10
Thriving on ambiguity	1 - 2 - 3 - 4 - 5- 6 - 7 - 8 - 9 - 10	Generosity	1 - 2 - 3 - 4 - 5- 6 - 7 - 8 - 9 - 10
Perseverance	1 - 2 - 3 - 4 - 5- 6 - 7 - 8 - 9 - 10	Honesty	1 - 2 - 3 - 4 - 5 - 6 - 7 - 8 - 9 - 10
Responsibility	1 - 2 - 3 - 4 - 5- 6 - 7 - 8 - 9 - 10	Good people judgment	1 - 2 - 3 - 4 - 5- 6 - 7 - 8 - 9 - 10
Problem solving	1 - 2 - 3 - 4 - 5- 6 - 7 - 8 - 9 - 10	Patience	1 - 2 - 3 - 4 - 5- 6 - 7 - 8 - 9 - 10
Persuasiveness	1 - 2 - 3 - 4 - 5- 6 - 7 - 8 - 9 - 10	Business knowledge	1 - 2 - 3 - 4 - 5- 6 - 7 - 8 - 9 - 10
Self-discipline	1 - 2 - 3 - 4 - 5- 6 - 7 - 8 - 9 - 10	Value appropriate control systems	1 - 2 - 3 - 4 - 5 - 6 - 7 - 8 - 9 - 10

Select three competencies in which improvement would be most beneficial to your future business. Complete the personal development plan below.

Personal development action plan

	Competency challenge	Action plan
1		
2		
3		

Entrepreneurial Myths

Learning Objectives

In this chapter, students will learn how to

- Identify common misconceptions and myths about entrepreneurs.
- Acquire the experience needed to succeed as an entrepreneur.

An abundance of myths about the entrepreneurial world prevail today. Entrepreneurs have once again become the American heroes. They grace the covers of business journals; they star in television shows; they write best selling books. And they perpetuate bigger-than-life myths. These Paul Bunyan myths can get in the way of an individual's decision making about whether or not taking an entrepreneurial step makes sense. Thus it is important to explore these myths and to examine the facts.

Common Misconceptions or Myths

Some common misconceptions or myths could affect attitudes toward undertaking any type of entrepreneurial ventures. These are explored one by one.

Myth: Business is risky.

Business is not intrinsically risky; the people are risky. If people choose to put their homes up as collateral for a new venture, this is their choice, not the business'. When a business is properly managed and set up, the risks are manageable. The wise and adept entrepreneur selects a business and organizes it in such a way that the risk is reasonable. The entrepreneur is the risk. It's surprising that more businesses don't fail, considering the skills of the people involved. What saves them is that people need all sorts of products and services and will suffer much ineptness to buy them.

To drive the point home: Hundreds of sound businesses making good profits have been subsequently ruined when taken over by new management. The business was not the risk—it was sound. The new people were the risk. They were inept, inexperienced, and unmotivated.

Common Myths:

Business is risky.

Entrepreneurs take
   big risks.

Entrepreneurs need
   great ideas.

Considerable experience
   is required.

It takes a lot of money.

Big business will ruin
   the small one.

Entrepreneurs get rich quick.

Entrepreneurs are born,
   not made.

Entrepreneurs are unethical
   because of their desire
   to succeed.

There is no universal law
dictating that one's rewards
in this life are proportional
to the risks assumed. Long-
shot players at the track
take big risks but generally
die broke. One must know
the difference between
rewards and risks.

Conversely, there are numerous turnaround situations in which failing businesses have been taken over by new, more adept management to great economic advantage. There was nothing wrong with the old business, but there was a lot wrong with the management. With new management installed, it was a new ball game.

Thus, the big risk is the people, not the business! High-risk businesses can easily be spotted and avoided.

Moreover, there's no relationship between the risks one assumes and the potential rewards for assuming those risks. Indeed, one of the most profitable types of businesses one can own is a government-granted monopoly in which there is little risk. Conversely, most extremely risky enterprises have very little real profit potential.

Myth: Entrepreneurs take big risks.

Closely akin to the previous myth that business is risky is the misconception that entrepreneurs take big risks. "Risk takers" is a term economists are fond of using in referring to people who start their own ventures. Many entrepreneurs love to think of themselves as "high rollers" and "wheeler dealers," thus adding to the legend. But studies and observation, when added to common sense, shatter this myth. Many studies have shown that entrepreneurial personalities are moderate risk takers when confronted with simulations in which they are asked to make a choice of risks and payoffs.

For some reason, economists harbor the quaint notion that the size of the profit is commensurate with the risk assumed. That is generally not so. Most huge risks offer little reward. Conversely, many low-risk enterprises pay off handsomely.

One managerial philosophy of the modern entrepreneur is to furnish the skill for the venture while letting other people furnish the money. Let others take the financial risk. The entrepreneur risks time, effort, and reputation.

Myth: Entrepreneurs need great ideas.

"I have hundreds of ideas. Get 'em all the time. They pop up like kernels of corn from a popcorn machine." The source of that statement must be credited as the inspiration for our designation of such people as "popcorn heads." They are so in love with their ideas and so impressed with their seemingly endless supply that they seldom do much more than dream. They are particularly unlikely to take one of their ideas and turn it into a profitable business. They often are so infatuated with their ideas that they are unable to perceive their lack of economic merit. They want nothing so much as to see their "brainchild" on the market. Never mind that no one wants to buy it.

The reverse of the "popcorn head" is the person who proclaims, "I want to start a new venture, but I just can't seem to be able to come up with a good idea." Such people are forever seeking the Holy Grail, the El Dorado—that one stroke of genius that will somehow transform them into millionaires. It seldom happens.

The reality is that an entrepreneur does not need a great idea on which to base an enterprise. All that is needed is an idea on which to make a profit—an idea that is doable.

There is also the inventor, the person who holds a special place in entrepreneurial folklore. Many people believe that the model entrepreneurial venture begins with an invention. In reality, relatively few new enterprises are based solely on inventions. Moreover, relatively few inventions ever make a profit. According to *The Wall Street Journal*, less than 1 percent of inventors ever make a penny from their inventions.

Most new businesses are based on a tried and true product or service whose markets are well established. They are carbon copies or improvements of enterprises with proven economic merit.

Entrepreneurs and investors are critical of ventures based on new inventions for several reasons.

- Inventors can be difficult to deal with and unrealistic in their business judgments. Inventors usually feel that the inventions are worth far more than they really are. Inventors seldom make good CEOs as they rarely have the managerial talents to make their inventions into successful businesses. Moreover, they usually have little desire to run a business. Their strength is in inventing.

- Normally, inventions will require large amounts of money to bring them to market. Thus, the financial risks are usually considerable.

- It's a long time from the inception of the venture to the cash break-even point, when the business can sustain itself without additional investments. Many years can be involved in this process.

- The market risk inherent in inventions is significant, even when the best research has been performed. No matter how excellent the invention might be, or how much it seems to be needed, the market has a way of making unexpected decisions on such matters and may not respond favorably.

    One of the classic mistakes in entrepreneurship is the product that is looking for a market. Entrepreneurial dogma insists that market-driven ventures are far more likely to be successful than product-driven ones.

Myth: Considerable experience is required.

Wrong! Experience is nice but not necessary. It is much more important for the entrepreneur to have the energy and enthusiasm to learn about a new field, its trade practices, and techniques than to have spent years in the field. Indeed, coming in with a fresh outlook and a willingness to learn often keeps the business from falling into status quo or stagnant traps that can immobilize the person who's had lots of experience in a particular area.

The case for experience

The following points support the case for experience:

- In every business, there is much to know. Trade practices and business know-how are often the difference between success and failure. Seldom can one learn all one needs to know by reading about it. It helps to have some "battle" experience. One of the main reasons for the success of many franchise systems is that they supply the needed experience in capsule form to the franchisee, who is taught everything the franchisor has learned through the years. When one is interested in buying a business, it is often wise to work in it for a while before purchasing it—at least to keep the seller around for a while to train the new owner.

- One of the keys to a funder's decision to finance an entrepreneur is the funder's appraisal of the entrepreneur's ability. And that is usually based on the entrepreneur's track record—experience. Entrepreneurs are not likely to attract much money from other people without some experience.

- Experience provides some maturity, which increases the credibility with the people with whom an entrepreneur must do business. Very young people, though they may be quite competent, report that they have to work harder to gain the confidence of potential customers who are much older than they are.

Advocates of the need for experience are uncomfortable when they read of successes such as that of Steve Jobs, one of the founders of Apple Computer; or Bill Gates, founder of Microsoft®; or Debbie Fields, whose cookies now enjoy worldwide distribution. These people had little business experience to support starting their enterprises, but this didn't seem to interfere with their success. The point is that they associated themselves with people who had the necessary experience.

Other ways the entrepreneur can gain experience are from mentoring, reading, research, college coursework, and seminars.

The case for timing

The following points support the case for going into one's own business as soon as possible:

- Years of experience might be of little use. Many people who work for 10 years do not have 10 years' experience. They have a month's experience repeated 120 times. Seldom does one really learn what is needed to know by working for someone else. But there are exceptions. Sales experience can be valuable, not only in acquiring certain techniques and work habits but in making valuable contacts in an industry.

- Energy and enthusiasm are key ingredients in entrepreneurial success. When people are young, they are more likely to possess them than they will in later years.

- Obligations are acquired—mortgages, families, and other demands on time. These inevitably conflict with a business. Starting a business usually requires large amounts of time. If people are not free to devote the time and energy required by their new ventures, their success is remote. Make the play before acquiring the obligations, when there isn't as much to lose should things not go well for the venture.

  A young entrepreneur founded a company that rescues boats at sea. He attributes much of his ability to nurture his foundling enterprise to its present successful state to his ability to live at home on $100 a month for the first two years of the venture's existence.

  It is often exceedingly hard for a new venture to generate sufficient cash to support the entrepreneur and his or her family in the first few years of its existence.

- It usually takes time for a business to become successful. Three to five years is often quoted as the time it takes to bring a business into sufficient maturity so it can survive. The sooner entrepreneurs start, the sooner they'll reach their goals.
- People can learn what they need to know in a relatively short time. Once they have the knowledge, they can be more effective. In the sale of a business, the former owner often is able to instruct the buyer about the business in a matter of weeks.

The enterprise decides how much experience

Naturally, the nature of the proposed enterprise strongly affects how much experience is needed to enter it. It would be folly to go into the semiconductor business without knowing a great deal about semiconductors. The famous last words of many bankrupt owners when starting their businesses were, "What's there to know about this business? There's nothing to it." There is always something "to it." It may not be much, but the entrepreneur had better know "it" or pay a price to learn "it."

Indeed, the entrepreneur often later admits that a large price was paid for "lessons from the school of hard knocks." Thus, the advice is often given to the young, would-be entrepreneur to let someone else pay for his or her education. There is merit in this advice.

Making the decision

The matter of acquiring needed experience is no simple decision. When should one take the plunge? Only the individual can make that decision. Here are some random observations that may help.

- Many entrepreneurs have said that if they had known everything they subsequently learned about the business they started, they would never have gone into it in the first place. Many businesses exist only because the owners were ignorant of what they were getting into. Once in the business, they were committed. They had to make it work. While self-confidence is comforting to the new entrepreneur, many people never achieve it. Their insecurities push them to greater efforts.

  Self-confidence may or may not be a virtue; it depends on how it affects behavior. Does the individual use it to advantage or does it lead to counterproductive behavior?

- An entrepreneur often can hire or associate with someone who has the experience he or she feels is needed in the enterprise. The firm needs sales experience—hire it. The firm needs control systems—buy them. A management team that has the experience the venture requires is put together. Indeed, one school of entrepreneurial thought holds that assembling the proper management team is one of the entrepreneur's main functions.
- A person who is determined to be an entrepreneur should get started. It is possible to write a good plan and enter business on a small scale if necessary. If the first venture does not do well, the entrepreneur will quickly learn from any mistakes.

Myth: It takes a lot of money.

It's surprising how little money is needed to start some ventures. Often an idea can be tried out on a small scale, on a test basis, for very little financial investment. Then, if the idea warrants it, larger amounts of money can be sought.

Indeed, there are some entrepreneurs who insist that having too much cash at the beginning of a company's existence can be disastrous. Management fails to develop needed controls and thus squanders the early capital that is so desperately needed later.

No one claims starting a business is easy. Money makes things much easier. But if entrepreneurs do not have much money, then they will just have to do without it if they want their own businesses. There are several strategies to doing that.

Low-investment business

Some businesses require such little initial investment that even those without resources can find sufficient funds to start. Many prospering landscape-maintenance services began with a borrowed lawn mower.

The principle is quite simple: If the entrepreneur does not have much money and cannot get money, then he or she should choose a business that can be had for the available money. This happens every day. Go into a business in which the key ingredient is labor—the entrepreneur's. It's called "sweat equity." Equity in the enterprise is built up by hard work.

A businesswoman decided to leave the world of medical administration and do what she'd dreamed of for 20-plus years—be a children's clothing designer and manufacturer. She started with the old sewing machine she had but soon acquired enough clients to afford the purchase of a cutting and sewing system. Her business venture was accomplished with determination and hard work every single day, but she's doing what she enjoys and gets paid for it as well.

Entrepreneurs not only can start a business with "sweat equity" and "bootstrap" financing, they can do it at just about any age, as long as they have the drive, enthusiasm, and physical stamina.

Take over a turnaround situation

For any number of reasons, a business can get into more trouble than its management can get out of. Some managements are inept. Some are tired. Some just don't care anymore. Whatever the reason, such enterprises present opportunities for the entrepreneur who wants to own a business without investing much money.

Usually someone cares greatly about the business. Perhaps it is the financial institution that has a large stake in it—a banker, venture capitalist, or a private investor. Perhaps it is an absentee owner. Perhaps it is a group of dissatisfied stockholders who fear for the future of their investment. Whoever they may be, they know the business needs new management. They want to throw out existing management and put in someone they trust. Thus, the key to this strategy is obvious: by some means gain the confidence of those people who control the company.

Raise money from other people

If entrepreneurs have sufficient credibility, some collateral, and a sound business plan, they can sometimes get other people to furnish the funds for their enterprises.

The management of Staar Surgical Company was able to raise $6 million from the public simply because the financiers were ophthalmologists. They recognized the company's product as possessing great profit potential and had great faith in the two founders, Dr. Thomas Mazzaco and Tom Waggoner, whom they knew because both had been active in the industry.

All sorts of entrepreneurs have raised money by selling securities of various descriptions. The method used depends upon market conditions and tax laws, but it's done all the time—entrepreneurs must know whom to work with in the money markets. They need to make contacts with the right people in order to play this game.

Myth: Big business will ruin the small one.

It is true that big business has great financial power. Large businesses have access to the money markets, which make huge amounts of money available to them at a relatively low cost. Such sums allow big businesses to buy markets, either through large advertising campaigns or by buying companies that have significant shares of a market.

Big businesses find it difficult to compete in the people market. Their managements prefer to invest in fixed assets, advertising, and things they can control. They have difficulty controlling people. Moreover, they prefer to engage in businesses in which size gives them a decided competitive advantage. Perhaps that advantage is in low production costs due to automation. Perhaps the advantage is in selling through mass merchandisers backed by large advertising programs.

A start-up company can compete if it maximizes its strengths: flexibility, speed of change, and closeness to the customer. Even then, it will be important to find the niche that positions the venture with a competitive advantage—niching is the insurance that protects the venture from any competitor, small or large.

One example is a small defense-electronics company that concentrated on short runs so small that its large competitors could not bid on the jobs because their overhead charges made their bids too high.

Another example is a specialty job shop producing a narrow line of goods in depth. Large retailers cannot carry lines in much depth because their inventory costs would soar. They must carry only the best sellers.

Here are some rules for competing with big business.

- Find a niche in the market that is being overlooked by large business.
- Seek businesses in which size is of little advantage in either costs or attractiveness to the market.
- Seek businesses in which additional added-value services are important.

Another way to look at big businesses is that possibly they're the entrepreneur's best friend. Many entrepreneurs exist because the big businesses are their customers. Big businesses feed the smaller subcontractors or outsource some activities. Moreover, big businesses that one fears may ultimately be one's exit; the entrepreneur will sell to them.

Myth: Entrepreneurs get rich quick.

It is a rare entrepreneur who makes a venture pay off rapidly. There are well-known stories of Internet company founders becoming millionaires or even billionaires in a few years. Yahoo's Jerry Chang is one of them. It is obviously possible, but it is rare. It takes time to develop a product, test it, market it, and develop and grow the market. Again, it is rare for an entrepreneur to reap immediate rewards of any significant size. It is very typical for a venture to take at least five years to break-even. Therefore, the business plan of the venture needs to be very clear in terms of financial projections. Many entrepreneurs are learning it takes dollars to make dollars, and it takes time.

However, the new businesses starting by using e-commerce to distribute their products or services could become a new model to shorten the time for a business to reach cash break-even.

Myth: Entrepreneurs are born, not made.

Myth
Entrepreneurs are born not made.

Reality
Most successful entrepreneurs are good planners and planning is a learned behavior.

Entrepreneurial patterns and techniques can be learned. Indeed, the many schools of business around the country that now teach entrepreneurial education have gotten great results in helping would-be entrepreneurs learn how to build successful enterprises. In addition, many courses are available to help those in organizations who wish to start and manage intrapreneurial ventures in the most effective ways.

Planning is a learned behavior that can be successfully taught. Writing a solid feasibility plan, business plan, strategic plan, and operational plan increases the chances that an entrepreneurial venture will be successful and profitable. By learning how to write these planning documents, the entrepreneur learns a new objective thought pattern and systematically analyzes each decision based on how it affects each part of the business, such as the management team, marketing plan, financial strategy, control and operating procedures, and potential growth of the business.

Myth: Entrepreneurs are unethical because of their desire to succeed.

There have been many stories in the media about unethical or immoral entrepreneurs who achieved success by any means. However, they are the exception, not the rule.

Entrepreneurs must be highly ethical and have moral convictions that parallel those of society. If they do not hold these convictions, their actions will be highly criticized and their reputations tarnished. Most will not survive. There are thousands of examples of entrepreneurs who live by a strict ethical code.

Conclusion

Many myths that stem from the early days of business in this country have been formed about entrepreneurs. These myths can be likened to those about the early gunslingers. Entrepreneurial myths are just that—myths that are misleading and often scare away potential entrepreneurs. The stories about entrepreneurs cause people to think of them as being mysterious and big risk takers. In reality, they are just driven by a burning need to control their own destinies and bring their dreams to the marketplace.

Identifying Venture Opportunities

CHAPTER 4

Learning Objectives

In this chapter, students will learn to

- Relate entrepreneurial success to the ability to identify market needs and spot trends.
- Identify how entrepreneurs find ideas for business concepts.
- Use specific activities to inspire creative thinking.

Innovative venture opportunities are springing up in both new and traditional industries. In the accelerated business environment, success as an entrepreneur is related to the ability to identify market needs. The number one source of ideas for a new venture is the entrepreneur's own work experiences. Because of their familiarity with their customers, entrepreneurs can often identify underserved market niches.

Entrepreneurs must be able to spot trends and distinguish those with staying power from flash-in-the-pan fads, to know what is happening in an industry, to look for expanding markets, and to predict where trends are heading. To succeed in the entrepreneurial world, it is important to continually recognize, monitor, and stay abreast of trends as well as technological, social, and attitudinal changes. Entrepreneurs who thrive seek out new trends and build venture opportunities based on them before everyone jumps on the bandwagon. The most successful venture opportunities exploit change.

Recent Trends

Some of the most recent trends creating new venture opportunities are based on the growing global marketplace, the increasingly diverse population of the United States, advances in technology, the changing workplace, the quest for weight loss, and the appreciation of a simpler lifestyle.

Following are recent trends, as well as associated products and services that could be explored.

Globalization

Small businesses operate in an increasingly global economy. No longer is it wise or correct to assume that a business need only be concerned or pay attention to one city, region, or country. What affects one country or industry affects all countries and businesses in that industry. In today's economy, world trade is crucial to America's economic health and the growth of many small companies.

A business does not have to be big to sell in the global marketplace. A small business cannot ignore international opportunities if it is to keep up with its competitors. In fact, the Small Business Administration reports that 97 percent of U.S. companies that export are small businesses.

In the last decade, the number of small businesses that export has tripled. The dollar value of exports has soared. To a large extent, technology has leveled the playing field for small businesses. Forrester Research, a technology research firm, estimates global online exports will reach $1.4 trillion in 2004.

Small companies can easily contact international customers and ship goods without establishing extensive offices overseas. A small business in Maine can export machine parts to 38 countries using the Internet. A woman in Mississippi can export food products to Canada. Handcrafts from Colorado can be sold in Japan.

With 96 percent of the world's population and 67 percent of the world's purchasing power located outside the United States, the potential for small business is significant. Small businesses that export or import include all kinds of enterprises in just about every industrial classification—both products and services. The fastest growth has been among very small businesses—those with fewer than 20 employees.

The top ten markets for U.S. small businesses are Canada, the United Kingdom, Japan, Mexico, Germany, Australia, Hong Kong, France, Taiwan, and Singapore, according to an SBA international trade report in 2000. Looking at the rate of growth in exports as a gauge of future market potential, the fastest growing markets for U.S. small business exporters are Brazil, Malaysia, China, the Philippines, Canada, Thailand, Israel, Argentina, the United Kingdom, and Hong Kong. The SBA has signed agreements with governments or entities in Ireland, Russia, Argentina, Mexico, South Africa, and Egypt to establish trade links between businesses in their countries and small businesses in the United States.

Some American entrepreneurs find it practical to start their business in another country and export their products to the United States. Examples are found in manufacturing and technology-based businesses.

An antiglobalization backlash due to economic slowdowns and political unrest in some countries can create instability in those markets. This reverse globalization, however, can lead to innovative thinking. Charles Tharp, president of Environmental Dynamics, a Missouri manufacturer of waste water treatment equipment, is focusing on regions where there will be strong growth, opening new sales offices in India and China. In *Entrepreneur Magazine*, Tharp states, "There has been a consolidation in our business, and the companies left will be the ones that export smart, control their costs, and develop connections overseas." Environmental Dynamics had 2002 revenues of $14 million.

Many of the same qualities that make a small business owner successful in the United States can make him or her successful in global markets. Entering the overseas market may also involve changes, such as new packaging and metric conversions. To succeed in exporting, entrepreneurs must identify the most profitable markets for their products and services. This process can be time-consuming and costly without outside assistance.

Entrepreneurs can find new global venture opportunities by contacting the Department of Commerce Trade Information Center at (800) USA-TRAD, the international clearinghouse on exporting, and ask for the desk officer who specializes in their particular industries. Federal programs through the Department of Commerce, the SBA, and the Export-Import Bank offer assistance to help businesses evaluate their export potential, identify potential markets, find export financing, locate distribution channels, understand trade regulations, and utilize technology. Additional information and resources are available at the Office of International Trade (www.sba.gov/oit), TradeNet (www.tradenet.gov), and the International Trade Administration at the Department of Commerce (www.ita.doc.gov).

Changing demographics

The demographics of this country are rapidly changing. Minority populations are now collectively the majority and are predicted to continue to expand in size, buying power, and political clout. Hispanics are the fastest growing ethnic group followed by Asians and African-Americans. At the same time, Caucasians are declining in the percentage make-up of the population.

Many opportunities abound in designing and marketing ethnically diverse products and services.

- Specialty lines of cosmetics
- Hair care products and salons
- Vitamins and dietary products
- Ethnic grocery stores and cookbooks
- Ethnic food mail-order catalogs
- Ethnic cafes, restaurants, and food courts

The millions of aging baby boomers also significantly impact the marketplace as their lifestyle and health needs dictate new products and services. Health and wellness centers and day spas are finding a lucrative market as aging baby boomers focus on remaining young and healthy.

As Americans gray and enter their golden years, many will seek independent-residential centers and assisted-living centers which operate like hotels and provide a homelike atmosphere. Residents have maid service, restaurants, dry cleaning, and salon services. These centers offer attractive alternatives to nursing facilities or living alone. Many people want parents living closer to them. The solution may be Club Meds for Seniors. Following are some opportunities for elder care ventures:

- Rent-a-grandmother services
- Products and services for the homebound

- Home health care providers
- Door-to-door transportation
- Homemaking services
- Personal services for the elderly
- Elder care consulting services
- Elder day-care centers and activities
- Senior travel clubs
- Independent-living centers
- Assisted-living centers

Technology

Technology continues to expand at a rapid rate and shows no signs of letting up. It has had a two-pronged effect upon business. Its development, production, and sale has spawned thousands of businesses and has affected how non-technical business is conducted.

The entrepreneur cannot be creative in a vacuum. Understanding the industry releases creativity.

The Internet, intranet, and similar developments have created an information explosion with traditional information sources such as books, magazines, newspapers, and reports readily available online. Information can be accessed anytime, anywhere in the world. Thousands of businesses are engaged in knowledge management: accessing, collecting, indexing, sorting, displaying, and disseminating this enormous amount of information. A 2002 Gartner report estimates that companies will invest more than $30 billion on information management systems.

The Internet continues to be a laboratory for new business ventures. Online retail sales or B2C (business to consumer) marketing has been replaced by B2B (business to business) marketing as the latest darling of Internet commerce. Forrester Research expects U.S. online business trade to reach almost $7 trillion in 2006. By contrast, traditional U.S. online retail revenues will reach $195 billion.

It's very difficult to build brand recognition in cyberspace. The companies that tend to succeed are the ones with brick and mortar in real life. People prefer to do business with the businesses they know. The good news is that B2B customers are more trusting and understanding of the Internet and more likely to try a new service provider if their own bottom line will be improved.

Wireless Internet capabilities are showing up in all sorts of devices. The electronics industry is focusing on how to best consolidate carry-around appliances into a single device.

Concerns over security and identify theft are other areas where technology can play a significant role. The Privacy Rights Clearinghouse reports about 90 percent of consumers are concerned about privacy which, according to director Beth Givens, "represents both a challenge and an opportunity for entrepreneurs."

The following are some opportunities which exploit new technologies:
- Information services
- Web services
- Online education

- Real-time consulting via streaming audio/video
- Content management services
- Online gaming
- Subscription services for content/information/media
- Web-based ordering for individualized vitamin combinations with auto-refill capability
- Wireless network security products
- Mobile devices
- Hardware that stops viruses and worms
- Personal security products and services
- Background check businesses
- Monitoring and tracking devices

Outsourcing

More businesses are relying on independent contractors rather than employees to perform a multitude of tasks, generally non-core functions. The resulting business structure includes a smaller staff, many of whom are dedicated to managing the work activity of an increasing number of temporary employees and independent contractors. This shift has not only resulted in employees being laid off but also created businesses and jobs for those providing these services.

Outsourcing lets a company focus on its core business while reducing operating costs by not having full-time employees, contracting for work only when it is needed. Outsourcing providers can bring specialized knowledge and skills that would not be available internally.

According to Dr. James Quinn, author of *Innovation Explosion: Using Intellect and Software to Revolutionize Growth Strategies*, "If you are not best-in-world in doing something, and doing it in-house, you are giving up competitive edge. You could outsource to the best in the world, up the value, and lower the cost."

Outsourcing is shifting to knowledge-based activities such as research, marketing, logistics, human resources, accounting, and legal work. Accenture surveyed 150 senior executives and found that 85 percent said they would outsource one or more of their human resources functions. Their primary reasons were lower costs and greater expertise.

It's not just big businesses that are outsourcing. Small businesses can achieve benefits too. StaffPay, a professional employer organization based in Irvine, California, provides small businesses with human resources administration, workers' compensation, risk management, safety training, benefits, and payroll. Small businesses contract with StaffPay to "employ" their workers. While the clients participate in the hiring and firing of employees and supervise the actual work, "StaffPay takes the responsibility and liability of being the employer," notes Vic Tanon, president. If an employee has a workers' compensation claim, it is against StaffPay not the small business. Employee paychecks and taxes forms come from StaffPay. By pooling the employees of their clients, StaffPay gets better rates for employees' health and retirement benefits.

The Outsourcing Institute (www.outsourcing.com) surveyed business executives that outsource functions about the criteria used to select vendors and contractors. Executives primarily consider these factors: commitment to quality, price, references/reputation, flexible contract terms, scope of resources, additional value-added capability, cultural match, existing relationship, and location.

The Outsourcing Institute sees opportunities for outsourcing in the following areas:

- Information technology
- Customer service field service
- Customer service telephone support
- Telemarketing
- Records management
- Printing
- Payroll processing
- Purchasing
- Transaction processing
- Accounting and taxes
- Recruiting and staffing
- Consulting and training
- Food and cafeteria services
- Facilities management
- Security
- Advertising
- Warehousing
- Freight consulting and brokering
- Fleet management and maintenance

Changing retail

Americans are changing the way they shop. Consumers, looking to save money and time, are making more purchases online. Retailers who focus on lifestyles are the big winners. The increase in teen spending power is also having a significant impact on the retail industry.

Today, buyers are increasingly hungry to find the best deal. Approximately 98 percent of online buyers report they comparison shop most, or all of the time. Today's consumers are more likely to show loyalty to price than store brand. Shoppers are likely to cross-shop. For example, they will purchase a dress at a designer store and shoes to match at a discount store. Consumers are looking for the best merchandise at the best price.

Consumers primarily use the Internet to shop for basics. The Internet is not as strong in shopping for fashion goods. Big online sellers are computer games and books.

"Shopping today is about time and convenience," says Tom Buxton, president and CEO of The Buxton Company, a retail market research firm in

Fort Worth, Texas. "Successful retailers are focusing on lifestyles," he adds. Lifestyle stores marry products, environment, and lifestyle.

Inside The South, a lifestyle shop in Jackson, Mississippi, shoppers find bedding, beaded lamps, leather and upholstered chairs, and original art displayed throughout. Further into the store, shoppers find china and flatware patterns, tabletop accents and even a selection of high-end menswear—all under one roof. This is not a department store, but a small business that celebrates and sells the genteel Southern life.

Some common examples of lifestyle stores are Aveda, Restoration Hardware, Old Navy, and Anthropologie.

Teenagers spend approximately $120 billion per year on clothes, electronics, music, and other items. This sector of the market is growing so fast and becoming so important, that small companies cannot ignore their spending power. In addition to their buying power, teens are the focus of clothing manufacturers because they are trendsetters, not only for one another, but also for the population at large. Younger children look up to teens to identify and adopt the latest fashion.

In a world dominated by big-box retailers, it's easy to feel like starting a retail business is out of the question. However, many entrepreneurs are finding ways to partner with or supply products to the larger retailers.

Entrepreneurs may find many opportunities to create new ventures in the following areas:

- Specialty lines of cosmetics for teens
- Lines of clothing for teens
- Resale shops
- Web stores
- Lifestyle stores
- Specialty items to sell to big-box retailers

Time scarcity

Double-income families and hectic daily activities for all members of the family have led to an increasing number of services designed to meet the needs of the busy and frequently weary household.

In *The Harried Leisure Class*, Steffan Linder shows that consumption in an affluent society is limited by our scarcest resource: time. The work week has actually increased for most American workers during the past decade. As a result, our time for personal activities and consumption is shrinking, even as our closets and garages fill with unused toys.

Make a list of daily nuisances that people experience. Then brainstorm creative solutions to these irritations and inefficiencies people face. This thought process will help you uncover hidden opportunities.

The result is a willingness to pay others to run errands and handle many time-consuming family and home tasks. Many traditional restaurants and grocery stores are offering carry out or delivery services and entirely new businesses have been started to meet this trend.

Personal errand and shopping services perform a variety of tasks: grocery shopping; picking up laundry, dry cleaning, theater tickets, and shoe repairs; taking cars for servicing and repair; taking care of pets; mailing packages; choosing gifts; and wardrobe consulting, to name only a few.

Many of these new venture opportunities can be launched as home-based businesses.

- Personal shopping and errand services
- House cleaning
- Lawn care
- Child care
- Tax preparation
- Home repairs
- Wardrobe consultants
- On-site customer apparel shoppers
- Gift services
- Corporate pickup and delivery service
- Messenger services
- Rent-a-butler
- Rent-a-chef
- Rent-a-driver

Obesity

The United States has become the fattest nation in the world. Over 50 percent of Americans are overweight. One in three adults is obese. More information and statistics are released daily about this unhealthy trend. A combination of other trends, such as growth in technology and time-saving services, has exacerbated this problem. Too many Americans are super-sizing their meals while reducing their day-to-day physical activity.

Products and services which may help consumers fight the battle of the bulge are flourishing. According to *Fitness Magazine*, the diet industry sells an annual $40 billion of products to American consumers looking for a way to shed excess pounds.

About half of all Americans are currently on a diet, reports the American Dietetic Association. Fad diets which prohibit eating certain food groups have created a market for specialized foods while hurting demand for the excluded foods.

Businesses are attempting to solve the problem of obesity by producing healthier foods. Leisure activities to reverse the effects of over indulgence are proliferating. Personal trainers customize workouts and target problem areas for clients.

New venture opportunities abound in the following areas:

- Low-fat foods and low-carb foods
- Cookbooks and diet books
- Nutritional supplements
- Diet programs and centers
- Videotapes and DVDs
- Exercise equipment

- Web stores and specialty retail shops
- Door-to-door wellness services
- Diet coaches and personal trainers
- Health clubs and fitness services

Shifting sports interest

Despite its self-proclamation as the national pastime, Major League Baseball is no longer the most popular sport in this country. The National Football League, NASCAR, NBA, and a host of other sports at the professional and amateur levels are commanding the attention of Americans.

Spectator sports such as these can create business opportunities related to the production and sales of licensed clothing, gifts, toys, novelties, and other merchandise. A product may realize greater demand and a higher price when it contains the colors or logo of a favorite team.

Extreme sports are the fastest growing participation sports in the United States. American youth are spending time and money on skateboarding, snowboarding, and off-road mountain biking. In addition to buying the actual sports equipment, some consumers are seeking the extreme sports lifestyle and demonstrate it by wearing hats, sweatshirts, and shoes that match their sport of choice.

Entrepreneurs who have a passion for a sport may find innovative ways to create a business that supports their passion. For example, iwindsurf.com provides subscribers with wind conditions reports for key windsurfing locations. Another company, Pro Designed, Inc., provides customized protective pads for extreme skaters. Customers enter several measurements into a web site, and the company ships pads that correctly fit the skater.

Business opportunities abound in the sports field:
- Clothing
- Novelties
- Catering for tailgaters
- Resale and consignment stores for sports equipment
- Repair shops
- Sports camps
- Sports photography
- Adventure travel
- Paintball fields
- Rock climbing facilities
- Corporate team building activities

Search for simplicity

In this increasingly frantic and complex world, many Americans are seeking to redefine how they live their everyday lives. They want their lives to be less busy, less cluttered, less complicated, or less expensive. Consumers who embrace the simpler lifestyle want to spend their energy and their money on things that truly matter to them.

This pursuit of a simpler life creates demand for products and services that provide inspiration, encouragement, motivation, and practical help. The magazine *Real Simple* and a number of books and newsletters celebrate the return of simplicity and frugality.

Many aging baby boomers are leaving the workplace early and opting for less demanding jobs or none at all. Some parents are deciding to homeschool their children. Consumers are enjoying activities representative of simpler times—eating pizza in front of the television set, playing board games, working on scrapbooks, quilting, and gardening. Home cooked meals are replacing dining out for this consumer group.

The focus on a better quality of life extends to an emphasis on health and healing both minds and bodies. Many people are showing a renewed interest in massages, herbal medicinal baths, and teaching self-healing techniques.

New venture opportunities are surging in the following areas:
- Spiritual and philosophical products
- Fitness products and services
- Yoga centers
- Homeschool materials
- Organizational products
- Organizational consultants
- Gardening supplies
- Crafts and hobby supplies
- Natural foods and organic produce
- Natural bottled water products
- Specialty coffee, tea, and wine shops
- Quaint hotels and boutiques with specialty services
- Aromatherapy (scented candles, bath oils, and lotions)
- Spa products for home use

Work at home

Thanks to technology, workers can perform many of their daily tasks without regard to location. As a result, more people are working both full and part-time in their homes. The shift to a service-based economy has encouraged this trend. Lifestyle and workplace changes will continue this trend. Serving and supplying this new home office market present numerous business opportunities.

Those employees who continue to work at a fixed centralized site are demanding flexible hours and other departures from the traditional 9 to 5 routine. When possible, employers are accommodating these preferences as a way of retaining their best workers.

In addition to the corporate world telecommuters who have opted for an office at home, a growth in home-based entrepreneurs has fueled the stay-at-home-and-work trend. As a result, people are creating a comfortable environment throughout the home including the accoutrements of a functioning home office.

Entrepreneurs can spin off new work-at-home ventures in the following areas:

- Home-office furniture and equipment
- On-site repair services for home office computers
- Home delivery for supplies and equipment
- Courier services
- Home video conferencing
- Digital imaging products
- Home decorating and furnishings
- Home safety and security devices
- Multisensory robotics
- Smart homes and appliances
- Voice recognition products

Creative idea source checklist

Entrepreneurs may find many ways to come up with ideas for business concepts. Following is a list of some activities in which entrepreneurs can engage to find inspiration.

❑ **Keep abreast of demographic changes.** Demographic changes are continual, but often their consequences are not noticed until too late. Population statistics change more rapidly today than in the past. Demographic changes regarding the numbers of births and deaths, age distribution, education, occupations, and geographic locations provide many business opportunities. For example, Peter Francese of American Demographics, Inc., points out that the fastest-growing age group in America is those folks 85 years or older. For this market, assisted-living centers, recreational activities, and delivery services are fertile ground for new ventures.

❑ **Look for the unexpected.** Unexpected successes or failures are often disregarded by business people. A sharp entrepreneur can harvest opportunities by observing these experiences in the marketplace and improving on the mistakes of others. Entrepreneurs scan business journals for unexpected business experiences.

❑ **Study problems.** Problems are fertile grounds for opportunities. Can something be done better … more quickly … more cheaply? People are perpetually looking for cost-effective solutions to their problems. Entrepreneurs are problem-oriented and good listeners. They are troubleshooters uncovering ideas that will make people's lives easier, more economical, or more pleasurable. They audit the media to determine what people are complaining about and try to discover solutions to their concerns. A list of daily nuisances that people experience, may yield creative solutions to irritations and inefficiencies that people face.

If the entrepreneur can solve a problem, the solution could lead to a new business concept.

- ❑ **Identify people's needs.** What is important to people today? What are their priorities? Entrepreneurs know their current and potential customers and find out what these customers need. They ask open-ended questions to discover dissatisfactions with today's products and services. A simple but most effective way to get such consumer information is utilizing a focus group. Another simple technique: Asking questions and listening whenever a chance to talk with prospective customers arises.

- ❑ **Engage in people watching.** Observing people can bring meaningful insights to stimulating new-venture ideas. Watching people's behavior and listening to conversations provide ideas on new needs and desires. Example: Walk into a hotel lobby, pick up a magazine, observe people by listening to their concerns, and conduct observation research. How good an observer are you? At social functions do you make more than small talk? Do you use the occasion as a focus group where you can ask questions about such concerns as: What is your greatest concern as you think about aging? In public places, such as malls and airports, do you observe patterns? For example, perhaps the increased use of motorized carts for transporting older and disabled people in airports might inspire a thought about the multiple uses of mobility carts. Are you noticing such trends as the increasing entry of women and minorities into the work force or more people eating at home because of health or cost concerns?

Borrow information from one industry and creatively apply it to another.

- ❑ **Monitor society, industry, and market.** Changes in tastes, lifestyles, and habits are constant and volatile. An example: Cajun cooking may be out, but low-fat ice cream is in. Another example: Jogging is no longer considered the best way to exercise; walking is better. Astute entrepreneurs observe various industries, such as banking, airlines, and communications, in terms of how they respond to deregulation and increased competition.

- ❑ **Examine new knowledge.** Entrepreneurs scan trade journals, browse in the library, and talk to people in their industries to discover what is new and exciting. They ask questions about other organizations, their markets, products and services, and challenges. They scan trade magazines from other industries.

- ❑ **Read, read, read.** Successful entrepreneurs spend a significant number of their nonworking hours reading and scanning publications. One study revealed that innovators often spend as much as a third of their business day just reading. They read intuitively, look for what is different, new, and exciting, make connections between seemingly unrelated events, and identify patterns. They read publications outside of their own industry as well as major metropolitan newspapers and local business journals, which cover community developments and trends in local markets.

- ❑ **Watch for new trends.** The secret of this technique is watching the media, the Internet, and professional associations for recurring themes.

Entrepreneurs scan junk mail for clues about new products and services introduced in the marketplace. They track the bestselling nonfiction books, which may contain trends they can exploit.

❑ **Utilize groups to exchange information.** Trading information among colleagues, competitors, and professionals in the community is a valuable exercise for spotting trends. Establishing a network of professionals who provide state-of-the-art information is an excellent way to spot trends and trade clues on opportunities. Entrepreneurs join associations that serve their industry. For new ideas and forecasts, they attend industry conventions and inventor trade shows.

❑ **Seek out recognized leaders.** Change is triggered by those who have contact with leaders outside their fields. Reading should be supplemented by exchanging thoughts with informed experts. Their feedback is often rich with insights. Periodically, entrepreneurs talk to these people or read their comments in the media.

❑ **Study the competition.** It is vital to know what the competition is doing. This knowledge is called market intelligence—gathering and analyzing data carefully. What are the competitors doing right? What are their weaknesses? What kinds of promotion and advertising are they using? Before launching a new venture, an entrepreneur must scour the marketplace to see who is there already and ask industry people, customers, and suppliers about present—and possible—rivals.

❑ **Talk to members in the infrastructure, academia, government, and journalism.** The entrepreneur's infrastructure—the accountants, the lawyers, the bankers—is a tremendous source of information about their industries and new trends. The academic world has to keep tabs on changes in the world so they can teach the next generation. Various government agencies, such as the Department of Commerce and Labor and the Census Bureau, compile data indicating new trends. An entrepreneur reviews the various publications from government agencies and contacts manufacturers, wholesalers, and distributors that service their industry to ask about market research they have recently done. These contacts, as well as leading research universities, polytechnic institutes, and professors, should be included in an entrepreneur's network.

❑ **Travel the information superhighway.** A great source for the latest information in various industries is online information. Entrepreneurs spot new trends on the Internet, exchange information on electronic bulletin boards, and shop various cybermalls.

❑ **Make use of commercial research sources.** Leading commercial sources include research and trade associations such as Dun & Bradstreet and RMA – The Risk Management Association, banks and other financial institutions, and publicly traded corporations. Commercial research sources generally charge a fee.

Conclusion

Discovering creative ideas and venture opportunities is a learned process. The Center for Creative Leadership, headquartered in Greensboro, North Carolina, for example, holds regular workshops that teach people how to unleash and enhance their creative skills. The key to creativity is the ability to discover new relationships and to look at subjects from new perspectives.

Becoming an entrepreneur requires becoming a trend spotter by analyzing sources of opportunities, going out and observing, asking lots of questions, and listening. The successful entrepreneur uses creative idea sources to help identify new business opportunities.

Trends Resource List

Books

Bishop, Bill. *Global Marketing for the Digital Age: Globalize Your Business with Digital and Online Technology.* McGraw Hill: 2000.

Carroll, Jim. *Selling Online: How to Become a Successful E-Commerce Merchant.* Kaplan Professional Company: 2001.

Feather, Frank. *Future Consumer.com, 2nd Edition.* Warwick Publishing: 2002.

Hedges, Burke and Steve Price. *Dreambiz.com.* INTI Publishing & Resource Book, Inc.: 1999.

Holden, Greg. *Starting an Online Business for Dummies, 3rd Edition.* John Wiley & Sons: 2002.

Izard, M.B., *Finding the Shoe that Fits—Business Ideas: Opportunity Identification and Evaluation.* Acheve Consulting Inc.: 2002.

Laermer, Richard. *Trendspotting: Think Forward, Get Ahead, and Cash in on the Future.* Cahners Business Information: 2002.

Long, Kim. *American Forecaster Almanac*, published annually by American Forecaster, Denver, CO 80210.

Martin, Chuck. *Net Future: The 7 Cybertrends That Will Drive Business, Create New Wealth, and Define Your Future.* McGraw-Hill: 2000.

Mazarr, Michael J. *Global Trends 2005: An Owner's Manual for the Next Decade.* Palgrave: 2001.

Popcorn, Faith, Lys Marigols. *Clicking: 17 Trends That Drive America.* Harper Business: 1998.

Popcorn, Faith and Lys Marigols. *EVEolution: The Eight Truths of Marketing to Women.* Hyperion: 2000.

Sawyer, Ben, Joe Cataudella and Dave Greely. *Creating Stores on the Web, 2nd edition.* Pearson Education: 1999.

Zaltman, Gerald. *How Customers Think: Essential Insights into the Mind of the Market.* Harvard Business School Press: 2003.

Zollo, Peter. *Wise Up to Teens: Insights into Marketing and Advertising to Teenagers.* New Strategist: 1999.

Newsletters

Consult *Oxbridge Directory of Newsletters* in the library; this resource lists more than 20,000 U.S. and Canadian newsletters in print and electronic format.

Springwise, a free online monthly newsletter (www.springwise.com)

Trendwatching.com, a free online monthly newsletter (www.trendwatching.com)

Magazines

American Demographics

Future Survey, a monthly abstract of books, articles, reports, forecasts, and trends, published by the World Future Society.

Associations

The World Future Society (www.wfs.org), 7910 Woodmont Ave., Suite 450, Bethesda, MD 20814.

Creativity Resource List

Ayan, Jordan E. and Rick Benzel. *AHA!: 10 Ways to Free Your Creative Spirit and Find Your Great Ideas*. Crown Publishing Group: 1996.

Browne, M. Neil and Stuart Keely. *Asking the Right Questions: A Guide to Critical Thinking, 7th edition*. Prentice Hall: 2003.

Godin, Seth. *Purple Cow: Transform Your Business by Being Remarkable*. Portfolio: 2003.

Higgens, James. *101 Creative Problem Solving Techniques: The Handbook of New Ideas for Business*. New Management Publishing: 1994.

Managing Creativity and Innovation, Harvard Business Essentials Series. Harvard Business School Publishing: 2003.

McCoy, Charles. *Why Didn't I Think of That? Think the Unthinkable and Achieve Creative Greatness*. Prentice Hall: 2003.

Michalko, Michael. *Cracking Creativity: The Secrets of Creative Genius*. Ten Speed Press: 2001.

Nadler, Gerald and John Farrel. *Creative Solution Finding: The Triumph of Breakthrough Thinking over Conventional Problem Solving*. Prima Communications: 1999.

Root-Bernstein, Robert Scott and Michele. *Sparks of Genius: The Thirteen Thinking Tools of the World's Most Creative People*. Houghton Mifflin: 1999.

Von Oech, Roger. *A Whack on the Side of the Head: How to Unlock Your Mind for Innovation*. Warner Books: 1983.

Weinstein, Matt and Luke Barber. *Work Like Your Dog: Fifty Ways to Work Less, Play More, and Earn More*. Random House: 1999.

Exercise 4a: Identifying Venture Opportunities

Using the newspapers, periodicals, and information from class members, identify three or four trends, and for each trend brainstorm two potential venture opportunities.

Trend	Venture opportunity

Entrepreneurial Entry Strategies

Learning Objectives

In this chapter, students will learn how to

- Identify the possible entry strategies for starting a new venture.
- Locate a franchise.
- Develop a home-based business.
- Form a nonprofit company.

Some people go into business with much deliberation and thought. Others find themselves in enterprises much to their surprise; they had neither planned for the business nor prepared themselves to run it. There are all sorts of ways—or entry strategies—for people to start new enterprises. Each has its own characteristics, problems, and success probability.

The entry strategy affects much of what entrepreneurs do to enter business. If they decide to go the route of franchising, they set in motion one set of activities. If they decide to buy a business, another set of activities is undertaken. If they decide to start a business from scratch, they find themselves engaged in almost a totally different set of activities. Thus, much consideration should be given to how one can best get into business, given the specific set of circumstances.

A young person might not hesitate to start some business from scratch based on some observed market opportunity. However, an older person who has just been laid off from a large company after 30 years of faithful service might consider buying a business or entering a well-established franchise system. The young person has the time and energy to start a business and yet not place great financial demands upon it during its early years. The older person needs a business that can generate some money almost right from the start.

Entering Business

How should an entrepreneur enter business? What is the entry strategy? There are many different entry strategies, ranging from chance and desperation to technical expertise and new inventions. The entry strategies listed are discussed in some detail.

Customer in hand

It is often said that in entrepreneurship, a person is not in business until there is a customer, until a product or service has been sold, or until someone wants to buy what the entrepreneur has for sale. Truly, the customer is the focal point for business. The customer is the reason the enterprise is created. It seems most appropriate to begin this examination of entry strategies with one of the best ways to get into business—there is a customer in hand who wants to buy something, and thus the entrepreneur creates a business to make that sale or to serve that need.

Why is this a good entry strategy? Because it removes many risks inherent in other types of start-ups. As can be seen in examining other entry strategies, it is often uncertain if a concept will be of interest to enough customers to make the enterprise profitable. With this strategy, customers are ready to buy. Perhaps they have already given the entrepreneur purchase orders for enough volume that the profitability of the enterprise is ensured.

Jack Blackson was a well-paid executive for a small New England firm that sold educational materials to public schools, as well as owned and operated a chain of trade schools. The trade schools needed books—lots of them. Jack negotiated deals with large publishers to supply the schools' books at discounts ranging up to 40 percent off the list price. Nevertheless, there were books that the schools had difficulty buying at a reasonable price. Jack spotted two particularly large courses for which adequate books were not committed. He formed a publishing company in partnership with a friend who had control of several properties (books) that could be used by the trade schools.

A solid, three-year contract was negotiated between the new publishing company and the chain of trade schools in which the schools agreed to buy sufficient volume to ensure that the new company would make more than $100,000 a year. Any other sales would be frosting on the cake, and the partners planned to partake of a lot of frosting, as well as a lot of cake. Why would the chain of schools agree to such a deal? Price. It was contracting to buy for 40 percent off list price books that it had been unable to buy elsewhere for less than 20 percent off. It was a good deal for all involved.

A word of warning is needed here. This situation is a blatant case of conflict of interest, for Jack was on both sides of the deal. He and his lawyer took particular care to cover Jack's liability in the case with full disclosure in writing to the buyer. A person working for a company must be very careful in any dealings with it, or in dealings any other company has with it, if the person has some interest.

Here's another example of a venture with a customer in hand. Two women wanted to start a catering business for corporate functions. The women did not have any money to start this new venture and needed some customers before they could launch their business. They began their customer search by visiting individual offices and giving the receptionists a plastic-wrapped chocolate brownie with a menu attached. They explained to the receptionists that they were starting a new corporate catering business and would appreciate their business, since they knew there was a demand for corporate box lunches.

Next, they looked for a licensed kitchen they could rent from a restaurant. They found a restaurant that closed at 10 p.m. and did not open for business until 11 a.m. the next day. They negotiated a low licensing fee to use the kitchen from 4 a.m. to 8 a.m. daily to produce their box lunches. They also sold their brownies to the restaurant.

For the next two weeks, they stopped by the same offices and gave away more brownies. By the third week, they started taking orders. Many firms ordered box lunches because of their loyalty to the "brownie girls." Today, they are still operating a successful corporate catering business and still sell their brownies to the restaurant.

Business is risk management. There are all sorts of risks inherent in any new enterprise. One of the largest risks is that there is no market for the firm's output. Market risks are so huge that they scare most investors away. One of the key questions asked by investors in new enterprises is, "Who is going to buy it?" They want solid evidence that projected sales volumes will be forthcoming. Too often they have been burned by glowing sales forecasts that turn out to be nothing more than pipe dreams.

There is tremendous advantage in gaining financial support when a good customer is in hand, ready to buy. Indeed, in many instances the customer is so ready to buy that it will furnish front money with which to start the business. An eager or needy customer can be a source of money. It is one of the ways entrepreneurs bootstrap their start-ups—use the customer's money.

The litany of customer-initiated start-ups could go on for some length. The key is that thousands of customers in the marketplace have serious needs that are not being satisfied by their existing suppliers. If entrepreneurs find such situations, they may be able to put together some sort of deal by which they can get into business with a modest financial risk.

Another word of warning. There are customers and there are customers. Some customers businesses don't want. Their word is no good, or their credit is less than bankable. Just because a venture has a firm contract signed by some company does not mean that other parties will place much value on it. How enforceable is the contract? What bailout clauses are in the contract? What seems to be a firm contract may not be if there are provisions in it by which the customer can bail out at any time. Even so, the document may have strategic value in getting a business started. Many people with whom entrepreneurs must negotiate will not examine the contract in detail. They will accept it at face value and will be more cooperative with the entrepreneurs in getting an enterprise started. However, astute investors are leery of customer contracts. Entrepreneurs who are careless with the truth have been known to make claims about having firm contracts in hand just to make other parties more receptive to their proposals. There is never any shortage of reasons why the contracts turn out to be unenforceable.

Another reason astute investors are leery of customer contracts is that they fear that the entrepreneurs will not be able to fulfill their part of the contract—deliver the goods as specified on time and for a profit. It's a long way from contract signing to the profitable culmination of the transaction. Thus, it is not surprising when the investing community is not immediately enthralled with a customer-based business proposal.

One enterprising person, who realized the advantages of going into business with a good customer in hand, began his career with Kmart in the buying offices. He reasoned that with this exposure, he should be able to spot some items the company needed, then arrange to supply them. He did so. Note the tremendous advantages he had. He knew the Kmart system and its requirements. He had the contacts, knew the people to see. They knew him. He knew their needs and their way of operating, and Kmart had tremendous needs for merchandise.

Moreover, this person encountered many interesting business opportunities while working for Kmart. All sorts of people with all sorts of deals approached him. He had made a good career move, for he had placed himself strategically in a location where lots of business opportunities would come past him. There are many such jobs. Bank officers, lawyers, accountants, purchasing agents, outside salespeople, and venture capitalists, among others, are exposed to many business opportunities. There are, however, many jobs in which people will be hidden away from the stream of business action. They must get into the swim of things if they want to see opportunities.

Hobbies

One of the key ingredients of success is the entrepreneur's dedication to the venture and willingness to spend time on it. Consequently, it is of great advantage if entrepreneurs enjoy what they are doing and know something about it prior to starting a business. Thus, hobbies can provide an excellent point of departure into the business world. People evidently enjoy hobbies. Why else would they pursue them? Enthusiasts have learned a lot about their hobbies if they have been the least bit attentive; thus they have a head start over someone who must learn the field from scratch. Consequently, a hobby can provide an excellent entry strategy into business.

Kim Kindred used her hobby to start a lifestyle business. She worked full-time for a corporation and used her free time during lunch hours, in the evenings, and on weekends to establish her business, American Gardenscapes.

American Gardenscapes sells a variety of standard—as well as antique, rare, and heirloom—plants, seeds, and fresh-cut flowers. Her primary customers are gardeners, landscape designers, business owners, and local nurseries and garden centers. An avid gardener, Kim enrolled in the Horticultural Science program at a community college to obtain a Master Gardener certification. In addition, she negotiated a contract with the Housing Authority and 4-H Youth Development Office to establish a community-based children's garden.

There is risk, however, in using a hobby as an entry strategy. Inherent in the entry strategy are some traps that the entrepreneur must consider. For entrepreneurs who are able to avoid these traps, a hobby may provide an excellent entry into business.

Technical expertise

If the entrepreneur is particularly adept at something, that skill can form an effective basis upon which to build a business. Such a skill can be an effective entry strategy because many people starting businesses lack the needed expertise or experience. They are unfamiliar with the industry or market,

---

Starting a business around a hobby sometimes ruins a good hobby.

Traps

1. Gaining a business but losing a hobby. What once was an enjoyable pastime may sour as it becomes a daily work effort.

2. Treating the new enterprise as a hobby, not as a business. A business owner must please the customers, the government, and the financiers.

3. Spending too much time on the hobby aspects of the enterprise and not enough on the business aspects, such as selling and control systems. Such tendencies can rapidly lead the enterprise into difficulty.

they lack contacts, and they are unaware of the pitfalls. Also, staffing the necessary technical skills can sometimes be the hardest part of starting a business. Having those skills and industry experience can be a particularly effective entry strategy.

The information technology industry, with all of its subsets and supporting technologies, provides many opportunities for the technically adept entrepreneur. Couple your skill set with a unique vision and your earning potential grows exponentially. Steve Jobs and Steve Wozniak knew that people would want a desktop-sized home computer that could be programmed by the user. They also knew how to build it and market it. Today, Steve Jobs' unique vision of style and functionality continues to keep Apple computers in front of the most passionate users of any product.

John Carmack, Adrian Carmack, and John Romero took computer gaming several levels beyond what anyone else was offering when DOOM hit the streets in 1993. Not only did they develop their own 3D gaming engine which took the computing world by storm, they also pioneered the idea of multi-player gaming on a computer network. If it's fun to attack computer-generated monsters, wouldn't it be even more fun to attack Bob in accounting? ID Software is the company these three programmers created and DOOM was followed by an even bigger hit, Quake.

But the Internet isn't just for playing games. This new communications infrastructure allows individuals and small teams of people to find ready markets for their products and services. Even a relatively simple understanding of the technology will allow entrepreneurs to use an Internet storefront site to put a catalog of distinctive products online. If their merchandise is particularly unique, they can sell it to the highest bidder at one of the many Internet auction sites. Entrepreneurs can offer consulting services via e-mail or online chatting to customers all over the world. One does not need to be part of a huge enterprise to take advantage of a global market.

A college degree is not a requirement. Both Bill Gates and Larry Ellison dropped out of college, so it seems unlikely that they would have spent the later half of the '70s founding software companies that are now number one (Microsoft) and number two (Oracle). These men did possess the technical skills, business acumen, and the vision to create these pillars of the software industry.

If the business requires technical expertise, the entrepreneur must acquire it or hire it. Suppliers or contractors can often furnish whatever technical help is needed. However it is critical that the entrepreneur take the time to identify the specific technical knowledge needed for the new enterprise and make certain that it will be available when needed.

Understanding the technology helps an entrepreneur understand the needs of a new industry. Pumatech founders Brad Rowe and Steve Nicol saw that the popularity of hand-held computing devices like the Palm Pilot or the Pocket PC meant that people were going to want to get data from their computer calendar and phone number lists into these mobile devices. Getting multiple devices to talk to multiple contact and appointment managers, not to mention all the various operating systems and types of computers, could be a nightmare. Pumatech set up key relationships with Palm and other manufacturers to include the IntelliSync™ software with the

Information Technology Opportunities
Application support
Databases
Programming
Computer repair
Networking
Telecommunications
Desktop publishing
Web authoring
E-commerce

product package. As a result, most data sent to PDAs today get there via Pumatech's technology.

Technical expertise is not relegated to the Information Technology field. Colonel Sanders fooled around for years with flavorings and spices for his chicken before settling on the particular combination that makes his birds so popular. Even seemingly simple businesses, such as fast-food restaurants, home and industrial cleaning or retailing require much more expertise than many people realize. All too often someone opens a store believing that there isn't much to know about running a retail outlet. One reason there are so many failures in retailing is that many merchants are not prepared technically for the business. Accounting knowledge, tax information, product expertise, equipment understanding all play a part in getting your business off the ground and growing.

When a certain amount of technical expertise is required for a business, many would-be entrepreneurs are advised to work in the industry before starting their own enterprise. Learn the business at the expense of your future competitor. Many new enterprises go broke solely because their owners failed to master the technical aspects in time to prevent disaster.

Friends and family

> "The trouble with hiring friends or relatives is that you expect more from them than you do of strangers, while they expect that you'll demand less of them than you would a stranger."
> —Bob Teller, owner of Bob's Old Fashioned Ice Cream

It's a classic situation. Two, three, or four friends, usually close, longtime ones, get to talking about some opportunity or deal one of them has encountered. They decide to go into business together. It seldom works. Neither the business nor the friendship endures for long. An entrepreneur who values friends avoids going into business with them. Naturally, there are exceptions, but the risks are high.

In the enduring enterprises in which friends are engaged, they pound out the ground rules and expectations early in the game. Moreover, they often establish a system for handling their internal grievances. Usually, each party has a clear-cut area of responsibility. A common arrangement is for one person to be in marketing, another in finance and control, while another is active in the production side of the business.

Fire and Ice, a biography of Charles Revson, provides insights into some of the problems that occur when family is involved in a business. Such situations can be emotionally tearing. For that reason, many astute entrepreneurs, as a matter of personal policy, just don't want any family in their businesses. Another interesting book on family business is *Bloodlines*.

On the other hand, often the only people who can be trusted in some situations are people in the family. Whether family members can work together depends largely upon the culture from which they have gained their values. Thus, the entrepreneur is the one best able to discern how well a family business will work for him or herself.

A notable success story of friends going into business together is that of Outback Steakhouse, winner of the coveted Entrepreneur Of The Year® Award in 1994. Chris Sullivan, Tim Gannon, and Robert Basham thought it would be a great lifestyle choice to open a couple of restaurants in the Tampa area, play a lot of golf, and just have a good time. Of course, everyone is aware of their great accomplishments. They remain close friends. The secret of their success, according to Sullivan, is their respect for the others' talents, clear roles and responsibilities, and shared goals.

Chance

The whims and vagaries of fortune, being what they are, often play a pivotal role in thrusting a person into business. There is no denying that an element of blind luck may underlie a move into business. More accurately, chance provides the opportunity to go into business. Whether a person accepts that opportunity or passes it by is a matter of discretion. The entrepreneur's resolution still dictates entry into business.

Fortune favors those who give it a chance to work. It favors people who are active, who meet and do things with other people. Two entrepreneurs, originally college professors, have for a variety of chance reasons found themselves in a long string of business endeavors.

One enterprise—Lawrence Home Builders—came about only because a student saw an opportunity to build some homes on a good tract of land and invited his professor to join him. He bailed out before the business ever got started, but the professor continued. Another time, two students talked one professor into buying an old Piper Cub with them so they could all learn to fly. They needed some hangar space for it, but the only available hangar at the airport was filled with boxes of baby walkers. To get the space, they had to sell the baby walkers for the owner. So there they were in the baby-walker business. They did too good a job of marketing them.

Chance will provide many opportunities to go into business, but care must be taken. Chance is random. The opportunities that chance offers are usually not the right ones. It is easy to be caught up in the emotions of the moment and the pressures of companions. A particularly persuasive social acquaintance can entice someone into deals that he or she has no business entering. A firm hand—great resolve—is needed to turn away those opportunities that are not right for oneself.

It would be easy to provide what might look like good advice on how to handle chance opportunities, but for each principle the exceptions are significant.

For example, it would be sound advice to say that one should never act on a chance opportunity without giving it considerable thought, so that the early emotions of the situation have waned and some semblance of rationality has been restored. But one can meet some entrepreneurs whose fortunes are founded on making quick decisions on a chance opportunity. Even a few hours' thought and the opportunity would have vanished.

In answer, purists maintain that the wise entrepreneur must learn to walk by an opportunity that won't wait. They are fond of saying, "There is no shortage of deals. You can't worry about all the good deals you miss. Just remember, in missing those good deals, you also miss a lot of bad ones." And that attitude is really at the heart of the entrepreneurial philosophy: Keep your bait. As long as entrepreneurs keep whatever money they have, they still have options on the deals that come their way. Once a bad deal leaves a person broke, he or she may be a long time getting back into the game. The importance of always coming out of a deal intact—no matter if the business prospers—cannot be overemphasized. Always try to get your bait back.

An 18-year-old student was thrown out of a prestigious Massachusetts prep school for hacking into the telephone system. After he had to leave school, he secured a job with Netscape where he helped develop the Netcenter Web portal that would become the company's hallmark product.

When Netscape was bought by America Online, he struck out on his own again. By now, he had more than a decade of high-tech experience under his belt. He began programming at 8 years of age, worked for an Internet service provider in high school, created web pages as a hobby, and worked for Netscape.

He had a chance to start a company with a former vice president of Netscape. The business, called Tellme Networks, brings the Internet revolution to the telephone. The company has raised $53 million from venture capitalists and has 51 employees. At 21 years old, the entrepreneur has an interesting entrepreneurial life ahead of him because he took advantage of chance opportunities.

Observation of a market need

Linda Diluco and Anne O'Callaghan envisioned a solution to a major problem faced by home-care professionals. When a home-care professional sees a patient, the professional may have to do 10 pages of writing; information goes to Medicare, the insurance company, the doctor, the agency, and the professional's own records. With NoteTime, the medical transcription and documentation company started by Diluco and O'Callaghan, the home-care professional calls into the company's digital dictation equipment, the notes are transcribed, and the information is sent via modem back to the home-care professional.

NoteTime Solutions, a second company, develops software to computerize the patient record in the home-care market. Professionals in the field work long hours doing clinical work only to come home to a mountain of paper-work. Diluco and O'Callaghan thought there had to be an easier way. Hospitals and medical practices were computerized and automated; ways existed to deal with the pressures of paperwork. In home care, however, these mechanisms did not exist. The two realized that dictation alone was not going to work without the software company. Although the two lacked knowledge of computer technology, they knew exactly what the software should do. They compensated for lack of technical knowledge by making a computer engineer a third partner in NoteTime Solutions.

Many industrial products are born of need.

Where a person works may be a particularly fertile place for discovering unsatisfied needs. Workers and managers are usually outspoken when faced with some task for which they are inadequately equipped or when they need something for their work. A roofer could not help but see the need for a shingle-nailing machine.

Sometimes this trait is called market sensitivity. Most studies of the characteristics of entrepreneurs quickly focus on this one trait as possibly being one of the most critical attributes an entrepreneur can possess. Indeed, a strong case could be developed that all business people should be sensitive to the needs and changes in the marketplace.

While market sensitivity is a critical skill, it can be a long way from recognizing a need to having a salable product. Normally, needed services are quicker and easier to develop than products. A lot of front money is often required to develop a product to meet an observed need.

Susan McCloskey, president of Office Plan, Inc., had been out of the job market for many years. "I was one of those stay-at-home moms, and I enjoy telling my story because there *is* life after your children go to college. It's just a whole different kind of life. It's not like I wanted to do this since I was 15 or anything like that. I ran political campaigns, and I think that has a lot to do with what I've learned about running a business. It's just maximizing resources to meet an objective."

Susan and two other women resigned from a new-furniture dealership and started a company that focused on providing services to people who had used furniture and equipment. "Really quite by accident, a couple of serendipitous things happened that just made us see there was an opportunity in buying and selling used furniture.

"We had a customer that was moving and wanted to sell its used furniture. I was working with a nonprofit that didn't have a budget for new furniture, and it needed some cubicles.

"Then, we had an employee who was working with another big end user who was relocating and throwing its furniture in the trash. The employee said, 'We've been looking all over town to try to find some of these for somebody and here these are in the trash.'"

The three women believed an opportunity existed in used furniture, so they rented temporary warehouse space, bought a load of used furniture, and began selling it to see if they could make a profit.

"We did everything with the idea that we were going to try it for 90 days, and pull the plug if it didn't work."

By the end of the 90 days, the three found that money could be made.

New inventions

Contrary to popular opinion, it must be said that new inventions are generally a poor vehicle for starting a business because of the high cost of research and development and the extreme difficulty in marketing them. Their track record is not great, since the market has usually not been proven, and designing an effective market-penetration strategy is perplexing. For this reason and the expense associated with marketing them, few inventions have provided the basis for a profitable start-up business. For every Polaroid, there are thousands of ideas and inventions that do nothing but lose money.

New ideas and inventions are not the easy way into business. Most money is made with well-recognized products in well-established industries.

Need. Many new ideas or inventions, which are exciting to their creators, are simply not wanted or needed. Nobody wants the thing. At least, not enough people to make the venture feasible. So entrepreneurs must first always check out the market need for an idea or invention.

Effectiveness. The idea or invention is needed but won't work in the real world. Labs are full of all sorts of marvelous technical gadgets that don't work well in real life. It is a long, long trail from an invention's prototype to a workable, commercially feasible product. A lot of money has been lost between the two points.

Business skill. Many inventors are excellent designers and idea people but often lack a basic working knowledge of how to start, market, and operate entrepreneurial ventures. They have wonderful technical expertise but have not had much experience in successfully marketing inventions.

They frequently turn to invention-marketing companies that take their money to prepare boilerplate marketing and business plans that rarely are successful in actually marketing and selling the invention.

It is, therefore, important for the entrepreneur to convince the inventor that there are many ways for them to partner. One possible solution is for the entrepreneur to license the product or service from the inventor and pay the inventor a licensing fee for all products or services that are sold. This frees up the inventor's time to do what he or she loves and does: invent new products or services. On the other hand, if the inventor would like to become part of the new venture, then the inventor could be in charge of research and development, in which case he or she would join the entrepreneur's management team.

Product line. The new idea or invention may be great and its creator cooperative, yet it does not provide the basis for an economic enterprise. One-trick ponies don't last long in show business. Similarly, one-product companies encounter serious obstacles to economic success. Institutions in the distributive trades have a strong dislike for dealing with new firms that have but one or a few products. They want to buy from established firms with many products. Moreover, short-line companies often cannot afford the overhead required to make and market the item. Furthermore, what can management do for an encore? The one new invention will surely become obsolete, often quite soon. New enterprises based on one idea or invention often fail when they are unable to follow their initial success with other products.

Market development. The money and time required to bring a new idea or invention to market, and consequently to a point of profitability, can be a lot of dollars and many years. The original idea for television can be traced to the years after the Civil War—yes, the Civil War—and considerable money was spent on its development in the 1920s, culminating in its public display at the 1939 World's Fair in New York. Still, profits from it had to wait for the 1950s. It is not for idle procrastination that most large firms fear pioneering new concepts—the price is too high for the rewards awaiting the pioneer. Bendix pioneered the automatic washing machine in the late 1930s, but Maytag cashed in on the idea in the 1950s. Bendix no longer makes washing machines. Maytag owns the market.

Various studies have indicated that it takes seven to eight years for a new venture to develop into a mature firm with some claim to success. It usually takes only one year for failure if that is to be its lot.

Finally, new inventions can be quickly copied if they prove successful. Lestoil, the first liquid, all-purpose detergent, found a nice market when it was first introduced by a small firm in the Southeast. But all of that quickly ended when Procter & Gamble brought out its "me too" product, Mr. Clean, and blew Lestoil out of its market share. Even so-called patent protection can be illusory, as people are able to design around the patent, ignore it, or successfully challenge it in court. Few companies are able to defend their patent positions successfully.

Salvage investment

Five friends invested equally in building a new theme restaurant. It was to be managed by an experienced restaurant manager, but the venture languished in losses from the beginning. Although facing bankruptcy from its inability to pay the bank loan, the five investors could not agree on what course of action to take. As their discussions turned ugly and bitter, one of the investors decided that the only way for the enterprise to be saved was to buy out the other four investors, bring in a new manager, and institute tight budgeting controls. He had to commit another $60,000 to the venture, but the turnaround plan he had developed indicated that it would be money well invested. It was; the venture became profitable.

However, not all such tales have happy endings. Often they are rat holes down which wealth is poured. One dictum seems to stand out—be cautious in giving the person who is losing money any more money to lose.

Investors who go into a business to salvage an investment must send more than money into the fray. New troops and new leadership are needed. Then they often put themselves into the managerial picture—they're into business instead of into an investment.

But having this entry strategy forced upon one is not all bad. At least there is a going enterprise and the person should have, by now, some knowledge of the business and some idea of what must be done to turn it around.

Moreover, there is the advantage of not being under any delusions—the entrepreneur knows he or she is in trouble and will have to do something fast. This position is in contrast to many beginners who are in big trouble but don't realize it until it is too late to do much about it.

Furthermore, if there are other people or firms who have invested in the business, the entrepreneur may be in a prime position to make a favorable deal with them to keep them off his back. They must agree to the entrepreneur's terms, or the entrepreneur walks away from the scene, and their investment is beyond salvage. At least, that is the position taken with them to get the necessary agreements to continue the enterprise. Trade creditors shouldn't be forgotten when setting the deal. The entrepreneur doesn't want any creditor pulling the string until there has been time to do what must be done to turn the enterprise around.

An entrepreneur who truly believes that he or she can save the business may be able to make a lot of money at this point by buying out creditors and other investors for a fraction of their claim. Many creditors are happy to get 25 to 50 cents on the dollar, if they believe the business is going to fail. But they shouldn't be paid off out of money needed to turn the business around. The business must come first, or all else is beside the point.

The working-capital needs of the enterprise must be given top priority.

Larry was in business with a partner for eight and a half years before the partnership ended. The partner had started the business in plumbing, then Larry bought half of the business and started a heating and air-conditioning division. Once he and his partner split, Larry had cash and an extensive inventory of heating and air-conditioning equipment. He had two choices: sell the equipment or start a business. The economy was too weak to sell the equipment, so his ultimate choice was to start the business. Six months later, the doors opened.

Larry wasn't a man without experience or education. He had been in the industry for 25 years and had a bachelor's degree in engineering and a master's degree in business administration. Even with his experience and education, he found that starting and operating a business has its obstacles.

"I'm here day and night. It's helped our growth, but it has taken a lot of my time."

Manpower to fuel growth has been another obstacle. Being nonunion, Larry didn't have a pool of labor waiting to be sent on a job, and finding good people was a challenge. The first year was very tough; Larry didn't even take a salary. He didn't even have a business plan, and Larry admits, "I never knew where we were going."

The bottom line is that Larry's company is successful and growing. Larry attributes this success to writing a business plan, quality of work, cash flow, timeliness, positive reputation, and the fact that the company now knows where it's going.

Expansion of part-time activity

People often develop successful enterprises from their part-time activities. A young woman developed a very profitable day-care center from her meager beginnings as a baby-sitter. A young man who was working part-time in a mini-warehouse complex saw the possibilities for several other such institutions in the area and branched out on his own.

The obvious advantage of this entry strategy is that while working part-time at something, people learn whether or not they like it, and they should learn something about what it takes to be successful in the business. Moreover, the time spent at such part-time endeavors can be used to do the research and planning needed to start a business. One of the advantages of this entry strategy is that often it can be an easy transition into a business, since activities just grow naturally with the expansion and demand. Entrepreneurs typically find themselves spending more and more time with the business to a point where it's no longer a part-time endeavor. Suddenly, they wake up and find they are in business for themselves, full-time.

Don Vinson was a professor of marketing to whom IBM came for consulting in an antitrust case. He developed a research technique that proved to be so effective in winning court cases that it made the national newspapers. It was called the ghost jury. Immediately, Vinson was deluged by other consulting contracts. As his experience and victories grew, so did the size of his business. Within two years, he was forced to retire from teaching in order to devote his full-time efforts to his new business, Litigation Sciences, Inc. A few years later, he sold his enterprise to Sache and Sache of London for a very attractive sum of money.

PROTEC Systems, Inc., is an Omaha-based employment screening firm that provides clients with access to information that can be used to verify applicants' skills and qualifications in the hiring process. The company offers a variety of services designed to improve the hiring process and reduce liability exposure. These services include verifications of social security numbers, criminal history checks, motor vehicle records, civil record checks, employment confirmations, worker compensation records, and academic or educational verifications.

Michael Matthews is a police officer turned lawyer turned entrepreneur. The idea for PROTEC came to him while in law school. He had two interests in law school: estate planning and employment law. "During my second year is when PROTEC Systems became an idea, and I did some research." Michael recognized the tremendous amounts of liability that our society has as a whole. He also recognized how rapidly employment laws were changing in comparison to the rest of the world.

Matthews began PROTEC Systems on a part-time basis and spent seven months on research and development prior to start-up. With a year left in law school, he had to decide between taking a law clerk job or opening his own business. So he gave himself a year, while still in school, to see if he could make PROTEC a money producer. By the time he graduated, Michael had created for himself a pretty good entry-level job as CEO.

Development of a home-based business

The economic and social scene is ripe for the rapid expansion of home-based businesses—enterprises that are operated out of homes. It can be an excellent entry strategy. Look at the advantages. Low overhead! Entrepreneurs are making fuller use of assets they already control. They can be with their families, taking care of their needs while still attending to business. This is a particularly attractive entry strategy for housewives and househusbands who want to generate additional money for the household.

Diane Kaminski loved to cook. She was a trained food technologist who had been forced to retire because of health problems. However, she continued making her muffins. She developed a highly nutritional muffin that was particularly tasty. As she began selling them in a few selected stores, her success came rapidly. Within three years, she owned a bakery and was operating a business, which she called "Mrs. Applegate's," on a highly profitable basis.

A great many food operations start out as home-based businesses. But a word of warning. In many areas, the local authorities strongly discourage home food operations. They have legitimate concerns over the health and safety of the business' customers.

One entrepreneur saw the potential of starting a home-based business by developing a web site that could be run out of her home. She started Webcertificate.com for people who like to shop online and want to give gift certificates. After signing up, a customer picks the amount he wants to give and pays a service fee of $2.95 to $4.95. Webcertificate then e-mails the recipient a gift certificate along with an identification number and a link to its site, where an account has been set up. The recipient can then use the account like a debit card, shopping at a range of web retailers. Online purchases are instantly deducted from the recipient's account, and the remaining balance can be viewed any time.

The Internet has been a boon to home-based businesses and will continue to be so in the future.

Desperation

One of the realities of life is that a large number of people became entrepreneurs out of sheer desperation. They didn't have jobs or money, but their appetites ignored their circumstances. The entrepreneurs were forced to go into business for themselves merely to eat. Most of these businesses start out in such service areas as mowing grass, doing maintenance service, land-scaping, and other such activities that require little or no capital investment. These businesses endure as long as the entrepreneurs' physical stamina holds up. From that desperate status, some enterprising people see attractive possibilities for establishing some sizable businesses. It is important to realize that many people go into business for themselves simply because they can't get a job anywhere else.

There is another type of desperation, perhaps just as real as that of physical needs. It is the desperation born of one's inability to achieve his or her financial goals through the established business system. Somehow the individual feels left out.

Marilyn Milne's life wasn't heading in the direction she had hoped. After returning from the Gulf War as a navy nurse corps officer, she had little money and only a part-time job. And the stress of Operation Desert Shield caused Marilyn and her husband to separate. Marilyn said she found herself lost, but not without hope. All she had to cling to was a single idea. The idea was to fulfill her dream of starting her own medical transcribing business.

Today, Marilyn's life is much different. She has fulfilled her dream to turn a single idea into reality and is the president of her own medical transcribing business, Boomerang Transcription, Inc.

Frustration with a current job can lead to desperate measures as well. An employee who worked for a company that did not believe in equity-based compensation became frustrated with its corporate policies. He quit the job and started a competing company. Great American Building Materials is not the first business started by John Amor. After college, he started and operated a painting business for four years. He admits it was on a much smaller scale than GABM. John had been in the building materials industry for 10 years. More recently, however, he was with a company for five years that did exactly what he is doing now, but that company didn't want to make him a part owner. As a result, he left the company and three weeks later decided to start his own. It took John three months to start up. He had enough money in two months, but he needed an extra month to commit to doing it.

John didn't take a lot of time to evaluate the opportunity. "I knew we were making money at the last place I was. I didn't do the projections. I didn't do a feasibility plan. I didn't do the stuff I should have done. I did some basic projections on what it was going to take, but I had no idea if the customers were going to come when we opened the door."

Well, he did it. He did it because he thought he could. "I'm able to make decisions here, where I couldn't at the last place. I was second-guessed all the time, and there was a lot of hierarchy in making decisions."

The customers did come. But so did the obstacles. "We really didn't have enough money to start." He didn't expect the payables to be as they were either. "We kind of have a rule of thumb around here that we are always to pay our suppliers on time. So I obviously expect to be paid on time. When that doesn't happen, I'm more forceful than most people, I guess."

Even with the unexpected occurrences, GABM has overcome adversity to succeed in business. According to John, success is due to service. "We pay more attention to customers. We solve their problems faster. We do some different things for our customers—delivery and other services for our market—that the competitors don't do and haven't bothered to follow us."

Commitment to growth industry

The trade press pinpoints certain industries that seem to be ticketed for abnormally rapid growth in the coming two decades. The future of telecommunications, cable television, home-maintenance services, the Internet, and several other industries have all been well recorded.

Scott Brown selected his enterprise with an eye to the future of genetic engineering and the great growth potential of the biophysics industry. His company is growing fresh water algae from which glycerol, beta carotene, and protein are extracted for animal food products.

The fundamental idea is quite simple: Position yourself in an industry that is going to grow rapidly in the next decade or so, and simply prosper with that growth. It sounds so simple and logically sound. Unfortunately, there are some problems.

The solar-energy industry is an example. Solar energy was seen as a growth industry during the oil embargo days in the late '70s and early '80s. Entrepreneurs and investors began to commit large resources to this industry. It seemed so obvious that solar energy met a market need. That trend began to cool as the oil flow increased and tensions lessened. It's a long way from recognizing a trend to the development of a profitable business based on some aspect of that industry. For example, there was the question of exactly what products were going to make money in solar energy. Of the products brought to the market that were positioned in solar energy, only a few have survived.

> A technologically chaotic industry poses real challenges to the entrepreneur to figure out just how to make money from it. Moreover, products that are pioneering new frontiers pose grave market risks.

While most people chant the virtues of solar energy, most of those same people are not willing to put their money where their mouths are. They opt for the old, proven ways, rather than spend their money on advanced solar technology.

One of the advantages in a growth industry is that there hasn't been enough time for a lot of competition to develop. Fighting over a declining market is much more challenging. Often, an entrepreneur is able to position a business as being the sole source for a certain item in that particular growth segment. Sometimes, the market is growing so fast that buyers have trouble finding suppliers. However, generalities are dangerous in discussing growth industries, as each industry is unique and must be carefully analyzed if the entrepreneur is to determine the economic viability of an enterprise in that industry.

> Overall, it is pretty good strategy to position oneself in an industry that is certain to be growing in the next decade. Essentially, it is necessary to look at the next 20 years and try to get into a business that will be prospering now and in the future.

Peyton Anderson, president and one of four cofounders of SciQuest says, "We cost-effectively and time-efficiently connect buyers and sellers in the life science market." The company uses the Internet as a vehicle for its service as a clearinghouse, connecting sellers of special equipment with the scientists who want to buy it. The Cary, North Carolina, start-up company generated more than $300,000 in its first three quarters and expected to be operating at break-even by the end of its fourth quarter.

When they were making sales calls for Baxter Scientific, Scott Andrews and Bobby Feigler, two of the SciQuest founders, learned that scientists wasted a lot of time thumbing through sales catalogs trying to find the proper equipment. The fractured state of the scientific equipment market coupled with scientists' familiarity with the Internet provided the inspiration that led to SciQuest.

Online shoppers who are looking for the best prices and good customer service are tapping into a growing number of web sites that offer consumers a helping hand through the confusing maze of e-retailers.

Comparison sites, such as My-Simon.com, bottomdollar.com, and Dealtime.com, are a fast-growing area on the Internet and many shoppers say they couldn't imagine braving the World Wide Web without them.

Many comparison sites use technology known as shopping bots—short for robots—that search the web looking for a specific product or types of products. These web sites are solving a problem that occurs in a rapidly expanding industry.

Although it is difficult to predict far into the future, it is wise to avoid industries where the future seems doubtful.

Personal preferences

There is absolutely nothing wrong with going into a business simply because one enjoys being in that business. All other arguments may be beside the point if their ventures are truly what they want to do. After being given all the warnings about the difficulties that lay ahead, a young man who wanted to open a restaurant quietly stated, "I know it's a rough business, and no one in his right mind would go into it, but that's the business I want to start. I like it." He did and prospered.

Another example of a company started simply because of enjoyment is Lotus Foods. "It's been the most incredible journey I have ever been on in my life," says Caryl Levine, equal partner and vice president of Lotus Foods.

The story is unique, and her passion is evident. Caryl and her husband, Ken, come from the East Coast where Caryl had been in higher education for 12 years. Ken was working in investments and insurance, but he was unhappy. In the early '90s, they started thinking about creating their own business together. Ken is Chinese-American, and in Rhode Island, where his family is from, Caryl and Ken met a woman from China who was attending business school. She spoke of China opening up and the business opportunities that existed. Caryl knew that if they were going to be doing business with the Pacific Rim, they needed to be living in California. She took a job at the University of California at Berkeley, and she and Ken moved to the San Francisco area.

"We took a two-month market research trip through China. We had some initial contacts from this woman, and we had some of our own. We just went on a search-and-find trip." In China, they had several business meetings. With every person they met, Caryl said, "We're not promising anything. Tell us what you need. Tell us what you want. Tell us where you think we can work best together, and then we'll take it under advisement." The two came back to the States with 90 ideas.

"The idea about grains was one we discovered ourselves when we were traveling in the southwest portion of China in Hunan province." They were in a village where every day they sat down to steaming bowls of black rice. "It was this black, raspberry color, and it had this nutty, earthy, mushroomy taste. It was absolutely delicious. We kept saying, with the proliferation of purple basil, purple potatoes, purple broccoli, and purple cauliflower, this would just go over so well in the States."

When the two returned from China and began going through all 90 of the ideas, Caryl remembered the black rice was the only idea that really excited them both. They began test marketing by going to the top gourmet restaurants in the San Francisco area. Each chef loved the black rice, but there was one problem—no supply. Throughout 1994, supply was a struggle, and black rice was not being shipped to Lotus Foods. Then in 1995, it continued to have supply problems because there was a ban on all Chinese rice exports. The first shipment of black rice from China was not until 1996.

In the interim, Lotus Foods found red rice from Bhutan. It is here that the story becomes a little eerie. Caryl continued to work at the University of California at Berkeley as the Director of Development for the Young Musicians program, which is funded in part by donations. To raise money, she decided to have a cocktail party. Catering the party was a young man named Christian. Caryl approached him: "Is this what you do for a living?" "No," Christian replied, "I'm trying to bring in this red rice from Bhutan."

Christian had been working on bringing the Bhutanese red rice to the States for five years, but he had no idea what he was going to do with it once it arrived. As a result of the meeting, Christian became Lotus Foods' master broker for red rice.

With the many supply problems encountered, Caryl knew Lotus Foods needed a domestic rice. While attending the National Rice Outlook Conference in Reno, Nevada, Caryl and Ken formed a relationship with a Texas long-grain rice farmer who used part of his acreage for harvesting organic jasmine rice. The relationship has blossomed, and Lotus Foods is selling its organic jasmine. Supply problem? Yes, Lotus Foods sold the entire 1996 harvest by October, but Caryl is urging the Texas farmer to devote more acreage to the organic jasmine rice.

An incredible journey it has been, and Ken and Caryl continue to look for products that nobody else is marketing. "These are exactly the types of products that chefs are looking for. Chefs are too busy; they don't have time to travel the world looking for unique, exciting ingredients to make their work easier. What Lotus Foods wants to do is have a reputation, so that when we bring in something new, chefs will listen and say, 'Send me 100 pounds of this, because whatever you guys bring in is high quality and exciting.'" Caryl and Ken are doing exactly what they want to do in pursuing their entrepreneurial dreams.

Inheritance

Many people find themselves in a business simply because they inherited it. This entry strategy often leads to difficulty if the heir does not really like or understand the business. The business graveyard is loaded with corporate corpses of businesses that were inherited by people who didn't know what to do with them or didn't care about them. Such developments should not occur in a well-managed business, as the entrepreneur should have foreseen the succession problems and made provisions for subsequent management. But often death gives no notice, and a business is suddenly thrust into the hands of the inexperienced or the uninterested.

A person who is likely to be the heir to an enterprise should begin learning something about it. If that person doesn't want any part of the business, then he or she should have some plan in mind to handle the problem if and when it arises.

Buying an existing business

Many advantages are gained when buying a going enterprise. It can be a good strategy. Although the advantages and disadvantages of buying businesses are examined in detail in a separate chapter, they are introduced here for an appreciation of this entry strategy.

Proven location. Often, the only way to obtain a good location in an area where a person wants to do business is to buy an existing business that has the desired location. It's not so much buying a business as buying a place in which to do business.

Fewer start-up pains. A great deal of time, effort, and money are involved in the start-up phase of all businesses. It takes time to get a business rolling. Many of these problems can be avoided by buying a going enterprise. It is true that other problems can be inherited, but at least there is an existing business with revenue flowing from an established clientele. There is an experience base upon which to expand. Buying a business can be a quick way to get to play the entrepreneurial game. It may reduce start-up time by three to five years. That is, if a person were to start a business from scratch, it might take three to five years to get to the point where the existing business already is.

Financing options. When buying a business, the entrepreneur will likely find a low-cost source of financing—the seller. Sellers, in their eagerness to make a deal, often give highly advantageous terms of sale to buyers with whom they have confidence. The deal allows the business to buy itself—the buyer pays the seller from the business' operating profits. This is a great advantage.

On the negative side, of course, is the matter of money. Often, the going business, with the desired location, costs more money up front than the entrepreneur has. He or she may sit down and crunch the numbers but then decide that starting a business from scratch is cheaper.

Here's an example: A man was trying to sell a yacht-service business for $35,000. When a potential buyer examined it, all the seller had to offer was a boat, a trailer, and a customer list. The boat was worth, perhaps, $5,000 on the open market. The buyer saw no reason to purchase the business, as he could buy similar equipment and go get the customers.

The success of this entry strategy depends a great deal upon how advantageously a person can buy the business. Typically, the best buys are in businesses that are unsuccessful but provide a good reason to believe that they can be turned around and made profitable. These issues are explored in Chapter 6, Buying a Business.

In buying a business, the question of price is always paramount. It's difficult to make money in an enterprise if the new owner pays too much for it.

Spin-offs

Perhaps one of the most highly publicized entrepreneurial entry strategies is the enterprise initiated as a spin-off from an existing company. Such spin-offs can take several forms, some friendly and some not so friendly. Paul had worked diligently in various productive capacities for a urethane-foam manufacturer in Los Angeles, but he harbored desires to have his own operation. Insightful management at the company provided him with just such an opportunity. The firm asked Paul if he was interested in beginning a separate company in Denver. The Los Angeles company would furnish know-how and initial capital for beginning operations in exchange for a piece of the action. That was its form of internal venturing. It had done so previously for another employee, and the venture had worked well. This was a good deal for everyone.

Why would a manufacturer cooperate in a spin-off operation? Simple! Money! Management was realistic enough to know that it would have eventually lost Paul to his own enterprise. Since he knew the urethane-foam-manufacturing business best, it was likely that sooner or later he would start his own operation. Entry requirements were modest. The only question was whether or not the parent organization would participate in the new spin-off. Management wisely decided to keep some control over the situation. It wanted to protect its Los Angeles markets by encouraging the new spin-offs to go elsewhere.

A more common type of spin-off, found in high-technology industries, is illustrated by Gene Amdahl, who left his high-ranking position with IBM to form Amdahl Corp., which subsequently developed a very large computer. The spin-off developed when IBM did not allow Amdahl to develop his computer for IBM, despite the fact that he had been instrumental in developing the IBM 360 series. IBM simply did not believe that there was a sufficiently large market for the monster computer to warrant its development. Amdahl proved IBM wrong.

Five people working for Texas Instruments spun off a company known as Mostek, a rapidly growing integrated-circuit manufacturer. High-technology industries are replete with examples of all sorts of little companies created as spin-offs from other operations. Sometimes, the spin-offs come about simply because the people are frustrated in the desire to do what they want under the existing corporate bureaucracy, and they must go into their own business to bring their ideas to fruition.

Other times, it is simply a matter of money. They see little use in working for some corporation and making it rich. They prefer to make themselves rich.

Some spin-offs take the form of legal divestitures of subsidiary operations by large organizations that, for one reason or another, no longer want the subsidiary in the corporate hierarchy. Thus, those people who have some contact with large organizations are often able to buy unwanted operations from them at very attractive terms. Note the word "terms," for it is the operative word. Corporate management usually must save its face by apparently disposing of the asset for an advantageous price in order to keep the balance sheet looking good. But the balance sheet does not disclose the terms of the sale—it may show a high price, but the terms are negotiated over a long period of time.

Another type of spin-off comes from one's job, but it is not a direct imitation. While working, a person may see an opportunity for a business from something in the company. An employee in the receiving department for an apparel manufacturer, for example, saw that the company was paying $400 a day in freight charges on linings made in a town 100 miles away. He did some quick figuring and made his boss an offer; he would deliver the linings each morning for $350. He made a lot of money on the little van he bought for that haul.

Spin-offs are a relatively sound strategy. They have a good track record, as there are several advantages. They do not happen overnight. The people have the opportunity to plan, and examine carefully, the technology and market for some time before they take the plunge. Armed with good information, the entrepreneur usually does not spin off until all aspects of the package are in place.

Joining a franchise system

Hundreds of franchise systems aggressively entice people to join their organizations. Undoubtedly, many people have successfully entered business by becoming a franchisee in some successful system. Equally true, many people have lost a lot of money joining the wrong system. The key is to pick the right franchise to buy into. That is not an easy decision. The highly successful franchise systems, such as McDonald's, AAMCO, and Midas, cost a lot of money to join. It is not always a low-cost way of entering business. The low-cost franchises are usually high-risk propositions that may offer the franchisee little in return.

A good franchise should offer the franchisee the following:

- Experience and know-how. Above all, the franchisor should provide the management training the franchisee needs to run the business. This is the key ingredient and major justification for franchising, and a big advantage for untrained people who are willing to work.

- Turnkey operations. Several top-flight franchise systems will locate and build the operation and turn it over to the new franchisee, ready to manage. Moreover, they will hold the franchisee's hand in the early stages of the business to make certain all goes well. Of course, it costs.

- Customers. Some franchisors, through promotion, have created a demand for their products or services that will come to the franchisee upon commencement of operations. The franchisee steps right into a ready-to-buy market.

The front-end cost of a franchise is often high, higher than what an entrepreneur would pay if he or she went into the business him or herself.

For these substantial advantages, the franchisee pays a price. An entrepreneur can start a fast-food hamburger operation a lot cheaper than one can buy a McDonald's franchise. A percentage of revenues is paid to the franchisor, thus lowering the franchisee's percentage take. Supplies often must be purchased from the franchisor at costs that seem higher than would be paid elsewhere, even though the courts frown on this practice. The franchisee is not free to manage it as he or she would like. The franchisor's policies and procedures must be followed. The business cannot be sold to just anyone. The franchisee has bought a job. This entry strategy appeals largely to people who are not able to build up their own business from scratch or do not want to do so.

Forming a nonprofit company

The first step to launching a nonprofit venture is to identify funding sources, such as private individuals, foundations, or corporations. Today, the demand for charitable donation is extraordinarily high and increasing. Competition for funding abounds among nonprofit corporations. Market research and a highly targeted game plan can be the competitive edge.

To be successful, a nonprofit venture must be seen as meeting a critical need in the community and, therefore, deserving of contributions.

For example, while day-care services are vital in most communities, such a venture may serve relatively few residents and may not attract enough funds. Fundability is a key question that must be answered before proceeding. If market research indicates that demand for a service's venture is high and obtaining funding is feasible, the next step is forming an independent 501(c)(3). This organizational structure qualifies a venture for exemption from federal income tax and enables donors to make their contributions tax deductible.

Nonprofit corporations can register with the secretary of state; however, registration does not grant tax-exempt status. Rather, a separate application must be made to the IRS. Numerous forms and documents must be completed. The IRS fees depend on the proposed project. In addition, it takes from three to six months to receive the 501(c)(3) designation. Local IRS offices are the best contacts for obtaining an application packet.

Because of the technicalities and complications involved in obtaining 501(c)(3) status, legal assistance from an attorney who specializes in nonprofit corporations and taxes is essential. The cost ranges from $2,000 to $5,000. These expenses can be reduced by doing much of the legwork and having an attorney review the entrepreneur's efforts.

In addition, some of the organizations mentioned previously as sources for funding information may also know of local management-consulting and training services available to nonprofit corporations.

Developing a constituency of potential donors takes considerable time and effort. Michael Seltzer's *Securing Your Organization's Future* offers a comprehensive workbook approach to acquiring funding and identifying potential donors. Two good funding resources include state community resource centers and local Junior League chapters. A state association of nonprofit ventures or a council of foundations can also prove to be invaluable resources. Local United Way agencies can assist with contacting such organizations.

Obtaining funding for nonprofit organizations is a challenge. Writing a sound and professional funding proposal can be a long process, since many donors review proposals only at certain times of the year. Their response is not immediate, and it may take six to 18 months to secure funding.

Many organizations use direct-mail solicitation with some success. However, direct mail is not a feasible funding source for every nonprofit. It takes time to build a constituency, and response rates average 1 to 2 percent.

The Internet has opened up many opportunities to start nonprofit companies. An example of this is 4charity.com, a site best described by its slogan: "Where shopping online raises money for charity." For consumers who are shopping online, doing it in the name of charity is a painless way to give. When they register at 4charity.com, consumers choose from a list of charities or supply their own favorites, and then link to e-shops listed, such as Amazon.com, JCrew.com, ibaby.com, OmahaSteaks.com, or cdnow.com— all of which give between 5 and 20 percent of the purchase price to the charity the customer has selected.

Another example is www.networkforgood.org. This site will help people organize their giving, as other sites do, but it also tells people how to donate their time. One can just click on Volunteer Match, enter a zip code, how far he or she will travel, special interests, and the like, and the person will get a list of charities that need help.

Company outsourcing

Today, companies of all sizes are increasingly outsourcing day-to-day management and support functions to entrepreneurial firms and focusing their internal resources on improving their primary products or services. In our globally competitive business environment, all organizations must control costs, enhance quality, and increase productivity to maintain their competitive advantages.

Outsourced services are now expanding beyond such simple clerical tasks as payroll and administering employee benefits. Now such services include internal auditing, back-auditing accounting, manufacturing, and customer services.

Coopers & Lybrand reported in the newsletter *Growing Your Business* that the most popular areas for outsourcing during 1996 were payroll, 68 percent; tax compliance, 48 percent; employee benefits/claims administration, 46 percent; maintenance/equipment, 35 percent; sales representatives or brokers, 27 percent; internal auditing, 21 percent; and accounting services, 19 percent.

Larger organizations benefit from outsourcing by obtaining outside skills and expertise that actually save time and money. Outsourcing also helps them keep their energies focused on their core business activities.

Managers of companies who outsource report that other benefits include greater efficiency and economies of scale achieved by outside providers, greater focus on core business products and growth, savings on cost of benefits and administration, less overhead investment or debt, a lighter regulatory-compliance burden, and avoiding the difficulty of finding skilled employees.

Outsourcing is an excellent entrepreneurial opportunity to pursue either through a contract or a strategic alliance with a large organization.

The success of any strategic alliance depends on selecting the right partners and developing that partnership. To make the partnership work, the entrepreneur must have

- relevant experience.
- credentials.
- financial stability.
- demonstrated commitment to quality.
- positive chemistry with the company.

Many entrepreneurs have thrived in a limited geographical niche. However, changes in technology, transportation, and communications have made what used to be a narrow marketplace into a global one. Outsourcing is a natural outcome of these changes and a great entrepreneurial strategy to use.

As companies reorganized and eliminated their in-house training function, Ada Kirby capitalized on the opportunity of outsourced training. CommTech International, Inc., helps organizations reduce operating costs by delivering customized training solutions to complex problems. These solutions can be as simple as creating a job aid or as sophisticated as building an interactive multimedia computer-based program to be delivered on CD-ROM, the Intranet, or Internet. The company primarily deals with human performance problems anywhere from employee productivity to sales training.

With approximately 25 employees, Ada is the president and CEO, and she considers herself the chief strategist. Due to the company's tremendous growth to $1.1 million in sales during the first year of operation, Ada finds that she must rely on many people. She has two general managers and a technical director that round out her core team. One general manager is responsible for the telecommunications area and the second covers all other industries. Because CommTech markets multimedia products and has all of the computer equipment in-house, she relies on her technical director to keep the company on the cutting edge of technology.

The field has become increasingly competitive since CommTech started up. "It's hard to say who the competitors are because no two companies are alike or offer the same kinds of services," said Ada. As a result, differentiation is important.

So what is CommTech's competitive advantage? In the telecommunications industry, it has subject-matter expertise that most competitors who perform computer-based training do not have. CommTech also distinguishes itself through art, graphics, and other production add-ons. Many companies use CommTech's services rather than try to build those functions in-house.

Strategic alliances, joint partnerships

The trends of increasing globalization, market complexity and instability, more competition, diversifying product mix, and technological advances have changed the way organizations are structured and do business. Overnight, new industries are created while traditional industries are being re-engineered. The rapidly decreasing product life cycle has shrunk from eight to 10 years to less than five years, making it more difficult to enter and expand a market. Consumers are pressuring corporations to be more responsive to their needs and deliver better service. All of these trends have led to corporate restructuring, buyouts, mergers, and foreign competition propelling many U.S. corporations into strategic alliances to be more productive and competitive.

Strategic alliances between entrepreneurial firms and large corporations involve inter-organizational relationships in the form of joint ventures, contracts, or stakeholder alliances between suppliers, customers, and employees. They usually involve some type of equity links, provide economies of scale, and the ability of partners to undertake large-scale projects for defined periods of time.

Entrepreneurial firms excel at getting to the marketplace more quickly with more flexibility, thus, outmaneuvering many corporate giants in commercializing innovations and new technology. On the other hand, increasing globalization makes it more difficult for smaller firms to act alone since their marketing and distribution channels tend to be inadequate. The continued need for growth capital also limits their expansion. Therefore, partnerships between large corporations and entrepreneurial ventures allow both to be more competitive and expand their businesses in an increasingly competitive global economy. Establishing strategic alliances increases valuable contacts in the business and financial community.

The success of any strategic alliance depends on selecting the right partners, capitalizing on complementary strengths as a competitive advantage, and developing the partnership. To make the partnership work, entrepreneurial firms must have relevant experience, credentials, financial stability, and goals similar to those of the corporation. Other important areas include a demonstrated commitment to quality and a positive chemistry between the partners.

Network (multilevel) marketing

Network marketing companies, sometimes called multilevel marketing firms (MLMs), have gotten a bad name because pyramid scheme stories are reported where people made money by recruiting others instead of selling

Benefits of Strategic Alliances

Faster access to new technologies

More rapidly diffused innovations

Reduction of risks and costs

Ironed-out bugs

Faster market penetration

Development of more customer-supplier relationships

Increased profitability

goods. Front loading is an illegal practice where distributors compel new recruits to purchase lots of inventory that they probably cannot sell. Companies that make money whether or not product is sold at retail are subject to prosecution.

However, there are many legitimate network marketing companies. Today, network marketing is an industry of more than $15 billion that offers aspiring entrepreneurs a chance to start home-based businesses with minimum costs.

Today, the hottest MLM companies are those that employ technology, distribution services, and innovative management to ensure long-term growth and stability. The top-ranking network marketing companies according to *Down-Line News* are Watkins, Amway, Herbalife, Nu Skin, and Shaklee.

As with any business opportunity, it is crucial to thoroughly investigate the company's history and its financial and legal records. Look for pending lawsuits, allegations of misconduct, or other types of business complaints. Check with the Better Business Bureau in the area and be cautious of start-ups that have a steep learning curve.

Licensing

A good entry strategy is to buy the licensing rights to a well-known product or name. Licensing is a $100 billion worldwide retail market with $70 billion in the United States.

Licensing offers several advantages. First, it gives the entrepreneur a unique selling advantage that the competitors don't have. In many cases, one can get above industry margins because of perceived value and the ability to charge a higher price than for a similar item that is not licensed.

The apparel industry is a natural for licensing opportunities, since most purchasers go for perceived value and reputation. Goods that have been licensed successfully include logos and products representing universities, sport teams, Disney and cartoon characters, toys, television shows, and artists.

A good source of licensing ideas is from trade shows and association meetings where entrepreneurs can meet distributors and sales representatives to learn about potential licensing opportunities and marketing trends. Other resources for licensing technology are colleges, universities, corporations, nonprofit research institutes, and information services such as the "American Bulletin of International Technology," "Selected Business Ventures" (published by General Electric Co.), "Technology Mart," "Patent Licensing Gazette," and the "National Technical Information Service."

Many corporations, nonprofit research institutes, and universities are involved in research and developing inventions or services that they do not exploit commercially since many do not represent sufficiently large markets or fit their missions. Some of these organizations license their technology through patent brokers, product-licensing information services, or their own patent-marketing departments. Some publish periodic reports containing abstracts of inventions they own that are available for licensing.

Obtaining a license can be challenging, since many licensors prefer to do business with companies that have strong financial backgrounds, manufacturing capabilities, and established marketing departments. Many license the marketing and the manufacturing for the property, or just one or the other. However, some large corporations prefer to work with smaller firms giving them a product line that enables them to spend more time with fewer wholesalers.

A word of caution—licensing a product or name does not mean instant success. The same due diligence should be performed on licensing that is required to start any kind of business. It takes detailed planning, good selling, and marketing to succeed. A solid licensing agreement can be a cost-effective marketing tool.

The key is to find a market niche and fill it with a unique product that has wide consumer appeal and will be profitable for both the entrepreneur and the licensor. It is critical to talk to prospects to see if the property being considered for license is something they would purchase. Scan consumer and trade publications to get ideas of various licensed items that might appeal to target consumers.

A good resource is the International Licensing Industry Merchandiser's Association (LIMA), which sponsors an annual show in New York City. Another key source is *The Licensing Resource Directory*, published annually by Expocon Management Associates, which lists alphabetically more than 3,000 owners and categories of products as well as tips, support organizations, consultants, designers, and other professionals specializing in licensing.

"The Licensing Letter" from EPM Communications publishes *The Licensing Letter Resource Sourcebook* listing the top 4,000 executives involved in the licensing industry. Adventure Publishing produces a weekly newsletter, *The Licensing Report*, and a monthly magazine, *The Licensing Book*.

If licensing is being considered as an entry strategy, information gathering should be started now. A licensing consultant could also be very helpful in launching this type of venture by identifying and acquiring a licensed brand or character. Some consultants represent the manufacturer seeking a license. This differs from a licensing agent who represents the property being licensed.

Most licensing consultants work by contract and receive a retainer. However, some negotiate for an additional percentage of sales agreements over and above the contract or retainer. To contact a licensing consultant, look through licensing resource directories or attend a licensing show.

Carts and kiosks

If selling in a retail location is important and if funds are limited, consider temporary retailing by locating in a vacant storefront, a pushcart, or a kiosk in a shopping mall.

According to a 2000 *Specialty Retail Report*, a Boston-based industry publication, the mall carts and kiosks segment has exploded into a $10 billion business over the past 15 years. Malls have found they can fill an empty space and generate lease income without worrying about whether a tenant can survive a long-term lease.

It's also an attractive arrangement for entrepreneurs with limited capital and business history since it's difficult to lease a prime, expensive retail location when the business is a start-up. There is no requirement to provide detailed sales and marketing plans, financial projections, and proof to a mall manager that the business can pay its bills and generate enough sales to pay a three-year, five-year, or longer lease.

Temporary tenancy is a low-cost way to test the market and product, and to more accurately forecast future sales. Start-up and operating costs are also lower. Less money is necessary on rent, decoration, stock, labor, and other costs.

However, it is important to find the right location by visiting various malls and counting the foot traffic and potential customers. The suitability of products to the specific mall and location within the mall should be determined.

Once a good location is found, the mall manager should be asked if the mall has a temporary-tenant program, and other entrepreneurs in the mall asked about their selling experiences and working with mall management. The best temporary lease terms can be negotiated by presenting the venture idea professionally: provide a sketch or picture of what the storefront or cart would look like; show the products and be prepared to explain how sufficient stock will be maintained; show the leasing agent a copy of the business plan. Temporary-tenant programs are attractive when a venture is selling inexpensive impulse goods that lend themselves to demonstration or sampling. Personalized merchandise also sells well.

To learn more about temporary retailing, contact the National Retail Federation, (202) 783-7971, the largest retail industry trade group.

If a person is prepared to work long hours and carefully plan for operating in a temporary location, this is a great way to launch a new business. It is also a good expansion and growth strategy to either move out of a home-based business or add new outlets to a permanent location.

Business Strategy

Strategy Considerations
What business do I want?
What is my exit?
How big should the firm be?
What is the profit source?
Who will own the enterprise?
What money sources
  will be used?
What marketing strategies
  will be used?

Most successful entrepreneurs have some general business strategy when they begin the enterprise. While there are a few common areas in which some strategic considerations should be made, the wide range of business situations in which people find themselves precludes any definitive coverage of the subject. The following are some of the general business areas that should be considered.

What business do I want?

Precisely, what will be sold and to whom will it be sold? Bob Teller has made a fortune selling ice-cream bars and lemonade from small stands located in shopping malls. That's all he sells. No soda pop, no hot dogs, no candy, or popcorn. Just ice-cream bars and lemonade! He knows exactly what business he is in and how to make money doing it. It would be easy to say that he is in the fast-food business, but that would only be one way of looking at his business. Another way is to consider him as selling rewards to thirsty or weary shoppers.

There are usually several ways of looking at a business, only one of which is to literally describe it by what it sells. Often valuable insights are gained if one looks at a business as a vehicle for delivering a package of buyer benefits.

What is the firm really selling to its customers? A carpet company does not sell some material that covers the floor. It sells an attractively decorated interior. A machine-tool maker doesn't sell an automated turret lathe. It sells profits. A garment maker doesn't sell clothes. It sells self-esteem, image, social acceptance, and career advancement. What package of benefits will the new venture sell?

Sometimes businesses define themselves by their operating or delivery systems. The fast-food retailers are into the speed business—cheap food, fast. Domino's Pizza is in the home-delivery business. A mobile poodle-grooming firm is in the convenience business: making it easier for people to buy from it.

Consequently, it is no small matter to define precisely what business one is in. The enterprise can be looked at in many different ways.

What is my exit?

Sooner or later the entrepreneurs will either want to get out of the business or will be forced out of it. They should plan for the exit now: make it be their choice, not someone else's. Many entrepreneurs, as part of their basic strategy, plan to build the company up to a certain level of operations and then sell it. They don't want to stick around to manage a large company. Consequently, much of what they do will be with an eye toward increasing the firm's ultimate sales price. If they want to sell their enterprises, then entrepreneurs must create something that is worth buying.

Other times, venture managers plan to take the new enterprise public once its size and profitability allow it. If the strategy is to go public with the venture, then managerial decisions and actions will be vastly different than if the plan is to keep the firm as personal property.

How big should the firm be?

Often, the market or the situation dictates how big a firm should be. There is an optimum size for most economic ventures, a level of operations that maximizes their efficiency and productivity. Some cannot survive unless they grow to a certain size. That level of operations is often called critical mass, a term taken from the field of physics.

Until the firm is so big, it just cannot be a serious player; often it cannot even operate. Owners of small businesses often complain about their inability to advantageously buy what they need. Many suppliers won't sell to small accounts. Often, there are carload or truckload minimum-order size requirements. One packaging supplier required its buyers to buy at least one day's production run. Thus, firms often have to get to a certain size just to be able to buy what they need at a competitive price.

Other times, certain enterprises should remain small. If they grow, they'll lose their advantages. Often the size of the firm is limited by the entrepreneur's inclinations and limitations. Some owners don't want a big business, while others are eager to reach for the sky.

What is the profit source?

Some firms plan to make their money by selling for high profit margins, while others strive to make profit from doing a large volume of business. Which will it be for the new business: profit margin or volume?

Who will own the enterprise?

Many entrepreneurs want no partners. They want the whole enterprise for themselves. Yet, many other owners plan to use other people's money; they aggressively seek outside investors and trade partial ownership (equity) in exchange for money.

What money sources will be used?

Whose money will be used to finance the enterprise? It can be a matter of strategy, although it is granted that often it is a matter of whose money can be obtained.

What marketing strategies will be used?

Much strategic thinking must be devoted to markets and marketing. Who is the target market? How will the market be penetrated? Much more about this appears in later chapters.

Conclusion

There are, obviously, many ways to go into business for oneself, some better than others. The preoccupation with one entry strategy should not be allowed to blind entrepreneurs to other opportunities that may come along. However, they should welcome those that allow them to reach the cash break-even point as quickly as possible with whatever funds have been invested.

Buying a Business

Learning Objectives

In this chapter, students will learn

- Reasons for buying a business instead of starting one.
- Why owners sell their businesses.
- Where to find a good business for sale.

The entrepreneurial trend is growing and here to stay. However, there is a new model of entrepreneurship emerging—the buyout entrepreneur. These are individuals who buy a business rather than start one from scratch. Many entrepreneurs are finding that big returns come from the growth and revitalization of existing businesses.

The number of businesses for sale as well as the number of buyers is increasing. This includes corporate acquisitions and larger corporations that are looking for smaller companies to provide innovative products in new markets. In addition, the impact of downsizing by larger corporations has encouraged corporate refugees to become entrepreneurs, and a good proportion find buying a business more appealing than launching a new one.

The often-quoted statistic "six out of every 10 new businesses fail during the first six years" represents the risk that is involved in starting a new venture. Overall, a successful business needs an operating history of five to eight years to sufficiently prove its concept, market, prices, location, and management.

In a start-up venture, all operational aspects are unknown. There is a high degree of uncertainty in starting a new venture from scratch. Some entrepreneurs estimate that they will break even in six months. However, it might take 18 to 24 months, during which time they need unanticipated operating capital. Typically, penetrating a market takes two to five times longer than originally projected.

Buying an existing business, on the other hand, is different. One can equate the differences to those of buying a pre-owned house versus building a new house. With a new house, owners worry about everything—putting in the lawn, other landscaping, and fencing; choosing the carpet and paint; installing the draperies. With the pre-owned house, all these things have been done, and new owners may make minor changes to get the house the

Purchasing a business without thoroughly evaluating the venture and its financial statements.

Accepting inadequate financial statements.

Purchasing a business within a shrinking market.

Purchasing a business in an industry with too many competitors.

Thinking you can manage the business better than the owner without any prior business experience in the industry.

way they want it. Similarly, when an entrepreneur purchases a business, there is an existing reputation, customer base, suppliers, equipment, leases, and cash flow. The infrastructure and management team are also in place.

Many entrepreneurs are more successful as turnaround artists. They grow ventures rather than start them. They are not creator types with ideas that could revolutionize the marketplace. Instead, they recognize good business opportunities and make an existing venture more profitable. One successful entrepreneur claimed that he had only two failures out of 10 ventures—the two businesses he started from scratch. The other business successes were all ventures he had purchased and grown.

Buying an existing business is a good entrepreneurial strategy when the business opportunity has been thoroughly evaluated and analyzed. It may take up to a year to find the right purchase. It is also a wise strategy to match one's interests and industry experience with an opportunity to purchase a business.

Smart Strategies

- Buying the right business to reduce the time involved in planning, organizing, and launching a new start-up.
- Negotiating with the seller to carry back debt and provide good terms so that the business can generate enough cash to buy itself back in five years.
- Asking the seller to continue working in the business for three to six months to help the transition and provide training.
- Seeking outside help from accountants, lawyers, and bankers to assist in assessing opportunities to purchase a business.
- Always asking for audited financial statements for the past three to five years. Keep in mind that for most small businesses the owner will not be able to provide audited financial statements. If this is the case, be sure to perform an adequate review of the financial information—starting with current and prior years' tax returns.
- Hiring a business owner of a similar business outside of the competitive area to help evaluate purchase opportunities.
- After analyzing historical sales and profits, preparing one's own projections of future profitability and growth potential.

Advantages

Overall, the risks associated with entrepreneurship are usually fewer in buying a business than in starting a new business. There are many advantages to buying an existing business, especially if the buyer knows the owner and the business. There are advantages to consider in purchasing a business, including lower risk, management training, and lower asset costs.

It is often easier to assess the risks involved in buying a going business than those inherent in developing a new venture. The buyer can evaluate a known quantity with an existing location, current customers, staff, suppliers, and a reputation.

The first two years of any business are the riskiest, and consequently, the failure rate is the highest. It can take two or three years to reach the break-even point with a start-up and another five years to become stable and successful. A business buyer should look for existing businesses that have already weathered that initial time frame.

Two major factors help limit risks. First, a buyer has better information on both the operating characteristics of the venture and its established market than an entrepreneur would have with a start-up enterprise. Much of the market speculation and sales forecasting are eliminated, since the business already has a track record. Therefore, better and more accurate forecasts can be made.

Second, and perhaps more important, the buyer usually is required to invest fewer dollars when purchasing an existing business. This relates back to the seller financing the majority of the venture. The more the seller is willing to carry back in debt, the higher the price he or she can expect to charge for the business. Lending terms negotiated with the seller of the business are usually better than those available from other money sources such as banks and lenders. The buyer should be as concerned with how the purchase can be structured as with the actual price involved.

Management training provided by the seller is another advantage of buying an existing business. Often, the seller will teach the buyer how to run the business. Much inside knowledge and expertise can be exchanged. Consequently, the buyer of an existing business may not have to learn those important start-up lessons the hard way. Additionally, a financially involved seller is motivated to hold the buyer's hand for a longer period of time.

> The business success a seller has achieved costs the buyer more money. Likewise, business failure costs the seller money.

Finally, it is usually cheaper to acquire assets by buying a business than it is to purchase them new. The buyer can often purchase the building and equipment for 10 to 20 percent of what it would cost new. Some businesses are purchased just for their locations or for the leases they have with the building owner.

Frequently, the assets of an existing business are not worth much, except for their use in that particular business. Thus, an entrepreneur may be able to get into this type of business with less capital than by starting a new venture. In essence, the buyer is purchasing used equipment at an attractive price. This happens more often when acquiring a firm that is in trouble.

Valid Reasons for Selling

One might wonder, "Why would anyone sell a good, profitable business?" Many good businesses are for sale, and for good reasons (although there are also bad reasons).

Retirement

There comes a time when many owners tire of their businesses and want to retire. They are looking for a way out, and often, it is not easy. An owner may have an entire estate tied up in the business. If it cannot be sold for a reasonable sum, he or she is stuck with it, unless the owner takes the loss and accepts a lower price to sell it.

> **Good Reasons to Sell**
> Retirement
> Other interests
> Illness or death
> Internal disputes
> Business too complex
> Inadequate capital
> Doubtful future
> Exit strategy planned

Owners who want to retire are not under much time pressure unless their health is failing. They can wait to get the deal they need, as long as the business generates enough cash. One seller spent 10 years trying to retire.

Other interests

Owners can lose interest in a business when something else grabs their attention. They want their money out of their businesses so they can put it into something else that either has more profit potential or is more fun. This motive can be compelling because they may feel an urgency not to miss out on the other opportunity. Perhaps another business has become available, and they need to act quickly. Often this motive can be strong because the owner has lost zeal for the business. Each day is a drag. Naturally, potential buyers should ask themselves if they would eventually react to the business in the same manner.

Unfortunately, this reason is often used to disguise other motives that are not good. The buyer has good reason to wonder why anyone would leave one business, proven to be good, for one that is unproven. All in all, a buyer has a right to be suspicious of sellers who claim that they want to sell because they need the money to invest elsewhere. Owners of successful firms usually are able to come up with funds for such acquisitions.

Illness or death

Owners get sick and owners die. When they do, their businesses will likely be for sale. Both the motive and the urgency to sell are strong. It's tough to go on in a business when one is ill.

Knowing that illness is a good reason for selling, some sellers feign sickness to disguise their real motives. While it can be touchy prying into such personal matters, there are ways to do it. If an owner is ill, other people will know it.

Internal disputes

At times, opportunities to either buy a business or buy into a partnership arise because of disputes among the owners. Naturally, the basis for such disputes requires careful examination lest the new owner become enmeshed in the same problems. A troublesome associate should be avoided. The entrepreneur may end up having to buy out of the trouble.

Business too complex

Strangely, people do sell businesses that have become either too difficult for them to manage or too time-consuming to suit their desires. The business, in its early days, may have been just what the owner wanted, but it grew beyond the owner's skills or interests. Naturally, such firms are not bought cheaply, nor is the owner usually pressed to sell them.

Inadequate capital

Some enterprises are for sale because the owners realize that they do not have and cannot get the capital needed to make the businesses profitable. If entrepreneurs have enough money to do the job, they may be able to buy promising businesses.

Doubtful future

Business owners become fearful of the future for one reason or another. A plastic injection molder for computer OEMs put his highly profitable ($400,000 profit on $1,000,000 sales) business up for sale. His stated reason was that he had lost interest in it and had other things he wanted to do. The truth: He was afraid a big depression was coming, and he wanted to sell while times were good. He wanted $1 million cash for the business; he would then walk off into the sunset. When a business recovery changed his outlook, he took the business off the market.

Exit strategy planned

Some entrepreneurs start a business with a plan to exit once they have hit a certain level of sales—often in only a few years. They enjoy and profit from starting and selling businesses, which makes better use of their skills. Many entrepreneurs have difficulty transitioning into the management role and prefer to exit, cash out, and start new ventures.

Problematic Reasons to Sell

While the previous factors would encourage buyers, there can be forces at work that would make the business unattractive to most buyers.

Deteriorating markets

Markets grow and markets decline. Astute managers have a feel for their markets and know what the future has in store for them. It is better to bail out before the market sours than to wait for the bottom to fall out. Naturally, a deteriorating market is a serious flaw that makes a firm an unattractive acquisition. Unless a buyer sees some way of reversing the market trend, knows something the owner doesn't, or can buy the business for a price that allows it to be profitable at the lower market levels, it's best to pass up such opportunities.

Problematic Reasons
Deteriorating markets
Product obsolescence
Loss of key people
Lease problems
Legal problems
Inefficient operations
Poor location
Competitive developments
Problems with key suppliers
Dependency on key account

Product obsolescence

Products come and go. A firm can develop a product that leads the industry for a while, only to fail when some other company designs a superior product whose attributes the firm cannot duplicate. The enterprise's research and development failed to keep the company abreast of the market. Unless entrepreneurs have the skills needed to remedy such weaknesses, they should avoid companies whose products or services are becoming obsolete.

Loss of key people

The owner of an electronics firm placed it on the market when he learned that he was losing his key design engineer, who created the company's most profitable products. He had no faith in his ability to replace the designer. He offered the design engineer a piece of the company to entice her to stay, but to no avail. It was too late. A buyer should beware unless he or she can bring someone to replace that departing engineer or can cut a deal with the engineer to stay.

Lease problems

Many a retail store owes its success to a fortunate lease. Either the location is good or the rent is relatively low. But leases end. When they do, firms may be forced to move, sell to the new lessee, or have the rent increased. In any event, the firms' operating characteristics may change for the worse.

Buyers must examine leases carefully. Will the landlords accept them as tenants? Will the terms change? Can they get leases extended? It is very difficult to sell a business in the last few years of a lease, if the landlord is not fully cooperative in writing a new lease for a buyer on attractive terms. Entrepreneurs shouldn't buy businesses assuming they can then renegotiate the leases.

Legal problems

The scope of potential legal problems is so vast that it precludes an exhaustive analysis. Perhaps a large liability suit is pending. Perhaps the company is about to be sued for patent or trademark infringement. Perhaps there are problems with environmental pollution. Astute entrepreneurs won't want to buy in on a lawsuit. Unless they can resolve the problem, they pass on it.

If the legal problem is the only thing blocking a purchase, a buyer might be able to make an offer with a contingency clause that requires resolution of the legal trouble before a final closing of the sale can take place.

Inefficient operations

Each economic unit has inherent operating characteristics that affect its costs. Some plants, because of design, equipment, or location, are relatively high-cost units. Typically, it is the high-cost plants in an industry that are for sale. The low-cost plants are so profitable that the owners are not eager to sell.

When Georgia-Pacific was buying fir plywood plants in the Pacific Northwest many years ago as its basic strategy for entering the plywood industry, it was offered many of the industry's inefficient plants or ones with marginal timber supplies.

Unless a buyer can spot the reason for a company's inefficiency and figure out how to remedy it, it's best to avoid structurally inefficient firms.

Poor location

A poor location is often the reason a firm is for sale. Upon realizing that the company's location precludes ever making a satisfactory profit, the owner hopes to unload the beast and go elsewhere. Poor locations should be avoided almost at any price. One will likely work hard to little avail trying to overcome a bad location.

Competitive developments

New competition ready to enter the market may pose some serious problems. The advent of IBM's PC microcomputer certainly affected the fortunes of all the smaller companies in the industry.

The competition from large supermarket chains has made many independent grocery stores change their business strategies. A Boulder, Colorado, supermarket operator sold her chain of three stores for $3 million upon learning that two large chains intended to invade the nearby Denver market. She decided it was time to cash in her chips while she still had some. National Tea bought her stores but was driven out of the market within two years by the intense competition.

Problems with key suppliers

Some businesses are totally dependent upon a vital supply of products and/or services from their vendors. Without them, the firm is out of business. Such sources of supply have been known to falter or become unavailable for one reason or another. Many importers rely on foreign suppliers whose continued existence is a matter of daily concern.

Perhaps the firm's profits have largely resulted from some low-cost input factors—labor, raw materials, or components. But prices change. Labor costs can go up. Raw material prices can increase. A firm's future profitability can be jeopardized by changing input prices. Sometimes these changes are sufficient to make an owner want to sell.

Dependency on key account

Often service businesses find themselves surviving due to one or two major accounts. Entrepreneurs should analyze carefully the client list and contractual relationships when buying service businesses. The seller may know something about a key account switching to another firm.

Where to Look

Astute buyers spend sufficient time evaluating potential businesses and analyzing the marketplace, thus avoiding hasty decisions. Many experts recommend that entrepreneurs spend at least one year to find and evaluate businesses that they would like to purchase. The following resources and checklist for buying an existing business can help in conducting a productive search.

Resources for buying a business

There are various resources available for information on buying businesses.

The following list is a starting place and demonstrates that there are many sources to tap during a search. Potential buyers answering an ad should present themselves as fully qualified persons in order to receive a response. They will probably be asked some qualifying questions to determine if the sellers want to continue the process. A successful search requires diligence and hard work.

Newspapers. The easiest place to start looking for a business to buy is in the classified section of newspapers under "Business Opportunities." The Sunday edition usually has the most listings.

The "Mart" section of the *Wall Street Journal* appears on Wednesdays and Thursdays. The *New York Times* Sunday edition contains several pages of diverse businesses for sale. There are also specialized newspapers, such as *The Business Opportunity Journal*. A local library may have similar publications to review.

Resources
Newspapers
Industry trade magazines
Banks
Business professionals
Business brokers
Business owners
Chambers of commerce
SBA and economic
   development agencies
Trade sources
Business bankruptcy listings
Friends

Industry trade magazines. Many of these magazines and trade papers contain a classified section with business opportunities that are industry specific.

Banks. Some banks publish newsletters of business opportunities. There may be a charge for some newsletters or catalog listings. Bankers can be helpful in a search, and establishing a relationship with them early on is a must. It might not be long before the entrepreneur will be asking them for lending assistance to help finance a venture.

Business professionals and members of the infrastructure. Talk with attorneys, accountants, venture capitalists, investment bankers, insurance agents, sales people, and others in the entrepreneurial infrastructure. These professionals often know of business opportunities that are never advertised.

Business brokers. These brokers have extensive lists of businesses for sale. They work for business owners and are paid a commission to market and sell businesses. A business broker's fee typically runs between 5 and 10 percent of the purchase price. A response to an ad may very well be to a business broker.

It may be possible to negotiate a buy-broker agreement, in which the broker agrees to seek out companies. The *Yellow Pages* may have listings of business brokers. A list of brokers who belong to the International Business Brokers Association (www.ibba.org) may be obtained by contacting the association at (888) 686-4222 or e-mail at info@ibba.org.

Business owners. Some potential buyers look for businesses they might be interested in purchasing and contact the owners to ask them if they are interested in selling. On the average, about three out of every 10 calls attract some interest. If they are not interested in selling, they might be able to refer buyers to someone else.

Chambers of commerce. Some chambers of commerce maintain buying and selling services for businesses in their areas.

SBA and state or county economic development agencies. The Small Business Administration and other economic agencies frequently know of businesses for sale and can provide referrals.

Trade sources. These include suppliers, vendors, distributors, manufacturers, and trade associations. Entrepreneurs check with these sources about potential businesses for sale, as they are an excellent resource for industry-specific businesses.

Business bankruptcy listings. Most local business journals publish a list of businesses that have filed for bankruptcy. For entrepreneurs who feel they have the skills to become turnaround artists, these listings may produce good leads.

Friends. One's friends have a wide network of contacts. Some buyers let their friends know what kind of businesses they are looking for and ask friends to notify them of any opportunities. Some might even offer an incentive to persons who provide qualified leads. Paying people for their time and effort is a good business practice.

Checklist for buying a business

There are both personal considerations and business factors to analyze and evaluate when thinking about buying an existing business.

❏ **Determine goals.** Identify goals for purchasing the business. Will the business being considered match these goals?

❏ **Evaluate expertise.** What are the entrepreneur's strengths and weaknesses? Do they complement the venture? Will existing knowledge and skills be of help in operating the business? No one is strong in all areas of entrepreneurship.

❏ **Consider lifestyle.** There is prestige in owning a business. Does this business fit the entrepreneur's status and image needs?

❏ **Review tax returns for the past three years.** A seller won't exaggerate the business's worth to Uncle Sam. If the seller cannot provide this financial information, then this is an indication of something amiss.

❏ **Research.** The Better Business Bureau can determine if customers have filed complaints about the business. For a fee, Dun & Bradstreet (www.dnb.com) will provide its estimate of the worth of the business. Local Dun & Bradstreet offices are listed in the *Yellow Pages*.

❏ **Assess the current employees.** A buyer is not only buying the company but also the employees. Who are they? Will they stay? Is there good chemistry among them? Do they appear to be ethical and honest? Personnel files should be checked for any disciplinary actions and poor evaluations.

❏ **Evaluate economic and political conditions.** What are the industry trends for this business? Is the market increasing or decreasing? What is the growth potential? What is the competitive environment? Is the market overcrowded with competition?

❏ **Meet with the customers.** What is their level of satisfaction with the business? If this is a service business, the buyer should ask for a complete list of customers during the past year and then call as many as possible. If this is a walk-in business, the buyer should talk to customers who come into the store and talk to former customers to find out why they are no longer buying from this store.

❏ **Choose the right seller.** This person should be both cooperative and willing to disclose all the financial, personnel, customer, and legal information related to the venture. If the owner resists sharing this information, a buyer has reason to be concerned.

These are just some of the key factors to analyze when considering purchasing a business. A good reference is C.D. Peterson's *How to Leave Your Job & Buy a Business of Your Own*, published by McGraw-Hill, Inc.

Evaluating this information is only half of the equation. Entrepreneurs should use a combination of both research and intuition in deciding whether a business is right for them and if they should make an offer to buy it. Although it may be a good acquisition opportunity, entrepreneurs will need good management skills and business experience.

Conclusion

The seller and buyer should come to a mutual agreement on the terms of buying the business, and then go to an attorney to have the agreement written in legal terms for the sale. Do not vary from the principles of the original agreement between the seller and the buyer.

While most potential buyers are obsessed with obtaining the seller's financial records and income tax returns, they must be careful when using such data. The records can be flawed. Perhaps the expenses were not as much as reported for tax purposes. Perhaps the seller has been charging many personal expenses as business items. Perhaps some cash income has been "forgotten." In any case, the seller may try to make a potential buyer believe that his or her business is actually more profitable than it appears to be on the tax return. Once the seller discloses that he or she has been playing fast and loose with the books, what can a buyer believe?

It takes investigation and careful reconstruction of a seller's financial statements, combined with the entrepreneur's plans for the business, to develop one's own set of projections for the firm.

Entrepreneur's Resource Checklist

Books

Honigmann, Ernest J. *The Arcane World of Buying and Selling a Small Business, and How to Deal with It*. iUniverse, Inc: 2001.

Honigmann, Ernest J. *Buying and Selling a Small Business: A Complete Guide to a Successful Deal*. Commerce Clearing House: 1999.

Paulson, Ed. *Complete Idiot's Guide to Buying and Selling a Business*. Alpha Publishing House: 1999.

Robb, Russell. *Buying Your Own Business*. Adams Media Corp.: 1997.

Tuller, Lawrence W. *The Small-Business Valuation Book*. Adams Media Corp.: 1998

Yegge, Wilbur M. *A Basic Guide for Buying and Selling a Company*. John Wiley & Son: 1996.

Contacts

World M&A Network, NVST, Inc. (www.nvst.com) 1100 Dexter Ave North, Seattle, WA 98109. (800) 843-9559. This organization publishes *The World M&A Network*, a monthly 100-page magazine that includes a listing of sellers, buyers, and financing information for $595 a year.

RMA-Risk Management Association (www.rmahq.org), 1 Liberty Pl., 1650 Market St., Suite 2300, Philadelphia, PA 19103, (800) 677-7621. *RMA Annual Statement Studies* is a valuable source of industry statistics and financial ratios on every industry. It is available in most libraries.

Business Valuation

CHAPTER

7

Learning Objectives

In this chapter, students will learn to
- Determine the market value of a business the entrepreneur's way.
- Use off balance sheet valuations to raise the price of a business.

After an entrepreneur has located a business that meets his or her personal criteria, it's time to figure out how much it's worth to the entrepreneur buyer. Notice the qualification—to the buyer. A business can be worth one amount to one person and another amount to someone else. For example, a consultant was looking at some golf courses to buy for a golf professional who wanted to own his own course. One of the major obstacles encountered was that most of the acceptable courses were grossly overpriced when analyzing their values based on expected cash flows and rates of return on investment. The prices had been bid up by rich golf enthusiasts whose marginal utility of the dollar was low. These people weren't buying on the basis of rational investment analysis. They were buying emotionally.

Nowhere was this principle more evident than in the Resolution Trust auctions of the Landmark golf and resort properties in Palm Springs, California. While the syndicate representing the former golfing members could bid up to $125 million for the course, it was far outbid by an outside company that was looking at the property from a different point of view. The company intended to turn the properties into public courses to maximize revenues. What the business was worth to the successful bidder was quite different than to the golfing members.

What's the Business Worth?

It doesn't make any difference if the seller wants thousands for a hot dog cart. The seller will either get what the market will pay for the cart or keep the cart. Naturally, if there is a large discrepancy between how a buyer values the property and what the seller thinks it is worth, the buyer will have some difficult negotiations ahead. A buyer should not be discouraged. Deals are made after lengthy negotiations bring two widely divergent parties together.

The seller's attention should be kept focused on hard financial data, such as profit projections that are based on the information supplied.

It is imperative not to react to the seller's initially high price. The buyer's position must be that the situation needs to be evaluated before he or she knows how much the business will be worth.

Later, the buyer may be able to develop ways of appearing to give the seller the asking price while, in reality, buying it for what he or she thinks it is worth.

Let the seller set the price if the buyer is allowed to set the terms. For example: I'll give $1 million for the car. The terms: I will pay in the year 2285. Ridiculous? Not really. Some firms are sold on essentially the same terms. The buyer never has to come up with any up-front money. The business furnishes the cash and the buyer pays the seller over a long period of time.

The Value of a Business

Value is a very complex issue. Economists and philosophers have argued value theory for centuries with little agreement. Thus, one should not expect a firm answer to the question of what a business is worth. However, the following methods seem to be the ones used by most entrepreneurs:

- Market value of net assets
- Value of future earnings
- Off balance sheet valuations
- Replacement cost

Market value of net assets

Often people confuse market value with book value. These are two entirely different concepts that must be thoroughly understood before proceeding. If someone wants to sell or buy a used car, he or she might have checked the "Blue Book" value of the car to give an indication of the market value or general going rate for the car. But suppose the car had new tires and fancy wire wheels. It would be worth more. Or perhaps, it had been painted a disgusting color. This would make the car less valuable.

The book value of a business is its value as indicated by the firm's accounting statements. It is the difference between the firm's total net assets and total liabilities. Accounting statements deal with historical costs. Seldom do they have any relationship with the market value of the assets. Sometimes firms are worth a lot more than their book values, often much less. Suppose some assets have gone up in value since their purchase but are carried on the books at their historical cost. The result is the company is worth more than its book value.

Such an error caused the owners of a small plywood manufacturing company in Eugene, Oregon, to sell their business for $15 million, a company whose timber stands alone were worth more than $50 million. The timber was carried on the books at $7 million dollars, the purchase price in 1970.

A firm may also carry on its books some expensive asset that is worthless. Perhaps a company's computer and software are obsolete but are shown on the books at original price.

Buyers can erase all thoughts that a firm's book value is relevant to a buyer's interests. They must develop their own evaluations of the firm's assets. The book value is only one piece of information. The first method for valuing a business is determining the market value of its assets, sometimes referred to as its liquidation value. If the business were dismantled and everything sold, how much money would be raised?

While the company's liquidation value is a value below which a rational seller typically will not go, it is not an easy figure to develop. Many assets have no real market value. Many assets vital to the business are worthless on the market. An insolvent ski manufacturer discovered this fact when forced to sell ski-manufacturing equipment for 10 cents on the dollar. There's not much demand for ski-manufacturing tools and dies. They are of value only to another ski manufacturer. So the buyer had all the bargaining power. The other ski manufacturer only had to offer enough to get the seller out of town. And that was how Phoenix Ski was started.

Even inventories and accounts receivable cannot be assumed to be worth what the books say. Many inventories are outdated, damaged, or unsalable. Owners may be lucky to get 10 cents on the dollar for them. Accounts receivable may provide a shock. One buyer discovered significant accounts carried on the books that were 10 years old. There was no way to collect them!

Valuing a business by painstakingly determining the market value of its assets is a difficult, time-consuming process. It is not surprising that most buyers avoid it. Fortunately, they happen to be right in ignoring market value in most instances. They are not buying a business to liquidate it. They are buying it to make money from its operations. The assets may or may not come along for the ride. Sometimes, a buyer will buy the business but lease the assets from the seller, who retains title to them.

The market value method usually establishes the lowest value for the business. It can be the starting point for negotiations.

Value of future earnings

What the buyer really wants to buy is the firm's earnings. He or she wants to buy a money-making machine. What is the cost of a money-making machine? It depends upon how much money it will make. Combine that with its reliability. A buyer will pay more for a company that has predictable earnings based on historical financials than for one with a volatile earnings pattern.

The business should make enough cash flow to return the entrepreneur's investment plus interest in three to five years.

The Basis of Valuation

Valuation begins with the interest rate, the prime rate, proceeds through the price-earnings ratios, and ends with an analysis of the firm's cash flow. Each of these matters deserve some consideration. They are exceptionally important in all business thinking. Understanding value theory is a vital part of entrepreneurial education.

First, the interest rate: All investment decisions rest on the interest rate. Suppose a buyer has $100,000. He or she could buy a business with it or buy some government bonds. The rate of return for government bonds has fluctuated between 3 percent to 6.5 percent over the past five years. So let's use a 5 percent rate of return for the purpose of this example. At a

5 percent rate of return, the price-earnings ratio of this type of investment is 20 (100 percent/5 percent).

Since a business is considerably more risky than a government bond, the buyer is usually going to pay a much lower PE ratio (price-earnings) for the business than he or she would for the government bond, unless inflation is a factor.

People don't buy the past; they buy the future. A business can be a great inflation hedge; a bond a disastrous one. Thus, the price of a business goes up as the buyer perceives its future as a great protector of purchasing power.

EBIT. Commonly, brokers and others connected with the sale of businesses use a concept called earnings before interest and taxes (EBIT) as the basis for applying a multiple for deriving the price of the business. For example, if a broker determines that the EBIT for a business is $250,000 and it feels a fair multiple for the business is four, then it will price the business at $1 million.

Multiples are statistics such as price-to-earnings ratios and sales multiples used to value a company. Determining what value to use as the multiple can be industry specific, but there is always room to negotiate.

Earnings after tax. Publicly held companies are valued on earnings after tax and interest. Therefore, if a public company has an after-tax profit of $300,000 and the analysis gives it a 20 multiple, then it has a value of $6 million.

Why would the public company have a higher multiple than the privately owned company? The higher PE ratios now being paid for many public firms have growth elements factored into them. People are paying now for higher earnings that they think will be forthcoming. They are betting on the future.

Many buyers feel that privately held companies should be valued on after-tax profits just as the public companies but with a lower multiple. Taxes and interest are costs of doing business if the buyer has to assume the owner's debt or borrow money to buy the business. The government will always want to take its fair share of the profits.

The seller likes to use EBIT and use a high multiple to establish the price of the business. It is to the buyer's advantage to determine the price of the business using after-tax profit and use a low multiple.

Here are some rules of thumb as a starting point. First, sellers are often shocked to discover that they are lucky to get three times last year's earnings for their company (PE = 3). Sometimes the PE ratio is 1 to 2, depending upon the buyer's view of the firm's stability of earnings and negotiating power. Everything is modified by negotiating skills and power. It matters little what a business is really worth if the seller is not in a position to bargain.

An entrepreneur bought a restaurant from an owner who was headed out of town just ahead of the IRS. The owner didn't even have time to say good-bye to his mother. It was time to grab the money and run. So, the price was very attractive to the entrepreneur at $130,000 for a business earning about $120,000 a year in cash flow. His PE ratio was just over one.

How much future to factor into the valuation of the business being considered is up to the buyer. Consider the following:

Why pay the owner for a future that the entrepreneur buyer will have to create? What does the owner have to do with the future when he or she is no longer involved with the business? If the seller stays on as a sort of investor or advisor, the buyer may have to pay for the seller's part of the future.

The buyer must have perspective about alternative investments. Quite commonly, independent businesses have sold for a PE ratio that is three to five times the reconstructed pre-tax earnings. "Reconstructed" means someone reworked the firm's financial statements to reflect what he or she felt were its true earnings.

Just as buyers cannot trust the balance sheet, they cannot trust the firm's profit and loss statements. They must develop their own. A woman asked a consultant to help her evaluate a bookstore she was interested in buying. The price was $77,500 with $27,500 down, and the balance at $10,000 per year for five years. The seller handed the woman copies of his federal income tax return for the previous three years.

After the consultant reviewed these returns, he saw it was evident that the seller should have won the Pulitzer Prize for fiction. The seller claimed a profit of $32,000 and said he paid tax on that amount, which was doubtful. Too many obvious and legitimate costs were missing. He had paid no wages, no FICA, no workers' compensation, no legal fees, no accounting, no supplies, no insurance, no auto expense, and many other normal operating costs were missing. He was obviously trying to cover up the bitter fact that the business was a disaster. It was not only worthless, it was also hopeless. No one could make money in that 1,000 square foot hole-in-the-wall. The business was worth only its liquidation value, perhaps $10,000.

Capitalization of future cash flows. Most valuations of businesses are based on their projected cash flow, commonly known as the capitalization of future cash flows. A projected cash flow analysis must be prepared with figures that have been developed from all gathered evidence and information, combined with knowledge of the business.

Once a well thought out projected cash flow statement has been prepared in which the buyer has some confidence, then he or she can multiply those earnings per year by the PE appropriate to the situation.

Suppose the buyer's figures indicate that a business will likely earn about $100,000 a year for the next few years. Moreover, the buyer believes that a PE ratio of four times the earning would be a bit high, and three would be a bargain. The bargaining range would then be $300,000 to $350,000. The buyer might begin by offering $275,000 and see what happens.

Why is cash flow stressed rather than profit after tax? Because those are the dollars buyers will have to work with in buying a business. Most of the time, they will be using part of that cash flow to buy the business. In fact, such a cash flow statement can be a powerful tool with which to persuade a reluctant seller to sell for the buyer's price. Many times, the seller will ask for unrealistic terms to pay off the business. A realistic cash flow projection prepared by the buyer from data furnished by the seller can show that there is no way those terms can be met. This gives the buyer a basis for negotiating realistic and fair terms.

Use of sales volume. The last method that has evolved to avoid some of the difficulties associated with using a firm's earnings as the base for calculations is the use of sales volume as the base, including appropriate adjustments in the multiple. For example, in some situations the sellers will say that the firm should sell for its annual sales volume: $1 million sales a year equals a $1 million value for the business. A multiple of one times sales is really nothing more than a roughly estimated multiple of earnings. If earnings in the business are about 10 percent of sales, then the one times sales formula is really a 10 times earnings figure. However, there is a problem with such simplistic formulas. The seller, knowing that he or she is going to be selling the business, can do many things to increase sales that adversely affect earnings.

A company hired a consultant to help it buy a radio station. The traditional way the industry values radio stations is one times the station's billings (sales). With the consultant's help, the company looked at 42 stations before settling on one in Montana. The station was worth about $2 million based on its previous year's billings, but the local manager, who was also a minority stockholder, already had an agreement in place with the owner to buy it for $1.5 million.

The purchasing company was negotiating to take over the manager's position in the deal but only wanted to put up $500,000 front money. The remaining million had to be financed over five years at 10 percent interest yearly with the principal paid at the end of the fifth year. Moreover, the note had to be without interest payments for the first two years.

How did the consultant arrive at those terms? The cash flow projections clearly showed that the business could not pay more and survive. Some high cash expenditures in the first two years were going to make $100,000 in interest payments impossible. When the owner balked, the consultant pulled out the cash flow and proved the business could not pay more. The sale was eventually made.

A business should be able to buy itself from its cash flow over a reasonable span of time. What's reasonable? Five years is often quoted. If a business won't buy itself, why would someone want it? There are a few other things that entrepreneurs should consider carefully.

- **Don't pay twice for the same goods.** One common valuation system advanced by many people, particularly sellers, adds the value of the firm's assets to the capitalized value of its future earnings. Suppose the assets are worth $250,000 in the market with $100,000 of liabilities against them; their net value is $150,000. Suppose that business appears to earn a pre-tax profit of about $100,000 a year. Furthermore, a PE ratio of three times earnings is agreed upon. These people would say that the business is worth $450,000 [$150,000 for assets + (3 x $100,000) pre-tax profit]. Make no mistake, this is a commonly used formula. But it is erroneous. The buyer is paying twice for the same thing. Either one buys the assets or the earnings, whichever is the most. But not both! After all, the buyer must have the assets to make the earnings; they are inseparable. When a person buys the money machine, he or she does get the machine. Consequently, the value of the concern is the highest of two values: value in liquidation or value as a going concern making a profit. But they cannot be added together. Many business brokers are using this formula. Naturally, it helps get the price of the business up. If a seller tries it, the buyer can just say, "I'll buy the earnings. You keep the assets." See how the seller manages to do that trick.
- **Don't confuse profits with wages.** Many sellers inflate their firms' earnings by not paying themselves enough salary. Buyers must not

confuse true economic profit with managerial wages. They should always make certain to plug in fair market wages for themselves and their management teams as an expense in projecting a firm's cash flows.

Off balance sheet valuations

In the reality of business, the greatest values in a business often do not appear in the firm's financial statements. Only dollars are recorded by accountants, but dollars often fail to represent the true value of the enterprise. Such factors as the people who work for the company, its distribution system, its patents and research, the economic setting in which the company operates, the location of its real estate, and other hidden values are often the true assets that potential buyers are most interested in acquiring.

In the reverse instance, suppose the company's plant is carried on the books at a depreciated value of $5 million, but, in reality, it is obsolete and in poor condition. The buyer would have to spend $10 million to modernize it. What looked like a $5 million asset is really a $5 million liability, which should be reflected in the projected cash flows.

Or suppose the plant sits on a former hazardous waste dump. The future cleanup costs are not shown as liabilities. Future product liability suits will not be shown, although pending litigation should be footnoted on the balance sheet. In California, sellers and everyone associated with selling a business, such as brokers and accountants, must disclose all known potential liabilities about the business.

People wonder why the buyers of the Hollywood studios paid so much for what looked to be mostly assets such as real estate and equipment. The hidden values of those firms were their huge film libraries that would bring in future rentals. Ted Turner wanted MGM's films, not the company or its studios.

Astute entrepreneurs start their ventures with the goal of building up off balance sheet items to raise the cash value of their businesses. Most sophisticated buyers examine the proprietary aspects of a business they are considering buying.

Off Balance Sheet Checklist

Advertising campaigns	Employment contracts	Litigation awards	Sources of supply
Advertising materials	Engineering drawings	Location	Subscription lists
Backlogs	Environmental rights	Mailing lists	Supplier contracts
Computer databases	Favorable financing	Manuscripts	Systems and procedures
Computer designs	Formulas	Mineral rights	Technical documentation
Computer software	Franchises	Non-compete covenants	Tooling
Contracts	Government programs	Packaging	Trade secrets
Copyrights	Joint ventures	Patents and applications	Trademarks
Credit files	Know-how	Permits	Training procedures (manuals)
Customer base	Laboratory processes	Proprietary designs	Unpatented technology
Customer lists	Leasehold interests	Rights	Use rights (air, water, land)
Distribution channels	Libraries	Royalty agreements	Work force
Distributorships	Licenses	Schematics and diagrams	
Easements	Literary works		

Source: The Geneva Companies, Irvine, California

Venture capitalists like to invest in companies that have such proprietary rights as patents, trademarks, trade secrets, and copyrights. The value of these proprietary items never appears on the balance sheet but they are usually the key aspect blocking competitors from entering the marketplace. Having strong proprietary rights gives the venture a higher cash value, especially when founders harvest from the company or when they sell its stock to the public.

Today's computer technology and database software have made it possible to design excellent databases that track customers' buying habits, preferences, and demographic information so owners can contact and market to their customers on a regular basis. Many marketing consultants advise companies that their most valuable off balance sheet asset is their customer lists, which should be treated like gold. To increase sales, it is more cost effective to cultivate existing customers than to try to develop new ones.

Replacement cost

When considering the purchase of a business, a buyer instinctively compares the asking price with the cost of starting the same type of business from scratch. The seller may want $1 million dollars for the business. The buyer may think, "I can start one for less money than that."

Starting from scratch is a viable alternative. Buyers need to be careful in estimating the costs of starting a business and the time and effort it takes to do so. It is easy to underestimate both. Recall all of the reasons for buying a business that were cited at the beginning of Chapter 6.

For bargaining purposes, however, it can be wise for a buyer to have a plan prepared for starting a business similar to the one being purchased. An unreasonable seller can be told, "Hey, get real! I can start a business like yours for this much. Why should I pay more?"

Some entrepreneurs think that it is easier to start a retail business than to purchase a business. They enjoy equipping their space with new fixtures and inventory, setting up a motivated sales force that can be trained, and molding the store's image to fit the founder. This is why owners of retail businesses need to build strong customer lists that contain complete demographic information, negotiate good leases, buy clean and desirable inventory, and develop strong sales forces to help them have an exit strategy.

Using Professional Appraisers

At the end of a successful negotiation, it is necessary to nail down all valuations of assets for the IRS, lest it challenge the terms of the deal. Thus, written opinions of professional appraisers are obtained to justify whatever it is clients want justified. And it works just about like that. What value does the client want? The appraisers have a great deal of latitude in their valuations, but there are limits beyond which they will not go. "I could not get on the stand and testify for anything more than…."

It can be seen that even the professional appraisers are more than somewhat loose on the value of many things. Buyers should not be swayed in their judgment on the value of a business by any document shown to them by the seller that is purported to be a professional valuation of the firm. It means nothing, other than someone got paid to do a valuation. Buyers must do their own valuations; they may use their own professionals, if they feel the need, but the buyers control the professionals. Moreover, they can reverse the tactics: "My professional says your professional is in error. The business is worth only…." This tactic is a part of the negotiating process.

Conclusion

Four methods of valuing a business have been discussed: market value of net assets; value of future earnings; off balance sheet valuations; and replacement cost. These methods can be used by both buyers and sellers to determine the value of a business. However, this is just the starting point. Once the facts have been reasonably ascertained, the negotiations begin. Much depends on the deal-making skills of the parties. There are hundreds of ways to put together a deal. The art is finding one that gives both parties what they want.

Once a deal is cut, the professionals take over to formalize it to the satisfaction of the IRS, the attorneys, and all other parties involved with the transactions.

The Art Gallery

A consulting client wanted to establish a favorable selling price for his art gallery in Carmel, California. The client needed to obtain a certain price for the gallery in order to retire. Using the four methods of business valuation yielded the following results.

Market value of net assets. Inventory for the art gallery was on consignment from the artist; therefore, there was no inventory value. The accounts receivable were secured by major credit cards. The fixtures in the gallery amounted to wall space and a few pedestals for sculptures. The building was rented under a 10-year lease. All together, the gallery's asset value minus its accounts payable showed a small net worth. Clearly, the seller would never want to establish the art gallery's sale price using the asset valuation method. The buyer, on the other hand, would certainly prefer to use this method.

The value of future earnings. The art gallery was formed as a sole proprietorship, and the owner took most of the excess cash flow as salary and benefits. The multiple of cash flow—three times for a cash payment and five to seven times for term sale—still left the selling price on the low side, though higher than the asset valuation method. This result still benefited the buyer far more than the seller.

Replacement cost. Starting up a gallery is not very expensive because inventory is on consignment, accounts receivable are on credit cards, and the fixtures and build-out expenses are minimal. Again, this method favors the buyer over the seller.

Off balance sheet valuation. The gallery had many valuable off balance sheet assets. The gallery had a permit to operate in Carmel, which had instituted a moratorium on all further licenses for art galleries within city limits. The gallery had been in business for 20 years and had established a list of wealthy clients and art buyers from all over the world. The gallery's 10-year lease secured a prime location that included heavy street traffic. The salespeople were well trained and exhibited a proven understanding of customers' needs and expectations. In addition, the gallery maintained exclusive rights to the sale of all the works produced by six of the most famous artists in Carmel. The customer service and connections the gallery had maintained for 20 years had earned the business a high level of positive name recognition. The off balance sheet method established a much higher value.

The art gallery owner then set up a five-year plan to build his off balance sheet through other intangible assets because this method will allow him to meet his retirement goals. All entrepreneurs should go through this valuation process to determine which method will work best for them as they plan for a high-priced exit. Entrepreneurs considering new concepts should always look at starting a business that can end up with a potentially high selling price.

Exercise 7a. Crowder's Jewelry Store Case Study

Introduction

The meeting was set for 3 p.m. on March 10, 2001, in the office of Sally Hornbein, a downtown lawyer. As the meeting participants began to arrive, the atmosphere became charged with anticipation. Mr. Reynolds, with his lawyer by his side, sat down and started looking once more through the stacks of papers in front of him. He wanted to make sure every detail was right. He had dreamed of owning a retail business for many years, and it could become a reality very soon. Mr. Crowder, an elderly gentleman, walked slowly in, greeted Ms. Hornbein, his lawyer, and looked nervously around the room. He had a right to be nervous; he was perhaps about to sell a big part of his life.

Store history

Crowder's Jewelry Store was started 25 years ago by Mr. Crowder, now age 72. This retail jewelry store has been operating in a suburban shopping center for the past 10 years. This has proven to be a very good location, since it is located in a well-established, affluent neighborhood. The store has a five-year lease in the present location at 6 percent of volume and two five-year options at no increase. Many of the customers have been shopping here for years, and Mr. Crowder has a very good reputation with his clientele. The store has a computer database of all its customers (name, phone number, past purchases, spouse's name, and the like.). The store is very attractive, having been remodeled about three years ago. The company owes a note of $20,000, with 10 percent interest on these improvements.

Crowder's Jewelry has always been operated as a family business. Mrs. Crowder occasionally helped in the store while raising their daughter, Alice, who worked there summers as a teenager and full-time until her marriage to Bill Roberts. Bill, Mr. Crowder's son-in-law, works in the store as a jewelry designer. He usually puts in about three days per week and sets his own hours.

Mr. Crowder has been having health problems, with high blood pressure and a heart condition. His doctor has advised him to retire from the business. Mr. Crowder reluctantly has put the business up for sale.

The buyer

Mr. Reynolds, age 42, heard about the jewelry store for sale through his accountant, who also does the books for Mr. Crowder. Mr. Reynolds has been designing and manufacturing fine jewelry as a hobby for the past 20 years. He presently is subcontracting the manufacturing and wholesales his designer jewelry to a few upscale jewelers nationwide. He has been thinking of expanding his hobby into a full-time business by opening a retail location so he can sell directly to the public at a high markup.

He has $100,000 in cash, does not own a house but has a good credit rating.

Mr. Reynolds has been doing research on Crowder's Jewelry to determine the feasibility of buying the business, the market potential of continued and growing sales and the value of the firm. Both he and his accountant have examined the financial statements. Mr. Crowder strongly hinted that he has been taking about $30,000 in cash out of the business per year without reporting that sum to the IRS.

Mr. Reynolds believes that, with good advertising, lower prices and good financing, he can increase sales to $1,500,000 in the existing location.

To become more comfortable with the true value of the assets of the company, Mr. Reynolds hired Jacobsen's Appraisals to analyze the assets and to give him a report on current market values of the assets. Here is a copy of the report Mr. Reynolds received.

Asset Appraisal
Statement of Value
February 28, 2001

Accounts Receivable

Accounts receivable	$92,000
Less: Estimated uncollected A/R	(15,000)
Net accounts receivable	77,000

Inventory

Inventory	$400,000
Less: Estimated obsolescence	(15,000)
Net inventory	385,000

Property, plant, and equipment

Office equipment	$14,500
Computer equipment	8,300
Furniture	5,400
Vehicles	24,000
Leasehold improvements	0*

A research of all liabilities of the company found the following:

Accounts payable	$70,000
Notes payable	20,000
Taxes payable	8,500**

Note: All other payables including the notes payable and wages were paid through the end of the month of February.

* The lease agreement stipulates that all improvements made to the property by the lessee are forfeited at the end of the lease when the property is transferred back to the lessor.

** A tax liability was discovered during a review of the prior three years of tax returns.

Crowder's Jewelry Store
Balance Sheet
February 28, 2001

Cash	$30,000	Accounts payable	$70,000
Receivables	92,000	Notes payable	20,000
Inventory	400,000	Current liabilities	90,000
Current assets	522,000		
		Owner's equity	547,000
Fixed assets	115,000		
Total assets	$637,000	Total liabilities and owner's equity	$637,000

Crowder's Jewelry Store
Income Statement
Years ending December 31, 2000, 1999, 1998

	2000	1999	1998
Sales	$950,000	$1,030,000	$1,150,000
Gross margin	437,000	463,000	529,000
Expenses	304,000	350,200	391,000
Pre-tax profit	133,000	113,700	138,000
After-tax profit	93,100	79,590	96,000
Mr. Crowder salary and expenses	70,000	60,000	50,000
Bill Roberts salary and expenses	40,000	35,000	30,000

Determine the price of the jewelry store using each of the four methods of valuation.

Method one: Market value of net assets

Assets		Liabilities	
Current assets		**Current liabilities**	
Accounts receivable	_____	Accounts payable	_____
Less allowance for		Notes payable	_____
doubtful accounts	_____	Interest payable	_____
Value of accounts receivable	_____	Taxes payable	_____
Inventory	_____	Wages payable	_____
Less obsolete inventory	_____		
Value of inventory	_____	**Long-term liabilities**	
Cash in bank	_____	Mortgage payable	_____
Total current assets	_____	<u>Total liabilities</u>	_____

Property, plant, and equipment (Market value)

Office equipment	_____
Computer equipment	_____
Furniture	_____
Leasehold improvements	_____
Vehicles	_____
Buildings and land	_____
Other assets	_____
Total property, plant, and equipment	_____

Total assets – Total liabilities =
Price of business   _____

<u>Total assets</u>   _____

Method two: Value of future assets

EBIT (earnings before interest and taxes)

Average last three years EBIT	Year 1	_____
	Year 2	_____
	Year 3	_____
	Total	_____
	Average	_____

Multiple _____ X average = Price of business   _____

Method three: Off balance sheet valuation

Assets

Current assets

Accounts receivable	_____
Less allowance for doubtful accounts	_____
Value of accounts receivable	_____
Inventory	_____
Less obsolete inventory	_____
Value of inventory	_____
Cash in bank	_____

Total current assets _____

Property, plant, and equipment

Office equipment	_____
Computer equipment	_____
Furniture	_____
Leasehold improvements	_____
Vehicles	_____
Buildings and land	_____
Other assets	_____

Total property, plant, and equipment _____

Off balance sheet items _____

_____
_____
_____
_____
_____

(see listing on p. 103)

Total off balance sheet items _____

Total assets _____

Liabilities

Current liabilities

Accounts payable	_____
Notes payable	_____
Interest payable	_____
Taxes payable	_____
Wages payable	_____

Long-term liabilities

Mortgage payable	_____

Total liabilities _____

Total assets – Total liabilities = _____
Price of business

Method four: Replacement cost (estimate costs not identified in the case)

Start-up cost:

Building lease deposits	_____	Supplies (cleaning, office, shipping, boxes, stationary, business cards)	_____
Build-out cost of space	_____	Training of employees	_____
Equipment (copy machine, etc.)	_____	Hiring employees	_____
Furniture	_____	Government licenses	_____
Carpet	_____	Printing (brochures)	_____
Shelving	_____	Auto	_____
Computers	_____	Pre-advertising	_____
Beginning inventory	_____	Three months' operating capital	_____
Telephone deposits	_____	Other costs	_____
Utilities deposit	_____		
Signage	_____		
Applicable city codes	_____	Total cost for start-up	_____

After reading the Crowder's Jewelry Store case, answer the following three questions.

1. What price should Mr. Reynolds offer Mr. Crowder for the jewelry store? Why?

2. What type of payment schedule should Mr. Reynolds offer Mr. Crowder?

3. Explain any other contingencies Mr. Reynolds should address to Mr. Crowder in the deal structure.

Plan Overview and Writing Tips

Learning Objectives

In this chapter, students will learn

- The sections of a feasibility plan.
- The sections of a business plan.
- Writing and formatting suggestions for producing good plans.

Every budding entrepreneur should understand the importance of planning and should carefully write a feasibility plan or business plan before investing any money into a new venture. The purpose of the feasibility plan is to determine whether an idea for starting a new business could turn into a profitable business venture. The purpose of the business plan is to investigate all aspects of a potential venture once it is determined to be feasible.

Too often the entrepreneur gets all wrapped up in and excited about a new venture idea without thoughtful consideration, research, and evaluation of its potential and pitfalls. Entering a venture without analyzing the feasibility can be an expensive shortcut. Later, the entrepreneur may realize that the idea was sound, but perhaps the market was saturated. Maybe the profit margin was too narrow. Maybe the management team was not in place. Or perhaps there was not enough capital. There could be many reasons the venture failed.

If entrepreneurs researched new-venture ideas and wrote feasibility or business plans before starting, many failed businesses would never have been started in the first place. Lack of planning and research is one of the basic reasons so many new businesses fail during the first, tenuous years of operation. This failure rate could be significantly reduced if properly structured research and planning were conducted in the beginning, preventing the start-up of ill-conceived businesses.

Deciding whether to start a new venture takes time to research the market, develop financial forecasts, and write a sound feasibility or business plan. Many entrepreneurs are reluctant to do all of these. Entrepreneurs are doers who want to take their ideas to the marketplace quickly. They know that the window of opportunity will probably be there only a short period of time. Consequently, they may avoid taking the necessary time to research and strategically plan their ventures, identify problem areas, and formulate plans to prevent potential roadblocks. Shrewd entrepreneurs understand the importance of planning and writing feasibility and business plans. The plans indicate whether ventures are likely to succeed. And if they take the time to plan, they can foresee problems and develop solutions before encountering disasters.

As entrepreneurs write feasibility or business plans, they will identify which areas pose the greatest threats. They will develop alternative solutions if a problem should occur. If the feasibility plan shows that the venture idea has potential, the next step is to write a business plan.

Writing a feasibility or business plan forces the entrepreneur to consider every facet of a business opportunity and write the results on paper. Then the entrepreneurs and others can objectively evaluate its potential. Knowing that every venture has both risks and opportunities, they can compare the risks to the opportunities, determine what potential problems exist, and determine whether potential problems can be either eliminated or minimized. Developing a feasibility or business plan addresses these questions. It allows for trial-and-error testing before any dollars are spent.

Writing a Plan

A feasibility or business plan should be written by the entrepreneur. The financials could be prepared with the assistance of an accountant, but the entrepreneur must understand every detail of the financial plan.

Many people have difficulty writing; they often express such concerns as: Where do I begin? How do I emphasize key points? How long should it be? How much detail should I include? What should it look like?

To help writers with each section and its subtopics, a series of checklist questions has been developed. These questions lead the writers through the process of writing a feasibility or business plan and provide a guide for them to include critical information. They are found in the *Venture Planning Workbook* and on *The Business Mentor* CD-ROM. *The Business Mentor* also contains samples of feasibility and business plans for use as guides in formatting plans.

Where to begin

The place to begin is to look over sample feasibility or business plans to get an idea of how the parts fit together to make a whole—to relate each part to the particular business idea. For every venture, the entrepreneurs must decide which topics are most important to the venture and which are not as important. Some questions may not apply, but it is advisable to answer as many as possible.

The writing style for both the feasibility plan and the business plan will be the same but the sections and questions to answer will be different. There are separate sections of the *Venture Planning Workbook* and *The Business Mentor* CD-ROM that relate to the two different plans. The writer needs to locate the appropriate section and follow the prompts to create his or her plan.

What to write about

The checklist questions help entrepreneurs decide what kind of information to include. The questions focus on various aspects of starting a business that should be addressed in the business planning process. All questions appropriate to the particular business concept should be answered, thus creating the content of the plan.

An easy approach is to start with the questions for which answers are already known. Those answers may lead to additional information and additional questions for which the information can be obtained.

Some redundancy will be found, because the same questions need to be addressed in more than one section. By answering the checklist questions in each section, the writer begins his or her feasibility or business plan.

Length

Length is a matter of judgment. Either plan should include only what is needed to provide complete information. Generally, a feasibility plan should not be more than 15 pages (not including appendixes), although a longer length is sometimes necessary. The feasibility plan is the skeleton plan that the entrepreneur uses to decide whether to go ahead with the concept and develop a business plan.

It is more difficult to generalize about the length of business plans. The primary purpose is to develop as complete a plan for the venture as possible. Several factors will determine the length. Depending on the complexity of the concept and the requirements of the potential funding sources, a business plan may be 30 pages, not including appendixes. It is much more difficult to write short, hard-hitting plans than to write lengthy ones.

Writing style

There is little need to worry about writing style. Since business planning documents are written for the purpose of planning, it is more important that they be accurate and provide the most complete information about the proposed venture. Language should be kept simple and direct. Sentences should be clear and concise with short, direct words. Most importantly, the writer should use a writing style that is comfortable for him or her.

Emotional pleas and flamboyant adjectives should be avoided. If terms like "best," "most complete," or "most advanced" are used, the writer should be sure to tell why this is true and include enough details to explain what is meant by the terms.

If it is necessary to use terms that are unique to an industry, each term should be defined the first time it appears.

> "I have made this letter longer than usual, because I lack the time to make it short."
>
> —Blaise Pascal

The 'Meat'

Many entrepreneurs think that if they have a great business opportunity that matches their experience and expertise, then the venture will be successful. In reality, finding a business to start is 10 percent of the work needed before opening up for business. The real work begins by writing a feasibility analysis to find out if the business could be profitable.

Sections of a Feasibility Plan

A feasibility plan explores whether venture ideas have potential to succeed. It is a first step in developing a detailed business plan to prove the venture idea. No effort should be wasted on pursuing a business opportunity if it does not have a growing market and the potential to earn a healthy profit.

The outline for a feasibility plan tells the scope of information that should be researched and included in the plan. Most of these sections can be used in the business plan if the concept is feasible.

Feasibility Plan Outline
Cover page
Table of contents
Executive summary
Product/service
The market
Price and profitability
Plan for further action

Cover page

Preparing the cover page seems simple, but often important items are either overlooked or given scant attention. The cover page should include the entrepreneur's name, address, phone and fax numbers with area code, and e-mail address. When possible, it is wise to show the product, or if the proposed business will provide a service, show the logo or trademark.

Table of contents

Often entrepreneurs neglect to include a table of contents, or if they do prepare one, they neglect to include page numbers. It is important that the reader be able to find information to review quickly and easily.

Executive summary

This section is a brief, concise overview of the key points that appear in each section of the plan and should be no more than one-and-a-half to two pages long.

The executive summary is the first section of the finished feasibility plan but it is the last section completed. As the entrepreneur develops a feasibility plan, he or she will uncover additional information that will change the original business concept.

Product/service

Before going any further in a new venture, the entrepreneur must determine if the concept has a working and tested product or service that is owned or can be licensed and is feasible. In this section of the feasibility plan, the entrepreneur fully investigates the potential for the venture's product or service.

Many nice-sounding concepts dealing with large markets fail for lack of a sound working product or service. Many business concepts just do not work. Dreaming is at its peak! Sometimes the technology is not there. If it is, sometimes it is not feasible technology. Sometimes it costs too much.

For example, solar energy, discussed in an earlier chapter, was very fascinating new technology. The concept was great, but it was hard to implement. First, the scientists had to develop small storage facilities that did not consume a large amount of space. They had to develop capabilities for giving the customer a quick payback with cheaper energy alternatives.

Often a proposed product or service has been previously tried and found lacking. Or perhaps the product or service is owned by other parties. If this is the case in a proposed venture, the entrepreneur will discover the risks before proceeding with the business.

The market

Market analysis is extremely important; it is critical to determine if there is a market for the concept's product or service and if it can be proven. The market may be so large and obvious that little needs to be done in the feasibility plan except to prove its size. In the feasibility plan, it is enough to prove that a large enough market exists for the concept and that further investigation of this opportunity is justified.

On the other hand, if no market can be found and proven, it may be futile to continue the pursuit of this concept. There is no need to waste effort if the concept does not have a sizable marketplace or a definite market niche.

It is also important to define the customer, identify various target markets, and determine if the product or service can satisfy their needs. The feasibility plan should explain the way the product or service will be sold to the customer and what kind of distribution channels will be used.

Price and profitability

In the feasibility plan, the entrepreneur examines the venture's profit possibilities, which are critical to the success of the venture. Will the customer pay enough for the product or service to make the enterprise profitable enough? Just being marginally profitable is not enough to survive in today's competitive environment. There must be a large enough margin for error. All too often the answer to that question is no. The venture fails because it cannot maintain a high enough gross margin to cover expenses and still yield a decent profit. If the profitability of the venture is suspect, the entrepreneur should pass on to the next possible venture.

It is essential to consider the venture's price/cost ratios. For example, in manufacturing, one rule of thumb to follow is that the product should sell for at least five times its direct cost. The venture that makes big profits has a much more favorable price/cost ratio.

The nature of the business generally dictates how much money can be paid out in salaries, benefits, and profits. It is difficult to outperform the well-managed firms in an industry. If a plan is based on doing a better job than competitors, the entrepreneur is making a serious statement about comparative management skills, and it is extremely difficult to beat industry averages.

Entrepreneurs should also consider whether the economics of the industry meet their personal criteria. For example, if an entrepreneur chooses to purchase an ice-cream franchise, according to industry data, he or she will likely make $50,000 after taxes. If that amount of profit is not enough to meet his or her personal needs and goals, then he or she should avoid that business venture.

Unfortunately, in their eagerness to go into business, entrepreneurs often start their businesses with concepts for which direct costs are too high to allow a profit to be realized. Their ventures are doomed from the beginning. The market won't pay the price to cover the expenses of the businesses.

Plan for further action

The last section of a feasibility plan focuses on the future. From the data that has been collected, the feasibility study can indicate several things: the concept is not feasible; the concept is good but not workable at this time; the concept is worthwhile but not for a new company; the concept is one on which the entrepreneur can build a business. Each one will dictate a different future action.

If the concept is found not feasible or not workable at this time, the entrepreneur has saved him or herself grief, time, and money by doing the feasibility study.

If the feasibility plan indicates that the concept is worthwhile but not for a new company, perhaps the concept should be sold or licensed to some existing firm.

If the entrepreneur proves that the business concept is feasible and a reasonable profit can be obtained, it is time to proceed to the business plan. This is a big step. It will require a commitment of time, effort, and, perhaps, money.

Many entrepreneurs will show their feasibility plans to potential investors, bankers, employees, friends, personal business advisors, and corporate strategic partners. Many times, this type of exposure will elicit useful information to further develop and better focus the original business concept.

Differences between a Feasibility Plan and a Business Plan

A business plan is built on the same foundation as a feasibility plan. As the table below illustrates, the marketing section is expanded and a more detailed financial plan replaces the price and profitability section. New sections included in a business plan are management and organization, operating and control systems, and a growth plan. An appendix contains supporting documents for the business plan.

Feasibility Plan	Business Plan
Executive Summary	Executive Summary
	Management and Organization Plan
Product/Service	Product/Service Plan
The Market • Industry Profile • Customer Profile • Customer Benefits • Target Markets • Market Penetration	Marketing Plan • Industry Profile • Customer Profile • Customer Benefits • Target Markets • Market Penetration • Pricing Profile • Competition Profile • Advertising and Labeling • Service and Warranties • Trade Shows • Future Markets
	Financial Plan • Budgets/Assumptions • Cash Flow Projections • Projected Income Statements • Pro Forma Balance Sheet • Financial Analysis Ratios
Price and Profitability • Pricing • Projected Profit and Loss Statements • Estimated Start-Up Costs	
	Operating and Control Systems Plan
	Growth Plan
	Appendix

Sections of a Business Plan

The outline in the margin provides some idea of what might be included in a business plan, depending upon the exact nature of the proposed venture. To a large degree it is common sense, planning the various aspects of a new enterprise. Entrepreneurs need to plan every aspect of their businesses, either formally or informally, as they proceed. One way or another, they must make a lot of decisions about what they are going to do in all phases of their businesses.

There is nothing sacred about the order of topics, although it does seem logical that one describe the concept first. Often that material is put into the executive summary.

After that, the plan should flow logically in answer to the readers' natural inclinations about what they would like to know next. It is advisable to lead off with the areas of most interest, which are usually the topics of finance and marketing. Naturally, the reader wants to know what the market is for the proposal. How much will be sold? Then, the questions are how much money is the venture going to make, how much money is it going to take to do it, and who are the people who will make this work.

Each of the sections of the business plan will be discussed in some detail to provide an idea about what to include in each. A rule of thumb is when in doubt, put it in; it's easy to take it out later if the material proves to be unneeded. The checklist questions on *The Business Mentor* CD-ROM and in the *Venture Planning Workbook* provide guidance for the kinds of information to include, and they suggest subheadings under which to organize the data.

Cover page

Preparing the cover page seems simple, but often important items are either overlooked or given scant attention. The cover page should include the entrepreneur's name, address, phone and fax numbers with area code, and e-mail address. When possible, it is wise to show the product, or if the proposed business will provide a service, show the logo or trademark.

Table of contents

Often entrepreneurs neglect to include a table of contents, or if they do prepare one, they neglect to include page numbers. It is important to be able to find information to review quickly and easily.

Executive summary

The business plan opens with a short synopsis of the scenario that is to follow. It summarizes what the entrepreneur proposes to do, how he or she intends to do it, what it will cost, and the potential rewards. It is a mini business plan that tells the story in a compelling way in two pages.

Interestingly, successful entrepreneurs are almost always able to articulate clearly and concisely the concept underlying their enterprises. If a person has difficulty telling others exactly what he or she proposes to do, it's a red flag that the person is not clear in his or her own mind exactly what he or she intends to do.

Business Plan Outline
Cover page
Table of contents
Executive summary
Management and
 organization plan
Product/service plan
Marketing plan
Financial plan
Operating and control
 systems plan
Growth plan
Appendix

Management and organization plan

One of the vital areas is the organization: Who is going to do all these fine things described in the plan? Who will be on the management team?

The success of the venture is largely up to the entrepreneur. But the entrepreneur will not likely do it alone. He or she needs to consider all the people that will be needed in the infrastructure of the venture. And he or she must be confident that the chosen management people can do the things the entrepreneur intends. What are the qualifications of the people on the management team? Does the entrepreneur understand who will be needed down the line as the enterprise matures?

Product/service plan

Depending upon the exact nature of the proposed venture, a certain amount of material must be included on the product or service that is being proposed. The product should be described just enough to demonstrate that its details have been sufficiently considered and that the bugs are out of it—it works and is ready to go. On rare occasions, funding has been secured on the promise of a working product. Much investment in biotech was based on potential workability.

If the entrepreneur intends to use the business plan to recruit potential investors, which will be discussed later, this section should not include an overwhelming amount of technical information. This is a particular hazard among technically oriented entrepreneurs. For those who want to know the technical aspects underlying a venture, the business plan can provide that information in an appendix. But the plan should not be bogged down with technical details.

Marketing plan

What industry will the business be in? Where is the industry on the growth curve? Entrepreneurs should carefully study the industries or customers to which their firms will sell. They should develop industry and customer profiles so they know the characteristics and behavior.

What is the marketing strategy? The overall plan in bringing products or services to market is a good beginning for this section. It sets the tone for what should follow. Who is the target market? What market segment will the firm seek? What is the timing of sequential market solicitation? Much of this is laid out in later sections on marketing. The business plan should detail exactly how the firm will market its wares.

Distribution system. Through which distribution channels will the firm market? What is the likely reception by those distribution entities? This is an important section because distribution is often the major obstacle the new enterprise encounters on its way to market.

If the entrepreneur can name names, so much the better. Precisely which distribution organizations have agreed to handle the product or service?

Sales force. Who is going to sell the output: agents or an internal sales force? Someone has to go into the marketplace and bring back some orders. How is this going to happen?

Promotion. What are the plans for promoting the enterprise? Advertising, publicity, trade shows, literature, and much more must be planned for. The market must somehow become aware of the firm's offer; what package of benefits has been assembled for the customers? By all means, numbers should be connected to promotional plans in order to show a constant awareness of costs.

Competition. Who will be the competitors? The competition must be identified. Simply naming the competitors will not do the job. It is important to know exactly how the new firm will compete with each of them. Which will pose major problems? How does each fit into the market? It must be evident that the entrepreneur knows the industry.

Pricing. How much will the market pay for the product or service? The entrepreneur has created a value; what is it? Some numbers are needed. The profits of the enterprise depend heavily upon the price it can get for its output.

> Price is the single-most important factor determining the profitability of an enterprise.

Many people question the ability of pure-play Internet companies to make a profit. Investors have poured billions of dollars into new economy companies without a definitive model for the sustainability of the company or its profitability. The new rules call for much more complex models. Pricing is even more challenging for these types of firms.

If an enterprise is selling into a commodity market, in which it must sell for a market price, then its profitability depends upon the ability to produce its product inexpensively. The enterprise needs a cost advantage. In such situations, the business plan should focus upon costs. But if there is no clear-cut market price for the output, then the entrepreneur has the problem of determining what the market will pay for it.

Generally, the proposed price list and price policies should be included in the plan. By all means, a break-even analysis should be included, showing the volumes needed to break even at various prices and trade discounts.

Financial plan

It is impossible to assemble any meaningful financial plan until all other plans have been formulated. This is because the amount of money needed depends upon what the founder plans to do.

Most of the financial plan focuses around the development of the cash flow plan. In it, all the cash flowing into and out of the firm is contemplated. The net result is an estimate of how much money will be needed to undertake the venture and how much money will ultimately be generated by operations down the line.

The financial plan should include how operations will be financed and where the required money will be obtained at the various stages of the venture's development. Businesses go through stages of growth: conception, start-up, growth, maturity, and innovation or decline. Financing at the various stages is usually necessary for successful companies. What are the plans for obtaining money at each stage? When will that money be needed?

Operating and control systems plan

The entrepreneur must understand the nature and importance of operating and control systems. The operating system ensures that everything that needs to get done does indeed get done. When a company receives an order for goods, it should set into motion all sorts of activities. Many people need to know about the new order if it is to be turned into a satisfactorily completed transaction.

A control system is critical to profit performance. Normally, one will rely heavily upon accounting professionals, whoever they are, for guidance on this aspect of operations. However, entrepreneurs must not think that they can totally abdicate responsibility for the control systems.

Recently, a major web consumer retailer, or e-tailer, has begun to slide. This company was backed by top-line venture capitalists, had a top management team, and was first to market. Failures in shipping product, poor customer service, and limited inventory line all led to its poor showing. Each of these factors was related to operational inadequacies. This section of the business plan should detail how careful operations will be designed and implemented, hopefully preventing costly errors.

Growth plan

By all means, the entrepreneur should plan for continued expansion of the enterprise. What additional products or services are possible? What other markets will be solicited? Where is the entrepreneur going to take the enterprise?

Appendix

All support documentation should be placed in the appendix so that the actual business plan remains uncluttered. While the three-year financial projections are part of the financial section in the business plan, the financial worksheets and assumptions can be included in the appendix. The appendix will vary in length according to the amount of detailed information needed to support the claims made in the business plan. If the appendix becomes too large, it can be made into a separate document. A table of contents for the appendix should be included to facilitate finding specific information.

The Look: Formatting

The purpose of formatting any piece of writing is to make it easier to read and to find specific sections. Legibility, smaller chunks of information, and visual aids like pointers make it easier for the reader.

With computers and word processing becoming so common, people have access to many type fonts. This has a downside; many try making their written pieces fancier and, in many cases, use inappropriate or too many type fonts.

Graphic designers usually limit type usage to two font families, a serif typeface and a sans-serif typeface (without serifs). A font family includes regular, italic, bold, and different sizes of the same style font.

Text is best in a serif typeface. Serifs are the short lines or strokes added to each letter. Studies have found that serif type faces are easier and quicker to read, probably because people are much more used to seeing such type. Studies have also shown that capital and lower case letters are easier to read

One mark of an incompetent entrepreneur is a disdain for all the details involved in operating a business and controlling its activities. This common inadequacy is the destroyer of many ventures.

than ALL CAPITAL LETTERS. Readers have learned to distinguish words more quickly by the varied shapes provided by the letters' ascenders and descenders. So all capitals should be limited to very specific purposes.

Common serif typefaces good for text include Times, Palatino, Century Schoolbook, and Bookman.

The sans-serif typeface is used for display purposes such as titles and sub-heads. It is also often used in tables and graphs, places where space is limited.

Common sans-serif typefaces good for titles and subheads include Arial, Folio, Futura, and Helvetica, which is probably the most commonly used.

Type size is another consideration for legibility. The most common size for text, used in magazines and newspapers, is 10-point type. A somewhat larger size, such as 11 point, makes for easier reading. Subheads are larger and bolder so readers can skim through and see the subtopics or even get an idea of an outline. Also, it is quicker to find a certain section that has a larger, bold subhead. Caution: Subheads that are too large can look bad and take up a lot of space.

Book chapters, as well as magazine articles, are broken up into smaller chunks with their own titles, or subheads. As mentioned, one reason for doing this is to make it easier to find specific sections. Another is aesthetics: A page of text broken up with subheads and other graphic elements is more pleasing to look at and, therefore, more inviting to readers. Graphic elements such as bullets make information easier for readers to find and understand.

Other Readers of the Business Plan: Potential Investors

Although the primary purpose of the business plan is to complete the planning of a new venture, entrepreneurs may wish to use it for obtaining investors. Chances are that these readers will be busy people who will want to find out quickly what the business is about.

The executive summary provides a brief, concise overview of the key points that appear in each section of the plan. It tells precisely what the entrepreneur proposes to do, how it will be done, what costs will be

Many times the executive summary is the only section a potential investor, lender, future employee, or strategic partner will read (at first, anyway).

Writing and Formatting Suggestions

- Look at sample feasibility plans and business plans to see how they are put together.
- Review and understand the objectives for each section of the plan.
- Write down any other issues or sub-issues that are related to each section.
- Begin with the questions for which answers are known.
- Include only enough information to be complete.
- Keep the language simple and direct.
- Write in a style that is comfortable.
- Have the plan reviewed for content by an entrepreneur who has expertise in the business concept.
- Have the plan proofread by someone well-versed in English grammar.
- Choose typefaces for their readability. Remember more is not better.
- Use charts, graphs, and bullets whenever possible to focus on the important aspects.
- Include a title page, a table of contents, and page numbers.

involved, and the potential rewards. It may even conclude with a statement of what is wanted of the reader.

The management and organization section should demonstrate that the entrepreneur and the chosen management people can make the venture successful. It will provide potential investors reasons to believe in the entrepreneur; it will show the qualifications of the people on the management team; and it will indicate that the entrepreneur understands who will be needed down the line as the enterprise matures.

Backers would worry if the entrepreneur showed signs that the venture will be a one-man band. It is understood that the entrepreneur is important and will be largely responsible for the success of the venture, but the entrepreneur will not likely do it alone. It is fine to have a one-person company, but it won't likely interest investors. Along with examining the background and credentials of the entrepreneur and top management team, investors look closely at the board of directors and advisors. Others will be impressed by the nature of the people with whom the entrepreneur associates. People aren't likely to invest with amateurs; they go with the pros. Resumes are often included in one of the appendixes.

The product should be described just enough so that the reader understands it and learns that its details have been sufficiently considered, that it works and is ready to go. How much about the product or service to include in the business plan can be determined by asking: "Will the reader need to know this to understand and appreciate the venture?"

Most astute financiers want to learn about the market or markets for the concept. Who will buy it? How large are the markets? What proof is there that someone will pay money for the item? A clear-cut delineation of target markets is a critical section for potential investors. Much hinges on the ability to convince the reader that there will be an adequate market for the output of the proposed enterprise. The entrepreneur who bases a venture on doing a better job than competitors is making a statement about comparative management skills. Potential investors will question the assumptions.

Backers will be interested in the promotion of the venture, including the costs. By all means, numbers should be connected to promotional plans in order to show a constant awareness of costs. Potential backers must be assured that the entrepreneur recognizes the reality of what is proposed.

Investors also need to be assured that the entrepreneur has studied the competition in detail and knows about the structure of the markets into which he or she is about to venture. The business plan must prove that the entrepreneur knows the industry.

Since pricing is a major factor in the profitability of the new venture, investors will look critically at the entrepreneur's pricing decisions. In the event there is no clear-cut market price, the reader of the plan will be interested in the entrepreneur's solution to the problem.

The financial section provides an estimate of how much money will be needed to undertake the venture and how much money will ultimately be generated by operations down the line. Financiers will want to see the point at which they can begin to retrieve their investment and get a return. Investors are eager to know when they will get their money back.

The cash flow analysis discloses much about an entrepreneur's management skills. If significant costs are overlooked, if the numbers are overly optimistic or even unrealistic, if there is a reason to doubt that the entrepreneur really knows the costs of running a business, then potential investors will doubt the entrepreneur's ability to manage a business. A good, realistic cash flow tells a lot about the entrepreneur's experience in business.

Financiers will look at the business plan for evidence that the entrepreneur understands the nature and importance of operating and control systems. While operating procedures must be detailed during the development of the business plan, many of the details need not be relayed to someone who is reading the plan for investment purposes. However, these readers should be assured that such details have been planned. They should know that the entrepreneur knows how important a good operating system is to the long-run success of the firm.

> Entrepreneurs aren't expected to have all the answers, but investors expect them to have identified the critical questions and have answers for these questions.

By all means, the entrepreneur should let potential investors know what is planned for continued expansion of the enterprise. They want some assurance that the entrepreneur doesn't have a one-trick pony. If the entrepreneur is seeking money from others, they are very interested in the future and what part the entrepreneur intends to play in it, if the entrepreneur plans on building an empire or if the entrepreneur plans on leaving once he or she has made some money.

The trend is clearly toward short plans. Financiers weary of long, dull ones. Length is usually determined by the plan's intended use. The "weight

---

Writing a Business Plan or Feasibility Plan

My entrepreneur students at the University of Southern California (USC) had to write a group business plan (four per group) the first semester. I assigned this to teach them the discipline of writing a business plan. In the second semester, they wrote another plan by themselves, and since they know the process, they can have more creativity in the plan. Being typical students, many of them wait until the last minute to complete the plan. They always underestimate the time involved in the completion of a plan.

USC has a large computer lab, and the entrepreneurs take over the lab the week before the plans are due. I sent a person whom the students didn't know to the computer lab at 2 a.m. the night before the plans were due. I told him to take a video camera and record some of the funny things that were happening, and then we would show the video in class the next day when the students handed in their plans.

One of the students, who was a real character, was sitting at a computer in the front of the lab. He yelled out to all the students in the lab, "Time to do my assumptions for my financials. What are my sales in January?" Somebody replied, "$40,000." He said, "OK. Now my expenses. How much will I pay in salaries in January?" The reply from another student was, "$8,000." The student proceeded to do all his financials by this method.

The person taking the video came to my office the next morning and told me that what we had gotten on video was priceless. Class started that afternoon, and I told the students I had a special video to show the class. My class was in a large amphitheater with aisles up each side. I turned on the video and there was the student doing his assumptions. The class just about died with laughter, and I saw the guilty student's backside as he was crawling on all fours up the aisle trying to escape.

But is that not typical of waiting until the last minute to complete a project? I always told this story to my classes, because the key to a good plan is detailed assumptions that have been researched.

—Mack Davis, *FastTrac* author

is quality" approach is erroneous. Too much information can be as damaging as too little. Lengthy plans only confuse, overwhelm, or discourage the reader. Nothing is gained by a lengthy, well-prepared plan if people won't read it. And many lengthy plans do not get read. It is easy to reject a long plan after a quick look at its summary. Writers should not make it easy for the reader to reject their plans.

How to Use The Business Mentor CD-ROM

The Business Mentor provides entrepreneurs with an electronic tool to use in the business-planning process. The CD-ROM includes computer templates for the text and uses Microsoft Excel for financial spreadsheets, which give entrepreneurs a jump start in producing business plans. They save entrepreneurs time by assisting with formatting, organizing, and presenting business decisions and information.

The electronic templates allow entrepreneurs to record decisions and enter them directly as they progress through the preformatted topics of the feasibility plan and business plan. There are also built-in helpful tips as well, to provide entrepreneurs additional business-planning assistance. Another alternative is to go directly to the Word templates to complete the feasibility plan or business plan.

Be sure to read the *Quick Start Guide* provided with *The Business Mentor* CD-ROM. It lists the system requirements and provides installation instructions. User information is also available on the CD-ROM by clicking the Technical Help button in the Mentor's Office.

The Business Mentor includes sample business plans, planning templates for feasibility and business plans, as well as features such as tips from entrepreneurs, a glossary, resources, and links to web sites.

It should be noted that the financial template assumes user familiarity with Microsoft Excel. For assistance in learning how to use Microsoft Excel, the following products from Microsoft Press are available through local bookstores or www.microsoft.com: *Running Microsoft Excel; Microsoft Excel Step by Step.*

Interactive questions and answer screens

The Business Mentor contains a series of questions and helpful hints for each of the plan's sections. Users can enter their responses to the questions in the area provided on the screen. Clicking the Need Help button on the left-hand side of the screen provides additional information to clarify the questions. Related Materials, found on the right-hand side of the screen, include a wealth of valuable support materials and can be accessed by clicking on Exercises, Examples, Sample Plans, Resources, and From Real Entreprenuers.

Saving and editing work files

Answers are stored in temporary work files as users advance from one question to the next. To save the answers to the computer's hard drive, the user must manually save their work by clicking on Save. It is important to periodically save work in progress. Users can edit their responses at any time by going to the planning document saved on the word processing or spreadsheet software program. Changes made directly to the documents saved on the computer's hard-drive will not appear in *The Business Mentor's* files. Detailed information on navigating *The Business Mentor* is included in the *Quick Start Guide*.

Excel financial template for the business plan

The financial template provides a Microsoft Excel workbook, which can save hours of time in projecting financial statements for the business plan. The financial template consists of worksheets (where data is entered) and projected financial statements as well as ratio analysis. The worksheets can be included in the appendix of the business plan. The worksheets are presented in a logical sequence for projecting financial information. Adjustments and changes can be made as the plan is developed.

The financial template consists of the following interactive worksheets.

- Introduction—provides valuable information on features of the financial template.
- Set-Up—records company information and the company's current financial position.
- Start-Up—compiles the costs involved in starting the business.
- Sales, Inventory, Operating Expenses, Capital Budget, Equity & Debt— records budget decisions for the next three years. Changes on these worksheets will automatically be updated on the financial projections.

The financial template utilizes the information entered on the worksheets to automatically generate the following documents:

- Monthly Income Statement
- Monthly Cash Flow Statement
- Year-End Income Statement
- Year-End Balance Sheet
- Financial Analysis/Ratios

Two additional functions are provided on worksheets:

- Amortization Schedule—figures principal and interest payments on loans.
- Print Options—with one click, prints instructions, worksheets, or financial statements.

Conclusion

After all of these questions are answered—as well as any additional questions that may surface—the entrepreneur is ready to begin writing and assembling the feasibility or business plan. These answers can be used as the basis for the plan.

The main purpose of a feasibility plan is to test the business concept and determine if it should be further developed. If the answer is yes, the entrepreneur must then consider developing and writing a formal business plan. One should not be disappointed if the completed feasibility plan indicates that the concept is not workable or profitable. Think of the money, time, and embarrassment of failure that can be saved by not pursuing a weak business concept. This is the reason that concept testing and entrepreneurial research and planning are so critical.

Only a small percentage of business concepts pass the test and justify writing a business plan. It is possible that some potential investor or lender may accept the answers to the questions provided in an entrepreneur's feasibility plan instead of asking for a formal business plan, but it is rare.

Many entrepreneurs try to write their feasibility and business plans like research papers or use an elaborate writing style. Instead, they should use short, clear sentences; break up and organize text with subheadings; use bullets to draw attention to important aspects; and take advantage of white space, graphics, or pictures to make the pages more inviting to read.

A good business plan not only takes much time and effort to develop but also will be modified many times as new information comes to light. As entrepreneurs mature as businesspeople, they find that more and more of their time is devoted to planning, for it is really the professional management that directs and controls a business's activities.

Exercise 8a. Feasibility Plan Checklist

This checklist can be used to critique feasibility plans.

Overall Comments

Readability

Strong Adequate Weak

❑ ❑ ❑ Language is concise (does not read like a novel or term paper).
❑ ❑ ❑ Each section clearly defines and satisfies its objective.
❑ ❑ ❑ Conclusions drawn from facts are reasonable.
❑ ❑ ❑ Facts are supported with sufficient charts and graphs.

Comments:

_____

_____

Spelling/grammar/math

Strong Adequate Weak

❑ ❑ ❑ Spelling is correct.
❑ ❑ ❑ Grammar is clean.
❑ ❑ ❑ Math is correct.

Comments:

_____

_____

Formatting

Strong Adequate Weak

❑ ❑ ❑ Font choice is readable.
❑ ❑ ❑ Spacing between lines is sufficient.
❑ ❑ ❑ Plan contains subheads.
❑ ❑ ❑ Formatting on heads and subheads is consistent.
❑ ❑ ❑ Plan contains page numbers.
❑ ❑ ❑ Formatting on page numbers is consistent.
❑ ❑ ❑ Plan contains enough white space for readability.

Comments:

_____

_____

Cover Page/Table of Contents

Strong Adequate Weak

❑ ❑ ❑ Cover page contains name of business.
❑ ❑ ❑ Cover page contains entrepreneur's and chief executive's name if different.
❑ ❑ ❑ Cover page contains address, telephone, and fax numbers.
❑ ❑ ❑ Cover page contains company logo.
❑ ❑ ❑ Page numbers in table of contents correspond correctly.

Comments:

_____

_____

Sections of the Feasibility Plan

Executive summary

Strong	Adequate	Weak	
❑	❑	❑	Has appropriate length (does not exceed two pages and only describes the new venture).
❑	❑	❑	Describes the business the venture is in.
❑	❑	❑	Specifies why the product/service is unique and what proprietary rights the business has.
❑	❑	❑	Gives an overview of the market section.
❑	❑	❑	Specifies how much money is needed to start the venture.
❑	❑	❑	Describes financing needs of the company.

Comments:

_____

_____

Product/service

Strong	Adequate	Weak	
❑	❑	❑	Describes purpose and unique features of product/service.
❑	❑	❑	Identifies stage of development for product/service.
❑	❑	❑	Identifies shelf life of product/service.
❑	❑	❑	Identifies proprietary rights.
❑	❑	❑	Describes the necessary government approvals and their status.
❑	❑	❑	Describes the liabilities the product/service may pose.
❑	❑	❑	Identifies the means of production.

Comments:

_____

_____

The market

Industry profile

Strong	Adequate	Weak	
❑	❑	❑	Addresses current market size.
❑	❑	❑	Addresses growth potential of the market.
❑	❑	❑	Addresses industry trends.

Comments:

_____

_____

Other marketing issues:

Strong	Adequate	Weak	
❑	❑	❑	Contains customer profile.
❑	❑	❑	Contains target markets and size of each.
❑	❑	❑	Addresses market penetration.
❑	❑	❑	Contains customer benefits.
❑	❑	❑	Describes nature of competition.

Comments:

_____

_____

Price and profitability

Strong Adequate Weak

Strong	Adequate	Weak	
❑	❑	❑	States the price the end user will be charged.
❑	❑	❑	Includes sales projections for the new venture by product/service for three years.
❑	❑	❑	Describes the cost for the product/service for three years.
❑	❑	❑	Identifies the gross margin for each product/service for three years.
❑	❑	❑	Identifies the sales, cost of goods, gross margin, operating expenses, and profit by year for the next three years.
❑	❑	❑	Identifies the start-up costs for the business.

Comments:

Plan for further action

Strong Adequate Weak

Strong	Adequate	Weak	
❑	❑	❑	Identifies specific pitfalls (not vague) of the business concept.
❑	❑	❑	Identifies the specific positives and strong points (not vague) of the business concept.
❑	❑	❑	Addresses how capital will be obtained.
❑	❑	❑	Clearly states what the entrepreneur's role will be in the business.
❑	❑	❑	States whether or not a business plan will be written and why.
❑	❑	❑	Addresses whether or not product/service will be licensed.
❑	❑	❑	Identifies possible corporate partners.
❑	❑	❑	Lists any proprietary rights.
❑	❑	❑	Identifies infrastructure members (involvement, cost).

Comments:

Summary Comments Overall

1. Strengths:

2. Weaknesses:

3. Suggestions for improvement

Exercise 8b. Business Plan Checklist

This checklist can be used to critique business plans.

Overall Comments

Readability

Strong	Adequate	Weak	
❑	❑	❑	Language is concise (does not read like a novel or term paper).
❑	❑	❑	Section stands on its own and clearly defines and satisfies its objective.
❑	❑	❑	Facts are supported with sufficient documentation.
❑	❑	❑	Conclusions drawn from facts are reasonable.
❑	❑	❑	Facts are supported with sufficient charts and graphs.

Comments:

_____

_____

Spelling/grammar/math

Strong	Adequate	Weak	
❑	❑	❑	Spelling is correct.
❑	❑	❑	Grammar is clean.
❑	❑	❑	Math is correct.

Comments:

_____

_____

Formatting

Strong	Adequate	Weak	
❑	❑	❑	Font choice is readable.
❑	❑	❑	Spacing between lines is sufficient.
❑	❑	❑	Plan contains subheads.
❑	❑	❑	Formatting on heads and subheads is consistent.
❑	❑	❑	Plan contains page numbers.
❑	❑	❑	Formatting on page numbers is consistent.
❑	❑	❑	Plan contains enough white space for readability.

Comments:

_____

_____

Cover Page/Table of Contents

Strong	Adequate	Weak	
❑	❑	❑	Cover page contains name of business.
❑	❑	❑	Cover page contains chief executive's name.
❑	❑	❑	Cover page contains address, telephone, fax numbers, e-mail and web address.
❑	❑	❑	Cover page contains company logo.
❑	❑	❑	Page numbers in table of contents correspond correctly.
❑	❑	❑	Table of contents includes contents for appendix.

Comments:

_____

_____

Sections of the Business Plan

Executive summary

Strong	Adequate	Weak	
❑	❑	❑	Has appropriate length (does not exceed three pages and wholly describes the new venture).
❑	❑	❑	Identifies company's unique features.
❑	❑	❑	Specifies what the management team hopes to accomplish.
❑	❑	❑	Specifies how much money the company needs and how funds will be obtained.

Comments:

_____

_____

Existing business

Strong	Adequate	Weak	
❑	❑	❑	Describes when and why the company was formed.
❑	❑	❑	Describes the marketing history of the product and service.
❑	❑	❑	Outlines the company's annual sales, profits, and overall performance to date.

Comments:

_____

_____

Management and organization plan

Strong	Adequate	Weak	
❑	❑	❑	Lists key management positions.
❑	❑	❑	Outlines primary job duties and responsibilities assigned to each position.
❑	❑	❑	Identifies the individuals who are expected to fill each position.
❑	❑	❑	Summarizes each person's prior business experience.
❑	❑	❑	Establishes credibility of the management team.
❑	❑	❑	Provides explanation of how deficiencies will be overcome.

Comments:

_____

_____

Product/service plan

Strong	Adequate	Weak	
❑	❑	❑	Describes product/service in plain English (not too technical).
❑	❑	❑	Describes product/service in specific terms (not too broad).
❑	❑	❑	Identifies unique features.
❑	❑	❑	Identifies special benefits.
❑	❑	❑	Wholly explains liability limitations.
❑	❑	❑	Identifies all fixed, variable and indirect product and service costs.
❑	❑	❑	Anticipates future development plans.
❑	❑	❑	Lists requirements from regulatory agencies.
❑	❑	❑	Provides evidence that the product and service is technologically feasible.
❑	❑	❑	Provides backup suppliers and subcontractors.

Comments:

_____

_____

Marketing plan

Industry profile

Strong	Adequate	Weak	
❑	❑	❑	Addresses current market size.
❑	❑	❑	Addresses growth potential of the market.
❑	❑	❑	Addresses geographic locations.
❑	❑	❑	Addresses industry trends.
❑	❑	❑	Addresses seasonal factors.
❑	❑	❑	Addresses profit characteristics.
❑	❑	❑	Addresses existing distribution networks.
❑	❑	❑	Addresses basis of industry competition.

Comments:

_____

_____

Competition

Strong	Adequate	Weak	
❑	❑	❑	Contains chart to illustrate competitive position in marketplace.
❑	❑	❑	Describes competitive advantage.
❑	❑	❑	Summarizes nature of competition.

Comments:

_____

_____

Pricing

Strong	Adequate	Weak	
❑	❑	❑	Contains price sheet.
❑	❑	❑	Contains volume and special pricing information.
❑	❑	❑	Contains pricing procedures for industry.
❑	❑	❑	Addresses gross margin potential.

Comments:

_____

_____

Other marketing issues

Strong	Adequate	Weak	
❑	❑	❑	Contains customer profile.
❑	❑	❑	Contains target markets and size of each.
❑	❑	❑	Addresses market penetration.
❑	❑	❑	Addresses advertising and promotion.
❑	❑	❑	Addresses packaging and labeling.
❑	❑	❑	Addresses customer reaction.
❑	❑	❑	Addresses warranties and guarantees.
❑	❑	❑	Addresses trade shows.
❑	❑	❑	Discusses future markets.

Comments:

_____

_____

Financial plan

Strong Adequate Weak

❑	❑	❑	Sales and profit projections appear reasonable.
❑	❑	❑	Assumptions/projections are wholly supported.
❑	❑	❑	All operating expenses have been included.
❑	❑	❑	Hidden costs have been identified.
❑	❑	❑	Salaries and other benefits are in line.
❑	❑	❑	Contingency plan seems reasonable if sales forecasts go unmet.
❑	❑	❑	Financial documents are mathematically correct.
❑	❑	❑	Figures on various documents (cash flow, income statement, balance sheet) are consistent.

Comments:

Operating and control systems plan

Strong Adequate Weak

❑	❑	❑	Demonstrates understanding and importance of control systems.
❑	❑	❑	Contains a contingency plan if schedule cannot be met.
❑	❑	❑	Identifies key goals and allows sufficient time to accomplish them.
❑	❑	❑	Identifies uncontrollable variables.
❑	❑	❑	Provides honest assessment of the downside risks involved.
❑	❑	❑	Addresses legal liability issues.

Comments:

Growth plan

Strong Adequate Weak

❑	❑	❑	Identifies the significant new products and services planned for continued growth.
❑	❑	❑	Identifies the market place for new products and services.
❑	❑	❑	Contains five-year projection for growth that agrees with financial section.
❑	❑	❑	Identifies the financial requirements for the new products and services.
❑	❑	❑	Identifies management personnel needed to support growth.
❑	❑	❑	Addresses how growth plan will enable owner and investor exit.

Comments:

Appendix

Strong Adequate Weak

❑	❑	❑	Contains three-year financial assumptions/projections.
❑	❑	❑	Contains resumes of management team/key personnel.
❑	❑	❑	Contains all employee contracts, stock option plans, retirement plans.
❑	❑	❑	Contains personal financial statements for each of the principals.
❑	❑	❑	Contains patent, copyright approvals.
❑	❑	❑	Contains all of the following applicable agreements: partnerships, sales, distributor contracts, noncompete/nondisclosure, corporate bylaws, and other legal documents.
❑	❑	❑	Contains copies of product and service brochures or other advertising samples.
❑	❑	❑	Contains copies of all logos developed.
❑	❑	❑	Contains copies of recent reference letters, recommendations, and endorsements.
❑	❑	❑	Contains copies of market studies or articles from trade journals or other media.

Appendix

Strong	Adequate	Weak	
❑	❑	❑	Contains professional photographs of the product.
❑	❑	❑	Contains detailed outlines of the operating/control systems.
❑	❑	❑	Contains customer-signed orders or letter of intent.
❑	❑	❑	Contains documents which support the industry study.
❑	❑	❑	Contains detailed description of high-tech products.
❑	❑	❑	Contains a map showing location of business.
❑	❑	❑	Contains a copy of credit reports.
❑	❑	❑	Contains tax returns for last three years.

Comments:

_____

_____

Summary Comments Overall

1. Strengths:

_____

_____

_____

_____

2. Weaknesses:

_____

_____

_____

_____

3. Suggestions for improvement

_____

_____

_____

_____

Concept Development

Learning Objectives

In this chapter, students will learn
- How to identify flaws in a business concept.
- How to identify positive traits of a business concept.
- What key questions need to be answered in order to write a concise concept statement.

A business concept is a set of thoughts that communicate to others the precise nature of the proposed enterprise. Or more formally, a concept is a set of cohesive ideas about how to create and deliver value to a market. A concept may be simple: To export used clothing to Third World countries. Or it may be complex: To develop, manufacture, market, and service a line of computerized devices that monitor and centrally record the usage of power, gas, and steam by individual tenants in large apartment complexes.

A dream is not a concept. Just about everybody dreams of economic success, but they do little or nothing to make their dreams a reality. True, a dream may be the beginning of a viable concept, but it takes much more than dreaming to be a successful entrepreneur.

An idea is not a concept. An idea is first cousin to a dream. All sorts of people come up with ideas and think they are entrepreneurs. James is now 42-years-old. While he was in college, he showed great entrepreneurial inclinations. He did buy a good business during his senior year, but he sold it within a few months when he tired of the work. James has at least one idea a day about how to make some money. Some of his ideas are really good. He could have made a lot of money with them, but he hasn't. James is what is called an armchair entrepreneur. He talks a good game. All sorts of engaging ideas will spill from his lips at cocktail parties, but nothing happens. They are just ideas, not concepts.

Entrepreneurs don't need a lot of ideas. They need just one that they can make a reality. People who are always looking for that one great idea that will make them wealthy seldom find it.

Successful entrepreneurs seem to be able to articulate clearly the precise nature of their businesses. If a person cannot do so, then others wonder if he or she really has a clear idea of what he or she wants to do.

It is not sufficient to say: "I want to open a restaurant." Such a statement tells the listener little. Instead, a potential restaurateur might say, "I intend to open a restaurant featuring moderately priced Mexican food served in an attractively decorated Spanish motif building located in the El Paseo Plaza of Palm Desert, California. We will have strolling musicians playing Spanish and Mexican music at mealtimes. In addition to the traditional fare served in such eateries, we will develop specialty dishes, appetizers, and drinks that will be ours alone." Now, readers have a better idea of what the entrepreneur proposes to do. And they get the idea that he or she has clearly in mind the precise nature of the venture and that much thought has already been given to it.

> A business concept is only an idea until a feasibility plan or business plan has been written to prove it has the potential to be a viable business.

Successful concepts tend to differ significantly in meaningful ways from those of competitors. A "me too" concept is weak. Perhaps, the concept is bigger or smaller, cheaper or more expensive, better or worse, or whatever. It is necessary to differentiate the concept from those of the competitors.

A Conceptual Model

While there are always some factors overlooked in the development of models, there is still some virtue in creating a conceptual model for a new venture. The model should precisely explain the following.

- What value is to be exchanged?
- To whom?
- For what?
- By what means?
- Where?
- Made by whom?
- Marketed by whom?
- Financed by whom?
- Conceptual flaws

Fatal Flaws
Won't work
No real need
Hidden traps
Unfortunate economics
No protection
Obsolescense
Installation
Education
Changing conumer
  behavior
Assumptions
Inconvenient
Service requirements

Many new enterprises are doomed from the start because the basic concepts upon which they are based are somehow fatally flawed. Perhaps the concept sounds good, but won't work in the real world. Perhaps the concept solves a problem that only exists in the entrepreneur's head; the intended customer has no need for it. Perhaps the concept contains a hidden snare, a trap not apparent to even careful thought. Or perhaps there just isn't a large enough market for it to make the enterprise successful.

It won't work

All sorts of great sounding inventions are used as a basis for starting a business. Many never get to market; the inventor cannot make the invention work satisfactorily outside the laboratory. One expert in water purifying began a venture to market his new concept in water purifiers. Supposedly, it would purify even sea water in agricultural quantities at a cost of 30 cents per 1,000 gallons. "It will revolutionize the world's food supply." So far, after five years and five million dollars, he has yet to do anything but play show and tell in his lab. Evidently, he has not been able to make it work right.

In evaluating high-tech business plans, one of the first things potential investors should do is get outside technical appraisals of a proposed product. Professional investors need to seek technological evaluations by established experts in the proposed technology. Will it work? Is the technology sound? Does this person really know anything on which money can be made? Such questions must be answered favorably before the investor has any interest in looking at a business plan. Investors have learned by bitter experience that the world is loaded with technical people who really don't know what they are talking about, whose ideas won't work. Just because someone has a long string of degrees from prestigious universities and has worked for some impressive people doesn't mean automatically that his or her concepts will work.

No real need

Businesses fail when they don't fill some need perceived by enough people to make operations profitable. Problems that loom large in some entrepreneur's mind may not be too pressing to other people.

When the Coca Cola Co. introduced a new Coca Cola to capture a greater market share, the customers said, "We do not need a new Coke, we like the old one." There was no perceived value for the new product.

Hidden traps

A product may threaten the career of the person who is supposed to buy it. Thus, a real barrier to its marketing lies hidden in the marketplace. When first introduced, the concept of interactive, computerized, company-specific video training programs was stifled largely because training and development people in companies saw it as a threat to their jobs. They rationalized that off-the-shelf training wasn't as effective as face-to-face training. Always assess the intended customer's reaction to the concept.

Most hidden traps lie in the minds of the intended customers, but not always. Sometimes they are physical. A line of 12 plastic disks called Astro Wheels encountered great difficulty obtaining distribution in the retail outlets it needed (supermarkets, drug stores, and gift shops), because the size of the disks required that they be hung on a wire rack that simply did not fit comfortably in those stores. There was no natural place to put them in the stores and potential sales were too small for any store to bother creating a place for the line. Moreover, shoppers would clog the aisles as they stood around the rack reading the astrological materials on the wheels. The dealers in the test markets were unhappy with the line despite its solid sales record. "It just isn't worth the bother" was an often heard comment.

Unfortunate economics

Some concepts will work and people perceive a need for them, but their costs are so high that they won't pay enough to make the venture profitable. If the customer won't pay at least five times direct product costs for an item, it is not likely to be profitable. True, there are exceptions, but few people are eager to go into business on exceptions. If the economics are not right, the venture is doomed. The market must be willing to pay a sufficient price for the concept before the venture can be profitable.

No protection

Some concepts, if proven sound, can be easily copied by other organizations capable of quickly exploiting the market, perhaps driving the entrepreneur from it. Investors are leery of new enterprises that have no protection, no patents, no copyrights, no trade secrets, no organizational or distributive advantages, no locational monopoly, or no cost advantage. If the nature of such a venture lends itself to the economies of size and the market has proven to be large and profitable, then entry into the industry by large competitors is likely. Sometimes, a venture's protection lies in the smallness of its market niche; it can make money serving some small segment of the market while larger firms cannot.

In other instances, the entrepreneur can prosper capturing only a small portion of the eventual market, while larger firms compete for the bulk of it. There are many ways to build profitable businesses, even in the most competitive of large markets. There are small specialty soap companies that do well with large soap companies as their "competitors." The key is to position such endeavors in a way that they really are not competing directly with the larger companies.

A woman started a company called Kids Only Taxi Service. She drives elementary students to and from school and will take them to their after-school functions. Working parents praise her service. Regular taxi services are usually more expensive and often will not take unaccompanied children. This leaves a market niche for someone who wants to perform a personalized service that solves a major problem for parents.

Obsolescence

How long is the concept's life? Many concepts are so faddish that an enterprise based on them has only a few months to make its profits. The pet rock didn't last long. Quiches and crepe restaurants used to be hot, but today soft pretzels, gourmet bagel stores, and coffee houses are in.

Some concepts have technological obsolescence. One large firm had to write off millions of dollars in research on a new type of microprocessor when a competitor leapfrogged over it technically with another approach to the same problem. Its concept, though sound, was obsolete before it was ready to leave the laboratory. The high-tech entrepreneur must be prepared to prove to backers that the new enterprise will have the capability to stay ahead of the market technically. Where will e-commerce be in 10 years? How will dot-com concepts of today fit in the marketplace five years from now? This is what investors will want to know.

Installation

Many concepts sound great until the realities of placing them into use are confronted. Customers don't buy products or services, they buy benefits. They buy solutions to their problems, which are not solved until the concept is in place and working satisfactorily.

All sorts of ventures have met with disaster when their products could not be installed and made to work properly. Many things that work well in the laboratory won't work at all in the field when installed. It's not smart to use factory people to do the installing in test markets unless the venture's plan is to do factory installations in the continued marketing of the product.

An innovative home heating unit was designed by some clever engineers. The first six units tested well when they were installed in the homes of company executives. The next winter, 200 units were installed in homes in Dallas. All 200 had to be replaced. The product's unique control unit was too sensitive to withstand the rigors of being installed by the heating contractors in the field, whose motto is, "If it doesn't fit, get a bigger hammer." The problem was never solved so the project was finally cancelled after a loss of several million dollars.

Education

If the new product will be successful only after the customer has been educated to use it, watch out. Education is a slow, costly process that poses great risks. Not many people welcome being educated to use a new product. Instead, it is much more comfortable to continue using old familiar products or ways.

Changing consumer behavior

Along the same line, consumer behavior is learned over time through numerous experiences in the marketplace. People have learned to institute certain actions to solve certain problems they perceive; experience has taught them what to do to solve that problem in the most satisfactory way. Consequently, consumer behavior has much stability and regularity.

Along comes a concept that requires a change in consumer behavior. It will be resisted unless the rewards are obviously sufficient to motivate the change in behavior.

All sorts of products have fallen victim to this trap. The developers of computerized grocery stores failed when they assumed that shoppers would prefer not to shop in supermarkets and, instead, telephone in their

---

Thinking "Outside of the Bottle"

As the entrepreneur learns more about the competition, the industry studies, and so on, the concept will change. Because it is nearly impossible to create innovations in a vacuum, the entrepreneur always is in an information-gathering mode. With more information in hand, the entrepreneur must then look beyond the conventional view.

For example, if an empty Coke bottle is placed in front of four or five people who are asked to name alternative uses for the bottle, they would list many. They might suggest that the bottle is a flower vase, a container for liquid, or a candlestick.

But what if the bottle is broken? Now how many ways could it be used? The base is an ash tray, the mouth is a ring or pendant, the smaller pieces can cover the bottom of a fish tank, and the ideas can go on indefinitely.

The entrepreneur needs to look outside the Coke bottle to see the possibilities. Good entrepreneurs are able to smash through conventional perceptions to find new ways to succeed. Domino's Pizza applied this idea to the pizza industry. The conventional way to get ahead in the pizza business used to be to create novel crust styles and toppings. However, the entrepreneur who started Domino's Pizza got "outside of the bottle" and saw a different way to satisfy the customer. Rather than revolutionize pizza, he revolutionized delivery, using a unique grid system to reduce delivery time. As a result, the pizza business was forever changed.

orders to a computerized grocery warehouse. In fact, studies show that most people like shopping in supermarkets rather than dealing with the problems posed by other grocery shopping systems, which have shown only limited success.

People are now doing what they want to do for reasons that are sound to them. They are not going to change just because an entrepreneur thinks they should do so. They will resist change unless the motivation is exceptionally powerful.

Assumptions

People can get into trouble with assumptions. One important procedure in evaluating a feasibility plan or business plan is to identify all of the assumptions it is based on and then severely question them.

All entrepreneurial endeavors are based on assumptions. Assumptions are unavoidable. Some, such as the entrepreneur will stay healthy, are simple. Others may be less obvious: It is assumed that the target market will continue its present state of prosperity. Some can be devastating: An entrepreneur may assume that the selected store locations can be properly zoned. If the locations cannot be zoned for the projected activity, then a new plan is needed.

After identifying the assumptions, the entrepreneur should try to find information that validates them. What reasons does the entrepreneur have to believe the assumptions are true?

Inconvenient

The principle of convenience is basic to marketing and when it is violated, difficulties arise. People tend to behave in ways that are most convenient to them. Convenience translates into time and effort. If a concept is a more convenient way for the intended buyer to do business, give it a big plus. If not, watch out.

Entrepreneurs who provide computer repair services in the customer's home or office with a quick response time save the customer the inconvenience and lost time involved with having a computer down as well as the hassle of bringing the CPU into a repair shop.

Legions of retailers have floundered when they assumed that their intended customers would go a little out of their way to patronize their out-of-the-way store (poor location) because of its superior offering, be it lower prices, assortment, or service. Sometimes, they will; sometimes, they won't, depending on a multitude of factors.

Many new products and services fail because they are inconvenient to use, such as car waxes that are too much work to apply.

Assemble-it-yourself products continually draw the ire of consumers who encounter great difficulty putting the things together. That is why new ventures have sprung up assembling these products for a fee. Many a customer is filled with trepidation upon seeing the words, "some assembly required."

Service requirements

Does the concept require service? If so, by whom? A service aspect to a concept greatly complicates it: costs rise, organizational difficulties multiply, and buyer resistance stiffens. Entrepreneurs have to be prepared to explain how they propose to handle whatever service requirements are connected with their concepts. Logistical difficulties have ruined many concepts.

Strong Attributes of Successful Products

There are some definite attributes that help a product or service succeed in the marketplace. Ventures that offer a product or service with the following attributes are looked upon with great favor.

Involves significant savings

Money is at the heart of business. If a concept saves either the customer or the seller a lot of money, the entrepreneur has the beginning of an interesting proposition. There is money to work with from the large gross margins that will result. Great concepts create products and services with clear-cut, recognizable values; people can see that they are better off financially with the product or service than without it.

One high-tech company, trying to sell a communications network for telemetering data from remote physical entities to a centralized control point via a satellite, encountered marketing resistance when it could not be clearly proven just what savings were realized by gathering the information that way. Everyone seems to be so in love with information these days that few people ask, "Why do we want to know it? How is the data going to make us money?"

Solves serious problem

The developers of the polio vaccine were not worried about its sale. If one can find a cure for the common cold, AIDS, or cancer, then obviously it will succeed. Concepts that deal with serious problems are given full consideration by the market. In fact, many faulty concepts are given the go-ahead just because they are dealing with serious matters.

Offers convenience

The lack of convenience was previously mentioned as a conceptual flaw. If a concept somehow makes life far more convenient for its intended customer, it will likely be given a successful hearing. Many people grapple with longer work hours, less leisure time, and killer commutes. Time-starved consumers need and demand quick and convenient solutions for routine tasks. Mobile psychological services, on-site custom apparel shopping services, personal fitness trainers, transportation coordinating (Mom's Taxi), and personal chefs are a few examples of new ventures providing conveniences to consumers.

Fits existing scheme of things

If a product or service fits nicely into the existing system, resistance to it will be much less than if it does not fit. Recall the Astro Wheels that did not fit the way the stores display their merchandise. Big screen TVs originally

Positive Attributes
Involves significant savings
Solves serious problem
Offers convenience
Fits existing scheme of things
Attracts media attention
Clearly identifies market
Captures a monopoly
Joins a rapidly expanding
   market
Promises a big upside;
   low downside

encountered acceptance problems because they did not fit into many homes. There was not a place to put one since it was too big and awkward. Today, many mega screen TVs are only six inches deep.

Attracts media attention

If a product or service will attract the attention of the news media, its promotion will be greatly facilitated. Is the concept interesting? Has it news value? If not, it's just another product fighting for a place in the market. Look at how much publicity there has been for new products and services for pets: doggie businesses providing day care, dog-goodie bakeries, cat furniture stores. New and novel ideas attract feature stories.

Clearly identifies market

Can the potential customers for the concept be clearly identified? Can they be named? Who will be the first customer? Who is next? Are there purchase orders? If so, the proposition becomes more interesting. If not, one wonders who will buy.

Captures a monopoly

Entrepreneurs love monopolies! That's where the profits come from. If the concept sells into a market in which it will be the only seller, a profitable business may be in the making. Venture capitalists love to invest in companies that have strong patents or copyrights because this can create a monopoly.

Joins a rapidly expanding market

An example of a rapidly expanding market is the gift market, which has experienced continual growth. It is attractive because it is large and is constantly seeking new products and services. It is receptive to new concepts, not resistant. Moreover, the gift buyer is not usually a price buyer, thus gross margins are not under severe pressure, as is the case in price-sensitive markets. The Internet is another example of a rapidly expanding market.

Promises a big upside; low downside

A concept that promises large potential profits with a modest downside risk naturally gains attention, just as the reverse repulses investors. If the odds are attractive, the concept may get attention despite some apparent flaws.

Writing a Concept

The acid test for a well-defined concept statement is to hand it to a stranger and have him or her relate back precisely what the proposed business is.

Even when the concept is clear, it will change over time as the entrepreneur learns more about the market and the economics of the new venture. It is perfectly natural, so most good business concepts do change. If they don't change, there may be reason to worry.

The concept statement will be reviewed and modified as additional information is gathered from the answers to other questions presented in the planning process. The last section completed in a feasibility or business plan is the executive summary, and the concept statement becomes the basis for this section.

Entrepreneur's Resource List

Books

Brabec, Barbara. *Homemade Money, Starting Smart!* M. Evans and Company: 2003.

Clark, Scott A. *Beating the Odds: 10 Smart Steps to Small Business Success.* HTC Group: 1993.

Edwards, Paul and Sarah, and Lisa Roberts. *The Best Home Business for the 21st Century.* Putnam: 1999.

Edwards, Paul and Sarah. *The Entrepreneurial Parent: How to Earn Your Living and Still Enjoy Your Family, Your Work and Your Life.* Tarcher: 2002.

Long, Kim. *The American Forecaster Almanac.* American Forecaster: 2004.

Mancuso, Joseph R. *How to Prepare and Present a Business Plan.* Prentice-Hall, Englewood Cliffs, NJ: 1992.

Rich, Stanley, and David Gumpert. *Business Plans That Win $$$: Lessons from the MIT Enterprise Forum.* Harper & Row: 1987.

RMA Annual Statement Studies, RMA-Risk Management Association, Philadelphia. (Published annually)

Magazines

American Demographics, P.O. Box 2042, Marion, OH 43306.

Brabec Bulletin, www.barbarabracbec.com. This online newsletter is dedicated to helping small businesses grow and prosper.

Contacts

Small Business Administration (www.sba.gov). The local SBA office in your area will provide you with a list of government agencies, trade associations, chambers of commerce, professionals, and counselors.

Small Business Development Centers (www.sba.gov/sbdc/). Contact one of the SBDCs in your area to assist you in starting a new venture. SBDCs are advisory centers located in more than 900 cities and are a partnership of the SBA, the local university and the local and state government. SBDCs provide free management-consulting services to current and prospective business owners. They also offer training, technical assistance, and business resource services. Counselors will match your needs with existing resources and identify consultants who have expertise in your specialty area.

Service Corps of Retired Executives (www.SCORE.org). SCORE provides free, confidential counseling for entrepreneurs. SCORE has 389 chapters in the United States. It also offers small-business workshops for a nominal fee. Local SCORE offices are listed in the blue government section of the phone book, under Small Business Administration or call (800) 634-0245.

Local Colleges and Universities. Many colleges and universities offer entrepreneurial courses or workshops on writing a business plan.

Chambers of Commerce. Many local chambers of commerce offer workshops and/or seminars on how to write a plan. Call the chamber in your area.

National Business Incubation Association (www.nbia.org), 20 E. Circle Drive, Suite 190, Athens, OH 45701, (740) 593-4331. The National Business Incubation Association can provide information and resources about any type of business incubator located in the United States. The association also publishes a useful newsletter.

Census of Business (www.census.gov), U.S. Bureau of the Census, Washington, DC 20233.

Census of Population (www.census.gov/population), U.S. Census of The Population, Washington, DC 20233.

National Association of Small Business Investment Companies (www.nasbic.org), 666 11th St., N.W., Suite 750, Washington, DC 20001, (202) 628-5080. SBICs, regulated by the SBA, license and provide loans to small businesses.

PRO.Net, Procurement Assistance, Small Business Administration (www.pro-net.sba.gov), 1441 L Street, N.W., Rm. 628, Washington, DC 20416. Through this agency, the SBA facilitates and promotes small-business procurement opportunities. It brings together federal agencies, major contractors, and entrepreneurs.

Small Business Administration, Publications, P.O. Box 46521, Denver, CO 80201. This organization offers both free and low-cost budget booklets to help entrepreneurs develop budgets, personnel policies, and business plans.

Small Business Innovation Research Program, U.S. Small Business Administration (www.sba.gov/sbir/), Office of Innovation, Research and Technology, SBA, 409 Third St., Mail Code 6470, Washington, DC 20416, (202) 205-6450. This agency provides seed funds for research and development grants.

U.S. Government Printing Office, Superintendent of Documents (www.gpo.gov), Washington, DC 20402, (202) 512-1800. This office prints hundreds of thousands of documents and booklets that help entrepreneurs start and operate their ventures.

Exercise 9a: Writing a Business Concept

Answer the following questions based on your business concept.

Function of product or service

1. What is the important and distinct function of the product/service? What are its strongest attributes, such as cost, design, quality, capabilities? Include any photographs or sketches.

Proprietary aspects

2. What are the proprietary aspects of the product/service, such as patents, trademarks, trade secrets, or copyrights?

Innovative technology

3. What innovative technology is involved with the product/service?

Position in industry

4. What position does the concept play in the industry, such as manufacturer, distributor/wholesaler, retailer?

Intended customer

5. Who is the intended customer? Include demographic descriptions such as age, gender, profession, income, and the like.

Customer benefits

6. What benefits will be delivered to the customer? Explain what problems you are solving for your customer.

Market-penetration methods

7. How will the product/service be sold to the customer? Explain which distribution channels will be used, such as sales reps, direct sales force, direct mail, telemarketing, other.

Who will make or supply the product/servivce?

8. Who will make the product or design the service? Will it be subcontracted to a manufacturer, or will it be produced in-house?

Exercise 9b: Write Your Concise Concept Statement

Use the answers to Exercise 9a, which provide an outline, to help in writing the concept. Be prepared to present your business concept in two minutes or less at the next class session.

Model Business

Learning Objectives

In this chapter, students will learn to

- Evaluate the characteristics of a perfect business.
- Rate a business concept against the model business to determine its positives and negatives.

Entrepreneurs evaluate a concept, write a feasibility plan, or develop a business plan so that they can continuously test the concept to determine if it can be successful after all the negative aspects have been considered. There is no such thing as a perfect concept. Entrepreneurs should attempt to discover the weaknesses and then develop solutions to solve potential problems. Some problems found in the concept may not have ready solutions, but the entrepreneur is at least aware of any negative aspects before continuing. Then realistic decisions can be made about whether to proceed further.

Model Business Characteristics

A hypothetical model business can be used to evaluate the positives and negatives of a business concept. This model features the 23 characteristics discussed in this chapter, which affect the chances of success for any venture. It is important for entrepreneurs to spend time matching themselves and their concepts to the list of personal and business criteria in Chapter 1. It is just as critical for them to spend time comparing their concepts to the model business characteristics. This is a method for objectively evaluating a potential venture. After completing both tests, entrepreneurs can be assured that their concepts have a better chance to succeed in the marketplace.

No investment

Obviously, if an entrepreneur does not have to put any money into an enterprise, then he or she can't lose any if it fails. Only the time spent is lost, assuming the entrepreneur has avoided personal liability for the failing firm's debts. The more money that must be put into an enterprise, the larger the risk. Thus, the less attractive that venture becomes to most entrepreneurs.

Model Business Characteristics

No investment
Recognized, established
   market
Perceived need for product
Dependable source of
   input supply
No governmental regulation
No labor
100 percent gross margin
Buyers purchase frequently
Favorable tax treatment
Receptive, established
   distribution system
Great news value
Customers pay in advance
No product- or service-
   liability risk
No product obsolescence
No competition
No fashion obsolescence
No physical perishability
Impervious to weather
Workable and feasible
   product/service
Proprietary rights
Continuous revenue flow
No legal entanglements
Exit potential

Some initial investments require so much capital that there is no way the venture can be a financial success.

Perhaps nowhere is this principle so tested as in the field of the now-popular theme restaurants. Owners often invest hundreds of thousands of dollars in fancy brickwork and designer interiors. Large initial investments make profitable operations difficult. Some make it, some don't. Those entrepreneurs who are infected with the restaurant bug are urged to select themes that are inexpensive to execute—a western saloon, with a sawdust floor and rustic motif, for example. Better yet, take over an expensive restaurant with a great location that has not been successful.

Some clever people manage to begin ventures in which they come away with money up front. They make money from the start by raising more initial investment than is really needed for operations. This is difficult, but it is done. If the venture has strong investment appeal, investors have been known to put up more money initially than is really needed.

Some builders have been able to borrow more money on a property than it cost to build it. They put cash in their pockets, while continuing to own the structures. Certainly, the property must be able to service the debt. During inflationary times, this is a good strategy.

The founder of a company that develops sports programming for the Internet, TV, and radio didn't have much money. He invited investors to participate in his venture for potential rewards—royalties instead of equity. A strategic partnership was formed with Sprint (which wanted to get into the sports market) as a result of the founder's persistence and openness to bartering.

Recognized, established market

The new firm should be selling something to a clearly recognized market that can be counted on to buy the product. No entrepreneur should be haunted by the fear that no one will buy. Would people buy a product that allowed them to access the Internet with the TV set already in their homes? Do people really want a joint system? Do they even need such a product?

It is not just happenstance that most major corporations sit on the sidelines during the pioneering stages of a new product. They are waiting for the market to confirm that it wants the new item. Those who don't wait often pay dearly for the adventure. The video disk disaster is such an example from the 1990s. The managements of the firms that introduced the video disks were convinced video disk players would become a standard appliance in the household, one for each TV set. They were wrong. On the other hand, DVD players have found broad acceptance by the consumer market.

The many chocolate lovers provide a ready market. A couple whose shop sells more than 100 varieties of homemade chocolates knew that they couldn't compete with the malls. With profits dwindling to the point that closing shop had to be considered, they launched the web site www.chocolatevault.com and dramatically increased their sales. About a third of their total business now comes from Internet sales. Despite the anonymity of the Internet, the couple stresses the personal touch: they are real people who care about their customers and their chocolates.

Perceived need for product

Ideally, the intended customers should perceive a need for what the venture intends to sell them. They should know they need the product or service, thus simplifying the selling task. If the customers do not realize their need, marketing becomes more difficult and expensive. Two sales are required instead of one. First, the customers must be persuaded that they need the product or service, and then they must be persuaded to buy it. This is known as educational marketing, which significantly increases marketing costs.

For this reason, products without a perceived need are more difficult to sell than products with a perceived need. Suppose the entrepreneur has a powder that would keep people from getting poison ivy. People probably would not buy it unless they were particularly sensitive to poison ivy and knew they were going to be exposed to it. But if a person had poison ivy, he or she would buy a product that would alleviate the misery. Perceived-need products sell easily.

Internet marketers found that they needed a source of e-mail addresses that hadn't been culled from areas of the Internet and then sold without the owner's knowledge or consent. Using such lists made them guilty of spamming, or sending unsolicited advertising messages. To effectively use e-mail as a marketing medium, online marketers needed the addresses of those who had chosen to receive advertising messages in exchange for points toward online purchases. Opt-in e-mail companies such as mypoints.com were built to fill this need.

> Adept entrepreneurs recognize that a product or service that requires educating the market has a higher cost than a product/service with an established perceived need.

Dependable source of input supply

Many concepts are never launched because there is only one source of supply for the material needed in the final product. For example, a pair of young entrepreneurs had a concept that involved producing and selling scented T-shirts that would withstand washings. The test market was to produce a T-shirt with a rose scent for the annual Rose Bowl football game played in Los Angeles. The process for adding the scent to the T-shirt was owned by a major corporation. The corporation demanded a large initial order that was unrealistic for these relatively young and inexperienced entrepreneurs to make. They were unable to overcome this barrier and were forced to drop the concept.

It is for this reason that the managements of most large corporations want to control their key input resources. They resist being held captive by sole-source suppliers. The American Hospital Supply Co. even went to the extent of putting a firm into the business of making the stainless steel micro tubes that are used for disposable hypodermic needles when it had only one supplier for them.

> Adept entrepreneurs make sure they have adequate supplies so they can provide what they sell.

The product/service section of a feasibility or business plan should always list backup suppliers for the product. Many investors will not give dollars to companies with one-source suppliers.

No governmental regulation

A true entrepreneur will quickly comprehend that the ideal business has no governmental regulation. Naturally, some governmental regulation is inevitable, but what is meant here is considerable governmental interference.

It is particularly difficult for new firms to enter any market requiring Federal Drug Administration (FDA) approval. The time and costs associated with FDA compliance regulations require a large capital investment to sustain the new firm for several years before the FDA rules on granting final marketing approval. Governmental approval is a large risk.

New environmental regulations have made many good business concepts difficult to launch. For example, new governmental regulations containing restrictions on storing fuel underground in tanks has made the cost of opening a gas station or truck stop much higher than in the past. In some places, the government has forced car washes to recycle their water, increasing the costs of the machinery to the owners and increasing the price of washing a car for consumers.

The founder of a retail wine firm took it online (www.sendwine.com). To solve the problem of the many state laws regulating sales of alcohol, the company built a nation-wide network of wine shops. With about 100 retailers, the Internet company can easily and legally arrange shipments to more than 80 percent of the nation's population. However, Congress is now looking more critically at the Internet and regulations could be forthcoming.

> If a business involves governmental regulations, the entrepreneur must understand how they will affect the business in both time and money.

No labor

Ideally, a business requires no labor force. Labor poses management problems and is expensive. Moreover, the government regulates how a company deals with labor. The instant an owner hires someone, he or she has all sorts of governmental paperwork to deal with. Unions may enter the picture. Few managers relish dealing with them. Labor-intensive businesses generally lack appeal to many entrepreneurs.

An owner of multiple McDonald's franchises said that the average turnover of employees is approximately two weeks. In addition, it takes an average of eight hours to train an employee at a cost in wages plus incurring the cost of a trainer, materials, and the like. This particular owner employs about 450 people. Therefore, if the turnover rate could be lengthened by one week, the profit margin would be greater. Instead of being in the fast-food business, the owner feels he is in the employment business. The high costs of labor and turnover can eat up profit margins.

> If a business requires many employees, the entrepreneur must be willing to accept the responsibility and challenge of managing people.

On the other hand, a savvy entrepreneur can make money by hiring people and then managing them wisely. The entrepreneur makes money from labor by hiring it at one price and selling it for a higher price. This is what temporary employment firms are doing today.

A woman who lost her job as a legal secretary used e-Bay, the Internet auction site, to parlay her part-time antiques dealing into a full-time income. She is more than halfway toward her hope of grossing more than $100,000 a year—without tapping her savings and by working alone.

100 percent gross margin

While it is not likely that a firm's gross margin would be 100 percent, the thought is that the larger the gross margin, the better the business. Gross margin is what businesses have left after they pay direct material and labor costs for whatever they sell. Service industries generally have larger gross margins than do product ventures.

The problem with low-gross-margin industries is that slight errors in calculations quickly result in losses. That's why so many discount retailers get into financial difficulty. A 1 percent error can result in substantial losses. Moreover, profits come fast in high-gross-margin businesses once they pass the break-even point. Businesses can make a lot of money on modest sales volumes. The venture's projected gross margin is the main key to profit and is a major factor considered by investors in making a commitment to a new venture.

Most tire stores sell their tires with relatively low gross margins ranging between 20 and 30 percent. However, they increase the stores' gross margins by selling the customer other accompanying products and services that have higher gross margins: valve stems, mounting and balancing tires, alignment, road hazard insurance, and more.

Intellectual capital can be a highly profitable product. Forrester Research conducts in-depth interviews of movers and shakers in the Internet economy and packages that information in research reports that it sells to its clients. Converting knowledge into a format that can be sold as a product to many different clients increases the profit margin.

Buyers purchase frequently

An ideal business has customers that purchase the product or service frequently. Take an extreme example: If a company bought Product XYZ only once each year, its seller would have to wait a year before the next order from that company. If a customer buys daily, the seller has a chance each day to make a sale. One reason the prepared-food industry is such a haven for entrepreneurs is that it is easy to make the first sale to a customer. The problem is getting customers to repeat. Moreover, a frequent purchaser is more likely than an infrequent one to try something new. After all, it's only a short time before an error can be corrected. An infrequent purchase has to be lived with for a long time.

A major manufacturer of razor blades gave razors with the Greek letters of each fraternity printed on the handle to fraternity members on major college campuses. The purpose of this promotion was to tap young male adults and get them hooked on using personalized razors. The only razor blades that would fit these razors were those manufactured by the company. As a result, the company significantly expanded its razor blade sales with this market segment.

An online drug store, planetrx.com, built its business around selling nonprescription items to customers when they returned to the site to renew prescriptions. Just like a traditional drug store, planetrx offers incentives and special offers on products that customers don't have to, but want to, buy.

Favorable tax treatment

Taxes are a fact of life for business. Ideally, a business will be given some tax moratorium, such as that granted to those firms locating in certain areas attracting industrial growth, such as Puerto Rico. Conversely, businesses that operate at a tax disadvantage should be avoided. Some of our states are particularly tax-heavy places in which to do business.

A good business usually has a high gross margin. However, if the venture has a low gross margin, methods can be developed to raise it. Every percentage point of increase in the gross margin will affect the profit of the business.

Investment in businesses that have high gross margins allows for a margin of error in projections.

A concept that has repeat customers after the initial sale is easier and cheaper to market.

The amount of money being invested in the stock market has increased since the government established the right for taxpayers to start retirement accounts and defer income taxes until they retire. This move has provided the opportunity for many new investment firms to start-up in the last few years.

If the business has some tax advantages, it is easier to attract investors.

Since 1986, different state governments have set up Enterprise Zones in economically distressed areas. Companies locating in those zones are granted attractive tax credits and other advantages that are hard to ignore.

A plastics injection molder located his business in an area in which the local government granted it tax concessions for five years. The city wanted to attract firms to provide employment opportunities for local citizens.

Receptive, established distribution system

It is beneficial if a venture can sell a product to an established distributor who is eager to handle it and who needs it. The advantage of tapping into an established distributor is that the company can immediately fill the pipeline. This means that the company is able to sell its product/service to the distributor for its opening inventories. Many founders have raised the money needed to operate their ventures by simply supplying the pipeline.

Whenever possible, adept entrepreneurs look for a concept with an existing distribution system.

If a product/service does not have an established distribution channel, then the entrepreneur may be forced to create more channels for moving products/services. This increases the cost of marketing because the entrepreneur must first identify and locate distributors, sell them on carrying the products/services, and then educate and train their sales staffs before a sale can be made. The entrepreneur without a distribution system spends significant time and effort to establish one. Time is money.

Amazon.com, the online bookseller, uses the same distribution and order fulfillment system as traditional bookstores—the only difference is that its customers browse online to buy books instead of browsing through the shelves of a regular bookstore.

Great news value

Publicity is a great promotional tool. Enterprises have prospered quickly with one good story in the right media. Usually the key to getting good publicity is to have something that is newsworthy, something that grabs the public's attention. The media is not going to get excited about the opening of another hamburger stand. But suppose the hamburgers were made from processed algae; the news media might pick up the story.

One big advantage of high-technology ventures is that they are usually very newsworthy. Some ventures may not have an apparent news value. It is important to find or create news value and then have the media feature the venture. This type of publicity is more credible to potential customers than paid advertising and does not cost money.

One entrepreneur started a temporary employment agency staffed primarily by seniors who wanted only intermittent work but had excellent skills to offer companies. Her business got off to a slow start until a major snowstorm hit her city. She had placed a 68-year-old woman to work for one week beginning on the morning of the snowstorm. The woman showed up for work but found the business closed down due to weather conditions. She called wanting to know why the business had closed and made a comment that workers today don't have a strong work ethic. Recognizing the news value of what occurred, the owner of the temp agency immediately called the newspaper. She spoke to a business reporter who jumped on the story, and the next day, the owner was featured on the front page of the business section in the newspaper. Immediately, her sales drastically increased; she had to install two more phone lines and hire three extra placement counselors.

Adept entrepreneurs find the newsworthy feature of a concept, such as fads, trends, and the like, and then write a press release or feature story to distribute to local news outlets.

FreePC.com made national headlines when it opened for business. An Internet service provider, FreePC offered to give away free computers to people who signed up for its service. In return for the free computer, the customers were required to provide FreePC personal data, which allowed it to offer higher quality demographic information to companies who want to advertise to FreePC's customer base. Unfortunately, advertising did not prove to be a deep source of revenues and support costs were underestimated.

Customers pay in advance

A business likes customers to pay for their orders upon receiving them, or better yet, when they place the order or contract for services. It happens! They need the product and understand that the only way they are going to get it is to pay for it up front. It is common for consultants to collect a nonrefundable retainer up front. Other times, customers are willing to give a deposit. If a business makes anything custom for the buyer, by all means it should get the money up front. Naturally, up-front money greatly reduces the capital requirements, not to mention bad debts.

The business with payments in advance is one of the easiest concepts to launch.

It is also ideal if customers pay in cash, not on credit. Cash businesses have many attractive virtues aside from avoiding bad debts. For example, most subcontractors that make products for other companies require at least a 50 percent cash deposit. This money usually covers their costs of materials and the labor necessary to fill the order. Therefore, they do not use any of their operating capital to fill orders.

An artist who paints portraits of people's pets charges the customer according to the size of the painting. The customer pays 50 percent down, and the balance is paid when the painting is delivered. It takes approximately one week to complete the portrait; however, the artist works on five or six paintings at the same time. The prepayments provide good cash flow while the artist completes the paintings. If by chance the customer does not accept the painting, the artist keeps the deposit and then sells the painting to an art gallery at a greater profit.

No product- or service-liability risk

Some products and services intrinsically have great potential liability. Any drug product or children's toy is loaded with potential product liability. Ideally, entrepreneurs should avoid products that might harm someone. As a general rule, any tangible product that comes into contact with people has the potential to hurt them, particularly anything that is taken internally. Service businesses face similar risks. For caterers, the potential liabilities are obvious.

In this litigious age, every product or service should be carefully evaluated as to its potential liabilities. Entrepreneurs can mitigate those risks by purchasing liability insurance or becoming self-insured. Due diligence is required when investigating the potential liability of a concept.

An entrepreneur who planned to manufacture children's clothing did not realize she would need to make children's sleepwear 100 percent fireproof and to obtain a comprehensive product-liability insurance policy. These requirements significantly increased production costs and reduced gross margins and net profit. After writing a feasibility plan, she decided to abort the concept.

Liability insurance is a rising expense for businesses today. Astute entrepreneurs look carefully at the liability potential for their business concepts.

No product obsolescence

The ideal product or service will not suffer technical obsolescence. Its demand will go on and on. The shorter its technical life, the less attractive it is. This is one of the major difficulties with high-tech ventures. Their economic life is often so short that there is no way for the firm to earn enough money on the product to make the venture profitable.

If the concept has a short product life cycle, adept entrepreneurs continue to add innovations, or add more spin-offs to replace the obsolete products or services.

Rapidly changing consumer-driven trends, new innovations, and technological advances can greatly shorten a product's or service's life cycle. However, some products and services have longer life cycles, such as popcorn and hot dogs. Notice how innovation enhances these traditional products. Today, popcorn comes in a multitude of flavors, and hot dogs are produced in many different varieties, such as kosher beef, turkey, and vegetarian.

In the world of computer technology, many hardware products become obsolete in a short period of time. Software has an even quicker life cycle, thereby increasing development costs. Even though packaging and disk replication costs for software are relatively low, the high retail cost of software programs reflects its shorter life cycle and high cost of research and development. Developers need to generate profits quickly to cover their costs.

The partners who started www.theknot.com thought the Internet would be a good place for couples to shop before they married. The web site offers one-stop wedding information and planning—including an online gift registry, a tool for locating the right gown, write-ups on honeymoon locations, as well as advice. Advertisers know that weddings trigger other purchases and prize the would-be-weds. The site generated ad revenues from the outset. The economic life of www.theknot.com is bright as every new couple that becomes engaged represents another potential customer.

When a company files for a patent and discloses what it is going to patent, if a patent is granted, the product has 20 years of protection from the filing date. A patent helps prevent obsolescence caused by other companies manufacturing and selling the same product, often at a lower price. A technology in the biotech industry can take 10 to 12 years to post FDA requirements, leaving a few years that the company can sell the product or drug with the protection of a patent. Companies in this situation may try to shorten the time it takes to get a patent and obtain FDA approval to lengthen the time it has patent protection. The price that the company sells the product or drug has to be high so it can cover the cost of development and make a profit.

No competition

Obviously, absence of competition makes life easier. But is competition absent because there is no market for the product or service? While little competition can be a double-edged sword, tough competition can mean lower profits. The nature of the competition should not go unnoticed. Is there price competition? If so, without a cost advantage, it is wise to proceed carefully.

If a concept is relatively new, the owner can take advantage of this newness and charge top dollar for its products or services. As more competitors enter the marketplace, the price will eventually be reduced, and so will profits. For example, weekend video rentals were first introduced into the marketplace priced at $6.95. Today, these same videos can be rented for 99 cents.

With no competitors at its start-up, the online gaming venture (www.gamesville.com) welcomes people to play free games—BingoZone™, a luck game, and Picturama™, a skill-based one—and win prizes. Advertising is the basis of the company's revenue and the advertisers love it; the company consistently attracts major advertising dollars from large and high-profile companies.

Competition is a double-edged sword. Too much or too little can be dangerous.

No fashion obsolescence

The whims of fashion being what they are, entrepreneurs are rightfully leery of ventures based on fashionable products. If they plan to compete in a fashion industry, they must create market-pleasing fashions season after season, and that is difficult to do. Fashion dictates success for the manufacturers of many products, such as cars, clothes, and watches, and those who can predict the right fad win big in the marketplace.

Fads have brief life cycles, so it is necessary to develop new adaptations or new ideas on a continual basis. For example, the Hula Hoop had new life when Wham-O added a ball bearing to the plastic tube that created a sound. The Shoop-Shoop was born and became a very successful fad.

A young man wanted to tap the growing gift business and offer an alternative to the usual flowers, balloons, and other standard gift items. He landed on the Internet (www.frangrancenet.com) and is on his way to becoming the largest discount fragrance retailer, carrying more than 1,000 genuine brand names with no knockoffs. An arrangement with a large distributor requires no warehouse and allows the company to carry virtually every available fragrance, including some that are no longer in stores. It can find customers' favorites that the stores have discontinued, allowing him to meet customer demand without carrying inventory that could become obsolete.

Fashion products and services usually have a short life cycle. Adept entrepreneurs will ensure that they can make a profit before the life cycle ends.

No physical perishability

Smart entrepreneurs watch out for products with a short physical life. This applies to more than just fresh vegetables, sourdough bread, and the like. Many products have a limited shelf life. A product with a long shelf life can be stored until a profitable market can be found for it. No such luck for a perishable one; its seller will have to take whatever the price is at the time. If a concept involves a product with limited shelf life, the perishable products must be delivered on a timely basis, and it is advisable to look for innovations, such as developing spin-off products.

An accountant purchased a bakery that specialized in freshly baked sourdough bread. The bakery was not profitable at the time of purchase. The owner's plan was to inject some capital into the business, buy more ovens, purchase more delivery vans, hire more sales people, and expand the sales territory. However, the owner did not recognize the importance of product perishability for sourdough bread. Sourdough bread has only a 24-hour shelf life. Delivery to new locations was time consuming. Sourdough that was not purchased the same day had to be thrown away. The business failed.

An online company (www.coastaltool.com) boasts an online inventory of more than 1,000 power tools and related supplies, from 45 cent screwdriver bits to $975 power saws. This company can afford to carry a large inventory because tools have a long shelf life and do not change often. The company's number-one priority is site navigation, allowing customers to easily browse subsections for the "hammerless" to experienced craftsmen, a Best of Category Tool List, and Ten Gift Ideas.

Impervious to weather

Consider the plight of the landscaper or the ski-area owner whose fortunes are in the hands of the weather. If the weather is right, they prosper; if not, they don't. It makes little sense to invest one's time and money in a venture that is little more than a gamble with the weather. The ideal business is not affected by changes in the weather.

For example, most ski areas have purchased snow-making equipment to keep their slopes open for business every day during the ski season. However, no snow-making equipment can generate snow without freezing temperatures. Coming up with a solution to this problem could be the next innovative concept for an entrepreneur in the ski industry.

The founder of www.igogolf.com wanted to offer the finest golf equipment worldwide at discount prices. He launched a multilingual site, with pages in French, Spanish, German, and Japanese, and staffed his company with golf experts instead of clueless order takers. By selling internationally, he can take advantage of the differences in seasons.

Workable and feasible product/service

Many new ventures encounter difficulty when their products or services fail to work well or are in some ways not feasible. Some concepts might not be feasible because they are prototypes and have not met governmental requirements or because high costs are involved in developing the product. Another reason could be that the concept has already been invented and patented by someone else. There can be numerous reasons why the product or service may not work or be feasible. The entrepreneur must carefully research the concept to ensure that these pitfalls either do not exist or can be overcome. The ideal concept sells something that works easily and has no service problems.

An inventor worked for two years in his basement developing a 3-D television. He was afraid that someone might steal his invention, so he would not discuss his product idea with anyone. When he decided that his working drawings and prototype were perfected, he contacted a patent attorney to start the patent search. During the patent search, the inventor found out the concept had been developed and tried four years previously and would not work. He wasted his time and money because he did not confide in other people and find out whether the product had already been invented and was workable and feasible.

If the product is perishable or has a short shelf life, adept entrepreneurs will find a method to sell the product quickly.

Adept entrepreneurs think of alternative uses for the product/service if weather is a concern. Products affected by weather conditions will greatly affect income projections.

Many inventions look good in the prototype phase but can never be mass produced.

In another example, the founder of www.expert-market.com launched a service that provides professional consultants a virtual home and potential clients an efficient way to find them. The company's revenues come from signing up consultants and their firms as affiliates and a percentage from the referrals it makes to the affiliates. This concept proved to work not just as a prototype but in the broader marketplace.

Proprietary rights

The ideal business owns some economically significant rights that can be protected from competitors. Such assets as protectable patents, trademarks, copyrights, and trade secrets are important forces in warding off competition. Proprietary rights add value and give the entrepreneur the right to prevent others from unauthorized use and/or production of protected aspects of the business. Even the right to distribute certain products in profitable markets can be valuable proprietary rights. Ralph Lauren, for example, built a business with a trademarked logo of a polo player on horseback. Most of his clothes are designed by his company but are manufactured by subcontractors. The perceived value of his products is in the logo.

New concepts that have proprietary rights have a much better chance of succeeding in the marketplace.

A woman in the San Francisco area secured the license rights from a famous water color artist for greeting cards. She paid the artist 10 percent of the wholesale price for the licensing rights. She has to sell a certain number of cards each year to keep the licensing rights. The greeting cards have been very successful, which is good for both her and the artist. She has also added great value to her business because other companies are trying to buy this proprietary right.

An Internet-based print shop (www.iPrint.com) offers a new way of creating and ordering professionally printed products—a WYSIWYG (what you see is what you get) publishing application. Customers enter the web site, select what they want to create, and choose from hundred of designs to create their final custom-designed layouts. With its proprietary technology, the company is creating a new printing paradigm.

Continuous revenue flow

The ideal business generates a continual flow of revenue after the initial expenditure of the marketing money used in soliciting a customer's business. It is an annuity. Spend money to establish a good restaurant and a dependable revenue flow will result if management is reasonably adept. No new heroic efforts are usually needed.

Adept entrepreneurs develop concepts that allow customers to return and make repeated purchases, such as buying additional supplies for the product/service, renewing an annual contract, or regular maintenance and service.

However, there are many one-shot businesses in which separate deals must be made for each sale. A construction company may have to compete for each contract. It can be feast or famine for these types of businesses. In such instances, marketing costs soar as management must continually seek out sources of financing.

One of the best examples of continuous revenue flow is the concept of fertilizing and weed control with an annual contract. Once the sale is made, the owner has a guaranteed 12 months of business without any additional sales costs. Another example is providing payroll services for small companies. Likewise, attorneys and CPAs like retainers because they can predict cash flow.

No legal entanglements

Lawyers are expensive and time consuming. Adept entrepreneurs avoid concepts that require extensive legal services, which result in higher operating costs and consequently higher prices.

Some businesses come with inherent lawsuits and legal harassments. Perhaps the founders or some key employees have signed a noncompete agreement that may pose some problems. Perhaps the technology will be challenged in a patent infringement suit. Perhaps there are environmental barriers. Such legal costs can kill a new business before it even gets its doors open.

As part of due diligence, the able entrepreneur investigates an entire array of potential legal factors that could affect the business concept. For example, airport shuttles that transport travelers to and from airports have run into continual legal battles with cab companies. The cab companies file legal suits and argue that airport shuttle services threaten to put them out of business. Legal fees can be quite significant, and the shuttle service owners have to be prepared to spend time and money in court defending their position.

A successful full-service grocery store had to close after three years in business because, as the owner stated, "Basically, we lost our lease." The business had 21 employees who lost their jobs; this created a hardship for everyone, including the small community where it was located.

Many entrepreneurs make the mistake of not securing a lease with options to renew when they open their ventures. Businesses don't always fail because of low sales volume, but sometimes fail for other operational and management reasons.

Exit potential

Entrepreneurs will exit someday—even if other family members become the new owners. Planning an exit strategy should take place simultaneously with planning to launch a new venture.

The ideal business builds wealth for its owners by accumulating assets that can be sold for more money than was invested. There should be a profitable way out of the business when the time comes for the entrepreneur to leave. Smart entrepreneurs always plan for their exit.

A trio of college students moved their Macintosh-equipped desktop publishing business from their dorm room to a storefront and became aware of a knowledge gap. Lots of people knew how to use IBM-compatible PCs but not many could use Macs. The three converted their business to a temporary employment agency that specialized in Mac-trained people. After 10 years, expanded services, and offices in 35 cities, MacTemps was sold to Aquent Partners.

The most common ways to exit a venture are to sell company stock into the public market, to sell the business for cash, or to merge with another public company, which enables the company to sell stock into the public market.

An often asked question is "Why would I design an exit strategy when I don't know if I will make enough money next week to meet payroll?"

Entrepreneurs cannot wait for success and then start building an exit strategy. The exit from the business should drive the concept and day-to-day operating decisions from the first day the business is open. Founders may wait 20 years to sell their ventures, but if a well thought-out business strategy of building assets, proprietary rights, customer databases, a strong management team, motivated employees, and solid leases has been created, the exit price will be high and rewarding.

Exercise 10a: Evaluate a Business Concept Compared to a Model Business

Model business rating scale: Evaluate your concept in comparison with a model business by indicating how well each of the ideal characteristics below applies to your concept. Use a scale of 1 to 10, where 1 means the ideal trait is not at all true for your concept and 10 means that it is perfectly true.

	1	2	3	4	5	6	7	8	9	10
1. No investment 1 = large investment; 10 = no investment	❑	❑	❑	❑	❑	❑	❑	❑	❑	❑
2. Recognized, established market 1 = no market; 10 = well-established market	❑	❑	❑	❑	❑	❑	❑	❑	❑	❑
3. Perceived need for product 1 = no customers; 10 = high perceived need	❑	❑	❑	❑	❑	❑	❑	❑	❑	❑
4. Dependable source of input supply 1 = only one source of supply; 10 = numerous sources	❑	❑	❑	❑	❑	❑	❑	❑	❑	❑
5. No governmental regulation 1 = highly regulated; 10 = no regulations	❑	❑	❑	❑	❑	❑	❑	❑	❑	❑
6. No labor 1 = many employees required; 10 = no employees	❑	❑	❑	❑	❑	❑	❑	❑	❑	❑
7. 100 percent gross margin 1 = low gross margin; 10 = 100 percent gross margin	❑	❑	❑	❑	❑	❑	❑	❑	❑	❑
8. Buyers purchase frequently 1 = one-time purchasers; 10 = customer buys daily	❑	❑	❑	❑	❑	❑	❑	❑	❑	❑
9. Favorable tax treatment 1 = heavy tax burden; 10 = minimum taxation	❑	❑	❑	❑	❑	❑	❑	❑	❑	❑
10. Receptive, established distribution system 1 = no established distribution; 10 = existing distribution system	❑	❑	❑	❑	❑	❑	❑	❑	❑	❑
11. Great news value 1 = no news value; 10 = highly newsworthy	❑	❑	❑	❑	❑	❑	❑	❑	❑	❑
12. Customers pay in advance 1 = 60- to 90-day dating; 10 = payment before delivery	❑	❑	❑	❑	❑	❑	❑	❑	❑	❑
13. No product- or service-liability risk 1 = high potential liability; 10 = no liability	❑	❑	❑	❑	❑	❑	❑	❑	❑	❑
14. No product obsolescence 1 = short product life cycle; 10 = no technical obsolescence	❑	❑	❑	❑	❑	❑	❑	❑	❑	❑
15. No competition 1 = saturated market; 10 = no competitors	❑	❑	❑	❑	❑	❑	❑	❑	❑	❑
16. No fashion obsolescence 1 = fad; 10 = classic style	❑	❑	❑	❑	❑	❑	❑	❑	❑	❑
17. No physical perishability 1 = limited shelf life; 10 = not perishable	❑	❑	❑	❑	❑	❑	❑	❑	❑	❑

	1	2	3	4	5	6	7	8	9	10
18. Impervious to weather 1 = weather affects sales; 10 = not affected by weather	❑	❑	❑	❑	❑	❑	❑	❑	❑	❑
19. Workable and feasible product/service 1 = unproven prototype; 10 = proven product	❑	❑	❑	❑	❑	❑	❑	❑	❑	❑
20. Proprietary rights 1 = no intellectual property; 10 = protected by copyrights, patents	❑	❑	❑	❑	❑	❑	❑	❑	❑	❑
21. Continuous revenue flow 1 = deals made for each sale; 10 = maintenance contracts, retainers	❑	❑	❑	❑	❑	❑	❑	❑	❑	❑
22. No legal entanglements 1 = inherent law suits; 10 = minimal legal problems	❑	❑	❑	❑	❑	❑	❑	❑	❑	❑
23. Exit potential 1 = nothing to sell; 10 = many exit opportunities	❑	❑	❑	❑	❑	❑	❑	❑	❑	❑

Total _____

Evaluation

200-230 = A concept: Take it to market. Customers cannot wait.

170-199 = B concept: You are almost there. Examine your low scores. What can you improve quickly and inexpensively?

140-169 = C concept: You have a 50:50 chance of succeeding. Examine the low scores to see if contingency plans can be developed to overcome negative aspects.

110-139 = D concept: The product or venture needs some major rework that could be costly. Do you have the time, capital, and energy?

Below 110 = Drop concept: Hit the drawing board and try again.

Building the Management Team and Infrastructure

Learning Objectives

In this chapter, students will learn how to
- Identify the management team that is needed for a new venture.
- Motivate and inspire the management team.
- Hire a good management team and avoid hiring mistakes.
- Build an infrastructure of outside people to support the management team.

The entrepreneurial mythology may glorify the individual who by sheer will power, cleverness, and hard work creates a profitable enterprise from little more than nothing, but the reality of most successful ventures of any size today is usually another story. It's a tale of teamwork with each person playing a vital role in the evolving enterprise.

The thousands of entrepreneurs who shun the team concept, however, cannot be ignored. Many people cannot or choose not to work with other people. Many smaller concerns simply cannot afford to pay for a management team. A business can support only so many people. Thus the owner must wear many hats. Anyone seeking to build a sizable business, however, will likely need a management team.

Even though the famous entrepreneurs love to relish the plaudits directed their way by admirers, to their credit most of them hasten to praise the teams of people who were really responsible for their enterprises' success. The simple truth is that it is difficult to build a substantial enterprise by oneself. It requires help.

Professional investors in new ventures consider the management team to be the single most important factor determining the attractiveness of the investment. Venture capitalists would prefer to back a second-rate concept put forth by a first-rate management team than a first-rate concept with a second-rate team. The thought underlying this philosophy is that a top-flight management team will somehow manage to turn the second-rate concept into a winner while the less talented management group will somehow mess up the great concept.

In many cases, businesses may operate for years with an incomplete or inappropriate management team. In these cases, an effective entrepreneur will want to evaluate the firm's management team as if the firm were a start-up.

Early in planning, entrepreneurs should give thought to the key roles they need to fill in their enterprises and who should fill them. It is not a matter to be undertaken lightly.

Avoid the Path of Least Resistance

One of the classic traps unwary entrepreneurs fall into is that of placing close friends and relatives in key positions either because they are convenient to hire or out of some sense of obligation. Entrepreneurs are not obligated to hire someone who cannot do the job and who will jeopardize the enterprise. The new-venture graveyard is littered with firms put there by inept relatives and friends.

This phenomenon is so well recognized that professional investors become immediately suspicious of a business plan in which the entrepreneur seems bent on furnishing employment for relatives. One must be prepared to defend the selection of the people who are to play key roles in the enterprise. There must be good reasons to support the hiring of each member of the team.

There are only two ways to justify someone for a slot on the team.

- The person has the track record to prove his or her talents.
- The person has the training and skills to do the job.

The Team

Depending on the nature of the enterprise, several common roles are essential to most ventures.

- Creator (R&D Director)
- Driving force (Chief Executive Officer)
- Organizer (Chief Operating Officer)
- Marketer (Marketing Director)
- Sales producer (Sales Manager)
- Watch dog (Chief Financial Officer)
- Maker (Manufacturing Director)

Each is discussed separately, but often two or more roles may be played by the same person. For example, the marketer and the sales producer may be the same person.

Team Roles
Creator
Driving force
Organizer
Marketer
Sales producer
Watch dog
Maker

Creator (R&D Director)

Perhaps an inventor, sometimes a researcher and often a production engineer are the venture's creators. Somebody must create the value sold to the customer. While creators are important, all too often they grossly overestimate their contribution to the enterprise.

Inventors and high-technology researchers often pose difficult obstacles to the successful culmination of a new-venture deal by insisting on a bigger piece of the pie than they deserve. Or they insist on assuming roles they are incapable of successfully fulfilling. One tragedy often encountered is the creator (inventor) who tries to play the roles of the driving force, organizer, and marketer combined. A few manage to pull it off, but not many. It is not the way to bet one's money.

Creators are best allowed to do precisely what they like and do best—create. Reward them for it. Praise them for it. But above all, keep them creating and keep them out of business affairs.

A temperamental creator scares professional investors. Is the management team prepared to continue with the venture if the creator leaves the scene? Does the creator hold the keys to the whole show? The venture should not be placed at the mercy of the technical side of the enterprise. There should be a contingency plan ready if the creator leaves. Creators often believe that the business is their baby and that others are adventurers trying to take it away. An enterprise should be able to show investors some people who can replace the creator. If not, it should be able to show them why the creator will not abandon the enterprise.

Driving force (Chief Executive Officer)

The key to a venture's success is the driving force—the person who makes everything happen, who puts together the resources to support the value and take it to market.

Without an able driving force, the venture will not amount to much. Time and again, promising concepts fail after squandering much money because there was no driving force. The inventor of a new water purifier with great potential, after four years and $4 million, was still muddling around in the laboratory. There was no driving force to push the project further. Experience has shown that most successful entrepreneurs are driving forces, not creators.

Organizer (Chief Operating Officer)

Call them the organizers, or the inside managers, or the operations people, or whatever, but an enterprise needs someone inside the office to make operations flow smoothly and economically. They make certain that the necessary work gets done on time and properly.

All too often these talents are precisely the ones missing from the makeup of the typical driving force who, more often than not, hates details. The organizer must relish details.

It is easy for the high-flying entrepreneur to hold the execution of details in contempt. Yet, it's the execution of those details that distinguishes the highly successful enterprise from the flash-in-the-pan venture that realizes early sales success but fails to deliver the goods satisfactorily. Steve Jobs, cofounder of Apple Computer, attributes the company's initial success to his fortunate hiring of an experienced organizer—Mike Markula. Mike was one of the early employees of Intel and was heavily involved in building Intel into a large computer company. His understanding of the computer chip was important to enhance the technology that led to the development of Apple's personal computer.

Marketer (Marketing Director)

No marketing capability, no deal! Few knowledgeable investors will look with favor upon a venture that does not exhibit an ability to market its products or services. Indeed, without a marketing capability, success is unlikely. One of the key elements to appraise in evaluating a new venture is its marketing plan and its marketing people. Can they sell? What reason is there for believing that these people can take the goods to market? All sorts of ventures create products with great adeptness. That's relatively easy. Selling the goods can be another matter.

Thus, the venture needs an experienced marketer because there is so much of marketing that is knowing the right people to see and getting through to them. That usually requires someone who has industry experience.

Sales producer (Sales Manager)

This person works hand in hand with the marketing director. The sales manager organizes the sales team or manufacturers' representatives to sell to the target markets chosen by the marketer. Sales drive the success of a venture and this function should be performed by people who understand the industry and benefits that motivate the customer to purchase the product or service.

Some companies try to recruit a sales manager from the competition. This reduces the amount of time it takes to make the initial sales because this person already knows the potential customers' needs and desires. In order to attract this type of person, some type of ownership in the venture can be offered, for example, warrants, stock options, phantom stock, pure grants of stock.

Watch dog (Chief Financial Officer)

It may be a CPA. It may be a bookkeeper. Often the money manager is the entrepreneur's spouse. Someone must watch the till to make sure that the employees are actually helping the venture and not themselves.

Outside investors often insist on putting their own money managers within the organization. They want to be sure that the money is spent on what was said it would be spent on.

Maker (Manufacturing Director)

Who's going to manufacture the products? Good production people are scarce. One reason entrepreneurs rely so much on subcontracting production is to be able to prove to both potential investors and customers that the production side of the business is in competent hands. Investors are not going to put money into a manufacturing venture without a good production manager in place.

Shaping the Team to the Mission

To a great degree, the people hired for each slot and the importance of each position depend a great deal upon the particular tasks that are critical to the firm's success. If the enterprise is involved in a situation that will require great marketing skill to be successful, then it follows that the marketing slot will have to be filled with someone who is up to the task at hand. Whoever is evaluating the prospective venture will be looking closely at the marketing clout being assembled on the team.

In a situation that requires production or technical expertise to be successful, then those slots on the management team will be critical. If an entrepreneur plans to open a bank, then some people on the management team better be sophisticated financially. One reason for the recent debacles in the banking business is that too many financially inept people were running them. Marketing considerations often overruled financial realities. The team must be matched to the needs of the company.

The Business Plan

Potential investors are keenly interested in knowing a great deal about the people comprising the management team. Thus, one should take care to provide full disclosure about their qualifications in the business plan. While capsule descriptions of the qualifications of the key people should be put into the body of the plan, a resume should be put into an appendix.

This is so important that some entrepreneurs stack the deck. They name their initial staff based more on how they look on paper than how they will perform. Appearances may seem more important than reality in the initial stages of a venture.

When one seeks public money, financial institutions will do a thorough investigation of management team members. They must be squeaky clean. Entrepreneurs should not include anyone in the management team whose record will not withstand scrutiny.

Motivating the Organization

Why will all these people come to work for the venture and perform all the needed miracles? Why will they work so long and hard? Different employees are motivated in different ways, including a belief in the strategic plan, the performance of the management team, or project evaluations.

Motivational and incentive programs can be designed to reward good work. Anyone who thinks he or she can get rich without properly rewarding the people who helped him or her do so will likely be disappointed. As one entrepreneur put it, "I want my people to get rich because I have set up a system whereby if they get rich, so do I."

Venture founders will have to share the wealth with their people. The only way to get and keep quality people is to make it worthwhile for them. Fortunately, they generally will not make immediate demands upon the firm's cash flow and will wait until they've earned it.

Few topics have been more discussed and written about than motivation. And rightly so! Wars are won, teams are victorious, and fortunes made by those leaders who have mastered the art of motivating their people to exert great effort in pursuit of their goals. There seems to be more variation in people's motivation than in their basic aptitudes. Given the proper motivation, skills can often be acquired. Without motivation, little happens.

This discussion will not delve into the standard motivational tools and tactics used by most American businesses, such as the compensation plan, fringe benefits, and the plethora of organizational-behavior material on the subject. Those require several books in their own right, and one can read about them in the standard works on each subject.

Instead, the discussion will focus only on a few thoughts commonly encountered by entrepreneurs and generally ignored by the traditional management writers on the subject. Some traditional thinking on a few subjects will be modified to conform with what is more commonly encountered in new enterprises: compensation, work environment and work rules, personal relationships, winning team, and promotional opportunities.

Compensation

Few new ventures can meet the pay scales used by their larger competitors. Management must often work for reduced pay for some time. The cash is just not there with which to pay generous wages. Thus, entrepreneurs must use other tactics to compensate their employees.

Stock options may not be the best way to provide incentives to people. Direct grants of low-price stock are often much better. Some firms have partially paid their people either in warrants to buy the stock at a low price or have paid them directly with stock. A warrant is an option to buy a certain amount of stock for a stipulated price that is transferable and can also be traded. Employee stock ownership and stock options have the added benefit of aligning the employees' interests with the owner's.

There are also some serious questions to contemplate about how much of the company the founder really wants the employees to own. In one extreme example, an entrepreneur gave each of his employees 100 shares of its stock (priced at about $12 a share at the time) after they had been with the company for six months and were past their initial probation period with the firm. The idea was to make everyone aware of the firm's stock price. It worked too well. As the price climbed past $20 on its way to $38 a share, the employees did little else than call their brokers to learn of the latest development. Morale soared. Then two downturns in the stock market dropped the price to $4 a share. Morale was shattered. Employees were bitter. The research director, who had exercised his management stock options, had borrowed the money on margin. When the margin was called he had a mental breakdown and never worked for the firm again. While the president was out of town, his wife was phoned by their broker and told to bring $875,000 in cash to the office in 45 minutes, or their huge stock position would be sold to satisfy the margin loan they had taken to buy a house. Such a forced sale would further drop the price. Those were not good times at the office. The point of this story is that using stock as an incentive is not without difficulties. It can backfire.

Traditionally, clever entrepreneurs let the financial market pay their people. "Make your money on our stock" is feasible since the income on stock can be taxed as capital gains instead of ordinary income.

The use of phantom stock needs to be mentioned here. Because the Securities and Exchange Commission (SEC) regulates the buying and selling of common stock by insiders, some managements that want their key people to work hard toward increasing the price of the company's stock devise incentive programs around the price of the firm's stock without the employee ever really owning any stock.

Suppose the CFO's employment contract contains a provision that he or she will be considered to own 10,000 shares of the company's stock, which is selling at the time for $10 a share. Furthermore, the CFO will be paid at some future time the profits that would have been made on that stock just as if it were really owned. If the price of the stock rose to $20 a share on the stipulated date, then the CFO would be due $100,000 profit on the phantom stock. Naturally, many contractual details must be worked out on such deals. What happens if the person quits or is fired? How long does the deal last? Such programs should not be taken lightly.

The problem with this arrangement is that the money comes from the company coffers, not the market. It is often used when management does not want to give voting rights when doing so would jeopardize its control of the enterprise.

Profit-sharing programs, while serving a purpose, thrust people into the firm's accounting policies, thus giving rise to some internal bickering over accounting policies.

More complex and varied incentive programs may be needed. Programs can be customized for each function. Marketers may be rewarded for the achievement of certain sales and gross profit goals. Deferred-compensation plans may be appropriate. Production managers may be rewarded on the basis of their output, cost, and quality performances. General managers may be rewarded on the basis of their budgetary performances. But the founder must be careful. It is much easier to administer grants of Founder's Stock or low-cost stock warrants. In any event, owners should be very cautious about the tax aspects of the incentive programs and how the employee will eventually cash out.

Should employees who resign or are terminated be required to sell back their stock to the company? The founder may not want the firm's stock in hostile hands. Then again, he or she may not care. Former employees may not be in a position to cause difficulty. It it is usually wise, however, to take possible troublemakers out of the game by repurchasing the stock, if it can be done reasonably.

Work environment and work rules

Many people are motivated less by the money they make than by the work they do and the conditions under which they must do it. Many new ventures have capitalized upon some people's desire to work in an informal organizational culture. One entrepreneur attributes much of her success at attracting excellent employees to the company's relaxed policy on manner of dress, which is roughly, "Don't get arrested." Occasionally, her salespeople have to put on a coat and tie to go see a potential corporate account, but that's expected.

Some new ventures have prospered by letting employees work flexible hours. Give them a key and let them work when they will. This policy will not be practical for all businesses. Certainly, flexibility in work rules is a big motivational force for many people.

Personal relationships

Ever have a personal relationship with a large corporation? Not likely! Large organizations are not conducive to an individual's ego. The smaller organization offers greater opportunity for close personal working relationships. Even simple tactics can work wonders.

An entrepreneur who owned a biotechnology firm set the first Friday of each month as a special day for the company. A potluck lunch was held, at which all workers, managers, and directors ate together. Management made a point to mix with the workers.

The entrepreneur gave out gag awards each month recognizing both good and bad performances. Two traveling rubber chickens were bestowed upon those who had somehow not met their goals that month. The chickens were awarded by the last month's holder, who gleefully gave up his or her ownership of the fowls. The entrepreneur then described the month's accomplishments and thanked the people individually for their particular achievements.

One director made it a point to get together with a production worker and learn what he or she was doing. One month, the lad who was molding the new silicon lenses was eager to take the director into his laboratory to show what he did and how the reject rates would go down once the FDA approved a change in the formula for the silicon mix. He was delighted that someone took time to see what he was doing to improve business.

And that is the key to motivating people in new ventures. Recognize them, know what they are doing, and praise their efforts. The cash payoff can be down the line. They know that. If they trust the founder, they'll wait.

Winning team

People love to be on a winning team. Thus, it is important to communicate to employees how the company is winning and the role they are playing in the victory. Growth is important, for it is one of the measures of winning in our economy.

Promotional opportunities

In a rapidly growing new venture, the opportunities for promotion are great. A worker in the factory, if proven competent, may become the production superintendent. The sales rep may become a manager in a very short time. There is never a sufficient number of management people with which to grow, so promotions can come fast, which is strong motivation to many people.

Initial relationships with associates

The entrepreneur is posed with a dilemma right from the start. Anyone at all knowledgeable about new enterprises has heard all sorts of tales of terror regarding the hazards involved in being associated with other people in the venture. Strong warnings are made against partnerships.

Corporate squeeze-outs seem to be the rule rather than the exception. Successful entrepreneurs report how often they were disappointed in the people with whom they were initially associated. Thus, one can build an exceptionally strong case that wise entrepreneurs are lone wolves who go their own way through the maze known as business. Then why do people choose to be associated with other people in a business? The answer is really twofold.

First, it's a lot more fun. People are social animals. They like company. They want relationships with other people. They like to do things with other people. It really is a lot of fun to build an enterprise in cooperation with associates whom one likes.

Second, the entrepreneur often needs the skills of other people in order to be successful. By associating with the right people, the chances for success are enhanced, and the total rewards may far exceed the rewards of the single entrepreneur. In other words, where one individual might make a certain amount of profit, the rewards to that same individual, if associated with two other able people whose talents are complementary, might be 10 times that amount. Thus, it can make good economic sense to be associated with the right people. Such associates leverage an entrepreneur's abilities tremendously.

Thus, the dilemma is neatly posed. One can go it alone and avoid the hazards involved with being in business with other people or take chances and have the fun and rewards that can be realized from successful relationships with other people. It is not just by chance that most new enterprises are formed by two or three people, even though down the line, perhaps only one or two of them stay in the business.

Hiring the Best Employees

Attracting and hiring the best workers are crucial to building a management team. If the right people aren't hired, it will directly affect productivity and bottom line.

> "… above all, I think it's a people factor that will be the secret of the success of your business in the future."
> —Ewing Marion Kauffman

Finding qualified candidates today is more difficult because of global competition, the economy, changing work force demographics and workers' values. Employers are learning to be open-minded and more flexible regarding employment policies and working hours. New strategies include providing for job sharing, working at home, using temporary help and contract labor, and hiring the disabled and retired seniors.

One way to begin is by networking with professional and technical people in the industry about potential applicants they know. Talk to larger companies that are downsizing and are trying to find employment for their laid-off workers. Ask current staff members for referrals of people they know and would recommend. Also elicit referrals from vendors, consultants, and alumni associations. Contact local college and university placement offices.

Some entrepreneurs use employment agencies and executive search firms because they neither have the time nor want to spend the time it takes to recruit. Always check references before contracting with these firms. Other contemporary recruiting methods include telerecruiting, direct mail, electronic bulletin boards, point-of-purchase displays, and retiree job banks.

An example of a web-based recruiting company is Monster.com, headquartered in Maynard, Massachusetts. Monster has developed a system that completely automates the application process. Applicants apply for various positions by entering relevant information on the web site. The applications are then sorted and e-mailed to employers who provide a suitable fit for the required skills. Employers have the choice of obtaining the capability of browsing through the resume database for a fee. This information can then be accessed at any time by the employer, including the printout of individual applications and resumes. This method of recruiting is said to be great for small-business owners and is expected continue to expand during this decade.

It is important to have all applicants complete and sign an employment application form, even if they have a resume. As a legal document, the application form must conform to state and federal regulations. For example, it generally must specify if employment with the firm is "at-will," which means that employment can be terminated at any time. Also, this form must give the employer permission to verify information submitted by the prospective employee.

Hours in interviews can be saved by screening applicants with the application form. Look for breaks in employment, omissions on the application, career changes, reasons for leaving other employers, salary history, and overall professionalism in completing the form.

All references should be checked by verifying the basic information provided and looking for gaps in employment. Such gaps can signal potential problems, such as being fired from a position or spending time in jail. Dates of graduation should be compared with dates of certification. Professional affiliations should be reviewed and those that don't quite fit identified.

People who overstate their job qualifications may cause future harm to an organization or be poor employees. Experts claim that 90 percent of all hiring mistakes can be prevented through proper background checks. Besides, claims of negligent hiring against employers make it essential to conduct thorough background checks on all potential hires. Studies show that about 30 percent of resumes contain some kind of false information.

Today, with disturbing and increasing frequency, disgruntled employees are taking out their anger and frustration on co-workers or customers. The injured party files a lawsuit claiming that the owner failed to thoroughly check an employee's background before hiring. Often, the owner is found negligent in hiring. Some states have laws requiring criminal-background checks on applicants for certain positions, such as those providing direct care.

Should criminal-background checks be run when they are not mandated by law? Yes. At a minimum, a criminal-background check provides critical information about a prospective employee. Rarely is that a bad thing. One can discover whether the candidate has been convicted of a crime and, if so, when, what crime, and perhaps what sentence.

Then the employer has important information to further explore with the applicant. The candidate can be asked to explain the details of the crime, including any mitigating factors, the employee's rehabilitation, remorse for the crime, and subsequent work or non-sentence, community-service activities.

Do not automatically reject an applicant because of a criminal conviction. Instead, evaluate whether and how the crime is related to the job sought. For example, a conviction for embezzlement is highly relevant for a position handling money. However, a conviction for failing to file income tax returns may have little relevance to a candidate's suitability for a clerical position.

A criminal-background check may also reveal whether an applicant is truthful. Many job applications ask if the person has been convicted of a crime. If the applicant answers no and the background check discloses a criminal conviction, the applicant would appear to have lied on the application. Then there may be grounds not to hire the applicant because of false or misleading information on the application.

There may be two disadvantages to running criminal-background checks: expense and delay. Depending on what information is checked, a minimal background check can cost between $15 and $100.

State police departments tend to charge less for the check but usually take longer. Private entities, such as Pinkerton's or other investigation agencies, usually cost more but have a shorter turnaround time. Look in the *Yellow Pages* under "Private Investigators" or in the directory of Public Record Providers by BRB Publications, Inc. Some agencies advertise through direct mail.

It is also difficult to obtain relevant job information from references. Legal ramifications of reference checks cause some employers to be cautious. Lawsuits have been won by applicants who discovered their previous employer gave derogatory job references. Therefore, many employers give only essential information about a former employee, such as dates of employment, title of last job, and salary.

Despite some employers' reluctance to provide references, listed references should be contacted to verify the information provided by the applicant. Under certain circumstances, legal ramifications may exist if reasonable care is not exercised in selecting staff, for example, if one employee later harms another during his or her employment.

Former employers should be asked about the applicant's dates of employment, title, duties and functions, stated reason for leaving employment, and whether the former employer would rehire the individual. Also inquire about the quality of work, attendance and punctuality, ability to get along with coworkers, and overall job performance.

A written record should be kept on all reference checks and the information obtained. One must be prepared to back up hiring decisions with written proof that they were based on relevant job information.

At least two references should be obtained on candidates being considered. If a job applicant does not receive a favorable reference from an employer, the candidate should not be automatically rejected. In this case, several employers should be interviewed in order to get a well-rounded view of the applicant's job performance. If possible, each significant employer should be called for references before making a final selection.

All information received through a reference check is confidential and should not be given to an applicant or referred to during the course of an interview. Note that a rejection decision cannot be based solely on a reference check.

Consider asking prospective employees to call some of the venture's business references and customers to get a true picture of the company. This process indicates how serious a prospective employee is about a job, since some may not follow through. Applicants can then decide if the position will be a good job match.

Then ask the references to comment about prospective candidates. Additional information will help in making a better hiring decision. A lot of grief can be saved by spending more time choosing the right applicant.

For more information on contemporary recruiting methods, refer to *The Employee Recruitment and Retention Handbook* by Diane Arthur (published by AMACOM, 2001).

Mistakes in Hiring

In interviews with entrepreneurs many report that, in retrospect, some of the biggest mistakes they made in the early years were in their selection of associates. They commonly report that they were not the best judges of character. Their disappointments lie largely in the areas listed below.

Inept associates

Typically entrepreneurs go into business with people whom they somehow know. Perhaps they are relatives or friends. Perhaps they are fellow employees where they presently work. Their relationship is based on factors other than skills. Perhaps one of the associates has been billing himself as a great marketing expert. He may even hold a job as a marketing manager of some other company. Thus, he is brought into the new enterprise as vice president of marketing.

A few months or so down the road, it becomes apparent that the marketing associate does not possess sufficient skills for the job. Such situations are always fraught with recriminations and bitterness. It is not pleasant from anyone's standpoint. After all, the parties were fairly good friends initially. There had to be some confidence in the person's skills or the association would not have developed. The entrepreneur not only is disappointed in the associate's ineptness but also does some soul searching of his or her own abilities to judge other people. It is difficult to admit when one is wrong about someone.

Of course, the tables sometimes are reversed. The vice president of marketing may be quite able, but the controlling entrepreneur proves inept. Thus, the minority associates are posed with the sticky problem of dethroning an incompetent leader.

Character defects

While there are occasions in which the entrepreneur has good cause to be surprised upon discovering that an associate is dishonest, more commonly the signs and red flags were up all along the line. It is amazing how many entrepreneurs confess surprising disappointment in an associate who proves to be dishonest when right down the line the individual has cheated all of his life.

An example: In one enterprise, the entrepreneur became associated with another aggressive entrepreneur who would regale everyone with endless tales about how he was cheating Uncle Sam at every turn, how he pulled one fast deal after another on this or that individual throughout life and would, at the drop of a hat, openly plot to do in some business associate. Now, how naive can one be to believe that the person would not immediately turn around and cheat another at the first opportunity? The person has clearly said that he is a man with few principles. He has taken advantage of everyone he has been in business with. He cuts corners and walks a fine line with the law. He is not going to change. He is going to do the same thing with anyone. What may seem cute and clever when it is done to someone else will not be when it is done to oneself. To judge the integrity of a potential business associate, his or her entire life should be examined.

Personality conflicts

If entrepreneurs take the time to really get to know the people with whom they become associated, personality conflicts are not likely to arise. They should know an individual long enough and well enough under a variety of circumstances in order to know whether they can work with him or her comfortably. Even so, conflicts can arise as conditions change.

Problems occur when a potential associate avoids developing a relationship to determine if personalities are compatible. In one such instance, two men were considering a venture together. One of them had invited the potential associate into his home several times and made great efforts to open himself up to the other person. The second party, however, at no time initiated any social contact whatsoever with the first party. No invitation was made to meet his family or see his home. The proposed business venture was canceled as it became rather apparent that the person seemed to be hiding something.

The bottom line is that unless entrepreneurs are really comfortable with the persons with whom they plan to go into business, they should forget it. It won't work out. Whatever little irritants are bothersome now will be magnified down the line.

There is an art to being a good business associate. One must work at the relationship. It requires tolerance and forbearance of the other associate's habits and mannerisms. Mutual respect is necessary. Compatible habits and common interests are helpful. But no matter the precautions, mistakes will be made, and people can change for the worse. No one is perfect. We all have our faults as well as our strengths. One thought: the adept manager tries to use people in such ways that their strengths help the company while their faults are somehow negated. Don't ask the detail-hating sales rep to do detailed paperwork; let the paperwork maven take care of the details.

A business relationship can be as close as a marital one. When parties cannot be open with each another, troubles are likely to arise later.

Policy disagreements

Honest differences of opinion arise over how a business should be operated. As long as the business is highly profitable, such conflicts are minimized, although disagreements do arise over growth policies. But if the company is having difficult times, rest assured that there will be many disagreements over what should be done about it and who is to blame. Even best friends will fall out in serious disagreements over what to do with a sick business. There are no magic solutions to this problem. About the only advice is that the associates should stay in close communication with each other and talk these things out almost daily. One hopes such disagreements would be resolved as quickly as possible with some consensus, but such is not always possible. Differences of opinion do arise that often cause relationships to break up. In these cases, a buyout agreement might be necessary. See Chapter 14: Contracts and Leases for a discussion of this type of agreement.

Evolution of the Team

Seldom does the entrepreneur begin business with a full slate of management people in place and ready to work. More typically, he or she is alone with some friends or family to help. As the venture grows, managers are acquired as the venture needs them and can afford them. Particularly in the early stages of the enterprise, the entrepreneur relies heavily on the huge infrastructure that stands ready to serve on call.

Infrastructure

Members of the Infrastructure

Lawyers
Accountants
Bankers
Risk-management advisors
Marketing consultants
Advertising/public relations agencies
Governmental agencies
Manufacturers' representatives
Manufacturing subcontractors
Engineering/design firms
Distributors
Human resource consultants
Lobbyists
Import/export brokers
Business consultants

Only a portion of the work that must be done for a company to be successful is performed by its own employees. Much of the work is done by outside organizations hired by the company. Fortunately for modern entrepreneurs, thousands of firms of all descriptions and skills stand ready to serve their needs. If they need an advertising program; there are firms ready to do it for those who have the money. If they need a production-control system installed in the plant; there are consulting firms eager for the job. Entrepreneurs have at their call whatever expertise they need, and they pay for it only when and if needed. They should learn to use the infrastructure well. The successful entrepreneur is effective in network building and continually works on this attribute.

Indeed, one of the reasons large metropolitan areas are so attractive to entrepreneurs is that they offer a vast array of firms that can promptly serve the market. As a young watch manufacturer in Hong Kong explained to his former professor, "In Los Angeles, when I want something, it may take a week or so to get it. In New York, a day or two. Here, I have it in 20 minutes. Everything I need is right here around me."

When an electronics manufacturer moved from Chicago to Raton, New Mexico, it encountered many unforeseen logistical problems in dealing with the infrastructure that served it. Each firm uses various organizations to sustain its operations. Smooth relationships with these firms are essential for a well-managed company.

While the large corporation normally enjoys the luxury of having on its staff a multitude of professionals such as lawyers, CPAs, real estate experts, insurance experts, and consultants of all kinds, the entrepreneur cannot afford such luxuries. Yet, highly specialized and technical advice is needed. Clearly, an entrepreneur needs legal assistance. Usually, one also needs accounting help and some expertise in various other problem areas such as advertising, research, distribution, and financial advice.

Consequently, entrepreneurs are heavy users of independent professionals who provide such technical advice. Therein lies a problem: whose advice to seek and whose advice to follow. Rare is the entrepreneur who cannot tell terrible tales of difficulties caused by using the wrong people. An inept lawyer can cause irreparable damage. Thus, the selection of the professionals is of critical importance and deserves considerable thought and investigation.

Lawyers

In this highly complex legal society, entrepreneurs need competent legal advice that is often the most difficult assistance to find. Where should entrepreneurs begin to look?

They cannot contact the local legal society and ask for recommendations because in most cases, it does not recommend attorneys. Instead, they can pay attention to other seemingly adept entrepreneurs. Who represents them? Who seems to win the court cases? They can also ask fellow entrepreneurs to describe any experiences in working with local lawyers.

How easy will it be to contact a business lawyer and receive an immediate response? One characteristic of the demand for legal services is that it is unpredictable. Rarely does one know in advance when various legal advice or assistance will be needed. For example, what if an entrepreneur has an opportunity to purchase a business on particularly advantageous terms, but a memorandum of agreement needs to be drawn up immediately? The entrepreneur cannot wait several days to meet at the lawyer's convenience. How quickly will the lawyer respond to the entrepreneur's request?

Should entrepreneurs look for a large or small law firm? One of the characteristics of the legal profession is that it is dominated by several very large firms that probably have dozens of partners. Many of these firms have substantial power and many contacts. A large law firm may have many advantages for the entrepreneur.

First, it can call upon expertise in many different fields. For the person who has a tax problem, the large law firms have tax experts. For the business owner who has a problem with the Securities & Exchange Commission, they have experts. If an owner is taking a company public, the law firm that represents him or her may add significant credibility to the venture. Thus, with one legal connection, the entrepreneur has rented expertise in just about every area of business. Many large law firms have connections and political power that can be very useful in some new ventures.

However, the large firm presents several disadvantages. A small business may not be important to it. Small businesses may be assigned to a new attorney who has little experience in small-business concerns. Second, it can be quite expensive. For example, a large firm might charge $3,000 to $5,000 for incorporating a business, while a smaller firm will charge $800 to $1,000. In addition, it may not be interested in a small business's account, or it may not be available when most needed. For these reasons, many entrepreneurs use smaller firms who are more eager for the business.

The process of selecting a business lawyer is a personal one. A good way to start is by asking friends and business contacts for recommendations. Perhaps a banker or CPA could recommend a competent business attorney. The lawyer who is hired should have considerable practical experience in small-business affairs.

After establishing a list of several potential business lawyers, the entrepreneur should make appointments and interview them, asking them for referrals of other entrepreneurs they currently work with. The entrepreneur should find out how many years of experience they have had working with entrepreneurial companies. Determine what their particular small-business expertise is. Describe a routine legal matter to take care of and evaluate how they would handle it.

Additionally, the entrepreneur should pay attention to how well he or she relates to the lawyer being interviewed? Is there some chemistry between the two? It is paramount that the entrepreneur and his or her business attorney get along and have a similar business philosophy.

Remember, this is an age of specialization, and there is far too much for any legal consultant to know. There are legal specialists in business, trial, Security Exchange Commission (SEC), Federal Communications Commission (FCC), Federal Drug Administration (FDA), intellectual property, taxes, and so on. Entrepreneurs will typically select an all-around general business attorney and then use specialists when the need arises.

There is an art to using a small-business lawyer advantageously. Legal advice is another form of outside expertise that must be managed effectively. Below are some guidelines to follow when contacting a small-business attorney.

Assist the attorney

Conduct a preliminary investigation and obtain necessary information in advance. The more legwork, information, and investigating conducted by the client, the more money can be saved. Provide the attorney with all the important documentation required to aid in the decision-making process. Use the lawyer's expertise to review the issues surrounding the legal matter and bring up potential risk factors.

Use standardized forms

Entrepreneurs use many different types of forms to operate their businesses, such as legal forms for organization and incorporation, lease forms, intangible-asset forms, intellectual-property forms, and so on. Using standardized forms can save expensive legal fees as well as time. However, the attorney should always review the forms that have been prepared so they can be structured to fit particular needs. One reliable form book is *The Complete Book of Corporate Forms* (2001). Lawyers do not regularly write original business forms for their clients. In some instances, they use standard business forms computerized in their offices.

When to involve an attorney in negotiations

When trying to buy or sell something, many entrepreneurs recommend not involving a business attorney until some common ground of agreement has been established. They suggest that parties initially discuss the deal together, since both the buyer and seller must discover whether an agreement is possible. Use a business attorney to review the situation, point out risk factors, and then draw up the legal documents to finalize the deal. The ultimate business decision must be the entrepreneur's.

Listen to the attorney's recommendations

There may be some instances when tax or technical problems in the deal require resolution. Good counsel should clearly tell clients what they are about to agree to do and what the implications are. Entrepreneurs may not be able to adequately judge the true impact of the deals they are considering. Lawyers are experts at pointing out the risk factors associated with business deals.

Beware of lawyers who are always in court

Although litigation is a cost of doing business, it does cost a lot of money. Entrepreneurs have discovered that sometimes the only winners in a court case are the lawyers. A competent lawyer should do everything possible to keep clients out of court. Litigation is time consuming, frustrating, maddening, costly, and hazardous to health, both mentally and physically.

Beware of lawyers who refuse to go to court

On the other side of the coin are the attorneys who lack the necessary skills to properly represent clients in court and do everything possible to avoid it. They will suggest settlements and compromises, sometimes giving away the client's position to the adversaries to avoid litigation. Many times one's position has to be, "Okay, this is the way it is going to be, or we'll see you in court." The posture has to be willingness to go to court to secure justice.

Never talk to the other side's attorney alone

One should always have a lawyer present when the other side brings its lawyer. This is because lawyers have superior knowledge about the law and may try to bluff the opposing party. An ethical attorney would never speak with someone directly without his or her attorney present. All correspondence should be handled through an attorney once his or her services have been retained.

Discuss fee arrangements up front

The costs associated with hiring the attorney should be determined at the beginning of the relationship. Many entrepreneurs negotiate a written fee arrangement with their attorneys before any services are rendered.

It would be wise to go to the public library and consult various directories that provide information about lawyers and their credentials. The most comprehensive directory is the *Martindale-Hubbell Law Directory*. It lists lawyers nationwide and provides detailed information on the backgrounds of firms and areas of specialization and sometimes includes major clients. It does give ratings for lawyers based on legal ability, ethical standards, professional reliability, and diligence. These ratings are based on confidential recommendations solicited from other lawyers. Other directories include *The Lawyer's Register by Specialties and Fields of Law*, the *Directory of Legal Employers*, and state-by-state Blue Books of lawyers. In addition, most local bar associations publish lists of local lawyers with some basic information about credentials and expertise.

Remember to develop a list of questions to use during the interview. There is an excellent checklist of interview questions in the book *100 Ways to Cut Legal Fees & Manage Your Lawyer* by Krasnow and Conrad. It is a good publication on managing legal affairs and controlling legal costs and runs the gamut from how to choose a lawyer to how to act as one's own.

In summary, select a lawyer with the experience and expertise that fits the needs, and collect any necessary information before meeting with the attorney.

Accountants

Fortunately, entrepreneurs usually can get excellent professional help from certified public accountants (CPAs), particularly within larger firms. But they still must understand what accountants know and their limitations. Entrepreneurs cannot expect accountants to manage their companies. Accountants are accountants, and that implies an entire way of thinking and approaching business problems.

There is great virtue in being able to afford the services of large CPA firms. They can do so many things for business owners that the smaller local company cannot. They are particularly useful in their worldwide coverage. Increasingly, they position their firms as consultants prepared to offer a wide range of services.

A few years ago the large CPA firms would not handle business affairs unless the businesses were sizable companies. Today, that has changed. The large CPA firms are very interested in acquiring emerging companies as clients and have separate divisions to promote the business. Several of them are doing some excellent work in helping new ventures mature. Entrepreneurs should definitely talk with some of them about their interest in new ventures.

If a venture plans on going public or using bank money to any significant extent, the founder will find it very helpful to have a large accounting firm auditing the books right from the beginning. The SEC may not accept the work of just any CPA for its purposes. Much time and money will be saved if things are done correctly from the start. Entrepreneurs can also use regional accounting firms that specialize in certain industries such as manufacturing, distribution, and the like.

Most entrepreneurs, however, use smaller accounting firms since the large ones cost much more. Excellent service can be obtained from small local CPAs. The key word is service. Don't stay with a firm that does not provide quick turnarounds on data.

Business owners want to know quickly how they are doing. They also want accountants who know taxes, as they may need a great deal of help in that area.

Bankers

Good banking connections are essential to entrepreneurs. A banking relationship should be established early—when founders begin to build their new ventures. Most of the time, start-up ventures do not qualify for a bank loan because they have no assets or collateral to pledge.

However, the bank can assist in setting up checking accounts, depositing employee payroll checks, and issuing bank cards such as VISA or Mastercard. They also can work with the founders to become bankable, that is, able to qualify for a commercial loan. Many entrepreneurs do not understand the functions of banking. They perceive that the bank helps new ventures with start-up capital. In reality, banks provide capital in debt form to companies that have an established track record: a company history, historical financial statements, and a good collateral base.

An entrepreneur shouldn't be disappointed if a loan request is denied if he or she has a start-up business. But he or she should realize that if good relations are established with a banker, the banker will become an important player in the infrastructure and a potential source of financing as the business grows.

The care and feeding of bankers takes time. They have to get to know the business owner, come to trust him or her, understand the operation, and get a feel for how good a manager the business owner is. One cannot expect to walk into a bank and get money. Moreover, it is important to understand what a bank can and cannot do. It cannot provide companies with equity money. That is not a bank's business. More about this is covered in Chapter 24: Money Needs.

Risk-management advisors

One principle of entrepreneurship is to avoid as much risk as possible in business operations. There are many risks inherent in business operations that can be transferred to others: liability loss from fire, flood, embezzlement, bombs, or theft, as well as many other types of legal liabilities. Entrepreneurs often fail to consider insuring their companies for such risks when starting a new venture. There are two major risks that owners need to cover-property loss and liability for injuries. Entrepreneurs frequently purchase packaged policies that cover both types of exposure.

The most popular package is a business owner's policy, often referred to as a BOP, which covers all major property and liability exposures in a single policy. The biggest advantage of a BOP is that the founder generally receives broader coverage at a much lower price than buying each type of insurance separately.

Even if an entrepreneur qualifies for a BOP package, he or she may have inadequate coverage for a disaster. For example, loss Loss of business income due to business interruption occurs when vital business equipment or other business property is unusable because of fire, explosion, or other property peril. A recent example are the wild fires in Southern California that destroyed small business offices and storefronts. Others lost hundreds of hours of productivity when workers were stuck on clogged highways or evacuated from their homes.

Overall, experts forecast that more than half of all small-business owners have not purchased business-interruption insurance. Finding and working with a good business-insurance broker to protect the company against risk is essential and an important part of the entrepreneur's infrastructure.

Marketing consultants

Consultants of many kinds abound in the world of business. One of the more common encountered is marketing consultants with all of their variations. Some will help business owners with total marketing plans while others specialize in certain fields such as direct mail, research, locational studies, product and brand positioning, and just about every other marketing area. Consultants may be able to bring existing specialized knowledge to an operation less expensively than a business could acquire it by itself. Perhaps nowhere is this so true as in the field of direct-response marketing, in which professional consultants and operational firms can execute an entire business-to-business direct-marketing program probably cheaper and more effectively than a business could for itself.

Advertising/public relations agencies

Advertising and public relations are two specialized fields in which the entrepreneur often needs help. Contacts and experience are usually needed, and good agencies will have both. Determining their competency is a problem common to all infrastructure organizations. The entrepreneur must look at their track records as well as their costs. New ventures may not be able to afford such help. Many entrepreneurs are forced by fiscal realities to become experts in advertising and public relations.

Governmental agencies

Strange that the government would be part of a venture's infrastructure, but it is. It can provide the venture with much help and information, and the costs are usually quite low, sometimes even free. These agencies include more than National Institute of Standards and Technology's (NIST) Manufacturing Enterprise Partnership (MEP) or the Small Business Administration (SBA). For example, the Patent Office can provide helpful technical information about products or processes in which a venture may have an interest. Also there are huge government data banks and research exchanges that contain information for those who will dig it out.

Manufacturers' representatives

In many industries independent firms can sell goods on a commission basis. Having its own sales force can be expensive for a new business. It may take $100,000 a year to keep a salesperson in the field. Thus if he or she can't sell at least $1 million worth of goods in a year, then selling costs soar to more than 10 percent of sales, a cost most firms can't afford. So it's smart to look for sales help, to rent a sales representative. To find one, the entrepreneur can talk to target customers to find out if manufacturers' representatives call on them and who the best ones are. The local Manufacturing Extension Partnership Center can work with the national network of MEP Centers to help find a sales representative that can represent specific product lines both nationally and internationally.

Manufacturing subcontractors

On the production side, thousands of firms exist solely to produce goods for others. Want to go into the vitamin business? Several excellent firms will make vitamin products to specifications. Want to market cosmetics? No need to make them; other firms will do it to a venture's specification. The entrepreneur just brings in the orders.

Engineering/design firms

If a new product looks a bit shabby for the modern market and the entrepreneur wants it spruced up, he or she can hire a designer. If a venture is having trouble with some technical aspect of its product, it can hire an engineering firm to solve it. Want to retrofit a manufacturing plant? There are firms that will design the whole thing. Some entrepreneurs believe in always hiring professionals to do a job rather than trying to do it themselves. They feel they get a better job at a lower cost in the long run. The local Manufacturing Extension Partnership Center has specialists in designing plant layouts to increase manufacturing efficiency. MEP can also help find architects and product design specialists to meet specific needs.

Distributors

A distributor can be many things and take many forms. However, in the end the distributor is an existing firm that will buy a venture's product and resell it to the intended market. It does just what the name implies; it distributes products for a venture, thus saving much time, money, and anguish. Attaining distribution for a new product is a difficult undertaking, one that often proves to be the entrepreneur's undoing. So a professional should be used, preferably a firm that has an existing system in the market.

Human resource consultants

Attracting and hiring the best workers are important steps for building a management team. If a venture doesn't hire the right people, it will directly affect productivity and bottom line.

Recruiting, hiring, and managing today's work force is a challenge. Finding qualified candidates is more difficult. That is why many entrepreneurs use employment agencies, executive-search firms, and employee-leasing firms. References should always be checked before contracting with these firms.

In addition, the legal environment and labor laws surrounding employee-employer rights and responsibilities are constantly changing and becoming more restrictive for business owners. For example, discharging an employee is one of the hardest and trickiest areas for most entrepreneurs to manage. This and other personnel actions can lead to headaches and lawsuits if not done properly.

A helpful book is *The Complete Do-It-Yourself Personnel Department* by Mary F. Cook (Aspen Publishing, Inc., 1998). This book is geared to entrepreneurs who must struggle with a myriad of personnel issues and who most likely do not have much training in this area. It provides numerous procedures, guidelines, checklists, sample policies, and personnel forms that can
be used.

Entrepreneurs may not be able to afford personnel managers on staff, but they are still required to comply with state and federal regulations. As the need arises, they can use human resource consultants or attorneys who specialize in personnel law to assist in handling complex personnel issues.

Lobbyists

Historically, entrepreneurs have not banded together against local, state, or federal legislation directly affecting them and their ability to conduct business. They have not taken advantage of lobbyists or trade associations to represent them on critical issues. This step is often worth considering.

Import/export brokers

To bring goods into the United States, entrepreneurs must comply with customs regulations. Import/export brokers, often referred to as customs brokers, will take the responsibility for such goods to clear customs in an orderly fashion. They charge a commission on the shipment's price, but usually this fee is not very expensive. Unless the business owner has previous experience in working with customs agents, he or she should use a customs broker. It will save time and money in clearing customs. To find a customs broker, look in the *Yellow Pages*. Hire a customs broker who has expertise in importing and exporting with the country the venture is dealing with.

Business consultants

Entrepreneurs use consultants because they are usually less expensive than hiring staff, especially when they need a specific problem solved or have a project that needs an outside assistant.

Choosing a consultant is an important decision that should be made only after carefully researching and interviewing potential consultants. Many skilled consultants can provide invaluable services. Nowhere are options so abundant and the quality so variable. The price paid for consultant services varies tremendously. Evaluate the consultants' performance by checking with other entrepreneurs they have worked for.

First, consider whether a generalist or a specialist is needed. There may be the need to have several different consultants. The person with expertise in finding a location for a business most likely will not have the skills necessary to assist in setting up the business' books. Be wary of can-do-it-all types.

Second, consider consultants' prior track record. Who else have they worked for and what services did they render? Obtain names of other entrepreneurs they have worked for and call to verify the results of their performance.

Ask for a written proposal based on needs. Evaluate proposals by looking for outcomes and objectives the consultants said they would accomplish.

The best way to find consultants is through referrals from bankers, lawyers, accountants, fellow entrepreneurs, and other associates. The government is also an excellent resource to find consultants. The local Manufacturing Enterprise Partnership Center can either provide consulting services directly at an inexpensive rate or help business owners find dependable consultants. The SBA provides consultants, sometimes at no charge. Some of these consultants are paid by the government, while others volunteer their services. Colleges and universities are another source for consultants on a private basis or sometimes through federally funded programs. Consultants might also be found in the *Yellow Pages* under "Management Consultants."

In the beginning, founders are usually short of cash and therefore try to find low-cost educational programs or government-funded management-assistance programs, such as those offered by the SBA and MEP. Typically, independent consultants charge anywhere between $300 and $1,000 a day.

Well-known consulting firms usually charge higher fees. Unfortunately, it is difficult to judge consultants based solely on the fees they charge.

The entrepreneur should choose a few consultants and interview them about their expertise and approaches. He or she must be comfortable with and communicate well with the consultants; evaluate their enthusiasm and openness; try to determine their interest level in the project; ask whether fee structure is hourly, daily, or fixed. The hired consultant should be one who works fast and effectively.

Don't underestimate the amount of time it will take to find a consultant who has the required expertise and the right chemistry. Books have been written on finding consultants: *Hiring Independent Contractors: The Employee's Legal Guide*, by Stephen Fishman (Nolo.com: 2000); *Selecting and Working with Consultants: A Guide for Clients (The Fifty-Minute Series)* by Thomas Ucko (Michael G. Crisp, editor, Crisp Publications: 1990).

Once the entrepreneur decides on a consultant, he or she should work out a written agreement specifying the consultant's responsibilities and objectives, including the compensation.

Dot-Com Companies as Advisors

Hundreds of dot-com businesses are starting up to help entrepreneurs run their companies better. Headlight.com, a San Francisco-based company, offers an extensive selection of online training courses for entrepreneurs who don't have the time or money to take outside classes. Another web site, www.onecore.com, provides people to help clients establish interest bearing bank accounts or set up payroll accounts costing less than the competition. The company functions as an electronic financial officer. Amazon.com invites small merchants to sell just about anything, for a modest fee, on the auction area on its mega-site.

In the future, as sites have more information on questions that entrepreneurs ask, the entrepreneur will be getting much of his or her advice online regarding how to run a company.

Conclusion

There is much to consider in forming a venture's management team. A good management team may be the ticket to success, while a poor one may provide only a one-way ticket to the poorhouse. Experience indicates that the selection of one's associates can be critical.

Some way must be developed to motivate the management team to do all the things necessary for the venture's success. Founders must be willing to share with their management people the success they have helped create.

Adept selection and use of the infrastructure firms loom as a large challenge to most entrepreneurs. Good professional help is often the difference between success and failure. Consequently, wise entrepreneurs spend much time working with support organizations.

Bankers, lawyers, accounting firms, and insurance firms are of particular importance; their use cannot be avoided. Entrepreneurs must have their services. The only question is the quality of the service they provide.

Exercise 11a: Management Team Assessment (Business Plan Only)

Evaluate your management team's competencies by scoring on a scale of 1 to 3 how well each of the ideal characteristics of an entrepreneur below applies to each member of your management team. 1–Needs improvement. 2–Satisfactory. 3–Good. Select three areas that need improvement and develop an action plan below.		Management team members						
C	Desire							
	Initiative/aggressiveness							
	Energy							
O	Low support needs							
	Thriving on ambiguity							
M	Perseverance							
P	Responsibility							
	Problem solving							
E	Persuasiveness							
T	Self-discipline							
	Belief in value of money							
E	Self-confidence							
N	Balanced ego development							
	Market awareness							
C	Generosity							
I	Honesty							
	Good people judgment							
E	Patience							
S	Business knowledge							
	Value appropriate control systems							

	Competency challenge	Action plan	Budget impact
1			
2			
3			

Exercise 11b: Management Team Challenges (Business Plan Only)

Identify management team challenges specific to your organization. After gathering information from qualified experts (management professors, team building consultants, successful entrepreneurs), develop a useful action plan for the organization.

Management team challenge	Action plan

Exercise 11c: Management Team Budget Assumptions and Impact (Business Plan Only)

What are some assumptions you might make about each of the management team-related expenses? For example, you may decide to have an external management consultant team (consisting of your attorney, accountant, and other experts) meet on a quarterly basis. Or you may decide to create an internal marketing department instead of using an advertising agency.

Management team budget assumptions

Evaluate the budgetary impact of your management team issues and implications resulting from establishing/developing/making changes to your existing management team plan. For example, the cost of each quarterly management consultant team meeting may be $1,500 for travel expenses, consultant fees, and meals.

Management team budget impact

Legal Forms of Organization

Learning Objectives

In this chapter, students will learn to

- Understand the five legal structures most often used for a new venture.
- Create a venture using the proper legal system.

Business must be done within some sort of a legal framework. The law insists on it. If an owner fails to take positive action to structure his or her enterprise legally, then the law will assume two things.

- The business is a sole proprietorship; that is, the owner and the business are legally one and the same thing.
- The business uses the owner's legal name as its own.

If the owner is associated in a business with other people, not including employees, the law automatically assumes that the venture is a partnership unless the business is incorporated.

For many reasons, it is unlikely that an ambitious entrepreneur really wants a business treated legally in such a manner. To keep the law from making decisions for the entrepreneur, he or she must make some decisions and take some legal actions.

In the hands of an informed, adept entrepreneur, the legal formats in which business is done can be a formidable offensive and defensive managerial tool. Entrepreneurs are advised to become well informed about the laws governing business organizations and then, in consultation with an attorney and accountant, make a decision as to which form is the most advantageous.

Most books on small business and entrepreneurship contain chapters on this subject. They recite the advantages and disadvantages of each legal form of organization. Unfortunately, those theoretical treatments of the subject do not reflect the realities of the business world. This discussion focuses on reality and how entrepreneurs organize their ventures into the legal forms of business organization discussed below.

As a business grows it might require a different legal structure to accommodate changing tax laws and the individual situations of its members. Tax accountants or business attorneys should be consulted for advice when such a change may be needed.

Sole Proprietorship

Legal Structures
Sole proprietorship
Partnerships: general and
    limited
Limited liability company
Corporations: C and S
Nonprofit corporation

In a sole proprietorship, it is the owner alone against the world. He or she owns the business lock, stock, and barrel. He or she can manage it or hire managers. All the profits are the owner's and so are the losses. The liabilities of the business are all the owner's which, of course, means that they are unlimited—a major disadvantage in this litigious age, a fatal disadvantage in almost any substantial venture. If the owner needs money, he or she will have to borrow on signature or put up collateral. However, the lender will be apprehensive about the loan, for should anything happen to the owner, the business will likely go down the drain. Thus, life insurance may be required for the amount of the loan. Clearly the owner will be severely limited in his or her ability to raise money, particularly large amounts of it.

Certainly sole proprietorships are simple and easy to form. Just hang out a shingle after the appropriate government hurdles are cleared. Even the income tax treatment is simple: Put it all in Schedule C of the 1040 form. No double-taxation dilemmas and no problems with excessive compensation or excessive retained earnings. It's as simple as it can be (if anything regarding our taxation system can be called simple).

It is also unfair. The proprietor is not allowed to deduct many items that are deductible to a corporation: defined-benefit pension plans, insurance expenses, health benefits, and other corporate goodies are not allowed.

As a practical legal vehicle for new ventures, the sole proprietorship suffers some fatal flaws besides the liability and tax drawbacks. First, the life of the business terminates with the life of the proprietor, which poses severe problems to estate planners, not to mention the disposition of the business. Second, exits are hampered. It is generally easier to sell a corporation than a proprietorship. Third, growth is usually restricted for several reasons related to financing and management motivation.

Finally, it is difficult to find good management for a proprietorship, which severely limits growth and performance.

Partnerships

General partnerships

Avoid being involved in a
venture that has a general
partnership as its legal
structure.

Despite all the admonitions about the dangers of general partnerships, they still exist in various forms, thus they need to be recognized. Most authorities strongly advise against using the partnership form of organization because its dangers are real and serious and consequences potentially disastrous. Liabilities are personal and unlimited. Moreover, each partner can be held fully liable for the actions of any other partner. For example, debt for the firm is a responsibility for the partner who has the ability to pay the debt. It is not necessarily divided equally between partners. This is also true for any liability claims against the partnership.

The business life of a partnership is precarious. A partnership ends upon the death of any partner or upon the request of any partner.

Limited partnerships

The limited partnership has become popular in the past two decades for some good and definite reasons. It solves some problems for the entrepreneur and some different problems for the investor.

In the limited partnership, the general partner is usually the entrepreneur, sometimes acting personally as a sole proprietor but more often as a corporation. General partners have full liabilities. A corporation can be a general partner. In addition to the general partner, there are one or more limited partners. Limited partners have limited liability. Often the number is limited to 35 to satisfy the laws that regulate the sale of securities. One needs expert legal assistance in forming limited partnerships for the purpose of raising money. While it is a way around the U.S. Securities and Exchange Commission's regulation for the sales of stocks and bonds, it still is not without its own stringent regulations.

The entrepreneur likes the limited partnership for several reasons. First, the problems of control of the venture are minimized. There are no stockholders. Limited partners are quite limited in what they can do to "guide" managerial efforts. About all they can do is sue for fraud.

Second, it used to be easy to sell interests in limited partnerships because of their income tax treatment. They were often a good tax shelter. The flow of values from the enterprise to the various partners is stipulated in the partnership agreement. Often all the tax goodies flow directly to the limited partners. These can be sizable, limited only by the amount of money the limited partners have at risk. The general partner may forgo participation in the tax goodies and may even waive rights to early income flow. It is not uncommon for the limited partners to be repaid all of their investments before the general partner receives anything. In essence, entrepreneurs position themselves as backing into the money, only after the enterprise has been successful and the investors have been made whole. This stance is most comfortable if the entrepreneur really believes in the deal. It tells investors a credible story. Some limited partnerships skim the income flow immediately to cover operating and management costs. Investors examine such provisions carefully.

Changes in the income tax laws have greatly reduced the attractiveness of limited partnerships to investors looking for tax shelters. They are now difficult to sell to passive investors.

Limited partnerships are mainly used for one-shot finite deals, such as real estate syndication, oil-drilling ventures, movie production—wherever the venture has a foreseeable life span. Seldom are limited partnerships used for ongoing, continual businesses.

Research and development (R&D) limited partnerships

The R&D partnership was a popular method of financing high-tech start-ups because of the favorable tax treatment formerly granted to such entities. Staar Surgical Company began as an R&D limited partnership so that the initial investors could write off all research expenses immediately. Once the research was completed, they exchanged their position in the partnership for Staar stock on a highly advantageous basis.

One form of the partnership, the limited partnership, was widely used in the past two decades as the vehicle for financing many real estate and R&D financing syndicates. It gave the investors the limited liability they demanded while allowing all costs and losses to be passed directly through to them. Such partnerships were tax shelters. Changes in the tax laws have nullified most of their tax advantages.

Limited Liability Company (LLC)

The LLC is neither a corporation nor a partnership. This type of business entity, when properly structured, is designed to combine the benefits of liability protection afforded to shareholders of a corporation with the favorable tax treatment provided to partnerships and their partners. In some states, LLC owners are called members, and people who operate the business are called managers. Managers are elected by members from their own membership or from the outside. The required number of members vary from state to state. Some states require at least two members to use this legal structure.

The principal advantage of an LLC is that for federal income tax purposes, the LLC is treated as a partnership unless members elect to have the LLC taxed as a corporation. Instead, like a partnership, the income and loss earned by the LLC are passed through to the members and reported by them on their respective tax returns. The LLC's advantage over the partnership status is that, unlike general partners (in both general and limited partnerships), the members' liability for the debts of the LLC are limited to the extent of their investment in the business.

The LLC also provides more flexibility in membership and organization than the S corporation. The LLC is not subject to the rules related to electing S corporation status. S corporations are inhibited by strict limitations on who can be shareholders (only U.S. citizens, resident aliens, and certain types of trusts). S corporations are also limited to one class of stock in which the allocation of profits and losses must be proportionate to shareholders' interests. In contrast, the LLC provides tremendous flexibility in planning distributions and special allocations of the profits and losses.

Forming an LLC is similar to forming a limited partnership or corporation. Articles of organization must be filed with the Secretary of State. In addition, there must be an operating agreement that resembles a partnership agreement. The operating agreement spells out the details of how the business will be operated and how the profits and losses will be shared. It is recommended that a business attorney be consulted to prepare the LLC's articles of organization and operating agreement.

Every state now has LLC statutes to permit formation of an LLC within its boundaries. A drawback of forming the LLC is that state law is still evolving to determine the treatment of LLCs formed in one state but doing business in another. However, business and other professionals are reacting favorably to the LLC.

Lastly, the LLC may have restrictions on admitting new members, permitting the transfer of a member's interest, and the LLC's ability to continue if a member withdraws.

The LLC is not the ideal legal structure for every business. Despite its disadvantages, the LLC is a good planning tool. Its simplicity and flexibility make it an attractive legal structure for some closely held businesses that operate in one or more states. This legal entity is also suitable for many real estate, oil and gas, and mining businesses as well as groups of professionals.

Corporations

There are many advantages to incorporating a business. The advantages may not be as great for small operations in which there is little likelihood of liabilities being created or ventures of such short duration or little importance that it makes no sense to create a separate legal entity.

C corporations

The founders of corporations—unlike sole proprietors who are personally liable for all debts of the business and all liabilities that may be assessed against it—have the corporate shield to help protect them personally from the claims of creditors.

Great care must be taken, however, to preserve the corporate shield by strictly observing all legal procedures and dealings with the corporation. Founders should always identify themselves and sign as officers of the company. They should never pay corporate debts personally and never pay personal debts from corporate funds. The corporation must be kept separate from personal life. If proper legal procedures are in place to keep the corporate shield intact, it provides peace of mind by keeping the founder's estate intact. Moreover, it is a deterrent to aggressive creditors who would go after the founder's assets if they knew the founder were personally liable for the debts of the business. An insolvent corporation with no money in the bank makes aggressive creditors easier to deal with.

Sole proprietors are also severely limited in financing options. They can't sell stock in themselves. Public money is blocked off from them. A corporation, on the other hand, has many more financial options than either the sole proprietor or partnership.

One of the fundamental principles of business is to create and keep open as many options as possible.

Indeed, as will be emphasized later, one of the great advantages of incorporating an enterprise is that it provides the legal right to sell many different types of rights.

When entrepreneurs want to sell their businesses, as they most likely will at some future time, the corporation provides a much more salable package.

A corporation can select a fiscal period other than the calendar year (which a sole proprietor must use), thus availing the owners of the business some latitude in delaying the payment of income taxes.

A corporation can set up much more generous employee benefit programs than can the sole proprietor. Moreover, the IRS, as a matter of policy, will allow many types of deductions to a corporation that would be immediately challenged if taken by a sole proprietor.

By law, a corporation must, at a minimum, hold annual stockholder(s) and director(s) meetings. Most states permit a corporation to have but one stockholder, one director and one officer, and they may all be the same person. In those states where more than one is required, the entrepreneur may select a trusted employee, family member or advisor to fill the other role(s) and still maintain control of the corporation. Among other permitted purposes, stockholder(s) must meet to elect director(s) and director(s) must meet to elect officer(s). Obviously, in those states permitting as few as one in each category, the sole stockholder holds a meeting at his or her convenience and elects him or herself as the sole director, then has a directors meeting and elects him or herself as the president of the corporation. The corporation must make certain that contemporaneous written minutes of each meeting are prepared, accurately stating the date, place, and time of each meeting; those in attendance (even if only one) and what business was conducted. Further, the corporation must make certain that it timely complies with all reporting requirements of the state of its incorporation and all others in which it is authorized to do business.

There are a few traps to beware of, but they should pose no problem to any knowledgeable attorney or CPA working with an aware entrepreneur.

The double taxation trap

The so-called double tax comes from the fact that if the corporation reports an income, it is taxed once at the corporate rate—which incidentally, is lower than the individual tax rates at low income levels. The second tax occurs when the corporate income is paid out to the stockholders as dividends. The stockholder pays taxes on it as fully taxed, ordinary income. Thus, the alert corporate entrepreneur pays out the corporate profits in the form of salaries, expenses, employee benefits, and bonuses prior to the end of the tax year. The IRS even cooperates by allowing a corporation a two-month period after the end of its fiscal year for paying employee and end-of-the-year bonuses. Entrepreneurs without an outside stockholder should never have to pay large corporate taxes unless they want to do so. There are some limitations, however, so one should consult with an attorney and CPA before paying relatively large amounts as bonuses. There are times when one may want to keep the money in the corporation. Remember, the corporate tax rate is usually lower than the personal tax rate. Entrepreneurs may want to take the profits at the lower corporate rate and leave the money there for use at a future time.

Key Rule
Keep control of as much cash as possible.

Or, founders may want to show a corporate profit because they hope to sell the business, either to the public or to another party. They will have to produce accurate records to prove to other people that the business is profitable.

If an enterprise is publicly held, then it is a different game. Founders will be somewhat limited in the amount of corporate profit they will be able to pass on to themselves and other investors who are close to them.

Nevertheless, entrepreneurs should not be discouraged by such regulations. There is still ample room for tax maneuvers completely within the law. Entrepreneurs can operate totally within the law and still gain great tax advantages by using corporations as the legal form of business.

The excessive compensation trap

As the corporation pays more and more of its "profits" to the founder as compensation, he or she runs a risk of the IRS declaring the salary unreasonable and taxing it as though it were a corporate dividend; that is, the corporation must pay the corporate tax first, then the founder will be taxed in addition.

Inc. magazine carried an article about a person who was challenged by the IRS on just this issue. A CPA wrote the following letter in response to the article:

> Mr. Howell's problems with the Internal Revenue Service sound like a case of an entrepreneur who thinks he knows it all. Apparently, he didn't have a tax advisor or didn't listen to him during the years he paid himself an unreasonable compensation. If he had been properly advised, Mr. Howell could have taken a number of steps that would have served him well when the IRS came 'round. In addition to points mentioned in the article, such as establishing a dividend-paying history and establishing his compensation policy early in the development of the business, he could have
>
> - Provided in the corporate bylaws that, to the extent compensation is found to be unreasonable, the employee is obligated to return the excess to the corporation. This would have eliminated the double-taxation problem.
> - Considered the use of an S corporation election, since it appears that he was draining all the profits out of the company anyway. This would have eliminated the double-taxation problem.
> - Established employment contracts between himself and his companies, setting his compensation package in writing prior to the time profits were known.
> - Paid himself reasonable interest on his loans to the company, rather than charging no interest and then attempting to justify his compensation partially on the fact that he had loaned money to the company (as it appears he did).
> - Treated the IRS representative respectfully and courteously when the first audit was begun. Better yet, his tax advisor should have handled the audit for him.
>
> I suggest that Mr. Howell's big problem was not that the IRS and the court dealt unfairly with him but that he was playing a game he knew nothing about.

S corporation

Mention was made previously of using an S corporation as a means for avoiding double taxation. The S corporation is such an important tool for the entrepreneur that some effort should be made to understand it, even though its use is recommended only with the direction of qualified tax counsel.

While the S corporation can be advantageous when the enterprise is losing money, problems arise when profits are made and passed on to the stockholders on which to pay tax, but no cash is passed on with which to pay the taxes.

The S corporation is not a legal form of organization but only a federal income tax provision that allows a corporation to be taxed as if it were a partnership when certain conditions are met.

The key to using an S corporation is foresight. The entrepreneur must anticipate the tax situation for the coming tax year. One cannot elect to be an S corporation after realizing that that form is needed. At that time, it is too late to change.

Not all companies are eligible to be S corporations. An attorney or tax accountant should review all the regulations of an S corporation before deciding if the legal structure is appropriate.

If the company is eligible, then it must file with the IRS by March 15 (all S corporations must be on the calendar year) form 2553, in which all stockholders give their consent for the company to be taxed as a partnership. After all, it does affect every stockholder.

The election to be treated as an S corporation can be negated automatically if a new stockholder refuses to consent to the election or if any of the other eligibility requirements are altered. Thus, it is easy to get out of an S corporation status.

The S corporation is limited in the kinds of securities it can offer: Only common stock can be in its capital structure. However, the new law does allow common stock with different voting rights. Thus, the S corporation can have voting and nonvoting common stock.

There are a few other technical details involving capital-gains treatments, but that's why tax counsel is necessary. One must look out for the details.

Nonprofit Corporation

A nonprofit organization, the most common form being a 501(c)(3), is an IRS classification for organizations that provide a service to the community for one or more of the following purposes: religious, charitable, scientific, testing for public safety, literacy, educational, fostering national or international amateur sports competition, or prevention of cruelty to children or animals. Generally nonprofits are prohibited from distributing net income to owners, members, directors, or officers.

There are two steps in becoming a 501(c)(3) nonprofit corporation. The first step is to apply to become a corporation in a state, deliver articles of incorporation, and pay the required filing fee. If the articles of incorporation conform to the law, the founder will receive a certificate of incorporation. This does not make the enterprise exempt from income tax. Exemption is accomplished by filing for tax-exempt status with the IRS, which is the next step.

The second step involves filing form 1023 with the IRS and a variety of other materials such as articles of incorporation, bylaws, and budgets, along with a nonrefundable IRS filing fee. Most entrepreneurs don't prepare their own articles of incorporation and bylaws. Instead they contact a lawyer who specializes in nonprofit corporations for assistance because of the filing complexities.

Since it is not always easy to determine whether a venture idea will be eligible under state and federal regulations for nonprofits, entrepreneurs usually schedule an initial meeting with the lawyer to determine whether to proceed.

The costs of a lawyer's and accountant's services will significantly vary according to the amount and accuracy of the paperwork initially provided, the complexity of the venture, and their individual fee schedules. The total costs to incorporate and obtain tax-exempt status for a nonprofit average from $2,000 to $10,000.

Before contacting a professional, the entrepreneur may obtain nonprofit incorporation information from local or national organizations. Many have start-up packages at little or no charge or offer seminars on incorporating as a nonprofit.

Today, it is more difficult to obtain nonprofit status. Therefore, entrepreneurs must carefully decide that this organizational structure is right for their ventures, and then find highly recommended legal and tax experts to file the necessary paperwork. Several months must be allowed to prepare the paperwork. It can take up to a year after the filing with the IRS before notification that the organization qualifies for this special tax classification.

Creative Capital Structures

Selecting a legal form of business will depend on several things, including the goals of the venture, the demands of investors, and how much liability the owner is willing to bear. One of the great advantages of the corporate form of business organization is its tremendous flexibility, its ability to provide its creators with the capital structure they believe they need to accomplish their aims.

An example is common stock. There are all sorts of things one can do with it. The only limits to the different types of common stock one may create are practicality, the state law, and what the investors will buy. It's fruitless to create a stock no one wants to buy.

While in theory, common stock represents ownership of the corporation, the real question always comes down to "ownership of what?" Ownership of rights is the classic answer, but then the question becomes "What rights?" Here is the nub of the matter: What are the various rights that are sold to the buyer of a common stock? The typical corporation, in which there is only one class of common stock, gives its owners rights to receive dividends from the company's profits, if and when dividends are approved by the board of directors; rights to vote for directors on some sort of pre-agreed-upon basis; rights to assets upon dissolution; rights to sell the stock to other people; the right to sue the officers or directors for any misuse of corporate assets or malfeasance; and perhaps the preemptive right to buy additional stock needed to maintain one's proportional share of the company.

Each of these rights will be discussed in more detail in order to gain a better perspective on how a creative entrepreneur can use them to his or her best advantage. However, all require professional advice and assistance before selection.

Stockholder Rights
Rights to income
Rights to sell the security
Rights to elect directors
Rights in dissolution
Rights to transfer stock
Rights to sue
Rights to buy stock
Rights to employment

Rights to income

Obviously, investors expect a return on investment (ROI). Depending on how the deal was structured, payback can come in several ways. The rights of certain stockholders to be paid dividends prior to other stockholders has long been established. Such securities are called preferred stock. They are preferred over other classes of stock in whatever way is promised. The income preference can be stipulated in either dollars or percentage, for example, $4 per share per year or 12 percent of the par value.

If the preferred dividend is promised only when and if the corporation earns enough to pay it and it is not carried over from one year to the next, it is called a noncumulative preferred stock. If unpaid dividends accumulate, the security is called cumulative.

In entrepreneurial ventures, the use of preferred stock is normally avoided. First, investors do not like a noncumulative preferred stock. The ability of a management to rig profits to suit its purposes is well recognized; thus noncumulative preferred stockholders could be cheated out of their fair share quite easily.

So that leaves cumulative preferred as a practical alternative to consider. Most entrepreneurs would not choose to create a cumulative preferred stock unless it represented the least threatening of several evils or they had some grand scheme in mind.

For example, it is normally considered good practice to always make a preferred stock callable by the corporation for a slight premium over par value, for example, a $100 stock might be callable after a certain period of time after issue for $105. By such means, entrepreneurs might be able to rid themselves of unwanted investors once a company is rolling. They just buy them out.

Most preferred stocks are created to satisfy investors' fears that they will not be paid the income due them from the company's good fortune. They know all too well that minority stockholders are often frozen out by a management that cannot be unseated from power. The cumulative preferred stock can be a powerful force to make management kick out dividends. However as dividends, the income was first taxed as a corporate profit and then as the individual's ordinary income. Uncle Sam loves preferred stock. Thus, most adept managements suggest to investors, who fear that they won't receive income, to take bonds instead. Therefore, the interest payments are deductible to the corporation, and only one tax is paid. For the investor who wants to participate in the corporation's good fortune, such bonds may have the privilege of converting into some sort of common stock at some pre-agreed-upon rate of exchange. Thus, convertible bonds can play a useful role in a capital structure.

Entrepreneurs should avoid issuing an income bond, one on which interest is paid only when and if earned, as the IRS will say it is really a common stock and will treat it accordingly.

The key question is to what extent a firm can stand to have claims on income against it. A founder does not want to create a security that will result in loss of control. Few start-up companies can afford to have fixed-income obligations accumulating against them. A founder would just be digging his economic grave deeper and deeper as time passes and the firm has yet to earn the cash necessary to buy back such obligations.

It is not enough that the venture is earning a profit. It must be throwing off enough cash from operations to pay out the interest or dividends. Not too many new enterprises generate such cash flows.

Consequently, one general rule is to create a situation in which the investor receives all cash returns not from the new venture, but from outside sources—the market.

Rights to sell the security

This right gives investors a security they can sell to other people when the time is right. The market pays the venture's equity bills.

The founders of some companies, from the inception of the venture, make it quite clear to everyone—investors, officers, directors, and employees—that all significant monies made from the venture will have to come from selling the stock for a large profit. This strategy lets the market pay the people.

Rights to elect directors

Most entrepreneurs want to keep control of the corporation; thus, they try to structure the deal so that outside investors have limited rights to elect directors.

Perhaps they try to sell a nonvoting common stock or at least one that votes for only a limited number of directors. Of course, the investor wants the right to unseat officers who do not perform as promised. So there is the basis of some serious discussion. How does a founder keep control over an enterprise?

Do not for one moment believe that a founder will not have control problems so long as he or she performs satisfactorily. In fact, the better the performance, the more problems the founder may have keeping control—unless the deal has been wisely set up. After all, the better the founder performs, the more the company is worth, and thus the more pirates will be attracted who want to take over the company. A bankrupt company usually is of little interest to investors. At that time, they want restitution, not control. Of course, if they feel that the venture can be saved, then they may want the founder ousted from control.

There are several control tactics available. Legal counsel is required, for their legality varies by state. First, there is the common stock that does not vote unless certain events either occur or fail to occur. So long as the founder performs as promised, the stockholders cannot elect the directors. Of course, this assumes the founder has had the foresight to select directors with care. Directors have been known to rebel. People can turn on founders, particularly in this age of director liability suits.

Second, there are voting trusts into which stockholders place their voting rights for the founder to vote. Such trusts usually dissolve under certain conditions.

Third, there are buy-back provisions by which founders can remove troublesome stockholders from the scene, if they have the money to do so, which is seldom the case.

Fourth, each class of stock may be allowed to elect only a few directors. Naturally, the founder's class of stock elects enough directors to control the enterprise. Why would investors go for such an arrangement? Because the founder has given them other protections for their concerns, and they have no real interest in controlling the company. They may realize quite clearly that the founder is the company's major asset and without him or her the deal is down the drain. This is especially true in high-tech ventures.

Fifth, the founder keeps some key assets, such as patents, trademarks, the ownership of vital property, or the rights for distribution or manufacture. The idea is that if control problems arise, the founder owns the real key to the company's future profitability.

True, others will likely contest the founder's desire to control such key factors. On the other hand, if the deal offered is attractive enough to them, the founder may be able to get the deal he or she wants. He or she may have to give up something else for sake of the control key. Such is the stuff of which tough negotiations are made.

A founder can do many things to maintain control over an enterprise, other than keeping ownership of 51 percent of the voting stock. Many entrepreneurs insist on owning all the stock. They want no possible interference from minority investors. At all times, they must keep in mind that the investor must be convinced to accept whatever deal is offered.

Rights in dissolution

Rights in dissolution should be considered. If investors are really worried about getting their money back should the venture go sour, let them own the assets into which the money is going and lease them back to the company. Thus, investors have title to the goods and avoid most of the hassle of creditor claims (it's also a good idea to get legal aid here). Moreover, they have good protection for income payout. If the rent is not paid, the investors can grab the assets.

Rights to transfer stock

Some closely held corporations, especially those in which the principal stockholders are crucial to the success of the venture, require restrictions on the rights to sell stock to prevent the beneficiaries of a deceased stockholder or perhaps the ex-spouse from obtaining ownership. This situation can be handled with a provision that stock may not be sold, given to or inherited by anyone without first being offered to the corporation at some fair value. The point here is not to cheat the other stockholder's estate, heirs or proper claimants but rather to permit the remaining stockholder to operate the business without interference by one whose only interest in the business is how much money they can get from it. In the case of death of one of the stockholders, a life insurance policy owned by the corporation can be the source of funds to permit the corporation to pay for the stock. The entrepreneur should thoroughly discuss this potential problem with legal counsel before forming the corporation.

Rights to sue

Generally any stockholder in any enterprise has the right to sue management for its misdeeds. Indeed, it is for this reason that many entrepreneurs refuse outside money.

Many entrepreneurs believe that so long as they own more than 50 percent of the stock, they can run the corporation as they please. This is true so long as management is exercising its judgment regarding a matter about which opinions, honestly held and commercially defensible, differ.

Management may not, however, operate the corporation to its benefit and the detriment of minority stockholders. Those minority owners may seek relief from a court through a stockholder's derivative action. If the court agrees with the minority owner, it may order curative actions be taken by management and award damages as well.

Rights to buy stock

In some closely held corporations, stockholders have a preemptive right to buy additional shares of all stock offered so that each investor's proportional share of the enterprise is maintained. Some states have laws dealing with such preemptive rights. This is designed to minimize the "watering" of the company's stock by selling large numbers of shares for a low price that results in the original stockholders' being squeezed out. The law can be very impatient with those promoters who try to swindle the initial investors out of their original share by selling subsequent stock at greatly reduced prices, but it does happen.

Sophisticated use of stock options, rights, and warrants gives the entrepreneur a valuable financial tool for accomplishing many things.

Unexpected, subsequent financing required because of managerial miscalculations or errors can be very expensive in both money and stockholder relationships. Often bitter fights evolve over the price a company has to pay for needed funds down the line, after management has squandered the initial financing.

Rights to employment

Not all rights are entitlements. One that is not is the right to employment. Today many of the founding investors in new enterprises are tacitly promised jobs in the company in return for their investment. What happens if they prove to be unsatisfactory employees? It's a touchy situation. Buyout agreements are nice but may not help if no one has the money to buy out the party.

Wise entrepreneurs usually avoid "selling" jobs in return for capital investments. It usually doesn't work out well. The two activities should be separate; simply say, "Look, there is only one reason I would hire you, and that is because I think you are the best person for the job. To do otherwise would be to violate my duties as president. If you were hired and did not do your job, I would fire you. Now, if you feel that putting your money into our venture is a sound investment, then, fine, we would be happy to have you as one of our stockholders. If you do not feel inclined to invest with us, then don't. We don't need any dissatisfied investors, and particularly, we don't need any dissatisfied employee-investors. If I held any other opinion, you should flee, for I would be an unworthy leader."

If people cannot see the logic in that policy, a founder wants nothing to do with them. Granted, it is often difficult to walk away from money that is desperately needed, but one must learn to do so, for there is money out there that founders want nothing to do with.

One case concerning rights to employment that worked well involved an entrepreneur who was starting a software production company. He needed to raise $250,000 in start-up capital but did not like asking people for money and did not understand various entrepreneurial fund-raising techniques.

The entrepreneur had a friend who had been successful in the outdoor-billboard advertising business and had sold his company for a sizable sum of money. He knew that his friend probably did not want to invest in his software company; however, his friend did know many retirees in Florida who belonged to an investment club for new ventures. His friend was not working and was getting bored being retired at a young age.

The entrepreneur made his friend the following offer: "If you will introduce me to the Florida investment group and help me raise the $250,000, I will give you an office, computer, and use of our receptionist to answer your phone and assist you in doing your correspondence. In addition, I'll pay for your health insurance and name you vice president of development, and I'll give you some shares in my company."

This offer was a perfect solution for the friend, since this provided him with an office to go to every day, interaction with other people, a title to put on his business cards, and health insurance for his family for no charge. The deal was accepted and the meeting was scheduled in Florida. It was successful in raising $250,000. The entrepreneur's friend was satisfied, and the entrepreneur was able to start a new software company.

Packaging the Rights

Security Packages
Common stock
Preferred stock
Bonds
Non-security rights
Licenses
Manufacturing rights

After the rights that entrepreneurs have to sell to their intended investors have been selected, the entrepreneurs need to package the rights in order to sell them to intended investors. There is a choice of several security packages: common stock, preferred stock, bonds, non-security rights, licenses, and manufacturing rights.

It is well to remember that, while entrepreneurs have at their disposal a tremendous assortment of securities with which they can weave together a capital structure to meet their needs, simplicity has great virtue. One shouldn't be complex just to be complex. There should be reasons for what is done. Founders do not want to create a capital structure that will somehow block what they might want to do in the future.

For instance, one inventor of a rather promising device set up his company originally by taking 80 percent of its common stock, plus a 10 percent royalty on sales for his patents. To furnish working capital, he loaned the company money. After four years of negative cash flow, the company needed outside capital on which to expand. Outside financial packagers uniformly told the man that unless he totally reconstructed the company's capital structure and the deals with himself, there would be no way to get the $3 million he was requesting. He refused to make any changes. The company foundered. It is difficult to get people to give up what they think is rightfully theirs, no matter how cogent the reasons may be for doing so. It is better to start out with a workable structure that recognizes the likelihood that additional money will be needed in the future, and not eliminate the possibility of future financing.

Common stock

Most firms are organized with one class of common stock, which enjoys all of the rights to income, assets, and control. This is simple and effective in most situations, but not all. On occasion, other classes of common stock serve a purpose. Some examples:

- The entrepreneur might create one class of "founder's stock" that has disproportionate voting rights in order to provide the founder with reasonable control over the situation. However, that stock may not participate in profits until other classes of stock receive a stipulated amount of money. Often the deal is structured so that outside investors get all their money back before the founders receive anything, much in the same way most limited partnerships are structured.

- The founder's stock might not be transferable except under certain circumstances, or the outside investor's class of stock might be redeemable for a certain agreed-upon price schedule. Thus, the founder would have a way of getting rid of the outside investors. Naturally, all such deals must be mutually agreed upon or nothing happens.

Preferred stock

The income tax difficulties of preferred stock were mentioned previously. Preferred stock is often used to buy out previous owners of a business who are fearful they won't receive any dividends from operations. They are usually retired and depend upon those dividends for living expenses.

Venture capital companies almost always buy or negotiate for preferred stock in companies they invest in or work with. This is because preferred stock allows them to control various parts of the company, such as assets, dividends, and anti-dilution provisions. If preferred stock is brought to the negotiation table, the entrepreneur should consult an attorney on all of the ways a venture capitalist can gain control.

Bonds

Convertible bonds are enjoying some popularity in new ventures, as they offer the investor some assured income, admittedly at a lower-than-market interest rate, while benefiting from the price action of the common stock on the upside. If the price of the common stock goes up, the bondholder can convert into the common stock at the agreed-upon exchange price. If the stock price goes down, the investor still has the bond and its interest. The entrepreneur likes convertible bonds for two reasons. It is a way of selling equity (the common stock) for a higher price than is currently possible in the market, because normally the convertible exchange rate is about 50 percent over the market price at the time of the bond's issue.

Second, it enables the company to borrow money at lower-than-market interest rates. A company sold $7 million of 9 percent convertible bonds to another company, convertible into common stock at $15 per share (the market price at the time was about $10).

Non-security rights

Often overlooked in the legal structuring of a corporation are various other types of rights that can have great value, such as distribution rights, licenses, and manufacturing or supply rights. There are people who believe that the smart operators in the high-tech arena are those who seek the rights to distribute the output of the high-tech manufacturer; their firms can deal with whatever high-tech firm is selling the most attractive product. They don't care who the winners are; they have the rights to sell the output. Often, the profits in distribution exceed the profits from manufacturing. Thus, some wise investors, as part of their initial deal to furnish the venture funds, seek the exclusive rights to distribute the firm's products in certain attractive market areas.

It can be a tempting offer to a hungry entrepreneur who sees not only money but a marketing outlet from the deal. It can work out quite well for all parties. On the other hand, what happens down the line if the entrepreneur wants to sell the operation to a large competitor that has its own distribution system? The distribution rights must be repurchased to make the deal. The price won't be inexpensive. What happens if the market proves much larger than anticipated, but the distributor won't tool up to take advantage of it? All performance quotas are being met in the distribution contract, but the firm is losing critical market share. The fact is that when such distribution rights are granted, some control over the enterprise is lost. Yet, there are times when it is still a wise move to make.

Entrepreneurs should be aware that distribution rights are valuable assets to the company. They shouldn't sell them cheap and should be sure it is possible to get them back with a reasonable payoff. There is no way to know what the future holds for a venture.

Licenses

The right to license to other firms the use of patents or technology can be very profitable. An optical-lens manufacturer licensed one of its silicon-lens patents to a large marketing company for a 6 percent royalty of sales, plus a 4 percent royalty for the technological know-how to use the patent. That agreement could be worth as much as $100 million to the optical-lens manufacturer's stockholders. The marketing company paid $3 million in cash as advance royalties. How is that for an inexpensive source of money? Why would the marketing company make such an agreement? Because the potential profits looked attractive!

Manufacturing rights

A venture needs someone to make its product. And it needs money. The founder runs into a supplier that likes the venture and makes an offer. In exchange for the rights to manufacture the product, the supplier will advance the needed funds. Does the founder accept the offer? That depends on the alternatives. In doing so, the founder has sold a valuable right to someone who has the power to control the venture. The founder needs protections in the deal. What about the price for which the venture buys the product? What about delivery guarantees, quality, and terms of payment? Does the venture need a second source? The fact is, such an arrangement is almost a partnership. How can the founder get out of it if it doesn't work out?

Playing the Legal Game

Entrepreneurs have no choice. They are totally enmeshed in a complex legal system. So complex, no one person completely understands it. And if entrepreneurs somehow master some part of it, it will likely change, either by statute or judicial decree. They must learn to play the game the best they can and to obtain astute, experienced legal counsel to assist them. Those who complain about the system's complexity must stop a minute to think. It is that very complexity and ambiguity that allows the clever entrepreneur much latitude in operations, particularly when corporate structure and operations are learned. Astute entrepreneurs use the legal system to their advantage.

Conclusion

There is no end to the possibilities available to clever entrepreneurs for devising the capital structure of their firms. The flexibility for the modern corporation is truly astonishing. Moreover, the sophistication of the money market now allows marketing many more types of security packages. It will pay well to master the art of corporate finance.

To understand the legal formalities of forming corporations there are several excellent paperback books that thoroughly deal with the subject: *How to Form Your Own Corporation Without a Lawyer for Under $75* by Ted Nicholas or the *Starting and Operating a Business in ... Series,* which includes a book for each state in the United States, published by The Oasis Press/PSI Research. Entrepreneurs are urged to read at least one of them if they are interested in forming corporations, even though they plan to use attorneys to do the work. By all means, an attorney should be used to form the corporations for entrepreneurs. But not all attorneys are adept at creating structures for effecting what entrepreneurs have in mind. Entrepreneurs may have to provide the attorneys guidance on what they want accomplished.

It is important to interview several attorneys to find the one who has the necessary knowledge and skill to guide the entrepreneur.

Exercise 12a: Legal Structure Assessment

Choose a legal structure, then evaluate advantages, limitations, and disadvantages of that structure in achieving entrepreneurial goals. This is important if you are writing a business plan.

Chosen legal structure proposed in feasibility or business plan:		
Advantages	**Limitations**	**Disadvantages**

Exercise 12b: Legal Challenges

Identify legal challenges specific to the structure chosen in exercise 12a; for example, buy-sell, employee contracts, 401k, intellectual property. After gathering information from all available sources, develop a useful action plan for the organization.

Legal challenges	Action plan

Legal challenges	Action plan

Intellectual Property

Learning Objectives

In this chapter, students will learn

- What a patent is.
- When patents are appropriate.
- What a trademark is.
- How to apply for a trademark.
- What a copyright is.
- What works are copyrightable.
- What trade secrets are.
- How to use a noncompete/nondisclosure agreement.

Protecting intellectual property (IP) is critical to the growth and stability of a company. IP gives a company a competitive edge in the marketplace and builds value. As a company is valued according to multiples, IP on the balance sheet directly translates to the bottom line. It is important for any innovator to have a basic understanding of the IP to understand all of the options available to protect and manage the IP as well as how to use IP strategically to create value.

This chapter discusses the familiar legal forms of intellectual property, such as patents, trademarks, copyrights, and trade secrets as well as noncompete agreements. Thinking of Coca-Cola is a good way to remember the differences between patents, trademarks, and copyrights.

- The artwork on the can or bottle can be copyrighted.
- The brand name and logo can be trademarked.
- The formula for Coca-Cola is a trade secret but could have been patented.

How can these intellectual property classifications be used strategically? When should an entrepreneur consider patenting versus getting a trademark or protecting a trade secret? Who owns the IP developed in the workplace? When should a company or entrepreneur consult an IP attorney if it does not have in-house counsel? Does copyright protection need to be federally registered? Becoming familiar with IP and some of the strategies behind using these legal tools will help entrepreneurs comprehend the ramifications of business decisions and strategically use IP to create new profit centers and increase a company's value.

When dealing with IP issues, the entrepreneur is thrown into the depths of the legal system and its minions, the lawyers. IP issues can quickly become expensive and time-consuming. A company may have its own legal department, or it may contract out with a law firm that specializes in trademarks, patents, copyrights, and the like. A corporate environment usually provides the luxury of in-house counsel. The entrepreneur, on the other hand, has to be very cautious about legal expenses. Having access to a corporate attorney is a real advantage for a corporate innovator. Intellectual property is a highly specialized field of law and most attorneys are not qualified to render legal advice regarding it. In fact, patent attorneys sub-specialize depending upon their background field of study. It is important to find an attorney who specializes in the type of IP law applicable to the entrepreneur's issue.

IP Battle in the Marketplace

Entrepreneurs can have very valuable rights stolen from them and yet be unable to do much about it for a number of reasons.

- The cost of correcting the problem is prohibitive.
- There is a lack of proof of theft.
- There may be no legal cause of action.

It costs money to file patent claims and even more money to protect a company's IP rights. One attorney advised that properly patenting an invention could easily cost as much as $15,000 or more. However, defending a patent against infringement is the true expense. Richard LaMotta spent $500,000 in court costs suing a large corporation that was infringing upon his registered trademark Chipwich. Staar Surgical paid its legal counsel $1.9 million in its Coopervision patent infringement case. This attorney worked on a contingency basis, which means he was paid a share of the settlement if Staar prevailed in court. This is a great way for an entrepreneur to manage his or her legal expenses. In-house counsel typically works on a salary. Contracted counsel usually bills by the hour.

If outside legal assistance is needed, costs can be kept down by requesting that new associates handle the "grunt work." In metropolitan cities, the difference between the billing rate of a partner and the billing rate of an associate is astronomical. Associates are billed out at around $140 to $180 per hour, whereas partners are billed at up to $400 per hour. One attorney believes: "The law is simple, it is experience that is valuable." While this is true, there is much that an inexperienced associate can do to cover the groundwork and research inexpensively. The experienced partner can be used to analyze the research and develop IP strategy.

The good news is that juries in patent cases are increasingly willing to recognize the true value of damage done by infringement. Today, damage awards are at an all-time high.

Cost: Benefit of defending rights.

The entrepreneur must always weigh the cost-benefit ratio of going to court when someone infringes on intellectual property. It is possible that while the entrepreneur is undertaking all of the cost and time to work with counsel to refine a patent, some other company satisfies the market demand with a similar product or service before that entrepreneur has rights to the idea.

This is particularly true of fad products. An attorney should be consulted to determine whether an IP strategy should be to get a patent, rush to market, or pursue a trade secret approach.

Another reason for patenting inventions is that the patent can then become a mechanism for transferring rights from one organization to another. That is a primary concern of universities. Students should find out who owns inventions and copyrights on what they develop in class projects and assignments, as teaching or research assistants, when researching thesis work, or on their own as part of extracurricular activities.

You snooze, you lose

Once IP is properly protected, a company must guard and maintain its rights zealously. "You snooze, you lose" is the name of the litigation game: in other words, if a company does not defend its rights, nobody will. If a company allow others to use its trademarks or copyrights without legal notice, its IP rights may slip into the public domain and become public property. Unfortunately, protecting IP rights takes time and money, but defending those rights is what maintains value for the company.

> Protecting IP rights takes time and money, but defending those rights is what maintains value for the company.

Another strategy some companies take is to license their property, by field of use or in total, or to sell their IP rights altogether. When a patent is licensed, the company that owns the patent may be responsible for defending the patent against infringement. By consulting an attorney, a company will be fully aware of the limits and liabilities of its IP strategy.

Patents

Patent law is highly complex, but it is critically important to have a working knowledge of patents to be able to make wise decisions regarding the possibility of patenting products, designs, or processes.

What is a patent?

A patent is a grant of a property right by the United States for a term of 20 years from the date on which the application for the patent was filed in the United States or, in special cases, from the date an earlier related application was filed, subject to payment of maintenance fees. (A maintenance fee is due 3, 7, and 11 years after the original grant for all patents filed on or after Dec. 12, 1980.) The right conferred by the patent grant is, in the language of the statute and the grant itself, "the right to exclude others from making, using, offering for sale, or selling" the invention in the United States or "importing" the invention into the United States. What is granted is not the right to make, use, offer for sale, sell, or import, but the right to exclude others from doing so. Any person who invents or discovers any new and useful (refers to the condition that the subject matter has a useful purpose and also includes operativeness) process (act or method), machine, manufacture (that is, articles that are made), or composition of matter (that is, chemical compounds or mixtures of ingredients), or any new and useful improvement thereof, subject to the conditions and requirements of the law, is able to apply for a patent. When a patent expires, anyone is able to use the knowledge contained therein. All of the inventor's rights are gone.

Design patents. Patent for designs are available under another provision of the act and are for a term of 14 years from the date of application. Unfortunately for designers, in many cases such protection has been to little avail because it is too easy to make slight variations in designs and thus circumvent the patent. Fashion designers have forgone trying to protect their work out of frustration with the system. An entire industry revolves around going to the haute couture fashion shows one day, copying the design that evening, and forwarding the knock-off design on to a manufacturer for overnight production of the latest look at a fraction of the price using less expensive materials.

Who owns the new invention? Every company owns the rights to the inventions that an employee develops within the scope of his or her employment if the employee was specifically hired to invent the product or process. The ownership of inventions developed by independent contractors and other technical inventions and patents developed by employees is not automatically transmitted to the employer as a matter of law.

As a result, companies require that employees and technical contractors sign a technology agreement that states that any inventions made within the scope of working for the company are the property of the company and will be assigned to the company. Technology agreements clarify and simplify the employer's ability to enforce its ownership rights and will avoid potential misunderstandings during the employment relationship.

At the time the patent application is filed, the employee or contractor should be required to sign a proper assignment with specific consideration recited and actually given to the inventor. Companies should realize that patents, in the absence of an assignment, are issued to the actual inventor, not the employer or the person who furnishes the money.

For domestic use only. The U.S. patent is only good within the United States and its territories and possessions. A company must obtain separate patents in each nation in which it wishes to have protection. This is a very expensive and time-consuming process, generally not economically feasible.

Use of "patent pending." The term "patent pending" may not be used until a patent application has been filed with the U.S. Patent and Trademark Office (USPTO or PTO). Since June 8, 1995, the PTO has offered inventors the option of filing a provisional application for patent that was designed to provide a lower cost, first patent filing in the United States and to give U.S. applicants parity with foreign applicants. Claims and oath or declaration are not required for a provisional application. Provisional application provides the means of establishing an early effective filing date in a patent application and permits the term "patent pending" to be applied in connection with the invention. Provisional applications may not be filed for design inventions.

The filing date of a provisional application is the date on which a written description of the invention, drawings if necessary, and the name of the inventors are received in the PTO. To be complete, a provisional application must also include the filing fee, and a cover sheet specifying that the application is a provisional application for patent. The applicant then has up to 12 months to file a nonprovisional application for patent as described later. The claimed subject matter in the later filed, nonprovisional application is entitled to the benefit of the filing date of the provisional application if it has support in the provisional application.

Provisional applications are not examined on their merits. A provisional application will become abandoned by the operation of law 12 months from its filing date. The 12-month pendency for a provisional application is not counted toward the 20-year term of a patent granted on a subsequently filed, nonprovisional application that relies on the filing date of the provisional application.

The United States Patent and Trademark Office has an award-winning web site (www.uspto.gov) which contains a wealth of information, phone numbers, addresses, frequently asked questions, forms, and searchable data bases. That office may also be contacted by mail at U.S. Patent and Trademark Office, USPTO Contact Center, Crystal Plaza 3, Room 2C02, P.O. Box 1450, Alexandria, VA 22313-1450 and by telephone to customer service representatives at (800)-786-9199 or (703)-308-4357.

Obtaining a patent

Before filing a claim. Prior to having discussions with a consultant or attorney about a new innovation, the entrepreneur should take the following steps to help protect the patentable idea:

1. Sign and date written descriptions of the invention. Include clear and concise descriptions of the invention along with photographs, if available, describing how it works, what it does, what its physical parts are, how the parts interrelate to each other, and how they are made.

2. Mark each and every page with "confidential." The burden of protecting the idea is on the entrepreneur's company.

3. Have at least one other person read, sign, and date each page of the description. Make sure that every person knows the material is confidential.

4. Obtain a nondisclosure agreement for people to sign who are going to see the idea.

5. Have every person with whom the idea is shared sign the nondisclosure agreement. The nondisclosure agreement strengthens the company's position should a court visit be warranted.

There is a one-year grace period from the time the invention is first made public or offered for sale to the time an idea has to be patented. Moreover, the description listed in number 1 above can be filed with the Patent Office under the Disclosure Document Program, which is maintained by the PTO for two years. (Write the U.S. Department of Commerce for its pamphlet *The U.S. Patent Office's Disclosure Document Program* for more information.) A disclosure document does not give a company any patent rights. Rather, the document establishes the date of conception and provides a description of the invention. The inventor who invents first and diligently works to reduce the invention to practice has the right to a patent.

A company's initial funding and scarce resources should be spent wisely during this time. The company should develop a marketing plan, test a prototype of the product with focus and consumer groups, research how much it will cost to produce the product, and perform a thorough competitive analysis. There should be some assurance that if a company decides to invest money in widespread protection of the idea, it will still have the resources to get off the ground.

Filing a patent application. A nonprovisional application for a patent is made to the Assistant Commissioner for Patents and includes the following:

- A written document that comprises a specification (description and claims) and an oath or declaration
- A drawing in those cases in which a drawing is necessary
- The filing fee; fees change regularly

The typed, one-sided application papers must all be the same size, with top, right and bottom margins of at least ¾ inch and a left-side margin of at least 1 inch. It is also required that the spacing on all papers be 1 ½ or double spaced and the application papers must be numbered consecutively (centrally located above or below the text) starting with page 1.

The application for patent is not forwarded for examination until all required parts are received. It is recommended that all parts of the complete application be deposited in the PTO together. If any application is filed without all the required parts for obtaining a filing date (incomplete or defective), the applicant will be notified. If the omission is not corrected within a set, specified time period, the application will be returned or otherwise disposed of. All applications received in the PTO are numbered in serial order and the applicant will be informed of the application serial number and filing date by a filing receipt.

The filing date of an application for patent is the date on which a specification (including at least one claim) and any drawings necessary to understand the subject matter sought to be patented are received in the PTO; or the date on which the last part completing the application is received in the case of a previously incomplete or defective application.

When and How to Use Attorneys

After running a search for prior art to make sure that the idea is patentable (see below), it is now time for an attorney to become involved. Patent law is an exceedingly complex field requiring the assistance of lawyers who specialize in intellectual property. Large firms have dedicated patent attorneys on their legal staffs. Those that do not can find several attorneys whose practice is totally devoted to the development and protection of patents. A list of the attorneys and agents authorized to practice before the Patent and Trademark Office can be obtained by sending $5 to the Superintendent of Documents, U.S. Government Printing Office, 732 North Capital Street, N.W., Washington, D.C. 20401. Any district office of the U.S. Department of Commerce has this information as well.

When Patents Are Not Appropriate

Usually an entrepreneur should retain the services of a patent attorney/ agent to determine if an idea should be patented. But the inventor should also be aware of a few of the realities of the patent world before hiring or engaging legal counsel.

The idea may not be patentable. For a number of reasons, the invention may not be patentable. For starters, some other party may already have patented the idea. Before investing in an idea, the entrepreneur should run an online search for prior art at (www.uspto.gov), (www.delphion.com), or, more traditionally, at the Patent Search Room which is located at Crystal Plaza 3, Lobby Level, 2021 South Clark Place, Arlington, VA 22202-3513. An attorney or agent can make such a search on the entrepreneur's behalf. Entrepreneurs who live near a law school can try contacting the administrative offices to see if there are students available to perform such work. The same materials are available in various libraries throughout the country.

Even if in-house counsel is available, performing a preliminary search can be of great help to entrepreneurs in learning about all other patents that may surround their ideas, some of which may be superior or complementary to it. Many companies get the *Official Gazette* of the Patent Office in which current patent activity is reported. The *Gazette* contains a wealth of ideas—some of which may stimulate the entrepreneur's thinking.

Not covered under the law. It is possible that the idea does not fall within the legally described limits of what is patentable. The idea may not be anything new as the law defines the word. Equally fallible, the idea may be some obvious improvement of an old idea. The idea may not be useful (the law says that a patent may only be granted for a useful idea). A large number of patent applications are rejected because they do not fit within the scope of the law. For example, one cannot patent an idea by itself, an inoperable device, or printed matter.

No matter how new or how useful the process, machine, manufacture, or composition, the inventor may not be awarded a patent if any of the following conditions exist:

- The invention was known or used by others in this country, or patented or described in a printed publication in this or a foreign country anywhere in the world, before the invention by the applicant for patent.
- The invention was patented or described in a printed publication in this or a foreign country or in public use or on sale in this country more than one year prior to the application for patent in the United States—even if it was described in print by the inventor him or herself. If over one year, the invention is not patentable;
- The differences between the invention and an existing patent are obvious to a person having ordinary skill in the area of technology related to the invention, the application will be refused. Substitution of one material for another or change in size is not patentable.
- The patentable idea was published. Prior publication bars patenting in most foreign countries.

Furthermore, laws of nature, physical phenomena, abstract ideas, and suggestions are not patentable.

Unenforceable in court. It has been reported that courts have invalidated as many as 70 percent of the patents that have been taken to court on infringement suits. It is an entrepreneurial reality that a patent is merely a license to sue. The courts ultimately decide whether a company has a viable claim to intellectual property. Clearly the risks of going to court are large in terms of time and money expended. While the costs and time spent obtaining a patent are substantial, in the range of $5,000 to $20,000 and two to four years, they pale in comparison to infringement suits which can easily run into the hundreds of thousands of dollars and three to five years.

Infringement is determined primarily by the language of the claims of the patent. If what the defendant is making does not fall within the language of any of the claims of the patent, there is no legal infringement. Oddly, the USPTO does not search for infringement when reviewing a patent application. Therefore, an improvement invention may be patentable, but it might infringe a prior unexpired patent for the invention improved upon and land the inventor in court.

In a licensing arrangement, the burden of enforcing a patent is often on the company that owns the rights. The government does nothing to enforce whatever rights an owner may have. The costs can be prohibitive. It is not without reason that many entrepreneurs believe that the patent game is reserved for large companies—small ones cannot afford to play it. Legal counsel for the Staar case mentioned earlier believed in the case strongly enough that he took it on a contingency basis. This percentage-of-settlement approach is often the only method available to smaller entities.

A patent can be designed around. A patent furnishes potential competitors with information they can use to design around someone's invention. An inventor must disclose a great deal of information in the patent application that is published with the patent. In doing so, a company may give away much valuable information for naught.

Competitors may use the patent illegally. One harsh example shows the reality of the patent world. A small chemical compounder obtained its products by stealing them from others. The company would spot a successful product on the market and copy it, sometimes with small changes. In one instance, the compounder spotted a particularly profitable product in the floral supply business that was patented. It obtained a copy of the patent, which provided all the procedures used to make the product. The company simply began production. The chemical compounder knew

1. The floral company was too small to institute suit.
2. The theft was too small for any effective remedy to affect it.
3. It would take years before anything would happen in court.
4. The company could lay down a smokescreen to confuse all issues so that nothing would be clear-cut.
5. The theft might be legal since the company slightly varied the chemical formula.

It is understandable why many people are critical of the patent system. For these reasons, many experts strongly urge companies to keep ideas trade secrets if at all possible.

Apply strategically with the aid of counsel. Because competitors can be ruthless, there is much strategy involved in properly applying for a patent. The name of a patented invention and the description of the process, machine, manufacture, composition, or any new and useful improvement thereof might be crafted just to hide the patent from searches on the one hand, or drafted with the utmost particularity on the other, depending upon the strategic objective. While an entrepreneur can save some money by creating a rough draft of what the patent ought to look like prior to meeting with the attorney, no attempt to draft the final patent application should be done without the assistance of legal counsel. For an example of a trap an innovator can fall into, without the aid of counsel an inventor may withhold relevant information concerning a patent. To do so is patent fraud and thus invalidates the patent if such withholding is proven in court.

Don't rush to the patent office. Occasionally the ambitious company will spend $25,000 or more patenting an idea in every conceivable country around the world. Entrepreneurs should think long and hard before taking this route, and then seek a second and third opinion before proceeding.

Helpful Resources

Since patents are granted by the U.S. Patent and Trademark Office, it is a good idea to obtain a copy of its publication, *General Information Concerning Patents*, available from the address above. Another resource that may be helpful is *Patent It Yourself* by David Pressman (Berkeley, Calif.: Nolo Press, 2002). The General Information Services Division is also available to answer questions about the filing process at (800) 786-9199.

Trademarks/Service Marks

Trademarks (™, ®) or Service marks (SM, ®) are important marketing tools in that they help distinguish a venture's goods or services from those of its competitors. They add value to a company as intellectual property. "Trademark" applies to goods and "service mark" applies to services. They are, in short, brand names. Throughout the ensuing discussion, even though "trademark" and "goods" are used, the same holds true for "service mark" and "services."

Trademarks can last indefinitely.

What is a trademark?

"A trademark is either a word, symbol, or design, or combination of words, phrases, symbols or designs, which identifies and distinguishes the source of the goods or services of one party from those of others. A service mark is the same as a trademark except that it identifies and distinguishes the source of a service rather than a product" (www.uspto.gov). Trademarks are usually written or artistic matter that includes a symbol, word, shape, or design. Service marks are often slogans or phrases used in the sale or advertising of services as opposed to products. A trademark is usually encountered on packaging and a service mark in advertising. Trademark rights may be used to prevent others from using a confusingly similar mark, but not to prevent others from making the same goods or from selling the same goods or services under a clearly different mark.

If properly maintained, a trademark can last indefinitely—in other words, as long as the life of the company and so long as it does not become generic; for example, aspirin, scotch tape, and xerox.

Trade dress. Brand names are but one form of trademark. Trade dress identifies products by distinctive containers or packages, by the way the name is written, by unique designs, by unique arrangements of colors, and by slogans or by some combination of these. These are all valuable recognizable symbols to people who may not be able to read. Children can recognize their favorite candy bar by its colors and packaging.

Origins of a trademark

Trademark rights arise from either actual use of the mark, which may be acknowledged by the ™, or the filing of a proper application to register a mark in the Patent and Trademark Office stating that the applicant has a bona fide intention to use the mark in commerce regulated by the U.S. Congress. Generally, the first party who either uses a mark in commerce or files an application in the PTO has the ultimate right to register that mark. Unlike the short, limited life of patents, registration designated by an ® runs on 10-year terms with 10-year renewal periods. Trademark rights can last as long as the owner continues to use the mark. In practice, trademarks continue for the life of the firm and are transferable. In the eyes of most business experts, trademarks are far more valuable than patents in protecting a firm's market franchise. The courts have dealt far more generously with the owners of trademarks than they have with patent holders. One can enforce trademark infringement much more easily and with more certainty than is true with patents.

The owner of a federal registration is presumed to be the owner of the mark for the goods and services specified in the registration and to be entitled to use the mark nationwide. Likewise, the owner of a registered mark has a significant leg-up on the competition in a court dispute over which user has the right to use the mark.

How to apply for a trademark

There are many benefits to trademarking a company logo at the federal level. Trademarks can be used to signify to customers who a company is. The following are steps to consider when applying for a trademark.

Classifications. Brands and logos may be trademarked as quickly as possible for very affordable protection. A domestic applicant may apply for federal registration in one of two principal ways.

- An applicant who has already commenced using a mark in commerce may file a "use" application, provided that the use is a bona fide use in the ordinary course of trade and not merely manufactured to reserve a right in the mark.

- An applicant who has not yet used the mark may apply based on a bona fide intention to use the mark ("intent to use" application).

Mark search. While a competing mark search is not required, such a search can possibly save money (as the application fee is nonrefundable) even if a competing mark prevents a company from registering. A search can identify marks that would prevent registration as well as marks that the entrepreneur may be infringing. Patent and Trademark Depository Libraries and local patent libraries have CD-ROMS containing the trademark database of registered and pending marks. On line searches may also be performed at www.uspto.gov/tmdb/index.html.

Filing. The following are required for filing:

- A written application form
- A drawing of the mark on a separate piece of paper
- The required filing fee
- If based upon prior use, three specimens of the mark in prior use in commerce (refer to the USPTO web site for specifics)

Trademark forms and information about applying for a trademark may be obtained by going to the U.S. Patent and Trademark Office website (www.uspto.gov). The forms may be downloaded, filled out and mailed to Mail Stop Assignment Recordation Services, Director of the United States Patent and Trademark Office, P.O. Box 1450, Alexandria, VA 22313-1450 . You may also use TEAS, the Trademark Electronic Application System (www.uspto.gov/teas). TEAS allows you to fill out an application form and check it for completeness over the Internet. Using e-TEAS you can then submit the application directly to the USPTO, paying by credit card or through an existing USPTO deposit account. You can also print out the application from TEAS. To obtain a hard copy of the Basic Facts About Trademarks brochure, call the Trademark Assistance Center at (800) 786-9199.

Competing marks. Any party who believes that it may be damaged by the registration of the mark has 30 days from the date of publication (in the *Official Gazette*) to file an opposition to registration. Opposition hearings are held before the Trademark Trial and Appeal Board.

Registration refused. Marks are most often refused for likelihood of confusion, or because the application is merely descriptive in relation to the applicant's goods or services, or a feature of the goods or services. Likewise, geographic terms and surnames will be refused.

Likelihood of confusion is determined by whether relevant consumers would be likely to associate the goods or services of one party with those of the other party as a result of the use of the marks at issue by both parties. The Office takes into consideration the similarity of the marks and the commercial relationship between the goods and services identified by the marks.

Copyrights

Copyright protection designated by © automatically subsists from the time the work is created in fixed form. The copyright in the work of authorship immediately becomes the property of the author who created the work.

Who owns copyrightable material?

Every company owns copyrightable material that an employee develops within the scope of his or her full-time employment. A company's ownership of copyrightable material comes into existence as a work-for-hire under the U.S. Copyright statute. The company files for the copyright and is considered to be the author. A company must obtain an assignment from independent contractors to own works created by the contractor.

Companies usually require that full-time employees sign an employment agreement. The agreement should contain language that the company owns copyrightable materials developed by the employee, and clarifies and outlines the company's ownership rights. Companies want new employees to understand from the start who owns the intellectual property developed during the employment.

What is a copyright and how does one give notice of its existence?

The copyright protects the form of expression rather than the subject matter of the writing.

Copyrights protect "original works of authorship" that are fixed in a tangible form of expression. A copyright is a form of protection provided by Title 17, U.S. Code, to the authors of "original works of authorship" including literary, dramatic, musical, artistic, and certain other intellectual works, both published and unpublished. The 1976 Copyright Act generally gives the owner of a copyright the exclusive right to reproduce the copyrighted work, to prepare derivative works, to distribute copies or phono records of the copyrighted work, to perform the copyrighted work publicly, or to display the copyrighted work publicly. Computer programs are considered literary works—some may be patentable. Initiators of such works should consult an attorney to see which is appropriate.

Notice. The notice for visually perceptible copies should contain all the following three elements:

- The symbol ©, or the word Copyright, or the abbreviation Copr.
- The year of first publication of the work
- The name of the owner of the copyright in the work (e.g. © 1999 John Doe)

The copyright notice should be affixed to copies in such a way as to "give reasonable notice of the claim of copyright."

What is the duration of protection?

The Sonny Bono Copyright Term Extension Act, signed into law on October 27, 1998, amended the provisions concerning duration of copyright protection. Generally, the terms of copyright are extended for an additional 20 years. For works after Jan. 1, 1978, there exists automatic protection from the moment of creation. The work is ordinarily given a term enduring for the author's life plus an additional 70 years after the author's death. For works made for hire, the duration of copyright will be 95 years from publication or 120 years from creation, whichever is shorter. Transfer of exclusive rights is not valid unless that transfer is in writing and signed by the owner of the rights conveyed.

What are the advantages of publishing original work?

While it is not necessary to publish copyrighted material, there are a number of advantages to publication.

- Publishing may effect the limitations on the exclusive rights of the owner.
- The year of publication may determine the duration of copyright in certain works.
- The material may bear the notice of copyright.

How does one register a copyright?

Applications for registration of a copyright are available at www.loc.gov/copyright. While it is not necessary to register copyrighted material, the following advantages should be considered:

- Registration establishes a public record of the copyright claim.
- Before an infringement suit may be filed in court, registration is necessary for works of U.S. origin.
- The registered owner may be eligible for statutory damages and attorney's fees in successful litigation.
- Registration allows the owner to record the registration with the U.S. Customs Service for protection against the importation of infringing copies. For more information, see publication No. 563 from Commissioner of Customs, ATTN: IPR Branch, U.S. Customs Service, 1300 Pennsylvania Ave., NW, Washington, DC 20229.

To research the copyright status of a work, request Circular 22, "How to Investigate the Copyright Status of a Work," and Circular 23, "The Copyright Card Catalog and the Online Files of the Copyright Office," or call (202) 707-9100, 24 hours a day. Send requests to the Library of Congress, Copyright Office, Publications Section, LM-455, 101 Independence Ave., SE, Washington, DC 20559-6000. Application forms may be obtained from the Copyright Office by telephone (202) 707-9100 or downloaded at www.loc.gov. Two copies of the work must accompany the application and filing fee. The mailing address for registrations is Library of Congress, Copyright Office, 101 Independence Avenue, Washington, DC 20559-6000. The public information telephone number is (202) 707-3000.

What is fair use?

Fair use, as defined in Section 107 of Title 17, U.S. Code, is best understood by examining a list of the various purposes for which the reproduction of a particular work may be considered "fair," such as criticism, comment, news reporting, teaching, scholarship, and research. Section 107 also sets out four factors to be considered in determining whether or not a particular use is fair.

The distinction between fair use and infringement may be unclear and not easily defined.

- The purpose and character of the use, including whether such use is of commercial nature or is for nonprofit educational purposes
- The nature of the copyrighted work
- The amount and substantiality of the portion used in relation to the copyrighted work as a whole
- The effect of the use upon the potential market for or value of the copyrighted work

Generally, courts have regarded the following as fair use:

- Quotation of excerpts in a review or criticism for purposes of illustration or comment
- Quotation of short passages in a scholarly or technical work, for illustration or clarification of the author's observations
- Use in a parody of some of the content of the work parodied
- Summary of an address or article with brief quotations in a news report

- Reproduction by a library of a portion of a work to replace part of a damaged copy.
- Reproduction of a work in legislative or judicial proceedings or reports.
- Incidental and fortuitous reproduction in a newsreel or broadcast of a work located in the scene of an event being reported.

What works are not copyrightable?

Unrecorded improvisation or choreography is not copyrightable, nor are the following:

- Titles
- Familiar symbols or designs
- Mere variations on typographic ornamentation, lettering, or coloring
- Discoveries
- Devices (as distinguished from a description, explanation, or illustration of a device)
- Works consisting entirely of information that is common property and containing no original authorship (for example, standard calendars, height and weight charts, tape measures)
- Names of products or services
- Names of businesses, organizations, or groups
- Names or pseudonyms of individuals
- Ideas, concepts, systems, procedures, processes, principles or methods of doing something. One may protect the description of his or her artistic rendering, but not the idea itself.
- Titles of works
- Catchwords, catchphrases, mottoes, slogans, or short advertising expressions
- Mere listings of ingredients, as in recipes, labels, or formulas. When a recipe or formula is accompanied by explanations or directions, the text directions may be copyrightable, but the recipe or formula itself remains uncopyrightable.

A work must meet at least a certain minimum amount of authorship in the form of original literary, musical, pictorial, or graphic expression to qualify as "original works of authorship." Title 17, Section 102, U.S. Code.

Trade Secrets

A trade secret is something an entrepreneur or firm knows that others do not know. What are they? What is required to protect them? How can customer lists be protected?

Trade secrets include techniques, designs, materials, processes, and formulas that are not known by the public and can be licensed in the same way as a patent. Naturally, a trade secret should be something that contributes significantly to the firm's profits or its success. That may be some manufacturing process or technique that one has learned from experience. Such trade secrets can be very valuable.

A venture's management may want to keep such a process, technique, or formula a secret to all but the upper levels of the venture—not allowing even the employees to learn them. For example, only a few top executives of the Coca-Cola Co. know the secret formula for the Coke syrup.

Company suppliers should be protected as a trade secret. Often, one of the advantages of purchasing a franchise is to obtain a supplier list from the franchiser.

Merchandising or promotional systems can contain secret information if a company knows how to promote something that others do not.

Requirements

The courts have been relatively generous in dealing with the owners of trade secrets who have had them stolen. The law recognizes a trade secret as a company's property and protects it as such. However, a few warnings are in order.

- The secret knowledge must be a secret. If another party can show that, in fact, the knowledge is known by others, the court will throw the case out.

- The company must take every precaution to keep the knowledge a secret. If it allows the information to lie around the office unprotected, the court is likely to say that the company does not consider the information to be of much value. The company must be able to show the efforts it has made to protect its trade secret.

- A company should place specific provisions in employees' agreements that they will neither disclose to others nor use for their own purposes any trade secrets they acquire while in its employ.

If an entrepreneur truly wants to keep something a secret, he or she must not tell anyone. If employees must know the secret in order to do their jobs, then the trade secret should be revealed only on an absolute need-to-know basis. Often, firms use different suppliers for different parts to a product so that no one supplier can gain total knowledge of the project. Some firms opt to keep in-house the manufacture of particularly secret processes or parts.

Courts generally grant the following three types of restrictions as legitimate provisions in employee agreements:
- *Use of trade secrets*
- *Solicitation of customers*
- *Use of customer lists*

Customers and customer lists

Customers may be a trade secret: A company knows where to sell the goods and other companies do not. Management may take pains to protect customer lists from suppliers and competitors. The courts recognize that a firm's customers and customer lists are valuable property. Often these are the most valuable asset of the business. Departing employees headed for work with a competitive firm often try to take such information with them. If they manage to obtain a list, they can do much damage to the former employer that may be hard to prove. The courts tend to take a dim view of such behavior, particularly if the act is in clear violation of the employee's agreement signed at the time of employment.

Such legal recognition would not be given to customer lists unless they were of significance and of great value. They are! A firm's customers are hard won and extremely valuable assets. They should be protected as the firm would protect its money with consistent, diligent, and systematic monitoring.

To protect itself from having employees leave with customer lists, a company should make the information a trade secret.

Defecting employees. Employees often come and go. They can be attractive to competitors or to firms trying to start in the industry. Entrepreneurs have been known to hire someone just to avail themselves of the person's specific knowledge of the market and the customers of some particular firm.

In some industries, firms are plagued with the problem of sales reps or other marketing people forming new firms—taking with them their favorite customers. The advertising agencies and consulting businesses have been famous for this market entry strategy. One big customer can be the beginning of a profitable business.

It is for this reason that some companies will not allow anyone in the firm to even have contact with the company's significant accounts. The boss keeps all of the most valuable contacts for him or herself. For example, the owner of a plant that made the dishwasher for Sears was the only person who dealt with Sears on a sales level. Entrepreneurs, on the other hand, should promote interaction with the customer as a method of determining true customer needs.

Employees should be advised that the information is secret and they should sign a confidential information agreement that prevents them from disclosing the information on these lists during or after their employment. Mark all lists "confidential." Courts will normally look at the extent to which the confidential lists were protected as a secret and the ease of obtaining the same information from another source.

Valuable employees

Employees can be the most valuable asset a company has. An organization occasionally hangs on the skills of just one or two uniquely talented employees. Without their skills, the organization would be in trouble. In any event, the management would have difficulty finding a replacement for the person.

Such people can be very attractive to someone contemplating entering the same industry. By one shrewd, albeit unethical move, a competitor may be able to put together a total sales or production program for a relatively low cost. Such tactics are common because often valuable employees are underpaid and unrecognized. Unsatisfied employees are just waiting to leave for a better opportunity.

Noncompete/Nondisclosure Agreements

The easiest way to protect proprietary rights is through the use of a written contract known as a nondisclosure agreement (also called a confidentiality agreement). Such agreements prohibit others from using a venture's confidential information or trade secrets for their own benefit or divulging that information to someone else. These agreements can be used to protect technical information, customer lists, methods of doing business, designs, formulations, and similar intangibles that provide a competitive advantage over competitors. These agreements, when properly structured, are legally binding. Such agreements should be used whenever proprietary information is shared.

Noncompete agreements protect a company when a valuable employee leaves to work for someone else. The agreements (frowned upon by courts) prevent an employee, by mutual agreement, from working in a similar field or within a certain distance for a specified number of months or years.

Noncompete/nondisclosure clauses and agreements are discussed in greater detail in Chapter 14 Contracts and Leases. For help drafting such an agreement, consult an attorney or read *The Complete Guide to Business Agreements* by Ted Nicholas (Enterprise/Dearborn, Chicago).

Conclusion

Protecting a company's intellectual property can take time, money, and considerable energy, not to mention frequent trips to an attorney's office. In most instances, the cost in both time and energy is worth the protection gained. The difference between the life and death of some companies hangs on only one or two recognizable ideas or a clever logo or product design.

The greatest barrier an entrepreneur can use to eliminate competition in a marketplace is having well-protected intellectual property.

Patents provide the ability to prevent others from making, using, selling, or importing an invention. Trademarks, on the other hand, can be a powerful marketing tool for distinguishing the owner's goods or services from those of competitors. They add value to an organization. Patents must be registered with the U.S. Patent and Trade Office to obtain protection. Trademarks originate through use and can be registered at the federal level with the U.S. Patent and Trade Office or at the state level. Federal registration provides broader coverage. Copyrights originate automatically upon production of the original work. Trade secrets also are created with the original, proprietary work.

It is important for the entrepreneur to understand the value of intellectual property and take steps to protect it. Some large companies are experts at protecting IP and have dedicated in-house legal counsel, which is an advantage to the corporate innovator. Entrepreneurs, on the other hand, often do not have sufficient working capital to protect their valuable IP. It is important to remember that IP creates value for a company and is an important asset on the balance sheet, and distinguishes a company's goods and services in the marketplace.

Exercise 13a. Intellectual Property

Identify which aspects of intellectual property are relevant to your business concept and explain how you can obtain them.

Intellectual property	How to obtain

Contracts and Leases

Learning Objectives

In this chapter, students will learn
- The key elements of a contract.
- How to avoid contractual problems.
- The important aspects of a lease for office and retail space.
- How to structure a buy-sell agreement and a noncompete clause.

Contracts are the very essence of business. Indeed, theorists visualize all business as a series of contracts. They see business as a set of transactions between a multiplicity of parties. Each transaction, of course, is a contract. From a practical standpoint, success in business depends upon the ability to make contracts advantageous. At least entrepreneurs should be able to protect their interests and not allow themselves to be cheated or placed at great disadvantage by the contractual skills of the other party.

Since a lease is simply a contract for the rental of property, it is included in this discussion of contracts. However, leases do have some unique characteristics deserving the special attention given them later.

Often businesses have been built around the procurement of one profitable contract. Perhaps it is a favorable contract from the government or some large corporation. Perhaps it is a favorable lease on a particularly attractive property. Perhaps it is a contract to buy some assets for a particularly low price. Whatever, the ability to procure good contracts for an enterprise will be one foundation for its success.

What Is a Contract?

A contract is an agreement between two or more parties in which each promises to do something for the other. The contract spells out the promises. The details must be sufficiently clear that a non-interested third party, perhaps a judge, can determine precisely what was promised by each party in the contract. This is no easy task if the parties have failed to make their intentions clear.

While the law requires certain contracts be in writing to be enforceable (statute of frauds), still a large number of valid contracts are made orally. Indeed, probably the bulk of the routine contracts made daily are oral ones. Two people simply agree to do something for each other. Usually, no problems arise as each party does what was promised. The subject of those contracts was trivial—not of much economic significance. Seldom does the oral contract go into litigation since the amounts involved are usually small. Nevertheless, some of them end up in small-claims court when the sums involved are for less than $5,000.

The problems with oral contracts are well recognized. First, the parties often fail to comprehend what was said. Misunderstandings are the rule, not the exception, in oral contracts. Moreover, an oral contract often ignores certain critical elements. A homeowner contracts with a gardener to weed his or her lawn. They settle on some amount, but fail to agree on the date of completion or what constitutes a successful weeding of said lawn. Most of the oral contracts that end up in court focus around what was really promised by each party. Was there a meeting of the minds? The results are usually unsatisfactory. The courts have taken the stance that they are not going to reconstruct a vague contract for two parties who were so inept that they couldn't make a binding contract. Judges are usually reluctant to play guessing games.

The second major problem with oral contracts is the matter of proof. What proof has one person that the other person made the promises claimed? The homeowner says the gardener promised to weed the lawn for $20. The gardener looks at the homeowner and says, "Who are you? I have never seen you before." Now how does the homeowner prove the contentions? Litigating such instances comes down to whom the court believes.

Thus, it is not surprising that business experts strongly advise putting all significant contracts into writing. Handshake deals sound fine, like a civilized way of doing business, but they suffer from vagueness. After shaking hands, one should casually mention, "I'll send you a memorandum of agreement on what we agreed upon today." Then, he or she should put on paper the substance of the oral contract and send it to the other party for agreement. Get things in writing. It is amazing how one's memory will improve when everything is on paper.

It sounds simple, but experience has proven otherwise. The need for the written contract is very simple. There are so many elements in any contractual relationship that are left unspecified by an oral agreement. For the sake of clarification alone, the written document is necessary. More importantly, a well-written contract helps ensure that there will be fewer misunderstandings down the road.

One of the tactics of people who have a penchant for being slippery in their business dealings is their avoidance of written contracts. They deliberately avoid signing anything. They flash a big friendly smile and put people off with such high-sounding statements as, "Ah, your handshake is good with me any day. We don't need to bring lawyers in on this." If the deal is significant, it should in writing, or it exposes people to great risk.

If the contract is for something significant and rather complicated, a lawyer should be used. Of course, in many common situations, such as the sale of real estate, standard contractual forms are available, which usually do a good job of covering the relevant points. But in anything out of the ordinary, an experienced lawyer will usually be worth the expenses by suggesting needed protections and ways to handle difficult contractual matters.

Unfortunately, such legal advice can cost much money. A contract with any amount of complexity can cost hundreds or thousands of dollars. In one recent deal, the preliminary draft of a contract setting out the terms under which two people were going into a joint venture cost $900 for a five-page document. The final cost had been capped at $3,000. It is understandable that lawyers are not used nearly as much as they need to be. It is just too costly to run to an attorney every time a contract is needed. On the other hand, it may be too costly not to do so. One must make that decision based on the lawyer's fees, the importance of the contract, and one's own skills at drafting good contracts. A few serious business people go to law school just to develop their legal acumen, not to practice law themselves.

The time devoted to developing contract-writing skills is well spent. It takes patience and thoughtful thoroughness. A place to start is with an outline of all the points that must be covered in the contract. It should not be assumed that the other party, or a judge, will understand what is meant. Then comes the difficult part—writing clear sentences that accurately convey the thoughts that must be communicated. It takes practice.

Elements of a Contract

Prior to entering into a business relationship, the parties informally negotiate the deal. A good strategy in contract negotiation is for the two sides to meet and discuss the terms of the contract without any attorneys being involved. Then, when the parties have agreed to the essential elements of the deal, one says he will have his attorney prepare a draft of the written contract for the other to review. This process avoids the costly and sometimes chilling involvement of attorneys from the inception of their discussions, yet provides to each the protection of a carefully written document of their agreement. Each is more likely to be satisfied by the deal, with less likelihood of later disagreement and litigation. A contract may result, depending upon whether the parties reach a mutual agreement—a meeting of the minds— and on the presence of several essential legal elements necessary before the law recognizes that a contract has been made, that is, offer, acceptance, consideration, capacity, and legal purpose.

Offer

From negotiations, one party makes a proposal in which some promises are made on what will be done if the other party does something or makes something happen. A contract is a set of mutual promises.

A book in contract law delves deeply into various aspects of an offer that are beyond the scope of this chapter, as are many of the other fine points of contract law. But entrepreneurs should be sensitive to when they are making offers and when someone else is making them bona fide offers.

A contract may begin with someone saying, "I'll buy that chair for $20." Sounds simple, but it isn't. The courts are filled with cases as to what constitutes a valid offer.

One must bear in mind at all times when dealing with legal matters that there are two fundamental purposes of a court. The first is to determine what the actual facts in the case are. The second is to apply the appropriate rules of

Elements of a Contract
Offer
Acceptance
Consideration
Capacity
Legal purpose

law governing those facts. Most court cases focus on determination of facts. What actually happened? What did the parties actually agree upon?

Most rules of law are well established. Most of the time, if two parties agree upon the facts, their lawyers can apply the law and tell them what the courts would do. That is the way most legal disputes are settled. There is no point in going to court if the outcome is predictable. Only when the dispute is in an area where the rules of law are not clear or have yet to be made do court cases involve matters of law. Consequently, most court cases are involved with determining facts. Naturally, this leads to a great deal of dispute as to what the facts of the case are. Each party brings forth its witnesses, and the most convincing presentation usually wins.

Back to the matter of the offer to buy the chair for $20—what if the manufacturer advertised that it would sell the chair for $20. Does that constitute an offer to which it can be held? The courts have generally ruled "no." It has a $20 price tag on the chair. Does that constitute an offer? What if it's mismarked? Thus, what seems to be a simple matter of making an offer can become a legal problem when someone changes his mind or when someone misinterprets what someone says or does as constituting an offer.

The obvious conclusion is that one must be careful in what one says and writes so that other people don't misinterpret intentions. One common situation involves job offers. It's easy for an employer to write a letter that the job applicant might consider to be a firm job offer. It should be made very clear in such letters whether a firm offer is being made to the person or whether negotiation with that person is being invited. It is sound business to state in clear-cut words, "This letter should not be considered an offer" or "I offer you…." Good contracts are noted for their clarity and leave nothing for the imagination.

Acceptance

There is no contract if the other party does not accept the offer. Again, this seems simple, but it isn't. Acceptance should be very clear and specific so that there should be no misunderstanding as to what is being accepted. The acceptance should be a mirror image of the offer. If the one to whom the offer was made says, "I accept but it is with the understanding that…"; such is not acceptance but is instead a counteroffer. The advantage of the written contract again comes to fore. A signed contract is rather solid evidence of acceptance. In a letter, the writer can actually state, "I accept your offer of…." then restate the offer as it is understood, or refer to the document in which the offer was made. Make it clear what is being accepted. Don't just say, "It's a deal."

Consideration

There can be no valid contract without consideration, which means that if one party promises to do something for a second party, the second party must give the first party some consideration (money or something of value) in return for that promise. Suppose George promises his next-door neighbor, "I'll fix your car's flat tire." The neighbor says nothing, makes no promise in return. George gets busy with something else and doesn't fix the tire. The neighbor has no recourse for damages, for there was no contract. George received nothing for his promise.

It's difficult in many long and involved contractual matters to determine exactly what each party promises to do for the other. In one recent contract negotiation, the first party was making some rather firm agreements to do certain things. He was clearly bound to perform. But the second party, despite a lot of verbiage about payments, rights, and what was going to happen, still promised absolutely nothing. The second party was not bound to do anything. There were no performance guarantees. There were no statements such as, "X will do…." There was no question as to whether the contract was valid, for there was no consideration. The law believes that when someone gives up something, that person should get something for it in return.

The signing bonuses given to professional athletes provide consideration for their giving up many rights. In signing the professional contract, the athlete almost submits himself into servitude for a number of years. What was he getting in return for signing the contract?

Indeed, contracts can be overturned in court for lack of consideration. In addition, if someone contracted to sell a building worth about $500,000 for $50,000, the buyer might have difficulty enforcing the contract in court. The judge would recognize that the deal somehow was not on the up and up. Either the seller was mentally incompetent, or there was some fraud involved, because no prudent property owner is going to sell a half-million-dollar property for $50,000.

Consequently, it is important to make very clear in contracts what the consideration is and to make sure that it is adequate.

Capacity

Certain people do not have the legal capacity to enter into contracts, underage children and the mentally incompetent, for example. The underage person can enter into a valid contract only for necessities of life. As to what constitutes a necessity of life, there is some dispute. It varies, depending upon the child, the culture in which the child lives, and the state whose laws apply.

The matter of capacity becomes more complicated when dealing with those who are acting on behalf of another person or another entity, such as for a corporation, an LLC, or a partnership. Does that corporation legally exist? Does the person negotiating and signing the contract have the legal authority to act on behalf of that entity? This question is of obvious importance to the other side. Why go to the trouble, time, and expense of a contract that cannot be enforced? If the contract performance is essential to the other's operations, perhaps that business will fail or suffer severe consequences by anticipating a performance from the other side that does not occur and cannot be compelled. Generally it is true that when a business is acting in the normal course of its business, anyone in a management or executive position can legally bind that entity to a contract. But do not assume that the one with whom you are dealing has authority to make a contract that is not in the course of the entity's usual business, insist on some proof of their authority, such as a resolution of the corporation's board of directors. These are the types of traps that a skilled attorney can held you avoid.

Suppose George enters into a contract with the XYZ Company, Inc. George goes to collect on that contract only to find out that the XYZ Company does not exist. The contract is not of much value, although George may now have a fraud case. Suppose the XYZ Company did exist, but the person who signed the contract was the shipping-room clerk, who was not authorized to sign anything for the corporation. Now George has a problem. Did he have good reason to believe that the person had the authority to bind the corporation? Such matters make interesting court cases.

The judge would take into consideration such evidence as prior behavior and trade practices. Had the shipping-room clerk previously signed contracts for the company that were honored? Is it traditional in this industry for shipping-room clerks to make such contracts for such things? Much contractual law relies on trade practices. Unless specifically stated otherwise in the contract, the courts assume that the parties will behave according to customary trade practices.

Legal Purpose

If the subject of the contract is illegal, the contract is unenforceable. One cannot contractually obligate someone to violate the law. The legality of the action is an essential element. Many things are against public policy and therefore, illegal. For example, if a father contracted to marry off his daughter to someone of wealth, the contract would be invalid, as it is against the law. In many states, gambling contracts are unenforceable.

Additional Contract Considerations

The matter of remedies is a difficult one for the courts. In many cases, a plaintiff demands what is called specific performance. It asks the court to force the defendant to specifically perform what was promised in the contract. For example, suppose Jane owned a very valuable painting. Jane made a contract to sell that painting for $50,000 to an art dealer. Later Jane changed her mind. She decided she didn't really want to sell it. She did not need the money that badly. The art dealer wants the painting so he sues Jane for specific performance. He asks the court to force Jane to perform her contract by handing over the painting in exchange for $50,000.

Courts are reluctant to require specific performance if money damages will provide relief. In this case, the courts would probably try to determine how much money the art dealer lost because of the defendant's breach of contract. Suppose the court determined that the painting was really worth $100,000 at retail; then the dealer suffered $50,000 damages. But suppose the plaintiff was an art collector, not a dealer; would the court then give specific performance, ordering the defendant to deliver the painting? Only the judge knows.

One of the real problems of going to court is that it is difficult to tell what a judge or jury is going to do in any given case. There are always tremendous risks involved any time one goes to court. Just remember that in any court case, one set of lawyers is wrong. People seldom go to court if they think they are going to lose. They try to settle out of court. Time and again, lawyers can relate how they walked into court with the strongest case, no question at all in their minds that they would prevail—but the court's decision proved otherwise.

One of the ways around the remedy problem is to specify in the contract the amount of liquidated damages, the amount of money due should the contract be breached, to set one's own damages rather than let the judge or jury do it. Bear in mind, of course, that the law will not enforce a contract if the provisions are inequitable.

The Role of Lawyers

While lawyers are often necessary to draw up the final drafts of a significant contract, it can be a mistake to bring them into contract negotiations too early. Most business people agree that the parties to a contract should have a meeting of minds before they go to the lawyers. They should be able to lay out to their attorneys exactly what they want in the contract, what it is they want to accomplish, and what has been agreed upon. Often they give the lawyers the memorandum of agreement and request a formal contract be prepared. A good lawyer will then be able to suggest ways of stating the intentions and also suggest some aspects that perhaps had not been considered.

Many lawyers are quite adept at negotiating contracts. There are situations in which one gains great advantages by using them. They can say things one would like to say but shouldn't for sake of future relationships or strategic positioning. For example, the lawyer can ask for some things that the client would feel uneasy about. If those things are refused, the client can be "the good guy" by backing down.

Professional athletes greatly prospered when they learned how well professional contract negotiators—the agents—can work for them. Their agents can say things about them and many situations that the athletes cannot gracefully mention.

One way for the entrepreneur to limit the role of lawyers is to have a terms sheet written and agreed upon by both parties. The terms sheet will explain in detail all the points that both parties want to be part of the agreement. The attorneys then take the terms sheet and write the agreement in legal terms.

Who Draws up the Contract?

There are advantages that accrue to the person who draws up the contract. In many ways, that party can make the contract favorable to him or herself. True, the second party can modify the first draft, but is modifying from the first party's base. Moreover, the first party will be able to get into the contract several little clauses that are advantageous to him or herself that may go unnoticed or unchallenged by the second party. If those clauses were later added to the contract, it would draw attention to them, and a discussion might ensue.

Relationships could disintegrate if one party were continually trying to add little clauses on this and that. Soon the other party might begin playing the same game as the first party's public posture is exposed as a nitpicker. But if the lawyer puts all the "nits" in the contract, the party will avoid looking fussy. In that way, if the second party objects to one of the nits, the first party can look good by deferring to the second party's desires. It is wise to project the image of the giver, not the taker.

On the other hand, if the contract ends up in litigation, courts hold the writer of the contract to a slightly more rigorous standard than they do the other party. In cases of ambiguity, the courts will interpret the contract against the writer. If there is any doubt as to the intention of a clause in the contract, it will be interpreted in favor of the person who did not write it. On balance, however, it would seem that the advantage is distinctly in favor of preparing the contract.

One word of warning: The initial contract should not be so outrageous that it infuriates the other person. Some people have been known to walk out of a business deal when the other person comes on with many unacceptable demands. They just don't want anything to do with someone who is trying to gain every advantage in the potential deal. Some people scare easily—show them a document full of barely understandable clauses, and they flee the project.

So-Called Standard Contracts

In situations where firms execute hundreds of contracts on essentially the same matter, they have their attorneys prepare a standard contract. One can go to many office-supply stores and bookstores to buy standard real estate contracts that have all the "ifs, ands, and buts" already in them. Most concerns have standard sales contracts, purchase orders, employee contracts, and leases.

However, do not be deceived by somebody else's standard contract. Anything in such a document can be changed. Most of those standard contracts have been drawn up to be grossly advantageous to the writer. That means one could be placed at a great disadvantage. Some of the standard contracts are so outrageous that they are almost unenforceable in court. For example, in some contracts, the buyer waives all rights to court action and actually signs an agreement that amounts to a judgment against him or her should he or she default on the contract. By signing such a document, the buyer waives legal rights.

Why, then, do people sign such documents? First, many signers never read the contract. They don't know the clauses are even in there. Second, if they do read the agreement, they don't know what the clauses mean. If they do know, they want what the other party is offering so badly that they'll sign anything. Or they they have nothing else to judge it against.

In many states, such clauses are unenforceable in court, but they are still used because they are tremendous bluffing material. That is, the aggrieved parties have absolutely no intention of going to court. They know the outcome won't be favorable. Instead, intimidation is used. "You signed this document and waived all of your rights. We got you. You can't go to court because you promised you wouldn't." People believe such threats. Regardless of the other side's statements such as "This is our standard contract, take it or leave it" or, "We don't need to spend a lot of money and slow this deal down by getting lawyers involved," if the matter is important to the venture, have your attorney review it. The fees to review a contract are far less than those to extricate you from a bad deal.

Avoiding Contractual Problems

One of the first things to do in judging a contract is to determine exactly what one promises to do and what the other party promises to do. Write those promises down and compare them. Do they balance out? Often contracts are written in which one party is bound to do a great deal, and the other party is bound to do little. To be bound means that the person must perform or suffer some consequences. In one recent contract, one party promised "to be responsible for the development of a series of management seminars." Just what does responsible mean? As the contract was rewritten, the other party was made to promise to put on two two-day seminars each month, guaranteeing a minimum dollar return to the performers.

Contracts may contain promises to "use our best effort to…", "assist in…", "reach a mutual agreement to…" or "…as later agreed to." Such phrases are difficult to enforce. There is no objective standard by which to determine what will constitute performance of them. Courts will not enforce agreements that amount to nothing more than an agreement to contract.

The following discussion focuses on common contractual issues.

Control

As a general principle, a contract should be structured so that in case of a dispute the other party is the one forced to go to court for remedies. The person who has to take action to remedy a breach of contract is in a disadvantageous position. It costs money to go to court, plus it often takes many months or even years before the matter will be litigated. Since time is money, such delays often make a mockery of the purpose of the contract.

For example, if John purchases some goods from a seller and the goods prove defective, then the burden is upon John to take action. If John cannot get satisfaction from the seller, then he will have to go to court. The seller has the money, and John wants it back. Chances are John wouldn't sue. But even if he did, he has many problems.

Suppose on the same sale, John buys the goods but doesn't pay for them. The other party must take action, at which time John erects a faulty-goods defense. The person who has the value in his or her possession has great contractual and legal advantages. Debtors are in the driver's seat, for the creditors have to take action to collect.

Price tags

Price tags should be considered for everything in the contract. This is particularly relevant to leases. While the rent is obvious, there are usually a half-dozen other clauses that will cost money. For example, the landlord may agree only to bring power to the meter. The renter will have to pay for all electrical costs past the box. Perhaps the renter is responsible for all repairs. Are there common-area charges? Must the renter pay a pro-rata share of taxes? Is there a merchants association fee? Landlords have many ways of slipping in levies in addition to the rents they charge. Entrepreneurs should learn to put price tags on everything a contract obligates them to do. They must always assume the attitude that a contract is a liability that they hope to turn into an asset.

Contract Issues
Control
Price tags
Bailout clauses
Role reversal
Liquidated damages
State laws
Arbitration
Loopholes
Time
Clear identification of intents
Clear identification of parties
Open-end checks

Bailout clauses

The future is unpredictable, and it is advantageous not to bind oneself irrevocably to certain promises. A party may want out of the contract because its performance would be disastrous. Common bailout clauses include those that make the contract void if performance is prevented by acts of war, God, or riots. Often, a venture must protect itself against labor strikes, not only in its own organization but also in those firms that supply it. The venture may not be able to perform on a contract because of labor difficulties. When inflation was rampant, wise businesspeople provided inflation-escape clauses in which prices escalated with the cost of living. Those are obvious bailout clauses and are usually acceptable.

However, there are other, more obscure ways of leaving the back door open on a contract. To the extent that a venture hasn't bound itself to do anything, it can get out of the contract any time. In essence, the contract is no contract. It is simply an agreement outlining the terms of a deal if a party wants to go through with it. In real estate, buyers will sometimes put a contingency clause into a contract where the offer is contingent upon some other event, usually the sale of the present home. If the present home is not sold, then the contract is void.

Let's take an example of an actual offered contract to purchase $20 million worth of electronic gear by the Pakistani government from a U.S. electronics manufacturer. The key clause in the 253-page document was a statement to the effect that the Pakistani government would pay the agreed upon sums upon delivery of the equipment in Pakistan to the Pakistani army and its acceptance of the equipment's performance after field tests.

The acceptability of the electronic equipment was totally in the hands of the designated officials in the Pakistani army. How much chance does the company have of ever collecting what was justly due it under such a contract? About zero! The equipment is in Pakistan, subject to its courts and subject to the army's acceptance. It is such an obviously stacked deck, one wonders why anybody would ever agree to such a contract. This company didn't, but there have been companies enticed into such bad terms. What is the bait? A high price.

A venture must always beware of people who willingly approve high prices for its goods or services. Such approval may indicate that they have no intention of paying when the invoice comes in. It is easy to agree to a venture's price when the buyer knows that later it will be able to negotiate that price downward in contractual disputes.

As entrepreneurs go through contracts, paragraph by paragraph, they should be sensitive to the net impact of each paragraph. They must be acutely sensitive to any clause that allows the other party a way out of the contract or a way to renegotiate price or terms.

Role reversal

It is often beneficial to play a little game called role reversal. Project oneself into the other person's shoes, and ask, "If I were the other person, what provisions would I want in the contract? What would be my fears? How would I protect myself?"

Liquidated damages

Often, in a sales contract, the buyer puts down a deposit with the contract, stipulating that if the buyer fails to go through with the contract, the deposit is forfeited as liquidated damages for the breach of the contract. The theory is that the seller has been harmed because of the buyer's failure to perform and is due some damages. Otherwise, the seller would have to refund the deposit and then sue in court for whatever damages might be awarded him in a civil action. Liquidated damage clauses can be used for a variety of contractual matters, all the way from total nonperformance to a slightly delayed performance. Such clauses save substantial costs and time if litigation is necessary since no time must be spent proving the amount of damages. Many times, in cases where there is no liquidated damage provision, there is no real dispute about whether a breach of the contract occurred, only about the extent of damages suffered as a result of the breach. Damages, since they must be measured in terms of money, often are very difficult to prove with the degree of certainty courts require.

State laws

The contract should make clear under which set of laws the contract will be judged. The laws of the states can vary tremendously. When parties from different states enter into contractual arrangements, such contracts should clearly say which set of state laws will be applicable to the contract. Sometimes it is appropriate to name the court and locale in which any contract dispute is to be settled. Entrepreneurs should make it inexpensive for themselves and stay at home.

This matter of jurisdiction is particularly critical in dealing with firms in other countries. Whose laws prevail? If a firm must use the other nation's court system, legal advice is necessary. Most countries have far different laws than we do.

Arbitration

Increasingly, parties to a contract try to avoid the costs and delays of court action by agreeing to submit to arbitration any disagreements or disputes arising from the contract. Arbitration can be a relatively inexpensive way of settling disputes if parties want them settled. Care needs to be taken with this arbitration alternative and legal advice obtained as to any arbitration provisions.

Loopholes

While contingency clauses are loopholes, they are rather obvious ones. A true loophole is something that is not in the contract, or something that is stated in such a way that it allows the party a way out. For example, many loopholes result from the failure of the parties to clearly specify exactly what was sold or when it was to be delivered. For example, suppose Sally buys a house furnished except for "personal items." When Sally gets in the house, she finds very little furniture there because the seller considered most of the things personal. The furniture to be included in the contract should have been itemized and identified. Pictures might have been used for particularly valuable items.

One approach to putting loopholes in a contract is to list all of the events that might occur that would make one want out of a contract and then try to include, in some manner, clauses that allow one relief if those events happen.

Time

A rather standard clause in many contracts is one stating that "time is of the essence," meaning that if things aren't performed on a timely basis, one of the parties is going to be severely damaged. Thus, failure to perform in a timely manner will subject the other party to damages. Without that clause, a court might not consider that it was really important for the carpenter to finish a room addition on time. So what if he was a month late?

Clear identification of intents

At the beginning, the contract should very clearly state what the parties' intentions are. What are they trying to accomplish by executing the contract? Later on, the courts will not listen to what one party thinks he or she intended to do or what one party thought was the intent of the contract. It will judge the intent of the parties on the contract itself and the facts surrounding its creation.

Clear identification of parties

While it might seem obvious to say that a contract should clearly identify the parties making it, visualize for a moment a document that states that this agreement is between John Jones, party of the first part, and Jack Smith, party of the second part. Now which John Jones are we talking about and which Jack Smith? It would be very difficult to bring such a contract into court because Jack Smith could say, "That wasn't me." Thus, not only should names be included in contracts, but addresses and/or other identifying facts. When in doubt, Social Security numbers can be used as a definitive identification of exactly who is making the agreement. While one might say the signature on the contract would identify the party, Jack Smith could maintain that it isn't his signature, that it is a forgery. That is one reason that on truly important contracts, notary publics are used to bear witness that Jack Smith did, indeed, sign that document.

Suppose Tom sells a copier to Management Services Company, Inc. Management Services signs the contract but fails to sign anything else, like a check the next month. Tom goes back to reclaim his copier only to find that Management Services is nowhere around. Tom has been defrauded. He failed to identify the parties. That is an extreme example, but it happens when one doesn't know the people with whom one is contracting.

Open-end checks

Often, people ask others for signatures on documents that are little more than blank checks. The signer's liabilities are unspecified. They could be anything. For example, a party may agree on the price of something but also agree to pay half of the legal costs involved in drawing up the contract. The party doesn't know what he or she agreed to do, and the legal costs might come in the size of the defense budget. Who knows? Instead, the party should specify a finite amount of money that he or she is willing to pay toward the legal costs. Always try to put a cap on every contingency cost. Limit losses.

Never sign a blank contract. It invites all sorts of mischief. Don't leave large open areas on a document. Things can be inserted into such space after the papers have been signed.

Leases

It was previously recognized that leases are a form of contract in which one party agrees to rent or lease some property to another. The reason leases loom large in business is that they can provide a valuable, useful way to finance a business. When an entrepreneur leases somebody else's property, he or she is really borrowing money. Someone is loaning the use of assets that the entrepreneur would otherwise have to buy with investment capital. Thus, a rental payment is really no different than an interest payment. The entrepreneur is renting money. By leasing the physical premises and equipment, the entrepreneur is able to get into business for a lower start-up cost than would be the case if the properties had to be purchased.

In finance, this is called off balance sheet financing. That is, if the entrepreneur purchased a property with borrowed money, the property would show as an asset and the debt would show as a liability on the balance sheet. The rental payment simply shows up as a cost on the operating statement.

One electronics company leased all of its equipment from Ute Corporation. The fact that Ute Corporation was wholly owned by the children of the electronics company's president was an interesting tax maneuver, but the tactic had far greater implications. It cleaned up the balance sheet of the electronics company to a point where it looked to be current and not laden with debt. Moreover, if the operating company encountered financial difficulty, creditors would have had a more difficult time making claims against it because all of the hard assets were owned by another company. The tactic of separating the debts of an operating enterprise that can get into trouble from the wealth used by the operating entity can be astute management.

Everything said about contracts is relative to leases, particularly those comments on making certain to put a lid on all of the cost elements in the lease. There are a few other aspects to leases that deserve special attention, including options, escalation, and tenant and landlord responsibilities.

Options

If a business leases a property that provides it a particularly advantageous location from which it can garner an attractive profit, the business does not want that profit confiscated by the landlord at the end of the lease period. One of the common strategies used by modern shopping mall owners is to give short-term leases, such as five years with no options. What kind of bargaining position will the merchants be in five years down the road (if they have successful operations)? They won't want to move from a winning location, so they will have to pay the landlord's higher rent demands. Rest assured the landlord knows exactly how much to demand. Of course, if the location proves unfortunate for the merchants, they will be long gone in any case.

> If the entrepreneur does not put ceilings on all the critical items of a real estate lease, for example rent, yearly increase, advertising allowances, common area maintenance, then the lessor has an open-end check from the lessee.

If an entrepreneur really has high hopes for a business in a specific location, he or she will want to make certain that the property is tied up for long enough to be worthwhile. The entrepreneur wants it to be his or her option to move, not the landlord's. Control the property! Don't let the property control the venture.

It is for this reason that it can be claimed that merchants in shopping malls have the landlord as a partner. The only difference is that their partner is taking a cut right off the top and not off the bottom line. Such landlords operating on short-term leases will confiscate a large portion of any merchant's profits.

In the pre-start-up stage of a new venture, the use of options can be advantageous. An option is a contract giving the right to buy or lease property at a specified price during a stipulated period. If an entrepreneur goes to an investor with a venture in which some piece of real estate is a vital portion of the deal, he or she is asked, "Do you now control the property?" If the answer is negative, the conversation ends, because there is nothing more to talk about. The entrepreneur doesn't control the essential ingredient of the deal. An option on the property would provide the needed control when the entrepreneur is putting together a deal that involves real estate. Tie up the property with an option long enough to get the money for the deal.

Escalation

As a hedge against inflation, landlords understandably insert many escalation clauses into their leases. First, they want to make sure their rents are not fixed but will vary with the inflation rate. Their favorite tactic for doing this is the percentage lease, in which the dollar amount of the rent increases right along with inflation, assuming that a firm's sales go up right along with the inflation (which is not always the case). Usually, there are escalation clauses on taxes, insurance, common maintenance costs, and who knows what. Be careful. If businesses agree to pay for all tax increases, why would property owners ever contest an unjust tax increase by the taxing authorities? As a tenant, a business has no rights in the matter and cannot fight the assessments. If it agrees to pay all increases in maintenance costs, what incentive is there for the landlord to try to control them? None. Realize that many so-called escalation clauses are little more than blank checks by which businesses have agreed to pick up all of the landlord's costs.

Tenant and landlord responsibilities

Considerable negotiations develop over who does what in regard to the property. Who fixes the roof? Who is responsible for plumbing repairs? What happens if the place burns down? In the matter of a fire, the tenant should be aware that a business might have some contingent liability to the landlord should a fire occur in the premises it leases. Thus, the lease should clearly cover the insurance obligation and liabilities of both parties in the event of a catastrophe.

The matter of who should be responsible for the repairs can be seriously debated and really depends upon the situation. Tenants might want the responsibility for repairs so that they can take quick action. Suppose the roof is leaking and water is puddling up on a merchant's floor? Clearly, some quick action must be taken. If it's the responsibility of the merchant, he or she can get on the phone and do something about it immediately. If it is the responsibility of the landlord, he or she may not act so promptly.

On the other hand, when the merchant agrees to do the repairs, he or she has signed a blank check. The merchant doesn't know what is going to happen to the property and might be saddled with some serious repair costs. The landlord is not going to be very keen on allowing the merchant to fix things and deduct the amounts from the rent because that provides the merchant a blank check.

These can be very important negotiations. As a general rule, entrepreneurs, as tenants, want as little as possible to do with maintaining the property owned by somebody else. It would be a blank check if they agree to keep someone else's property in good repair.

The foregoing discussed provisions for repairs of a fairly minor nature. Of even more concern are matters dealing with substantial damages to the premises. What happens to the rent while the premises remain untenable? Is the lease terminated if the premises are damaged or destroyed or merely suspended? How long does the landlord have to decide to rebuild or to make the repairs? Where does the tenant conduct business until the premises are once more usable, and is the tenant obligated to return to the repaired premises? The answer to these questions can have a profound effect upon the success of a business. Such provisions are usually found in long, painstaking-to-read commercial leases. It is astounding how many entrepreneurs enter into such leases without reading and understanding what they mean. Seek professional legal assistance in understanding and negotiating such leases.

Employment Contracts

The basic law in most states is that management has the right to fire any employee at its discretion. However, that basic "right" has been severely abridged in many instances. If the employee claims discrimination, the employer must be ready to document the reasons for the termination.

Since the courts have been strongly leaning toward protecting employees from discriminatory firing, many employers have tried to protect themselves by creating an employment policy that spells out the conditions under which the employee can be terminated. Usually such policies specify the time period during which the employee is on probation and can be discharged for any or no reason at all. Three types of employment contracts should be considered: buy-sell agreements, noncompete clauses and contracts, and nondisclosure agreements.

Buy-Sell Agreements

The buy-sell agreement is used to protect the principal parties in a new venture from undue financial loss should the personal or business relationships disintegrate.

Entrepreneurial history is replete with cases in which the several founders of a new venture later fell into serious disagreement with one other. About the only thing they could agree upon was to disagree. Naturally, under such circumstances one faction usually wants to expel the other from the enterprise. The controlling faction in a corporation can essentially exclude minority interests from participation even to the extent of depriving them of their investment in the firm. It is strongly urged that the founders of a new enterprise should always agree at the beginning what they will do

Employment Contracts
Buy-sell agreements
Noncompete clauses
 and contracts
Nondisclosure agreements

should they want to disassociate someone from the venture. They need an agreement on how to buy out the interests of each party should the problem arise: It's called a buyout or a buy-sell agreement.

Buy-sell agreements also make provisions for a death or disability of a partner and possibly a court ordered ownership allocation to a divorced spouse. They typically provide for redemption by the company of that person's share, possibly paid for by a life insurance policy carried by the company on the person. Or they provide for cross-purchase of the person's shares by the surviving partners, possibly paid for by insurance carried by the surviving partners. The preferable provision depends largely on tax considerations. A lawyer and accountant should be consulted about the best type of buy-sell agreements for a particular situation. Regardless of how the evaluation is made, the agreement should have a provision for pricing the shares of the venture.

About all that can be done here is to point out the problems that require consideration and discuss some of the traps into which the unwary can fall. Precise recommendations are impossible because each situation is unique, requiring a unique buy-sell agreement.

The difficulties of buy-sell agreements

When sitting down to compose a buy-sell agreement, the parties will be immediately faced with some serious issues, some of which can be easily resolved. There is the difficulty of knowing precisely the circumstances that will prevail when they will want to exercise the provisions in the agreement.

- Will there be an instigator or victim of the buyout?
- Has the company prospered, or has it failed?
- What will individual circumstances be?

The instigator of any buy-sell would want a lenient agreement, one that would put few pressures on him or her. Indeed, a person certain of power in the situation might try to avoid having any buy-sell agreement at all, for he or she would be protected by the basic power position. It is the people who do not have power who need the protection of a buy-sell agreement.

However, a strong case can be made equally well that even if a person holds the power, buy-sell agreements can save much aggravation and legal expense, not to mention the goodwill of the people he or she wants out.

The serious disagreements arise when there is a lot of money at stake. If one believes that his or her holdings in the company are worth $1 million dollars, but is being squeezed out for the cost of the investment, say $25,000, then he or she will be outraged and demand some means of redress. The buy-sell agreement must create a system by which the value of one's holdings can be realized upon departure from the company.

When the time comes, is the entrepreneur being forced out, or does he or she want out? Does the entrepreneur need cash or can he or she take someone's promissory note? Difficult to predict! So, assume that cash will be needed; one can always settle for less later. Assume that someone else will be in control of the situation, for if the situation is otherwise, one can usually protect one's interests; the buy-sell agreement is usually to protect the person who doesn't have control.

Who will draw up the buy-sell agreement?

It's easy to say, "A lawyer will draw up the agreement." Yes, ultimately an attorney will likely draft the final agreement. And one may want advice of counsel on the matter. But there is the nub of the problem. The first party will have a lawyer, the second party will have a lawyer, any other parties will have lawyers, and they together will point out all of the conflicts of interest that exist in the situation. Exactly who will be represented by the lawyer who draws up the agreement? Whoever it is, rest assured that the agreement will favor that lawyer's client. So the parties think, "Let's get all the lawyers together and pound it out." They need to consider the costs and the likely results before plunging into that mode of operation.

More likely, the founding group will have to develop the essential elements of their agreement, what they want the buy-sell document to reflect, and then take it to the company lawyer for drafting.

How will the enterprise be valued?

At the heart of the buy-sell agreement must be some system by which the enterprise is to be valued. There must be some basic value of the firm to serve as the basis for the buy-sell. Here is one of the most difficult problems in business. What is the value of the company? The question implies one answer when in fact there are several of them. Value to whom? Under what circumstances? Strictly construed, the value of a company is exactly what someone will pay for it, no more and no less. But how much is that? There is no way of knowing without putting the property on the market. In addition, there are firms that entrepreneurs can hire to evaluate the business's value.

Certainly, the accounting book value of the enterprise represents little more than a base from which to start. A firm can be worth far more or far less than its book value. The entrepreneur's investment in the company, while of interest to the entrepreneur, may not be relevant in the matter.

Profits are certainly an important factor in valuing a firm; buyers purchase a firm's future profits. But three questions immediately arise: Exactly what have been the firm's true profits? What will those profits be in the future? How much should be paid for those profits? (What multiple of earnings should be used?)

The buy-sell agreement must find some solutions to these problems. It must recognize the possibility that the firm's reported profits may be somewhat less than its true economic profits. It must recognize that most closely held businesses do not sell for high multiples; the owners might be lucky to get three times earnings for such a firm. And it must recognize that the past is a poor predictor of the future.

To provide insights into how one group solved its valuation problems in its buyout agreements, its procedures will be examined. The few stockholders of a manufacturer met at the first of each year and agreed upon a figure that represented the value of the company at that time. For the rest of the year, if any one of the stockholders died or wanted to sell, that figure was used to value his holdings. Since no one stockholder knew if his interests would be buying or selling, it was to each of their best interests to try to place an accurate value on the concern. The system worked rather well.

"I set the price. You choose to buy or sell."

One common method partners use to settle their buy-sell conflicts is to have one partner set a price for which the other partner decides to either buy or sell. Some groups hold sealed bids for the company. The associate who bids the most buys the firm for that price.

One problem with this technique is that it assumes the people have equal buying power. They seldom do. The stockholder who has no money is at the mercy of the person who does.

Elements in the buy-sell agreement

A model can be developed entailing the major factors that must be considered in formulating a buy-sell agreement. The following circumstances must be considered:

- Who is to be a party to the agreement?
- What initiates action under the terms of the agreement?
- How is the seller's price to be determined?
- Who is the buyer?
- What is the transferability of the other parties' interests?
- What are the terms of purchase?
- Is the bought-out partner prevented from competing with the remaining business?

Noncompete clauses and contracts

It is a good tactic and precaution to require founders, staff and freelance contractors or consultants to sign employment agreements, including a confidentiality agreement stipulating they will not leave or enter into competition with the employer using his confidential information at any time or place.

It is reasonable to assume that employees and agents, in the course of working for a company, will be exposed to and acquire valuable confidential information. Such agreements allow the company to put a lock and key on its confidential business information.

Most states stipulate that a business can only require partners, owners, executives, managers, and their staffs to sign noncompete agreements, and their enforceability depends on the reasonableness of the restrictions in the document. However, all employees can be bound to maintain the trade secrets that have been established in the business.

Noncompete agreements should be signed at the beginning of the employment or contract relationship. They may be separate agreements or provisions contained in the employment agreement. Unfortunately, many entrepreneurs do not have or use employment agreements. They should be a key part of the employment package and policies.

These agreements specify that confidential business and technical or other proprietary information will not be divulged, disclosed, or used for the benefit of that person or outsiders without the company's written permission. Such provisions also can appear on an invoice or job-order form for contractors.

The confidential provisions of an employment noncompete agreement serve several important functions. First, they identify what information is confidential or protected. Second, the provisions inform employees of their rights and obligations regarding such information and alert them of the company's ability to enforce its rights. In addition, they invest in the development of information capital in the company.

Courts usually determine the validity of noncompete agreements based on the validity of the protective interest, the geographical area covered, and the time period the agreement is to be in effect. They determine the protectability of trade secrets based on the steps taken to identify these to employees and agents, by the steps that are taken to protect them, and by showing that they are not readily available from public sources.

Protectable interests usually include trade secrets, technical information, customer lists, or other legitimately confidential business information. Customer contacts can be protected by restraining a former employee from contacting those customers in direct competition subsequent to employment. The more frequent and direct contact that an employee has with customers and the more unique the customer list is, the greater likelihood of establishing a protectable interest on behalf of the company.

The provisions of successful noncompete agreements vary widely by state and profession and should be drafted by an intellectual property business attorney. He or she can become a valuable resource to the venture's management team. Also, exit interviews should be conducted with every employee, whether or not he or she has signed a confidentiality agreement, to review benefits and remind the employee of his or her duties concerning proprietary information.

Nondisclosure agreements

The best and easiest way to protect proprietary rights when working with contractors is to have a written contract, known as a nondisclosure agreement, (also called a confidentiality disclosure agreement) governing the disclosure. Such agreements prohibit others from using a venture's confidential information or trade secrets for their own benefit or divulging that information to someone else.

Use a nondisclosure agreement with employees and with third parties, if the venture's confidential information needs to be shown to others outside the company. These agreements are often used to protect technical information but can also be used to protect client lists, methods of doing business, designs, formulations, and similar intangibles that provide a fair advantage over the competition.

Nondisclosure agreements cover situations in which valuable information is presented to people who, in the absence of a promise not to use the information, might use it in a manner that will hurt the business or for their own financial gain. The agreements are legally binding contracts that obligate the person signing it to hold the venture's information in confidence.

When the agreement is signed, it becomes a binding contract giving the originator of the idea the right to file a lawsuit to stop the unauthorized use of the information or to sue for damages for breach of contract if the information disclosed is used without the originator's permission.

Nondisclosure agreements should be used whenever proprietary information is shared. It is appropriate when the information is in the idea or concept stage as well as when the originator has a copyright or pending patent application.

In the agreement, there must be a definition of what are considered to be the company's specific trade secrets or proprietary information. It should contain language strong enough to show a court that the proprietary information is considered a vital part of the business and that an injunction or monetary damages should be in order.

Once the nondisclosure agreement is signed, a firm can go to court for a restraining order or an injunction on a simple breach-of-contract theory to enforce its terms.

In order to be entitled to protection for proprietary information, it must be treated in a protective manner, for example by stamping all relevant information "confidential," keeping the material secure, and advising all persons who have access to it that it is confidential.

Furthermore, even in the absence of a contract, many states have both civil and criminal statutes regarding the protection of trade secrets which have been protected and treated in a proprietary manner.

Using a nondisclosure agreement increases the chances of protecting a venture's proprietary rights. Preparing a strong document now can help avoid a messy court case later.

Conclusion

Entrepreneurs need to be sensitive to the pitfalls that can await the unwary contract signer. While hundreds of contracts can be successfully completed in routine daily operations, it is the few exceptions that can prove to be so costly and time consuming.

The entrepreneur should be aware of the international complications related to contracts, especially with respect to their enforcement, courts, and partnerships. International agreements can lead to a major downfall if the entrepreneur naively enters into agreements that are similar to American agreements but are to be enforced in foreign courts. Many foreign laws are not compatible with American laws; therefore, the agreements are not binding.

Protecting Business Interests

Learning Objectives

In this chapter, students will learn
- What causes one person to squeeze out another person.
- How one owner squeezes out other owners.
- How to avoid squeeze outs.

Entrepreneurs must be aware of the need to protect the interests of both themselves and their businesses. There are legal problems inherent in starting a business. All too often, naive entrepreneurs make serious legal blunders that cost them dearly, even to the extent of losing their businesses. The more valuable a business becomes, the more likely the owner will be under attack by other employees who seek to steal the results of his or her efforts, using whatever openings have been provided them.

The message is clear: Don't give them anything to work with, and don't be naive. There are many unscrupulous people, some quite possibly within a business, who want what the business owner has. If many businesspeople seem paranoid about contractual relationships, the reason is that they have collected a lot of costly scars from experience. So much for warnings. This chapter examines one of the premier issues—protecting one's position in the enterprise.

Forces Causing the Squeeze Out

In some ventures, founding people have been squeezed out somewhere along the line. As time passes, relationships change, fortunes come and go, talents and skills become apparent or change, the needs of the business change, and greed develops. Things change. When they do, entrepreneurs want things to change their way, not in some other direction.

Although there are defensive measures that can be taken to protect one's interests in an enterprise, it helps to understand the basic forces causing squeeze outs: greed and power. Recognizing these forces and their warning signs can help entrepreneurs avoid a squeeze-out situation.

Greed

Unquestionably, greed heads the list of reasons underlying squeeze outs, despite the protests to the contrary of the person wanting to take over the business. The mind of the squeezer is always able to conjure up a noble justification for eliminating some business associates. Experience uncovers fascinating tales of how a person's behavior and attitudes change. It is easy to be a good friend and an understanding associate when there isn't much money on the table. Let the price for keeping a good friend around go to a million dollars, and then examine the relationship. Some examples of greed in action may provide a few insights that will allow entrepreneurs to appreciate the jeopardy with which minority stockholders hold their positions in an enterprise. Frank owned 40 percent of the rock quarry north of a small town in Indiana. The remaining 60 percent was owned by Ralph, a multimillionaire building contractor who was by far the rock company's number one customer. The rock company prospered mightily. While Frank drew a salary for his work as general manager, the board of directors, totally controlled by Ralph, declared no dividends. The ostensible reason that went into the corporate minutes was that the money was needed for future expansion. Privately, Ralph made it clear that he didn't want any cash dividends from the company because Uncle Sam would take most of them in income taxes.

Since Ralph was already extremely rich, he didn't need the cash. Frank, on the other hand, had a growing family and wanted to enjoy the financial fruits of his work. Ralph refused. After several years of continual discussion on the matter, Ralph finally, in private, looked Frank squarely in the eye and said, "Frank, you can't be this stupid. Hasn't it dawned on you that you'll never get any money out of that rock company? I control it. The only way you are ever going to see a dime is to sell your stock to me. I'll give you $200,000 for your stock right now."

That represented selling out for the equivalent of about 5 cents on the dollar, since the company was worth about $4 million. Frank objected, of course. Then he headed as fast as he could for his lawyer's office. After all of the available options were examined, Frank was advised to take the $200,000 and be happy that Ralph was even that generous. Not only was Frank posed with some serious legal obstacles in the Indiana courts to forcing a dividend payout, he was reminded that Ralph had the power to fire him as general manager, thus causing him to lose his reasonable salary. Moreover, Ralph's company was the rock company's biggest customer. Consequently, the reality was that Ralph had Frank in a situation he couldn't do anything about.

This actual case clearly identifies the problems minority stockholders can have in a profitable company under the control of one major stockholder. The brutal truth is that the minority stockholders' interests are generally worth only what the majority stockholder says they are worth. Granted, there are occasions in which a minority stockholder can successfully obtain relief through court action. Such instances, however, are rare exceptions for a number of reasons.

First, if the majority stockholder is legally astute, he will see to it that there is no cause for legal action. Second, the majority stockholder often has other strangleholds on both the corporation and the minority stockholder.

Many entrepreneurs think if they own 51 percent of the company, they control the company. This is not true. The person who controls the money controls the business.

Third, the costs of litigation are large and are particularly questionable in light of the odds of success combined with the time required to go through the legal process.

Typically, the minority stockholder is not wealthy and is pressed for money; thus, legal remedies are often not a choice. The individual needs the money quickly and therefore will settle for a fraction of the value of the company. For example, Frank was willing to settle for his $200,000 in hand rather than gamble on a larger sum years down the road. With the logjam in the courts, Frank's decision was probably sound. Applying time and probability factors to an eventual court outcome, the $200,000 probably exceeded the statistical answer to Frank's problem.

It should be pointed out that a minority stockholder does have some nuisance value. The ownership of that stock does give rights to initiate a number of court actions to force the majority stockholder to account for the proper use of the company's assets. The most vulnerable point at which to attack a majority stockholder is the issue of how he or she is using the corporation's assets. If it can be shown that the majority stockholder is using the company's assets for personal benefit, that he or she is not dealing at arm's length with the corporation, then the minority stockholder gains some legal leverage in the situation.

The courts' general attitude toward minority stockholders and their rights could be puzzling. The following may help explain the law's reluctance to meddle unnecessarily in the affairs of a corporation:

- Minority stockholders are not necessarily more virtuous than their majority counterparts. There are scoundrels who would use the courts to do their dirty work if the courts would listen. Don't jump to the conclusion that some minority stockholder who is grousing about his or her treatment by the majority is justified. The minority stockholder could be the villain.

- Basic legal premise is that the majority rules. Thus, the court reasons that the majority has the right to run the business as it desires so long as it does not violate the law in doing so.

- The law generally considers stockholders to be prudent businesspeople who buy the stock with their eyes open, knowing full well the limitations of their minority position.

Consequently, from the majority stockholder's point of view, entrepreneurs should once again realize the importance of dealing with their corporations at arm's length. Smart entrepreneurs do not provide minority stockholders with the ammunition needed to go to court to claim that the company's assets have been used improperly for personal benefit.

In another case, three men joined together to start manufacturing a line of clothing. Their stock ownership was 60 percent, 20 percent, and 20 percent. One of the 20 percent stockholders was allowed his position initially in exchange for labor. The second 20 percent stockholder paid $25,000 for the stock, which was used to finance the venture. The majority stockholder paid $40,000 for his 60 percent interest. Three years later, a large manufacturer initiated contact with the majority stockholder to purchase the company, which had grown into a highly profitable business. The initial offering price was $1 million. The majority stockholder became greedy. He openly made the statement to the working minority stockholder that there was no way that he was going to let the $25,000 investor receive $200,000 for his stock after only a three-year investment. He considered that an excessive rate of return for the nonworking investor.

Consequently, he began squeezing out the $25,000 investor. A few years later he bought out the remaining stockholder and is now sole owner of a company worth about $3 million. Bear in mind that these three men were the closest of friends and that the minority stockholder who was originally squeezed out had done many favors for the majority stockholder. But greed has a way of overriding all considerations. In that instance, it was fascinating to observe the behavioral changes in the majority stockholder when he learned how much money was on the table. In essence, the reasoning was that for $3 million he could find a new friend.

This case is used routinely as one of a series to emphasize that even the deepest friendships can come apart under the pressures of greed. Many times, in the organizing phases of a business being started by three or four friends, the chorus is always loud and repetitive, "We don't need all of these protective arrangements. We are good friends and nothing can pry us apart."

If people bet money on those emotions, they will most likely lose, because greed's batting average in destroying such close friendships is staggeringly high.

Don't be misled by the protests of the squeezer that greed had nothing to do with his actions. Rest assured that squeezers always have rationalized away in their own minds all thoughts that they are doing in their friends. A horde of other excuses can always be found.

Power

Closely akin to greed, but still sufficiently distinctive to deserve separate mention, is greed's twin—power. Power, a common motive underlying much behavior, is usually cloaked in other trappings, for it is socially unacceptable in many circles. To openly covet power is somehow repugnant to most people. Yet, most of the leaders in business and politics hold their positions largely because of tremendous power drives. These leaders want to be in control. There is nothing wrong with this. Only when the drive for power overshadows others' values does it become an issue. Powerful people are admired and receive all sorts of benefits, but only if they do not openly strive for power.

Seemingly, the way to get power is to appear not to want it too badly. The position often should be that one would be willing to accept the power in order to do all sorts of good things that need to be done. Power is fun, power is ego gratifying, and power is rewarding.

There have been cases in which minority stockholders who sought power in the organization were able to squeeze out the majority stockholders. The ownership interests in small corporations are often evenly divided. The situation in which three owners each own one-third of the business is often encountered. Then, one of the owners manages to get rid of the other two. It is often a two-step maneuver. First, the squeezer joins with one of the others, who is gullible, to squeeze out the third person. Now, there are two owners. And by some means, the power seeker manages to gain control over the remaining party.

Three men came out of the Vietnam War as buddies whose bonds of friendship had been forged under fire. Nothing would ever pry them apart, or so they claimed when they started a small chemical compounding business in Denver shortly after the three graduated from college. Each owned one-third of the business. While the product and concept were sound, the initial sales manager wasn't. As a result of his lack of knowledge about the industry into which they were trying to distribute their product, the company lost $100,000 in its first year of operation. It was insolvent. If it was to continue operations, it needed some cash.

Fortunately, one of the three had some money available from his wife, which she was willing to loan to the company on a one-year note at a reasonable rate of interest. The sales manager was fired and replaced with someone with the needed experience in the industry. Operations were turned around during the second year but not to the point where any cash was available for paying off the note. At the end of the year, the stockholder who had loaned the company the money and who was also its president quietly made the board of directors what seemed to be a reasonable proposition. "As you know, the note for $100,000 is due this week. The company does not have the cash to pay it. The banks are unwilling to lend us the money. My wife is unwilling to extend the note. Naturally, she has no desire to take this company to court for collection. As the company's major creditor, she could take over ownership of its assets, which would include the product patents and trademarks. She doesn't want to do that. What my wife is willing to do is accept more stock in this company in exchange for the note. Right now the book value of the stock is negative, as you well know. However, she would be willing to trade the note in exchange for 100,000 shares of common stock. That's the proposition for you to consider."

It was all very quiet and polite. The other stockholders realized they had no bargaining position. She could go to court and do exactly what she said. The company had no funds with which to defend itself. The remaining two stockholders had been given their positions as production manager and treasurer in exchange for their modest initial capital inputs. The offer was accepted. The net result gave the president control over roughly 60 percent of the stock. He was now in total control. The next week, his production manager buddy was invited to leave the company. The remaining buddy accepted the reality of the situation. He recognized the power of the president and followed orders. His minority stockholder position was worth whatever the president ultimately decided it was worth.

The reason for going deeply into these situations is to illustrate that almost inevitably in this type of arrangement, the parties refuse to set up their business relationships in a way that recognizes the possibility that they may later have a falling out. Yet, experience indicates that a very high percentage of such relationships eventually crumble as the interests of each party diverge. Consequently, it is simply stupid not to organize a company properly from the start in a way that will protect the interests of the people contributing to it.

Warnings

If business associates insist that such mutual-protection arrangements are not needed, an entrepreneur might have reason to ponder their motivation for such naivete. Is the entrepreneur being set up for a later time? Following are some signals in shareholder relationships that stockholders should be wary of.

Inactive shareholder. Not uncommonly, a new enterprise is formed by one, two, or three people who intend to work in the company in addition to contributing some money. But they need some money from outside investors who will not be active in the firm. The working investors, through hard work and long hours, make the enterprise prosper. It is now worth a lot of money, and all because of their efforts, they believe. Often they come to resent the outside investor who is profiting so handsomely from their hard work.

Thus, the squeeze is on "the person who didn't contribute anything except a few dollars, but now look what we've done for him." So the rationalization begins. Never mind the fact that at the beginning those "few dollars" were the ones that allowed them to go into business. Such memories are short and rationalized away: "We could have borrowed the money somewhere!" Why didn't they? The outside investor must go. Such squeeze outs are easy if the investor has not used some protective tactics.

It is for this reason that outside investors should not stay too far outside the company. They should consider participating to some degree and trying to appear as if they are part of the team. Such investors should always provide the potential squeezer with a buyout price that meets the investors' goals. Otherwise the investor may get nothing by being frozen out— no dividends, no benefits, no market for stock.

Death or change in status among stockholders. One group begins a business. The associates are happy with their relationships, but one of them dies. The survivors don't care to be in business with whomever inherits the stock. Thus, the need for buyout arrangements is apparent, as well as life insurance to furnish cash to execute the buyout. Similarly, especially with divorce being so common, the situation occurs where one of the originators of the business is involved in a divorce in which interests of the couple in various property is at issue. The spouse of the originator is awarded some or all of the interest in the business. Imagine how smoothly that business now operates with owners who have just been through a divorce and possibly acrimonious property dispute. Entrepreneurs should consider restrictions on transferability of interests and/or a buyout arrangement with triggers to permit those in the business to force a buyout of spouses. Also, imagine the prolonged illness or disability of one of the founders. The success of the business is dependent on the daily involvement of all the founders. For how long will the other founders do the work of the ill or disabled one and continue to pay salary and/or continue that person's interest in the business? Perhaps they need to hire others to take up the slack or to induce another to become an owner to obtain his or her talent. Entrepreneurs should consider agreements before this happenstance so that authority exists and all are aware of and have agreed to it. It is important to clarify that buyouts are not designed to cheat anyone or treat them unfairly, rather to provide for changes in business and personal situations which can and do happen everyday. If agreements are reached at the inception of the business when relationships are good, parties tend to treat all parties in the changed circumstance fairly. After all, one never knows which side of the transaction one will be on. Without reasonable buy-sell arrangements, the survivors will likely initiate a squeeze out to remove the unwanted people from the firm.

The close corporation is really a closed corporation—closed to all but those people who are wanted in it. Anyone who isn't wanted must watch out.

The aged founder who hangs on. As the song goes, "You gotta know when to hold 'em and know when to fold 'em." Too many aging entrepreneurs don't know when to fold 'em, when to leave. They love the game too much or just don't see any reason for giving up anything. Why should they?

Often younger people in the organization could furnish some reasons. The older person is getting in the way of progress or at least their concept of it. So a squeeze out is undertaken. Henry Ford discovered the folly of giving stock to his wife and family; they combined to force the old gent out of the Ford Motor Company in favor of Henry III. Of course, had they not been able to do so, the company most likely would have gone under.

The drive of superior talent. Cream rises to the top! Talent demands its rewards. Should ineptitude, or the appearance of it, seem to block talent's rise, then the talent may try to squeeze out the blockage.

Three men founded what was to become a highly profitable industrial plastics molding company. Profits were large. The two vice presidents decided that the president was worthless and had to go. The VPs told him that at the next board meeting they were joining forces to oust him from the company. They each owned 10 percent of the stock. The remaining stock was owned by various investors around the country.

The president got on a plane and visited enough of those outside investors that he was able to walk into the board meeting with sufficient proxies to control the day. The two would-be squeezers suddenly became the squeezees. They were on the street. Why did they warn the president? Who knows! The two formed a competitive company and did rather well, as did the original company.

More needs to be said about this ego drive based on a perception of talent. Those people who perceive themselves as being talented at whatever they do often become overbearing and intolerant of people whom they consider less talented than themselves. Given the power in a business, they often drive out other people at an alarming rate. It seems that no one can work for them for long. Moreover, often such talent can be unreasonably jealous of other talent and will squeeze out anyone who threatens the throne. Entrepreneurs who associate themselves with such people need to take extreme precaution to protect their interests.

Unreasonable minority shareholders or stockholders. Many squeeze outs are the results of the minority stockholders' own behavior. They give the majority stockholders so much trouble that no rational person would tolerate them for long. In a close corporation, the stockholders are not adversaries. They are on the same team. If one or more stockholders cannot play team ball, then some changes will be made.

Sometimes such behavior by a minority interest is designed to force management to settle with it on favorable terms. In one case, from the very beginning, a minority stockholder who was also a director was very obnoxious. No one could understand how he ever became involved in the venture. He had put up $200,000 of the $3 million initial capital. He disagreed vigorously with everything. On two occasions, other directors almost came to blows with him. Each time he would offer to sell his stock back, there were no takers. It was apparent that the company was failing due to their inability to work together. He was blackmailing the directors. The price for his ouster was giving him his money back. The directors at the table were sufficiently wealthy that they could have agreed to his offer if so inclined. But they didn't. He could go down with them.

Divergence of business interests. In the beginning of an enterprise, the initial entrepreneurs are usually possessed with one overriding interest—that of making the new venture successful. They bring to the venture an assortment of talents and money. Each is aware of the others' outside business interests and tends to accept them as one of the conditions that exist when they start operations.

The reality of close corporations is that the founders tend to regard themselves as partners. There is a strong feeling of camaraderie. They view their relationships as closer than that of being fellow stockholders in a new corporation. They spend more time with their business associates than they do with their families. Thus, it is not surprising that such relationships erode when one or more of the partners violates the implicit rules of partnership by excluding one of the others from some business opportunity. It happens in many ways.

Perhaps one of the partners simply invests some money in an outside venture that does very well without providing his partners with an opportunity to share in the venture. In one instance, one of the partners was made president of the local country club, to the great consternation of his golf-fanatic partner, who became so jealous that he couldn't stand it. The squeeze out was on.

Or one of the minority owners begins another business, perhaps even a competing one. Woe to the offender, for few things will upset a majority stockholding position in a company more than to have one of the minority stockholders begin a competing company. That is considered to be disloyal, if not a conflict of interest. If the person is only a stockholder in the enterprise, legally there is nothing at all inappropriate with starting a competing business. Just because George owns stock in General Motors does not mean he cannot also be a manufacturer of automobiles. If he were part of the company's management, then he would have legal problems. Great care must be used in distinguishing between the roles people play in a corporation: employee, officer, director, or stockholder. Each has different legal obligations to the corporation and to the stockholders.

Popular shareholders in a group often will be offered business opportunities around town that are not offered to less popular members of the same group. Such situations are loaded with explosive content, for they signal a beginning of the end of their old relationships. Typically, what happens is that as the individual spends more and more time on the outside business deals, the offended shareholders reason, often with justification, that the stockholder is no longer playing a team game. He is not fully committed to the interests of their business.

In one such situation, the two offended partners said, "Well, if he wants to play the lone wolf and go it alone, let's accommodate him." And they did very easily, for the close corporation had been drawn up without any view to protective tactics, even though excellent sophisticated legal assistance had been used initially. In that case, the two simply fired the third party from his job as treasurer of the company and excluded him from all managerial participation in the company. Since no dividends were paid in the organization (the stockholders were all employees of the firm and withdrew their profits disguised as salaries and expenses), the net result was that the third party was stripped of his investment. They did not even bother trying to buy back his 33 percent stock ownership.

Consequently, small groups of people going into business for the first time should understand that they are becoming members of a team and that thereafter they need to do everything possible to make certain that their interests coincide. The minute a serious conflict of interest develops between the stockholders of close corporations, a squeeze out will be forthcoming.

Discovery of duplicity

Duplicity can occur in many forms. The squeeze out can work both ways, with the person being either the squeezer or the squeezee. In one example, an inventor of a chemical compound that was designed to temporarily fix cracked automotive engine blocks was able to begin a company to manufacture and distribute the product with money furnished by three investors, who were business professors at a Big Ten university. The company prospered through a large contract from the Army. The firm made a lot of money, which was kept in the corporation to finance its growth. Then, suddenly, at a board meeting, the inventor told the majority investors that unless they sold their stock to him for a sum equivalent to about 10 cents on the dollar of what it was worth, he would not renew the license he'd given the corporation for manufacturing and marketing the chemical compound.

It seems the professors had been a bit negligent in doing their due diligence. They had failed to check that the inventor had assigned all of his patents and trademarks to the corporation. Instead, he had merely licensed them, and the license was running out. They felt they had no alternative but to give up their positions in the company, for it had no future without the rights to make and sell the product. Unfortunately, this was a case in which the duplicity paid off for the deceiver to the detriment of the majority stockholders. In other instances, such duplicity so infuriates the adversaries that they go to extreme lengths to punish the inventor. There were ways the professors could have fought and won, but they weren't tough enough. The inventor bought the investors' stock.

In a small manufacturing company, a minority stockholder who was in charge of manufacturing operations and purchasing had covertly set up a small machine shop in partnership with a machinist. He subsequently gave all of the company's business to his machine shop at noncompetitive prices. Upon discovery, the minority stockholder was quickly fired and squeezed out of the corporation by the threat to press litigation to recover the profits and take over ownership of his position in the other company. In this instance, it was a blatant conflict of interest, which the courts are prone to deal with rather harshly.

In another instance, the chairman of the board, who had invested $160,000 of the company's $3 million initial capital, was discovered by his fellow directors to have illegally diverted money into his own pocket. When one of his friends wanted to invest in the company, instead of selling him company stock, he would sell him some of his own stock. He was divesting himself of his position in the company, which appeared to have a problem, while on the surface telling all his friends what a great buy it was.

Since the stock had not been registered with the SEC, it was not transferable without restriction. Moreover, the proper legends had not been put on the stock certificates to warn people not to transfer it. Because of several violations of the law, the offending minority stockholder was quickly forced to rectify his errors. Up to that time, most of the directors had considered him to be the good guy in the scenario. With the disclosure of his duplicity, relationships changed.

Part of the motive for duplicity among inventors is that initially the financiers demand the lion's share of the stock for financing the company. The inventor gets a substantial block of shares for transferring his patents and trademarks to the corporation. But under what terms and exactly what patents? The inventor has an advantage over the financiers in that he may be aware of other patents and other ways of getting around the patents; thus, he keeps some aces up his sleeve in dealing with the financial people, whom he regards as having taken control of "his baby." Often inventors reason like this, "Okay, I'll go along with you now and give you what you think is control of the company, but when the time comes, I've got a few aces to play that you don't know about."

What the inventor is thinking about is keeping control of some key bits of information, without which the corporation cannot exist. Patents don't tell the whole story. Thus, it is not by accident that financiers are wary in their dealings with such technical people, for they realize their vulnerability. In a high-tech venture, if the technical people walk out, the majority stockholders often will have nothing left because the real business was in the minds of the technicals.

Legal arrangements made during the organization of the company may provide that future inventions be turned over to the company and may specify how the inventor will be rewarded. It might prevent some disputes from developing.

It is the practice of most experienced lawyers to include in the contract or other pre-incorporation agreements a clause covering future inventions. Yet, there is real doubt about how well inflexible arrangements work when entered into at a time when the inventor is in an extremely weak bargaining position. It's very difficult for outside investors to force their way into the privacy of the inventor's mind and obtain the fruits thereof.

Squeezing Out Business Associates

One of the reasons that squeeze outs are so common is that they are so easy to do. The parties have done little or nothing to protect their interests. Often, it is simply a matter of firing the person from his or her job in the company and then freezing the person out from all participation in the fruits of the enterprise. The common squeeze-out techniques are discussed below.

Termination as employee

In many new enterprises, the stockholders all intend to obtain their rewards through salary and expenses. There's no intention of ever making sufficient profit that dividends can be paid. Thus, when the majority stockholders want to oust a minority stockholder-employee, all they have to do is fire him or her. There are a few cases in the courts charging wrongful discharge. However, for the most part, when majority stockholders want to get rid of an unwanted stockholder-employee, the real reason is that they are unhappy with the person's performance. (Or at least they can find reason to be unhappy with it.)

Defensive tactic. If a person enters into a relationship with the intention that the investment also buys a job with the company, then such a person would likely want the initial agreement to clearly state that if the person is discharged for any reason, the stock must be repurchased at an agreed-upon price. An ability to recover the investment immediately upon termination should definitely be in writing.

Of course, such an agreement might be unwise from the company's viewpoint, for the agreement might place a cash demand upon the company when the company could ill afford it. Wise management should be wary of tying its hands in dealing with employees. It would be very awkward to have to retain an unwanted or inept employee just because majority stockholders or the company did not have enough cash with which to buy out his or her stock interest. Thus, these matters can be difficult to solve. There is no easy solution to the problems created when the various roles of the people are mixed in the enterprise.

Withholding dividends

The classic way to squeeze out unwanted minority stockholders is simply to withhold dividends. They can sit on their stock to the end of time, but they'll get nothing for it. Moreover, sale of the stock is restricted. It has little value. This tactic, when properly executed by a majority management that knows what it is doing, is almost unassailable in court, for there are many ways that it can be made to appear as if the company has only nominal earnings. Accumulated retained earnings have to approach truly gargantuan size before the courts will move to action. Some minority stockholders attack this freeze-out tactic by trying to get the IRS to declare the corporation has excessive accumulated earnings, thus forcing a dividend payout. Again, this is not likely to happen if management has availed itself of reasonable legal assistance, and in most squeeze-out undertakings, it usually has.

Defensive tactic. If a minority stockholder truly expects dividends to be paid on his or her stock, then perhaps he or she should be thinking in terms of receiving a preferred stock in which the dividends are cumulative, if the company earns them. Convertible bonds on which interest must be paid are another investment medium that avoids the problem. However, these securities can create some additional problems for the company. Stock dividends create a double-taxation situation, thus losing the firm's cash to Uncle Sam. The convertible bond not only has to be repaid at some time, but it goes on the balance sheet as debt, not equity, and thereby reduces the firm's ability to borrow money elsewhere.

Investors in the new enterprise often decline investing through the medium of buying stock in the company, preferring to purchase assets for the new enterprise and then leasing them to the company, thereby getting their income through rental payments rather than dividends. This has several attractive tax advantages to both the company and the investor.

Removal from board of directors

It is often implicit in closely held corporations that all stockholders will be on the board of directors, thus privy to the inside workings of the corporation. A director has many legal rights and responsibilities not bestowed upon the stockholder. Minority investors often insist on a seat on the board as one of the conditions for making the investment. Therefore, in squeezing out minority stockholder-directors, one of the first moves is to remove them from the board. Management doesn't want them around where they can learn anything about the company.

Defensive tactic. Obviously, the major defensive tactic here is to place in the bylaws of the corporation a stipulation that each stockholder is to be a director of the corporation. If there are too many of such stockholders, then each minority investor will have to make a separate deal. Often a separate contract is made in which the minority investor is granted a seat on the board so long as he or she owns stock in the operation. The stock must be repurchased if for any reason the person is not elected to the board of directors.

Mergers

On a vastly more complicated level, minority stockholders can often be squeezed out, in effect, by merging the company with another company that is wholly owned by the majority stockholders. The terms are not favorable to the stockholders of the old company. But what difference does it make to the majority stockholders of the old company? Since they own all of the new company, they are the beneficiaries of the merger. Such squeeze outs take a lot more legal finesse and are far more costly than the previous tactics but are often necessary when squeezing out a number of small minority stockholders who are neither employees nor directors of the company.

Defensive tactic. The key defense to merger tactics is to make certain that the corporation's bylaws state that such mergers cannot take place without the approval of the minority stockholders. In a company with relatively few stockholders, the bylaws might even require unanimous approval of stockholders for any such mergers. In other instances, perhaps a two-thirds or three-quarters stockholder approval would be necessary for any such merger. The whole idea is that the minority stockholders must block the majority stockholders in their plan to transfer the assets of the company into a legal framework that they own entirely.

The importance of every section of a company's bylaws cannot be stressed enough. Despite warnings that entrepreneurs give serious thought to each and every provision in the corporate bylaws, many have not done so. Only after it's too late do they start reading the fine print. Be warned that most of the standard bylaw provisions and provisions of most state laws, particularly those of Delaware and New Jersey, are set up for the benefit of the majority stockholders. There are few provisions in such statutes for the protection of the minority stockholders.

Redeeming the shares

Again, this tactic requires some extensive legal maneuvering but has been used successfully in instances in which a number of minority stockholders are to be squeezed out. The game plan is something like this: Under some form of reorganization, merger, or recapitalization, the common stock of a company is converted into preferred stock for some ostensibly sound business reason. One of the provisions of the preferred shares is that they can be redeemed at par value at the company's discretion. Once this legal maneuver has taken place, then the majority stockholders have within their power to take the minority stockholders out of the picture. Often the common stock is converted into preferred stock during troubled times. The minority stockholders, at the time, are only too happy to have their positions seemingly improved.

Defensive tactic. Again, the defensive tactic for this squeeze-out maneuver lies in controlling the bylaws to such an extent that the majority cannot make the reorganization without the minority stockholders' approval.

Use of veto provisions needs to be mentioned. In some extreme cases, minority stockholders have insisted upon and gained a veto power over all actions of management in regard to sale of assets, mergers, reorganizations, recapitalization, and the payment of all salaries and expenses. Naturally, management hates such constraints and is thus motivated to skirt them in some fashion. It is usually not smart to give people such a stranglehold. Wise entrepreneurs walk away from investors who insist on such veto provisions. This is money they don't want.

Watering the stock

The classic squeeze-out maneuver from the early days of corporate capitalism was the watering of the corporation's stock through the issue of additional shares of stock to the majority stockholders, thereby diluting the minority's interest. Because this tactic was so widely used in the past, many corporations require that all stockholders have the right to buy such additional shares of any stock offered that allow them to keep their proportional interest in the company.

Thus, the preemptive option clause that exists in many corporate articles of incorporation and bylaws is designed to prevent the squeeze out of stockholders through the issuing of additional corporate stock. However, note that it applies only to newly authorized shares. In many states, treasury stock and shares already authorized may not fall under these provisions. These are highly technical legal matters that vary state by state and should be carefully examined by minority stockholders whose positions might be threatened by such tactics. An entrepreneur simply must know, in detail, what the law provides in the company's state of incorporation.

While the preemptive option clause sounds well and good, the reality may be something else. How many minority stockholders want to put additional money into a company whose management is obviously trying to eliminate them? Moreover, astute managements often execute the stock offering at a time that is financially inconvenient to the minority stockholder. If one doesn't have the money, one can't buy the stock. Therefore, even with the preemptive option clauses in the bylaws, the tactic of issuing additional shares can be successfully used to dilute the position of unwanted stockholders.

Defensive tactic. Play the role of a venture capitalist and ensure that an antidilution agreement is executed stating that if additional stock is issued, one's percentage of ownership cannot be diluted. Therefore, the stockholder would receive additional shares that would ensure that he or she still had the same percentage of ownership.

Selling corporate assets

One of the more devilish ways by which majority stockholders can defraud their minority colleagues is by arranging the sale of the key corporate assets to a company that they totally control. In some of these instances, all of the assets, trade names, and customers are neatly transferred to another corporate body for inadequate consideration. The money is then distributed to all stockholders in proportion to their holdings.

Naturally, such sales may be regulated by corporate bylaws that require the approval of a certain percentage of the stockholders. However, the courts have not always dealt kindly with this tactic if it is apparent that management has appropriated the company assets unfairly. Such litigation usually comes down to appraising the fair market value of the assets. Nevertheless, within limits, the majority is able to sell off valuable portions of a corporation to other entities in which it has a more substantial interest.

Minority stockholders who have been victimized by this tactic have a stronger case in court, if it is worth their time and money to pursue it. Naturally, such transactions are often difficult to prove, and the problems of evaluation always hang heavy on the plaintiff.

Defensive tactic. As in many of the previous cases, one defense against such sales is to require such a high-percentage stockholder approval that the minority stockholders can block such unwarranted sales. Another is for the minority stockholder to hold title to some key asset and lease it to the company.

Dissolutions

While it might seem strange that dissolving the corporation is a way of squeezing out unwanted stockholders, still the tactic has been used in situations where certain stockholders felt they could acquire the assets of the corporation out of the action and be able to operate the enterprise once again without the unwanted stockholders. Naturally, this tactic is fraught with legal problems.

Defensive tactic. If the bylaws are of no help, about all the aggrieved minority stockholder can do is try to assert his or her claims in court and trust in the legal system. In other words, the minority stockholders could be in trouble.

Change the state of incorporation

Often as a prelude to squeezing out unwanted stockholders, management moves the state of incorporation to one whose laws are more permissive to the subsequent squeeze-out actions. Without a doubt, the majority stockholders will always have noble and high-sounding reasons for changing the state of incorporation, thus luring the potential minority stockholders into relinquishing many of their legal rights. Still, the end result is that the unwanted stockholder will be eliminated.

Defensive tactic. This ploy can be thwarted by a bylaw provision that prevents changing the state of incorporation without the unanimous approval of the stockholders.

Appropriation of business opportunities

Being in control of a corporation, the majority stockholders (management) are able to appropriate for themselves particularly attractive business opportunities that would otherwise be made available to the company. Properly executed, such tactics are difficult to fight. It's just not feasible to devise legal blockages to force other people to make all of their business opportunities available to the corporation. The fact remains that the management holding the majority interest in a company can, in hundreds of small and large ways each day, damage the interests of the minority stockholders, and little can be done about it.

Defensive tactic. It is for this reason that potential investors in an enterprise focus keenly on the integrity of the entrepreneur. If the majority owners of a business are of such a bent that they're out to cheat their colleagues, they will find a way to do so. The general advice given people is if they haven't got complete confidence in the integrity of their business associates, they should stay away from the investment. That is easy to say but difficult to do.

Siphoning off the money

The target is, after all, the company's money. The people controlling the money are normally in a position that by various means they can siphon it off through their salaries, expenses, and other means to the point that the minority stockholders' interests are confiscated in the end. Unless the minority investor is able to institute and enforce real controls over the flow of money and goods out of the corporation, there is little that can be done to stop such tactics, if management has been clever and reasonable about siphoning resources for personal benefit.

Defensive tactic. Investors, worried about this problem, often insist on total control over bank accounts and insist on active participation in the financial management of the concern. But if there is reason to worry about it, why invest?

Corporate meeting maneuvers

Most shareholder meetings are routine. While the bylaws provide that proper notice must be given and the agenda provided, a clever management is often able to place on the agenda seemingly innocuous items whose end result can be devastating to the minority stockholders' position. Moreover, they often hold such corporate meetings at inconvenient times and places. If management knows its problem stockholders live in Los Angeles, it may decide to hold the corporate meeting in Burlington, Vermont. While the corporation may pay the transportation costs for the management, the minority stockholders are left to pay their own way. If they happen to show up at a potentially explosive meeting, the matter is passed by until the next meeting. Management will keep it up until the minority stockholders finally slip up or wear out. It is simply not feasible for most minority stockholders to attend the corporate meetings called by a hostile management.

Defensive tactic. Key to defending against such tactics is to state in the bylaws that all such meetings be at corporate headquarters at reasonable times. Simply remove the freedom of management to dictate location and timing of such meetings. Most corporate bylaws allow management to name the time and place of all meetings.

Buy-sell agreements

Throughout this discussion on protective tactics, there was mention of the existence of buy-sell agreements as one way of protecting the minority stockholders' position. It may seem peculiar that these same buy-sell agreements can be one of the majority stockholder's major tools for cheating the minority stockholder out of his or her just due. It works quite simply by the stockholders agreeing to a seemingly fair pricing arrangement in the beginning. The minority stockholder is bought out later, after the firm has prospered, for a price lower than the true worth of the stock.

Defensive tactic. Make sure that the buy-sell agreement is reviewed annually by the shareholders who should set the price for the shares. This business-valuation figure should reflect the true worth of the business.

S corporation

Situations in an S corporation deserve special treatment, for they can pose squeeze-play problems for both the majority and the minority stockholders. Recall that the whole idea underlying the selection of the option to treat the corporation as a partnership for purposes of federal income taxation was to avoid paying a corporate income tax and to pass on directly to the owners whatever tax credits have been earned, as well as operating losses. Two key aspects of the law pose problems for the stockholders. First, while they must pay tax personally on whatever income is declared by the corporation, they do not necessarily receive any cash with which to pay the tax. A bad cash flow problem can be created. Minority stockholders can be placed under pressure by the majority, who are able to pay the taxes with money borrowed from the company.

Second, all stockholders must agree in writing to the S corporation treatment and can void their selection each year or have it rendered null and void by committing any one of several acts, such as selling their shares to a corporation (one possibly owned by themselves). The minority stockholder can block the majority by threatening to negate the S election. That might cause some tax problems for the majority stockholders. Consequently, S corporations pose some real problems among stockholders who are not getting along well.

Defensive tactic. Minority stockholders should execute a written document that stipulates that the corporation will pay their tax burden on the S corporation's distribution of profits. Also, all stockholders should have a written agreement stipulating that the S corporation cannot be null and void unless there is approval by 100 percent of the stockholders.

Partnerships

Since a partnership is a relationship by consent, it can be dissolved at any time by any of the partners simply declaring it so and asking for an accounting and settling up of accounts. A financially strong partner can get rid of unwanted weaker ones at any time by settling up accounts according to the articles of partnership and moving them out.

But the partner must be paid off. The courts are willing to examine the internal affairs of a partnership closely. If substantial money is involved, the squeezer-partner may use other, more devious tactics. It has previously been shown that the corporate form of organization is readily amenable to all sorts of squeeze plays. Therefore, the squeezer often suggests to his or her partners that their enterprise should be incorporated. A rational case can usually be built for doing so. Once incorporated, the squeeze out begins. Of course, the squeezer has seen to it that the corporate setting and bylaws are such that the squeeze out poses few problems.

Defensive tactic. If partners do incorporate the partnership, avoid becoming a minority stockholder by owning 50 percent or more of the stock.

Avoiding Squeeze Outs

For each squeeze-out technique, appropriate defensive tactics were suggested. Some additional defensive tactics are available to minority stockholders for protecting their interests: refuse minority positions, control bylaw provisions, participate in management, and specify buy-sell agreements.

Refuse minority positions

At the top of the list must be one's refusal to be a minority stockholder. Some people have a policy when investing in small, closely held companies to play the game only with 50 percent ownership or more.

Defensive Tactics
Refuse minority positions
Control bylaw provisions
Participate in management
Specify buy-sell agreements

Many venture capitalists also demand majority control for all the reasons that should by now be apparent. Why would an entrepreneur give up control of a venture for money? The answer is simple. It is the only option left. The person has tried to get money on other terms everywhere. It is that or nothing.

However, in most of such cases, the factor that sells the deal is the provision of buy-sell clauses by which the entrepreneur can get rid of the financier by paying him or her off. Naturally, the price is high, but that is why the financier put in the money to begin with.

Always remember that the financier may be at the mercy of the entrepreneur who is operating the company and has the technical expertise and contacts that underlie the firm's success. Most venture capitalists are not prepared or inclined to manage the enterprise. They just want profits.

Control bylaw provisions

Minority stockholders can protect themselves by controlling the following key factors in the bylaws:

- Location of meetings
- Notice and agenda of meetings with provision that any deviation must be by unanimous consent
- Effective veto power over such matters as mergers, sale of corporate assets, payment of salaries and expenses, reorganization of the company, the state of incorporation, the issuance of securities, and the retention of earnings

Participate in management

As a minority stockholder, one should not be an outsider. Try to get control of the money. It does not take much time to write checks. As a condition of investment, the stockholder should make a place for him or herself on the management team. If removed, he or she must be paid off by a previously agreed upon formula. The condition should avoid fixed prices that, if the company is quite prosperous, can invite a squeeze out in which the others can buy the stockholder out at a fraction of the worth of his or her holdings.

The minority stockholder should consider an employment contract to assure him or herself access to the corporate coffers (to avoid being frozen out of the payoffs). As a condition for making a minority investment, the stockholder is to be given a contract that provides for employment at a stipulated salary doing stipulated things. Settlement conditions should be spelled out in the event employment is terminated. If the stockholder really does not want to work daily in the company, he or she might become a well-paid director.

Such long-term employment contracts should provide for flexible compensation—based on some index of what others in the corporation are being paid. It is not easy to draw up such a contract; legal assistance is needed.

Specify buy-sell agreements

Minority stockholders must realize that if a majority of the stockholders are dedicated to getting rid of them, the majority will do so one way or the other, no matter how well the minority stockholders have tried to protect themselves. Thus, what the minority stockholders want to do is make certain they get money for their position, to let the buy-sell agreement be the only way the majority can remove them.

Conclusion

The minority stockholder is in a difficult position in many cases. But the controlling majority needs to pay careful attention to legal matters lest it provide opportunistic minority stockholders a chance to gain the advantage.

Governmental Regulations

Learning Objectives

In this chapter, students will learn

- What assistance the federal, state, and local governments can provide for the entrepreneur.
- What an entrepreneur must do to gain governmental approval to begin business.

The very existence of new enterprises depends upon political license and forbearance. Simply put, people can't go into business unless the government allows them to do so. In the United States, there are several governments to satisfy: the federal, the state, the local, as well as any of their agencies. Entrepreneurs must clear the hurdles governments have created before beginning operations. Most of these requirements were created for the purpose of putting people on the various tax rolls—income, sales, Social Security, workers' compensation, unemployment, personal property (inventory). Other requirements were established to prevent a person from doing some things that some people don't want done.

While the federal regulations are the same for everyone in the United States, each state and locality poses a different problem. For example, while most states have a sales tax, each state's method for handling the tax differs. Thus, an entrepreneur will have to contact local authorities for precise information about requirements. Fortunately, they are eager to provide information. Often it is as simple as looking in the telephone book for the state taxing agency. The local chamber of commerce or Small Business Administration will likely have the information. Often such agencies publish a kit containing the needed information. Also books are published locally in most large cities that outline what must be done to start a business in the area.

For the purposes of this discussion, we will use California laws, a state that many entrepreneurs consider hostile.

The selection of the state and city in which to locate a business is not a minor matter. Where an entrepreneur chooses to do business greatly affects the cost of operations, markets, and profits. Granted, circumstances are often beyond control and force a person to do business in a high-cost state. Still, the adept entrepreneur is keenly aware of the added costs that are borne by doing so.

Governmental Concerns

Businesses not only are regulated by governmental entities—federal, state, and local—but they also can obtain some assistance from governmental agencies.

Federal government

Entrepreneurs who own 100 percent of their businesses do not realize that they still have partners—the federal, state, and local governments.

Unless an enterprise plans to make or sell alcohol, firearms, explosives, pharmaceutical drugs, nuclear devices, or other controlled substances, its main concern is with the Internal Revenue Service. The IRS wants to know where a business is and what the business does so that it will know where to look at tax time.

To that end, a business owner must file form SS-4 with the IRS. These forms can be obtained from any IRS office or from an accountant. Upon filing the form, the owner will receive an "employer's kit" that tells all about the taxes that must be paid, when to pay them, where to pay them, and how to compute the amounts due. Forms and helpful information are also available at the IRS web site (www.irs.gov).

The Employer's ID (EID) number (or social security number for a sole proprietor) will be needed on all future communications with all governmental agencies. It will also be needed to open bank and brokerage accounts and in dealing with others who must report the business's actions to any governmental agency. From this point forward, the government knows the venture by its EID number, not by name. The IRS forms also cover FICA (Social Security) contributions.

Assistance

Many nations can be aggressive if they believe that a business will hire a significant number of people. The governments of Northern Ireland and the Irish Free State are particularly noted for providing financial and other incentives for locating plants in their countries. Ventures that entail a high labor content may find such arrangements to their benefit. They are worth examining with care. For example, entrepreneurs considering a move to another country should ask if sharing rights to their intellectual property is a pre-condition.

So many isolated governmental grant programs are aimed at helping various types of businesses that entire books are written on them. The Small Business Administration has booklets describing most of these programs.

State governments

Most states have a sales tax. A business must register with the appropriate state agencies that administer that tax. If business is conducted in several states, the venture may have to be registered in all of them. A quick check in the telephone book will disclose the nearest office. The higher the sales estimate, the more front money the state is likely to demand as bond for the business's sales tax payments. And that bond money is lost for the life of the enterprise.

Sometimes, if the amount of projected sales tax is not large and the entrepreneur owns property in the state, the state will not demand money up front. But if it does, there are usually two choices: put the demanded amount into an escrowed bank account for the benefit of the state, or give the state a check. Naturally, entrepreneurs should choose the bank account, as they can collect some interest there. When applying for a state sales tax number without putting up a deposit, an entrepreneur should be conservative in estimating expected sales. Remember, no one really can forecast the future, and there are no penalties for poor forecasting skills.

Entrepreneurs might wonder why they should pay attention to the sales taxes so early in starting ventures rather than waiting until later. The reason is that the number is needed when buying goods for resale without paying sales tax on them. Generally, once a business has a sales tax number, it does not have to pay tax on the things it buys for the purpose of reselling. The business must still pay sales tax on the things it buys to use, such as plant equipment, office supplies, and plant-maintenance supplies.

Naturally, a few games are frowned upon by the authorities. Some business people buy personal items they consume under the guise of buying them for resale; one druggist placed some antiques for sale in his store as a cover not only for making his hobby of antique collecting deductible for income tax purposes but also to avoid paying sales taxes on his purchases. If a venture were buying jewels for investment, it generally would have to pay sales taxes on them unless it purchased them in a state without sales tax or purchased them out-of-state and had them shipped to the founder's home. In such a case, technically, the venture would in most instances owe the state a use tax on such purchases (which it is supposed to report and pay). On large retail sales, such as automobiles, the licensing authorities collect the sales taxes due just to defeat out-of-state buying for tax-avoidance purposes.

Indeed, the California authorities are keenly interested in all cars driving in California with Oregon plates, because more than a few purchasers of expensive cars buy and license them in Oregon to avoid the California sales tax. On a $50,000 car, the tax would be about $4,000, which pays for some effort to arrange such a setup. Should the driver of an Oregon-licensed car be stopped and the owner found to reside in California, consequences of attempting to avoid sales taxes become expensive and time consuming.

This matter is brought up because the thought occurs to many entrepreneurs that they should buy their expensive equipment out of state to avoid sales taxes. Be advised, there are problems in doing so. Of course, what is equipment to one company is inventory to another; an equipment distributor that buys equipment to resell pays no sales tax on it. Bear in mind that the burden of proof that a sale is tax exempt generally is placed upon the seller. To protect themselves, sellers require the buyers to sign a statement declaring that they are buying the goods to resell and require the buyers to provide their sales tax numbers, which incidentally are coded to provide the tax examiner with an idea as to what kind of business the ventures are in. If an entrepreneur is in the restaurant business and has bought a party dress from a wholesaler in the garment district, by giving her sales tax number to avoid the sales tax, she might need an explanation if ever questioned about the transaction.

To aid them in their enforcement, the tax people enlist the support of the financial community. It is important to understand that unpaid taxes are a continual lien against the property, which precedes all other claims against that property.

Suppose a person buys a boat from a private party for $100,000; $7,500 sales tax would be owed on the deal. Since no retail outlet was involved in the deal, the buyer might be tempted to allow the state to remain ignorant of the purchase. But if the buyer borrowed money from a bank with which to buy the boat, the bank's lending officer will make certain that the sales tax is paid. After all, the bank loaned the money that was being spent, and the bank does not want the state to have a future lien against the boat. The loan officer wants a clear, unencumbered title against which to file a mortgage. Thus, financial institutions help administer tax collections.

In most states, registering with the sales tax people also alerts whatever agency administers the labor laws. The labor agency sends the founder information on the required workers' compensation insurance. Workers' compensation is not inexpensive; it can run up to 3 percent (sometimes more) of the payroll, depending upon the nature of the work the people do.

Other governmental hurdles must be cleared, depending upon what other actions an entrepreneur decides to take. If the goal is to incorporate, then another governmental system must be satisfied. That topic is covered separately in the chapter on legal forms of organization.

States may regulate franchises. California law requires registering all franchise operations with the state corporation commission.

State assistance

Many states are now so eager to develop new business (more payrolls and more taxes) that they provide a great deal of assistance to firms that want to locate there. Not only will they provide much information and do considerable lead blocking for a venture, but often they offer tangible financial incentives for locating in those states. Most states have so-called industrial development commissions that new businesses can contact. These development commissions can be of great assistance if they believe that anything of substance will likely come of the activity.

Many states have established various agencies or offices to assist the aspiring entrepreneur. Some have one-stop shops where the entrepreneur can obtain *How To* booklets, forms, and guidance. Many states have websites designed to assist in starting a business with downloadable forms, step by step guides and links to the appropriate governmental offices and agencies. Browsing the Internet using "business assistance centers", "starting a business" or similar key words should locate the proper site.

Fictitious names

If an entrepreneur does business under any name other than his or her own or that of his or her corporation, a statement may need to be filed with the designated authorities in the state or county. Each state has slightly different arrangements for this requirement. In California, entrepreneurs file with the county clerk, who then provides the legal forms to take to a bank and the newspapers for publishing the DBA (doing business as) name. The newspapers' rates vary, depending on circulation. Most states do not require such publication and only require filing the legal form.

Trademarks

While trademarks are registered with the federal government, many states also maintain trademark registries for firms doing business within the state. An entrepreneur should be sure to clear any proposed trademarks and trade names with the state. If they are already owned by another person, there is likely to be a serious problem rather soon. Trademark conflicts are common. Obtaining clear-cut rights to use the name of choice can be difficult. Generally federal registration should be obtained as well.

Local governments

Local governments regulate licenses and zoning. Licenses are largely creations of the cities. A call to the local city hall is frequently necessary to identify local requirements. Usually, they cost nominal amounts, but not always. They can become burdensome in areas such as Los Angeles, where a company might do business in 20 different cities and legally have to be licensed in each one of them. In Southern California cities, some people will not do business because of the local regulations. Some of this local complexity is caused by the local businesses who want to keep out potential competition.

Typically, when applying for a local license, the new business is immediately brought to the attention of the fire and zoning authorities. The fire department wants to know all about the business: Is it doing anything that poses the department potential problems? Does the place of business meet the fire codes? These officials can cause a business owner much grief if the business is not in compliance.

A new plant that was built completely to the local building-code specifications was forced to cut a large hole in the middle of its floor for another stairway from the basement, even though the basement was not used for anything. The stairway to nothing in the middle of the plant area added a significant expense of $9,500.

As a general principle, it does not pay to fight with the zoning authorities. The authorities don't lose many fights, and the cost of the fray comes right up front in cash flow. Entrepreneurs who see real zoning problems and no apparent solution should see if third parties have a vested interest in having the enterprise locate there. People who may help change the laws include landlords, people selling the property, bankers, and local officials that have some interest in the venture.

An example: For a long time, by every means at their disposal, public officials in one large city, discouraged businesses from entering town. So much so that one large manufacturer fled the area to open up in a nearby town, thus shifting considerable employment opportunity with it, much to the consternation of some local people. There are numerous examples of small entrepreneurs who were discouraged by zoning regulations. Yet, when IBM wanted to come to the area to build a huge complex, local officials could not do enough. When a small electronics manufacturer wanted to move into town, it had no problem at all with local people because the person who wanted to sell it the land and build its plant was well-situated politically. The term of the deal was that the seller had to provide all clearances, or the deal was off.

The moral is rather simple. When trying to start a business in an area that is difficult, an entrepreneur must ally him or herself with local political clout to clear the way. A lead blocker is needed. Often it is an attorney who has the right political connections. Sometimes it is the local banker. The entrepreneur must do some homework to discover the power structure of the area, then ally with it.

In Texas, businesses must obtain an occupancy permit to do business at a certain site. After that permit is filed, the fire, zoning, and local tax people are alerted to their operations. The officials want to know all sorts of things about the inventory businesses will be keeping and what they will be doing. Most states tax inventory.

Perhaps it is easy to understand why some entrepreneurs choose to operate from their basements and garages without official sanction from local governments. This is particularly prevalent among people who live in areas in which the zoning authorities stringently prohibit all business activity.

Other entrepreneurs avoid such problems by locating in rural areas or small towns without excessive requirements.

Checklist for Governmental Clearances

The following list provides a summary of what an entrepreneur may have to do to gain governmental approval to begin business. Several states have instituted one-stop registration centers to streamline the process.

❑ Go to the IRS for Form SS-4, which will assign an Employer's Identification Number.

❑ Go to the state sales tax authority for a sales tax license and number.

❑ Get appropriate licenses from local, state, and federal agencies. Usually a local license is needed for doing any business.

❑ Obtain the proper zoning clearances. Make sure this type of business can be operated in the selected location. Some local governments require occupancy permits before any business premises can be occupied.

❑ Register trade names with the state or federal government.

❑ File a Fictitious Name Statement with local authorities if business will be conducted under a name other than the entrepreneur's or the actual name of the corporation.

❑ Food and drug businesses require special permits. Discuss requirements with people in the industry and the FDA.

❑ Toxic-waste-generating businesses require special permits.

Conclusion

Entrepreneurs should be mindful that states and local governments have different regulations and requirements for starting and operating new ventures. It is important to check with each state and locality in which one plans to conduct business. Numerous sources provide information about such requirements, such as Small Business Administration's local or regional office, state offices of regulatory reform, chambers of commerce, and so on. Most states also have extensive information on web sites to help entrepreneurs.

Market Research for New Ventures

Learning Objectives

In this chapter, students will learn how to

- Identify sources of information needed to research the industry of a venture and determine what the collected information means.
- Gather information on the competition.

Central to the skills necessary to develop, write, and implement feasibility and business plans is an understanding of the market research necessary to complete the plan's market section. In researching the market, entrepreneurs are trying to determine if anyone will purchase their products. Likewise, they consider whether their products meet customer needs. Is there a difference between their products and those of the competition? How many and what kinds of competitors are there? How can entrepreneurs differentiate their products? How large is the market?

To thoroughly research their markets, entrepreneurs must uncover numerous sources of market information. These include libraries, trade associations, government reports, and university bureaus of business research. Mountains of data are available from the Census Bureau, Department of Commerce, the Small Business Administration (SBA), Standard & Poor, Moody, and the Internet.

One resource is EntreWorld, the web site of the Kauffman Foundation (discussed on p. 277), which lists current information of all types for entrepreneurs. Another resource is *The Business Mentor* CD-ROM; click on the Resource Center in the Mentor's Office.

It is important for all entrepreneurs to understand and know how to use all of the marketing resources and studies available. An excellent resource for locating good marketing information is *Find It Fast* by Robert I. Berkman 2000, published by Harper & Row. This paperback book explains how to uncover expert information on any subject. The more entrepreneurs know about industry trends, market statistics, customer needs, and competition, the greater their chances of launching successful ventures and continually adding innovation to their business concepts.

Market Research Tools

Entrepreneurs usually have limited funds available to operate their ventures and equally limited funds to hire personnel devoted to market research. Most entrepreneurs do not have the time to carefully research market possibilities and customer needs. As a result, it's important to be creative when identifying sources of information, choosing target markets for research, and determining what the collected information really means. Limited resources also mean that gathered information must be used for multiple purposes. For example, a market survey that indicates demand for a particular product or service needs to be compared in different market segments and in different geographical locations with the actual use of that product or service.

Getting Started

The entrepreneur usually has access to secondary research, which is prior research conducted by others. Reviewing such research may provide a wealth of information applicable to his or her needs. The following information sources can be used to prepare the market sections of feasibility or business plans.

Local sources

Secondary Research
Local sources
Trade associations
Government reports
Demographic information
Computer and Internet
    searches

Local sources of market information include the local library, university research centers, and local chambers of commerce. The first step is to go to the library, talk to the business-reference librarian, and ask about abstracting services, specialized bibliographies, *Reader's Guide to Periodicals*, technical-digest services, and so on. General business journals such as *Business Week, Fast Company, Forbes, Money, Fortune, Inc., The Wall Street Journal,* and others provide good sources for market research. *Entrepreneur, Success, Home Office Computing,* and *Nation's Business* are some other good entrepreneurially focused publications. Most periodicals have web sites searchable by keyword. Articles in these publications report on products, services, companies, competitors, and proposed products. Also, the U.S. Patent and Trademark Office has designated libraries around the country to conduct patent searches.

Check the shelves for the *Small Business Sourcebook*, edited by Carol A. Schwartz and published annually by Gale Research. It is an excellent guide for sorting through the many business references and data available. For example, it profiles 224 types of business resources for everything from accounting services to beauty shops.

Working with the business librarian, an entrepreneur can obtain financial information and statements from competitors in Dun & Bradstreet corporate reports and the Standard & Poor's Profiles.

If this form of research seems overwhelming and time consuming, one might consider prepay search firms that will do the legwork. Or graduate students or library research assistants can be hired to obtain the information needed from these sources. If the local library is small, perhaps information can be found at a university or larger public library. The local newspapers may also offer research-information services on a variety of topics that have been printed in their papers.

Most colleges and universities have research centers that gather a wealth of information for dissemination. Some of these research centers have venture divisions that assist aspiring entrepreneurs and business owners in reviewing the technical feasibility of an idea or new business. If the college has a Library and Information Science program, the students have access to research tools and databases not commonly available to the public.

Many local chambers of commerce either provide already collected market research information or could refer people to some local sources that might have information about their specific markets, including sales data. Some provide more detailed assistance and information to their members.

Trade associations

Almost every industry has a trade association that publishes a journal that represents one of the best sources of market statistics, demographic information, and financial data for its market. Trade associations furnish industry guidelines that can assist entrepreneurs in tracking their businesses.

The trade associations provide information on gross industry sales, which are broken down further into major product categories. Much of their information is reported in percentages, which is even more helpful in comparing one business's performance to that of similar businesses. These percentages are broken down by size of business, sales volume, and geographic area. For example, they can tell the average inventory turnover for a particular type of business, typical gross and net margins for comparable ventures, and average sales and marketing expenditures.

In contacting the trade associations relevant to a business, the key is to find the appropriate association for that business. Most libraries have available the *Encyclopedia of Associations* (published annually in three volumes).

By writing or calling the identified trade associations, one can find out the type of data they publish and whether there will be a charge. Some associations do charge, while others will send free information. If entrepreneurs can befriend someone on the staff, they may be able to obtain meaningful industry information that the association has not published.

Trade associations are membership-based and they usually get very excited about new businesses joining their industries. They will try hard to convince people to join their associations so they can collect membership dues, which pay for their overhead and operating costs.

Customarily, joining the appropriate trade association is money well spent. It has membership lists of similar businesses and it publishes trade journals that contain excellent information on current trends, market surveys, and forecasts in its particular industry. Such trade journals are a good source for obtaining free publicity for a business. Editors write feature stories about entrepreneurs, new products and services, and other human interest stories.

Entrepreneurs should try to get to know the trade magazine editors who might write about their ventures and who can provide internal information about the industry. Advertisements in trade journals provide an excellent source of information about competitors and their products. It is a good idea to go to the library and review the *Gale Directory of Publications and Broadcast Media.*

The entrepreneur cannot be creative in a vacuum. Understanding the industry is the knowledge that releases creativity.

Trade associations conduct national and regional meetings, where it is possible to obtain other types of industry statistics. One can identify major competitors, discover leaders in the industry, meet suppliers and distributors, and learn about the future direction of the industry, as well as spot new trends and preview the newest products and services.

Attendees of such meetings can talk to experts in their field. Attending some technical sessions will reveal information about future products and new technology. All this information can be obtained for the price of a ticket to the annual meeting. In conjunction with their annual meetings, many organizations hold trade shows which can provide additional market research information.

Government reports

The U.S. government offers tons of data in print and online which can be used in researching a market either free or for a small fee. All governmental publications are summarized in the *Statistical Abstract of the United States* (2003), which provides basic information about income levels, employment figures, industry outputs, and so on. It is available through almost every library.

The U.S. Government Printing Office (GPO) is the largest publisher in the world. Tens of thousands of books, pamphlets, and magazines are published annually. Governmental organizations can be looked up with Yahoo, Lycos, Excite, Alta Vista, or other search engines on the Internet. Also, ask for a listing of GPO bookstores, which are located in most major cities. They carry the most popular of the government's published materials.

Information prepared specifically for entrepreneurial ventures is available from the SBA. The local Manufacturing Extension Partnership Center (start at www.mep.nist.gov to locate the local Center or call (800) 637-4634) can assess a manufacturing business' marketing needs, and then help develop a marketing strategy to meet those needs. The SBA (www.SBA.gov) also has hundreds of publications containing marketing information that may be of help. These publications are free or available for a small charge. The Small Business Development Center (SBDC) in one's area might also be able to assist with collecting needed marketing information. Usually its assistance is free of charge, and most have business libraries.

The U.S. Department of Commerce (USDC) covers all 50 states and has 47 offices throughout the country. It has a vast amount of data at its disposal, both published and unpublished. Typically, it can provide information by industry, size, and geographic location. The USDC can be contacted directly and staff members asked for assistance in collecting needed information. They may charge for preparing this data or do it for free, depending on the amount and complexity of one's needs.

A call can be directed to the appropriate agency if the caller specifies local, domestic, or international data. Also, every state has a commerce department that provides similar information for its area, including lists of businesses categorized by industry, size, and geographic location.

Demographic information

Entrepreneurs frequently need specific information about their target markets within a specific geographic area. First, they need to find out how many people are living in their market areas. Next, they need to determine how much money people are spending on their products. It is also important to find out how much of that money is being spent in the area and how much is being spent in surrounding locations.

Demographic information can be collected by visiting the local library, obtaining the latest U.S. Census population data, or visiting the local chamber of commerce web site. One can determine the number of people in a market area, age range, household income, or other demographic information. This information may need to be adjusted to project any changes that have occurred since the data was collected. Another source is *State and County Business Patterns*, which lists businesses' sales, annual payroll, number of employees, and other useful data.

Another helpful publication to consult is the *Sales & Marketing Management* magazine published by VNU Business Publications, New York. This magazine publishes an *Annual Survey of Buying Power*, which contains useful information about retail sales and population statistics by metropolitan area. Simmons Market Research Bureau (SMRB) and Mediamark Research Inc. (MRI) also list product categories and demographic characteristics for varying levels of consumption. Brand consumption within a product category is also reported in many cases. These sources do not describe specific markets and do not report on service industries. They should be used as inputs in the data-collection process.

Computer and Internet searches

Internet. For the entrepreneur, the Internet is a powerful information tool. There is no greater source of timely information than the Internet. Tens of thousands of pages of information are being added to the digital-information archives *every day*. Through the Internet, one can electronically access major publications, periodicals, company home pages, information clearinghouses, and interactive discussion groups. One can browse or order items from thousands of consumer and industrial product catalogs, which include pictures, technical specifications, and drawings.

The EntreWorld web site of the Kauffman Foundation (www.entreworld.org) is a good place to start. Designed specifically to serve the needs of entrepreneurs, it pulls together the best information from other web sites and organizes it according to a business plan format. Whether entrepreneurs are looking for market research data, or just want to read what other entrepreneurs write, or talk to others, they will have access to one of the most powerful tools on the Web.

Databases. Many different databases are available online for rapid browsing and searching on a computer, both free and fee based. These databases come from a variety of sources, including associations, government agencies, private publishers, and other organizations. These databases are accessed by subscription to an online database vendor, who sells access to databases over the Internet. Some databases are available in the library which may charge a small fee to cover their own out-of-pocket expenses.

Another good database to check is the Dow Jones News/Retrieval Service, which specializes in economic and business information. Also, the Lexis/Nexis database and the Dialog information service allow access to legal and business information. Look for these and other databases at local municipal and college libraries. Another source of business information is the Compuserve online service, which originated as a business-oriented service, and has business database and professional forums, as well. Other online services, such as AOL, are geared more toward personal use. The Internet itself also has a wealth of information online, accessible through search engines and search engine collections.

Some organizations, especially government agencies, make databases available either very inexpensively or free. For example, for a nominal fee, the Department of Commerce's Office of Business Analysis and Economic Affairs offers the *Economic Bulletin Board* (www.ita.doc.gov/uscs/uscsebb.html), which gives the latest releases from the Bureau of Economic Analysis, the Bureau of Labor Statistics, and other federal agencies. It can be contacted at (800) USA-TRAD. More information on free government databases can be found in the *Federal Database Finder*, published by Information USA, or its web site.

The world of cyberspace is changing constantly, and the best way to keep on top of it is through the Internet itself. Search engines can be used to search the Internet. In addition, there are several Internet Yellow Pages collections of site addresses published annually. While the addresses may change, the organization names and other phrases from site descriptions can be used as keywords for an Internet search.

Analysis of Competition

Primary Research
Analysis of competition
Customer surveys
Focus groups

To find competitors, entrepreneurs can look in such sources as the *Yellow Pages* and *Thomas Register* and count the number of competitors listed. Information about competitors may also be available through the local chamber of commerce, especially if it has a research division.

Learning as much as possible about one's competition is an excellent entrepreneurial strategy. It is recommended that this data be obtained while the entrepreneur prepares a feasibility plan or business plan.

One can also conduct primary research by visiting competing stores. Some entrepreneurs will work for their competition before starting a competing new business. They try to learn all the ins and outs of the business ahead of time.

One of the best strategies to learn more about the competition is to locate a competitor at a distance. Often, direct competitors will not divulge much information about their operations. One will be more likely to obtain significant industry and competitive information from a competitor outside the immediate geographic area. Preferably, one should find several competitors in other states that operate corresponding businesses in a similar demographic area.

The industry trade association can be contacted to learn about industry leaders with comparable businesses in another part of the country. Those entrepreneurs can be called or visited. Because they will not view one as a direct competitor, trade association members may share important information.

Another strategy to follow is to contact competitors' customers and determine what they like about the business and what they do not like. Some entrepreneurs will interview their competitors' customers by conducting a telephone survey or attending a meeting where they will be present.

Other entrepreneurs will try to contact their competitors' employees, asking questions about the services offered, pricing discounts, areas of improvement, and so on. Some entrepreneurs hire their competitors' employees.

Suppliers are another source of information about competition. They may be willing to share inside industry information. Ask the banker, accountant, and attorney whether they have any information about competition or the industry.

Entrepreneurs must become detectives to learn as much as possible about their competition. They will be one step ahead if they collect and analyze information about their competition and the industry and continue accumulating it. Projecting market trends and determining competitors' strengths and weaknesses is an ongoing activity that can provide a competitive edge in the marketplace.

Always keep an eye out for the possibility that competitors will move into your target markets.

Customer surveys

In order to operate a venture successfully, the founder must identify actual and potential customers. A good way is to brainstorm and develop a list of these customers by answering the following questions:

- Who are the potential customers?
- Given scarce resources, what are the target markets with the highest rate of return for the product?
- Why would potential customers use these products?
- What products does the market really want?
- What distinguishes my product from those of the competition?
- Where would my customers purchase the product?

Another is to ask potential customers questions and listen carefully to their answers. Researching customer needs is often the missing ingredient in marketing efforts among new business owners. Customers have strong views, unmet needs, definite preferences, and good ideas, but they are seldom asked.

A common, inexpensive, and effective way to research customers is to use customer surveys. Customer surveys involve asking customers about a product either in person, by telephone, or by questionnaire. One can research customers directly and learn about their needs, problems, and opinions regarding a proposed product. This form of market research is up to date and helpful in preparing a business plan and convincing others that there is a market for a product. Also, it can result in future sales.

The first step is to select key questions and then decide whether the best method to query customers is by telephone, face to face, or through the mail. For example, if the product is a food product that is purchased in grocery stores, the customers for that product would probably be intercepted at the grocery store. It is important not to use leading questions or introduce bias.

Minimize leading or assuming questions that will result in skewed answers.

After collecting enough data, it is time to summarize and evaluate the information that has been gathered. Are there similar responses that indicate a trend in responses? Many times, survey information may be suspect because the respondents are not committing to purchase the product; rather, they are just giving their opinion. Second, since most surveys are very brief, it is not possible to collect in-depth information.

Focus groups

Focus-group sessions can provide more customer insight and identify hidden needs of future customers. All entrepreneurs can benefit from using this marketing technique with potential customers, especially to identify niche markets and forecast potential market share. Focus-group interviews are an easy research method to gain fresh perspectives on customer views and ideas, as well as obtain new ideas to improve market position and penetration methods.

Conducting focus groups is a market research technique traditionally used by industrial and consumer product firms. This technique is growing quickly in popularity and is widely accepted because it produces useful information at a reasonable cost.

In its more sophisticated version, marketing experts will use one-way mirrors, closed-circuit videotaping, and exhaustive analyses of the recorded sessions. Most entrepreneurs are using simpler focus-group interviews, which still provide a richness of data for entrepreneurs on a limited budget. Essentially, it is a get-together with about eight to 12 people who are typical of potential customers and who are unfamiliar with one other.

Most people enjoy participating in focus-group sessions and endeavor to give useful feedback. In fact, entrepreneurs will probably find that potential customers appreciate being asked their views. They feel important that they have been chosen and that some effort is made to listen to them. In addition, they will realize that the entrepreneur is trying to design a good product and launch a new venture. It is recommended that members be paid an honorarium or be treated to breakfast, lunch, or a gift for participating.

The moderator plays an important role in the focus group, leading the focus group through in-depth and freewheeling discussions. Consider using a skilled outside moderator to prevent bias. However, good moderators are not inexpensive.

A typical focus group takes about one-and-a-half to two hours, scheduled at a time convenient to the people involved. The atmosphere should be relaxed to ensure an informal discussion of participants' opinions and feelings. Some light refreshments should be served at the beginning of the discussion. The discussion format and interview questions should be carefully prepared ahead of time. Respondents should be prescreened to ensure quality. The moderator asks broad questions at the beginning and then focuses the group's discussion on the specific information the entrepreneur wants to obtain. Moderators skillfully probe the group, stressing the importance of sharing different points of view and emphasizing that there are no right or wrong answers.

Moderators can take notes during the discussion or have the discussion taped. Self-administered surveys can be used to collect additional information. Findings are then analyzed to interpret feedback from participants and relate it to a business.

Focus-group moderators can be located under "marketing consultants" or "market research" in the *Yellow Pages*, or through the marketing department at a local university. The local chamber of commerce may have recommendations. Not only can focus groups be an excellent source of generating new ideas on how to increase sales, they can also help initially screen new ideas and concepts. Entrepreneurs should get in the habit of continually researching customers' needs and opinions. They can gain a renewed sense of clarity and purpose that will guide them through the ever-changing marketplace and intense competition. If a moderator cannot be located, the entrepreneur can run the focus groups, but the drawback of doing this is the difficulty of remaining objective.

Focus groups are rapidly becoming a major entrepreneurial marketing tool for gaining insight into customers' thoughts and feelings. They can be a relatively inexpensive way to maintain quality in a business.

Conclusion

Entrepreneurs must become detectives to learn as much as possible about their markets and their industries. The legwork done gathering market information will yield great returns in helping them grow their businesses. It will also increase their credibility to reviewers of their business plans.

Entrepreneur's Resource Checklist

Books

Albrecht, Karl. *The Only Thing That Matters: Bringing the Power of the Customer into the Center of Your Business.* Harper Business: 1993.

Anderson, Kristin, and Ron Zemke. *Delivering Knock Your Socks Off Service.* AMACOM: 2002.

Burwell, Helen. *Online Competitive Intelligence: Increase Your Profits Using Cyber-Intelligence (Online-Ease).* BRB Publications: 2004.

Cohen, William A. *Developing a Winning Marketing Plan.* Wiley: 1987.

Dychtwald, Ken. *Age Power: How the 21st Century Will Be Ruled by the New Old.* Tarcher: 2000.

Encyclopedia of Associations, 41st edition. Gale Research Inc. This reference lists national organizations, including trade, business, and commercial.

Fox, Jeffrey. *How to Become a Marketing Superstar: Unexpected Rules that Ring the Cash Register.* Hyperion: 2003.

Fuld, Leonard M. *The New Competitor Intelligence: The Complete Resource for Finding, Analyzing, and Using Information about Your Competitors.* John Wiley & Sons: 1994.

Gross, T. Scott. *Outrageous: Guilt-Free Selling, Unforgettable Services.* AMACOM: 1998.

Hamper, Robert J. *Strategic Market Planning.* Passport Books: 1991.

Hester, Edward L. *Successful Marketing Research: The Complete Guide to Getting and Using Essential Information About Your Customers and Competitors.* John Wiley & Sons: 1995.

Household Spending Who Spends How Much on What? 2003, 8th edition. (www.newstrategist.com)

Kahaner, Larry. *Competitive Intelligence: How to Gather, Analyze, and Use Information to Move Your Business to the Top.* Touchstone Books: 1998.

Keller, Edward, Jonathan Berry, and Douglas Reeves. *The Influentials: One American in Ten Tells the Other Nine How to Vote, Where to Eat, and What to Buy.* Simon & Schuster: 2004.

Lescher, John F. *Online Market Research: Cost-Effective Searching of the Internet and Online Databases.* Addison-Wesley Publishing Co.: 1995.

Mackay, Harvey, and Kenneth H. Blanchard. *Swim with the Sharks, Without Being Eaten Alive: Outsell, Outmanage, Outmotivate, and Outnegotiate Your Competition.* Ballantine Books: 1996.

National Trade & Professional Associations of the United States, Columbia Books: 2001.

Ross, Marilyn and Tom. *Big Marketing Ideas for Small Service Businesses: How to Successfully Advertize, Publicize and Maximize Your Business or Professional Practice.* Communication Creativity: 1994.

Sourcebook of Zip Code Demographics. CACI: 2002. Variety of demographic and consumer market statistics and information arranged by zip code.

SRDS Direct Marketing List Source (www.srds.com). Variety of targeted marketing lists. Available online by subscription.

SRDS Lifestyle Market Analyst (www.srds.com). Demographic and lifestyle profiles from more than 7.5 million U.S. households; profiles arranged by city, gender, age ranges, etc.

Standard and Poor's Industry Surveys. Multi-volume set covering 52 specialized industry groupings.

Zemke, Ron, and Dick Schaff. *Taking Care of Business: 101 Ways to Keep Your Customers Coming Back (Without Whining, Groveling or Giving Away the Store).* Lakewood Publishing: 1998.

Computer Databases

Business & Industry ASAP

Comfind (www.comfind.com). Worldwide directory of company web sites.

Dow Jones News Retrieval Services

Dun and Bradstreet Million Dollar Directory (www.dnb.com). Information on over 1,300,000 U.S. public and private companies with sales greater than $1 million. Subscription database, publicly available in some libraries.

Regional business journals from across the country (www.bizjournals.bcentral.com)

10k wizard.com. SEC filings (www.10kwizard.com)

Thomson Research

Websense Company Locator (www.websense.com/locator.cfm) Comprehensive directory of company web sites

Internet Resources:

    EntreWorld (www.entreworld.org)

    Google (www.google.com)

    IMRmall (www.imrmall.com)

    Marketresearch.com (marketresearch.com)

    Mindbranch (www.mindbranch.com)

    Northern Light (www.northernlight.com)

    Yahoo (www.yahoo.com)

    Web Crawler (www.webcrawler.com)

Magazines

Advertising Age (www.adage.com)

American Demographics (www.americandemographics.com)

Business Week (www.businessweek.com)

Fortune (www.fortune.com)

Sales & Marketing Management (www.salesandmarketing.com)

Value Investment Survey (www.valueline.com). Financial and investment analysis and advice on companies and industries. Information available online by subscription.

VNU Business Publications (www.vnubusinessmedia.com)

Contacts

Information Industry Association (www.infoindustry.org/index.html), 1625 Massachusetts Ave., N.W., Suite 700, Washington, DC 20036, (202) 986-2080. The association is involved with the creation and distribution of information services.

Mediamark Research, Inc. (www.mediamark.com), (800) 310-3305. This group also lists product categories and demographic characteristics for varying levels of consumption.

Simmons Market Research Bureau (www.smrb.com), (212) 598-5400. The bureau lists product categories and demographic characteristics for varying levels of consumption.

Trade Show Information

There are three major publication sources for trade shows: *Tradeshow Week Data Book*, *Trade Show and Exhibit Schedules*, and *Trade Shows Worldwide*. These publications should be available in the local library.

Trade associations: directory (www.marketingsource.com/associations/)

Trade associations: high technology (www.aea.org)

Trade show associations (www.exhibitions.org.hk/amass.htm)

TSNN.com: resources for the trade show industry, the database has information on more than 15,000 trade shows and conferences (www.tsnn.com)

The Center for Exhibition Industry Research (www.ceir.org), McCormick Place, 2301 South Lake Shore Drive, Suite E1002, Chicago, IL 60616, (312) 808-2347. This organization is the industry's resource center, providing information about the latest industry trends, successful practices, and hot topics of interest. It has a catalog of publications that assist entrepreneurs with exhibiting at trade shows.

U.S. Department of Commerce (www.doc.gov). The department publishes extensive data and demographics on various industries. Bureau of Economic Analysis (www.bea.doc.gov).

Exercise 17a: Market Research and Analysis Challenges

Identify marketing research and analysis challenges specific to your business concept. After gathering information from qualified experts (business school librarian, library and information science majors), develop a useful action plan for the organization.

Market research and analysis challenge	Action plan

Exercise 17b: Research Scavenger Hunt

You will have a set time to hunt for the answers to the following questions or questions designed specifically for your resource location. Your objective is to find the information, answer the questions, and note the source for the information. Return to the designated location at the specified time. Good luck!

Question	Answer	Source
What is the SIC or NAICS code for your business concept?		
Is there a company offering a similar product/ service over the Internet? How much does it sell its product for?		
How many competitive producers are there for your business concept in the city you are currently in or the nearest large city?		
How much would it cost for you to advertise in the local newspaper?		
What is the median household income for the city you are now in or the nearest large city?		
Make a copy of the key business ratios for your business concept using Dun & Bradstreet or Robert Morris Associates Key Business Ratios.		
Identify the trade association for your business concept.		
How many trade magazines are there for your business concept? List two specific trade publications.		

Exercise 17c: Competitor Analysis Matrix for Your Business Concept

Competitor analysis matrix

Product/Service	Price	Production/ quality	Unique features	Distribution system	Marketing/ advertising	Geographic location	Strengths/ weaknesses	Market share
Competitor A								
Competitor B								
Competitor C								
Competitor D								
Competitor E								
Competitor F								

Exercise 17d: Market Analysis—Identifying Potential Competitors: Direct, Indirect, and Future

Direct competitors

Direct competitors are businesses that sell similar products or services in the same target market. Who are yours?

Examples:	Burger King and Wendy's
	Rite Aid and Walgreen's
	Reebok and Nike

Future competition

Entrepreneurs should always look to the future and think about how much time they might have before a competitor competes for their existing customers and locations.

Indirect competitors

Indirect competitors are businesses that sell similar products or services as a sideline to their normal business. Who are yours?

Examples:	Major grocery chains sell cards and flowers, indirectly competing with card shops and florists.

Sometimes customers will create the product or perform the service themselves or decide to eliminate the purchase when times are tough financially. This is a form of indirect competition.

Could this kind of competition apply to your product or service?
❑ Yes ❑ No Explain.

Examples:	Housecleaning services Lawn-care services Businesses that choose to use training videos instead of hiring a training consultant

Exercise 17e: Analyzing Potential Competitors

List potential competitors in each of the three categories: direct, indirect, and future. What are the competitors' advantages and strong points? In what area can you capitalize on the weaknesses?

Direct competitors

Competitor's name	Strengths	Weaknesses

Indirect competition

Competitor's name	Strengths	Weaknesses

Future competition

Competitor's name	Strengths	Weaknesses

Analyzing the Market

Learning Objectives

In this chapter, students will learn how to

- Identify the customers for a venture.
- Determine how customers buy and why they buy.
- Define target markets.
- Recognize marketing traps.
- Understand the competition's marketing strategies.
- Care for customers.

Entrepreneurship is often defined as the development of market opportunities. Chapters 4 and 17 stressed the importance of identifying and researching market opportunities. Many new enterprises are primarily concerned with marketing; they allow others to make the goods. Indeed, marketing is at the very heart of a successful business. Marketing is based on people and their wants and needs—the customers.

All business begins with a customer. Until a company has a customer, it isn't in business. And unless the company gets and keeps enough customers, it will not stay in business for long. Truly, the most valuable asset of any business is its customers, from whom everything flows.

It is often difficult to detect much concern about the customer in many organizations. Who hasn't contacted a business where the clerks seem to avoid serving the trade, preferring instead to do paperwork or talk on the telephone? Yet, top-flight firms instill in their people that there is nothing more important one can do than serve a customer. This is one critical area in which the entrepreneur has a tremendous advantage over larger concerns. The entrepreneurial enterprise can give customers better service than larger firms. In many competitive arenas, such service is a vital factor in getting and keeping customers.

Not only is business captive to the customer's desires, but marketing efforts, in particular, are planned and based upon a careful analysis of consumers and their buying behavior—their buying habits and motives. Thus, market analysis begins by studying the consumer—the customer. If entrepreneurs understand the consumer, they'll go far in business. If they don't know their customers, they'll fail in business. It will pay them well to do a lot of studying and thinking about consumer behavior.

Moreover, what would a potential investor think of an entrepreneur who demonstrated an ignorance of the market and its consumer?

Consumer and Market Analysis

Some minor semantic difficulties often arise in discussing markets and their analysis. On one hand, the market analyst often describes markets in aggregate terms, such as how many people or firms are potential customers or how much sales volume can be sold into each identifiable market. Such information is helpful to the extent that it is based on some hard data and not on wishful thinking.

Unfortunately for many new ventures, such hard data is difficult to obtain. It may not even exist. Who knows how many truly new widgets people will buy? Sometimes only market experience will provide sufficiently accurate information. Market analysts can also describe potential consumers in subjective, descriptive terms. Often demographic and psychographic classifications are used to aid in understanding customers, because the quantitative measurement of markets is a function of the particular venture at hand. Moreover, a market cannot be quantitatively measured until the people or firms in it are identified. Consequently, market identification is an important step.

Identifying Customers

The customer may not be the consumer. In the practical business world, the customer is the person who pays the enterprise for its products. Customers may be far removed from consumers. Indeed, entrepreneurs may have little to do with the people who ultimately use or buy their wares.

Marketing theorists may focus their attention on the ultimate consumer, but entrepreneurs are more concerned with the people they deal with directly: the customer who buys the product or service.

The first task is to identify who will be the most likely customer for the enterprise. While markets for consumer and industrial goods and services are distinctly different, in many respects their analysis is much the same. Thus, discussion of the two will be combined where possible and then the differences will be emphasized.

Fortunate is the firm that will sell to only one type of customer—for it has to do research only on that one buyer. Pity the firm that sells to dozens of different types of customers, each of whom buys a significant portion of the firm's output. It must research all of them.

The Whos of Marketing

Who is the most likely customer for the product or service? There is no single answer, as there are four roles to consider. There four whos in marketing are the user, the decision maker, the buyer, and the influencer.

Each plays a different role in the marketing process. Naturally, there are transactions in which all four roles are played by one person. A snacker sees a candy machine, puts in money, takes out the goods, and eats; this snacker is the user, the decision maker, and the buyer; there is no way to know who the influencer was. Perhaps it was some celebrity who vouched for the product.

In other transactions, many people may be involved in each role. There may be several users, several decision makers, several buyers, and many influencers. In such instances, marketing becomes quite sticky. Any combination of roles and people may be encountered.

Experience indicates that in any one enterprise, one commonly encounters a few clear-cut patterns around which a marketing program can be built. Entrepreneurs must plan on the basis of frequently encountered patterns, not exceptions.

The user

The concept must be designed primarily for the user. Diapers must fit the baby, not the mother. However, the mother's wishes cannot be ignored; she is both the user and the decision maker. The baby does not particularly care whether the diapers are cloth or if they have pink polka dots on them, but the mother does. Disposable diapers were successful not because the baby needed them but because the mother found them convenient to use.

Many products have failed when they did not take into consideration the user's needs and preferences. Steve Jobs, one of the founders of Apple Computer, stressed this point as one of the foundations of the firm's success. He was obsessed with making his computer as user friendly as possible.

Generally, too little attention has been given to this aspect of product design. In the menswear industry, experience proved that the firms that gave attention to how their garments fit their targeted customers stayed around, while those that did not pay attention to fit did not last long. To make a well-fitting garment, the manufacturer has to study closely the dimensions of the intended customer. Old men are built differently than young men and need different products. Automakers are another example. Have they paid much attention to how their cars fit their women customers?

Entrepreneurs should study carefully how users interact with products in order to spot ways they can make the products more convenient. Donald Norman's *The Design of Everyday Things* (Doubleday, 1990) can help sensitize entrepreneurs to the usability aspect of product design. Motion-analysis techniques, for example, can pay large dividends to clothing manufacturers.

Customer Roles
User
Decision maker
Buyer
Influencer

The decision maker

Marketers study the decision maker for the obvious reason that unless the firm can get a favorable buying decision from that person, no sale will be made. Naturally, promotion is aimed at the decision maker. Sales representatives are taught the importance of seeing the right person in the organization, the person who has the power to buy. In many situations, the decision-making power is shared, so several parties must be contacted. Much motivational work is directed at trying to find out why the decision maker behaves in the manner he or she does. Marketing probably spends more effort on the decision maker than on any of the other parties in the transaction.

The buyer

Who will make the actual purchase? Often the decision maker and the buyer are the same person, particularly with consumer goods. Industrial buying is different. Often the decision maker is hidden somewhere in the organization. The actual buying, however, is usually done by a purchasing agent.

Channels of distribution are largely determined by the buyer's desires. Where does the buyer want to go to buy a product? Successful entrepreneurs find out and are there. It is that simple.

The influencer

There are many influencers. The boss may be strongly influenced by what some professional athlete or celebrity says about using the product. Or, perhaps, the next-door neighbor's opinion counts for something. This type of influence is often called word-of-mouth advertising and is one of the most effective forms of influence. Influencers can be used as lead blockers (discussed in Chapter 20) whenever possible. An astute entrepreneur selling smoke detectors would try to get the fire chief to recommend his or her detectors.

Industrial Markets

While the potential buyers of an industrial item are often quite obvious and easily identified, at other times the task of identifying them can be quite puzzling. If a company is selling a new type of power roofing hammer, the potential customers arc roofers and roofing firms. But what if a company has developed a new way to control production processes using optical-recognition equipment and bar codes? What firms are the most likely customers? This is not a question that can be answered offhand. One is likely to answer, "All large manufacturers," but that would be incorrect. Many have no need for the expense. In such situations, the entrepreneur goes fishing by contacting firms that might be potential customers.

Often the entrepreneur allows potential customers to identify themselves. The firm goes to various trade shows patronized by a wide range of likely customers and makes it easy for the potential customers to come to it. Sometimes clever advertising of a product's benefits will bring forth inquiries from firms that recognize their need for those benefits. Much attention is paid to a firm's first buyers. Who are they? When the entrepreneur knows that, then he or she should go see their competitors. Astute entrepreneurs check out who buys from their customers' competitors! Those same firms are probably potential customers.

The Customer Profile

Entrepreneurs should develop a profile of the potential customer or the target market, so that all personnel in the company know who they are trying to serve. This profile usually is a description of the target market based on demographics, psychographics, and user-team characteristic terms.

Demographics

Markets are usually first described in such demographic terms as age, gender, education, occupation, geographic location, nationality, race, income, religion, and other commonly used census classifications. Perhaps some of the demographic classifications are not relevant to one's product; for example, perhaps a customer's occupation is not relevant. However, the consumption of most items is strongly affected by demographic characteristics.

Religion alone can knock out markets; no attempt is made to sell alcoholic beverages in Islamic nations. If an entrepreneur is making a women's apparel product, he or she must know the target customer's age brackets, income, location, and possibly nationality.

Psychographics

While far too little is known about the psychological makeup of customers and there are few tools with which to measure accurately what is suspected, there is still the belief that what people buy is strongly affected by their psychological characteristics. For example, new products are first purchased by people who think of themselves as innovative, open-minded, and adventuresome. Many people are reluctant to try new things; they lack self-confidence or possibly do not like to project themselves to others as being avant garde. Whatever the situation, the entrepreneur frequently must deal with the innovative-minded, for others want no part of the new venture's output.

There are many other dimensions to the target market's psyche, too many to cover here. It may be helpful, however, to describe customers in terms of their desires for comfort, security, adventure, physical pleasures, and the like. Several marketing books delve into this topic.

User-team characteristic terms

Sometimes target markets are described in terms of how they use the product. One common classification scheme is based on product usage, that is, heavy users versus light users. There are obvious advantages for targeting heavy users as one's customers. They buy more than other people!

Other characteristics might be the site of consumption: the at-home market versus the away-from-home users. Or the purpose of the use might be relevant: professionals versus amateurs. There is no end to such classifications, depending upon the situation. One must perceive the classifications that are relevant to a concept and use them to develop a profile of the target market.

Buying Behavior

Once the who of marketing is established, the where, when, what, how, and why of it need to be determined. Several questions require answers: Where do the buyers want to buy? When do they buy? What do they buy? How do they buy? Why do they buy?

Buying Behavior
Where
When
What
How
Why

Once entrepreneurs have answered each of these five questions, they should be able to clearly convey in a business plan the precise nature of the target market. An entrepreneur should be able to provide customer profiles of the customers the venture seeks to satisfy. Then they should show an understanding of how target markets behave, how they buy, and why they buy.

Where do the buyers want to buy?

"Where" determines channels of distribution. A manufacturer must place its goods where people want to buy them, where they expect to find the goods. Similarly, middlemen are determined by where the dealers want to buy. If a retailer wants to buy from a distributor, then the manufacturer probably should use one. If the dealer wants to deal directly with suppliers, then the manufacturer should be prepared to sell direct. "Where" is one of the easiest questions to answer.

Often there is great temptation to test some new "wheres" for a new venture upon encountering resistance from the old "wheres." Direct-response marketing or the Internet are often tried to determine if it will work. Sometimes it will; sometimes it won't. Testing is usually required to find out.

When do they buy?

"When" answers two main questions: when to promote and when to have goods available. Timely promotion is one of the keys to effectiveness. A venture must promote when the market is about ready to make a buying decision. Understanding the budgeting cycle of potential buyers is vital. Often there is money at year-end that needs to be spent. Entrepreneurs must make themselves available!

But "when" can refer to dimensions other than calendar progressions. It may refer to the customer's stage in life: Entrepreneurs may plan to sell to young marrieds or to senior citizen markets.

The concept of demand triggers is a helpful one. Think a moment of how many items are purchased because of an event such as a birthday, a wedding, a holiday, a promotion, an anniversary, an accident. Try to identify the event that will trigger the demand for the product.

What do they buy?

"What" do people want to buy? Naturally, every entrepreneur wants to answer, "My product," but, people don't buy products, they buy benefits. What is it that the target market really wants to buy: safety, lower costs, comfort, status, fun, self-esteem, security, power, exhilaration, a reward?

What other things do they want to buy with the new product? Often, a purchase is a package of things in which the product is only one item. A person decides to go on a vacation: perhaps 100 items will be sold to fulfill that decision. The vacation decision triggered the demand for a large number of things. Understand just what people are buying when they purchase a product or service.

How do they buy?

How do people go about buying a venture's goods? Do they take it with them, or is delivery needed? Do they spend a lot of time shopping, or is it an impulse purchase? Do they buy in multiple units? Do they buy it alone or in a group? Will they buy it over the Internet, by mail, over the telephone, or from catalogs? How and where naturally overlap and work in conjunction in affecting the distribution problems for a venture. The answer to such questions obviously affects how a firm will market its wares.

Why do they buy?

"Why" will people buy from a company? That question sounds simple, but it isn't. The determination of buying motives is perhaps one of the most difficult tasks in marketing. People give the obvious reasons for why they buy things—

lower costs, better products, certain features, customer service. The real reasons are usually hidden. Why does an overweight person continue to buy ice cream, knowing full well its eventual resting place? Perhaps they buy it as a reward for accomplishing something. Perhaps to recall in some small way the pleasures of childhood. Perhaps to punish someone! Motivation is not as apparent as it might seem. The industrial tycoon who claims he bought his Lear jet because of its total long-run low costs is either lying or a fool. He bought it for reasons of status and convenience. Or perhaps he could not stand to have someone else one-up him. Or perhaps he is trying to impress some other business people with whom he deals. Perhaps it's a symbol of power.

Identifying Markets

Market planning begins by clearly identifying the markets to which a company will sell products. Sometimes it is easy. The firm has a product that is sold only to obvious customers—a new golf ball sold to golfers. A venture is indeed fortunate if its markets are so clearly identifiable and delineated.

But even the new golf ball's market requires additional focusing. Few products will appeal to all segments of a market. Certainly, a new golf ball is not one that would. What segment of the golf-ball market is it aimed at: professionals, high-handicappers, women, municipal golf course players, the low-price buyers, the status golfers?

At the other end of the scale are entrepreneurs who want to sell something but don't know who will buy it. Their customers are not apparent. When Edwin H. Land first developed his Polaroid camera, its markets were hidden. He originally thought of it as a consumer product, but that market rejected the first models because of poor picture quality and high costs. But salespeople, particularly real estate agents, found the Polaroid very useful. Its costs and quality were not fatal defects. Polaroid backed into the huge industrial markets for its invention.

Industrial markets are so huge and complex that it is difficult to learn facts about their needs that are relevant to a product. Suppose an entrepreneur develops a new adhesive. Who can use its characteristics? Much research is required to identify the markets for products that can

Table 18-1 Golf-ball markets and desired features	Low cost	High cost	Durability	Balata cover	Long distances	Trajectory	Customized to gender	White	Color
High-handicap players	✔		✔		✔			✔	✔
Public course players	✔			✔					
Private course players	✔	✔	✔	✔	✔	✔	✔	✔	✔
Skilled amateur players		✔		✔	✔	✔		✔	

be used by a wide range of firms and people. One of the advantages of starting a business with a customer in hand is that one's first market has been identified and somewhat quantified.

It's helpful to construct a matrix that displays the various identifiable markets for a concept. As an illustrative exercise, the matrix in Table 18-1 was constructed for the golf-ball market, assuming a firm has developed a new golf ball. Depending upon the market being studied, such matrices can be simple listings of market segments or two- or three-dimensional tables that coordinate the segments with some relevant characteristic such as buying motive and price.

Here the matrix will be kept simple. It shows four potential markets. Each of those markets could then be classified as to its demands. For example, the high-handicap golfer might be most interested in a durable golf ball of low cost. The skilled amateur golfer might want a long-distance ball, but with a Balata cover—not as durable and gets less distance but has a better feel when it is hit. The corporate market might want a ball with a recognizable brand name. The driving-range market wants a low-cost, durable ball.

Each market would be studied carefully for its demands, size, and potential profitability, with an eye to how the new golf ball fits into the picture. For example, after studying the market, the maker would probably conclude that the professional market would be most unlikely to accept the innovation. Moreover, without the professional market, the maker might conclude that other markets that follow the professional's lead would likewise be unlikely markets. Perhaps the new ball would be most appealing, however, to the hacker. Thus, the base of the marketing strategy would be established.

Entrepreneurs should try to pinpoint the markets in which their ventures will most likely be well received.

Target Markets

Once the possible markets have been identified, priorities must be set. The targets must be selected. Target marketing is the fundamental strategy used by most successful businesses today. Seldom does a firm try to be all things to all people. Instead, market segments are selected for attention. Some segments of the market may be totally ignored. Perhaps the segment is too small to bother with. Perhaps a product does not quite fit its needs as well as some competitive products, putting the seller at a competitive disadvantage. Perhaps the competition for that segment is too stiff for comfort. Perhaps that segment will not pay a sufficient price for the entrepreneur's wares. A company can't make any money in that market. There are all sorts of reasons for ignoring many markets. There is just some business that a company doesn't want to solicit.

The market segments that seem attractive are then targeted for attention. Special marketing tactics are developed for each target market; marketers call this strategy market segmentation. It is the basic marketing strategy used by most good marketers.

Target markets should be selected and a marketing program developed for penetrating each of them. The business plan should clearly identify all markets and then provide the basis for their selection. Each of the target markets should then be treated almost as a separate marketing program.

Entrepreneurs are often urged to seek niche markets for their output. A niche market is some small market or a small segment of a large market that, for some understandable reasons, other firms in the industry are ignoring. Many markets are too small to be attractive to large competitors, yet a firm can do quite well with a small niche market. The theory is to locate some niche market in which the firm can enjoy some exclusivity.

Some observations:

- Pick for the first target market the one that is the easiest to sell. Don't begin business with backbreakers. In one case, the president of a company targeted General Motors as its first customer. He had reason to believe that he would get a large order from GM because one well-placed person "owed me one." It didn't happen. That failure affected all subsequent events. Start out a winner. Pick targets that will make customers. Go after the easy pickings first. Get experience before heading for the major leagues.

- Don't bother with markets that are not right for the company. Don't try to operate in arenas in which the company is at a competitive disadvantage. Pick markets in which the venture's products are superior.

- Go for markets that are not price sensitive. They will pay for the benefits provided by the product. Gross margin is needed during a business start-up, and it won't be achieved by selling into price-competitive markets.

Sequential Marketing

Another strategy is sequential development of the markets. It is usually unwise to try to develop more than one market at a time. Each market requires much attention. A company should not invite failure by diluting attention to the market's demands. A schedule of market penetration should be planned carefully. Enough time should be allowed for each market to be developed sufficiently before beginning to develop a new market. The efforts required to open up a market should not be underestimated. It takes a lot of time and hard work, not to mention money.

Market Positioning

How does the company want the market to think of it and its product? Positioning a product necessitates understanding how a product meets the needs and wants of its customers relative to the competition. To a large extent, by promotional activities, entrepreneurs can position their products in the buyer's mind. Continuing with the golf-ball example, perhaps the manufacturer decides that it wants the golf-ball-buying public to think of its product as the best value in durable long-distance balls. It should try to develop a product that stands for one thing and make the product mean something to its potential customers.

Basis for Positioning
Customers' needs
 and wants
Product's strengths
Competitors' weaknesses

Planning Timetable

Plans change as time passes. Entrepreneurs begin with a plan and it evolves. As a firm gains financial strength, it can develop new markets. The owner should be able to articulate the plans for the first few years at least.

The Entrepreneurial Education Foundation (EEF) received a grant to disseminate its business-development program, Premier FastTrac®, to entrepreneurs throughout the country over a five-year period. EEF had developed an initial plan to accomplish this goal that specified having 10 to 12 centers responsible for large areas of the country encompassing several states. By the end of the second year, EEF discovered that this dissemination strategy was not practical or feasible. Instead, it was determined that an individual center could disseminate a training program only in the region where it already worked and was recognized. The initial dissemination plan was revised to accommodate this change.

Planning by its very nature is a look at the future. True, the look may be blurred, but experience indicates that such planning is still beneficial. The entrepreneur's followers want to believe that the entrepreneur knows where he or she is going to lead them.

Custom Market Strategy

While target marketing and market segmentation are broad, widely used strategies, most successful firms generally develop some particular strategies to take advantage of their situations. These strategies are so diverse that they defy generalization. Only by considering them case by case can we gain some insights about the role of marketing strategy in a firm's success. So let's examine some marketing strategies in action. Entrepreneurs should be able to articulate strategies quite lucidly and defend their wisdom.

Wave Craze Wake Board Inc.

Upon graduation, Bob Lasser decided to launch a wakeboard manufacturing facility in California to take advantage of this fast-growing sport.

He wanted to develop a marketing strategy that would make his boards unique among wakeboarding retail outlets. He wanted not only to be different, but also to develop a marketing strategy that would be hard to duplicate. Any time an entrepreneur launches a venture in a fast-growing industry, many competitors will spring up. The best way to stop competition is to erect an intricate entry barrier to overcome.

Since his target customers were young people, Bob knew they would relate to sport celebrities. Bob, an accomplished pole vaulter in college, knew it took courage to wakeboard, as it does to pole vault. He decided to work hard on becoming an excellent wakeboarder by performing difficult tricks, and thus to become well known and admired by potential wakeboarders.

Next, Bob raised start-up capital from friends and relatives, secured a location, bought inventory, and opened his new manufacturing location. After the plant opened, he began executing his market strategy. In just two years, he won the U.S. Wakeboarding Championship and the Pro World Wakeboarding Championship. Today, he is a successful wakeboarding manufacturer, with all of his competition certificates well displayed on the walls of his sales office. He personally autographs wakeboards for all his young customers, and he makes public appearances and talks to them about the sport. His customers are impressed, and his cash register keeps on ringing.

Chipwich

After Richard LaMotta spent three years perfecting his chocolate chip cookie ice cream sandwich (the cookies kept crystallizing when frozen), he began distribution on the streets of New York, using vendors who pushed unique carts specially designed for Chipwich. The price was $1.25 a bar. Thus, his strategy consisted of four essential elements: quality product, premium price, convenient distribution, and aggressive salespeople. He sold his company to a large firm in 1983.

ZDC, Inc.

An entrepreneur, in marketing the Energy Sentry product line, chose to do so through power companies. His entire marketing program for that line involves working closely with the local power companies. With their help, he sells the devices in large batches. One Rural Electric Association power company bought 9,000 units for its customers. Selling to the individual customers would have been prohibitively expensive.

Cranium

Using a virtual development team, Whit Alexander and Richard Tait developed a board game that exercises different parts of the brain. After spending a vacation weekend playing Pictionary and Scrabble, they noticed that those who did very well at one did not do so well on the other.

Cranium did not advertise. They initially decided to by-pass the traditional game retailers and the annual toy trade show. Rather, they decided to sell their game through other retailers where their potential players shopped. This more unusual positioning has resulted in their largest sales coming through Starbucks stores, an unconventional channel. The game also sells well on Amazon.com, and through Virgin Megastores, and Barnes and Noble.

Gateway Computers

Historically computers were generally purchased from computer or electronics stores. Gateway decided that they could successfully combine the increase in consumers' interests in mail order purchasing with a "build it your way" approach and apply it to personal computers. The direct sales to the consumer circumvented the middleman and allowed them to price competitively and acquire a significant piece of the market share.

This approach also allowed them to remain in South Dakota, where they could build an infrastructure less expensively and labor was cheaper compared to the more traditional Silicon Valley area. They highlighted this point to their customers through their now well-known cow design.

Glow Dog, Inc.

Beth Marcus was consulting for Reflective Technologies Inc. a manufacturer of a glow-in-the dark fabric called IllumiNite. Reflective Technologies targeted nocturnal joggers, when Marcus considered the opportunity potential of the four-legged market. Positioned to leverage the growing markets for pet supplies and services, Glow Dog Inc., which Marcus started, has 100 wholesale customers, including PETsMART, the largest pet superstore in the country.

Naut-a Care Marine Services Inc.

Applying the concept of Jiffy Lube to watercraft, Naut-a-Care Marine Services, Inc. started by three principles is expanding as a franchise. Using custom-designed boats, the company provides services such as oil changing, steam cleaning of marine bilges and maintenance of systems to boat owners. By going to the customers' boat via water, they can service the boat without even needing to pull into a dock. By operating from a boat, they also avoid the high expense of water front real estate needed for most successful marine-oriented businesses.

Strategy Traps

Several traps are so commonly encountered in market planning that a separate mention of them is warranted.

The "everybody will buy one" trap

There is nothing that everyone buys. Yet, time and again, some entrepreneur claims that his product is so great that everybody will just have to have one. Beware of this thinking. Instead, isolate those people who will really buy the product and customize marketing materials to them.

The 1 percent of the market trap

Too often entrepreneurs decide to start a business because only 1 percent of their target market needs to become customers for the business to succeed. The arithmetic may be correct, but the reality isn't. That 1 percent ultimately proves to be more difficult to sell than anticipated. Such statements prove nothing but that one can multiply and divide. Don't say how much of the market the company needs—prove how much it can get. Let others decide the likelihood of attaining that market penetration.

The armchair strategy formulation trap

A young graduate from a famous business school that focuses on marketing strategy purchased a business that was developing a patented method for making higher quality metal diecastings. He spent countless hours developing a complex matrix showing the structure of the metal diecasting market by kinds of metals and end-use markets.

From this matrix, he spotted an opening in the large-volume aluminum-castings business. While the company had a small market developing for brass castings from the sprinkler head industry, the aluminum-casting business seemed to hold promise for more profitable operations. So the firm's marketing efforts were directed to that market. Orders were ultimately obtained from Ford and Scovill. Unfortunately, four realities had been overlooked in selecting the marketing strategy.

First, the company could not possibly fulfill the orders from those firms. It did not have anywhere near the plant capacity—nor could the company get it. Second, the quality of the company's castings did not meet the requirements of the target market. Third, the company never perfected its technology to the extent that it could operate efficiently. It always had breakdowns and difficulties. Fourth, the company ignored the only market from which it had received any positive encouragement—brass castings.

So much for selecting strategies sitting in a chair. The market must be allowed to forge the strategies. The strategies must be in alignment with the realities of both the market and the firm. The target market may not want what the company has to sell. Or the company may not be able to furnish what the target market wants to buy. Strategy must fit into the reality of the world in which it will operate.

Finally, it is important not to become so fixed in thinking about strategy that great opportunities are ignored that do not fit into the strategic design.

The unrealistic expectations trap

Little purpose is served by developing elaborate marketing strategies that the firm cannot execute. They must be achievable. Money definitely limits strategic marketing alternatives. A company must live within its budget.

The entrepreneur also must live within his or her own capabilities and make the strategies fit the talents. If he or she is a great manager of salespeople, then those skills should be used in the entrepreneur's corporate strategy.

Strategy alone will not make entrepreneurs successful. Great strategies will fail if not adeptly executed. Often it matters not so much what entrepreneurs do but how well they do it. They can be successful using any one of the many strategies so long as it is well done. Don't think that there is one ultimate grand strategy that will take a company to victory.

Competitive Strategy

"We have no competition. There's nothing like it on the market." "Competition? No problem!" Most investors in new ventures have repeatedly heard such statements by enthusiastic entrepreneurs who choose to ignore the realities of the marketplace. Competition is a force to be reckoned with, and those business people who refuse to do so usually regret it. Entrepreneurs should know the competition, basis of competition, potential legal problems, and the economics of the industry.

The competition

Business owners should know the names and locations of every significant competitor. It is particularly helpful to know the key players in each firm with which a company will be competing: know their personalities, how they think, how they react, and their political strengths inside their organizations. Some people are keen competitors who will react aggressively to any challenge of their market position. Other managers may take a more tolerant view of newcomers in the industry.

Strategy Considerations
The competition
Basis of competition
Potential legal problems
Economics of the industry

Basis of competition

How do the firms in the industry compete for business—price, product, service, convenience, location, promotion, finance? What tactics seem to work best in the target market? If the basis of competition is price, then entrepreneurs know what must be done and the problems their firms will encounter. Do the competitors meet price competition? In many situations, various competitors compete with different tactics, some going after the price-sensitive segment of the market while others seek the business of those who want customer service, quality, and so forth.

A vice president in charge of business development of a Fortune 50 firm said that winning a multibillion dollar bid, with a proposal several inches thick, would really depend on "relationships." If it is true for Fortune 50 companies to stress the importance of relationships to make a big sale, it should be true for entrepreneurial companies.

Some observations are in order at this point. First, using price as a competitive weapon is fraught with danger unless one enjoys a significant cost advantage that allows the company to make a profit even at lower prices. Second, the firms that seem to stay around longest are the ones that provide excellent products. Third, the most profitable firms somehow develop a way to sell for premium prices.

The entrepreneur should comprehend exactly how each competitor competes in the market and how each will react to the intrusion of a firm into the market. Often the new firm only threatens one or two competitors; the others couldn't care less about the new firm because it won't affect their markets.

It is particularly important to identify which firms will provide the most significant competition and what they will likely do.

Potential legal problems

In some instances, competitors have a history of threatening some sort of litigation to keep out new enterprises. Two examples, one small and one substantial: An entrepreneur, while in school, started a little specialty business by making customized buttons for university groups. A small production company sent him a nasty letter threatening to sue the student for violation of its copyright on some product of a similar nature. One look at the two items removed any question of copyright infringement. The student's lawyer replied with appropriate observations, yet the harassment continued. It made no sense, yet the tactic had its effect, and it increased the student's legal costs.

A large medical-supply firm had a reputation of automatically threatening to sue every new firm in the industry for some violation of its patents or trademarks. The management was infamous for such intimidation tactics. The board of directors of a smaller medical-supply company was, therefore, not surprised when it received such a letter. It chose to totally ignore the letter, not even answering it. The board only hoped that the competitor would sue, as it had some surprises in store. Its lawyer had discovered some fraudulent statements that the other firm had made to the Patent Office. A suit was filed. When the dust settled, the large firm gave two checks for a total of $10 million to the smaller company. The large firm's personnel hadn't done their homework.

The point of these stories is that in some industries history shows that the new firm can expect legal harassment as a competitive deterrent. Companies need to be ready for it if they are venturing into such a competitive climate.

The economics of the industry

Much useful information can be acquired by studying the history of the industry. Entrepreneurs should know where it started and who started it; they should understand what the industry has been through so they can talk intelligently to people who have been in it for years; they should do some library work; and they should scan the industry's trade journals from the industry's inception.

Every industry has a set of economic forces that affect its fortunes. The entrepreneur should understand them and how they affect his or her firm.

Strategic Positioning

Usually, each firm in an industry occupies a unique position in the minds of the industry's market and infrastructure. One firm will be seen as the leader in innovation while another is seen as a tough marketer. Some of these positions develop over time as a result of what the company has done. Entrepreneurs should understand how each of their competitors is positioned in the market and determine a distinct position for their product or service.

Monopoly

While society often values competition as a desired economic state of affairs, most business people continually seek a monopoly. And they do so for good reason. Profits come from monopolistic positions. In theory, there are no profits from pure competition; only wages—and low wages at that. Fortunately for most companies, purely competitive situations are seldom encountered. In most situations, there are some monopolistic aspects such as location, managerial expertise, or product differentiations. Thus, the term monopolistic competition was coined years ago to describe the economic system.

An entrepreneur needs somehow to develop some sort of monopolistic position in the market. This is sometimes called a differential advantage. The theory is that each firm in an industry must have some sort of differential advantage over its competitors, if it is to survive. Most investors want to know what the differential advantage will be. Why will people buy from one company rather than its competitors?

Learn from Competitors

Often entrepreneurs, as part of their plan for entering business, spend some time working for their future competitors to learn about them and the industry. This can be time well spent.

Outside investors can be particularly impressed if the proposed enterprise is being formed by people who have had successful experience in the industry.

Caring for Customers

One of the real secrets of business success lies in the cultivation of customers: forging long-lasting commercial and personal ties between a company and the people to whom it sells. It's been said many times, "It's not what you know, but who you know that counts." Henry Rogers, the founder of Rogers and Cowan, one of the nation's leading public relations firms, stresses this point in his book, *Rogers' Rules for Success*. He recalls that he spent about 10 years beginning his business, operating at a subsistence level, just meeting people, making contacts, and developing relationships.

Contacts and relationships are the essence of marketing and business.

People have to learn who the entrepreneur is, what he or she can do for them, and that he or she can be trusted. That takes some time. This is one of the reasons underlying the time it takes to get a business off the ground: It often takes time to develop the relationships needed to make a business successful.

But it is in this realm of customer relationships that the entrepreneur can prosper and far outdistance large competitors. It is difficult to have a close business relationship with a large corporation. Its people keep changing. By the time the customer gets to know the firm's sales representative, a new one appears.

The following section suggests some ways to building customer loyalty.

Building relationships

The art of fostering relationships is not mystical. It simply requires a bit of subordinating one's own ego to that of the other person while being aware of a few basic principles and using good interpersonal skills.

Providing mutual benefit

Most business relationships are built on mutual need. Each party believes that the other may be of some use to him in the future.

The root of business relationships is money—profit. Somehow the entrepreneur must plant in the other person's mind that the entrepreneur can help him or her make some money. As cruel and cold as it sounds, a large number of successful business people build their lives around relationships only with people who can somehow help them. Every party they have is a group of people in their business lives. They use each other for mutual benefit.

Eliminating loneliness

One of the prices paid for a highly mobile industrial society is a longing for close personal relationships—social contacts. New computer technology has enabled more people to work from home and communicate electronically through e-mail and over the Internet, which contributes to the loneliness syndrome.

Work relationships have become the focus of many lives. If, somehow, a person is able to be a good companion to people, they will cherish and nurture a relationship with that person. Even a few minutes of social contact every so often is important to people.

Being a good playmate

People may grow older, but they change little from childhood. As has often been observed, the only difference between men and boys is the price of their toys. People wanted playmates when they were kids. It's not much fun playing alone. It still isn't. Grown-ups need playmates too. But with whom does a corporate president play? Other corporate presidents, of course. But even this poses some problems. It is not for idle reasons that salespeople often serve as playmates to presidents and other decision makers. Time for golf? Tee it up with somebody who is a good golfing companion. Want to fish? So it goes.

Of course, not everyone is a good playmate. Some people won't play by the rules. They somehow threaten the other person or fail to provide him or her with an enjoyable experience. They don't know when to talk business and when to talk of other things. They may try to exploit a relationship, which is usually a no-no.

If an entrepreneur has a good relationship with someone, the benefits will be forthcoming without the need to be pushy. People resent and react when they feel that the only reason someone likes them is for their business. It is indeed an art to cultivate friendship with a client and not appear to be business-oriented. Yet, an entrepreneur does not want to be so retiring that a friend is unaware that the entrepreneur wants his business. It is a difficult line to walk.

Making customers feel important

Perhaps the art of making other people feel important is the key to developing relationships. People want to feel important. Yet, society does its best to make them feel unimportant. Trying to gain recognition is difficult, particularly in large cities. People buy mansions, hire public-relations firms, give charity balls, and spend money on all sorts of activities to gain recognition.

Entrepreneurs must learn the art of making others feel important. Some simple little techniques such as really listening to what they say and agreeing with them can work wonders. A sales representative, when talking with a customer, was overheard to say, "You know, Leigh, I was thinking the other night about what you said the last time you were in here, about the price of oil. You know, you're right...." Now, look what this one statement does.

1. It tells Leigh that the sales representative knows her name. It's difficult to think one is important to another person if one's name can't be recalled.

2. It tells Leigh that the sales representative remembers her from the last time and recalls what she said. The sales representative must have been listening.

3. Not only had the sales representative been listening, but he thought about the conversation later. Now how often does that happen?

4. The sales representative thinks Leigh's right. Not many people tell someone that he or she is right about things.

Oh, what a lovely sentence, what a delightful way to begin a sale!

Providing good service

Entrepreneurs will not have customers for long if they fail to provide the customers with the services they need. What is service? Everyone talks about it, but few define it. Service means that a person must work for the customer's convenience, not his or her own.

Each customer is a valuable asset of the entrepreneur and should be treated with care.

A men's custom clothing company distinguished itself from competitors by offering to drive to a customer's house and rearrange closets with both existing and newly tailored clothes. Old clothes were weeded out and then donated to Goodwill Industries. This provided an excellent opportunity to offer a customized service, while identifying new clothes needed in the future to complete the wardrobe.

The same store installed a soft-drink machine, which produced fountain-mixed soft drinks in 4-ounce cups for customers. Children accompanying customers would later ask their parents, "When are we going to the Coke store again?" It cost the company about $60 a month for this service, while it differentiated the store from competitors and was a hit with the family.

A founder and builder of Master Fence ascribes his fantastic success to building relationships with fence dealers by giving them unheard-of service. He would deliver needed fence or fencing products on weekends or late at night—wherever the dealer wanted them.

Service is doing things on time. Service is helping customers make more money. Service is helping customers solve problems. Service is being available. Service is providing needed information. Service is promptness. Service is living up to one's promises.

Service is a lot of work and costs money. How much service must a company provide its market? How much service can it afford to give? There is a limit. Some customers demand so much service that they are not economical to have as clients. Some business a company doesn't want. If a company can't service an account properly, it shouldn't take on the account.

Customer Service for Web Sites

In the early stages of e-commerce, many web sites didn't interact with customers, viewing Internet shopping as a self-serve operation. And customers didn't expect a whole lot. Online shoppers were frustrated when they experienced lags in download times, slow responses to questions, and sluggish product delivery.

The magic formula for success today is customer service. It's a mix of mechanical and human efforts. The web sites will have to have fast Internet connections, answers to customers' questions, low cost or free shipping, good return policies, and low, low prices, and the site must be easy for customers to use.

Scott Nilson, director of business development for eSupportNow, which outsources staffing for dot-com firms, said there's a strong argument for customer service from a cost standpoint. "Companies need to invest in the whole customer service piece, because it's a lot less expensive to retain customers than acquire new ones."

As is true elsewhere on the Internet, speed is crucial. Companies are overinvesting in capacity because they don't want to disappoint their customers.

Web Considerations
Speed
User interface
Contact information
Brand recognition
Adequate staffing
Return policy

Second in importance to speedy access is the user interface. The first screen people see must be attractive and easy to understand. The site's interface needs menus that are simple and comfortable for the customers. This means good help selection and the ability to find what they are looking for.

The third part of a friendly site is communication that provides several ways to contact the company. A response within twenty-four hours is a must because if customers don't get answers quickly, they will go to a competitor.

The site needs to build brand recognition because once consumers are familiar with a company's brand, they will make purchases from that company. Web sites have greatly increased their advertising in the conventional media. Big ad spending poses a risk for start-ups because some of the advertising will be successful, but a lot of it will not. The smaller companies have to be very careful in placing their advertising.

Web sites must have adequate staffing during the peak times. Knowing how many employees are needed is difficult to determine. Many sites are outsourcing to temporary employment companies that specialize in employees who are trained to work for companies' web sites. These temporary agencies have people trained in multiple programs and can allocate staff based on needs of different clients. Some companies have trained every employee in the company in a customer service capacity so the company can quickly respond to surges in site activity. This includes the CEO.

The web site venue should provide a fair return policy. Thirty days, no questions asked is being used by many sites. Sites that also have bricks and mortar stores allow web purchasers to return items to these stores.

Purchasing from the Internet is still in its infant stage, but is growing fast. Many web sites will not be successful, but those that have good customer service will increase their odds for success.

Conclusion

This chapter must end with the same emphasis with which it began: The key to success in entrepreneurship is the ability to cultivate customers. A firm must be oriented toward the marketplace and focus its efforts on a targeted segment of its identified market.

True customer orientation is difficult to institute and maintain throughout an organization. The entrepreneur must work hard to develop it and work continually at keeping it. It does not just happen. It reflects a basic attitude. Enrepreneurs cannot expect their people to adopt attitudes other than the entrepreneurs' own. If they berate customers, how are their employees going to react to customers?

Exercise 18a: Current Customer Profiles

Write a customer profile for two potential customers for your business concept.

Customer group	Profile

What research do you need to complete to compile these profiles?

Exercise 18b: Potential Target Markets and Customer Profile

Brainstorm a list of currently untapped potential customer groups for your concept, write a customer profile for one of these, and identify possible tactics.

Potential customer groups

Selected customer group profile

Possible marketing tactics

Possible marketing tactics (continued)

Pricing

Learning Objectives

In this chapter, students will learn how to
- Prepare a break-even analysis.
- Determine the selling price for a product.
- Select a pricing policy.
- Set pricing for services.

Pricing presents a paradox in business education. Unquestionably, pricing is the single most important factor affecting profits. Also unquestionably, less is known about pricing practices than any other phase of business.

Key to Profits

Business people are keenly interested in pricing because it determines profitability. The extent to which a business makes a profit depends on how much above costs it can sell its products.

But price is even more important to profits than that simple statement indicates. It involves:

Profits = Revenues – Costs

Profits = (Unit sales x Price per unit) – Costs

Yet, unit sales are a direct function of price, as are costs. Usually, the lower the price, the more units a firm will sell. And the more it sells, the lower are its costs.

Thus, the price obtained for what is sold affects each factor in the profit equation.

Every sales dollar received over break-even costs goes directly into profits. The difference between the product's marginal revenue (the actual money for which the product is sold) and its marginal costs (the producer's out-of-pocket costs) goes into profit once the break-even point is reached.

This formula has great implications, for it means that if a firm sells something with a relatively low marginal cost, profits come quickly after it reaches the break-even point. If marginal costs are relatively high, profits come much more slowly. This may help an entrepreneur determine which type of business to launch.

It is easy to understand why entrepreneurs fight for pennies on many orders. If a business is selling 100,000,000 buttons, 1 cent per button represents $1,000,000 profit. One-tenth of 1 cent is $100,000 profit. Profits are often counted in pennies. The profits of many operations are less than the cash discounts they take. Often a business fights for price on each order.

Why is an extra $25 on the price of a new chair so important to the manufacturer? If the dealership sells 100 chairs a month, that is $2,500 extra profit for that month.

That doesn't sound like much when the trade press bandies around sums in the millions and billions of dollars. But the entrepreneur sees $2,500 a month as additional money in his or her pocket to spend.

The ability to obtain and sustain a relatively high price for a product reflects total managerial skill. It means a company has developed a product that the market values highly and it has backed that product with sound marketing. Price is the market's barometer for telling how it values a business's offering.

A firm that must continually cut price to meet its goals has some serious defects in its operations.

Included in pricing strategy is perceived value. Perceived value is when a customer believes that a product or service has an intangible value, such as DKNY® brand clothing, or a haircut at Vidal Sassoon's salon. Many entrepreneurs design products that have perceived value, so they can charge a desirable price for their goods or services.

Break-Even Analysis

Most skillful entrepreneurs make extensive use of break-even analysis in making judgments about entering a business or venture or bringing out a new product or service. Break-even analysis not only aids in making pricing judgments but it also helps the entrepreneur decide whether or not to undertake a venture.

Simply put, break-even analysis is a mathematical formula that discloses how much output must be sold for the firm to break even: that is, the cash coming in equals the cash going out. It is the point at which the firm's revenues equal its costs. It is a rather comfortable feeling to learn at what level of activity the enterprise is no longer losing cash, but rather it is beginning to make money.

In many types of ventures, profits come fast once sales pass the firm's break-even point. This is particularly true in companies in which variable costs are a small portion of the selling price. Break-even charts enable an entrepreneur to glance over potential profits.

The formula for the break-even point is:

$$Break\text{-}even\ point\ (in\ units) = \frac{Fixed\ costs}{Sales\ price\ per\ unit - Variable\ cost\ per\ unit}$$

Break-even point: When total revenues are equal to total costs. The break-even point in units is the number of units that need to be sold to cover all costs, both fixed and variable.

Fixed costs: Costs that remain constant over the entire range of output. These costs typically include rent, insurance, interest charges, executive salaries, and the like.

Variable costs: Costs that vary directly with the sales level, manufacturing labor, materials used in production, sales costs, and the like.

For example, if the company's fixed costs are estimated at $50,000 and variable costs of $.20 per unit with a $1 retail price per unit, the break-even point would be 62,500 units.

Fixed costs = $50,000, Sales price/unit = $1.00, Variable costs = $.20
50,000/(1.00 – .20) = 50,000/.80 = 62,500

Now the entrepreneur starts thinking: "Can I sell that many?" What would happen if the price were increased to $2 retail with the same variable cost per unit of $.20? So recalculate:

50,000/(2.00 – .20) = 50,000/1.80 = 27,778

Now the entrepreneur ponders: "Would it be easier to sell 27,778 units for $2 or 62,500 units for $1?" The entrepreneur would likely do many such calculations to help figure out which pricing strategy to undertake. The entrepreneur would keep in mind the profit picture that would develop at each price after the break-even point has been passed. Successful entrepreneurs do a lot of calculations.

Sometimes it is extremely helpful to chart the break-even relationships. It can be seen at a glance what happens to profits as prices and volumes are changed.

It is most desirable for the projected sales to be larger than the break-even sales to avoid losses. Entrepreneurs should not assume a sales volume and then determine the profits. They should do it in reverse: first determine the sales volume necessary for the business to break even. Above the break-even, the company makes money; below break-even, it loses money. The ability to control costs accurately can be enhanced by forecasts of the effect on the break-even point.

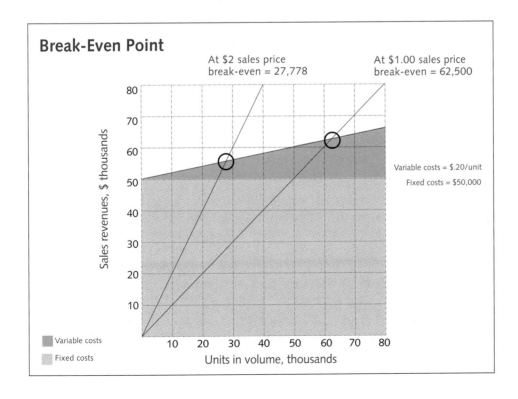

Break-Even Point

At $2 sales price break-even = 27,778

At $1.00 sales price break-even = 62,500

Sales revenues, $ thousands

Variable costs = $.20/unit
Fixed costs = $50,000

Variable costs
Fixed costs

Units in volume, thousands

Evaluating Pricing Constraints

Pricing cannot be done in a vacuum. There are forces that govern the price a company can get for its products. Note the wording: The price the venture can get.

Price is what the venture gets, not what it wants. A producer can put a tag of $500 on its widget, but that is only a hope. If the customer pays $300 for it, that is the price. In many industries, such as real estate, the so-called prices are but invitations to negotiate. In other industries, asking prices are firm. But many "firm prices" are not firm. There are all sorts of ways to cut price when the seller needs to do so.

First, in many industries there is a market price for a company's products. It's difficult to get much more for a product than what the market price dictates.

An owner of a fuel station with a convenience store was forced to sell his gasoline at the same price as his larger, corporate competitors to keep current customers and attract new ones. He didn't make money on the gas, but by selling products and services in the convenience store, he made money on the products his customers purchased when they came in to pay for the gas: check cashing service, ATM machine, fax services, copy machine, soft drinks, and sandwiches.

Much entrepreneurial effort is devoted to avoiding markets in which one has little control over price. They are called commodity markets. A business is selling a commodity for a fixed-price market. Profits are difficult to come by in such situations unless the business has some distinctive cost advantages.

Second, the government sometimes regulates prices. Sometimes that's good and sometimes not. The airlines might prefer to return to the good old days when their prices were set by the government. They made more money that way. Now that they must compete, many airlines have discovered they can't. Some have gone bankrupt. Competitive prices have been distressful to many airline managements.

Can a new business whose basic strategy is to cut price to capture some market segment do so without competitive retaliation? The risks are obvious. The ones that have gotten into trouble have been those that miscalculated the volume they would realize on certain runs with their low prices. When they are wrong, disaster quickly follows. Low prices leave little room for error. High prices cover up many miscalculations.

Finally, the prices of other products limit pricing freedom. Both directly competitive and substitute products affect what a business can get for its product. In most markets the buyer confronts an array of products that vary from expensive, top-of-the-line products down to cheap junk that may be barely acceptable. All of these items affect price. An entrepreneur will have to fit a product's qualities and features into this spectrum of prices. It is usually difficult to charge more for goods than a competitor charges for a somewhat superior item. While there may not be any direct competition, there are always substitutes seeking the customer's dollars. Prices of ski lift tickets have become very expensive. People have other options for engaging in outdoor activities at less-expensive prices, such as cross-country skiing, backpacking, and camping. There is always a point at which a product is simply priced out of the market. It costs too much for the benefits received.

The Internet, via new trading models for business to business and auction sites such as eBay, can lead to the entrepreneur's having little or no control on pricing.

Pricing Procedure

A four-step procedure is recommended for setting prices: determine the relevant price range, evaluate the price sensitivities, select a strategy, and set the price.

Determine the relevant price range

First, determine the reasonable range of prices in which a price must be set. In other words, know the limits.

Price floor. The bottom of the range, the floor, is usually set by costs. Just how little can a business sell its product for and still stay alive? Don't hasten to the conclusion that costs set prices; the market always determines price. The costs determine whether an entrepreneur will stay in business or go out of business. Customers control the price. Costs determine profits.

Market price. The price is what a seller is willing to sell the product for and what a buyer is willing to pay. Market price is not set in concrete.

Of course, if customers want a business' products, they'll likely have to pay at least the costs or the business won't sell. But not always. It depends upon business acumen.

Of course, a market price may set the price floor. There is no need for a business to sell below market. By definition, it can sell its entire output at market price. That's what a market price means.

Ceiling price. Just how much can a product sell for? That is a far more difficult question to answer than the one concerning the price floor.

Six major factors should be studied before deciding on an item's price: savings, competitors' prices, prices of substitutes, role of complementary products, market's perceived values, and distributive-network pressures.

Savings. When a business sells something that saves the buyer money, its price can be based on those savings. The business can confiscate a good portion of proven savings. That was the source of the Hughes Tool Company profits. Its oil-well drilling bit saved drilling contractors a great deal of money over the older cable drilling technology. As a result, it was able to charge a large rental fee for its bits.

Always analyze any potential savings for the customer first, for those savings can provide a very profitable pricing base.

Competitors' prices. Early in their investigations, entrepreneurs should have closely studied the prices of competitive products. Competitive prices clearly affect the entrepreneurs' prices. They will likely base price on those of the competitors one way or another. Perhaps they feel that they can sell their products or services for a premium price over the competitors'. Perhaps they intend to sell at a lower price. In any case, the price of directly competitive products and services must loom large in a pricing analysis. To ignore competition is to invite disaster.

Prices of substitutes. Like competition, substitutes can limit how much a venture can get for its goods. The OPEC nations ran into substitutes as they

Pricing Procedure
1. Determine relevant range
2. Evaluate price sensitivities
3. Select strategy
4. Set price

Price Factors
Savings to buyers
Competitors' prices
Prices of substitutes
Role of complimentary products
Market's perceived values
Distributive-netowrk pressures

increased the price of their oil. The oil-buying nations were fleeing to other fuels as fast as they could switch over. As copper prices increased, the preference for substitutes knocked copper out of some of its markets. As the price of hard-surface flooring increased and carpet prices decreased, carpet took over a huge share of the flooring market. This is called pricing oneself out of business.

Entrepreneurs should recognize the potential substitutes for their products and understand the effects the prices of those substitutes have on the market. If entrepreneurs want the market, they must stay under the switch-over price.

Role of complementary products. Often an item is not really bought separately but is purchased as part of a package of products and services. A housewife wants draperies for her new house. She contracts for them with a draper. That sale is a package of material, drapery rods, hardware, and labor.

If an item is but a minor part of a larger package, then its price may not be too important to the buyer. Why worry about the price of hooks when buying material for $30 a yard?

The car buyer pays scant heed to the price of its radio. What's $500 in a $20,000 package? Yet $300 could be saved by buying the radio elsewhere. High profits can be made when selling products that are small in the total package of benefits purchased by the buyer.

Market's perceived values. Here is an elusive factor. What values does the buyer impute to a product? In the end, it matters not what the product costs or what other products sell for, but rather what the buyer will pay for an offering.

One can buy blue jeans for as little as $5 a pair in a thrift store, but on Rodeo Drive in Beverly Hills, some people pay $200 for them. The extreme of this situation is referred to as an inverse demand curve. Normally, the economic theory of demand dictates that fewer goods will be sold as the price increases and vice versa. That is logical. But people are not always logical. Often they will buy more at a higher price than at a lower one. Suppose a cosmetologist produces a marvelous cream that makes facial wrinkles disappear. She could sell it for $5 a jar and be profitable, if people would buy it. But would they? Would they believe that anything that could do what was promised could cost only $5? How could it really be worth anything if it is priced at only $5? But if it were priced at $75, would people believe in its benefits? One of the attractions of the entire cosmetics industry is that many of its wares enjoy inverse-demand situations. Customers are more likely to buy if the product is expensive than if it is inexpensive. The bestselling perfumes are the most expensive ones.

Make no mistake about it, people rely on price to help form their value judgments. If the quality of a product is not apparent, which is often the case, price is often the major element by which the buyer determines the quality of an item. It is assumed that the highest-priced article is the best. Thus, the pricing policies affect the market's attitudes toward entrepreneurs' products and their organizations.

Distributive-network pressures. Often price will have to conform to the attitudes of product distributors. For example, in buying an automatic gate closer from Sears, the Sears' buyer felt that it should retail for $5.95 with a 40 percent margin; thus, the factory price was $3.57 f.o.b. factory. The buyer resisted a lower retail price of $5.69. His price point for the item was $5.95, not $5.69. He did not want to leave any money on the table. Naturally, this conversation was informal during the early start-up stages of the venture, when the firm's pricing structure was being formulated.

Evaluate price sensitivities

Investigate the price at which the middleman wants to have some product to offer the trade. A menswear merchant might have three price points for his suit department: $195, $250, and $325. He would go to market to buy suits to fit into those price points, sometimes called price lines. With a 50 percent initial markup as his goal (sometimes called keystone), he would then try to buy suits for a cost of approximately $97.50, $125, and $162.50 to fit into those price points.

Retailers have developed a rather delicate touch on how much their customers will pay for various things. They have paid dearly for the knowledge. They have tried to charge more only to have the goods sit in inventory. So when dealers look at an item and tell the manufacturer that it will sell for $20, the manufacturer should consider their opinions carefully. As a group, they generally know what they are talking about. Even if they don't, the fact that they believe they know what they are talking about will make them resist a product if it does not fit into their perceived-value structure for it.

If by good fortune, an entrepreneur can offer them something they think is a bargain, a good value, distribution will be facilitated.

Select a strategy

There are two basic pricing strategies: price skimming and penetration pricing. Price either at the top of the range or the bottom of it. In some instances it makes sense to price somewhere between the extremes.

USC Taffy: Perceived-Value Pricing

This example illustrates how perceived value can be used in product pricing.

First, the retailer starts with a package of taffy that normally sells to the consumer for 89 cents. Are there any noticeable differences among taffy candy? Has anyone ever tasted taffy and said, "That's the best taffy I have ever had?"

Taffy is just sugar and water. Not much can be done to a batch of taffy to make it different from other taffy. But the retailer can sell this taffy for a higher price by adding perceived value to the product.

The candy maker takes basic taffy and makes the candy in different colors. The school colors for the University of Southern California (USC) are crimson and gold, so the taffy is made in those two colors. The cost for this specially colored taffy is the same as for regular taffy.

The next step is to use a mason jar with a snap-on lid as a container and put the USC crest on the side of the jar in gold leaf. Finally, a gold tag is designed to hang around the lid of the container. The card will describe how taffy was the favorite candy during the Roman Empire days and how Tommy Trojan, the USC Mascot, still loves taffy today.

By adding a small cost to the product, the perceived value to the consumer is greater because it is a perfect gift for a USC alumnus. Most people will spend $10 to $20 on a gift of this type. USC taffy sells at the campus bookstore for $15.95. The 89 cent bag of taffy has turned into a high-profit item.

Price skimming. Some new ventures begin by trying to price skim. That is, they price their wares or service at the top of the relevant price range. The reasons for doing so are several and persuasive.

This strategy guards against errors in estimating the cost of the product or service. It is far easier to lower a price set too high than it is to raise one set too low. If entrepreneurs are in a position to lower prices, they can do many creative promotions to stimulate sales that escape entrepreneurs who must increase prices. And cost mistakes often occur. It simply costs more to make the product than was anticipated. There is good reason to want to limit sales, and thus production, early in a venture. A venture doesn't want more business than it can handle satisfactorily. Typically, there is much learning early in a venture that is best done at low levels of activity. A low price may attract more activity than the organization can handle, leading to an unfortunate reputation for poor service just at the time the company is trying to impress the market otherwise.

Naturally, a price skimming strategy increases gross profits, and that brings in money at a time when it is needed.

Over time, this strategy maximizes total revenue for the item as each market segment is charged what it will pay. By starting high and progressively lowering price, each segment of the market buys in on the proposition when the price hits its value scale. Thus, each market segment pays what the item is worth to it.

Finally, a price skimming strategy is called for if there are hints of an inverse-demand situation. To price low in face of an inverse-demand curve is to invite disaster.

Success always attracts the attention of others.

The major disadvantage to price skimming is that it attracts competition. Other firms noting a high price can figure out the costs and act accordingly. High profits attract competition. There is no question. But a new venture may not really be all that concerned with competition if it sees the items as a short-run fad in which it will make money and run to the bank. Let the competition come in and be left holding the bag.

If the venture sees a good long-run demand for its products, however, and it has no way of keeping competition out, then it may want to consider another strategy.

Penetration pricing. For the entrepreneur who thinks an item will have a good long-run market and he or she really doesn't have any way of restricting competition, then a low price may do several things. First, it will definitely discourage competition. Firms do not like to go into ventures in which the prices don't look profitable. Second, the low price will facilitate distribution and market penetration. By getting into the market first and obtaining the best distributors, entrepreneurs do much to help block competition from the market.

By pricing an item to penetrate the market quickly, a venture must be prepared to deliver the goods. And that is a huge task for most new concerns.

Financial requirements for a penetration-pricing strategy are often higher than the new venture can afford. Moreover, the organization may not be able to accommodate a penetration-pricing strategy.

If this discussion frightens entrepreneurs into thinking that pricing is some kind of magic, they can relax. Most of the time pricing will be easy. The market will quickly indicate what the price has to be. With the help of the distribution networks, entrepreneurs will be able to set reasonable prices with which to begin operations. If they are wrong, they can rectify the mistake quickly. If a price proves to be too high, it can be lowered.

Set the price

The price list is an unappreciated marketing tool. When a distributor or dealer or industrial buyer needs to buy a certain product, a trip to the files produces some folders with sales materials and price lists of the products under consideration. That material is a sales representative at the time the decision is being made. A price list does far more than disclose prices. A price list should

- Sell the goods.
- Clearly identify the products.
- Clearly inform the buyer how much each item will cost and the terms of sale governing it.
- Tell the potential buyer where the goods can be purchased.

Some Policies to Consider

The list of pricing policies is so lengthy it is possible to present only some of the more common ones entrepreneurs will likely encounter.

Motivate large orders

Most firms offer quantity discounts because it is highly profitable to do so. All studies show that small orders are costly; many are even sold at a loss. Many firms refuse to accept small orders. The customer must order a certain minimum amount. Consequently, entrepreneurs should study costs carefully to determine how much they can afford to reduce price in order to encourage large orders.

One must be careful not to confuse the market with too many price brackets. A firm should have in mind some specific buying behavior it is trying to encourage, such as a dozen units or a case of goods or a truckload of merchandise—whatever makes sense for the intended market. It is useless to offer a truckload price to a buyer who can only handle a dozen units. If a typical customer buys only one unit at a time, perhaps the quantity discount would be designed to reward the buying of two units, a 100 percent increase in sales volume from that account. If accounts normally buy a dozen units, perhaps the firm would try to extend their commitment to two dozen.

If an analysis of the customer's buying habits indicates a finite set requisition, that is, the buyer is going to buy only a certain amount no matter what the price discount is, then it is pointless to offer one. For example, if a lawyer needs a word processor, there would be little sense for the vendor to offer a better price for buying two of them because the buyer needs only one. Quantity discounts should be offered only if there is real opportunity to sell more with the lower price. If not, then quantity price reductions are usually handled differently on an individual basis.

A large firm wants to buy 500 word processors and inquires about quantity discounts. A manufacturer submits a bid for the business. It would not handle such orders with a price list.

Lock in the customer

Patronage discounts are given as rebates, after a period of time, based on the total purchases a customer makes from the vendor. For example, a large dress-shirt manufacturer gives patronage discounts based on the merchant's total sales of its products for the year. Some retail shops used to get about 4 percent of their purchases returned to them each year as a rebate check. That's a lot of money that goes right to the merchant's bottom line.

Avoid price conflicts if possible

Price wars are generally stupid and costly. Unless a venture has a definite cost advantage and believes it can win the price war, it shouldn't start one. If a price war develops, a firm should try to handle it in an oblique way and not try to match penny for penny the competitor's price cuts, for they are too easy to copy. A firm must think up different ways to achieve the same results. Admittedly, sometimes a price war may seem unavoidable. Entrepreneurs might have to discourage some competitors who are trying to drive them from the business by matching the competitors' prices right down the line.

Disguise price cuts

It is usually wise to disguise price reductions so that the previous price structure is not destroyed. A firm may want to go back to an early price structure when the difficult market conditions are over. After all, there is only one reason for cutting price. The firm isn't happy with the sales volume at the existing prices. It isn't selling enough. So instead of cutting price, perhaps the firm gives some free goods. A gypsum company might offer some free sacks of plaster in every load of wallboard when it wants to shade prices.

Don't lower price without a signed order

When an account demands a lower price, the seller should not agree to it immediately. The response should be, "Let's submit your order for that price to the boss and see if he'll go for it. He just might."

The boss should then say, "Do I understand that you are ready to give me an order if I meet your price requirement? Give me a firm purchase order to consider." A venture shouldn't lower price without a firm commitment to buy, or it will likely have just started a progression of price pressures as the buyer keeps applying more and more pressure to see just how low the venture will go to get the business.

One of the problems with published quantity discounts is that they tell everyone something about a venture's costs. Published discounts disclose how low the venture will go to get business. So tough buyers will begin demanding the lowest price quoted for whatever quantity they want to buy, disregarding quantity limits.

Tough buyers can really put on the squeeze. They know a firm wants the business badly, and they want to make it buy their business. It's a difficult situation, for a firm may be starving for business and will do anything to get some volume into the shop. But if a firm starts playing these games with the buyers, how will it ever sell anything to them for a profit? Once the buyers know a firm has no backbone, that it will fold under pressure, they will push for lower prices. If a business owner can't handle price pressure, then he or she should not try to do so. He or she should send in someone who can, someone who does not have the authority to cut prices. There are advantages if the boss is not present in the buying office where buyers can really put the deal under the gun.

Creative pricing

Some of the biggest fortunes have been made by those people who have been able to develop slightly different ways of pricing their goods to the market. Some examples:

Leasing is but a pricing policy in which a venture sells the goods to a customer over time while retaining title to the goods. The venture sells the goods and keeps them. IBM, Xerox, United Shoe, Hughes Tool, and many more firms made their fortunes leasing, not selling, their goods. Leasing can be highly profitable.

People don't buy products, they buy benefits. One tire company sold aircraft tires to an airline on a per-landing basis. It agreed to keep the tires on the planes in good shape for so much per landing. After all, the airline company did not care about the tires. The airline was buying safe landings and takeoffs.

Don't sell the product, sell the benefits.

Push high-margin products

Different products usually have different gross margins. Often a firm will have some products on which profit margins are slim. The high-margin articles are usually more difficult sales. Consequently, a venture must design its marketing program to push those with high margins.

There are people who refuse to sell low-margin products just as they refuse to do business for a loss. They maintain that it is pointless just to move goods through a warehouse. If there isn't profit in the order, they don't want it.

Some customers are not wanted

Some accounts are so troublesome or refuse to pay a sufficient price that there is little profit in dealing with them. So why do it? One of the real keys to profitable operation is to develop a base of customers who are somewhat insensitive to price. In selecting target markets, an entrepreneur should pay special attention to each customer's market-price sensitivity.

Don't make money on price and lose it on terms

Some clever buyers will not argue about a price because they are fully aware that a firm is girded for battle on it. Rather they will try to gain more favorable terms; for example, the firm pays the freight, delays dating, or allows a larger cash discount. Whatever they think the firm will accept. Be careful. Cost out any concessions.

Use price list to win orders

An enterprise's price list is one of its most neglected marketing tools. It is common to open a business without having developed a price list. Then when customers call asking about quantity discounts, the entrepreneur doesn't have the answer. Yet, featuring quantity discounts on the price list can be one of the most highly profitable marketing strategies.

Motivating a customer to purchase a product by reading a price list is key to continued success. Whenever a potential customer, distributor, or dealer needs to buy, he or she automatically looks through files containing sales materials and price lists. A firm's price list is its sales representative at the time the purchasing decision is being made. It needs to be attractive, informative, easy to read, and easy to order from. Most entrepreneurs make the mistake of including only their prices on the list. To begin with, a price list should clearly identify all the different products. Brief product information may also be appropriate. The price list should indicate how much each different item will cost and the terms of the sale.

Often missing from the price list is information on where and how the goods can be purchased. Many price lists fail to include the seller's address and phone number.

Never forget the one basic principle of marketing—make it as easy as possible for the customer to buy. The easier it is to buy, the more goods will be sold.

Here are some other ideas to transform a price list into an effective marketing tool that can more easily sell goods.

- Use easy-to-mail order blanks that can be dropped into the mail. If possible, obtain a toll free telephone number and feature it on the price list so customers can immediately call in the order.

- Whenever possible, display goods on the reverse side of the price list. Using attractive pictures of products can enhance the price list and encourage sales.

- Try to keep the price list out of the customer's files by placing it on some useful advertising-specialty item that will be placed on the customer's desk, such as a calendar, business card holder, or Rolodex card. Contact an advertising-specialty business and solicit its ideas on unique ways to display a price list.

- Make the price list simple to read. Some price lists are extremely complicated and confusing to all but people experienced with the product line.

The price list should be updated frequently to stay up with the trends in the industry. Entrepreneurs should be flexible and try different pricing strategies until one that works best is found. They can run monthly or quarterly specials for featured products, or offer customers a deal they can't afford to turn down.

Pricing for Service Businesses

Pricing is one of the most complex challenges entrepreneurs face when starting a new venture. Yet, pricing is the single most important factor affecting profits and the entrepreneur's ability to be successful. Usually the lower a product or service is priced, the more that will be sold. In some instances, however, customers associate a lower price with lower quality. In such cases, a lower price can actually hurt sales. And the more that is sold, the lower the costs. But developing a pricing strategy is not that simple, especially with a service business.

Many entrepreneurs price in a vacuum based on what they want to charge. Certain factors govern the price that can be charged for services, namely, the marketplace. Both the potential customers and the competition directly affect pricing strategies.

The first step is to determine what price the potential customers would be willing to pay versus what the entrepreneur wants to charge. Here are several ways to obtain pricing information: call on several potential customers and ask them what they would be willing to pay for the services; hold a focus group with potential customers and ask them how much they would be willing to pay for different services. Keep in mind that some potential customers would be willing to pay more than the price they share with you.

It is a good idea to talk to other entrepreneurs offering similar services outside the immediate geographic area and ask them what they charge. A professional association can be contacted and asked what type of pricing is standard for the industry.

The second step is to find out what competitors charge for similar consulting services. Both directly competitive and substitute services affect what one can charge for services.

When obtaining pricing information from potential customers and competitors, entrepreneurs will find a range of different prices, from the very expensive to the more reasonable. They should price their services within this range. Services could be priced at the high end, at the normal market rate, or at the lower prices to create more demand.

Entrepreneurs can consider incorporating the principle of perceived value into the pricing strategies. Perceived value is when potential customers believe that services have some type of intangible value and are willing to pay more for it. For example, look at the higher prices that Abercrombie & Fitch charges for its shirts or the higher prices for some perfumes and jewelry. Many entrepreneurs design products or services that have perceived value, so they can charge a higher price for them.

Experts report that professionals who charge fees in the upper range are usually the most successful. That's perceived value—charging more based on expertise, reputation, and referrals from satisfied customers.

When an entrepreneur is starting a new venture, communicating credibility is the biggest challenge. For example, to attract new customers to a training company, an entrepreneur could offer a pilot training program at a greatly reduced price or free of charge. If the customer is satisfied, then the entrepreneur could contract to conduct more training sessions.

Other Pricing Factors

Other factors, such as taxes, daily and hourly rates, and nonbillable time, should be considered in pricing. It is necessary to calculate taxes when pricing a service in order to cover federal income taxes, state income taxes, and unemployment taxes. The price will have to include enough to pay these taxes. The entrepreneur will have to estimate the amount based on their individual tax situations.

The owner of a business will spend a certain number of hours each week managing the business: networking, marketing, billing customers, doing professional development, and preparation. These hours are not billable time, but are necessary to do business. Most owners of service businesses plan on working 15 days per month, with the remaining five workdays dedicated to managing the business in those nonbillable activities.

After estimating the nonbillable time needed to operate the business, the next step is to calculate daily and hourly rates for pricing. A full-time employee works 40 hours per week, 52 weeks in a year, or a total of 2080 hours or 261 days. The entrepreneur must decide whether to develop an hourly rate, a daily rate, standard fees for specific services, or a pricing structure that includes more than one of these rates.

Fees for services will also be affected by the entrepreneur's reputation, years of experience, amount of competition, length of time as a service provider, and what the market will bear, in other words perceived value and what customers are willing to pay. In the service industries, prices are often invitations to negotiate. The entrepreneur must be careful to avoid the trap of negotiating away too much and working for less than he or she wants.

Conclusion

Pricing deserves a great deal of attention. It is not only the key to profits, but often the key to sales. While costs are important in determining the price floor and ultimate profits, the market usually sets the price. Unquestionably, aggressive pricing tactics are often used to invade established markets, but smart business owners avoid being destroyed by a competitive price war.

Exercise 19a: Pricing Formulas

Markup: The percentage amount of the retail price on an item over and above the cost; this figure is always related to the retail price. Then, the markup is the difference between retail and cost.

Remember: Markup relates to the retail price, not to what was originally paid.

1. Markup $

    $ Retail – $ Cost = $ Markup

For example, if the retail price of a product is $64.99 and cost to manufacture is $13, the markup is $51.99.

2. Markup %

$$\frac{\$ \text{ Markup}}{\$ \text{ Retail}} = \text{Markup \%}$$

For example, markup of $51.99 divided by retail of $64.99 gives a markup of 80 percent.

3. Retail $

$$\frac{\$ \text{ Cost}}{100\% - \text{Markup \%}} = \$ \text{ Retail}$$

For example, if the cost of the product is $115 and the markup is 35 percent, then $115 divided by 65 percent results in a retail price of $176.92.

4. Average inventory

$$\frac{\text{Sales for the year}}{\text{Stock turn}} = \text{Average inventory}$$

For example, sales of $300,000 for the year divided by stock turn of 3 gives an average inventory of 100,000. (Refer to Chapter 23 for more information on inventory turnover or stock turns.)

Calculating markup

1. The retail price of an item is $74.50. The cost of the item is $53. What is the markup in dollars? Using this information, calculate the markup percentage.

Pricing a product

2. The cost of the item to you is $14.90. Your markup is 45%. What is the retail price?

Checking a competitor's markup

3. Tootsies Toodlers (your competitor) is selling corduroy overalls that you would like to carry also. The retail cost is $48. Her cost (from checking with the distributor) is $23. What is the markup percentage?

Projecting sales

4. Hot Tomato plans to sell $400,000 its first year in business. From research, the storeowner feels stock turns of 4 are obtainable. What is the average inventory of Hot Tomato?

In completing a feasibility or business plan, the right price is what potential customers are willing to pay for the product or service. The real question is whether the business can make a satisfactory profit at this price.

Exercise 19b: Pricing Strategies

Given the goal in the column on the left, what pricing strategies would you employ to achieve that goal? Write the pricing strategy in the column on the right.

Goal	Pricing strategy(s) to determine goal
Maximize profit	
Ensure adequate cash flow	
Increase sales volume	
Increase market share	
Meet or beat the competition's prices	
Maintain or create a certain image	
Improve customer relations	

Exercise 19c: Pricing a Product

Below are some questions to help you determine expenses so that you can, in turn, develop the correct price structure. The questions will help you understand what kind of information you need.

Question	Formula	Enter amount
What is your cost of product per unit?	Enter unit cost	$
How many units do you estimate you will sell in one year?	Enter estimate of number of units sold in one year	
What is total product cost?	Cost per unit x units sold	$
What are your estimated yearly operating expenses (excluding your salary)?	Actual or estimated monthly operating expenses x 12	$
How much salary per year do you want to make?	Salary per year	$
How much profit do you want to make?	(Total product cost + salary per year + yearly operating expenses) x profit percentage	$
What is your yearly estimated tax liability for federal and state taxes?	Salary per year x 50%	$
How much revenue will you need to generate?	Total product cost + estimated yearly operating expenses + salary per year + desired profit + yearly estimated tax liability	$
What's the wholesale price for your product?	Annual revenue required/ estimated number of units sold	$
What's the retail price for your product?	Wholesale price per unit x 2*	$

*The 2 is called a "multiplier." Some industries have established multipliers which create standard pricing. Research will uncover if there are multipliers for your industry.

Exercise 19d: Pricing a Service

Use this table to determine the level of sales you would have to obtain to be profitable and the amount of billable hours necessary to meet that level of sales. Use a service business concept to complete these questions.

Question	Formula	Calculation
How much money do you want to take home?	Annual net income	$ Annual net income =
What are your total annual expenses?	Estimate your monthly expenses and multiply by 12	$ Operating expenses =
What about taxes? Calculate 50% or half of your desired income.	Annual net income x 50%	$ Taxes =
What amount of sales or annual gross income will you need to cover operating expenses and taxes?	Annual gross income = Annual net income + annual operating expenses + amount to cover taxes	$ Annual gross income =
How many billable hours will you work in one year?*	Number of billable hours per day x number of days per week x number of weeks per year	Number of billable hours =
What is your hourly rate?	Annual gross income / number of billable hours	Hourly rate =

* Be sure you are only calculating time that you will be able to bill your clients. Do not include nonbillable administrative time, sales and marketing, etc.

Exercise 19e: One More Look at Pricing a Service

Use a service business concept to complete these questions.

1. What standard services will you provide?

2. How long will it take to provide each service? _____ hours

3. What is your hourly rate? _____

4. What prices will you charge for each service?
   (Hourly rate multiplied by the number of hours to provide services = price of service.)

Services	Number of hours	x	Hourly rate	=	Price
		x		=	
		x		=	
		x		=	
		x		=	
		x		=	
		x		=	
		x		=	
		x		=	

Market Penetration

Learning Objectives

In this chapter, students will learn to

- Identify different methods to sell products and services to customers.
- Evaluate strengths and weaknesses of market-penetration methods.

Penetrating the market involves specific methods ventures use to sell products and services to customers. The first mistake made by most entrepreneurs when developing a concept is failing to carefully define potential customers.

As mentioned in Chapter 18: Analyzing the Market, great care is taken to identify direct and indirect customers. Who will make the buying decision? Will the venture sell directly to the end user or to someone else? A limousine service has identified executives as its end users but knows that secretaries make the buying decisions. Its market-penetration tactics will be aimed at the administrative staff, while providing excellent service to executives. The same is true of catering companies that target corporate clients. Different market-penetration methods are necessary to reach secretaries rather than executives.

Market-Penetration Methods

A variety of methods exist for penetrating markets. The most common and effective methods will be discussed here.

Direct-sales force

A direct-sales force is a group of salespeople who work directly for a company and are paid either straight salary, salary plus bonus, or straight commission. The advantage of using a direct-sales force is that the company can control them as full-time employees. The entrepreneur has more control in training them how to sell, price, and service the product or service. The disadvantage is the expense involved in maintaining a full-time sales force. The company has to pay salary, travel, office support, and benefits for each salesperson.

Salespeople require substantial incentive programs to provide the continual motivation required to keep them pushing for more sales. A common problem is that most salespeople work unsupervised. How does the employer know if they are working? What they do goes on in private conversations, interfaces between them and the customers. Consequently, sales managers install several automatic supervisory tools that are at work constantly to try to get the salespeople to do what management wants them to do. They assign territories, accounts, quotas, and budgets all designed to control the salesperson's activities. But the most significant automatic supervisory tool of all is the compensation plan. It affects the salesperson every hour of every day of the year. It can be quite potent and, one would hope, helpful. It can also be counterproductive if improperly designed.

There is one school of thought in entrepreneurial circles that all one has to do is pay the salespeople substantial commission on the sales they make and forget about them: commission is all it takes to get sales. If it were only that easy. While a straight commission plan sounds like a logical way to get the sales force to do its job, there are some problems with it that must be resolved.

First, in many situations it may be inappropriate. The salesperson may not directly take orders or may have to work in a team over a period of time to get the order. Commissions work best in situations in which the salesperson goes face to face with a potential customer and gets an order— or not—depending upon the skills used.

Second, just because someone is paid by commission does not mean that he or she is willing to work. A commission plan does not mean that management can abdicate responsibility for managing the sales force. The commissioned salesperson still needs strong support from management. Sales materials, home-office support, training, and close communications with management are still needed.

Third, often salaries or other forms of payment can provide the desired incentives. The clear message is that the salaries are closely tied to the salesperson's performance —do a great job, get a great salary; don't do the job, don't get a salary.

The root of the problem is human nature and its evaluation of rewards. Psychologists say that the more immediate the reward, the more effective it is. If an employer wants to see a sales force hop, he or she can offer to give the salespeople who accomplish the specified sales two free tickets to some hot event that is coming up—a concert, the Super Bowl, a play, a vacation.

One retailer on a slow day about noon would say, "When you have sold $600, you can go home." Customers who walked in right after that were subjected to the finest selling tactics that could be mustered for service.

It may be difficult for a manager get the salesperson to make that one extra sales call in the late afternoon or early morning when the rewards for doing so may be delayed for a year or so. But when the salesperson is thinking, "I need $500 in sales for that TV set, so I am not going home until I get it," the extra call will more likely be made.

The sell or starve aspect of commission plans provide such incentives. Really good salespeople prefer to be paid by a straight commission because they can make more money doing so. The more they sell, the more they make.

One question will arise: Should the salespeople be paid a larger or smaller commission as their sales increase? There are no definitive answers because there are advantages and disadvantages to both progressive and regressive commission rates. While a progressive rate makes much sense in providing incentives for the salespeople to sell more goods, it can lead to many bad selling practices, such as overloading customers with goods, bunching sales orders into alternate pay periods, and pooling of orders between salespeople. The employer must give much thought to the pay system, for many serious problems lurk for the unwary manager. Usually, the pay practices of competitors will provide some guidelines for setting policies.

Recruiting and selection

Someone must go into the market, locate people who need what the firm is selling, and then persuade them to buy. Not many people want to do it. Even fewer can do it. Good salespeople are not plentiful. It is a challenge to find and recruit effective salespeople and persuade them to join a fledgling company.

Hire selectively

Too many entrepreneurs are so eager to get salespeople so that needed revenue will start flowing into the company's coffers that they hire anyone claiming to be a salesperson. They can hire a lot of bad salespeople that way. If customers are the firm's most important asset, it makes little sense to place their patronage at the mercy of people who may be inept. Founders want assurance that a salesperson will do no harm before unleashing him or her on the trade.

Two problems hinder the entrepreneur's efforts.

- The time and effort involved in hiring quality salespeople
- Not knowing what to look for in potential salespeople

Entrepreneurs must be willing to spend whatever time and effort it takes to find the right people for a sales force. If one can afford a sales manager, then efforts must be directed toward hiring that individual in whose hands the sales effort is entrusted. Few new enterprises can afford, however, to hire a sales manager in the beginning. The firm is fortunate if one of its founders has the needed marketing and sales skills to guide its sales program. Indeed, professional investors often demand that someone with marketing clout be on the management team before they will invest in the firm. Without marketing skills, success is usually elusive.

But how does one select the right people? Many managers in despair hire everyone and let the market select the producers. It's like the "push them off the dock" school of swimming. The problem is too many people drown, and they may take the company down with them.

While even the best of sales managers will at times err in hiring someone, informed sales management can do a much better job of hiring salespeople than random chance.

Look for accomplishments

All sorts of people talk a good game. But what have they actually done? Do their resumes show a record of achievement? Resumes should be checked out carefully. People have been known to fabricate an outstanding career. Good salespeople have records to prove it.

Entrepreneurs usually have little money. The faster they can penetrate the marketplace, the quicker their companies will produce sales revenue.

Hire salespeople with good contacts

It's not likely that new ventures can afford to hire and train inexperienced, raw sales recruits. They need salespeople who can get into the field and produce revenue quickly. New businesses are in a race to reach the cash break-even point before they run out of money. They don't have time to develop a sales force from raw material.

A good way to start is to hire a sales force from among the salespeople who are now selling to the people the new venture wants to sell to: to hire experience and pay for it. It may be the best investment a venture will make.

One reason for hiring proven, experienced salespeople is to avoid extensive training. While some training is needed in product and customer knowledge, most new firms are unable to do extensive sales training. But it is critical that ventures do not send unprepared salespeople to call on customers. The salesperson must be professional and knowledgeable. The firm will be judged by the sales force that represents it.

One of the hidden traps for the entrepreneur in starting a new venture is the cost of the ramp-up. Ramp-up includes all the costs the company incurs from researching and developing the product or service, office and supply overhead costs, and the training time involved before the first accounts are set up. Lead time to establish a new venture can run up to one year. One way to reduce the ramp-up costs is to avoid hiring and training a new sales force. Instead, use sales agents and lead blockers.

Manufacturers' reps or sales agents

Manufacturers' representatives will be referred to as sales agents for simplicity. A sales agent works as a subcontractor for a company to sell products or services. Agents are paid by commission, which is calculated as a specified percentage of the wholesale price. They receive their commission after the company collects from the customers. The sales agent pays for expenses such as product samples, travel, office, telephone, and supplies that are incurred in selling the product or service.

The founder assigns a specified territory to a sales agent where he or she can sell the product or service. In addition, a performance contract is used and signed by the sales agent, which outlines a minimum number of units to be sold annually. The minimum usually increases every year for the next five years and then is frozen. The founder is responsible for providing training to the sales agent and leads for potential new customers.

The advantage of using sales agents is that the company does not incur any sales costs until it has been paid for the product or service sold. The company is able to quickly build a large sales force and have the product/service sold nationwide in a relatively short period of time.

The primary disadvantage of using sales agents is that they usually sell other products or services, meaning that any product or service is just a part of a complete line handled by the sales agent. Sales agents tend to push the easier-to-sell products and services and those that have already established a large customer following. The founder has no control over the sales agents since they are subcontractors and do not work directly for the company. Therefore, they can be extremely hard to manage in regard to pricing, follow-up, and service.

Sales agents sometimes work for other organizations known as sales associations. These companies employ many different sales agents to cover different parts of the country. Some entrepreneurs hire a sales association instead of dealing directly with many different sales agents. The advantage is that all sales agents can be trained at once, and the founder has to deal with the sales association only for the commission structure, receiving the order, collecting the account, and supplying new product or service information.

The best way to find sales agents is to talk to the intended customers and ask them which sales agents they have dealt with and find helpful. They know who is good and who isn't. They also might know which sales agents might be interested in carrying the firm's line. Another way is to attend industry trade shows, where there will be many sales agents to evaluate. Entrepreneurs could also contact industry trade associations, which often have directories of sales agents who service particular industries.

Once a sales rep is found, the entrepreneur needs to regularly contact him or her by phone or in person to ask what is happening and keep track of performance goals and accomplishments. The entrepreneur should offer to help reps in their marketing efforts and continue to supply the reps with any qualified sales leads.

Successful firms provide reps with a detailed sales manual that includes competitive comparisons, photos, and any other type of product information that can be helpful, such as journal articles.

Firms also need to furnish reps with demonstration kits, point-of-sale displays, training sessions, and other support materials. Oftentimes, the entrepreneur will sell the demonstration kit to the rep at cost to recoup the dollars invested in it. Reps can later sell the merchandise and make a profit.

Possible customer objections should be listed and countered with good arguments for purchasing the product or service. A list of happy users should be provided for customer references. It is important to furnish reps with all the ammunition they might need to make selling easier.

Sales representatives can be motivated with newsletters describing new company developments, territory sales volume, or new spin-offs. This is an inexpensive way to keep the communication lines open. They should receive copies of all prepared press releases and marketing packages. Sales contests, prizes, incentives, monthly discounts, or double commissions can be used. The new venture is competing for their time with the other product lines they carry.

Someone in a new company should go out in the field with the reps. Sales reps need to be supported all the time, especially when they ask for assistance.

Successful entrepreneurs follow up on sales leads to determine how the sales rep interacted with the customer. The sales rep should know the firm is interested in both successful and unsuccessful sales leads. New customer lists should be developed continually.

Commissions must be paid on time. Nothing distresses a rep more than to wait for commission checks. Some entrepreneurs, when experiencing cash-flow problems, defer paying their reps. This trap should be avoided. Loss of a key rep could cripple sales volume for many quarters.

Quarterly or annual sales meetings can be held with the firm paying for the hotel, meals, and other rep expenses, but often the reps cover their transportation costs. Sales sessions can be held and reps' input asked for. They function as part of the management team and are recognized for outstanding performance.

A firm should always deliver on product promises and avoid late delivery and unresponsive warranty servicing. Reps need the long-term goodwill of their customers more than they need the firm. Sales reps can usually find another source for products they want to handle.

House accounts should be avoided if possible. These are accounts that the entrepreneur has personally established and sometimes sells to at a lower profit margin. Reps are leery of lucrative accounts the boss keeps. They do not like to see large shipments of product going into their territories without commissions being paid to them.

An option is to offer the sales rep the house account as soon as his or her total sales volume from other customers in the territory reaches a certain amount. Then, the rep has a good incentive, and the entrepreneur is not risking paying a commission check to a mediocre rep.

Whether a firm uses sales reps or hires its own sales force depends on the product, rep quality, market characteristics, and its financial condition.

Lead blockers

In football, a wise coach sends a very large lineman barreling into the intended area into which the runner is destined to carry the ball. This lead blocker is supposed to knock down the first thing that looms in the way. In a similar vein, it is often highly advantageous to have someone in a target market who can open the right doors, someone whose sales reputation is such that his or her credibility in that market rubs off on the company. A new company needs someone who can provide that lead block, who can knock down the barriers in that market.

To get lead blockers, a company often must make an offer they can't refuse. The firm may have to buy its way into a market. Following are some examples of this tactic.

A company in Colorado makes computerized energy-management devices for the conservation of power, gas, and steam. Mastered-metered apartment houses are its main target market. The company proved the viability of its devices with two years of successful experience in the nearby Denver market, during which it sold more than $1 million of product while learning a great deal about the end user. The company was able to raise capital to allow expansion into other markets, particularly the large eastern ones and Chicago. But a small firm in Colorado can't waltz into the huge eastern markets with much chance of success without years of hard work trying to persuade key accounts to buy. The company needed a lead blocker.

Out of the East came just the man for the job. The owner of a large manufacturer of steam pumps contacted the company to learn about its products. The device that monitored the BTUs delivered to each apartment in a steam-heated system interested him for its obvious fit into his steam-pump line. He also sat on the board of directors of a large eastern bank-holding company that controlled 186 banks. He was a highly respected businessman.

After several weeks of considering the product, the Easterner called and said, "I'm flying to L.A. today. I'll stop in Colorado and see you at 8 a.m. on Saturday morning." The firm's president canceled his fishing plans, and the meeting was on. Entrepreneurs work when there is work to be done.

The Easterner's opening remark was, "Your products are exciting, but I don't think we are interested. The numbers just don't work out for us."

Now, people don't fly to Colorado just to tell company managers they are not interested in the company's product. It had to be an invitation to dance. Having just returned from a lecture by one of his mentors on the need for a lead blocker in entering a market, the president blurted out, "I'm going to make you an offer you can't refuse." He proceeded to concoct the following offer:

The prospective lead blocker would be allowed to buy 80,000 shares of the company at the then-going price of 50 cents a share. The stock would likely go public within the next three months at a price that would make the stock worth about $3 a share. The thought of having his name on the stock prospectus and having him front for the company when it conducted due-diligence meetings in the East was not overlooked. He would be given distribution rights for the products in the East, for which he would receive a 20 percent commission on all sales. He would set up the sales agency that would sell to the same distribution network through which he was selling his steam pumps. He would place his top man in charge of the operation. It was an offer the Easterner could not refuse. The deal was made.

Did the president give away too much? Who knows! The proposal did the job. Moreover, it would have cost the firm a lot of money to try to penetrate those large eastern markets on its own—probably more than what it paid the lead blocker, and with less likelihood of success. The lead blocker set up 13 large eastern distributors for the products, and the race was on to penetrate the eastern markets.

The role of time in an initial marketing thrust cannot be ignored. Time is money. Time is lost opportunity. Time is risk. The longer it takes to become established in a market, the more it will cost, and the more risks that the market will disappear or be enticed away by new technology. One must move with appropriate speed in high-tech ventures. The market may not wait around. Thus, if necessary, an entrepreneur must spend some money or give some equity away to enter the market in a timely manner.

The lead blocker strategy for penetrating a market is to select as an initial key account the firm that is the leader, the firm whose behavior is copied by others in the industry, accounts whose names mean something. Nicole Frank, in selling her new line of children's luggage, used the big retailer of children's toys, F.A.O. Schwartz, as a lead blocker. If she sold to the market's leaders, the others will follow.

A second example: A large maker of word processors in its struggling days assigned the responsibility for penetrating the San Francisco market to one of its young marketers. Upon arriving in the area, he discovered that a large local insurance company was planning to buy 500 word processors. He made an appointment to see the person who would make the buying decision. His deal was simple, but direct. "I'll bring you 500 word processors. You don't have to pay for them for six months, and you don't have to pay for them then if you don't like them. That's a deal you can't refuse. But, in turn, I ask only one thing of you.

"When I refer potential buyers to you, I want you to tell them that you looked at all of the word processors on the market and decided to buy ours. For every 10 calls you answer, I'll take you and your wife out to dinner at any restaurant in San Francisco."

The deal was made. After 92 calls, both the salesperson and the buyer had had their fill of eating fine food. But the market had been penetrated. The public endorsement of a large, recognized buyer was enough to allay the fears of potential buyers.

Consignment sales

Consignment merchandise, like every other element of business, has both positive and negative aspects to it. Consignment merchandise means that a retailer does not take title to the inventory but tries to sell it for another person. As a result, the profit margin is much lower, but inventory cost is zero. As a rule, the retailer will receive 40 to 50 percent of the sales price for consigned merchandise. Following are some of the positive and negative aspects of consignment merchandise.

For the retailer. There are many more positives for retailers carrying consigned merchandise in their stores than retailers who purchase the merchandise.

Most importantly, there is no financial investment. However, the retailer should choose to carry only a quality product or product line that has good sales potential. These types of products may be hard to find. Ventures must be selective in the type of products they carry on consignment. They need to determine beforehand if there is a market for this product, and try to determine if customers will buy it.

A second advantage is that consignment merchandise offers the opportunity to carry goods that ventures might not otherwise be able to carry. Because of cash-flow restraints, they may be limited in the amount of inventory they can offer. Consignment goods may allow ventures to carry a complete line of merchandise without tying up a penny of their operating capital. This enables companies to expand product lines without additional dollars. It is a real advantage to carry top-quality merchandise without any additional investment or owning the goods.

In some cases, the manufacturer placing the consigned goods in a store will be involved in its promotion. Most manufacturers are interested in selling their products as rapidly as possible so they can earn a profit.

Consigned goods can allow retailers to carry the latest and most popular models of a product line without risking obsolete-inventory problems. For example, if the manufacturer introduces a new or improved product, the retailer will not be left with old inventory or out-of-date merchandise that is hard to move.

For many retailers, consigned merchandise means that they can offer greater quantity and variety of products. In some industries, consignment merchandise is the norm. For instance, in an art gallery, the majority of the artwork will be sold on consignment. It would be to the owner's advantage to try to obtain as many salable pieces as possible on consignment.

However, consignment is not without its problems. On the negative side, the goods may not move but take up valuable shelf and inventory space. Another disadvantage is that buyers may return the consigned merchandise for full credit after the retailer has paid the manufacturer. An agreement should be negotiated up-front on how returned goods will be handled. Consignment merchandise can be a real plus for retailers if they select quality products to sell.

For the consignee. If an entrepreneur is trying to market a product, putting the goods on consignment has both advantages and disadvantages. Overall, consignment is not recommended unless the product is new and untested in the market.

One of the key problems is that middlemen or distributors may not give consigned merchandise as much attention as the goods in which they have invested their own money. The profit margin for retailers is less on consigned merchandise, so their motivation to sell the product may be lower. They are usually more concerned with selling products that cost them money if not sold. Whenever involved with consignment, entrepreneurs should consider offering incentives to retailers to motivate them to sell the goods more quickly.

Another issue with consignment is to avoid counting delivered merchandise as sales. Consignments should not be recorded in the ledgers as sales. It is not known whether the transaction is actually a sale until it is either paid for or returned. All that has occurred is that some of the goods are being stored on someone else's shelf or warehouse.

Consignment merchandise causes accountants numerous problems. Since consigned goods are not sold, they cannot be counted as income. If these goods are shown as accounts receivable, income statements are falsely inflated, and the financial statement becomes distorted. Consigned merchandise should be tracked separately to avoid such problems.

Once the goods are sold, it may be difficult to receive payment for them. Recordkeeping and sales reporting must be verified regularly, and periodic inventory counts must be made to ascertain sales payments due. Handling returns must be considered. Auditing consigned merchandise is an administrative headache.

What happens to the merchandise when the retailer is cash-poor and is unable to pay for sold merchandise or declares bankruptcy?

Damaged merchandise can also be an ordeal. Oftentimes, employees are not as careful with consigned stock. If any of the consigned goods are damaged, the supplier must take them back and absorb the damage costs.

If entrepreneurs decide to put merchandise on consignment, they should obtain insurance coverage. The goods remain their merchandise and not the property of the retailer selling them. They must consider what would happen if merchandise were damaged by flood, hurricane, or fire. Insurance can represent a significant added expense, depending on the value of the goods and conditions under which they are sold and warehoused.

On the positive side, placing goods on consignment may allow wider distribution. Distributors do not have to pay to carry the goods and might be willing to add them to their product lines at no cost. This could be an avenue of additional sales.

Various lenders, such as bankers or venture capitalists, will look at consignment merchandise with skepticism. They prefer to see solid sales in which the money comes back, not the goods. An entrepreneur may be painting a weak image of his or her company if many of the goods are on consignment.

Companies are also able to control the pricing of their products when sold on consignment. This might be a way to avoid price-cutting in the marketplace.

If the goods sell, the makers should be able to convince the retailer to purchase them outright on a regular basis. This might enable makers to establish a solid market position.

There are also situations in which there may be no choice but to place goods on consignment: if the merchandise is going to sell at the retail level, a consignment deal must be accepted. This is especially true when introducing new, untested products.

Also, if entrepreneurs want retailers to stock a large inventory in anticipation of forthcoming demand, consignment may be the only option.

Instead of consignment, the entrepreneur can consider giving the retailer delayed payment terms with generous return privileges. Astute entrepreneurs should carefully consider the pros and cons before deciding to place their goods on consignment. Consignment is great for the retailer but could be a disaster for an entrepreneur.

Media advertising

The largest media advertising for entrepreneurs includes newspapers, magazines, radio, and television. Advertising in large metropolitan newspapers has become quite expensive for the new start-up business. Entrepreneurs who are considering advertising in one of these papers must be able to ensure that the ad will yield the desired results. Many regional and local newspapers, however, may reach the intended customers. Advertising in these papers is less expensive and may produce good results. The trick is choosing the right newspaper. Most entrepreneurs cannot afford institutional advertising to build their name recognition in newspapers because the costs are prohibitive.

Magazines are a type of media advertising that has longevity and remains in the home or place of business longer than a daily newspaper. This can be a good medium for reaching a larger geographical area and for testing the acceptability of products and services. However, the cost of space and the costs of producing a professional ad can be high. Entrepreneurs may also encounter a 60- to 90-day lead time just to place an ad in a magazine. In addition, research has shown that any ad must be run a minimum of six times before a purchase can be anticipated. This requires a larger advertising budget and more time than other market-penetration methods. Founders must carefully choose media advertising for market penetration because of price constraints and the need for quick results and rapid sales.

Entrepreneurs who have determined that radio or television advertising could be an effective way to reach their customers try to purchase small blocks of local radio or television time at a reduced rate. This will depend on the supply and demand for radio- and television-advertising time in the local area.

Entrepreneurs usually work with a radio or television sales rep, a media-buying service, or an advertising agency. Media-buying services usually charge 5 percent of the total bill and provide expertise in buying various types of media. Advertising agencies charge in a variety of ways, such as a fee, a per-project charge, or a commission based on the media rate. Sales reps have detailed demographic information that helps to match target customers with various audiences, listening and viewing times, and programs.

Preemptable time costs less but can be bumped. Most stations will avoid losing revenue and will try to schedule commercials at a later, and possibly better, time. If timing is important, preemptable time is not the right buy. If commercials are part of an image campaign, then preemptable time will probably satisfy marketing needs.

Options for advertising in media are enormous. Such journals as *Advertising Age* provide more information. Local advertising associations can probably provide a media start-up kit.

The fast-growing industry of dot-com businesses is using established media to promote company web sites. Advertising by Internet companies in traditional media such as newspapers, magazines, radio, and television surpassed $1 billion in 1999. This shows how companies doing business online are turning to established media as they try to make consumers aware of their brand names and compete for customers.

Fliers and handbills

Fliers consist of handouts that a person finds under the car's windshield wipers or stuck in the handle on the front door, giving the recipient some reason to purchase a product or service. Fliers often contain a discount coupon to attract potential customers.

Many start-up ventures, such as pizza deliverers, car washes, and housecleaning services, use this market-penetration method to establish and grow a repeat-customer base. With all the new software programs and quick copiers, this can be a cost-effective way to reach a small market area. The entrepreneur can also trace how many customers are attracted by counting the redeemed coupons.

The disadvantage of using fliers is the difficulty of trying to cover a large geographical area. Founders who need to cover a large geographical area would be better off using print media and running an ad that contains a coupon.

Many beginning businesspeople with little money to spend on advertising have to use guerrilla marketing tactics. They bootstrap their promotional efforts by placing on parked cars in nearby parking lots fliers or handbills they have printed themselves. These can be inexpensive, yet effective, if done properly. The fliers must quickly tell the person something he or she wants to learn.

Fliers cost just pennies to produce, can be read quickly, provide more flexibility than other print media, and keep a sales message alive. They have many different applications: informing, explaining new information, and selling. Fliers are used to supplement other sales literature and catalogs.

Fliers are most effective when announcing a sale or a special offer, or augmenting an existing promotion. Most fliers are $8\frac{1}{2}$ x 11 inches printed one color on one side. But there are many varieties, such as printing on both sides and folding it in half, making a standard mini brochure. Another variation is using a 4 x 9 inch flier that fits into a standard business envelope. This size is effective when put into standard display racks, placed on counters, or used as a mailing insert.

Color can be added by printing on colored paper with no additional charge. Or add color by using colored ink. Pictures, graphics, or clip art provide a stronger visual impact.

The format of a flier isn't as important as the content and its appearance. The message should be simple, making a timely offer, and tied in with other promotional materials. An attention-getting headline that highlights the most important benefit of a special offer catches the reader's eye. The message should be believable and catchy and should ignite the impulse to buy.

Some tips:

- Make the sales message sound like a one-to-one conversation with the reader.
- Include all information the reader needs to make a buying decision.
- Personalize the sales message by handwriting a note to the recipient.
- Include all relevant information: full address, directions for getting there, telephone and fax numbers with area code, credit cards accepted, hours of business.

A good, creative printer can assist in designing a flier at little or no additional charge. Or a graphic designer can provide assistance.

There are several ways to distribute a flier, including giving them out at the business or to other business owners. Offer to distribute other businesses' fliers. Fliers can also be used as bag stuffers, self-mailers, or business-mail inserts in someone else's mailings. They can be handed out in shopping centers, at sporting events, at trade shows, or on street corners, as well as slipped under doors, placed under windshields, or placed in sales racks or on counter displays.

The most successful distribution methods bring in the most sales and can be tracked by asking customers where they heard about the offer. Satisfied customers can pass on fliers to their friends and neighbors. Costs can be minimized if several different versions of fliers are printed, since they cost as little as 3 to 4 cents each in quantities of a thousand. If prepared and distributed properly, fliers can be an effective but inexpensive sales tool.

Signs

Numerous local, state, and federal regulations control the use of signs. Companies must comply with such regulations; penalties can be significant.

Today's modern technology has provided many different sign options, such as neon, reader boards, computer-operated messages, roadside billboards, windows, and awnings. While storage costs can be expensive, this market-penetration method can reach many potential customers for a long time. Signs must be in good taste and unoffensive and have a strong marketing message. The entrepreneur should carefully research potential customers and surrounding neighbors to determine if a sign will be a welcome addition to the community.

Web billboards. The high-tech Internet commerce industry has turned to low-tech outdoor advertising for old-fashioned results. In 1999, the use of highway billboards by companies that sell their products on the Internet increased dramatically.

The major reason for the explosion of e-commerce businesses advertising on billboards was the settlement of the national lawsuits against the tobacco industry in 1999. The settlement prohibited the tobacco industry, which had long dominated outdoor advertising, from advertising on outdoor billboards.

If entrepreneurs are selling products on a web site, the first thing they must do is make people aware that they exist. Dot-com companies are turning to conventional outdoor advertising to create this awareness.

Direct mail

Direct mail is sending marketing information and sales literature to potential customers by mail. From the standpoint of size alone, direct-mail marketing provides a medium to reach a large number of customers quickly. It is selective and accountable because it allows owners to easily measure the response.

The economic significance and size of the direct-mail industry is staggering. People love the convenience of being able to order by telephone or mail and the guarantees that process offers. Thoughtfully designed direct-mail pieces can produce desired results. Research has shown that more than 90 percent of Americans have bought at least one item as a result of direct mail.

The disadvantage of using direct mail is that the cost is front loaded. The mailing piece, mailing lists, and postage are paid for up front without any guarantee that sales will be generated. The effectiveness of a direct mailer is only as good as the actual mailing list, followed by the right offer. One of the best mailing lists is one compiled from customers by keeping track of their names and addresses via receipts and order forms. Asking customers to sign a book or list in a store and holding sweepstakes that attract people into the store to sign up and register continue to enhance a customer mailing list.

While the response rate on direct-mail pieces varies by business, it tends to be very low, averaging about 1 to 3 percent per mailer. This can become a very expensive market-penetration method for the new start-up business. To increase the response rate, most experts recommend that the target be contacted at least seven times. The timing of a direct-mail piece is important. Studies have also shown that prospects are more receptive to mail pieces in the middle of the week and least receptive on Mondays and Fridays. Other research declares that January, February, and October are the best months for direct mail. Toll-free numbers also increase response rates, especially when mailing to individuals. After evaluating and compiling the results from direct-mail pieces and testing different formats, the founder can increase the response from direct mailers into more profitable areas.

The entrepreneur with a new concept and limited marketing funds can test the market by sending a smaller number of action letters (10 pieces of direct mail) to a selected mailing list. Then the entrepreneur can make an individualized personal follow-up. The sample letter should tell the prospect the date and time for the follow-up call on the message in the direct-mail piece. The follow-up should take place no later than one week after receiving the piece. Another method is sending direct-mail postcards, which if effective, can limit costs and provide an avenue to keep in communication with customers. A series of postcard mailings is most effective.

Sales can be increased not only if the mailer is followed up with a telephone call shortly after the customer receives the mailer but also if the mailer contains something of value, like $1. Using direct mail can be a convenient way to purchase a product or service. This medium allows the seller to make a thorough sales presentation to the intended customer.

Another direct-mail device is postcard packs, which are packages of 15 to 30 postcard coupons wrapped in transparent plastic and sent to people with specific demographic characteristics.

Catalogs are an expensive direct-mail method and are primarily used by companies with large marketing budgets. Entrepreneurs can try this strategy on a small scale if they have a ready supply of merchandise and a mailing list of known customers of their products or services. Success is dependent on repeat customers who have had at least one or more satisfactory transactions with the company. Catalog operations are discussed later in this chapter.

Mail-order advertising

Mail-order advertising refers to the advertisements that are placed in magazines and newspapers to sell a product. Many companies have made fortunes using such direct promotional tactics. There are essentially three elements in mail-order advertising that must be satisfied: the medium, the message or advertisement, and the offer.

The medium

Mail-Order Elements
Medium
Message
Offer

As the mailing list was to direct-mail marketing, the medium is to mail-order advertising. If a company advertises in the wrong medium, it will draw a blank. If it picks the right one, it may have a winner. The key is to place the ad in media that will be read by the target market. Note the two operative words: target and read. The media must go to the intended target market, and the potential customers must read it. Many magazines and newspapers may be delivered into the hands of potential customers, but they are not read. One of the reasons that advertisers are particularly fond of magazines with large newsstand sales is that if a person actually pays money for a magazine, the likelihood is quite good that it will be read. Many subscription magazines may be delivered to the home yet not read. Currently, the in-flight magazines published by the airlines are quite popular among mail-order advertisers. The reason for their effectiveness is that air travelers read those magazines cover to cover, looking carefully at the products advertised in them. They don't have anything else to do while flying.

Consequently, mail-order companies spend a great deal of time studying the different media available to them. Again, they will test extensively. They will put trial ads in a magazine or newspaper just to see how it pulls. The term pulls refers to the ability of an ad to generate sales. There are some ways to tell whether or not a magazine or newspaper is highly regarded by other mail-order advertisers. Do the same advertisers appear in the magazine issue after issue? If a mail-order seller is advertising continually in some magazine, it means that the firm has found it effective. It won't keep advertising in a media that is not bringing in sales volume.

The presence of a lot of mail-order advertisers in a magazine is a good sign. It means that they have found the magazine to be an effective seller. More important, a large number of mail-order advertisers in one magazine actually make it into a catalog. All studies show that people love catalogs and will buy from them. Ads placed in certain magazines can be highly effective for certain sellers.

The mail-order advertiser is greatly concerned with the costs of advertising in various media. There are great qualitative differences among the media, which can justify differences in their prices. Many magazines have a far greater impact on their readers than others. But failing all else, the advertiser falls back on the advertising rates per 1,000 readers.

The message or advertisement

Naturally, some advertisements are more effective than others. Some of the most famous mail-order ads in history have run for years unchanged, with a simple format. It is not necessary to change a proven winner as long as it is winning. Typically, only one thought can be communicated in a mail-order ad. So the ad should be focused on the best shot.

There is much debate over whether it is better to have one big ad or many small ones. It has been proven that if a company has the right offer in the right media, a small ad can do the job. Moreover, the advantage of many small ads is that it provides better coverage of the market. Obviously, the big ad has the advantage of gaining the attention of a larger percentage of readers. Developing an effective ad requires long, hard work.

The offer

As with any aspect of business, there are always some basic principles that affect the outcome of an endeavor. Mail-order advertising is no exception.

First, the principles of recognition and perception play a critical role in successful mail-order advertising. The intended customer must be able to recognize and perceive what the offer is. The product should be immediately recognizable. If a company tried to sell some truly innovative item by advertising, a large percentage of the readers would fail to comprehend exactly what the company is trying to sell. One must be able to communicate the benefits that are offered.

Second, mail-order advertising is usually far more effective when it is trying to sell an item that is not generally available in retail stores. If people can easily pick up a product at a dealer, they are not likely to buy by mail.

Catalog operations

The catalog industry has grown by leaps and bounds. Firms like L.L. Bean, Orvis, and Land's End have all enjoyed tremendous growth and success. There is even a catalog for left-handed golfers and a catalog of catalogs. The strength of catalogs is that people love to look at them. They will carefully study a company's offering if it is presented properly. What more can one ask of a promotional piece?

There are four considerations in a successful catalog operation in addition to the business's ability to fulfill the orders. A catalog company is involved heavily in the logistics of business. The four considerations are the catalog, the catalog recipients, the use of e-commerce, and the assortment of goods.

The catalog

Catalog mail-order businesses differ significantly from other types of direct-response marketing programs in one extremely important way. A great deal of money must be invested up front in producing the catalog. Catalogs are not cheap. Not only are printing costs high, but the photography must be first rate. Moreover, it is no small task to put together a catalog. Much work goes into its preparation. The lead times necessary for planning are long.

Catalog recipients

Building and maintaining a list of potential buyers for a catalog is the secret of starting a successful mail-order business. No matter how attractive the products or services are or how effective the catalog is, without the right mailing list of target customers the business is doomed from the beginning.

A company can either build its own mailing list or rent one. Typically, it is better and less expensive to develop the mailing list, referred to as a house list, rather than to rent a list. This may be impossible if a company is just starting out and doesn't have current satisfied customers. More risks are involved if a company rents a list because it has no guarantees that the names will generate any sales. A 1.5 percent response rate is considered good from a rented list versus the average of a 10 percent rate from a house list.

A rented list of names usually contains between 2,000 and 5,000 names, which are needed to test the response rate of the list. If a company rents 5,000 names and receives only 50 orders, it could lose much money taking into consideration the costs of producing the catalog, renting names, and mailing. Also, no copies can be made of that list to use at a later time.

There are two different kinds of mailing lists. A mail-response list contains names of people who have purchased products within six months or a year. A compiled mailing list consists of people who have something in common with the target customers. Mail-response lists usually produce more sales.

Mailing-list companies that are listed in the telephone directory can be asked for a copy of their latest mailing-list catalogs. One resource for purchasing mailing lists is the Best Mailing List Company at (800) 692-2378.

Regardless of the mailing list that is rented, the names should be sorted by different characteristics, such as the time since their last purchase and amount of purchase. Then a company should test which characteristics work best for it. The company does not have to mail to all the names at once. This can be expensive. Most mailing-list companies provide free consultation on choosing the best list for a business.

Another alternative is to place small display ads in magazines or newspapers that the company's target customers read and send them a free catalog if they write or call by a specific time. To further entice readers, a small gift can be offered for those requesting a catalog. Then a company can build its own house list of people who enjoy shopping and buying by mail.

As the mailing list is built, the origin of orders should be analyzed so the company can continue to advertise in magazines or papers that generate most of the sales. The key to success in mail order is making money on repeat orders.

Mailing lists age quickly as consumers' tastes change and people change their places of residence. Statistics show that a one-year-old mailing list is only about 30 percent accurate. Therefore, names of customers who move or fail to order need to be deleted.

Contact the National Mail Order Association at 2807 Polk St. N.E., Minneapolis, MN 55418-2954, (612) 788-1673 (www.nmoa.org). Membership includes a subscription to *Mail Order Digest* and the *Washington Newsletter*. It sells a variety of mail-order books and reports. Other resources include *Home-Based Catalog Marketing* by William J. Bond, McGraw-Hill, Inc. (1998) and *Mail Order Moonlighting* by Cecil C. Hogue, Ten Speed Press (1988).

E-commerce catalogs

The Internet has introduced another way for catalog companies to reach new customers. Electronic catalogs can be available to customers on company web sites. This method has allowed companies to attract new customers that see their catalogs while surfing the net. Advantages of the electronic catalog: there are no printing and mailing costs, prices can be changed at anytime, and products can be added or deleted at any time.

Assortment of goods

People look at catalogs to see merchandise that they cannot otherwise view conveniently. Thus, it is not surprising to learn that the eventual success of a catalog operation depends upon the assortment of goods that can be assembled. They should be unique. It helps if they represent good values. People have come to expect that they will be able to buy better values from a catalog than they can at a store. However, in recent years many catalog operations sell products for premium prices. They no longer are trying to represent that the products are good values. Also many firms specialize in offering goods to people in some interest group: golfers, fishermen, knitters, cooks, for example.

One problem with print catalog sales is that the prices must be fixed for the life of the catalog. A company must have firm buying prices from vendors for the term of the catalog since the company has promised to sell the goods for the advertised price. In inflationary times, that is risky business.

Tremendous sales-forecasting issues confront the catalog operator. Potential demand for each item in the catalog must be accurately estimated. Then management must make sure that the vendor can supply it. Few things will discourage a catalog buyer more quickly than inability to obtain an ordered item. Thus, good vendor relationships are key to the catalog operator's success.

Telemarketing

Pure telephone selling has emerged as a major sales tool with the advent of automatic dialers and computerized-screening sales pitches. No matter the scale, the modern marketer should make maximum use of the telephone.

Telemarketing programs take several forms. First, they can be used as an alternative to an outside sales force. It is too expensive and time consuming to make personal sales calls without some positive evidence of the prospect's interest in the product or service. The telephone is a low-cost method of screening prospects. Moreover, many industrial buyers prefer to deal over the telephone rather than be bothered by someone's presence in their office. Why bother making a sales call in person when the order can be obtained over the phone?

Second, some telemarketing programs are prospecting systems, much like direct mail, that are intended to generate names and addresses of qualified prospects upon whom a salesperson will call. The telemarketers will call a list of likely prospects and then make a pitch from a tested script. Again, testing is used extensively.

Sales can be increased with the use of qualified leads—people who already have requested information or those with whom the business already has a relationship. Telemarketing success improves if the person first receives a letter stating that someone will be calling with marketing information.

Third, there are inbound telemarketing programs in which prospects can call in, usually using a toll free number, to place an order or get information. Such inbound programs are often tied into customer-satisfaction programs.

Staffing and managing a telemarketing salesroom is a continual, stressful job. Rejections are encountered often, and people are not always pleased to be summoned to the telephone for a sales pitch. Timing calls is important in order to ensure that someone is there to answer the phone. The script must immediately make the listener want to hear more, so it leads off with a major benefit. Early in the script, the rep tries to establish some sort of rapport with the listener.

One advantage of telemarketing is its low cost. It costs little to get started, and the marketer can choose the scale of operations. Perhaps the program initially is to make 10 calls a day.

Using 900 numbers can also be a good option. It's the immediacy that entices callers to initially dial 900 numbers for either information or service. What keeps them calling is the currency, professionalism, and uniqueness of the information being offered. If the venture can provide quick, convenient, and accurate information, a 900 line may be a good supplement to the business.

However, it is important to thoroughly research 900 lines to determine if a venture could be successful using one. A business's credibility and reputation in the industry impacts whether potential customers will call its line.

Customers pay a per-minute fee to receive the information the business is selling on the 900 line. It is also known as pay-per-call service and has experienced tremendous growth in recent years, totaling nearly $1 billion in revenue a year.

Telephone companies act as carriers of the lines and handle the billing of 900 calls on the consumer's regular phone bill. Calls are charged at a predetermined rate, and the carrier is paid a percentage of each call or sale. The balance is sent to the information provider within 30 to 90 days of billing.

Three phone companies that provide 900 numbers are Sprint, MCI, and AT&T. They offer similar services but charge and bill somewhat differently, and each has different polices on processing collectibles. These companies offer discounts for volume usage.

Check with the state attorney general's office to find out if no-call laws prohibit certain telemarketing calls to consumers.

Telemarketing programs are not easy to develop which is why outsourcing should be considered as an option.

Standard charges for businesses using a 900 number are about $3 for the first minute and $1.50 for each additional minute. On the average, 900 calls are 10 minutes per call. These figures can vary, depending on the type of information being sold.

Entrepreneurs may find that the setup and equipment charges associated with establishing 900 lines are extremely high. Start-up costs vary tremendously depending on the type of information being provided. That's why many owners contact a legitimate telephone service bureau that has a good reputation and reliable references from both the carrier and other customers. Typically, a service bureau has a pre-equipped and staffed facility that services a number of different information providers.

There are several service companies that help owners start and operate 900 lines. One reputable service is Call-Interactive (402) 498-7000 in Omaha, Nebraska. Entrepreneurs should look for other service bureaus that do business in the industry and ask their industry associations for referrals—always get referrals.

Resources include *Entrepreneur Magazine's* business guide, *900 Know-How: Operating a 900 Number for Profit*, and a book on how to use 900 numbers, *How to Succeed with Your Own 900 Business*, by Robert Mastin, Aegis Publishers, Newport, Rhode Island (1996).

There are ongoing marketing costs associated with a 900 line. Experts suggest that entrepreneurs allocate enough dollars to market their 900 numbers for at least six months without relying on incoming revenues. As with any other business, customers do not beat a path to a company's doorway. How a venture markets and advertises a 900 line significantly impacts its success.

Infomercials

Another method of market penetration is to buy one-half to one hour of cable television time for a set price. Then produce a television show, usually using a celebrity demonstrating how a product or service works. During the television show, commercial spots are run, enticing viewers to buy the product or service by calling a toll free number and charging the purchase with a credit card.

The advantage of using this market-penetration method is that many satellite networks or cable television channels can reach large population bases, where high sales can be made. Also, their costs are relatively low. Infomercials are available for as little as $200.

The disadvantage is that all the marketing expense for the production of the program, setting up the toll free number, and purchasing the television time is incurred before knowing the results and number of sales generated.

However, if a venture has a product or service with a defined demographic market segment that wants the product or service and to whom certain cable television stations appeal, then the risk of up-front marketing costs is reduced.

It is advisable to investigate and experiment with many different market-penetration methods. Failure should be expected with many of the tests. The entrepreneur should look for the methods that produce the best results and continue to refine and improve them.

Distributors

Distributors will be responsible for warehousing, selling, billing, delivering, and servicing the product or service produced by a company. Some distributors do not provide all of the above functions. For example, the distributor may market and bill the customer, but the manufacturing company is responsible for shipping and servicing. A venture should always have a formal agreement with the distributor on who will perform which duties.

Advantages of using a distributor as a market-penetration method are many. First, distributors give the entrepreneur's new company some credibility and fast movement of products or services to the target customer. Second, the distributor usually has many assets in place to service the customer, such as a sales force, delivery trucks, a service department, a customer hot line for complaints, and warehouses. Third, a newly founded company can have nationwide or worldwide coverage in a short period of time by persuading a large distributor network to stock and sell its product or service. Fourth, as mentioned earlier, the new company gets immediate sales by selling the original inventory to the distributor.

The disadvantage of using a distributor is loss of control because the salespeople work for the distributor and not for the entrepreneur's company. Also, the distributor will require the company to have backup inventory so it can have quick delivery and keep its inventory low. If the product or service does not sell at the estimated sales level, the company will end up with the inventory and without a market-penetration method to sell the product or service. The smart entrepreneur always has a backup market-penetration method when using a distributor as the marketing arm of the company.

Companies that are having their product or service produced by a subcontractor can use a distributor for the market-penetration method; however, this can make the product or service more expensive to the customer because each company has to make a profit. For example, the consumer price could include the subcontractor's 30 percent profit, the entrepreneur's 30 percent profit, and the distributor's 30 percent profit.

Franchising

Franchising is a business-expansion strategy for entrepreneurs to consider if they have an innovative yet proven concept that can be replicated with consistent success. Entrepreneurs have been franchising their ventures at increasing rates for the past decade. Franchises currently account for nearly one-third of all retail sales. On the average, about 300 businesses are franchised annually.

Why has franchising been such a popular and successful means of expanding a business? It can be an excellent way to quickly expand businesses. The key is to prove that the concept works, the product or service is widely accepted, the business has a steady record of success, and the success can be repeated in other locations.

The franchisor must provide potential franchisees with a predictable way of doing business. The business must be assembled complete with planning, management-control, and operating systems accompanied by continual management support and training.

In a franchise system, facilities are duplicated and equipment is purchased in bulk. Inventory is provided through established procurement systems. The franchisee has only literally to turn the key in the door, step in, and be in business.

This is not an expansion or distribution strategy that makes sense for every successful business. It is extremely important to evaluate whether this is an appropriate market-penetration and expansion strategy. Does it make sense to franchise a business? Will the entrepreneur be getting value for his or her business? Can the franchisor give value to potential franchisees through his or her experience, knowledge, and continual support? To be successful, franchisors must have productive franchises that provide a steady stream of income to the franchisor.

Franchise types. There are several different types of franchises to consider for expanding a market. These include trademark and brand-name franchises, product-distribution franchises, business-format franchises, and affiliate or conversion franchises.

Franchise Types
Trademark/brand-name
Product-distribution
Business-format
Affiliate or conversion

In a trademark and brand-name franchise, the franchisee pays for the right to use the franchisor's established trademark or brand name, usually for marketing purposes. By marketing products or services under a well-known trademark or brand name, the franchisee can gain market visibility and market share more quickly by capitalizing on the credibility and recognition of the franchisor. An example is Ralph Lauren's Polo brand clothing.

In a product-distribution franchise, the product manufacturer establishes a distribution network by contracting with dealers who distribute the product. The manufacturer stipulates how the franchisee will operate. For example, the distributor may not be allowed to sell competitive products or purchase parts or supplies not expressly authorized by the franchisor. The franchisee receives support in terms of capital, advertising, or discounts on purchases and managerial support. As a specific example, many car dealerships are set up this way.

In a business-format franchise, the most common type, the franchisee pays a fee and often a royalty to receive the entire business format. This includes trademarked products or services, operations systems and manuals, site selection, training, accounting, and other managerial support services. This type of franchise operation is attractive to the individual who is not familiar with business or does not want to take the time to launch a new start-up. It is the fastest-growing segment of the franchise industry today. An example is McDonald's fast-food restaurant chain.

In an affiliate or conversion franchise, the franchisees ally themselves with like ventures. This often occurs in a fragmented industry where there is little opportunity for large-scale visibility. By forming such a system under one name, individual affiliate franchises pool funds for marketing and advertising campaigns that are designed to capture greater consumer attention and recognition for their businesses. Remax, Century 21, and many other real estate companies are organized this way.

Franchise considerations. The big misconception about franchising is that entrepreneurs think they have a great idea and therefore should franchise their concepts. They believe it will involve only signing a contract and selling to potential franchisees. Franchisors just sit back and count the royalty checks and deposit them in the bank. Many entrepreneurs have no idea of the legal contracts and operating criteria that are required to franchise a concept. Franchising procedures are much more difficult and complex than some may imagine.

Before franchising a business concept, entrepreneurs should determine if they really have a product or service that is franchiseable. Does the product or service have any proprietary ingredients, a distinctive manufacturing or operational system or unique service-delivery system that could be franchised? Having one of these ingredients is key to launching a successful franchise business.

Deciding whether to franchise a successful business concept is a complicated decision that takes careful consideration. A franchise is a partnership in which each party has a close and continuing legal relationship, almost like a marriage. It is a constant give-and-take relationship, and it is extremely important that both sides win.

One of the key differences between starting a franchise and starting an independent business is the extensive training franchisors must provide to franchisees on all phases of operation, from production to sales and from employee relations to buying supplies. Franchisees must be taught to run and control every aspect of the business and its operating system. It takes a great amount of personal involvement and tremendous preparation to franchise a concept and assist franchisees with opening multiple locations.

Another franchising consideration is whether the entrepreneur has a successful flagship operation that has all the operating systems in place and earns a profit. This is one of the major reasons for buying a franchise. The franchisee purchases a turnkey package that has a proven product or service and established management procedures to operate the business and attract customers. The franchisor must provide continual managerial and technical assistance as well as quality control of the product or service. A recognized brand, logo, or trademark provides buying power that is not available outside of the franchise. Providing a proven, turnkey business concept costs money that the franchisor must pay before any fees can be collected from potential franchisees.

There are several attractions and pitfalls in franchising a successful business concept. The major attraction to the franchisor is the extensive and rapid expansion that can occur without borrowing or taking significant financial risk for growth capital. Franchise systems require fewer investment dollars by the franchisor to attract the same widespread distribution. Most franchise systems require the franchisee to put up significant amounts of money in the beginning, which reduces the total investment of the franchisor in the system. This allows for faster growth on a limited capital base. Many lenders are reluctant or unwilling to provide capital for expanding new businesses. Franchising opens the door to low-cost financing not available through traditional money sources.

Franchising provides another financial attraction with the income from franchisee operations. This revenue is derived from royalties on ongoing sales, profits from sale of supplies and equipment, and management fees. This income can provide both a healthy ongoing profit stream and an exit strategy to the franchisor. However, it takes significant up-front capital to package a franchise business before the franchisor collects any money.

Another attraction is that it is easier to find competent franchisees than to hire competent managers and staff to expand the business. Many businesses, especially fast-food, experience high personnel turnover. The franchisee has an investment in the venture and is more likely to be motivated to work hard and manage the unit successfully.

Pitfalls of franchising include fragmented markets with limited demand, national expansion without prior regional concentration, and the difficulty of establishing name recognition and maintaining quality control.

Many entrepreneurs overestimate market penetration and embark on a large-scale expansion strategy only to find there is a limited demand and fragmented market for the product or service. Expanding to these types of markets will cause franchisees to become disgruntled and antagonistic. If the franchisor's image is no better than that of the competition, then the franchisor must stimulate demand through more advertising and promotion, which is an expensive proposition. Building a strong regional identity allows the franchisor to better penetrate other regional markets with the capital needed for more sophisticated marketing programs.

> Many franchisors make the mistake of trying to expand nationally before penetrating regional markets, which would strengthen image and name recognition.

Maintaining quality is one of the most challenging aspects of franchising because the founder cannot personally oversee each franchisee's operation. The pitfall is in assuming that putting out a product or service is a routine matter. Many customers may have already lost faith in the franchisor's operation, and sales decline.

Licensing

Many entrepreneurs seek companies or people to license their products to. The first step in licensing is finding a company or person interested in the product idea. The best place to begin is the local library, looking through the *Thomas Register of American Manufacturers* (www.thomasregister.com) for potential names of companies in the industry. This resource book lists industry manufacturer names, addresses, and thousands of different businesses. Also Dun & Bradstreet's *Reference Book of Corporate Managements* gives a detailed biographical description of many leading companies and their principal officers. All communications with a potential licensee should be directed to top management.

Next, a list of competing companies can be developed by looking at competitors' products displayed in stores. Most packages give the name and location of the producer. These companies may be interested in expanding their product lines and may be good prospects for a potential license. Because these companies are competitors, however, care should be taken to avoid disclosing information that could later be used by the company to compete with the entrepreneur.

It is advisable to find out as much about licensing arrangements as possible. Some organizations that deal with licensing issues include the Licensing Industry Merchandisers' Association, The National Association of Small Business Investment Companies, and The National Venture Capital Association. The local chamber of commerce, small business development center, venture capitalists, or banks can also assist with licensing leads.

After locating businesses in the industry that might be interested in a license agreement, entrepreneurs must determine what they want from such an agreement. Will they ask for any up-front money to pay for out-of-pocket expenses for developing, prototyping, patenting, or other associated costs? Success in negotiating for up-front money will depend largely upon how badly the company wants to license the product.

What royalty percentage will be requested? Five percent is generally a good starting point. What type of exclusivity will the entrepreneur be willing to negotiate for? One must be cautious about bargaining away exclusivity rights. Exclusivity rights should be considered as a bargaining wedge. In most cases, if an entrepreneur can find one licensee, he or she will probably be able to find more.

How much does the entrepreneur want to be personally involved in marketing the product or overseeing its production? Should a lawyer be retained to represent the entrepreneur during negotiations? If the potential licensing agreement is complicated, it is wise to have legal counsel.

After these questions have been answered and licensing arrangements researched, the entrepreneur can begin writing query letters to potential licensees. The entrepreneur should consider obtaining a confidentiality agreement before disclosing information that may be protectable under patent or trade secret law.

The query letter should include several things: information on the demand for the product, including any marketing research or testing results; identification of potential purchasers; a description of applications and alternatives for the product; a list of any proprietary rights, such as potential or existing patents, trademarks, or copyrights; and the entrepreneur's qualifications and business background.

Most importantly, the letter should demonstrate how the licensee will benefit from the product. Writing query letters can take considerable time, and the result will probably be a number of "we're not interested" letters.

The entrepreneur shouldn't get too excited about receiving a letter of interest. Often, the first interested party will not be the last. Hasty decisions in signing a contract should be avoided. A sound licensing agreement will benefit both the entrepreneur and the licensee.

Exporting

Another market-penetration method is to expand marketing and sales efforts to foreign markets. Although there are slightly higher administrative costs and more documentation involved, a company can usually charge more for its products or services. Therefore, exporting can yield higher profit margins.

Modern technology, communications methods, and speed of travel allow entrepreneurs to better compete in world markets. Time, not distance, is now the important factor in international sales and service. Direct dial telephone service, fax machines, computers, printers, copy machines, e-mail, and the Internet make it possible to communicate and send information electronically to almost all countries at a relatively low cost. Air freight can be delivered in a few days. International-standard container shipments by trucks, railroads, and ocean freighters allow delivery to major countries within a few weeks.

To determine if its products or services are suitable for exporting, a firm must first consider several key factors. If it has plain "vanilla" products that are no different from the competitors', it will be difficult for a company to be successful at exporting. However, if the company has created a niche in the marketplace by selling innovative products or services with unique benefits, it has a chance. The product or service must have distinguishable features, and the company must be able to guarantee quality. If the product or service meets these requirements, a venture could be successful at exporting.

Also to be considered are government standards and regulations, local customs, electric-power requirements, and so on. All these factors will affect design, production costs, and suitability for exporting. Therefore, to explore exporting opportunities, a company must design its product or service so it can be easily modified to meet foreign requirements.

Marketing materials and brochures must also be designed with foreign markets in mind. These materials should show both American and metric units and also use language and symbols that are universal English and not unique to the United States. Then a company can look for expanding markets that are easy to enter, such as Canada, Mexico, Northern Europe, Hong Kong, South Korea, Singapore, and Australia.

There are many community resources that offer exporting assistance for little or no cost. One place to start is by contacting the local chamber of commerce and the international department of a bank. Entrepreneurs could also contact the local small business development center, a freight forwarder, a local international trade club, or local entrepreneur groups. The state's department of commerce, the Small Business Administration, and the U.S. Department of Commerce also provide exporting assistance. Any of these organizations can help entrepreneurs or refer them to private consultants and agencies that have expertise with the entrepreneurs' particular exporting needs.

Feature articles

Getting a feature article written about a business is an excellent way to obtain free publicity and promote its services. As all entrepreneurs realize, promoting a business can be extremely costly. Considering the skyrocketing costs of advertising and traditional promotional tools, such as direct mail, trade shows, and selling, new ventures are usually hard-pressed to maximize the results realized from a limited promotional budget.

One feature article in a newspaper or an appearance on a television or radio talk show can generate hundreds of inquiries and a substantial amount of new business. In fact, many say that feature coverage is at least twice as credible as advertising.

The first step is to target specific media that reach the same audience with whom the entrepreneur would like to communicate, to single out the media most advantageous for the venture. Astute entrepreneurs observe the various stories covered by their target media so they understand what these media are looking for. There might be several trade magazines that would be more appropriate to contact than the local newspaper. Editors of newspapers and magazines, as well as producers of radio and television programs, are constantly under pressure to deliver news and feature stories that appeal to their audiences. It is smart to research what the target media needs.

The best way to increase the chances of getting publicity is to develop an angle or a newsworthy hook. It is key to convince the media that the company has a good story or a feature item of interest to their specific audience. What is different or unique about the service? Is there a special benefit or community activity involved with the service? Has the company received a recent award or sponsored a seminar or contest? Does the company have any trend forecasts or industry overviews of interest? Can someone on the team write a "how-to" article? Is the founder a colorful entrepreneur with a fascinating background or unique personality profile to offer? Be interesting, timely, and factual in the angles presented.

Determine which writer or editor is responsible for the type of story being pitched. Having a referral as well as establishing a working relationship with the editors are helpful. Suggested approaches: call to schedule an appointment; take them out to breakfast or lunch or for a cup of coffee.

Because media people are exceptionally busy, they may just ask people to send their information. Have it ready before you contact the media. Some media outlets prefer to write their own stories while others will use stories written by the business owner. Ask them for their preference. One never knows when media people need to fill space and will use a story because it is convenient. After sending the story, it is wise to follow up after the editor or writer has an opportunity to review it, making sure the person is not under a deadline. E-mail is less intrusive than a phone call to stay in contact with the media.

If the editor is not interested, he or she should be queried about what types of stories he or she is looking for. It might be possible to reconstruct the angle to suit the editor's needs. It is always good to leave the door open for another try.

Entrepreneurs may want to consider whether a newspaper article is the best promotional vehicle for their products or services. The advertiser pays to have a specific message conveyed to the public and, therefore, controls the message and the manner in which it is presented. The advertiser tells the public what it wants them to know about its product or service.

With publicity, there is no such control. A company provides the media with the information about its product or service that it believes is worthy of coverage. The media people will decide whether to cover the story and what to write about the business. The company has no control over what is written.

One of the best kept secrets to guerrilla marketing is using public relations strategies to obtain sales publicity. Public relations is different than marketing or sales. The purpose of public relations is to manage various communications between a company and different target markets.

Obtaining news and feature stories about a company and its products and services in selected media viewed by potential customers is worth thousands of dollars from a marketing budget and is free to the company. Sales publicity opens doors and can increase sales besides educating prospects about products and services. Its effectiveness is based on the power of an objective third-party evaluation of the offerings that gives a company credibility. Sales publicity is similar to having thousands of word-of-mouth referrals occurring simultaneously. So other market-penetration strategies, such as advertising and brochures, become more effective. One of the secrets in obtaining sales publicity is contacting editors first to determine if they have an interest in the story or angle about the company before sending any information.

Stationery and business cards

Most entrepreneurs regard their stationery and business cards as just props needed when launching a new venture. A company's business cards, letterhead, and stationery should reflect the image it is trying to portray.

Most business cards are simple, plain, and unimaginative printed paper rectangles that are handed out without much thought. Business owners often fail to realize that they can use their business cards as an effective and inexpensive marketing tool.

Business card designs are becoming more creative. Why not design a card to sell particular products or services rather than just providing information about contacting a company? Distinctive business cards range from those made with unusual materials and imprinting methods to those that convey solid messages and establish their own identities.

To determine how effective a business card is, the entrepreneur should observe what others do when he or she hands them his or her business card. Do they look at it and comment or put it directly in their pocket? If it goes in their pocket, the entrepreneur has failed to catch their attention and may want to redesign the card. Looking at other business cards can provide a good idea of what catches the eye. To attract attention and create an impact, a variety of sizing, type fonts, and spacing can be used.

A card that is memorable and highlights the uniqueness of the venture should be designed. The business card should have the same typeface as the company's letterhead and stationery to present a consistent image. The business card should directly communicate to the target market. It may be necessary to design several different business cards that appeal to different segments of a market.

The card should be considered as a mini billboard. Some experts suggest including the services and benefits offered. Many times business cards only give the basics—that is, name, address, and phone number. They fail to indicate what kind of business the person is in and what special services and products the business offers. When glancing through cards, people frequently forget where they received the card and what business the company is in. This should not be allowed.

Creative entrepreneurs use design alternatives. Instead of using an average-sized business card, they might consider using a card that fits into a Rolodex or one that folds in half. A folding card can feature products or services and becomes a brochure, a wallet-sized advertisement, for a business. The outside of the card can contain standard business information, while the inside contains a headline followed by a list of features and benefits.

Color can be used as background or to make type stand out. Adding another color may raise the printing bill but may be worth it. Also, various textures, such as a high gloss, matte, or rag content, might enhance a card.

Astute entrepreneurs make the most of their business cards to help with referral business. They are never without one. A good business card can be as effective as a TV commercial. Cards can be mailed with letters and other brochures.

Yellow Pages

The attractiveness of advertising in the *Yellow Pages* is that most homes have a copy, and people who look there are usually in a buying mood. Studies show that about 50 percent of the users purchase products or services.

The businesses that get the most customers from the *Yellow Pages* are those whose customers are local, whose business is used in an emergency (such as a plumber or a locksmith), and whose business is retail sales. Other businesses attract few new customers from the *Yellow Pages*, especially if their market is narrow, with a limited number of customers. It is a good idea to determine whether a venture's prospects look in the *Yellow Pages* and if the *Yellow Pages* are appropriate for its product or service.

Is there a clear-cut heading under which to place the company's ad? If there isn't, the company might not get many customers from a listing. It is possible that there is more than one *Yellow Page* category that classifies what a business does, such as word processing services, which are listed under both "Secretarial Services" and "Typing." In such a case, it is reasonable to assume that the category containing the most large display ads or boldface listings is where customers look most often. In some instances, a company might want to advertise under more than one category.

If lots of competitive businesses advertise in the *Yellow Pages*, it may be worth a try. If there are only a few listings, the company should find out if that is because this advertising attracted few new customers. A company should try to determine what percentage of its competitors' business comes from people who have located them through the *Yellow Pages*.

If a company decides to advertise in the *Yellow Pages*, it should be part of the local telephone company and part of the local telephone book. Anyone can publish a directory, which may or may not be distributed widely.

Smart ventures advertise in telephone books that blanket their target areas. If they market nationally, then they use *Yellow Pages* in all appropriate cities, including those where they don't have offices. There are also specialized *Yellow Pages* such as *Silver Pages* for seniors, ethnic *Yellow Pages*, and business-to-business *Yellow Pages*. Today many large metropolitan areas have these editions. A company's ads should be in all the books its target customers regularly use.

Customers obtained through other advertising should not be directed to get a company's telephone number from the *Yellow Pages*. That will send them straight to the competition. Instead, they should be referred to the *White Pages*. Two good references are *Yellow Pages Advertising, How to Get the Greatest Return on Your Investment* by Jeffrey Price, Idlewood Publishing, 1991, and *Getting the Most From Your Yellow Pages Advertising* by Barry Maher, Aegis Publishing, 1997. These books list the most often looked-up headings—such as cleaners, physicians, department stores, television dealers, taxicabs, beauty shops, and air-conditioning contractors —and other invaluable information.

If advertising in the *Yellow Pages* makes sense for a business, it needs to consider how to design an effective ad. A study of other ads in the *Yellow Pages* provides ideas on the types of approaches that attract attention, which headlines, graphics, and copy appeal to readers. The ad should be an attention grabber.

Specialties can be emphasized by describing the market niche, that is, what distinguishes the company in the marketplace. The ad should give brief, attention-grabbing information and include key benefits. Readers should be able to find out all the key reasons why they should buy from the advertiser. A good rule to follow is not to put too much information in too little space. It is important, however, to include everything a company sells, especially if prospects shop for specific brands.

If potential customers are expected to come to a company's location instead of calling, the ad must include the address, the days and hours it is open, telephone number, and availability of parking. If the location is difficult to find, the ad should provide brief directions or include a map. Other useful information can be included, such as whether the company delivers, accepts credit cards, or finances purchases.

Size and price of the ad are important considerations. Large display ads generate more response than standard line listings. The size of competitors' ads may influence a company's ad size; it wouldn't design a small ad if competitors use big ads.

The cost of *Yellow Pages* ads is assessed monthly and can be steep. The best guideline is to start at a price level a company can afford and track responses. No financial strain should be put on the business. Keep in mind, though, that the smallest business can look big-time with a good *Yellow Pages* ad.

If a product or service can be represented by a picture or graphic, then a display ad might be worthwhile. People looking in the *Yellow Pages* are usually attracted first to display ads.

If a company decides to purchase a listing, simple boldface-type listings are twice as effective as plain ones. Color can double the costs and is not always cost-effective. On the other hand, color usually helps draw attention to smaller ads.

A company should track the results of its *Yellow Pages* ad: ask callers how they heard about the company. If it has multiple phone lines, one number can be used just for the *Yellow Pages*. It is important to have a backup telephone answering machine. If potential customers call the company's number and no one answers, it will lose potential business. Name, address, and telephone number in the ad should be double-checked before the directory is printed and after it comes out.

Telephone books list names alphabetically. Therefore if an entrepreneur has not yet named his or her business, he or she might consider a name that will put it as one of the first listings.

Designing an attractive and effective *Yellow Pages* ad takes time, effort, and careful attention. Although the telephone or *Yellow Pages* company will be of some help, contacting a professional designer could be considered. The *White Pages*, which are heavily used, are often neglected by many entrepreneurs as a good marketing strategy. Listings can be upgraded with the use of boldface capital letters, super boldface letters, rules, color, and other options offered.

Coupons

Today, many entrepreneurs are using coupons, and more than 3 billion coupons are distributed annually. However, less than 3 percent are redeemed, indicating that many consumers don't clip or use them.

A marketing study found that the critical factor in the effectiveness of coupons was not whether they were redeemed but whether they were seen by potential customers. People who do not clip or redeem coupons may still make a mental note of the item and later purchase the product or service. Even when coupons are clipped, the customer often forgets to take them to the store but purchases the item anyway.

Coupons raise awareness of a product even after they have expired. Many business owners redeem expired coupons to create goodwill and accommodate their customers. Others honor the terms of the offer without the actual coupon in hand.

Experiment with different ways of using coupons to determine what works best. Coupons should be coded so the company can track what is most effective.

Coupons can be distributed through various print media, in a direct-mail packet, a postcard pack, web sites, or a retail location. Small coupons can also be printed on the back of cash register receipts. The main advantage of advertising on store receipts is the ability to hit a specific audience. Other store owners whose products might be complementary might print a company's coupons on their receipts. It is possible to trade or barter when using other merchants' store receipts. Entrepreneurs shouldn't forget to use the backs of their own receipts for coupons. Coupons can also be included in invoices, statements, or other outgoing mail. People can be hired to distribute coupons on busy streets or at public events or fairs.

It might be possible to team up with a noncompetitive business with a special promotion. Giving coupons to another business can be an added bonus for its customers. The key is to find a business whose goods appeal to the target market. Good customers or those who provide referral business can be rewarded by giving them a one-shot special coupon.

Coupons are also a great way to build a company's mailing list by asking recipients to fill out their addresses and other specific demographic information. Markets can be segmented into specific areas and a composite of best customers developed. Ventures can also chart how much business comes from repeat sales.

Last, it is good business to accept a competitor's coupons, or give an additional discount if customers bring in a rival's coupon.

Patience is key. As with other advertising, a potential customer needs to see a coupon several times before taking action. A coupon often motivates a prospect to come to a store. This provides an opportunity to explain other products and services that are offered. Businesses get to know their customers better. Coupons are usually cheaper than most other forms of advertising, and they do not need to be redesigned often.

Postcards

Postcards can be a powerful marketing tool and can increase sales. Sending postcards has many advantages over other types of advertising and direct mail. A large percentage of direct mail is never opened. A postcard overcomes that obstacle. Direct-mail pieces often contain several pages that the recipient has to sort through before deciding whether to read the information. A postcard simply has to be turned over to have the information read.

Postcards are less costly to design, print, and mail than other direct-mail pieces. In addition, there is a quick turnaround time from design to mailing. A firm can almost get a mailing out overnight.

Another advantage is that if the recipient does not immediately need the product, he or she may pin it on a bulletin board or keep it until ready to make a purchase. This means the company could experience a delayed response before receiving orders after sending a promotional mailer.

It is critical that a postcard be unique and compelling and that it communicate a strong message. An advertiser only has a few seconds to attract attention and to have the postcard stand out in the mail. Testimonials from customers, clever phrases, or catchy words can be used. Pictures, cartoons, or other graphics can be included to attract and hold customer interest. Adding color is another technique.

A strong headline followed by a few condensed bullet points should complete the message. The limited amount of space dictates that the number of words be limited and still make a memorable impression. The recipient should be encouraged to take immediate action by including an incentive. Contact information, such as phone, fax, and address, must not be forgotten.

The right mailing list is *the* number-one priority for direct mail success.

Another way to have a postcard noticed is to use a size larger than the standard 4-by-6-inch format. Rates for larger sizes should be determined. Enlarging the card costs more but not as much as an envelope mailer. A company can benefit from the impact of the increased size, and it provides more space to communicate the message.

As with other direct mail, typically it takes five to seven contacts before the recipient takes action. Therefore, a series of postcards might be developed to keep the company's name and product information in front of potential customers. The effectiveness of the postcard campaign and the response rate should be tracked. Postcards can be a good marketing tool, turning leads into sales and developing new and repeat customers.

Fax marketing

Fax marketing can be an effective and unique direct-marketing tool as the business marketplace continues to move toward phone, e-mail and web-based transactions. In the past few years, use of the fax machine has leveled off and in some cases fallen as other forms of electronic communication have been seen as more efficient. It's certainly curious that a twenty-year-old technology can make a company different in the eyes of its customers.

While voice-mail and e-mail boxes fill up with unsolicited junk, and the paper inbox contains piles of envelopes, a carefully addressed fax can rise to the top of a customer's awareness.

The two most important things to remember about fax marketing are the personal address of the message and the message itself. The message should be sent to the number of the fax machine nearest the person to be reached and not to a generic job title. Businesses are familiar with junk faxes and will often simply throw away a fax sent to "Director of Purchasing." Entrepreneurs should check to see if there are any local, state, and federal regulations covering the fax marketing they are considering.

Smart entrepreneurs take advantage of the fact that faxes will be retrieved and placed in front of the customer "ready to read." They use that 8.5 x 11 inch real estate to sell their message. With e-mail, customers will see the subject line and with regular mail, they'll see the envelope, but with a fax, they see the whole thing, especially if the message is clear and to the point.

Faxes can be used when speed is important to get out the message fast. One of the advantages of using the fax to market goods and services is its cost efficiency. The cost of faxing is offset by rising postage rates, printing costs, and handling charges. A fax user should, however, remember who pays for the fax in terms of printing costs: the recipient. The savvy entrepreneur avoids ill will caused by overusing this method of communication.

An enterprise should also consider using the fax machine as a method of receiving orders from customers. It should be as easy as possible for them to check off the products and services they need, sign the order and send it in. Faxes can be a great way of documenting purchase requests, eliminating claims such as "we never ordered that."

Some tips for using fax marketing:

- Computers can generate and send faxes. Special fax software allows the sender to address multiple faxes to individual people (similar to a form letter), making each fax seem personalized. Computers also treat the remote fax machine like a printer. This feature eliminates the loss of resolution inherent in the scanning process normally used to send a document to a fax machine. The message is personalized and crystal clear.

- Fax design should be pre-tested and the response rate tracked before the fax is sent to multiple customers. Order forms should be designed carefully and small type avoided. If the fax does not bring in the number of anticipated responses, it should be redesigned. In addition, the fax should be checked for clarity to determine if it is readable on poor-quality fax machines, which some customers may have.

To gain further insight into fax marketing, obtain a review copy of *E-Tactics* by visiting their web site at www.e-tactics.com. It's a monthly newsletter featuring fax broadcasting, fax on-demand, videotext, cellular communication, and the latest information on marketing technology, including a marketer's resource catalog.

Electronic media

If a business is deciding among any of the marketing strategies mentioned earlier in this chapter (fliers, signs, catalogs, infomercials, feature articles, coupons, and postcards), an interactive floppy disk or CD-ROM brochure can be considered instead or in addition to these ideas. This relatively new marketing technique allows customers to view diverse forms of information at their leisure and at their desk.

By booting up the program on the disk, targeted customers are led through an interactive program in which the desired messages are presented and orders can be placed, either by printing out an order form for mailing or faxing or by designing links to a web-based or e-mail order. Since it is a novelty item, customers will probably be curious and want to look at the disk the company has mailed to them.

Almost any form of digital communication can be represented on a CD-ROM. An enterprise may want to use video for customer testimonials, product demonstrations or training. Another business may want to offer a searchable catalog of products or services. Or they may want to have 3-dimensional model of a unique product that the viewer can rotate around or zoom in and out to see all the details. All of these technologies are available for delivery on electronic media.

Because they can incorporate so many different communications technologies, interactive disks can initially cost more than paper to design and create. But once completed, interactive disks are relatively simple to update or revise for specialized needs. Special features such as printing out an order form or adding links to a web site can be added.

The delivery of electronic interactive disks offers multiple options. If the message fits, a floppy disk can be the least expensive option. CD-ROMs come in two sizes and a new technique is to "cut" the smaller size into a calling card format while still retaining enough circular area for the digital message to fit. Finally, more and more people will be getting DVD support on their computers and in their homes if a message either requires the enormous amount of storage or an enterprise want to really impress its customers with advanced quality or modern technology. But if the customer doesn't have the ability to play the message, the process could backfire and create ill will or a technical support headache.

Although not designed for mail without a special packaging, electronic media can be distributed in inexpensive covers if placed in retail outlets or handed out at conferences or other situations where there is direct customer contact.

When comparing the cost of producing a four-color print brochure and an interactive brochure, there are two big differences. It's cheaper to prepare the paper brochure than a fully interactive media disk. Both require graphic artists and content providers. The digital media usually also requires computer technologists or at least advanced graphic artists who understand the modern tools for creating interactive media. The good news is that reproducing the disk (CD or floppy) can be a lot cheaper than a four-color brochure, and the equipment to create and label CDs is less than $8,000, so a company can afford to do production in house for smaller runs. Since the response rate is currently greater for interactive digital media due to its novelty or the richness of the message presentation, the cost per customer reached is can be substantially lower.

To maximize dollars, all marketing efforts should reinforce and build upon one another.

A company needs to establish a well-defined, forceful image that will strengthen its identity. Knowing the audience is the key to success, whether a print brochure or an electronic disk is used.

Interactive kiosks

Many malls have kiosks that shoppers can use to locate the stores and products they want to examine. These units respond to the shopper's requests for information using interactive computer programs.

Content for the kiosk can come from monthly updates on CD or DVD or from direct interaction with the kiosk. If a business can afford the additional expense or its location offers it, a connection to the Internet will allow it to remotely update the content. Customers will then have access to the most current information. A connection to the Internet also allows the kiosk to accept orders, send e-mail or even chat online with a customer representative.

With the growth of the Web, kiosks should only be considered for unique circumstances. For example, in Circuit City, kiosks are available for customers to custom build computers by choosing components from onscreen menus. The customers' selections are shipped shortly after. The advantage of kiosks versus the Web is that customer will need to be directed to or otherwise be able to find the web site, when a carefully placed kiosk essentially puts interactive content directly in front of them.

Kiosks can be an expensive way to penetrate markets. Companies will charge upwards of $20,000 for a kiosk with Internet and fax capability. A business should make certain a kiosk makes sense compared to using the Web or other forms of customer interaction.

Internet

The Pew Internet and American Life Project (www.pewinternet.org) estimates that

- Over 60 percent of Americans now have Internet access.
- Women and men are online almost equally with the highest usage in the 12-to-25 age range at 80 percent.
- 63 percent of all Americans expect a business will have a Web site that gives them information about a product they are considering buying.
- Nearly half of all Americans said that providing product information online makes them more likely to go the physical store to buy this product.

Who uses the Internet? The young, the educated, and the wealthy. The many research companies that track Internet usage statistics for both the number of servers and individual Internet users agree on one thing: Internet usage numbers are going to continue to grow for the foreseeable future. As businesses continue to expand online, consumers are increasingly expecting businesses both large and small to offer their products and services over the Internet. According to the Pew study, 72 million Americans, 62 percent of Internet users, have purchased a product over the Internet.

Businesses should think of the Internet as an integral part of their company. While Internet-only companies have struggled to create brand and loyal customer followings, bricks-and-mortar companies have found success in supplementing traditional marketing methods with the Internet. Internet users simply expect a company to have a web site. The vast majority of Internet shoppers don't purchase products on the Internet, they use the Internet as an information-gathering tool before choosing a method of buying and accepting delivery of a product.

No matter what the product or service, entrepreneurs can explain it, show it off, take orders for it, update customers about it, support it and in some cases even deliver it over the Internet.

The Internet has become so important that many startup enterprises pick a company name based on the availability of the Internet domain name. The entrepreneur should check www.networksolutions.com to find whether a combination of letters or an exact company name is already registered. Research has shown that the easiest names to remember are three to five letters in length. The cost of keeping and maintaining an Internet domain is relatively inexpensive—hundreds of dollars per year. Having an easy-to-remember Internet presence can and will have an effect on the bottom line.

Internet marketing, when used as part of a comprehensive marketing plan, can build sales and target a large customer base very inexpensively, when compared to more traditional marketing methods. Remember the lessons of the dot-coms: using the Internet as the only marketing tool should be avoided, even for businesses that only do business online. All company materials such as business cards, catalogs, and brochures, should include e-mail addresses and web site addresses.

Entrepreneurs are using the Internet as a marketing tool to sell products, as a research tool to look at changes in the industry and competitive companies, and as a communication tool allowing smaller businesses to do business on a national or international scale. The most frequently used Internet capabilities are electronic mail (e-mail) and the World Wide Web (WWW or Web).

While it's true that the number of commercial web sites has skyrocketed, most have had trouble generating revenue for the company. A quick survey of web sites shows why—too many sites appear to be an afterthought of the enterprise. Just because a college or high school intern can throw together a web site doesn't mean that's the best method. In the world of higher education, the Web is now a fundamental part of the organization. Mark Milliron, the President and CEO of the League for Innovation in the Community College says a business owner should think of the web site as he or she would a new building. The effort, the cost, the amount of time, and planning will all be just as important for a location in cyberspace as it would be in any retail location.

Another key aspect of an Internet presence is customer service. E-companies are quickly recognizing that customer service is a key differentiation for an online business, leading to the implementation of integrated customer call centers and vastly expanded Internet development and maintenance budgets.

E-mail marketing

E-mail is by far the most popular use of the Internet, both because of its ease of use and wide accessibility. Not only do people have access from home through local Internet Service Providers (ISP) or access providers like America Online, most businesses are now providing an Internet e-mail address as a vital part of the organization. Entrepreneurs can contact new customers, promote products and services, and build their reputation as experts in their fields online.

E-mail marketing has a variety of uses. Past and potential customers can be targeted with e-mailed marketing messages that offer special discounts or

Integrating online marketing with other marketing efforts is key.

E-Mail Benefits
Immediacy
Low cost
Efficiency

remind customers about a specific product that is now available. Individuals with problems or questions can contact the business via e-mail for help. By creating a list of media e-mail addresses, entrepreneurs can send press releases or pitch articles to journalists. A company can also reduce its toll free number or other customer service costs by using e-mail.

In addition to the e-mail programs that individuals use for retrieving e-mail, there are also bulk mail programs that allow the same message to be sent to a mailing list of hundreds of addresses. Many such programs are available on the Internet as freeware or shareware, or may be available as part of a business software package. These programs automate the mailing process, and can be used in the same manner as a traditional mailing list to contact customers, journalists, and vendors.

Some organizations offer an e-mail service called a mailing list (listserv). These are free or for-fee services that make it easy for members of the list to communicate with each other. The way a mailing list works is simple: the customer subscribes to the list and his or her e-mail address is added to the list automatically. Members on the list receive e-mail that is sent to the list, either by the organization or by any member of the list. This is a simple way to encourage a sense of community regarding a product or service. An ISP can provide information on how to create a mailing list for any enterprise.

E-mail mailing lists can be a low cost way to post useful information in front of hundreds or thousands of key customers. Depending on number of subscribers and daily activity, it's possible for one mailing list to have hundreds of messages, and thousands of readers, each day. If a mailing list has so much useful interaction on a topic central to the business, the entrepreneur might subscribe to a list and monitor it on a long-term basis. The typical pattern for using mailing lists is to locate a list through a search engine, subscribe, monitor postings for a brief period, then post to the list. Responses to a posting can go to the list and all subscribers will see them or they may be sent privately. It's important to understand that most mailing lists are non-commercial in nature, even those that are offered by for-profit organizations. Because of this, it is particularly bad form to attempt to promote products or services in the hope that it will target the message. Even if a company is selling medicine that can help cancer survivors, it will do the business more harm than good by posting a message hawking products to a cancer support group mailing list. The smarter thing to do is to create good will by setting up the cancer support group mailing list and promoting its existence.

Different mailing lists and individual e-mail recipients have different standards on what is acceptable and what is not, which is why monitoring the discussion is very valuable prior to posting to a mailing list. If an entrepreneur is managing the mailing list, he or she will periodically find customers who want to be removed from the list. Refusing to remove these addresses from a mailing list can cause major problems for a business online, so respecting the wishes of those on the mailing list is paramount.

Using e-mail to communicate with customers, suppliers, employees, and colleagues can be a good marketing and communication tool because of its speed, lower costs, and efficiency. There is no extra charge for each message sent, unlike phone calls or mail. No long-distance charges are incurred as with using the fax. It takes only a little extra work to send an e-mail message to thousands of customers. And the messages can find their way around the world in seconds.

Another advantage is that e-mail can increase productivity if the business centers around documents. E-mail content can be quickly transferred into a word processor or database rather than retyped. Five e-mail messages can be answered in the same amount of time it takes to answer one phone call. And people usually read their e-mail messages soon after they arrive as opposed to mailed correspondence, which can stack up for days.

One of the main advantages for entrepreneurs is directly and quickly communicating with customers. Customer newsletters can show up within minutes of being sent electronically. Job quotes can be returned rapidly and payment time increased if an electronic bill-payment service is provided. With e-mail, it's possible to do business internationally without leaving one's own backyard. As U.S. markets become saturated, world markets can be tapped instantaneously.

There are, however, important drawbacks to consider. Spam, security and privacy issues, technology problems and the casual nature of e-mail can be disadvantages.

Spam is unsolicited e-mail. Just as customers hate junk mail in their physical mailbox at home and at work, they hate junk e-mail even more. Too many people have decided that they can get customers by blasting e-mail to as many addresses as possible in the hopes that some small percentage will answer. A unique strategy in the late 90s, it is now largely a waste of time and could be the reason that a customer never does business with that enterprise again. If a sender isn't certain that a recipient of an e-mail message will appreciate hearing from her, she shouldn't send it.

Security can be a serious problem. E-mail travels across a public network, unlike the confidential path taken by paper correspondence. Technicians, hackers, supervisors, and co-workers may have access to and read other people's e-mail. While the odds are in favor that no one will see any particular message, senders should be careful about putting confidential information in an e-mail message.

If a computer or network link goes down, it could take several days to reach the intended address. Another, more frequent problem is the use of a wrong e-mail address. If the recipient has changed his or her address and senders don't know it or have somehow mistyped the correct address, the message will be undeliverable. Different e-mail systems use different rules for undeliverable mail. Sometimes it will be returned and sometimes it will be sent to a systems administrator at a remote site. If a business owner is expecting a response to an e-mail message and hasn't heard anything, a timely phone call is the best remedy.

Some large bulk e-mail services have tried to short circuit consumer complaints by using fraudulent e-mail addresses, either invented or stolen from others, leaving the recipient of a message with no way to respond to the actual sender. There are movements to make such junk e-mail practices illegal, but regardless of the legality of such practices, they are unacceptable to the Internet community. Many ISPs and all the online services have strict policies against sending junk e-mail, and such behavior can result in being permanently barred from the service.

E-mail is an absolute necessity in today's fast-paced world, and spam is an absolute abomination. Never waste anyone's bandwidth with unsolicited e-mail.

Overall, e-mail is easy to use, inexpensive, and interactive, and it has a great degree of geographic independence. When assessing various electronic communication tools, an entrepreneur must consider the importance of immediacy, costs, and confidentiality.

Web site

People who use the Internet assume all businesses have web sites. Statistics show that young, educated people with money make up the bulk of users on the Internet and a business will be irrelevant to them without a web presence of some kind. Anyone can have a site that describes the products and services. Many businesses have online catalogs where customers can order merchandise. Some businesses offer interactive web experiences that entertain, educate, sell and support. Whether the business requires a full-fledged e-commerce system, or it plans only to post useful information for traditional customers, establishing an Internet presence can be an expensive and difficult process, and the entrepreneur should proceed with caution.

The entrepreneur has two choices when setting up a web presence: She can do it herself or pay someone else to do it. Doing it herself means she either has the technical skills or the ability to recognize and hire them. These skills include a grab-bag of talents: computer networking, graphic design, complex systems administration and web-page authoring. Very few entrepreneurs have the necessary skill sets or the desire to hire in the team at the beginning of the enterprise's existence, unless the business centers on an e-commerce initiative.

Many organizations use outside contractors or service providers to develop and run the company's web site. Internet Service Providers (ISPs), Application Service Providers (ASPs), E-Commerce Service Providers, and well-known technology companies like IBM will assist any size organization in the creation of anything from a few web pages to an e-commerce site complete with shopping carts and online chatting with customer representatives.

For small organizations with a catalog of products to sell, companies like Yahoo (http://smallbusiness.yahoo.com/merchant/) or Bigstep.com can do everything an enterprise needs. Yahoo charges $100 a month for online catalogs of 50 products or less all the way up to $300 a month for 1,000 items with each additional 1,000 items then costing another $100 per month. Check their web site for current pricing as this market is volatile. Yahoo can even register and host a domain name (www.mybusiness.com) for $35 a year. For these fees an entrepreneur can set up an on-line shop without needing any real technical experience. They support shopping-cart technology and allow credit card transactions.

When a business hires another company to produce a custom, interactive, full-blown web presence that connects with its accounting systems and provides detailed customer resource management, it can easily spend $50,000 to well, unfortunately, there is no upper limit. One corporation can do all of the tasks, or the work can be spread among e-commerce specialists, graphic design firms and web site hosting companies.

There are usually more technical requirements, and thus additional costs, associated with e-commerce sites. Some hosts are not equipped to handle all the technologies an enterprise may want to use, while others may provide programming services with a range of fees. Long before a company even produces its web site content, there are important issues to address. An investment of some time in detailed planning of the real needs, versus wants of the business web site, may end up saving thousands of dollars in direct costs as well as avert Internet-related headaches.

Someone must design the web site look and feel, create graphics, and write content for the web site. Programs, such as Microsoft FrontPage, Claris Home Page, and Macromedia Dreamweaver, make this process simpler, but in order to compete with other sites by making a site eye-pleasing and easy to use, especially those produced by larger companies, the investment in a web design firm may be worthwhile.

In looking for a design firm, a buyer should look at other competitive sites and find out who designed them. Frequently sites will have credits and an e-mail link to the design firm that created the site. He or she should look at sites that are eye-catching and simple to use, and contact those creators as well. One difficulty in working with web design companies is that their prices can vary wildly, from a few thousand to more than $20,000 for the same amount of work.

The planning that takes place up front with a web design consultant can save dollars and headaches in the future. Buyers will want to decide who the primary audience is: customers, employees or suppliers. Then, they will choose a style that fits the business: stately, fun, informal, business-like, etc. They'll pick technology features for the visitors to interact with: shopping carts, online chat, training or demonstration animation, forms to fill in, search engines, site maps, contact information, help and support, streaming audio or video, and connections to existing systems or databases within the organization. While web site features may always be added or deleted at any time, some changes may require a significant amount of money or equipment or personnel to implement.

In addition to the up-front creation costs, maintaining and publicizing a web site requires money and time. In order to maintain an interesting site to which customers return again and again, new content, graphics and other interactive features must be posted regularly. Navigation on the site may need to change in order to better direct customers to products, or to highlight new or sale merchandise. And any messages from site users must be answered promptly.

Once a site is ready for visitors, how should it be publicized? Unfortunately, building brand recognition on the Internet is no different (and may actually be more difficult) than building brand recognition in real life. Though once threatened by the existence of the Internet and web sites, traditional advertising media outlets now benefit from the need of web sites to promote themselves. Of course a web address should appear on all printed material for a company (business cards, stationery, envelopes, product packaging, etc.), but it should also be placed in tag lines on traditional advertising and maybe even run specific ads promoting the site. Every e-mail sent from a company has a signature block from the sender that includes the web address. The company fleet (cars, trucks, airplanes) all have the address printed on the side of the vehicle. Brand is built in the real world and will spill over into the online world.

But what about building brand in cyberspace? The conventional wisdom of the early adopters of the Internet was something like this: pick a product to sell on the Internet (fishing lures); get a dot-com established (www.getfish.com); register the site with some web search engines; people searching for the product at the search engine see the site in the search results; people come and spend millions on those products.

What actually happens is that many people do locate things using search engines, but it needs to be a part of the over-all strategy for site recognition. Here's a tip: Yahoo (www.yahoo.com) is such a popular web index, all of the top search engines store the contents of the Yahoo index with great frequency. A site registered at Yahoo will (within a month or so) be showing up in search results from most search engines. A web design consultant knows how to improve placement in search results which is critical as a site should appear in the first 10 or 20 listings, not hidden back in the 100s.

Placing banner ads (small rectangles of colorful content pleading "click me" to anyone who sees them) on other web sites has been shown to be a mixed bag. Best results come from the careful placement of a banner ad on a related web site. If a company is selling fishing lures, it should consider sites for sportsmen, hunting and fishing, related magazine web sites, etc. The ad should be quick and to the point and take the visitor directly to the offer. The downside of banner ads is that most web surfers simply ignore them. "Click-through" numbers, which represent people who actually followed a banner ad, continue to fall and the concern is that unlike a television commercial, which interrupts viewing and takes over the entire screen experience, web banner ads are simply noise on the web page that is easy to ignore.

Internet security issues are also important to address in web site design. Online purchases continue to grow, but a large number of Internet users continue to voice concerns about submitting their card number on a web page. The commercial site must meet these concerns, or the site will not be an attractive e-commerce site for at least some of its users. A successful tactic is to explain in detail to customers how the company is assuring that their transactions are encrypted and secure. Placing an "Is my information safe?" link on the ordering page allows customers to educate themselves about the technology involved. Secure servers are used to encrypt and transfer sensitive information online, which also increases the cost of the web site. Alternatives to the secure server include printing out an order form and having the purchaser fax it; taking orders online and following up with a phone call to take credit card information; or offering the user the option of sending a check and shipping the order when payment is received. Each of these options makes the ordering process more cumbersome and may decrease the number of orders, but ignoring security issues will cost even more in lost sales.

Another issue in using the Internet is the privacy of user information. A poll conducted by Harris Interactive found that Americans believe the Internet is where their personal information is most vulnerable (46 percent), compared to a distance second place finish for "dishonest phone order agents" (26 percent). Some companies gather information online and sell it to other companies. Good sites have a clearly written privacy statement that details how the company plans to use any information collected from site visitors or regular customers. TrustE (www.truste.org) provides information on how to create a privacy statement.

The power of the Internet to market a business can be harnessed in more ways than can be covered in more detail in this introduction. In using the Internet for marketing, issues the entrepreneur should consider include the time, effort, and budget to invest in the online segment of an enterprise. The most current information on online marketing will be found online, and local colleges may have courses on using the Internet, as well as topics like Internet research techniques and E-commerce. To find the best books on Internet marketing, visit Fatbrain (www.fatbrain.com).

Trade shows

For a relatively low cost, a large number of high-quality prospects can be reached by spending a few days attending or exhibiting at the right trade show. Thousands of trade shows are held all over the world. It takes some time to determine which trade show to attend to meet target customers.

Studies indicate that 50 percent of the people attending trade shows do so for the purpose of seeing new products and services. Thus, trade shows are ideal marketing opportunities for entrepreneurs. Many founders claim that the success of their ventures is largely attributable to the effective use of attending trade shows.

The advantages of exhibiting at trade shows include a method of quickly identifying many prospects because they come directly to the exhibitor. It is an excellent chance to meet people in the industry whom one would otherwise never have an opportunity to meet.

Another advantage is the opportunity to display and demonstrate product quality or superiority. Questions from prospects about the product or service can be answered. In addition, this meeting can be used to establish business relationships by inviting potential customers to a follow-up breakfast, lunch, or dinner meeting. These are just a few of the immediate benefits that entrepreneurs can take advantage of while working a trade show.

There are several dos and don'ts of exhibiting at trade shows.

Do select the appropriate trade show, where the right prospects will be attending.

Do visit as many other exhibits as possible.

Do preplan marketing strategy and set some specific objectives to achieve while attending the show. Develop some quick screening questions to ask, so solid prospects can be identified quickly. Follow up on all leads and contacts immediately after returning to the office.

Don't wait until the last minute to sign up for booth space. Instead, try to secure prime exhibit space early. Don't run out of a product to sell or samples to give away. Don't use giveaways that have nothing to do with the products or service.

Don't run out of business cards.

Don't allow anyone representing the venture to wear inappropriate clothing. Ensure that they are properly trained to answer all questions from prospects.

A good exhibit is, in a sense, an opportunity to make a special kind of sales call.

In certain circumstances, by displaying a product at a trade show, entrepreneurs may lose their ability to maintain information about the product as a trade secret or to obtain a patent on the product. If entrepreneurs are considering obtaining intellectual property protection for the product, they should consult an intellectual property attorney before attending the trade show. An adept exhibitor promotes products or services in advance of participation by sending out invitations to visit the booth and talk to exhibitors before the show to determine possible tie-ins.

A meeting should be held with everyone who will be covering the booth and specific responsibilities assigned to those involved in the exhibit. High achievers who get the most orders can be rewarded.

News releases should be available to give to reporters and editors who visit. Some seasoned entrepreneurs prepare press kits to disseminate at the shows. After the show, results should be evaluated while the experience of participating in the trade show is fresh. What worked best should be determined, and the most productive approaches should be reused.

Successful entrepreneurs learn to work trade shows for all they are worth. Nowhere will they have a better chance to meet the key players in the industry and learn what is happening. The contacts they make can ultimately provide significantly increased business that will better establish

---

Super Sales Calls

As the people at *California Magazine* wrote in a handout on trade-show usage: "Trade shows are the super sales call." As an exhibitor, an entrepreneur can experience several advantages.

- Prospects come to you.
- In an exhibit, you can control the environment. It's not somebody else's office, plant or store. It's your territory—one that you can design to serve your needs.
- You can demonstrate product quality or superiority. You can create a laboratory to prove product strength, durability, flexibility or special quality.
- You can answer every question from a prospect because you have backup expertise—product specialists, designers—right in your booth.
- You can have top company executives in attendance and introduce them to your prospect. "Let me introduce you to our chief engineer in charge of product quality," says the salesperson. "Meet our marketing vice president" or "Why not ask that question of the man who invented it?"
- You can show the product in operation in most cases. You can arrange for such special needs as power, or water and drainage, or gas.
- You can dramatize your story, your message, through exhibit design.
- You can call attention to significant points to reinforce the salesperson's presentation.
- You can use the exhibit exposure as the start of a successful business relationship. During the run of the show, you have more opportunities for follow-up contact.

Unfortunately, many exhibitors don't understand that an exhibit is an opportunity for a super sales call and may muff the opportunities. Whatever a salesperson can do in the field, he or she can do better at a show if properly trained and if the exhibit is designed for the super sales call.

and increase their market share.

Trade show into a bonanza

Robert Letwin of the Trade Show Bureau identified the following 20 essentials that could turn a so-so trade-show experience into a bonanza.

1. **Before you go into a trade show, make sure you know who attends.** Are they mostly engineers, technicians, high-level executives, purchasing agents, what? You have to have some idea of the numbers of the specific kinds of people you want to reach with your message. It may be that only 10 percent are important contacts, but it is important you know that in advance. Ask show management for attendance breakdowns. If management can't or won't tell you, don't go into the show until you visit it first and have an opportunity to see who comes and can talk to other exhibitors about the audience.

2. **When you know the number of important people to expect, then you must set an objective.** The objective should be in numbers. Examples: We want to sell three systems at the show; or we want to sign up 12 new dealers at the show; or we want to have 240 people who express interest in our products and want a salesperson to call. Your objective can be a combination of expectations, but it should always be in numbers. Otherwise, how would you know if you were successful? How else could you measure success objectively? You set your objectives based upon the number of prospects that normally come to the show, the competition, the economy—whatever factors can affect a good sales call.

3. **Buy enough space at the show to accommodate all the people you are trying to reach and all your sales, technical, and executive personnel.** Since a trade show is an opportunity to make sales calls, you need room for people to talk to your prospects. With show management's help, you can estimate how many of your prime targets are going to be walking down the aisles every hour. Don't be stingy with spaces for your own personnel if the figures indicate there are a lot of important prospects they should be talking to.

4. **Before the show opens, hold a meeting with everyone who is going to be in your booth—salespeople, engineers, company brass, others.** Often, 30 minutes or so before the show opens is time enough. At this meeting, make sure everyone knows what your goals are—in numbers. Don't assign specific hours to be on duty, but instead consider how many of the objectives each of your booth personnel is responsible for reaching every day of the show. Let them role play how they will handle prospects.

5. **Consider an annex to your exhibit in the headquarters hotel or a nearby hotel where special prospects and customers can be given special attention.** This is not a "hospitality suite" but a workshop or business environment where you can negotiate in private, examine equipment in fine detail—whatever will help your prospect make a wise buying decision.

6. **Avoid games and unrelated giveaways (items that have nothing to do with your product).** They attract crowds of the wrong people. The serious prospect is not interested in a 10-cent ruler or rolling the dice to win a 50-cent prize. The job of your exhibit design and operation is to

limit the idle curiosity of spouses, children and other non-buyers, not attract them.

7. **Assign responsibilities to those involved with your exhibit program.** Examples include selecting personnel and training them for booth work; ordering an exhibit booth designed to fit your objectives; supplying directives to everyone involved so they know your objectives and their assignments before, during, and after the show.

8. **Reward high achievers.** At your daily meetings, give away a small gift to those who beat their quotas and a gift to the person who did best for the day. The gift can be small; it's the recognition of high achievement that counts.

9. **Check on other exhibits at the show.** Take time to examine which are getting the right kind of audience and which are failures, and analyze why. It will help you plan next time. Don't be fooled by big crowds. The key to exhibit success is to attract only those people who could buy or recommend purchasing your products or services.

10. **Have news releases in your booth for reporters and editors who stop by.** Make sure there is always someone on duty who can talk to someone from the media. Shows attract media people, and you miss important exposure if you are not prepared with the right people and information.

11. **Promote, in advance, your participation in a trade show. Send out invitations to visit your booth or annex.** Have your ad agency alerted to include an invitation in your advertising long in advance—magazines go through the mail so slowly these days.

12. **Make sure the message your exhibit conveys is directly related to your prospect's needs.** It's more important to address your prospect in the exhibit header than to have a startling logo in 17 colors. Tell your prospect how you can solve his or her problem in a few words—big and prominent. Company ego trips (names in big type, maps of plant locations, pictures of the founders) are of little interest to a buyer who is looking for an answer to a problem.

13. **Consider the Fiddle Factor.** Engineers and technicians love to touch equipment and examine parts minutely. They simply love to fiddle with things. Plan your exhibit so that they can turn dials, look through a magnifying glass, feel the parts. If you are not trying to reach engineers and technicians, the "fiddle factor" is not as important.

14. **Have a telephone in your booth to be used for business only.** Make it a hotline to the home office. You can handle a customer's complaint immediately or check on a delivery or get an answer to a technical question that no one in the booth can answer.

15. **Use a demonstration in your booth.** Show the superiority— or difference—of your product. Find something it does better and demonstrate it. Demonstrations are the most cost-effective ways to attract a worthwhile audience. Use a sledge hammer to pound a part to show its strength; run a tape through boiling water and then into ice water to show it will still function under extreme environmental conditions. Demonstrate anything that could make a difference to a buying decision. Don't use young women in bikinis to do it. Use technicians and engineers in white lab coats. Make the demos professional in appearance.

16. **Monitor your booth's activity daily.** See what works and what doesn't. Maybe a sign should be changed because nobody is reading it, or maybe the main features should all be on one sign instead of placed around the booth on several signs. Be flexible! Change hours of duty if booth personnel are getting too tired or if the traffic pattern at the show is not what you intended. Don't consider your plans as set in concrete. Look for clues of success or failure, and use this knowledge constructively.

17. **Meet with your booth personnel each day of the show—preferably right after the show's closing hours.** Discuss what each one did and what was learned. Share experiences so you can improve booth operations the next day.

18. **Assign booth personnel in advance to seek out specific prospects or buyers who are visiting the show.** Have salespeople make appointments in advance to meet with VIPs at your booth or annex. Don't trust to luck that important prospects will find you; arrange for them to meet with your people.

19. **Talk to exhibitors in advance of the show to seek possible tie-ins.** Sometimes you can get dozens of other exhibitors to use your product with extra exposure at a show.

20. **After the show, evaluate everything you did and what happened.** Do it immediately or soon after the show, when everyone's experience is fresh. A post-show meeting is valuable. It doesn't take long, and it dredges up many ideas worth pursuing next time to give you sound reason for dropping the show or being more prominent.

See, says Letwin, there's no trick to having success. There is a lot of hard work. Those who try to wing it are usually those who complain about high costs and poor return. Those who know what to do, and do it, seldom complain on their way to the bank.

Conclusion

Although most entrepreneurs use multiple market-penetration methods, they begin by trying to determine which methods will be most successful and then experiment with a couple of methods. Market research will indicate which methods are likely to be the best for the venture. Customers' buying habits should be examined and the competitors' market-penetration methods should be observed.

Market-penetration methods will change as a business matures. For example, sales reps are often used in the early stages of development, but as the business grows, a direct sales force is usually hired.

Market-penetration mistakes are costly. One or several methods can be chosen for the venture based on research done while the entrepreneur writes the feasibility plan.

Exercise 20a: Designing Advertising

For your business concept, select a product or service. Write and design an advertisement for this product or service that could be used (1) in a newspaper, (2) in a radio advertisement, (3) on a billboard, or (4) in a direct-mail advertisement. Be sure to sketch out any illustrations you think would be useful in explaining your ad copy. Also list the suggestions you might make concerning such features as the color of the ad, the headline style and size, the "action" wording you might use, or the music you might select. For a direct-mail advertisement, also select an appropriate audience to receive the material.

Exercise 20b: Case Study

After reading this case study, answer the four questions on page 380.

The pizza shop owned by V. Johnson has been doing business in the city of Morris for 35 years. Johnson chose to start a pizza shop in Morris because there was relatively little competition, and this proved a wise decision. Sales have grown steadily through the years.

Morris has a population of 75,000 (22,500 households) and is the largest city within 160 miles of an urban center with a population of 1 million. Morris was formerly the center of a farming area, but today farming is less important to the city's economy.

Sales are estimated at $750,000 for the current year, off $50,000 from the preceding year. The reason for this decrease is the sharp increase in competition. The opening in Morris of two new pizza shops owned by a large chain last year affected business severely.

Johnson has done well, however, because he has kept the prices competitive and has excellent customer service. Johnson has continued to update his menu and add additional items.

Local advertising media consist of the following:

Newspaper
> *Morris Times*. Published evenings except Saturday and Sunday. Circulation: city zone, 14,370; trading zone, 16,572. Rate: $50 an inch for display ads.

Radio
> WBZL, local station. Programming is generally directed to adults. Station estimates 60 percent of households tune in for at least one program daily. One-minute spot announcements cost $50 in the evening hours; $35 all other times.

Shopping guide
> Free local weekly newspaper, limited editorial content. Claims 10,000 circulation, unsubstantiated. Rate: 15 cents a line, flat.

Television
> No local station. Three stations located in nearby metropolitan area cover Morris.

Direct mail
> At initiative of local merchant.

During the preceding year, when the retail sales volume was $800,000, the advertising budget was $15,000. Johnson cut the budget in the current year. The competition, however, advertises in every media available and takes advantage of national discounts. It is now December, and a budget for the coming year is being discussed.

A five-inch display ad has been consistently run in the *Morris Times* twice a week. No experiment of schedules in other media has ever been tried. Johnson has no knowledge of the demographic characteristics of his customers, nor has he attempted studies of where his sales come from. Additionally he has not concerned himself with the growth rate of the city, the income level of local wage earners, or any other basic research data.

1. If you were developing Johnson's pizza shop advertising program for the coming year, what decisions would you make about the selection of media?

2. Should research be undertaken, and if so, what kind?

3. What would you feature in your ads?

4. What size budget would you recommend? If other media besides the newspaper are to be used, on what basis would you use them, and what percentage of the budget should be allocated to them?

Exercise 20c: Promotion

List the promotional activities you are considering for your business concept. Then develop a list of methods for evaluating those promotional activities. List as many methods as possible.

Promotional activity	Evaluation methods

Exercise 20d: Market-Penetration Challenges

Identify market-penetration challenges specific to your proposed venture. After gathering information from qualified experts (marketing consultants, marketing professors, other successful entrepreneurs), develop a useful action plan for the venture.

Market-penetration challenge	Action plan

Exercise 20e: Marketing Assessment

For two specific targeted customer groups for your business concept, list proposed market-penetration tactics and evaluate their appropriateness/effectiveness.

1 = inappropriate/ineffective; 2 = appropriate/effective; 3 = extremely appropriate/effective

After completing the assessment, develop an action plan.

Targeted customer group:				
Marketing tactic	Rate			Action plan
	1	2	3	
	1	2	3	
	1	2	3	
	1	2	3	
	1	2	3	

Targeted customer group:				
Marketing tactic	Rate			Action plan
	1	2	3	
	1	2	3	
	1	2	3	
	1	2	3	
	1	2	3	

Exercise 20f: Linking Target Profiles to Tactics

Identify two target customer groups and list three market penetration tactics for each group.

Targeted customer group:
Future marketing tactic

Targeted customer group:
Future marketing tactic

Budgeting

Learning Objectives

In this chapter, students will learn to
- Define the benefits of budgeting.
- Budget by using assumptions.
- Determine start-up costs by using the "walk through" method.

The budget system is one of the two major control tools for a business. The other is the cash flow plan, which will be discussed in Chapter 22.

A budget is simply a tool, a financial guide, which a manager uses to plan profitable operations by anticipating and allotting the revenues and expenditure of funds. Thus, the budget is the basic source of information fed into the cash flow plan. Once the various budgets have been developed, the cash flow plan naturally follows.

By adopting various budgetary procedures, management hopes to guide the operations to a predetermined end—a certain amount of profit from a certain volume of sales. Without a budget, management could never be certain whether operations were going successfully.

Benefits of Budgeting

Budgeting plays a major role in business planning. Five major benefits are realized by using a good budget system. Each of these benefits is discussed below.

Control of expense-revenue ratios

Maintaining the desired relationship between expenditures and revenues is the key to profits. Losses result when expenses exceed revenues. The objective of business is to buy revenues in the market at a reasonable cost, and the budget establishes what that cost should be. Thus, the budget helps keep expenses in line with revenue. In theory, a firm can make money at almost any level of sales if it keeps its costs proportional to its revenues.

It takes great discipline and mental toughness to abide by a budget, particularly in new enterprises, in which expenditures are often chaotic and unpredictable.

The new enterprise's irregularities cannot be used as an excuse for not diligently developing a good budget system. Entrepreneurs resort to all sorts of excuses for not budgeting. "We can't budget. Our revenues are too uncertain. We haven't time to budget. That's something big business does." Such excuses are not only nonsense, but are dangerous to the firm's solvency.

Coordinating activities

The budget helps top management coordinate the activities of all departments. If $500,000 in sales is to be shipped, then the shipping department must be allowed enough money to do the job. Production must be coordinated with sales. The firm cannot ship $500,000 worth of products if they have not been produced. The production budget tells the factory what is to be made. If products worth $500,000 in sales are to be made, the finance department must be prepared to finance the operation.

Establishing performance standard

Once the budget is established, it becomes the standard of performance for all departments. Marketing is expected to sell $500,000 and spend $25,000 doing it. The budget becomes the goal. The name of the game in business is meet the budget. Those people who fail to do so seldom last long in most organizations.

Evaluation tool

Naturally, if a group fails to meet its budget, it is not looked upon with favor by top management. Thus, the budget becomes a means for evaluating each unit's performance.

Obviously, this aspect of budgeting causes some problems. Knowing that the budgets they submit may be the rope that hangs them, the department heads can become cautious by asking for far too much money and promising far too little output. Budget meetings can be interesting as final budget figures are pounded out between departments and the management.

Triggering remedial action

The month's budgetary performance is on the entrepreneur's desk. The telephone budget was $2,800; the actual was $4,700. That's too much variance. What happened? The entrepreneur calls for the bill and either scans it himself or hands it to someone else to do it. It is important to know who spent the $1,900 and why. Was it necessary? If so, the money will have to be made up elsewhere. But if the calls were not necessary, they must be stopped.

Effective cost control dictates that quick action be taken to remedy unnecessary cost overruns. Allowed to go unchecked, they not only accumulate a large sum of money, but they tend to accelerate in amount as employees learn that cost overruns don't seem to be important and the staff does not focus on the bottom line.

By quickly and forcefully coming down on offenders, several messages are delivered to staff members. First, they learn that management is watching what is spent and is on top of operations. Second, they learn that management means business about staying within budget. Third, they learn what happens to people who misuse company money. Once the proper tone

Budgeting Benefits

Controls expense-revenue ratios

Coordinates activities

Establishes performance standard

Serves as evaluation tool

Triggers remedial action

is set within the company, controls become much easier to administer. The staff learns that the very survival of the enterprise depends on staying within and meeting the budgets.

The Budgeting Process

The budget begins with the sales forecast, since all activities must be tied to the anticipated level of sales. Once the sales forecast has been set, then that figure is given to each manager of a budgetary unit—such as marketing and production. In many smaller new ventures, the entrepreneur works up the entire budget with the help of the accountant.

Obviously, the more reliable the sales forecast, the easier it is to budget operations. As the sales forecast becomes increasingly suspect, the budget-making process becomes more tentative. It is difficult to budget a large sum of money for advertising in advance of sales if sales are uncertain. It is difficult to budget for hiring new employees in the shipping room if the volume of shipments is in doubt.

When developing budgets, the entrepreneur should consider the following key factors.

The role of assumptions

A word needs to be said about the need for making assumptions in developing the budget. For example, the sales forecast is developed based on several assumptions about economic activity, new products coming on line, levels of competitive activity, prices, and so forth. These assumptions should be clearly stated in the budget document.

Various assumptions underlie many of the figures in the budget. These should be footnoted in the budget so readers will know how each figure was derived. The validity of these assumptions affects all planning because a plan can be no better than the assumptions upon which it is based. The cash flow projections are similarly based on many assumptions; a company must assume many things in projecting its sales and costs. Management must make certain those assumptions are clearly recognized and stated.

Underlying all planning are some implicit assumptions that often go unrecognized, such as the state of the economy, the state of world peace, political or regulatory developments, the continued good health of the entrepreneur, unforseen technological developments, and so on. In general, most planning assumes a static environment. Any significant changes in the environment often cause plans to go astray.

Forecasting sales

When management cannot forecast sales with any degree of confidence, two budget approaches can be used. First, the minimum-budget approach can be used when forecasting sales is difficult, such as when the venture is introducing a new product to the marketplace. For example, the owner can draw up a minimum budget that would indicate the least money for which each function can be performed. He or she would start out with the minimum amount of money needed for each expense center, and then allocate more funds to the budgets as sales warrant. Budgets can be flexible, thus allowing for changes in a firm's fortunes.

Key Budget Factors
The role of assumptions
Forecasting sales
Expense lead time
Budget periods
Line-item budgeting
Program budgeting
Budget accounts
Start-up costs

A plan can be no better than its assumptions. These assumptions should be clearly stated in the financial section of a feasibility or business plan.

The second approach involves developing a must-do budget. Sometimes the founder, in the absence of good, hard data on which to base the forecasts and the budgets, sets the budget on the basis of what must happen if the company is to make it. It's pointless to set budgets that result in failure. Set budgets that result in success. No founder wants to budget his or her venture into failure.

Two methods used by many entrepreneurs are the bottom-up and top-down methods. With the bottom-up method, the entrepreneur develops budgets for all expenses and cost of goods, therefore, showing what sales would have to be to cover these costs. Example: If expenses are $100,000 and cost of goods is 50 percent of sales, then a break-even sales forecast would be $200,000.

With the top-down method , the entrepreneur projects sales volume first, then develops cost of goods and expenses and projects whether the company can make money. Example: If the sales volume projection is 300,000, cost of goods is 50 percent, and expenses are $100,000, then the company would make a profit of $50,000.

Expense lead time

The flexibility in a budget depends greatly on how much time is involved between the expenditure of funds and the receipt of sales dollars from those expenditures. At one extreme is a project in which all funds must be spent long before any sales revenues can be realized. If a venture is building oil rigs, management must spend a lot of money before it ever knows whether the venture will earn a dollar of revenue from a well. For this reason, oil adventurers prefer to use other people's money to drill wildcat wells. Let people who want to take such gambles put up the money.

At the other extreme, there are businesses in which revenues are received before much money is spent. Perhaps a customer pays up front, such as in the cases of insurance, magazines, many direct-mail promotions, and custom manufacturing. Such instances are fortuitous, for the venture's management knows its sales volume on which to plan its budget system, and all it must do is stay within budget for fulfilling the contract.

If sales volume follows expenses by a short time, a month or so, then the budget can be quickly reduced or expanded to reflect sales experience. Risks are minimized. The longer the lead time of expenses over sales, the larger the risk of losses due to spending too much money because of over-budgeting by the various expense centers.

Budget periods

Most often the budget is prepared for the coming year in monthly increments. Sometimes, in strongly seasonal businesses such as the apparel industry, each budget will be for a season. Sometimes, in project-management types of businesses such as defense manufacturing and contracting, a budget is prepared for each contract.

Line-item budgeting

Most budget systems start out by identifying expense centers for those areas over which management wants controls established. Thus, department budgets are set up for such departments or activities as production, marketing, and general and administrative items. Each department's budget details specific budget accounts. Or budget accounts may be built along the lines of more traditional accounting systems of accounts.

Such budgets are often called line-item budgets because each expense category is a separate line in the total budget. Obviously, line-item budgets go into great detail, so much so that it is their weakness. Seldom can anyone plan expenses in that much detail. Thus, in operations, such budgets are conducive to all sorts of budget games, as managers rob one budget to pay for costs incurred elsewhere.

Program budgeting

In a system of program budgeting, larger sums of money are dedicated to programs, with their expenditure and distribution left to the discretion of the program manager. The marketing program would be budgeted for $500,000 in total; how that amount is spent is up to the marketing manager. Obviously, management must have great faith in its marketing manager, although the breakdown of marketing expenses is usually reviewed by top management.

The theory of program budgeting is that management should not tie the marketing manager's hands by dictating how marketing funds will be spent, while holding the manager responsible for the final sales results. However, after the program has been awarded its budget, its manager must then apportion the total among the traditional line-item expense categories.

Budget accounts

The number of budget accounts and the kinds of costs lumped into each account are solely matters for managerial discretion. However, there are some general guidelines.

Do not use so few accounts that all sorts of costs are lumped together. If advertising-media costs are lumped together with direct-mail costs, then it becomes more difficult to tell which expense is out of control. Enough detail should be budgeted so that when the manager looks at the performance of a budget, he or she is judging a single activity that needs control. For example, if both postage and telephone costs are included together in a communication budget, the manager would not know whether someone was stealing stamps or making unauthorized telephone calls. A large budget variance should focus attention to one area of expenditures.

Budget accounts should parallel the ledger accounts so that posting results is easy. With the advent of computerized accounting, the monthly output for the budget book is a simple matter.

Start-up costs

One method of determining how much money a venture will need at start-up is to do a mental walk-through of what the business will look like. The following questions should be asked to determine start-up costs:

- Where will the business be?
- What size will it be initially?
- What will the office or retail space look like?

- What types of walls and fixtures will it have?
- What type of equipment will be needed, such as computers, furniture, carpet, copy machine, shelving?
- What types of signs will be required?
- How much of an opening inventory will the business need?
- How will it be paid for?
- What kinds of deposits will be required? For instance, how much will deposits cost for telephone, utilities, and rent—first and last month?
- What city codes must be complied with, and are there any costs involved?
- What types of government (local, state, federal) business licenses will be required?
- What types of supplies will be needed for cleaning, office correspondence, shipping, boxes?
- What kinds of marketing costs will be incurred before opening the business for items such as brochures, advertising, stationery, and business cards?
- What are potential costs for recruiting and hiring initial staff?
- What type of staff training is necessary before opening?

When estimating these expenses, entrepreneurs should be as realistic and accurate as possible. They always discover hidden costs that are incurred but not planned for. Other owners in a similar business can be queried about what their start-up costs were and how much money they suggest be reserved before opening doors for business.

Most lenders recommend that entrepreneurs have a minimum of three-months' operating capital on hand.

Avoid forcing the budget process or trying to underestimate start-up costs. Let the budgeting process indicate how much money the business concept needs.

For example, one entrepreneur wanted to launch a venture that involved manufacturing submarines and selling them to operators of underwater ocean tours at island resorts. The idea seemed feasible. After estimating his start-up budget, he discovered that he needed about $1.2 million for operating capital to launch the venture. He could raise only about $10,000. After estimating start-up costs, he determined there was no way he could start this business himself.

There is no lack of ideas for launching new companies, but venture ideas must match the entrepreneur's personal and business criteria as well as his or her pocketbook. Problems, such as running out of money or realizing enough money cannot be raised to launch a venture idea, can be avoided by accurately estimating start-up costs and preparing an initial start-up budget.

The Budget Book

When some entrepreneurs managed the budgetary system of their company, they developed an effective yet simple way of monitoring the chain's monthly budget performance.

First, the entrepreneurs developed a budget book, a loose-leaf ledger or computer program containing information for each budget account. Each sheet showed the budget and actual figures for that account for the previous 12 months, the projected budget for the year by months, the current actual performance, and the variance of the actual figures from the budgeted figures.

The bookkeeper prepared the data for the entrepreneurs by the 5th of each month. Each account that was over or under budget was circled in red. The entrepreneurs would glance at the red circles and decide if the difference was significant. If so, was it explainable? Did they know why it happened? If they did not know the reason for the significant variance, the entrepreneurs would call for the checks or other documents that supported the out-of-line expenditures. If problems were identified, plans were made to take immediate action. Many entrepreneurs claim this system is the only way to manage a budget for their businesses. It takes only 15 minutes a month to survey the organization's budgetary performance.

Customize the Budget

No two budget systems should be alike. Each venture should develop one that meets its needs, not the needs of the accountant. The accountant is hired to accommodate the venture, not to dictate his or her wants. A venture needs an accounting and budgeting system that its personnel can understand and that provides the needed information in a usable form.

Timeliness is essential. Budget information two months old is of little use. A venture should have its accounting information within two weeks after the end of the month. One big advantage of having an in-house bookkeeper in addition to an outside accounting firm is that access to needed information is much faster.

Management by Percentages

At the heart of most budget systems is a basic philosophy called management by percentages. For most businesses, experience has established that a firm can afford to pay only a certain percentage of its sales for each expense. For example, in the menswear manufacturing business one owner found it difficult to make a profit if he paid more than 8 percent for rent, 10 percent for sales compensation, or 5 percent for management salaries. Naturally, these expenses depend upon the particular philosophies and plans of management. Where one manufacturer may rely heavily on advertising, budgeting perhaps 10 percent of sales for it, another may rely on trade shows to bring in the business, thus budgeting only 4 percent for advertising. The budget that the owner eventually arrived at left him 9.8 percent of sales for profit. Most percentage budgets are built on operating experience. This owner was copying the operations of another similar business.

Department Budget Accounts

Sales-reps compensation
Field-selling expenses
Sales-office expenses
Advertising
Printing
Communications
Sales-management salaries
Trade show expenses

Traditional Accounts

Travel
Auto
Entertainment
Supplies
Telephone
Salaries
Printing

If a venture is just starting out, it is much better off making up the budget in dollar amounts based on actual field determination of what the expenses will be. This is the reason that good budget building requires considerable time and effort. Of course, the entrepreneur's experience bears greatly upon the amount of work that must be done. An experienced operator knows the costs and percentages and can develop a meaningful budget rather quickly. The inexperienced person must work at it or find some experienced operator to do the budget.

Composite Budgets

Some managers prefer to develop several budgets, one for each separate significant segment of the business, and then combine them into a composite overall budget. For example, a menswear merchant developed three budgets: sales, capital, and expenses. The sales budget was developed in great detail by lines and months. It was used not only for developing the cash flow statements and financial budgets but was also used by the merchant as the basis for his buying. If separate budgets are developed in detail, then the overall budget is a simple one, consisting of a few lines.

Some companies will develop a best-case/worse-case projected budget. The best-case scenario represents the budget with which the management team thinks it can run the company. The worst case is usually the budget that reflects the break-even projection. Bankers like to see a company use this approach, so they know what the company has to do to stay in business.

Conclusion

The need for entrepreneurs to master the development and use of budgets cannot be stressed too strongly. They will find that following budgets is really the only way they can run businesses of any substance with any degree of confidence. Without budgets, some expenses will run out of control and the managers will know nothing about it until it is too late.

Exercise 21a: Projecting Start-Up Costs

Start-up costs are the costs incurred before the opening of the business and before the business generates enough cash to cover its operating expenses. Below is a partial list of potential costs associated with starting a business. Disregard those that are not associated with your business concept and add any costs not listed.

What and why	How much
Legal and other professional fees	
Advertising and promotion for opening	
Rent	
Starting inventory	
Fixtures and equipment	
Deposits	
Training	
Licenses and permits	
Decorating and remodeling	
Installation of fixtures and equipment	
Accounts receivable	
Cash	
Supplies	
Total estimated cash you need to start	

There are many costs related to starting a business, such as rent and utilities deposits, fixtures and furniture, computers, signage, office supplies, and insurance. If the entrepreneur has not realistically projected start-up costs, the business could start with a negative cash flow and run into immediate financial difficulties.

Cost is an expenditure incurred to obtain revenue. Cost information is imperative for the decision-making process and is necessary for operational and control purposes as well. It is important that entrepreneurs understand the different types of costs found in a start-up situation, how to classify them, and how to accurately obtain cost information.

Costs, for the purpose of this exercise, are broken down into two types: one-time costs and ongoing costs.

One-time costs are costs that are required to get the business up and operating. These costs are considered one time if, as a rule of thumb, the venture probably won't have to spend on this item again for the next five years. Examples of costs considered one-time costs are leasehold improve-ments, advertising signs for the business, the initial supplies of the business that will last a significant period, deposits, equipment purchases, grand-opening celebration costs.

Ongoing costs are costs that are incurred in the day-to-day operations of the business. These can be fixed or variable costs. Examples of ongoing costs are inventory purchases, rent, utilities, insurance, and wages. Don't overlook

- Expenses such as licenses, payroll, taxes, delivery expenses, postage for mailings, participation in trade shows, insurance, trash removal, property/equipment maintenance, or sacks to wrap and bag customer purchases.
- Budgeting for miscellaneous expenses.
- Escrow for all forms of taxes.

Don't create just one budget. Alternative scenarios help look at worst case and better than expected cases. In both the worst-case and best-case scenarios, operations are affected and different decisions need to be made. Preplanning for those situations allows the entrepreneur to make changes.

Exercise 21b: Projecting Operating Expenses

After determining the business expenses required to get a business started, you can begin thinking about how these expenses will continue as operating expenses. One way to begin determining operating expenses is to do a mental walkthrough of what it will be like to operate the business. Consider the following questions:

- Was the start-up cost a one-time expense?
  Example: Installing an alarm system
- Is there an ongoing expense associated with operating the business?
  Example: Monthly service fee for the alarm system

Determining the projected operational costs for the intended business is an important reality check. While it is hoped that sales will take off once the door is open for business, the reality is that it often takes several months for a business to generate enough sales to cover all of its expenses, let alone make a profit. How much money will you need to help cover these initial months of operation?

Below is a partial list of potential costs associated with operating a business. Disregard those that are not associated with your business concept and add any costs not listed.

What	Monthly cost	Quarterly cost	Annual cost
Salary of owner-manager			
All other salaries and wages			
Rent			
Advertising			
Delivery expense			
Supplies			
Telephone			
Other utilities			
Insurance			
Taxes, including Social Security			
Interest			
Maintenance			
Legal and other professional fees			
Total operating costs			

Exercise 21c: Projecting Sales

Projecting sales estimates is one of the most critical issues in financial planning for a business. Estimated sales directly affect all expenses and determine profitability.

However, remember estimated sales are just that—an estimation!

There is no crystal ball that can show you the future of a business. Projecting sales requires that you look at the issue from a variety of perspectives and test what each might mean for your business.

Sales can be projected with either the bottom up or top down methods (discussed on p. 387–388). Both methods can also be used to run best-case, worst-case, and most likely scenarios.

Section I: Bottom up

Question	Formula	Calculation
Project all expense for the year, including salaries.	Use operating expense projections; monthly expenses x 12	Annual expenses =
Estimate cost of product/ service per unit	Identify and add all costs. Calculate the per unit cost. Do not forget the value of your time.	$
Estimated sales for one year	Annual expenses divided by the cost of product/service per unit.	Number of units you need to sell =

Section II: Top down

Question	Formula	Calculation
Estimate how many units you will sell in one year	Use competitor's sales volumes if necessary	Estimated number sold =
What is your total cost of product/service for one year?	Estimated # sold x cost of product/service per unit	Annual cost of product/ service =
What are your total expenses for one year?	Estimate your business expenses if you sold this many units	Total annual expenses =
What are your total dollars needed?	Annual cost of product/ service plus total annual expenses	Total $ needed =

Section II: Top down (continued)

Question	Formula	Calculation
Estimate how much revenue your sales estimate will generate in one year	Unit price x estimated # sold	Revenue generated =
Compare total $ needed with revenue generated	Will you lose money, break even, or make a profit? Revenue generated minus total dollars needed.	$

Financial Statements

Learning objectives

In this chapter, students will learn how to
- Construct the financials for feasibility or business plans.
- Use the income statement, balance sheet, and cash flow statement to make business decisions for a venture.

Financial statements are tools, as essential to business management as the wrench is to a machinist. Does a machinist only have one wrench? Do all the wrenches work the same way? No—different jobs require different tools and the knowledge to know which one is the right tool for each job.

Financial statements are a reflection of management decisions over a period of time. Every day business decisions are made that will have an eventual, if not immediate, impact on the financials of the business.

Suppose a company implemented a new ordering process that reduces cycle time by two days. That decision means there is less inventory in the warehouse and fewer employees "touching it," and the cost of goods went up. Why? The company's managers will need to be detectives for a few days to examine the effects of the new process.

Often entrepreneurs don't understand the full impact of their decisions. Sometimes they don't understand the impact of not making a decision or dragging their feet. Financial statements not only show the expected outcomes of decisions but the unexpected outcomes as well.

For example, a company found a new vendor who can supply an essential part for 50 percent less per piece than the previous supplier did. But after a few months, the company's overtime is increasing. Why? The new piece has a failure rate 25 percent higher than the last one. That means more rework. Which costs the company more, the item or the employees' time? How long would it have taken this information to come to the attention of company management by other means?

The two primary business objectives of every company are profitability and solvency. Profitability is the ability to generate income. Solvency is the ability to pay debts as they become due. Financial statements provide the tools for company managers to examine and forecast a company's ability to achieve these two objectives. The income statement reflects the profitability of a company; the balance sheet its solvency.

When reviewing or comparing financial documents and statements, it is important to remember that different businesses and industries may use different terms to describe the same numbers. That's why it is important to understand what the numbers mean and where they come from regardless of what they are called.

The financial statements play a significant role in business planning. By reflecting on the current and the past financial statements, the entrepreneur makes decisions for the future. This chapter begins by looking at two primary statements: the income statement and the balance sheet.

The Income Statement

The income statement shows how much a company made or lost for a given period of time—in other words, a company's performance. This financial statement displays the amount of revenues (sales) earned by the company and the expenses that were incurred to generate those revenues. To some this statement represents the company's grade card, in that it will communicate whether the company's business strategies are working. Although this statement does reflect the profitability of the business (revenues – expenses = net profit or net loss), be sure to understand that net income or profits don't always indicate positive cash flows. One reason is that some non-cash expenses such as depreciation and amortization are included in the income statement. In some instances, particularly in real estate and other high-investment enterprises, large depreciation or amortization charges can result in a loss—no profit—yet the firm is flush with money. Another reason for the disconnect between the income statement and the actual cash flows of the business is that there can be significant cash outflows for debt repayments, purchases of inventory and payments to the owners of the business (dividends or draws) and cash inflows from borrowings from banks and other lenders that are not accounted for as income or expenses and therefore will not show up on the company's income statement.

A case can be made that the income statement is largely a tax document developed according to IRS regulations and is not intended to provide management with the information it needs to operate the venture. The company's tax obligation is determined by the profit or loss on the income statement.

Balance Sheet

The income statement reflects the income the company makes, but note that the income statement says little about how much the company is worth. If the company owns a building (an asset), it probably still owes money to the bank (a liability), and of course, the company may have some retained earnings (equity); none of these are reflected in the income statement. The income statement does not show the tangible worth of a company. This is the function of the balance sheet: to show what a company is worth at a given point in time. It is a reflection of how much the company owns and how much is due to it and how much it owes to both creditors and the owners. It shows the company's assets, the liabilities, and the owner's equity. Here's another way of looking at the balance sheet:

Formula for the balance sheet
Assets = Liabilities + Owners' equity

On the balance sheet, the assets are divided into current assets, which includes assets either currently in the form of cash or expected to be turned into cash within one year. Examples include cash, accounts receivable and inventory. All other assets are considered noncurrent such as plant and equipment (also known as fixed assets) and any other assets not expected to be converted into cash within a year (long-term notes receivables and intangible assets, such as goodwill and patents). The liabilities are divided into current liabilities and long-term liabilities. The stockholders' equity is the difference between assets and liabilities and it represents the owners' rights to the value of the company.

Sample Statements

The following pages show examples of income statements and balance sheets. All businesses are different, and sometimes one will use names for accounts that are different from those used by others. There is no definitive template for financial statements. As entrepreneurs review more statements and have a greater understanding of the contents of the various line items, navigating from one statement to another or one business to another becomes easier.

Financial study

Duke's Manufacturing Inc.

Duke's Manufacturing Inc. (DMI) is a family-owned toy company established in 1980 with an initial investment of $15,000 by C.V. Duke. DMI began as a distributor with 15 employees in Cleveland. In 1988, DMI started manufacturing competition yo-yos.

In 1992, DMI expanded its product lines by producing yo-yos for the beginner and intermediate users. In 1994, DMI became a national name when it contracted with a fast-food restaurant to produce a yo-yo for its children's meal.

In response to the increasing demand of the national toy market, DMI opened a new factory in Memphis. The financial statements below reflect DMI's 20xx performance.

Duke's Manufacturing Inc.
Income Statement
For the year ended December 31, 20xx

Sales		$3,000,000
Cost of goods sold		1,800,000
Gross profit		$1,200,000
Marketing expense		300,000
Administrative expenses		300,000
General expenses		260,000
Earnings before interest and taxes (EBIT)		$340,000
Interest:		
Short-term debt	$37,800	
Long-term debt	80,000	
Total interest charges		117,800
Earnings before taxes		$222,200
Federal Income Tax		88,880
Net income		$133,320

Duke's Manufacturing Inc.
Balance Sheet
As of December 31, 20xx

Assets		Liabilities and stockholders' equity	
Cash	$240,000	Accounts payable	$380,000
Accounts receivable	320,000	Notes payable	420,000
Inventory	1,040,000	Other current liabilities	50,000
Total current assets	$1,600,000	Total current liabilities	$850,000
		Long-term debt	800,000
Plant and equipment	1,000,000	Total liabilities	$1,650,000
Accumulated depreciation	(200,000)	Stockholders' equity	
Net plant and equipment	$800,000	Common stock	650,000
		Retained earnings	100,000
Total assets	$2,400,000	Total stockholders' equity	$750,000
		Total liabilities and stockholders' equity	$2,400,000

Reading the income statement

Below is the income statement for Duke's Manufacturing Inc. The income statement reflects a company's performance during a specified period of time.

Remember that the income statement reflects how profitable or unprofitable a company has been. Use the income statement, as well as all financial statements to help monitor the business. If after reviewing the financial statements, you notice something out of the ordinary. Take the time to research the reason for the unexpected difference. This could possibly save a lot of the business' precious resources, such as time, energy and cash flow.

Duke's Manufacturing Inc.
Income Statement
For the year ended December 31, 20xx

Sales		$3,000,000
Cost of goods sold		1,800,000
Gross profit		$1,200,000
Marketing expense		300,000
Administrative expenses		300,000
General expenses		260,000
Earnings before interest and taxes (EBIT)		$340,000
Interest:		
Short-term debt	$37,800	
Long-term debt	80,000	
Total interest charges		117,800
Earnings before taxes		$222,200
Federal Income Tax		88,880
Net income		$133,320

Cost of goods sold includes all the costs allocated to the inventory sold during the period, including labor, materials, and overhead. This line directly affects inventory on the balance sheet as the amount of cost of goods sold is a withdrawal from the inventory account.

Gross profit is the first cut. Can the company's sales price cover all of the costs to manufacture the items being sold?

Earnings before interest and taxes (EBIT), also known as operating income, is the income generated from conducting business.

Net profit is also called net income or earnings after taxes (EAT).

Reading the balance sheet

Below is a balance sheet for Duke's Manufacturing Inc. The date line in the heading reads "As of" a point in time not a period of time. A balance sheet is a snapshot of a company's worth on a given day.

Some intangible assets are not seen on the balance sheet, such as brand loyalty. Although earning loyalty from customers obviously is valuable to the company, attaching a dollar value to that loyalty cannot be accurately and consistently done—therefore it shouldn't be included on the balance sheet.

As we learned earlier, the formula for the balance sheet is:

$$Assets = Liabilities + Owners'\ equity$$

Duke's Manufacturing Inc.
Balance Sheet
As of December 31, 20xx

Assets		Liabilities and stockholders' equity	
Cash	$240,000	Accounts payable	$380,000
Accounts receivable	320,000	Notes payable	420,000
Inventory	1,040,000	Other current liabilities	50,000
Total current assets	$1,600,000	Total current liabilities	$850,000
		Long-term debt	800,000
Plant and equipment	1,000,000	Total liabilities	$1,650,000
Accumulated depreciation	(200,000)	Stockholders' equity	
Net plant and equipment	$800,000	Common stock	650,000
		Retained earnings	100,000
Total assets	$2,400,000	Total stockholders' equity	$750,000
		Total liabilities and stockholders' equity	$2,400,000

Assets
Always on the left side of the balance sheet.

This line shows how much cash DMI has in the bank.

How much is owed to DMI from its customers.

How much DMI has in inventory. (Caution: If much of this inventory is old or obsolete, its value is obviously impaired. Be sure to verify the marketability of inventory included on the balance sheet.)

How much the plant and equipment are worth. (Again, if the plant is old and in need of extensive refitting to make the company competitive, then this asset may not be as valuable as it looks.)

Liabilities and stockholders' equity
Always on the right side of the balance sheet.

This line shows how much DMI owes for expenses incurred on credit. Generally due in 30 to 60 days.

How much DMI has in short-term debt (loans due in less than one year).

How much long-term debt DMI has committed to.

The owners' stake in the company. It is often made up of combinations of the owner's investments (stock and additional paid in capital) and retained earnings.

Linking Financial Documents

The income statement and the balance sheet, while serving very different purposes, are linked together. Table 22-1 shows how changes in daily transactions affect the balance sheet. The table is read as a sentence. For example, the first line (under the heading) would read "An increase in sales on the income statement increases the accounts receivable on the balance sheet."

Financial statements should be considered as tools for managing a business. Each type of statement has its own job of keeping track of money matters and has specific links to the other statements. When business owners look at the financial statements for more than one year, however, it is difficult to get a true picture of performance by comparing one year's numbers with another's. These comparisons are done by ratio analysis which is covered in Chapter 23.

A change in inventory may only appear as a change on the balance sheet. But don't forget inventory carrying costs—warehouse, shrinkage, shopware, and depreciation—will affect the income statement.

Table 22-1: How Daily Transactions Can Affect the Balance Sheet

Income statement	Change	Balance sheet
Increased sales	Increases	Accounts receivable
Increased cost of goods sold	Decreases	Inventory
Increased operating expenses	May increase	Accrued expenses
	Or increase	Accounts payable
	Or decrease	Cash
	Or decrease	Prepaid expenses
Improved net income	Increases	Retained earnings (owners' equity)

Percentages of Revenue

Entrepreneurs will have good cash flows if they can
- Produce the sales forecast.
- Produce the projected gross margin.
- Control expenses.
- Control capital expenditures.
- Control accounts receivable and inventory.

There are two types of expenses, fixed and variable. Fixed expenses are those that do not change in relation to the number of items produced. For example, rent expense is the same every month no matter how much the company produces. Variable expenses are those expenses that change based on production. As a paper mill produces more paper, it buys more lumber.

The percentage of revenue figure tells exactly how much of each dollar of revenue is expense and how much is profit. Calculating the percentage of revenue helps owners to know if the company's variable expenses are consistent with its production and sales. It also tells how the company is managing its fixed expenses. Simply because they are fixed expenses does not mean they are uncontrollable. Administrative salaries are fixed expenses (they are not tied directly to each item produced) but the lights can be turned off at night to keep the costs down.

To calculate the percentages of revenue, simply divide the line item on the income statement by the revenue line and multiply by 100. Below are the calculations of percentages of revenue for Duke's Manufacturing Inc.

Each item is divided by DMI's sales of $3,000,000. For example the costs of goods sold = 60 percent of revenue or ($1,800,000/$3,000,000).

It can be stated another way by saying that for each $1 received, DMI spent 60 cents on labor and materials (COGS).

$$Percentage\ of\ revenue = \frac{Income\ statement\ line\ item}{Revenue\ sales\ line}$$

Duke's Manufacturing Inc.
Percentages of Revenue
For the year ended December 31, 20xx

Line amount	$ amount	% of revenue
Sales	3,000,000	100
Cost of goods sold	1,800,000	60
Gross profit	1,200,000	40
Marketing expenses	300,000	10
Administrative expenses	300,000	10
General expenses	260,000	9
Earnings before interest and taxes (EBIT)	340,000	11
Short-term debt	37,800	1
Long-term debt	80,000	3
Total interest charges	117,800	4
Earnings before taxes	222,200	7
Federal Income Tax	88,880	3
Net income	133,320	4

Building Cash Flow Projections

Unquestionably, the cash flow analysis is by far the most important document in the business plan for a venture. It is also the most important tool management has for contemplating and controlling the enterprise's financial affairs. If entrepreneurs master it, it will serve them well.

The need for cash flow analysis comes from the time discrepancy that usually exists between the time funds are expended to generate sales and the time it takes to actually receive the cash from the sales. The cash flow projection reflects the basic business principle that the entrepreneur takes cash, buys some assets, and then sells those assets for more money than they cost, thus generating some surplus cash. However, the cash-back-to-cash cycle takes time, during which more cash-to-cash cycles are started. Thus, additional funds are needed to keep the business running while waiting for a previous cycle to finish.

Fortunately, cash flow planning is simple in concept, although it can take some effort in execution. Coming up with the numbers can involve considerable work. Cash flow is exactly what its name implies: It is the anticipation of cash—cold, hard cash—as it flows into and out of the firm's coffers. Only cash is included in this analysis! Non-cash accounting entries, such as depreciation, amortization, and asset transfers are ignored. The cash flow plan positions receipts and expenditures in a span of time.

Time is the critical ingredient in cash flow planning; the firm may have a lot of money coming in the future, but that may not save it from insolvency if it must pay out a lot of money in the present. At any time, a negative difference between the cash that has come in and the cash that has been paid out must somehow be financed—either borrowed or raised as equity.

The positive difference (cash surplus) between the cash received and the cash paid out is available for management's use—to pay back debt, pay dividends, or whatever.

Enough theory—it's time to work through some cash flow plans. A cash flow plan is the entrepreneur's projection of the cash flow for his or her business. While the cash flow projection for Kareem's Manufacturing, Inc. (Table 22.2) may be relatively simple, those of a real venture may be as complex and detailed as the enterprise requires. The plan is designed for the needs of the venture and the entrepreneur. Perhaps a business is simple, and the entire cash flow plan can be put in detail into one document. Or the business may be substantial enough to require that the cash flow plan show only the cash results of large blocks of expenses and cash receipts, with each line backed up by a supporting document.

Thus, the cash flow plan can be a summary of all other cash budgets, or it may present a complete picture of all cash flows in and out of the firm.

All figures are calculated for the end of the month. While the cash flows presented start with sales figures, sales should never be confused with cash unless they were made for cash.

The cash received line shows other cash income that might be from the proceeds of a loan, proceeds from the sale of stock, cash from the sale of assets, cash from vendor rebates, or whatever. But only cash is counted. No promises to pay.

Cash flow projections should be as self-explanatory as possible. After all, the entrepreneur may not be present when someone is studying the document. It should be explained how a figure was obtained whenever it appears necessary. All assumptions should be clearly stated.

Table 22-2: Kareem's Manufacturing Inc. Cash Flow Projection

	Month 1	Month 2	Month 3	Month 4	Month 5
Cash in:					
Sales revenue	195,000	205,000	187,000	172,000	207,000
Other cash received	10,485	5,500	8,900	7,500	1,200
Total monthly	205,485	210,500	195,900	179,500	208,200
Cumulative cash	205,485	415,985	611,885	791,385	999,585
Cash out:					
Administrative costs	108,002	104,564	106,574	105,679	107,645
Manufacturing costs	27,512	29,987	28,001	28,893	27,991
Raw materials cost	35,000	28,750	5,754	3,479	37,987
Marketing programs	5,000	8,003	15,000	350	11,730
Principal portion of debt	1,300	1,287	1,254	1,229	1,193
Other cash paid	325	800	1,000	1,200	1,000
Total monthly outgo	177,139	173,391	157,583	140,830	187,546
Cumulative outgo	177,139	350,530	508,113	648,943	836,489
Cash in less outgo	28,346	65,455	103,772	142,442	163,096

The cash received is totaled for each month as shown in the line labeled total cash monthly. A cumulative cash income (total cash received to date) is developed on the next line. This is a very important calculation. It discloses how much cash in total will come into the company coffers by that time.

Now for the outflow of money—the cash expenditures. Again, the stress is on cash. It is not when something is purchased that is important, it's when it is paid for, when the cash leaves the bank account.

If something is paid for with goods or stock, then it does not show on the cash flow statement per se but only as a cash expenditure when the venture pays for whatever it traded off.

The section labeled cash out provides the information on how much money a venture actually plans to pay for the goods and services it will use in the business.

The next six lines present various expenses that are expected to be paid. In some cases, more detail might be desired by the reader. For example, one might want to know more about administrative costs. They cover a wide variety of expenses that many investors would like to know more about. They should be supported by other tables. Most prospective investors are sensitive about overhead costs. They fear that the entrepreneur may have hidden a lot of benefits in such a catch-all category.

Other cash paid might reflect dividend payments, income taxes, employee loans, or whatever. Of course, separate lines could be used for each of these cash outflows.

Total monthly outgo shows the total cash paid out each month. The next-to-last line is the cumulative outgo, the total amount of money paid out at the end of each month for the year to date.

And now the key line—income less outgo—results from subtracting the cumulative outgo for each month from the cumulative income for that month.

Cumulative cash income less cumulative cash outgo equals one of two things, depending upon whether the balance is positive or negative. If cash out has exceeded cash in, then the figure represents the amount of money management must somehow raise. This money might come from the owner's personal funds or from an outside entity, such as a bank, friend or family member.

If the money cannot be raised, then the plan will have to be altered somehow to accommodate the financial realities of the situation. If the resulting balance is positive, then that is the cash that management will have at its disposal to use as it wants.

The cash flow plan is an ongoing management tool that requires constant updating as new information becomes available from operations. Many business owners will update this analysis with actual information once a month has been completed. By doing this the analysis can show the actual inflows and outflows of the business, the current cash balance and the projected cash inflows and outflows. Management can use this tool to analyze if changes in strategy are needed.

The cash flow plans put into computer programs, such as Microsoft Excel, are most flexible. If the file is set up to do so (as the Excel templates on *The Business Mentor* CD-ROM are), as a new number is plugged into the plan, the computer changes all other numbers in the plan that are based on it. Thus, it becomes quite easy to play around with the figures, to determine what happens to financial needs when some of the basic input assumptions are altered. Using computerized spreadsheets is strongly recommended for developing cash flow plans.

Mr. G's Recording Promotion

Many entrepreneurs are not involved with ongoing enterprises. Rather they are interested in one-shot deals. Such is the case of Mr. G., who had come into the possession of the rights to distribute an excellent-quality recording of Pope John Paul II's statements on peace when he visited the United States. The recording had the official approval of the Vatican as well as the support of the Church in its distribution. Mr G. had in his possession a letter from the head of the Vatican Library attesting to its support.

The venture was to have begun financially in August with the bulk of the sales volume realized during the fall. The deal was to be terminated in January.

Mr. G. was looking for an investor to back the entire deal. He was unwilling to commit any of his "meager" resources to the venture.

Table 22-3 presents one of Mr. G's cash flow plans. While the cash flow plan Mr. G. submitted was considerably more detailed, many expenses here have been lumped together when little was to be gained by itemizing them.

The cash flow plan Mr. G. submitted reflects an initial payment of $125,000 to the person who created the CD as a licensing fee. In fact, the person was broke and owed that money to various people who helped finance the recording of the Pope's speeches. They were putting pressure on him for repayment.

That item caused more than its share of problems with potential investors, who refused to allow their new money to take any of the old money out of the deal. It proved to be a big barrier in the deal, as the owner of the copyright refused to license it without the payment, and the financiers balked at letting the person out of the deal with his money back right up front while still profiting nicely from the results. Their attitude toward the creator was, "Either stay in or get out, but it isn't going to be both ways."

His attitude was, "It's going to be my way or none at all." In the end, it was none at all. After three different private investors rejected the deal, Mr. G. dropped the project to pursue another deal. The administrative-costs projection included $80,000 for a salary to Mr. G.

The cash flow plan can be reworked to minimize the money needed for the deal.

What are some of the approaches that could be tried to do the deal? Some possibilities:

1. Try to get the CD maker to wait for payment until the cash comes in.
2. Let the promoters wait for their money.
3. Delay paying some of the marketing costs. Item-by-item examination would be required to see what and who could be put off.
4. Don't pay the copyright up front.

Table 22-4 reflects some of the possible changes. Payment for the CDs has been delayed into the month following sale, and $50,000 was eliminated from the administrative costs by telling Mr. G. he would have to wait for his money just like everyone else. He did not like such a noble attitude. The Church royalty was adjusted, as it was well in excess of what was required by the contract. The copyright payment was delayed until the end.

It can be seen that under this arrangement, only $3 million would be needed in month three with which to finance this plan.

The profits from the deal appear to be around $2 million. The cash flow would have to be carried out for a few more months to determine how the deal would finally end up. In one-shot deals, it is important to cut off administrative costs as quickly as possible after the action is over. Costs should not be allowed to run on and on.

One of the aspects of this format that should be stressed is the need for playing around with prices and sales. In reality, dozens of these cash flow sheets should be developed for various prices and sales rates. Table 22-5 illustrates what would happen if the price could be increased to $10.25 net to the company and sales not be affected. About $1 million more would be made, but the amount of money required to finance the deal in month three would remain unchanged.

Table 22-3: Mr. G's CD. Cash Flow Projection

	Month 1	Month 2	Month 3	Month 4	Month 5
Cash in:					
Units sold, thousands			575,000	1,250,000	300,000
Price, 9.75					
Revenue			5,606,250	12,187,500	2,925,000
Cash received 30 days later			5,606,250	12,187,500	
Other cash					
Total monthly				5,606,250	12,187,500
Cumulative cash				5,606,250	17,793,750
Cash out:					
Copyright license	125,000				
CD costs		787,750	1,712,500	411,000	
Fulfillment costs				287,500	625,000
Administrative costs	150,000	180,000	210,000	250,000	150,000
Marketing programs	50,000	800,000	1,500,000	1,500,000	500,000
Royalties to church				2,300,000	5,000,000
Other					
Total monthly outgo	325,000	1,767,750	3,422,500	4,748,500	6,275,000
Cumulative outgo	325,000	2,092,750	5,515,250	10,263,750	16,538,750
Cash in less outgo	−325,000	−2,092,750	−5,515,250	−4,657,500	1,255,000

Table 22-4: Mr. G's CD. Cash Flow Projection

	Month 1	Month 2	Month 3	Month 4	Month 5
Cash in:					
Units sold, thousands			575,000	1,250,000	300,000
Price, 9.75					
Revenue			5,606,250	12,187,500	2,925,000
Cash received 30 days later				5,606,250	12,187,500
Other cash					
Total monthly				5,606,250	12,187,500
Cumulative cash				5,606,250	17,793,750
Cash out:					
Copyright license					125,000
CD costs				787,750	1,712,500
Fulfillment costs				287,500	625,000
Administrative costs	100,000	130,000	160,000	200,000	100,000
Marketing programs	50,000	800,000	1,500,000	1,500,000	500,000
Royalties to church				1,150,000	2,500,000
Investor royalty					
Repay investors					3,000,000
Total monthly outgo	150,000	930,000	1,660,000	3,925,250	8,562,500
Cumulative outgo	150,000	1,080,000	2,740,000	6,665,250	15,227,750
Cash in less outgo	−150,000	−1,080,000	−2,740,000	−1,059,000	2,566,000

Table 22-5: Mr. G's CD. Cash Flow Projection

	Month 1	Month 2	Month 3	Month 4	Month 5
Cash in:					
Units sold, thousands			575,000	1,250,000	300,000
Price, 10.25					
Revenue			5,893,750	12,812,500	3,075,000
Cash received 30 days later				5,893,750	12,812,500
Other cash					
Total monthly				5,893,750	12,812,500
Cumulative cash				5,893,750	18,706,250
Cash out:					
Copyright license					125,000
CD costs				787,750	1,712,500
Fulfillment costs				287,500	625,000
Administrative costs	100,000	130,000	160,000	200,000	100,000
Marketing programs	50,000	800,000	1,500,000	1,500,000	500,000
Royalties to church				1,150,000	2,500,000
Repay investors					3,000,000
Other					
Total monthly outgo	150,000	930,000	1,660,000	3,925,250	8,562,500
Cumulative outgo	150,000	1,080,000	2,740,000	6,665,250	15,227,750
Cash in less outgo	−150,000	−1,080,000	−2,740,000	−771,500	3,478,500

Table 22-6: Mr. G's CD. Cash Flow Projection

	Month 1	Month 2	Month 3	Month 4	Month 5
Cash in:					
Units sold, thousands			300,000	900,000	200,000
Price, 15.00					
Revenue			4,500,000	13,500,000	3,000,000
Cash received 30 days later				4,500,000	13,500,000
Other cash					
Total monthly				4,500,000	13,500,000
Cumulative cash				4,500,000	18,000,000
Cash out:					
Copyright license					125,000
CD costs				411,000	1,233,000
Fulfillment costs				287,500	625,000
Administrative costs	100,000	130,000	160,000	200,000	100,000
Marketing programs	50,000	800,000	1,500,000	1,500,000	500,000
Royalties to church				1,150,000	2,500,000
Investor royalty					
Repay investors					3,000,000
Other					
Total monthly outgo	150,000	930,000	1,660,000	3,548,500	8,083,000
Cumulative outgo	150,000	1,080,000	2,740,000	6,288,500	14,371,500
Cash in less outgo	−150,000	−1,080,000	−2,740,000	−1,788,500	3,628,500

Table 22-6 increases the price to $15 with sales dropping as shown. Note that the profits remain about the same. Now the question comes down to strategy and probability. Which scenario would be most likely? Neither affects the amount of money needed for the deal.

Also it should be noted in this deal that the key to the financing was the CD manufacturer. All other cash costs paled in comparison. Mr. G. would have to locate a cooperative, eager replicator or come up with an additional $3 million dollars. It is important to learn to spot the key items that need to be worked on to lower financial requirements. Time should not be spent on matters that are of little significance. Rather, the entrepreneur should go right to the big numbers first.

An update to this project is in order. The recording was dusted off when the Pope again visited the United States. Another group put together a syndicate to market the CD by direct-response advertising on cable television. The group had reasonable marketing credentials but still lost a lot of money. Only 1,500 CDs were sold at $15 each. Evidently, there is a hidden trap in the concept. The recording is now passé.

Financial study

Libby's Custom Tile

Libby's Custom Tile started as a service business in 1979 when Libby Kelsor, began creating a custom hand-painted tile mural for one of her husband's clients who was remodeling his home. At first it was just a simple flower border painted on the edge of the counter top, but after seeing the results, the client decided to include two murals for the backsplash.

Libby set up her studio in the back room of her husband's office. At first she sent her clients to different showrooms in the area to pick out their tile.

As the business developed, Libby felt that she could better serve her clients if she could help them by creating their tiles. Finally one day, Libby came to work and announced, "I want to manufacture tile on my own!" A few months later, Libby's Custom Tile had a 3,000-square-foot plant north of Chicago.

Providing unique made-to-order ceramic tile to the upscale, northern suburbs of Chicago, the business has grown to the point where Libby is now entertaining purchase offers from national tile manufacturers.

The following statements reflect Libby's financial results for 1999 and 2000.

Libby's Custom Tile
Income Statement
For the year ended December 31

	1999	2000
Sales	$2,700,000	$3,065,000
Cost of goods sold	1,485,000	2,000,200
Gross profit	$1,215,000	$1,064,800
Marketing expense	270,000	239,000
Administrative expenses	240,000	244,000
General expenses	240,000	242,000
Earnings before interest and taxes (EBIT)	$465,000	$339,800
Interest:		
Long-term debt	40,000	40,000
Earnings before taxes	$425,000	$299,800
Federal Income Tax	170,000	119,780
Net income	$255,000	$180,020

- Libby's sales increased, cost of goods increased, and gross margin decreased in 2000.
- Expenses decreased in 2000 by $25,000.
- EBIT decreased in 2000 mainly because of increase in cost of goods sold.
- Net profit decreased in 2000 with higher sales.

Libby's Custom Tile
Balance Sheet
As of December 31, 1999

Assets		Liabilities and stockholders' equity	
Cash	$100,000	Accounts payable	$180,000
Accounts receivable	125,000	Notes payable	300,000
Inventory	300,000	Other current liabilities	45,000
Total current assets	$525,000	Total current liabilities	$525,000
		Long-term debt	400,000
Plant and equipment	900,000	Total liabilities	$925,000
Accumulated depreciation	(150,000)	Stockholders' equity	
Net plant and equipment	$750,000	Common stock	300,000
		Retained earnings	50,000
Total assets	$1,275,000	Total stockholders' equity	$350,000
		Total liabilities and stockholders' equity	$1,275,000

Libby's Custom Tile
Balance Sheet
As of December 31, 2000

Assets		Liabilities and stockholders' equity	
Cash	$150,000	Accounts payable	$200,000
Accounts receivable	100,000	Notes payable	300,000
Inventory	350,000	Other current liabilities	50,000
Total current assets	$600,000	Total current liabilities	$550,000
		Long-term debt	400,000
Plant and equipment	960,000	Total liabilities	$950,000
Accumulated depreciation	(160,000)	Stockholders' equity	
Net plant and equipment	$800,000	Common stock	350,000
		Retained earnings	100,000
Total assets	$1,400,000	Total stockholders' equity	$450,000
		Total liabilities and stockholders' equity	$1,400,000

- Assets increased $125,000 in 2000 but $50,000 was in inventory and $60,000 in equipment
- Liabilities increased $25,000 in 2000 and net worth increased $100,000, therefore giving the company more value on its balance sheet.

Sample financial statements for a service organization

Gleaning Cleaning provides professional cleaning services in the Salt Lake City area. Established in 1985, Gleaning Cleaning was started by two sisters initially focused on seeking a way to earn additional cash by offering basic housekeeping services. They have since expanded into some commercial cleaning opportunities. The business has grown into a large full-time operation, with billings of over three-quarters of a million dollars each year. The company has more than 20 full- and part-time employees and nearly 300 clients.

As noted previously, financial statements of different companies may use different names to reflect the same type of financial information. Additionally, depending on the type of business, there are some line items used in manufacturing businesses that are rarely if ever used in service businesses.

For example, the balance sheet for Gleaning Cleaning, a service business does not have an inventory line while nearly all manufacturing businesses will have one. Other differences include more investments and securities assets, and significantly higher fee incomes with a lower cost of goods sold (COGS) for service businesses. In a service business this can be called cost of sales or cost of service. The cost of service is any cost directly related to providing the service and expenses are all of the costs of doing business not directly related to providing the service.

Gleaning Cleaning
Profit and Loss
For the year ended June 30, 20xx

Ordinary income/expense	
Income	
Cleaning fees	793,455.30
Total income	793,455.30
Cost of goods sold	
Labor	323,004.31
Chemical purchases	18,187.01
Supply purchases	6,121.79
Equipment rental	1,664.20
Total cost of goods sold	348,977.31
Gross profit	444,477.99
Expense	
Salaries	45,966.51
Other salaries and wages	
Bonus	4,455.79
Vacation	4,230.40
Total other salaries and wages	8,686.19
Administration and general expenses	270,061.53
Total expense	324,714.23
Net ordinary income	119,763.76
Other expense	
Interest	1,603.33
Taxes–Federal Corporate	4,000.00
Taxes–State Corporate	0.00
Total other expense	5,603.33
Net income	**114,160.43**

Gleaning Cleaning
Balance Sheet
As of June 30, 20xx

Assets		Liabilities and equity	
Assets		**Liabilities and equity**	
Current assets		Liabilities	
Checking/savings		Current liabilities	
Cash	49,103.55	Accounts payable	30,403.58
		Other current liabilities	18,868.45
Total checking/savings	49,103.55	Total current liabilities	49,272.03
		Long-term debt	45,966.51
Other current assets		Total liabilities	95,238.54
Investment account	10,000.00		
Shareholder advances	34,518.86		
Receivable from shareholder	145,613.14	Equity	
Accrued interest receivable	16,180.79	Common stock	1,000.00
Employee advances	1,690.00	Retained earnings	70,929.57
Receivable–Federal income tax	283.00	Net income	114,160.43
Total other current assets	208,285.79	Total equity	186,090.00
Total current assets	257,389.34	**Total liabilities and equity**	**281,328.54**
Fixed assets			
Furniture, fixture, & equipment	15,211.96		
Accumulated depreciation—FF&E	(12,493.27)		
Equipment	45,053.51		
Accumulated depreciation—equipment	(31,751.60)		
Net fixed assets	16,020.60		
Other assets			
Deposits	3,824.00		
Note receivable	2,094.60		
Receivable	2,000.00		
Total other assets	7,918.60		
Total assets	**281,328.54**		

Conclusion

It is necessary for entrepreneurs to master the use of the cash flow projection. They will find it to be the single most important planning tool. Astute business owners know that positive cash flow is a critical ingredient to the success of their business. In conjunction with planning for a positive future, a business owner must continually analyze the financial outcomes that result from his or her business decisions and strategies. These results will be presented to the owner in the form the financial statements (balance sheet and income statement). Remember that the income statement is disclosing the profitability of the company and the balance sheet explains how many assets a business has versus liabilities. Every decision the entrepreneur makes on cash expenditures affects the income statement, the balance sheet and most importantly, the cash flows of the business.

Financial Ratios

Learning Objectives

In this chapter, students will learn to

- Calculate the four types of financial ratios: profitability, liquidity, risk, and efficiency.
- Use the four types of ratios to help make decisions in managing a business.

As discussed earlier, financial statements are management tools. Ratios help to leverage their usefulness. Just as a vise can hold something steady while it is being worked on, ratios provide stability. They allow a company to judge its relative performance and see relationships or correlations between items on different statements.

By measuring performance in percentages—rather than raw numbers—ratios allow the owner to evaluate a company's performance over a period of time, to compare the company to other companies of different sizes, and to plan for the future.

Like the percentage of revenue calculation, ratios allow accurate comparisons of performance from one time period to another.

Is it reasonable to assume that the costs of operating a plant that produces 5 million yo-yos a month and one that produces 2 million are the same? Probably not, but they should be *relatively* the same. If the net profit margin for the toy industry is normally 6 percent, then it should be about 6 percent no matter how many yo-yos the company produces.

Ratios are a ballpark estimate. They cannot consistently provide complete, detailed, and accurate data nor can they determine one's course of action, but they can provide invaluable insight necessary to the effective management of a company.

There are four types of ratios: profitability, liquidity, risk, and efficiency.

- **Profitability ratios** measure and help control expenses. These ratios provide measures of profitability in a number of ways. A profit margin shows profit as a percentage of sales. Profit on owner's investment measures net profit in relationship to equity and can be used to help determine how the investments or funds are working. Profit on net working capital shows the manner in which capital is used in the business and any returns realized on it. Unfortunately the ratio name is not always descriptive of what the ratio measures or how it is calculated.

- **Liquidity ratios** measure the amount of cash or investments that can be converted to cash to pay expenses and short-term debts. Liquidity ratios determine the entrepreneur's ability to meet current liabilities. The two ratios most commonly used are the quick ratio and the current ratio. The quick ratio is the ratio of current assets (excluding inventory) to current liabilities. This information determines if there are sufficient cash, receivables, and marketable securities available immediately to pay off current debts. Current ratio is based on all of the current assets and current liabilities, and a 2:1 ratio is usually considered ideal. In other words, a business has twice as much available in current assets as it has in current liabilities.

- **Risk ratios** measure what portion of the company is leveraged or financed (how much the owners could lose to creditors).

- **Efficiency ratios** tell how well business is being conducted.

Ratio Analysis

Whether the change in the ratio is considered positive or negative is dependent on several factors.

- Does the change move the business closer to or farther away from the industry norm?
- Was the change expected, based on the management team decisions made during the period in question?
- Does management calculate the ratios often enough to know if the change is significant? In other words, is the change indicative of a systematic issue or a single event?

Industry Comparisons

Ratios that are important in making financial decisions should be reviewed every month.

It is useful to compare a business' ratios with the average ratios in its industry. Industry ratios can be found by contacting industry associations, contacting the reference desk of the local library, or checking business sites on the Internet.

Conclusion

Financial ratios have little meaning unless they are compared over a long period of time or compared to industry averages.

While the four types of ratios will meet the needs for most occasions, the entrepreneur should not be reluctant to develop whatever ratios that could have meaning to his or her own business. Ratios need not have textbook sanctions to be useful. Entrepreneurs need to understand their businesses well enough to use the ratios that will have the largest impact on their business decisions. Bankers will use ratios to analyze a business for a bank loan; therefore, the entrepreneur must be able to discuss these ratios in an intelligent way.

Profitability ratios

Gross margin

What it measures	The profit a company enjoys on the goods it sells after direct costs are subtracted out.
What it tells	This is a rough measurement of overall profits; gross margins tell companies how well they are controlling direct costs. If the COGS are increasing faster than sales, then the direct costs are out of control. Owners of the business would want to do some research to determine why the costs are increasing.
How it is calculated	Gross profit / Net sales

Operating margin

What it measures	The percentage of costs that are generated by overhead.
What it tells	Operating margins show how well a company is managing its overhead costs. If the company's gross margins are rising while its operating margins are falling, management knows immediately that the company is having difficulty controlling indirect costs.
How it is calculated	Operating income / Net sales

Net margin

What it measures	Profitability.
What it tells	How many cents on each dollar of sales are profit. A falling net margin may signal problems in controlling costs or prices.
How it is calculated	Net income / Net sales

Return on assets (ROA)

What it measures	Profits against assets.
What it tells	ROA can be used to compare the profitability of companies of different sizes. Assets remain fairly stable; so an increasing ROA indicates greater profitability while a decreasing ROA indicates less profitability.
How it is calculated	Net income / Total assets

Return on equity (ROE)

What it measures	Income against stockholders' equity.
What it tells	Whether or not the company is a good investment. As ROE increases, generally the company becomes more attractive to potential investors. Generally, improving net income will also improve shareholders' equity as the profit will become retained earnings.
How it is calculated	Net income / Shareholders' equity

Liquidity ratios

Current ratio

What it measures	If the company has enough liquidity to pay its short-term obligations.
What it tells	If there is enough cash in the bank (or relatively available) to pay the bills. Theoretically, a current ratio of 2.0 is preferred for most companies. It is important to watch this ratio closely. If it begins to go down, then a company's cash position may erode quickly. The quickest way to increase cash is to improve sales.
How it is calculated	Total current assets / Total current liabilities

Quick ratio

What it measures	If the company's assets minus inventory will provide enough liquidity to cover its short-term obligations.
What it tells	Also referred to as the acid test. This ratio shows whether the company has enough cash to meet its short-term obligations. If this number is going down, then sales are not strong enough to meet daily cash obligations. Quick cash management intervention is required.
How it is calculated	(Current assets – Inventory) / Current liabilities

Risk ratios

Debt ratio

What it measures	The proportion of assets that are financed by creditors' funds (debt).
What it tells	A debt ratio of more than 1 means negative net worth. This means if a company could sell all of the assets for full value, there would still not be enough money to meet all the company's obligations.
How it is calculated	Total liabilities / Total assets

Debt to equity

What it measures	How much the company relies on debt versus equity financing.
What it tells	The more a company's debt exceeds its net worth, the less likely it is to obtain financing. As this number increases, the company's ability to obtain financing decreases. Additionally, the owner's position is weakened and those that own the debt (banks, large suppliers) can establish control of the company.
How it is calculated	Total liabilities / Shareholders' equity

Efficiency ratios

Inventory turnover

What it measures	Shows how often inventory turns over.
What it tells	How popular the merchandise is. High turnover is generally good. However, high turnover may also indicate that there is not enough merchandise and sales are lost.
How it is calculated	Cost of goods sold / Inventory

Days sales outstanding (DSO)

What it measures	Average number of days it takes customers to pay their bills.
What it tells	How effective a company is at collecting money and how much "float" it must finance. DSO also shows how effective its credit policies are. Remember, the tighter the credit policy, the fewer the DSO. That policy, however, may also reduce sales.
How it is calculated	Accounts receivable / (Net sales / 365)

Investment turnover ratio

What it measures	The amount of sales generated by the assets.
What it tells	How efficiently a company uses its assets. This measurement shows how quickly and how often an asset (piece of machinery or investment) pays for itself. If an older piece of equipment works more slowly but pays for itself three times in a year, while a newer module takes two years to pay for itself, the owner must reflect on whether the payoff is worth the greater investment.
How it is calculated	Net sales / Total assets

Duke's Manufacturing Inc.
Income Statement
For the year ended December 31, 20xx

Sales		$3,000,000
Cost of goods sold		1,800,000
Gross profit		$1,200,000
Sales and marketing expense		300,000
General expenses		260,000
Administrative expenses		300,000
Earnings before interest and taxes (EBIT)		$340,000
Interest:		
Short-term debt	$37,800	
Long-term debt	80,000	
Total interest charges		117,800
Earnings before taxes		$222,200
Federal Income Tax		88,880
Net income		$133,320

Duke's Manufacturing Inc.
Balance Sheet
As of December 31, 20xx

Assets		Liabilities and stockholders' equity	
Cash	$240,000	Accounts payable	$380,000
Accounts receivable	320,000	Notes payable	420,000
Inventory	1,040,000	Other current liabilities	50,000
Total current assets	$1,600,000	Total current liabilities	$850,000
		Long-term debt	800,000
Plant and equipment	1,000,000	Total liabilities	$1,650,000
Accumulated depreciation	(200,000)	Stockholders' equity	
Net plant and equipment	$800,000	Common stock	650,000
		Retained earnings	100,000
Total assets	$2,400,000	Total stockholders' equity	$750,000
		Total liabilities and stockholders' equity	$2,400,000

Duke's Manufacturing Inc.
Ratios

	Calculation	Result
Profitability ratios		
Gross margin		
Gross profit / Net sales	1,200,000 / 3,000,000	40.00%
Operating margin		
Operating income / Net sales	340,000 / 3,000,000	11.33%
Net margin		
Net income / Net sales	133,320 / 3,000,000	4.44%
Return on assets (ROA)		
Net income / Total assets	133,320 / 2,400,000	5.56%
Return on equity (ROE)		
Net income / Shareholder equity	133,320 / 750,000	17.78%
Liquidity ratios		
Current ratio		
Total current assets / Total current liabilities	1,600,000 / 850,000	1.88
Quick ratio		
(Current assets – inventory) / Current liabilities	(1,600,000 – 1,040,000) / 850,000	0.66
Risk ratios		
Debt ratio		
Total liabilities / Total assets	1,650,000 / 2,400,000	68.75%
Debt to equity		
Total liabilities / Shareholder equity	1,650,000 / 750,000	2.20
Efficiency ratios		
Inventory turnover		
Cost of goods sold / Inventory	1,800,000 / 1,040,000	1.73
Days sales outstanding (DSO)		
Accounts receivable / (Net sales / 365)	320,000 / (3,000,000 / 365)	38.93
Investment turnover		
Net sales / Total assets	3,000,000 / 2,400,000	1.25

Exercise 23a: Financial Ratios

Using Libby's Custom Tile's 20xx income statement and balance sheet calculate the profitability, liquidity, risk, and efficiency ratios of the business. Enter your answers on the next page.

Libby's Custom Tile
Income Statement
For the year ended December 31, 20xx

Sales	$3,065,000
Cost of goods sold	2,000,000
Gross profit	$1,065,000
Marketing expense	239,000
General expenses	242,000
Administrative expenses	244,000
Earnings before interest and taxes (EBIT)	$340,000
Interest:	
Long-term debt	40,000
Earnings before taxes	$300,000
Federal Income Tax	119,780
Net income	$180,220

Libby's Custom Tile
Balance Sheet
As of December 31, 20xx

Assets		Liabilities and stockholders' equity	
Cash	$150,000	Accounts payable	$180,000
Accounts receivable	100,000	Notes payable	320,000
Inventory	350,000	Other current liabilities	50,000
Total current assets	$600,000	Total current liabilities	$550,000
		Long-term debt	400,000
Plant and equipment	960,000	Total liabilities	$950,000
Accumulated depreciation	(160,000)	Stockholders' equity	
Net plant and equipment	$800,000	Common stock	350,000
		Retained earnings	100,000
Total assets	$1,400,000	Total stockholders' equity	$450,000
		Total liabilities and stockholders' equity	$1,400,000

	How it is calculated	Calculation	Result
Profitability ratios			
Gross margin	(Gross profit / Net sales)		
Operating margin	(Operating income / Net sales)		
Net margin	(Net income / Net sales)		
Return on assets (ROA)	(Net income / Total assets)		
Return on equity (ROE)	(Net income / Shareholder equity)		
Liquidity ratios			
Current ratio	Total current assets / Total current liabilities		
Quick ratio	(Current assets – inventory) / Current liabilities		
Risk ratios			
Debt ratio	(Total liabilities / Total assets)		
Debt to equity	Total liabilities / Shareholder equity		
Efficiency ratios			
Inventory turnover	Cost of goods sold / Inventory		
Days sales outstanding (DSO)	Accounts receivable / (Net sales / 365)		
Investment turnover ratio	Net sales / Total assets		

1. How do Libby's profitability ratios compare to DMI's?

2. How secure is the stockholders' position at Libby's?

3. Is Libby's liquidity position better or worse than DMI's? How can you tell?

4. Are Libby's liabilities greater than the equity (debt to equity)?

5. How can Libby's improve its days sales outstanding?

Money Needs

Learning Objectives

In this chapter, students will learn
- What types of capital are needed to finance a business.
- The factors that determine the financial needs of an enterprise.
- The difference between debt and equity financing.

As soon as planning for marketing, management, and production is completed, financial planning can begin. Until the entrepreneur has decided what he or she is going to do, there is no way of predicting how much money will be needed to do it.

Moreover, after the first financial plan, most likely the operating plan will need to be revised to bring it into the realm of financial reality. Each change in the operating plan will affect the financial plan.

This chapter discusses the determination of initial capital requirements, the manipulation of capital needs and the planning of future capital requirements. One of the first questions asked by any financier is: "How much money do you need?"

That is a simple question to ask, but one that is not so simple to answer. The money needed depends upon decisions. It depends upon how the entrepreneur plans to do business. Thus, it is necessary to understand the factors that affect financial needs.

The emphasis is on how much money is needed, not how much money is wanted. In one case, a young graduate of a famous business school put together a business plan for a custom touring bicycle manufacturing business that required $250,000 initial financing. After much effort in contacting many venture capitalists and wealthy investors without success, he was facing ruin. He had proceeded with the venture assuming that he would have no trouble raising the money. After all, he had majored in making connections at the school. Faced with failure, he put a sharper pencil to his major financial planning tool, his cash flow plan, and figured out that he really needed only $100,000 to do the job. The rest was just padding and comfort for his own peace of mind. With the smaller amount to raise, he divided it into units of $5,000 each and sold them to his friends. His fund raising was successful.

When faced with the bitter reality of raising money, entrepreneurs must appreciate penetrating analysis of their true needs for money. There are many factors and many decisions that combine to determine money needs.

Much depends upon the circumstances and how the entrepreneur wants to, or must, play the game. One bootstrap entrepreneur said, "Your measure as an entrepreneur is your ability to do what you want with whatever you have to do it with." Financiers report their frustration with entrepreneurs who not only don't know the amount of money they need but don't understand the financial side of business operations.

Bear in mind that there are great advantages in being able to finance a venture without outside capital. If the entrepreneur can figure out a way to finance the operations without seeking outside money, life will be much simpler and nights more restful. The decision to go after other people's money is a serious one, loaded with implications and responsibilities. One's management style must accommodate outside investors' requirements.

Kinds of Money Needed

Traditionally, entrepreneurs need four different types of capital: seed money, start-up capital, working capital, and growth capital. A good cash flow plan accommodates all four types of money.

Seed money

Seed money can vary from a few dollars to rather large sums of money; it all depends upon the nature of the venture. The seed money to develop a new invention might run into the millions. Nolan Bushnell spent millions of dollars of his own funds as seed money for his various ideas as well as raised additional millions of dollars from the public. Such was the public's faith in his ideas.

Typically, seed money must be furnished by the entrepreneur, the family, or some friends. Few investors are interested in seed-money investments, though the returns for getting in at this stage can be quite attractive. An investor must have a great deal of confidence in the entrepreneur to be willing to furnish the seed money for the new venture.

Seed money goes for research and development of the prototype. It is often spent over a long period of time, usually on work done in the basement or garage. Thus, it often comes from the entrepreneur's current income stream. Calculating how much seed money is needed can be difficult, if not impossible, depending upon the concept. Some concepts require little seed money; some money for researching the market and writing the business plan may do the trick.

In the world of high technology, some new ventures have raised seed money by using the so-called R&D limited-partnership tax shelters. In the right circumstances and properly used, such tactics can be successful. Staar Surgical has made extensive use of R&D partnerships for funding the initial research on its products.

Congress seriously hampered the use of the R&D limited partnership when it amended the income tax laws in 1986. These tax shelters did serve a purpose in the entrepreneurial world when appropriate.

Start-up capital

Again, depending upon the concept, start-up capital can vary from relatively few dollars into millions. Start-up money pays for the initial equipment, initial expenses of getting the enterprise under way, and the initial working capital needed to finance the first sales.

The amount of start-up money needed can be manipulated by the entrepreneur by various means. Start-up money is not a fixed, immutable sum. It can be managed. Clever entrepreneurs find a way to do what they want with the money they have available. They buy used equipment rather than new. Perhaps they even borrow the equipment. If a customer is in hand, deposits on the first orders can provide some of the needed start-up money. Vendor terms of sale can even provide some start-up money. Some private investors and a few venture capitalists will furnish start-up money but only if the concept and the management team look particularly good.

Do not make the mistake of settling for too little money to get the job done. It is usually a mistake to start up knowing that there is not enough money but hoping somehow it will be provided. If the necessary start-up money cannot be obtained, then it is time to go back to the drawing board and develop an alternative business plan that will allow the business to begin with the money on hand.

Few things make an entrepreneur look as foolish as the inability to figure out just how much money will be needed to start the venture. Underestimates throw doubt upon his or her knowledge of business.

Working capital

Working capital is the money used for financing inventories, accounts receivable, and the cash operational fund. It is money that is needed for financing sales. Traditionally, it is the area in which successful venturers entrap themselves. The scenario goes like this: The venture is off to a roaring start. Sales far exceed expectations: they are $200,000 over forecasts. Suddenly, the entrepreneur must buy additional inventory to satisfy the unexpected demand: With what? Not only is the cash for those sales still tied up in accounts receivable, but profits are insufficient to finance the rapid inventory buildup.

Fortunately, working capital is the easiest money to attract. Banks are the traditional suppliers of working-capital loans; entrepreneurs can borrow on inventory or accounts receivable. If the banker won't approve a working-capital loan, then there is either something wrong with the banking relationship or something wrong with the goods and customers. Owners should be prepared with a sound business plan that shows how the loan can be paid in a reasonable time. Some bankers can be reluctant to make loans to entrepreneurs.

Now, other lending institutions and programs can help finance working capital, such as micro loan programs, SBA 504 certified development companies, leasing companies, and factors. Traditionally, factors purchased a company's accounts receivable at a discounted price. In today's market, they offer lines of credit for working capital, lending money for large purchase orders, and giving other financial assistance. For more information on factors, refer to Chapter 25: Traditional and Alternative Money Sources.

If one is entering a business for which some financial data exist, the calculation of working capital needs is not difficult. Generally, managements compute all financial requirements from the level of sales. They know it takes a certain amount of money to finance each $1,000 of sales volume.

Classic Squeeze
Many new businesses die because they grow faster than their ability to serve the market. All sorts of bad things happen with such unexpectedly high sales: quality control can slip, customer service sags, credit ratings suffer, and operations run out of control. Fortunate is the entrepreneur whose venture grows according to plan.

Keeping in mind that money is not needed to finance the profit in a sale, each time a sale is made on credit the variable cost of making that sale must be financed. The entrepreneur invests money in the sale, in the customer. It's called accounts receivable. For practical purposes, most managements plan their receivables as so many days' sales, for example, they might plan to carry 45 days' sales as receivables. Thus, if monthly sales volume is anticipated at $100,000, the accounts receivable would be planned for $150,000. That $150,000 contains both costs and profit. Most managements ignore the profit component both for convenience and for some margin of comfort.

Inventory is treated the same way. Perhaps the firm needs to carry four months' sales in inventory. If four months' sales are $400,000, then the inventory would be that amount multiplied by the cost-of-goods-sold percentage. If the firm's cost of goods sold ran about 50 percent of sales, then the inventory plan would be $200,000.

Then, a firm always needs a certain cash balance in the bank to absorb the differences between cash inflows and outflows. Perhaps the entrepreneur would like to have a minimum cash balance of $10,000. This cushion might need to be financed.

By using a cash flow plan with actual cash outflows and incomes, there is no actual need to figure the inventory and receivables by the above method, for they are all incorporated in the cash flow. Nevertheless, most business people develop certain rules of thumb for their firms about how much money is needed to finance sales. It is a convenient way to think about the problem.

Study the financial statements of similar businesses for guidance about how much money is needed to finance sales. See how much they carry in inventory and receivables for their sales volume. To go even further: How much investment is needed overall to support each $100,000 sales volume? How much investment is needed for every employee? Such indices can provide some idea of the needed working capital.

Growth capital

The business is under way and has proved its marketability and the entrepreneur's skills as a manager. There is great potential for growth, but more money is needed if the venture is to realize that growth potential. Perhaps new plant and equipment are needed. Perhaps some people must be added, a lot of people, and they must be trained.

Growth takes money. Traditionally, growth was financed from the profits of operations. If the venture wasn't making enough money to finance the growth, then it did not deserve to grow. However, that has changed somewhat. Some markets move so fast that to take advantage of them requires an infusion of capital, lest competition get to those unserved markets first.

Fortunately, the venture has been proven. The public may want to buy in at this stage of development. Venture capitalists stumble over themselves to invest in such winners.

It is sometimes helpful to develop a five-year growth plan so that the entrepreneur can communicate to others the venture's long-run money needs and the fact that he or she is on top of the situation. Show them what the future looks like. In this case, management would be forced to evaluate its plans for plant expansion to support its sales growth. The company is growing and profiting, but it's a money hog. It is taking too much additional capital to support the growth. The entrepreneur must figure out a way to get the growth without the additional plant and equipment.

In today's marketplace, many ventures have a long lead time before they can reach cash break-even and eventually profits. Examples are Amazon.com in terms of its massive investments in brand development and infrastructure while still losing money and biotech firms in terms of the long lead times for R&D and FDA trial costs before reaching pay dirt.

Factors That Determine Financial Needs

A number of factors determine the financial requirements of an enterprise. Fortunately, entrepreneurs have considerable control over each of those factors; thus they can control the firm's financial requirements.

Sales volume

Very simply, the more that is sold, the more money is needed in the business. It takes a certain amount of capital to finance each thousand dollars of sales, depending upon the industry and the situation.

Consequently, some entrepreneurs find it advantageous to limit their sales volume to a level that they can finance with whatever money they have available to them. Fortunately, one of the best ways to limit sales is to raise prices, which increases the gross margin. This in turn lessens the amount of money that will be needed, as will be shown. A venture shouldn't go after new markets or more sales if it doesn't have the money to finance them.

Yet, many entrepreneurs believe that somehow everything will work out if more sales are made: "Sales cure everything!" Well, they don't! Many firms have sold themselves right into bankruptcy when needed funds did not materialize. True, sales volume does attract the attention of money, but on what terms will it be made available if a venture is desperate for it?

Growth rate

Closely akin to the level-of-sales factor, the firm's growth rate greatly affects its money needs. Fast-growing firms are money eaters. It's called the burn rate. Rapidly growing firms burn money in frightening amounts. They must continually go back to the money market for additional rounds of financing, even if they are earning high profits. True, this is the financier's dream, a real winner, but still, the rapid growth rate creates the need for continual infusions of additional capital. One hopes that the entrepreneur has the financial skills that allow him or her to obtain these rounds of financing without paying too much for them. Far too many highly successful entrepreneurs created fast-growing firms and lost control of them to the new financiers in the quest for more money.

At times the entrepreneur must say, "Enough is enough!" It may be pointless to grow if the end result is that everything is lost. Real conflicts can arise between the interests of the entrepreneur and the firm that was created.

Factors Determining Financial Requirements
Sales volume
Growth rate
Gross margin
Conversion cycle of assets
Lead times
Terms of sale
Buying policies and terms

Gross margin

Financial requirements increase as the gross margin drops. Contrast two extreme cases for illustrative purposes: Company A does $100,000 sales with an 80 percent margin, while Company B does the same volume with a 20 percent gross margin. All other factors remain the same. Assuming an inventory turnover rate of four, Company A would need $5,000 to finance its $20,000 cost of goods, while Company B would need $20,000 to finance its $80,000 cost of goods. Naturally, this would vary, depending upon the terms of purchase.

Moreover, with the larger margin, a larger profit should be made, thus generating cash for the business. Early in a new venture, large gross margins are needed. Normally competition erodes such high gross margins.

Operating entrepreneurs report that one of their biggest continual problems is that of maintaining their gross margins. Even the venture's own salespeople are often an opponent in this battle. Lower prices make it easier for them to sell the goods.

Conversion cycle of assets (turnover)

Often called capital turnover, turnover combines with the net-profit margin to determine a firm's rate of return on investment.

> *Rate of return (ROI) = Net profit/Investment*
> *Net profit margin = $ Profit/$ Sales*
> *Rate of turnover = $ Sales/$ Investment*
> *Thus: ROI = Profit margin x Turnover*

If the firm generates a 10 percent profit from each dollar of sales and has a turnover of four times a year, then the rate of return on investment is 40 percent. If the turnover rate could be increased to five times, then not only would the ROI be increased to 50 percent, but the additional 25 percent sales would be financed by the same amount of money.

Suppose sales were $1,000,000. The investment would be $250,000, with a net profit of $100,000. Increase the turnover to five times, and the same investment would finance $1,250,000 sales. Or if sales remained at $1,000,000, only a $200,000 investment would be needed.

Clearly, capital-short firms strive for high rates of turnover. A venture must do a lot of business on little money, and that is precisely why shrewd investors love ventures that are lean and mean. They realize a high rate of return on their invested capital.

Lead times

It takes time for things to happen in business. The more time it takes, the more money it takes. As they say, "Time is money!"

The main reason capital requirements are so large in the medical-drug-biomed fields is that it may easily take three or four years to gain approval from the federal Food and Drug Administration before the firm can sell its product. That's three or four years that must be financed before there is any hope of revenue flow. No wonder profit margins must be high in these businesses. It's the only way they can attract capital.

Everything possible should be done to shorten lead times if the venture is short of money. It may mean renting buildings rather than constructing them. It may mean buying a business rather than starting it. Whatever, it is important to remember that time is money.

Terms of sale

The amount of money needed is severely affected by the terms granted to the buyers. In order to minimize capital requirements, the venture could request payment when the product or service is delivered. The sooner it gets paid, the less money will be needed. If a venture must finance its customers for 90 days or more, terrible things happen to its cash flow. The entrepreneur will begin to wonder if he or she is in the banking business.

Buying policies and terms

Sometimes delayed terms or usage rates can be effectively used to lower money needs. When buying, the entrepreneur should try to get extended terms from vendors. For example, a shirt maker's company gave a clothing store a $5,000 credit freeze when it began operations. That is, the clothing store only had to pay the shirt maker's bill down to $5,000. The shirt maker was financing $5,000 of the clothing store's shirt inventory or about $15,000 of the store's shirt sales (shirts turned over about three times a year).

Even landlords can help. If they want to rent the premises badly, they will give a lease that is loaded on the back end. That is, the rent increases at the end of the lease and is lower at first. Sometimes a venture can get a month or two free as it is setting up for business: it pays when the venture opens.

Capital Structure

Some business fundamentals are often overlooked in the fascination with the complex financial structures in today's business world.

It is necessary to first understand what is to be achieved with the firm's capital structure. The ideal capital structure provides sufficient money for financing operations; money is available when needed. Moreover, that money is obtained at a cost that is affordable, if not minimal. Some firms cannot afford to pay even the minimum costs for funds.

In addition, the structure should be flexible enough to easily accommodate rapid expansion or contraction of operations. The capital structure should not block management from undertaking whatever actions are necessary in the future. In particular, it should not impede or block needed future financing.

Finally, the structure should provide the control the entrepreneur wants while giving the investors and lenders the protection and return they require. Compromises must be made, for the achievement of these ideals is difficult.

Since capital is obtained by either incurring debt or selling equity, the discussion will be organized into that dichotomy.

> **The ideal capital structure provides sufficient money for**
> - Operations.
> - Capital costs.
> - Flexibility.
> - Control.

Debt

Debt takes many forms, some more rigorous than others. The essence of debt is that the borrower must repay the funds along with service charges (interest, fees to originate a loan) that were agreed upon. If the money is not repaid as promised, and this is most important, the lender can start collection proceedings, and this can become very uncomfortable for the entrepreneur. He or she could lose the business.

The reason for this apparently simple approach is that many business people seem oblivious to the fact that when they borrow money, they are playing a game that could be called Bet Your Company. The entrepreneur makes a deal with the lender in which he or she uses the company to bet that he or she will be able to perform according to plans. If the plans are wrong, the entrepreneur loses the company.

This point is stressed to emphasize the seriousness of borrowing money. It is not something to be done lightly. The borrower assumes a serious obligation. This should be apparent to any reader of the business trade press who follows the plight of companies that borrowed a lot of money and could not repay it. It is a basic lesson of finance that money should not be borrowed unless those funds will earn in excess of their cost. Many managers forgot that lesson in finance. There are several ways to borrow money, some of which are not generally recognized by the average person: direct loans, suppliers, leasing, and bonds.

Direct loans

Debt
Direct loans
Suppliers
Leasing
Bonds

By directly borrowing money from a bank or other financial institution, a private party, another company, or the government, a liability is created, which is recorded as a note payable in the liabilities section of the balance sheet. If it must be paid back within a year, it is a current liability. If it is due after a year, it is put into the long-term liabilities section.

Depending upon the deal that is negotiated, the note is either secured (collateralized) or unsecured (signature loan). On an unsecured signature loan in default, the lender sues in court for a judgment against the borrower in the amount of the note plus legal costs.

If the borrower fails to meet the terms of a secured note, the lender asks the court to take possession of whatever asset was pledged as collateral and sell it. The proceeds of the sale are then applied to the amount due on the note. Notice that the loss of collateral may not release the borrower from all liability on the debt. Suppose the owner borrows $20,000 from the bank, using the company's injection-molding machine for security. For some reason the owner doesn't pay. The bank goes to court and proves its case to the judge. It proves that the note is legal, that the owner is in default on it and that it wants from the court a legal document that will allow the sheriff to take possession of the molding machine.

So the bank gets the right paper from the court, and the sheriff comes to the owner's plant to haul off the molding machine. It brings only $5,000, some of which goes to the lender and some to the attorney. The owner still owes the lender $15,000 plus legal fees and court costs, depending upon the initial agreement. Most lenders insist that borrowers pay all legal costs incurred, which can be substantial. In the owner's case, the $5,000 might be just enough to pay the legal costs.

For those reasons, most lenders are wary of collateral that is not almost liquid—securities and accounts receivable. Or they want collateral that can be located easily and for which there is a recognized market value. They want collateral that has some liquidity.

These details of note collection are discussed so that entrepreneurs can appreciate the extreme reluctance and great caution exercised by lenders of money. They know how difficult it is to collect on a note, so they are not about to lend money unless they feel certain that it will be repaid. Seldom will they lend money in the hope of getting the collateral when borrowers default. They want their money and interest, not the property or business.

Who borrowed the money? Be prepared to sign the note as a corporate officer as well as a personal guarantor. Many entrepreneurs recommend avoiding personal guarantees whenever possible. Most banks, however, will insist on a personal guarantee if the company is closely held by the entrepreneur and a few people. There may be cases when the bank could waive the requirement for guarantees, depending on the strength of a company's financials, the nature of its collateral, the loan structure, and so forth.

Suppliers

Most businesses use their suppliers' money to finance operations. It appears on the balance sheet as accounts payable. It is usually the cheapest money that can be borrowed so it should be used liberally. Sometimes suppliers are so eager to have the entrepreneur as a customer that they will go out of their way to help finance the new venture.

Many manufacturers will allow dating; that is, they will extend the length of time for payment. A retail clothier had a supplier agree to ship its fall sweaters in August, but the clothier did not have to pay for them until October. The supplier wanted to get the sweaters out of the warehouse to reduce the rent it was paying for the space.

Leasing

Leasing is a form of borrowing. A lease is a liability. Once the entrepreneur signs the lease, he or she is obligated to pay the lessor some money in exchange for using whatever asset is being rented. The obligation taken upon signing a lease should appear on the balance sheet, but it seldom does. Sometimes it is footnoted.

Leasing is a great advantage to entrepreneurs since they can reduce the large up-front expense of purchasing assets by paying only a much smaller monthly charge. However, founders must strike a balance between owned and leased assets.

For example, a restaurant had great success in its first location. The founder was anxious to expand but had not accumulated enough retained earnings to finance a second location. Instead, he decided to lease all kitchen equipment, furniture, fixtures, utensils, signage, computers, and the like. The second restaurant was also very successful and even more profitable than the first. Next, he wanted to expand and open up a third location and use this same method of financing assets—leasing. The last restaurant was not profitable, therefore requiring the founder to borrow money to make up for the cash flow shortfall. The bank turned down his loan request since he had no collateral assets and insufficient retained earnings. The failing restaurant finally depleted the positive cash flow of the other restaurants, and he was forced to file Chapter 7 bankruptcy.

The lesson learned is to remember that leasing is borrowing money that has to be repaid. The business is not building up assets to use for collateral to support expansion loans. Leasing should be considered an option to reduce start-up and expansion costs, but an entrepreneur should continue to build the venture's assets.

Bonds

The bond is a more formal instrument than other notes and contains many formal provisions that must be observed lest the trustee who oversees the administration of the bond declare the company to be in default.

While most people think that bonds are something for big companies only, this is not the case. Small concerns can also use bonds effectively. They provide the financier with some advantages not enjoyed by a note holder.

- They tend to be more negotiable than a note.
- There are third parties involved to see if the payments are made on time.
- Courts are more likely to be responsive to the pleas of a group of bondholders than they will to the complaints of note holders.
- The inclusion of options, warrants, and conversion features in the bond can give its owner many, if not all, of the advantages of ownership, thus letting the creditor enjoy the enterprise's prosperity. The investor can have the virtues of both debt and equity.

The company, while having a more flexible instrument to use in raising money, will find the costs of floating a bond issue usually exceeds the costs of raising money by note. Yes, it can cost money even to sign a simple note at the bank. The bank may want the borrower to keep an offsetting balance in its account of 20 percent of the loan, thus effectively increasing costs. The bank may insist on some additional accounting audits periodically, again incurring some costs. Thus it should be noted that all of the costs of borrowing money are not paid as interest.

It is not uncommon for bonds to be sold to investors in new ventures in combination with some sort of equity instrument. For example, one unit for $2,000 might consist of one $1,000 bond and 100 shares of common stock. The stock might be of a special class that gives the investors certain preferences in income or claims on assets, or restricted voting rights under some circumstance. One of the advantages of the corporate form of business organization is the tremendous flexibility it provides for financing it.

Equity

Equity means ownership—the owner's equity in the business. And it is well-known that the owners get everything that is left over after everyone else gets paid—suppliers, employees, the bank, the government—everyone.

Late one evening, an entrepreneur of a publishing house was depressed and venting his anger over the antics of some of the people with whom he had been dealing. He screamed, "I'm tired of being last in line. Everybody gets paid before me. I'm selling out to someone who will have to pay me first."

Sounds most unfair, but that's the way it is. Of course, it is hoped that what is left over at the end is ample. Entrepreneurs are playing for all the marbles. They hope the upside gains are far more rewarding to the owner than the negotiated gains of the other parties, whose participation in the company's prosperity is limited.

Equity is a complicated concept, it is much more than simply common stock. Equity is a combination of the three factors: right to control, right to income, and right to assets.

Right to control

Control is gained through the ability to elect the majority of the board of directors—the officers who run operations. The majority control of the voting stock is the key to control. True, majority control may not be necessary if the stock is dispersed widely enough among people who are not likely to get together to replace the entrepreneur from his or her job. But unexpected things can happen, particularly when the stakes are high.

Equity Factors
Right to control
Right to income
Right to assets

Right to income

Control is one thing, income is another. Sometimes one class of common stock has voting rights but little else. Another class has the rights to income on some preferential basis but without voting rights unless certain provisions are not met. This means entrepreneurs can keep control of their ventures as long as they meet the stipulations of the preference stock.

So-called preferred stock has puzzled business experts for years: Is it equity or debt? The IRS says it is equity and considers all money paid to its owners as dividends, thus not deductible to the corporation for income tax purposes. Thus, the use of preferred stock has been unpopular, for it gives the government tax money unnecessarily. A bond has many of the same provisions but the payments are called interest and are thus deductible to the corporation for purposes of determining its income.

Many times the tax owed comes down to what something is called and some small, inconsequential provisions in the instrument. Again, expert tax counsel is needed for these matters. The IRS is aware of entrepreneurs trying to have equity money appear to be debt. It is a way of getting money out of the corporation without having to declare it as income; the money is the repayment of a debt.

If an entrepreneur puts $100,000 into a company as equity, the only way he or she can pull it out is either as dividends or by selling the stock. Neither is an attractive alternative. If the entrepreneur buys $10,000 worth of stock and loans the company the other $90,000 on a repayable note, he or she can pull out $90,000 as loan repayment, tax free. In theory, the entrepreneur wants $1 as the investment and $99,999 as a loan. But the IRS will take note.

The issue of thinly capitalized corporations is one that the IRS looks at closely. For years, most accountants used a 10:1 ratio as the minimum acceptable of debt-to-equity ratio; for example, for $10,000 of equity, there can only be $100,000 debt. Now that has been challenged in a number of instances. Most entrepreneurs today are using 20 percent equity and 80 percent debt.

Right to assets

Rights to assets in dissolution can vary according to the financial instruments used. Usually entrepreneurs are not all that interested in what happens to the firm in dissolution because they figure that they would have left the company by then.

Moreover, if they have control, they figure that they can get their assets before dissolution. Thus, investors who are worried about their claims on assets can be given preference over the other stockholders.

If investors are really worried about their rights to assets upon dissolution, the entrepreneur may choose to allow the investor to own the assets and have the firm rent their use. In that way, title to the assets remains with the investor, which is great legal protection if the company runs into trouble.

Use of Debt and Equity

The theory of debt and equity is fine, but the key question remains, "What are the factors to consider in financing your enterprise?" The following major factors must be weighed and balanced when determining the capital structure.

Investor preferences

Unquestionably, the preferences of the money market play a large role in determining a company's capital structure. The founder must usually provide investors with what they want to obtain their money. If they are playing the capital gains game, then they want some stock or the rights to buy some. If they want assured income, then the founder must think in terms of giving them some debt instrument or lease some assets to them.

The investment bankers can tell what their customers are buying and what the founder will have to give them. It's easy to find out what the investor wants. The key question is, "Can you go along with it?" The founder may not want an inappropriate capital structure, one that will jeopardize future plans. There are times founders should say "no" to investors, if they can afford that luxury. But first, they should examine the market closely.

It is easy for investment bankers to say that convertible bonds are hot in the market; after all, like everyone else, they want goods that are easy to sell. However, rest assured that other forms of financing are also selling, but to other investors.

Founder's preferences

As the entrepreneur, the founder hopes to control his or her own destiny. If the founder cannot live peacefully with some type of financing, then it would be wise not to use it. It really is a matter of philosophy. What types of financing are most comfortable?

In particular, the use of debt is a matter of great concern to many entrepreneurs. Even though many modern financiers love the concept of leverage and urge the utmost use of debt in a capital structure, a founder may not like creditors or their hold over the business. Perhaps a founder loses sleep over the pressures of debt. Be comfortable—avoid debt!

Time constraints

When is the money needed? It takes time to get money, and some kinds of money take longer than others. If an entrepreneur wants to raise capital through a public stock issue, he or she is looking at a minimum of six months, more likely nine to 12 months, depending upon how much time is needed in preparing the documents for a public stock issue.

Thus, if it is the intention to take a firm public at some future time, the entrepreneur should by all means make contact with an investment banker early. Let the investment banker guide him or her in structuring the company so that it will take a minimum of effort to go public when the time comes. More important, the entrepreneur should let the investment banker have time to get to know him or her and the operation. In a very real sense, when an investment banker takes a company public, the investment banker is giving some testimony about the company's credibility and what he or she thinks of its future.

Even a bank will take some time, a week or so, to pass on a loan, unless it knows the borrower well and the amount fits within its lending limitations. Again, entrepreneurs should let their banks know about needs ahead of time. They should get to know their bankers and make sure that the bankers know the entrepreneurs and their operations.

If the founder needs money quickly, he or she will likely have to borrow it. Most equity takes more time to develop.

Amount of money needed

How much money is needed? A small amount may be easily borrowed, but if a founder needs a large sum of money, he or she may be forced to think in terms of a public sale of securities.

Banks have definite limits to what they will lend any given company. They usually feel that the founder should own more of the company than the bank does. Banks are also limited by law as to how much they can lend to any one borrower.

Thus, if an entrepreneur foresees the need to borrow a substantial sum from the bank, he or she should start a relationship with a large bank, one that can bank the operation, or have a smaller bank share the loan with a larger bank.

Venture capitalists have certain limits on what they want to invest in any one company. They also have certain minimums. If an entrepreneur needs only $50,000, there are few venture capitalists who will talk with him. They cannot afford to take the time to consider a $50,000 investment. Normally, they are looking at investments from $500,000 to $5 million.

Entrepreneurs who are looking for small amounts of money need to seek private investors. An insurance company might not be interested in anything less than $1 million. Insurance companies have huge sums to invest and cannot do it in small amounts. Few investment bankers are willing to take a company public for less than $5 million. It isn't worth their time to do so. And the more the entrepreneur needs, the more they like the deal. Thus, the amount of money that an entrepreneur needs will affect the type of financial institution that will deal with him or her.

Control aspects

There are all sorts of ways to maintain control of an enterprise. In some high-tech ventures, the talents of the entrepreneur are so critical to the venture's success that without that individual's knowledge, the firm would likely be unsuccessful.

Certainly, the average investor knows that he or she is incapable of managing the company, so there is no threat of a takeover from investors. Instead, they are afraid the entrepreneur will leave the firm for another company. In such cases, the entrepreneur might sell a good deal of equity with little worry about losing control, particularly if the deal is wisely structured.

On the other hand, there are deals that look so profitable and easy to do that it would not be smart for entrepreneurs to allow absolute control out of their hands. After all, the entrepreneur is the one doing all the work to set up the deal. One entrepreneur with a particularly attractive venture went to a venture capitalist for a needed $500,000 expansion. The venture capitalist not only wanted a controlling interest in the venture, but also wanted to put in his own chief executive officer. The entrepreneur declined and quickly got her money elsewhere.

Costs

As one financier says, "The most expensive money is the money you don't get." Opportunity costs are the profits the entrepreneur forgoes when he or she can't go into business because he or she doesn't have the needed money.

Some money costs more than other money. Going public may cost a minimum of $150,000 in up-front legal and accounting fees just for developing the prospectus. If the stock does not sell, and it is not a guaranteed deal, the founder is out $150,000. Not many firms looking for money can afford that kind of loss.

The investment banker may want between 10 and 15 percent of the money raised. The founder may have to pay out another 5 percent in finder's fees to various people who helped find the money. Even a private placement costs money: finder's fees, attorney costs for preparing the private placement document, and accounting costs.

Banks are the cheapest source of money. There are few front-end costs, and the interest rate will likely be the least expensive.

While the venture capitalist seems to have gained some sort of foothold in modern entrepreneurial lore as the financial savior of entrepreneurs, research of how start-up companies raise capital does not support this notion. In total, they finance a very small portion of new ventures and do so at high prices. They are relatively costly.

Confidence in the plan

As previously stated, when entrepreneurs borrow money they are betting on their companies: betting the loans can be repaid as promised. If they are wrong, they lose. Those who are not quite so certain of their futures may prefer equity, which does not have to be repaid on any schedule.

Ability to service debt in early years

Once money is loaned, the lender wants to start receiving interest fairly quickly. At times lenders will give borrowers a little breathing room. The borrowers must pay the interest. Will they be able to do so? Many new enterprises do not have sufficient money in their early months, or even years, to pay much of anything—salaries, expenses, rent, interest.

An entrepreneur with a business that will be slow to get off the ground must be cautious when borrowing money. Equity may be a better alternative.

Glamour of venture

If a proposed new venture is in a glamour field with excellent publicity and news value, it may be able to go public right from the start with little substance to show—the dot-com ventures in 1999 are a prime example. Many other high-tech ventures successfully went public far before their time because their stories captured the investing public's imagination.

Try raising $50,000 for a dry-cleaning shop. Only someone in the dry-cleaning business would appreciate that investment. And that was who financed one entrepreneur who wanted to open up a dry cleaners—a dry-cleaning equipment dealer.

Purpose of funds

How will the money be used? Fixed assets? Inventory? Accounts receivable? Research and Development? Each of these requires different kinds of money. The banker will help design the type of loan that will fit into its loan portfolios.

Using short-term debt to finance long-term fixed assets is a common mistake made by corporate financial officers during periods of high interest rates. When they go to the money market to finance some long-term fixed assets, they discover the interest rate is far higher than they want to pay over the long haul. So they borrow short-term money, anticipating that they will refinance the debt as long-term when the interest rate returns to normal. Normal never happens. Rates keep going up. And then the short-term notes start coming due. How can they repay the money? They have put the borrowed funds into assets that cannot be liquidated, except with much loss and difficulty.

That is called a money crunch! Entrepreneurs do not want to experience one. Thus, they shouldn't borrow short-term money unless they know they can pay off the note. They shouldn't rely on the lender's inclination to refinance the note when it comes due. It is not just happenstance that when a note comes due is the same time when the lender needs money and when the borrower is most unable to repay it.

Short-term loans are usually made for financing seasonal inventory and accounts receivable. They are often referred to as asset-conversion loans by bankers because the funds are invested in assets that will be subsequently converted into cash again within a year to pay off the loan. The bankers want borrowers to pay such loans each year.

Term loans, an increasingly rare breed, are made for financing equipment. Suppose an entrepreneur buys a machine with a five-year payback: Then five-year money would be needed. If he buys that machine with three-year money, then he will have to take money from some other part of the business when payoff time rolls around. The money would most likely come from the firm's income flow. Thus, bankers call this type of loan an income-repayment loan, inasmuch as the bank must look to the firm's income for liquidation of the loan. As a general rule, bankers much prefer asset-conversion loans to income-repayment loans.

Contacts

Undeniably, contacts play a role in financing plans. If entrepreneurs have excellent banking connections, they will likely rely heavily on bank borrowing. If they have a connection with an investment-banking house, then they will likely sell some securities. If they know some private investors well, entrepreneurs will likely look to them for financing.

Management skills

It takes more managerial skill to operate an enterprise on borrowed money than on equity. Unlike lenders, stockholders cannot put the company into bankruptcy. Stockholders can make noise, but once the company has their money, their legal rights are limited largely to whatever voting rights they have.

Nature of the industry

The economics and stability of an industry strongly affect the financing of the firms in that industry. Utilities borrow a lot of money. They can because of the dependability and stability of their income flow.

It would not be smart to operate on borrowed money in an unstable industry. Most apparel manufacturers can borrow money only by factoring their receivables. When the future is uncertain, equity is usually required.

Putting It All Together

Now that the fundamentals of capital structure have been examined, some applications by real companies will illustrate how practice differs from theory.

The BBQ Rack

An entrepreneur wanted to produce barbecue sauces but had little capital to spend on launching this concept. He explained his dilemma to his banker, who informed him that a customer of the bank who owned a commercial kitchen just filed for Chapter 7 in a bankruptcy proceeding. The bank was in the process of repossessing the company's fixtures and equipment and was looking for a buyer.

The banker arranged for the entrepreneur and the customer of the bank to meet with the landlord of the failed business to see if a deal could be negotiated. The entrepreneur was able to make a deal for the leased space and received three months' free rent. Then he negotiated with the bank to sell him the fixtures and equipment on a five-year note with no principal payment due the first year. After that, he would be responsible for principal and interest payments.

Next, the entrepreneur contacted the company's previous suppliers and negotiated a 30-day line of credit on purchases of supplies. He then decided to make minor remodeling changes to the plant. He kept his expenses low by using scrap materials and by doing the remodeling himself with his family's help.

He opened his business in a way that afforded him time to generate his cash flow before he incurred many expenses. The entrepreneur's total start-up cost was $8,000.

ZDC, Inc.

Originally, ZDC, Inc., was formed by an IBM computer engineer who second-mortgaged his home and cleaned out his savings account to come up with the $60,000 seed money needed to begin the company. The firm developed a line of computerized energy-management devices. The two target markets were apartment houses on master meters and home owners whose power bills depended upon their peak usage. Within a year, two products came from the lab: Fair Share for apartment houses and Energy Sentry for the home market.

While Fair Share was marketed in the Denver area initially, Energy Sentry was marketed initially in Ohio, where Ohio Edison charged its customers on the basis of their peak demands for power.

By the end of the first year, sales were slightly less than $1 million with what was thought to be a $160,000 profit. It was time to expand. The product had been proven and debugged. It was time for second-stage financing to expand into eight new markets.

A consultant, after studying the firm, introduced a financial packager to the entrepreneur. The financial middleman proposed raising $500,000 by a private placement to individual investors. The financial plan included paying off the mortgages and amounts owed by the founder, who was still active in the technical side of the business.

The owner had been president, but he made little effort to disguise his preference for technical work. The financier suggested making the consultant president as a way of building up the credibility of the company's management team. After much soul searching by the founder, it was done.

A pitch was made to eight wealthy investors in Florida, who immediately wrote out checks for the needed funds from their personal checking accounts. The expansion was on.

Within a year, sales were approaching a profitable $3 million when an investment-banking house approached the company with a firm offer to raise $3.5 million by selling 25 percent of the company's common stock: the price would be $4.25 per share. The eight private investors had paid 50 cents a share for their second-stage financing.

Thus, third-stage financing valued the company at $14 million, while it had been valued at only $1.68 million five months earlier. This is not a bad return for a five-month investment. Note the difference in returns, depending upon what stage in the venture the investor buys. The earlier, the better, assuming all goes fairly well.

The new president had not planned to take the company public until sales had reached the $10 million mark, which was planned in two years. Thus, the underwriting offer surprised him. But not for long. He thought he had to go for it while the "window was open." That is, sell the stock when the market would buy it.

Anyone who has tried to cash in a winning ticket at a race track when the payoff window was closed got no money. Financial windows have a way of slamming shut suddenly. One adverse economic announcement can do the trick. Thus, the old adages—strike while the iron is hot, make hay while the sun shines, and grab the money and run—seemed applicable. Or so he thought. But one point of this story is to relate how quickly markets change and how unreliable investment bankers can be.

After spending about $100,000 for legal and accounting costs connected with the initial public offering (IPO), the investment banker found reasons to drop the deal. There were some fine-printed paragraphs in the firm letter of commitment that allowed the banker not to do the deal. So how does the president get the needed funds for expansion?

A venture capitalist provided so-called bridge financing for some stock at a reasonable price. The fact that the same venture capitalist already held an interest in the company from the second-stage financing of $500,000 played some role in the decision. This venture capitalist was the financial packager, and he had been given a finder's fee in stock options for 50 cents a share.

Still needing access to public money for its expansion, the firm agreed to be purchased by a publicly held, high-tech firm that needed not only new management but the company's marketing clout. Thus, the company became part of a public company with the consultant-president becoming president of the new firm. The merger made even more sense because the public company had the physical plant and R&D capability badly needed by the company for its expansion.

Note how the company was financed with equity, except for the initial debt of the founder, which was, in reality, equity to the company—the founder borrowed the money to buy equity in the company. Also note the use of private money early in the venture. Finally, the rapid change in the company's capital structure should be noted.

The Clothes Line

An entrepreneur wanted to start a mother/daughter clothing line made with unusual fabrics from different parts of the world. Her business plan showed that her start-up costs would be about $50,000. She decided to form a corporation and sell 40 percent of her stock to an investor. Because clothing is mostly a lifestyle business, it probably would not command a large exit price. Most likely, it would be difficult for her to attract outside investors.

She had a friend who was consulting with her on how best to launch this new venture. He designed a four-part deal to offer to a potential investor:

1. $50,000 would purchase 40 percent of common stock in the corporation.
2. Of the money raised, $10,000 would be used to purchase 40 percent of the common stock and $40,000 would be a loan to the corporation at 8 percent interest to the investor.
3. The investor would be given the title of Buyer.
4. The investor could also purchase any product for cost plus freight.

What the entrepreneur was really offering a potential investor was the following:

1. The $40,000, used as a loan to the corporation, could be paid back with no tax consequences because it is a return of the principal. The interest on the note would be taxable to the investor but used as a tax write-off to the company. If the total $50,000 was used to purchase stock, then in order for the investor to recoup the investment, it would have to be paid back in a dividend, therefore creating a double tax. The corporation would be responsible for paying corporate tax on the earnings, and then the investor would be responsible for paying taxes on earned dividends.
2. If the corporation failed, then the investor could write off both the $10,000 stock investment as either a short-term or long-term capital loss, depending on how long the business had been operating. The $40,000 note could be written off, since it would qualify as a nonbusiness bad debt and be reported as a short-term capital loss on the investor's individual tax return. The tax write-off received would offset some of the loss.
3. As soon as the note is paid, the company could switch its legal structure to an S corporation and pass all profits directly to the owners in proportion to their ownership. Therefore, the corporation would not pay taxes on the profit. The investor would be taxed on the money received as ordinary income. This structure would avoid double taxation. However, the business could not be sold for 10 years after becoming an S corporation.
4. The title of Buyer, given to the investor, would allow this person, while traveling abroad, to purchase fabrics for the corporation and have the corporation pay for these trips. The expense would result in a tax write-off to the corporation if the investor properly documented the business conducted in each country in accordance with prescribed IRS regulations.
5. The investor could purchase clothing at a 50 percent reduction, which would be much less expensive than buying from a retail store.

The entrepreneur then looked for potential investors who liked to travel internationally, enjoyed buying exotic fabrics, and would have an interest in being associated with producing a line of clothing. One month later, she raised the money from a doctor who was looking for a business to get his wife involved with. The couple's youngest child had just graduated from college, and the doctor wanted to reduce his office hours to one day a week. The two were ready to start a new life traveling the world, and this business concept fit their investment desires and their personal criteria for a new venture.

Conclusion

Entrepreneurs have considerable control over the amounts of money they will need, depending on how they intend to do business. A firm's capital structure can range from a very simple one consisting solely of the entrepreneur's own equity to a complex blending of debt, equity, and operations. Entrepreneurs should use capital structure to their advantage; it is a management tool.

Traditional and Alternative Money Sources

Learning Objectives

In this chapter, students will learn how to

- Obtain money to start and run a new venture from banks, governmental agencies, venture capitalists, and investment bankers.
- Obtain money from alternative money sources.

Raising money is an art. Fortunately, it can be learned, and all entrepreneurs should become experts at raising money. Some business owners become so adept at finding capital through their knowledge of the money market, the people in it, and how to deal with the money market that it may appear as if they are in the business of raising money. It's an art that entrepreneurs should study even though they may not be concerned now with obtaining outside capital.

Repeatedly, hard-pressed entrepreneurs say that if they could only get some more money they would be able to get their enterprises rolling. Entrepreneurs are prone to blame the lack of money for most of their problems.

Money alone solves few problems; still it is important and often critical. The entrepreneur needs to know about sources of money, how to find them, and how to relate to them. There may come a time when he or she will need money. Whether the entrepreneur is able to get it depends on what he or she has done long before the money is needed and how he or she goes about dealing with its owners.

It is interesting to note that the majority of financing for entrepreneurial ventures comes from private investors, including family and friends. Table 25-1 depicts where entrepreneurs get their funding.

Sources of money can be classified several ways. In this chapter, they are divided into two major categories: traditional and nontraditional or alternative sources. But before the discussion of those sources, first consider the advantages of self-financing.

Self-Financing

The advantages of selecting a business which one can finance oneself must be appreciated after observing the agonies, frustrations, and results of those entrepreneurs who use outside financing. Four major considerations must be recognized: time, cost, control, and mental anguish.

Time

The person who goes to the money market for funds spends much time doing so. It may take months of almost full-time effort to get money from outsiders. If an enterprise is in its early stages of development, that time is usually taken at the expense of other critical activities. The time spent finding money might be better spent finding customers.

In seeking funds, the entrepreneur often neglects the business. After all, there is just so much any one person can do. If an entrepreneur takes a company public, he or she must plan on spending several months in preparation. The company had better be able to run well by itself, for there will be weeks during which the entrepreneur will be absent. The business owner will find out how well he or she can manage over the telephone. The time it takes to raise outside money should not be underestimated.

Cost

The entrepreneur raising money for a new venture must be prepared to contact at least 50 people. If a person does not want to participate, ask him or her for a referral to someone that might be interested.

Money is expensive. Its price is often shocking. Being familiar with bank interest rates, entrepreneurs may become upset when some private investors, investment bankers, or venture capitalists want 25 percent to 100 percent return per year for their funds. A private investor in a computer manufacturing company invested $50,000 and was bought out three years later for $350,000, a high rate of return. The hard-asset lender wants the prime rate plus 10 percent, and that's cheap money in many circles. One of the reasons for the bank's continued popularity is that it is the cheapest source of money. Many enterprises are not profitable enough to afford outside financing, and thus they have limited access to the money market.

Most money people demand a highly profitable venture before investing. A marginal business that may be attractive to a person because it would provide a good living will not be attractive to the money people.

Control

In many instances, control over the enterprise may be jeopardized if the entrepreneur obtains outside money. The venture capitalist may want voting control. After several rounds of financing, the entrepreneur's portion of the firm may dwindle to only a few percent. Gene Amdahl, founder of Amdahl Corporation, was left with only 3 percent of his computer business after

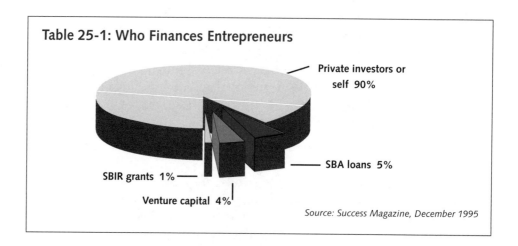

Table 25-1: Who Finances Entrepreneurs

Private investors or self 90%

SBA loans 5%

Venture capital 4%

SBIR grants 1%

Source: Success Magazine, December 1995

several fund raising stages. Why bother getting the money if the enterprise is lost in doing so? The old cliche that "It is better to have 10 percent of something than 100 percent of nothing" has a few flaws in its logic; it is not that simple.

There are alternatives. Many entrepreneurs feel that one of the main reasons they are in business for themselves is to control their own destiny; using outside money may negate that goal, as the investors may control the future of the enterprise.

Mental anguish

Anyone who has ever borrowed money and then not been able to repay it knows that lenders will likely do things to force borrowers to pay. Outside investors can place great mental pressure on entrepreneurs.

Consequently, many advantages are gained when the entrepreneur chooses to do business in such a way that outside investors are not needed. The venture may not grow as fast and as big as the big-money players. But the owner may have more fun and sleep better at night.

Traditional Sources of Money

The traditional sources for obtaining money are banks, governmental agencies, venture capitalists, investment bankers, money finders, and other lending institutions.

Banks

Banks are the most important professional money supplier in the financial system. Entrepreneurs need good banking connections. Ready access to quick money can create advantages in many situations. For example, deals arise in which cash can gain substantial leverage in the transaction.

A furniture manufacturer had an opportunity to buy a $70,000 note he had given to the person he had bought the company from—if he could come up with $40,000 within 24 hours. Fortunately, the manufacturer had good banking connections. He phoned his banker, related the tale, and had the money within the hour. The quickest and least expensive source of money is usually a commercial bank, if it will make the loan. The problem is that banks usually won't loan money to a new enterprise unless the entrepreneur has collateral to support the loan or has someone else who has sufficient collateral to cover the note.

Banks are not interested in an equity position in companies; they are in the debt business. Their profits come from the interest borrowers pay after they deduct the costs of operation, which are substantial. On a $100,000 loan at 10 percent interest, the bottom line profit may be only $1,000 after operating expenses are deducted. Consequently, one loan that goes sour can wipe out the profits of 100 other loans. That's why bankers are very careful in lending money. They can't assume risks. They will not make the loan if there is risk in the picture. They must be reasonably assured that the loan will be repaid on time.

Banks have different criteria, different markets, and different lending policies. Entrepreneurs must search for banks that fit their needs and lend to

Traditional Sources
Banks
Governmental agencies
Venture capitalists
Investment bankers
Money finders
Other lending institutions

businesses in the same industry. For example, some banks solicit SBA-backed loans, while other banks do not process many SBA-backed loans. Some banks may prefer to work with companies in the clothing-manufacturing business since they have experience with lending to these types of companies.

After selecting a bank that wants to work with the entrepreneur's type of venture, he or she should cultivate a good relationship with the loan officer. For example, entrepreneurs will probably have the opportunity to meet bankers from the community at civic events, school meetings, church, and so forth. They can usually establish both social and business relationships.

Once an entrepreneur has identified the bank he or she wants to do business with and the contact there, he or she can invite that person to see the business in operation. Such a visit will let the banker know who the entrepreneur is and what the entrepreneur does. If the entrepreneur has assets, the banker can see them. If a product is made, he or she can see how. This visit should occur before the time the entrepreneur asks for money.

These are some general guidelines to consider when dealing with bankers. Bankers seldom furnish start-up money for a venture. Any money entrepreneurs are able to borrow from banks at the beginning of their ventures will be loaned personally on some other basis than the businesses. They may be able to borrow on general credit rating or on some personal assets. But that is money entrepreneurs could borrow whether or not they were starting businesses.

If a person is buying a business, the bank may be willing to make a loan against some of the company's assets, that is, the leveraged buyout. The buyer can look closely at accounts receivable and inventory to support such a loan.

Banks prefer to make working-capital loans. For example, seasonal inventory expansions and increases in accounts receivable would be appropriate for working-capital loans. For established businesses, banks may make equipment term loans but for not more than five years' maturity. As a general rule, banks like short-term loans, no more than three years and preferably one year. They prefer asset-conversion loans.

The interest rate will be a floating one: prime plus a few points. If the entrepreneur is a good customer, he or she may have to pay prime plus 1 or 1.5 percent. If the entrepreneur is asked to pay prime plus 4 or 5 percent, he or she knows that the banker thinks that the company has some risk. Typically, the entrepreneur will pay it just the same because it will still be the cheapest money that can be found.

Governmental agencies

One of the lesser-known facts of business is that there is a lot of money, some of it at relatively low cost, available from various governmental agencies. Books have been published providing comprehensive lists of the governmental agencies that can help finance new ventures; an example is Laurie Blum's *Money for Small Business and Entrepreneurs* (New York: John Wiley & Sons, 1995).

Many entrepreneurs have used governmental sources of money successfully. The paperwork and time-consuming procedures, while a bother, are not insurmountable obstacles. In all fairness, other types of money people can

> A banker might go a long way down the road with a venture if convinced that the owner were trying to work out a difficult situation.

be equally slow in responding to an urgent call for capital. And they all make the entrepreneur jump through their hoops. Today, many governmental agencies are trying to reduce the amount of paperwork and respond in a more timely manner to requests for funding.

The following discussion surveys some governmental-financing sources that entrepreneurs are successfully using today.

Small Business Administration (SBA)

The SBA offers the 7(a) bank-loan guaranty program and the SBA 504 certified development company fixed-asset loan program. The following information was obtained from www.sba.gov/financing/.

The 7(a) bank-loan guaranty program is available to existing businesses as well as start-up ventures to finance working capital, accounts receivable, inventory, equipment, machinery, leasehold improvements, and real estate.

Depending on what the loan is used for, the terms are as follows: working-capital loans, five to 10 years; equipment and real-estate loans, up to 25 years. The banking institution, however, will usually choose the term of maturity that coincides with the bank's formal loan policy.

Guaranty amounts. For loans of less than $100,000, the SBA will guarantee up to 85 percent. For loans greater than $100,000, the SBA will guarantee up to 75 percent.

Interest rate. The banking institution and the borrower negotiate the interest rate subject to SBA maximums which are pegged to the prime rate published in the *Wall Street Journal*. For example, on loans of $50,000 or more with a term less than seven years, the rate must not exceed prime rate plus 2.25 percent. Loans for a smaller amount or a longer term would have slightly higher maximum interest rates.

Special 7(a) loan guaranty programs. SBA also offers the following specific-use loan programs:

CAPLines loan guaranty program

This program provides small businesses with a way to finance their cash cycles. Over a period of up to five years, the SBA provides a term commitment to a commercial banking institution for a loan that supplies the capital for the cyclical, recurring, and short-term lending requirements of small businesses. This program can be used as a revolving line of credit, in which case the business utilizes the amount of the loan dictated by the immediate cash needs of the business. This line can be fully drawn, paid off, and drawn on again during its maturity cycle. The program can also be used as a term vehicle for the consolidation of short-term debt.

The lender can use the CAP*Lines* loan as a general revolving-line-of-credit vehicle in which the SBA can generally guarantee up to $1,000,000. The lender will request a maximum of 75 percent of the loan to be guaranteed by the SBA. There are loan programs that have specific purposes and that fall within CAP*Lines* loan program parameters. These CAP*Lines* programs are listed below.

- **Contract line:** This program provides loan guarantees for short-term lines of credit to finance projected costs of the labor and materials needed to perform a specific contract. Loan funds cannot be used for the financing of receivables and inventory outside of the specific contract.

- **Builders line:** This program offers loan funds to small general contractors or builders to finance construction or renovation of residential or commercial buildings for resale. Loan funds are available for direct labor and materials costs.
- **Asset-based line:** This asset-based revolving line of credit is designed to assist businesses in need of a short-term line of credit to finance cyclical growth, recurring, and short-term needs. Repayment comes from converting short-term assets such as inventory and accounts receivable into cash.
- **Seasonal line:** This program offers loan guarantees for short-term lines of credit to finance seasonal increases in inventories and accounts of small firms.

SBA export working-capital program

This program provides a revolving line of credit under a loan guarantee to assist businesses in exporting their products and services abroad. Loan proceeds may be used to finance labor and materials needed for the manufacture or purchase of goods and services for export. The loan proceeds may also be used for businesses to develop in foreign markets (for example, advertising and trade-name registration). The proceeds may not be used to fund existing domestic debt obligations or to purchase fixed assets. The SBA can guarantee up to 90 percent of a secured loan.

International trade loans

Businesses that are preparing to export or to increase their export sales may be eligible for an international trade loan. The SBA can guarantee up to $1,250,000 for a combination of fixed-asset (facilities and equipment) financing and export-working-capital-program assistance. The fixed-asset guaranty cannot exceed one million dollars and the non-fixed-asset portion cannot exceed $750,000. Loans for facilities can have maturities of up to 25 years and may be combined with an export working-capital loan which has a maturity of 12 months with two annual reissuances allowed for a maximim maturity of three years.

SBA pollution-control loans

The SBA guarantees loans to small businesses for financing the planning, design, or installation of a pollution-control facility. A pollution-control facility is defined as real or personal property that will reduce pollution. SBA will guarantee loans of up to $1 million under this program.

SBA prequalification loan program

This program allows low income borrowers, disabled business owners, new and emerging businesses, veterans, exporters, rural and specialized industries to receive prequalification from the SBA before going to a bank. The SBA will issue a commitment letter, indicating the SBA's willngness to guarantee the loan, that the business owner can take to a lender. Businesses applying for this program must meet SBA standards for business ownership as well as maximum annual sales and number of employees.

Low documentation program

This program is designed to help small businesses simplify the loan-application process for loan requests of $150,000 or less. With the LowDoc program, an applicant completes the front of a one-page SBA application form; the lender then completes the back. In addition to the form, the lender will require additional information (for example, personal financial statements, tax returns) from the borrower to substantiate the lender's credit decision. Once the lender sends in the form, the SBA processes the application within 36 hours. Eligible businesses include start-ups and businesses whose average annual sales for the preceding three years do not exceed $5 million and that employ 100 people or fewer, including affiliates.

SBAExpress program

The SBA allows selected lenders to use their own documentation and procedures to approve loans to small businesses using the 7(a) loan program in return for a 50 percent guaranty and other modifications to SBA's normal lending practices. The SBA provides a 36-hour response after receiving the application package.

SBA 504 certified development company fixed-asset loan program

Through certified development companies (CDCs), the SBA provides financing for a portion of a small firm's fixed-asset purchases (for example, land, buildings, machinery, equipment). The 504 program provides businesses with long-term (for example, 20 years) fixed rates for a portion of the total loan. The structure of a loan would be as follows:

Total loan size	*$1,000,000*	
Bank participation, 1st Deed of Trust	*$500,000*	*50%*
SBA Participation, 2nd Deed of Trust	*$400,000*	*40%*
Owner participation	*$100,000*	*10%*

There are two separate loan payments: one made to the bank for its participation and the second loan payment made to the CDC for the SBA participation of the loan. A 504 loan request should generally not fall below $400,000. Fees will be paid by the borrower to the bank and to the CDC packaging the SBA portion of the loan.

To be eligible, the business must be operated for profit and fall within the size standards set by the SBA. Under the 504 Program, the business qualifies as small if it does not have a tangible net worth in excess of $7 million and does not have an average net income in excess of $2.5 million after taxes for the preceding two years. For some SBA programs (for example, 504 program), the size standards for individual Standard Industrial Classification (SIC) codes have been increased. A knowledgeable SBA lender will be able to determine those size standards pertinent to a venture's SIC code.

Small Business Investment Companies (SBICs)

SBICs are a good source of seed and expansion capital for small ventures that meet predetermined investment criteria. SBICs are privately owned and managed investment firms that are licensed and regulated by the SBA. They use their own capital, plus funds borrowed at favorable rates with an SBA guarantee, to make venture capital investments in small business.

SBICs provide equity capital or loans for working capital, expansion, research and development, and acquisitions. An SBIC loan is not fully collateralized and usually is backed by equipment collateral. Loans to minority and disadvantaged entrepreneurs are available through Specialized Small Business Investment Companies. SBICs were established in 1958 by the federal government to provide venture financing and management assistance to small businesses. SBICs are either partnerships, corporations, or bank subsidiaries and are required to have $1 million in capital.

SBICs can borrow from the SBA up to $3 for every $1 of private capital available. They use a variety of financing methods, such as purchasing debentures convertible into company stock, purchasing capital stock, purchasing debt securities, using traditional instruments of equity financing, or making long-term loans to the business. The majority of their transactions are equity related, although they are legally prohibited from taking control of a company.

For the fiscal year 2003, SBICs reported financing $2.5 billion to approximately 4,800 ventures. The SBIC investment per company ranged from $100,000 to more than $1 million. The 442 SBICs in the U.S. are a good source of long-term capital for small businesses that lack the potential to become a major business.

SBICs can raise new funds to invest in small firms by issuing securities backed by the SBA and sold on the bond market. The proceeds from the sale of the bonds go to the SBICs, who will buy stock in small firms in exchange for ownership. When the companies are sold or go public, the SBICs and the SBA will receive a return on the initial investment. Each SBIC establishes its own investment criteria.

To be eligible for SBIC financing, a venture must qualify as a small business, defined as a business that is independently owned and operated, has a net worth no greater than $18 million, and has an average after-tax net income of less than $6 million for the prior two years. In addition, it must be able to meet the business-loan guidelines under the traditional SBA guaranty-loan program.

For the most current SBIC list, contact the local SBA office or the National Association of SBICs (www.nasbic.org), 666 11th St. N.W., Suite 750, Washington, DC 20001, (202) 628-5055, fax (202) 628-5058.

State programs

State, regional, and municipal development agencies are also good sources for financing. Governments want jobs for their constituents and therefore are willing to guarantee or supply loans, work out venture-capital deals, or act as resources for financing sources. States such as Michigan, Wisconsin, and Pennsylvania have attractive start-up funds available to entrepreneurs.

Consult with the National Association of State Development Agencies, (703) 490-6777, to obtain information on what specific states offer.

State pension funds are also taking a more active role in helping minority business owners obtain financing. In addition, municipal or community development grants may be available, especially if the business is located in an economically depressed area. For more information, review a copy of *Free Money From the Federal Government for Small Businesses and Entrepreneurs* by Laurie Blum, John Wiley & Sons, 1995.

Venture capitalists

The term venture capitalist or VC was coined not too many years ago to describe a financial institution that specialized in making investments in new ventures. One of the first VCs was American Research and Development, which was formed by General Doriot, the famed Harvard professor of New Enterprises. One of its early investments was Digital Equipment Corporation, which quickly became a sensational winner. Perhaps, because its success was widely heralded, American Research and Development was used as a model for future VCs.

Since that time, venture capitalists have proliferated not only in number but in form. Today, there are more than 1,000 firms that purport to make investments in new ventures. Moreover, these many firms take all sorts of forms and follow all sorts of policies. Some specialize only in leveraged buyouts, while others will furnish seed money. Some want only to make an investment, while others want to participate in management. Some want control, while others don't.

Generally, venture-capital firms are grouped into the following categories: divisions of large corporations, family funds, and private investment firms. Because of the number of mergers and acquisitions during the past two decades, venture capitalists have expanded into other fields such as investment banking, asset-based leasing, exploration, and international projects.

In 2002, venture investments in emerging businesses totaled $21 billion, according to the National Venture Capital Association (www.nvca.org.) A study conducted in 2000 estimates that venture capitalists have helped create 7.6 million jobs and over 1.3 trillion in revenue since 1970.

Another study by the U.S. General Accounting Office (GAO) followed 72 public companies (developed with venture-capital investments of only $209 million in the 1970s) showed that they produced, by the end of that decade, the following impressive results:

- Aggregate sales of $6 billion, growing at an annual rate of 33 percent
- An estimated 130,000 jobs created
- More than $100 million in corporate taxes paid
- More than $350 million in employee tax revenues paid
- $900 million in export sales generated

Not a bad return on $209 million investment. Too bad the GAO didn't go on to find out how much money the investors and entrepreneurs made from the actions.

When thinking about contacting venture-capital firms, entrepreneurs should consider their minimum investments, propensity to get involved in managing the business, and types of investments they make.

Minimum investments

VC Considerations

Minimum investments
Management participation
Types of investments

Many VCs like to claim that they are interested in looking only at deals for more than $500,000 and cannot afford to evaluate a smaller venture. But most actual investments range between $100,000 and $500,000; one VC said that a $250,000 investment was more typical for his firm than the $1 million figure given in the firm's brochure.

In any event, if a venture's financial need for funds is under $100,000, the venture capitalist is not the way to go.

A founder of a large venture-capital firm in Denver says emphatically that any worthy entrepreneur could raise up to $100,000 on his or her own.

VCs want to look at sizable deals, but they seldom want to invest more than $5 million in any one new venture. They feel that any company needing more than $5 million should be looking at a public stock offering. Diversification is critical to their investment policy. They often hedge their positions in an investment by inviting other firms into forming a syndicate to help finance the deal.

Management participation

While a few VCs will make an investment in a new enterprise and then sit back to await results, that is not the pattern of most big VCs today. They want active roles in the new firm. This value-added investing style brings more than money to the venture. They typically want a seat on the board of directors, and may even want to place one of their people as CEO of the firm. Others will demand control over the company's finances and control systems. Most keep close watch over, and constant contact with, their investments.

In a very real sense, when an entrepreneur takes a venture capitalist's money, he or she takes on a partner. One should not rush to the conclusion that this penchant of the VCs to participate in the enterprise is necessarily bad. It is often quite good. They know people; they can open the right doors. They know a lot about business and thus can help the entrepreneur with things about which he or she knows little. They can also serve as a task master, forcing the entrepreneur to do things that he or she might be reluctant to do otherwise. A good VC will force the entrepreneur to be successful if the entrepreneur has the right stuff; if the VC can't, the entrepreneur will probably be out of business.

Types of investments

For the most part, the venture capitalists are interested in technology-based ventures. If an entrepreneur has some concept that appears to have a technology component in it, the venture capitalists will talk to him or her; however, they avoid revolutionary technology. They want developmental technology on proven products with proven markets. They would not have financed Fulton's steamboat or Henry Ford's automobile.

Investment bankers

Investment bankers vary in sizes and ways of operating. They are primarily located in large cities, particularly New York. Some focus on taking firms public, often refusing to look at any deal of less than $10 million. Some specialize in new ventures while others prefer to deal with firms that have several years' seasoning. It has been said that a firm must have three years of solid profitable performance before an investment banker will talk to its management, but that rule has been waning in recent years.

Many new ventures without a profit performance have attracted the eye of investment bankers in recent years. Amazon.com is a good example of such a company. After all, investment bankers are in business to sell stock, which is how they make their money. And many of their customers are interested in some of the new ventures that have done well in the market. As has been mentioned, investment bankers cost money. In the end, the entrepreneur will pay about 15 to 20 percent of the raised money for their services.

Using an investment banker depends upon having an exciting story to tell the investor. The investment banker must be able to make its customers believe that there are great fortunes awaiting those people who can see the virtues in an entrepreneur's company. The deal must scream growth, future, profits, and other such good things.

> If entrepreneurs think they will ultimately use the services of an investment banker, the sooner they make contact with an excellent house, the better. They should let the investment banker know their plans and have the investment banker help guide them. They don't have to pay the investment banker until it raises the money.

Money finders

Aside from the formal investment banking houses, there are numerous financial consultants who will not only help an entrepreneur package a deal but will also put him or her into contact with potential investors. This will usually cost money up front plus finder's fees. Typically, these people work with firms whose capital requirements are below the minimums required by investment bankers. Money finders are flexible in their operations and vary tremendously in their abilities.

> Entrepreneurs should check credentials and ask for and call all references. They need to find people who are interested in and understand their businesses and have good reputations.

One should beware of

- Frauds who pass themselves off as financial consultants. They promise to raise the needed money but demand an advance payment or finder's fee. Many such deals are cloaked in quite clever scams involving loans from foreign countries at low interest rates.
- People who cannot be trusted. It is not easy to spot these types of people. They often have the best addresses and the best-looking offices. And they can be very persuasive.
- Incompetents who will promise money but cannot deliver. They don't have the contacts they profess to have.
- Dreamers who really think they can do something for entrepreneurs, take a company public or whatever, but they are wrong. Many of these people are simply unrealistic. They are easy to spot, but unfortunately, entrepreneurs may not want to spot them. The entrepreneurs want what the dreamers say to be true.
- People working around the fringes of the money market who just don't know what is going on.

Other lending institutions

The money business has seen its share of entrepreneurial activity during the past two decades. At one time the traditional commercial bank was the main source of money for most people. Now there are many firms offering to "sell" money on various deals and terms. A few that deserve some attention are savings and loan associations, credit unions, commercial finance companies, and hard-asset lenders

Savings and loan associations

Not many years ago, the savings and loan companies made loans on real estate only; that was the purpose for which they were created. Then, with deregulation in the 1980s many savings and loans rushed to resemble commercial banks and aggressively sought to make commercial loans. The S&L scandals of the early 1990s dried up this source of money. It probably won't return for a long time, nor should it.

Credit unions

Initially created to serve the financial needs of the workers of large organizations, particularly for the financing of cars and home improvements, the more aggressive credit unions have branched out to help their members finance other activities. In some instances, people don't even have to work for any one company to join a credit union. One in Richardson, Texas, accepts members from any company in town.

The big advantage in dealing with credit unions is that their terms are often more reasonable than those offered by other financial institutions. Their money, however, is short-term and limited. They usually do not lend a large amount of money, such as $50,000, but they would be far more comfortable with loans of $10,000 to $20,000. Thus, they can be used mainly for small personal loans.

Commercial finance companies

Names such as Beneficial, CIF, Household, GMAC, Associates, and The Money Store are some of the well-known commercial finance companies. They are interesting entrepreneurial endeavors, for they have prospered by lending money to people with whom bankers refuse to deal. And where do they get the money to lend to such questionable risks? From the very commercial banks that refuse to take such risks.

While these firms are known for their activities in consumer credit, they still do considerable business with commercial institutions. Some of their loans are quite large and in the three- to five-year range of payback. They are worth the time to investigate. But they do cost more than loans from a commercial bank. They are professionals and can examine specific situations and perhaps provide some ideas. When entrepreneurs go hunting for money, they often get a good education in finance and business.

Hard-asset lenders

Certain firms will lend money against so-called hard assets such as equipment and machinery, tangible assets with a recognizable liquidating value. Most of the firms with which they deal have exhausted other avenues of borrowing, largely due to poor credit ratings. Now nearing the end of the road, they pay dearly for the money. Prime plus 10 is a good deal in this segment of the money market.

On the other hand, hard-asset lenders are usually excellent business people who can provide quick, decisive action and much good advice. They must be adept lenders or they would not last long in this business. But they are sometimes misled by the market into believing that some asset thought to be hard is, upon market testing, found to be soft. The liquidation value was not what it was thought to be when the loan was made. The problem is that when a loan goes bad, the whole market is likely to be bad; times are depressed. Thus the hard asset has to be liquidated in a poor market.

Alternative Sources

There are many different types of alternative money sources that entrepreneurs should become aware of and learn how to use. Because of the current credit crunch for business loans and tighter banking regulations, business owners are being forced to use more of the following alternative money sources.

Private investors—angels

One of the fascinating unknowns in the world of entrepreneurial financing is the amount of money private investors place directly into new ventures. It is tremendous. Much private investing is done by people of wealth who become interested, for one reason or another, in putting money into some enterprise.

While it is easy to say that the desire for a high rate of return is the motive impelling the deal, that would be an oversimplification. Much private investing is motivated by nonfinancial motives: a desire for perquisites, a craving for some action that promises to be interesting, a need to do something, or simply having fun.

Angels like to invest in start-up ventures, and this type of money is easier to acquire than venture capital. They generally offer better interest rates than banks and have fewer strings than venture capitalists. Many do not want voting rights in the company. They may want to take on an advisory role. But they do expect returns of three to five times their investment after two to five years.

In addition, angels are hard to find. The place to start is within the specific industry by contacting the trade association or professional group. Local economic-development governmental agencies should also have lists of potential investors.

Another way to find angels is to use intermediaries who are advisors to angels. Merchant bankers, boutique bankers, financial consultants, and financial planners are typical intermediaries who specialize in raising small amounts of capital. They develop small networks of angels who invest in the deals they find and recommend.

One can also look in the *Yellow Pages* under "investment management," "financing consultants," or "financial planners." Financial consultants and financial planners usually work through a brokerage firm and are involved in managing the investments of angels.

Alternative Sources
Private investors—angels
Private placements
SCOR
Credit cards
Family and friends
Customers
Factoring
Joint ventures/strategic alliances
Suppliers
Employees
Professional advisors, business acquaintances
Leasing companies
Sale of distribution rights
Microloan programs

Venture-capital clubs in the area can be a good place to learn about the local angel community. Another source is US Investor Network (www.usinvestor.com), which provides access to capital, contacts, and information. One must be cautious when working with intermediaries: check their references and track records. One should seek referrals from lawyers, bankers, accountants, and insurance brokers.

Universities are making their vast network of alumni angels available to new ventures that have developed through their entrepreneur programs in business and engineering schools.

More information about private investors can be found in *Finding Private Venture Capital for Your Firm* by Robert J. Gaston (1990) or *Guerrilla Financing* by Bruce Blechman and Jay Conrad Levinson (1992). Both are excellent entrepreneurial resources on financing tactics.

Private placements

A private placement may take the form of either debt or equity or a combination. Private placement differs little from any other security flotation except it is often quicker, easier, and encumbered with fewer legal hassles.

There are two distinct segments to the private-placement market. One requires that a formal legal document be created to give to qualified investors prior to taking their money. The other requires no legal documentation. Thus, there are two topics to discuss: the document and the qualified investor.

The document, known as a private-placement memorandum, requires legal assistance, which takes time and money. In many respects, it resembles the prospectus needed to sell securities to the public. Full disclosure of all relevant information is required by the law. It may cost anywhere from $3,000 to $20,000 or more to prepare a private-placement memo, depending upon the complexity of the venture.

Private placements can be done by the entrepreneur directly, but more commonly investment bankers, financial packagers, or venture-capital organizations handle these matters much as they would handle other types of financing. It depends on how much money is being sought and from whom it is being solicited. Good investment bankers have a huge clientele interested in buying a part of their private deals.

Private placements are exempt from scrutiny by the Securities and Exchange Commission (SEC) so long as they do not use any form of public advertising or display and the investors are fully qualified to evaluate the risks inherent in the enterprise and can bear the economic risks involved. There should be documentation of the investor's qualifications to judge the venture and bear the risk. For example, when a venture sells its securities to a venture capitalist, the sale is exempt from SEC scrutiny; it is assumed that the venture capitalists are able to take care of themselves.

While there is no stated limit to the size of the private offerings, there is some uncertainty about how large a private offering can be without incurring SEC scrutiny.

A program for raising money from qualified private investors usually involves a number of cocktail parties to which potential investors are invited by some lead blocker with whom they are acquainted.

Such contact people are usually paid a finder's fee for the money they raise. Normally, such fees begin with 5 percent for the first million and decrease 1 percent for each subsequent million raised. However, it is all negotiable and will depend upon the circumstances. The entrepreneur must make certain that he or she has firmed up the deal with the money finder.

Lawyers or accountants often know private investors who are looking for a good deal. If the entrepreneur has something that holds great promise, they'll likely be able to help. One advantage of using professional people who frequently deal in new ventures is that they have a clientele interested in new enterprises.

Often, the entrepreneur is looking for only one or two private investors—angels. In such cases, it is a matter of making a deal that gives both parties what they want. However, the entrepreneur must be certain that he or she can live with the investor. It is advisable to try to insert into the deal some way to get rid of the investor on some reasonable basis should difficulties arise. Buy-sell agreements are needed. The founder of the computer manufacturing company previously mentioned paid dearly for this oversight when he had to pay $350,000 to get rid of a partner who had invested only $50,000 three years previously. An agreement signed beforehand could have reduced the amount of money needed to buy out the private investor who was blocking the firm's growth.

One mark of naivete is an expectation that someone is going to find money for the firm for nothing. The entrepreneur will have to pay for help in raising money just as he or she pays for legal and accounting assistance.

Small Corporate Offering Registration (SCOR)

SCOR is a simplified and relatively inexpensive stock offering that is administered on the state rather than federal level. SCOR provides several advantages for entrepreneurial firms. First, it is far less expensive than a regular initial private offering, and there are no high fees to an underwriter. Companies can also establish a trading market for their common shares on NASDAQ's electronic bulletin board.

The size of the offering is relatively small—a company can raise up to $1 million in a given year. The company must have $25 million or less in annual revenues. Companies must also register to do business in each state in which they want to offer stock. SCORs can be a great opportunity for entrepreneurial firms to raise money.

Credit cards

Although one of the least-preferred financing options, modest use of credit cards for financing short-term needs has been used by some entrepreneurs. This is an expensive and risky method of raising capital. It can be used as a short-term alternative when more traditional sources are not available. Entrepreneurs must be certain they have sufficient cash flows to make the payments. It is preferable to repay the credit cards in full within 30 days. Credit cards should not be used to finance start-up costs. Any late payments on credit cards may affect the ability to qualify for future loans.

One entrepreneur started a snowboard manufacturing business. The challenge with operating this type of seasonal venture is that the owner hires temporary workers, pays them after the work is completed, and then sells the product later, resulting in a serious cash flow problem. Some companies might pay within 10 days, while others pay within 30 days.

She was looking for a way to finance her cash shortages. Her banker, however, turned down a request for a line of credit. She was forced to use her personal credit cards to cover her cash shortages.

Her company continued to grow, and her business has expanded. She needed more financing to support her growth, but was again turned down for a line of credit from her bankers. She created her own line of credit by finding a partner to join her business who had many credit cards. Once she developed an 18-month business history, the banker agreed to give her a line of credit, and she no longer used credit cards for financing growth.

Family and friends

Often oneself and one's family are lumped together as a source of money, but there are some significant distinctions between the two. One is sorely tempted to turn to family money for financing a venture. At times it's all right, but there are problems involved. Families can be even rougher than outside creditors.

> If an entrepreneur loses family money, he or she will pay for it forever—not in money, but in respect and relationships.

Many entrepreneurs advise not using family money. The advice is: Be very careful with family money. Bankruptcy will not save the entrepreneur who loses it. About the same advice can be given with respect to friends. Borrowing money from a friend is a good way to lose a friend, even though the entrepreneur will ultimately get the money back to the friend.

It is true that many business deals are made between friends. And it is equally true that the entrepreneurs must be careful in such deals. Friends are not that easy to come by. Naturally, all of this depends upon the deal. Some friends will be offended if the entrepreneur does not let them into a deal, but as one man put it, "Better they be offended outside the firm than inside it. There is no way I can run a business without doing something that would make an investor mad at me. Sooner or later, my expense account would be too large, or I would be paying myself too much, or something. The minute you let anyone into your company, the rules change." Social relationships differ from business ones. Friends cannot be treated the same way an outside stockholder would be treated. Many business people prefer to keep everything on a businesslike, professional basis by dealing only with the professional money people.

An entrepreneur who just graduated from college wanted to start a tent production business with another friend and needed $20,000 for his share of the venture. The only place he knew he might be able to raise this kind of money was from his parents, who were retired and living off 6 percent interest earned from their savings. He knew they would not spend their principal, and, someday, he would inherit half of their estate, with the other half going to his brother.

He struck the following deal with his mother and father. First, they would loan him the $20,000 at 8 percent interest. He would obtain a $20,000 term life insurance policy, with his parents serving as the beneficiaries. He would pay the interest monthly to his parents. If the business declared bankruptcy, he would still be required to pay the 8 percent interest. Upon the death of his parents, the first $20,000 would go to his brother, and then they would split the remainder of their inheritance.

This deal structure enabled the entrepreneur to acquire the $20,000 investment to start his new venture, while paying only $1,600 in interest annually. He covered the risk his parents took if he died before paying off the debt with the life insurance policy. His parents would still receive $1,600 annually if the business went broke. His brother was taken care of because he would get the first $20,000 of the inheritance when the parents died.

He convinced his parents to lend him the money to do something with it while he was young, rather than later, when he might be too old to start a business. The business was a success and all parties benefited.

Customers

It seems unlikely that intended customers would finance an operation, and usually that is the case. However, there are instances when customers want products so badly that they will either put a deposit down with their orders or supply the money an entrepreneur needs to get the job done. Customers can be a inexpensive source of money. Even if they must be given a discount for paying COD, the entrepreneur may be money ahead.

A farming entrepreneur in eastern Colorado spotted an opportunity when he recognized a problem that affected home builders. Environmentalists and government regulators complain that the increase in home building has a negative effect on wildlife, such as the prairie dog. Capturing the animals and moving them to uninhabited areas resulted in higher costs to the developers, as well as presenting potential danger of bites and spread of infectious diseases.

The entrepreneur obtained agreements from developers and contractors to pay him in advance to remove and relocate the prairie dogs. He re-engineered the large compressor on an old wheat truck to pull air in instead of blowing it out and added a hose large enough in diameter to pull a prairie dog through it and into a cage. With the customers in hand, Dog Gone Inc. removed the prairie dogs effectively and efficiently. The farmer claimed the ride made the little animals dizzy, but they quickly recovered unharmed.

Customers, as a source of funds, do not pose the control and time problems of outside investors. The real question is whether the entrepreneurs are going to finance customers or the customers are going to finance the entrepreneurs. If the entrepreneurs extend credit to customers, the entrepreneurs are the source of money for the customers. If the customers pay the entrepreneurs prior to delivery of goods, the customers are the source of funds for the entrepreneurs.

Factoring

Factoring accounts receivable is another alternative financing source available to entrepreneurs experiencing a cash crunch. Factoring is short-term financing by selling accounts receivable to a commercial financing company called a factor.

Many entrepreneurs use factoring when more conservative lenders, such as banks, turn down loan requests and when the entrepreneurs have tried to guarantee the loans with their accounts receivable.

Factoring does not use accounts receivable as collateral. Instead, accounts receivable are sold directly at a discounted value to a factoring company. Factoring discounts usually range from 1 to 5 percent of the face value of the

Factoring is not a credit transaction and therefore does not appear on the company's balance sheet. Therefore, it shouldn't affect the company's ability to use other collateral to obtain other types of loans.

invoice. Some factors discount according to a schedule, paying a smaller percentage up front and then paying an additional percentage, depending on whether the receivables are collected within 30, 60, or 90 days.

Factors do all the collection work, which includes mailing the invoices and doing the bookkeeping. This means that customers will be notified that their accounts are owned by and payable to the factor. The factor often advances to the client a portion of the face value of the invoice and pays the balance, less the discount, after it receives payment from the debtor.

Primarily, there are two different types of factoring arrangements, depending on who assumes the risk of a bad debt: recourse and nonrecourse. If a company assumes the risk that its customers may not pay, then the factoring is recourse. If the factor assumes the risk, then it is nonrecourse. Factors need to be assured that customers will pay their bills. Typically, they make substantial credit checks on each debtor and carefully analyze the quality and value of each invoice before buying it. They will analyze the strength of the receivables and creditworthiness of the invoices the company wants to sell them.

Factors usually establish credit limits for each customer, since they want to feel comfortable that a business has the necessary margins to absorb their factoring discounts. For example, if the factor uses a one-time charge and discounts 5 percent for every $1,000 of a company's receivables, the company will receive $950.

It is not unusual for factors to require business owners to establish a reserve for bad debt of approximately 5 percent of the business's account. Then, if the account is not collected within 120 days, the factor will draw against the reserve. If the receivables eventually are collected, the factor's return on investment far exceeds that of conventional lenders.

A company can obtain cash as soon as proof of shipment is provided to customers or on the average due date of the invoice. The job of collection is borne by the factor. Most factoring arrangements are made for one year.

Normally, it is difficult for newly established businesses to work with factors, since they have a limited credit history and their accounts receivable may be evaluated as marginal credit risks.

Factoring is becoming more available to smaller and medium-sized businesses. In the past, it was used primarily by large clothing and furniture manufacturers. Today, a majority of factors do business with a wide range of different industries.

Check with trade associations for recommendations or with an accountant, who may be able to help establish a working factoring relationship.

Joint ventures/strategic alliances

Sometimes other firms that have an interest in what an entrepreneur is trying to do will form a strategic partnership with that entrepreneur to help him or her accomplish the tasks. They want to benefit from the entrepreneur's work.

Suppose an entrepreneur is working on a new toxic-waste-disposal method. A waste-management firm might finance the work so that it could license the resulting technology from the entrepreneur. Who benefits from the work? Answering that question provides a clue as to who might be willing to furnish money for the job.

Some entrepreneurs using factoring companies find it necessary to increase the price of their products to cover the discount they must pay to factor. That's the main disadvantage of using factoring.

In other cases, entrepreneurs can use a joint-venture arrangement to help finance their operations. Two or more firms can share the same assets such as plant, offices, and people, thus lowering their capital needs. The new-venture incubators are based on this principle: Help the new firm get started by furnishing some of the fixed assets that it needs on some basis it can afford.

Suppliers

If an entrepreneur doesn't pay for the purchased items when they are received, then the vendors are helping finance the operation. The longer one can delay paying the vendors—it's called extended terms, if the vendor agrees to them—the more the venture is being financed by the suppliers' money. Thus, suppliers are a source of money; the cost of the money may be another matter.

If a business must forgo attractive discounts for paying early, the money may be costly. Missing a 2/10, Net 30-day discount costs 36 percent on an annual rate. A business can lose 2 percent for using the money an extra 20 days. The computer manufacturer was unable to take the 6 percent cash discounts offered by his suppliers because his private investor refused to pony up the needed funds. For 30 days' early payment, 6 percent is a 72 percent per year rate of interest. That's a hefty price to pay for money. So another private investor was found who would lend the money for half of the discount—a 36 percent return on the investment.

One person who wanted to start a roof tile manufacturing business had an excellent location but lacked the $50,000 needed for equipment. The traditional sources of money rejected his overtures even though he had an impressive background and was apparently a responsible person. He was able to get the money from the company from whom he intended to buy the equipment, a used-equipment supplier. Today, the business is not only highly profitable, but also another outlet has been opened. The equipment supplier was easily repaid.

Sometimes a key subcontractor believes in the concept and wants to participate in it sufficiently so that it will provide funds in exchange for manufacturing rights. Again, look to the people who will benefit from the business. It is called off-balance sheet financing because often such money does not directly show up as loans on the balance sheet. The debts are semi-hidden, either as accounts payable or as part of the firm's costs of goods sold.

A Generation-X entrepreneur developed several different accessories to be used with a variety of different Jet Skis, including a work bench, trailer, storage rack, and display fixtures. All of these products required a supplier who specialized in bending metal tubing. The entrepreneur located several suppliers and found an expert in metal tubing. The owner was excited about his products, and during the next two weeks, he negotiated the following business agreement.

The metal shop would build the prototypes at no charge but required the entrepreneur to sign a manufacturing agreement with the metal shop to be the sole supplier for the accessories at a preset price. The entrepreneur would be primarily responsible for marketing the products to potential buyers. He attended industry trade shows and convinced Yamaha to purchase his accessories and sell them through its dealers.

This business venture was started with the supplier furnishing the start-up capital, manufacturing the prototype, and producing the Jet-Ski accessories. The founder did not have to pay the supplier until Yamaha paid for the products. The owner of the metal shop was interested in this deal because he realized the upside of the Jet-Ski industry and saw an opportunity to be the sole supplier of these accessories and create another income stream. Currently, this business is a multimillion-dollar Jet-Ski accessory business.

Employees

Employees, whether they are past, present, or prospective, are often a good source of financing. Prospective employees can be offered an opportunity to "buy" their job. The worker-owned cooperative plywood plants in the Pacific Northwest were financed by having each of the approximately 100 employees that would be needed buy a working share for $20,000. The working share entitled the person to a job in the plant. Naturally, a set of problems arises when the employees are also the owners, but there are ways to handle those problems.

Firms in financial trouble are sometimes helped financially by employees who believe in the owner and the company and are willing to invest some money to keep it going.

Even past employees who have left under positive circumstances may be willing to put money into the venture—if they still believe in it. Naturally, the owner must make it worth their while for making these investments. All too often the real reason people don't invest is that the entrepreneur failed to make it really worthwhile for them to do so. An entrepreneur may think he or she is giving them an attractive proposition; potential investing employees don't see it that way, but they won't say how they feel for fear of looking greedy.

Professional advisors, business acquaintances

Lawyers, CPAs, other business professionals, and business acquaintances have been known to invest in enterprises if the prospects look bright enough. After all, they have money and have investment interests of their own, so they are usually on the lookout for a good investment.

However, many entrepreneurs caution against ever taking money from a lawyer, as they have the capacity to make one's life miserable. Their legal costs are much lower than an entrepreneur's, and they know how to play a very rough game if the need arises.

Sometimes a business acquaintance has contacts that make him or her helpful in nurturing the new firm. This type of investor is often strongly motivated to help the firm prosper.

Leasing companies

Leasing is becoming a more popular financing strategy. Equipment/asset leasing—including the sale and subsequent lease back of an asset—is a major source of capital for entrepreneurs as an alternative to taking a company public. Entrepreneurs can significantly reduce cash outlay and expand operating capital with asset lease arrangements.

Generally, it costs less to make lease payments than it does to make payments on a loan used to purchase equipment. However, leasing requires analysis of tax, accounting, and financial situations.

Leasing allows a business owner to accommodate short-term expansion without much capital outlay and leave the risk and rewards of ownership with the lessor.

Leasing can free a business from obsolescence and changing needs. For example, a computer expected to have a 20 percent residual value in five years could be worthless in three years. The lessor accepts this risk. Many lessors provide takeouts, rollovers, or upgrades for technological changes, so a business can have state-of-the-art equipment.

Additionally, leases provided by the vendor are usually simple to execute. The flexibility of these types of leases allows the entrepreneur and the lender to negotiate a deal that meets both their objectives.

More importantly, traditional leases are treated in financial statements as executory contracts. This means no assets are recorded and no liabilities are shown except payments as they become due. This treatment reflects lower liabilities and lower expenses to a company, especially in the first, low-cost years of the lease.

Leasing equipment is a viable way to pay down bank loans and increase cash revenues. One should consider leasing before purchasing hard assets.

Leasing can positively affect a company's balance sheet and present a more favorable picture of a company's financial condition. The cash flow benefits can be greater than purchasing equipment with borrowed funds.

Sale of distribution rights

Much money can be made distributing the output of the new enterprise. Often people will pay money for distribution rights. Franchisees do just that in franchising systems. Naturally, to get a lot of money from a distributor, entrepreneurs must be prepared to give a lot in return. The person may ask for the distribution rights for a large area, such as everything east of the Mississippi. Before selling such rights, the entrepreneur needs some performance guarantees. Also, be aware that if the distributors are the major investors, the entrepreneur will be making many decisions to favor their interests over those of others.

Microloan programs

Essentially, microloans are small-business loans to help entrepreneurs start or expand a business. Some start as low as a few hundred dollars and go up to about $35,000. Some lenders go up to about $75,000 for these loans. A number of banks are beginning to make these types of loans, realizing that they can be profitable. However, nonprofit groups have been increasingly active at the lower end of the market. The Small Business Administration is now helping fund microlending programs. Loans are typically made for purchasing inventory and other working-capital needs. Neither the SBA nor banks have any blanket restrictions on how the funds are used other than they cannot be used for retiring old debt.

Some of the microlenders charge interest rates roughly comparable with those on consumer credit cards, while nonprofit lenders tend to charge a couple points lower and extend credit for longer periods of time than traditional lenders. Lenders usually require less collateral than conventional business loans—recognizing that borrowers are just beginning to establish credit.

For a list of SBA's microlenders, call the district SBA office or the agency's answer line at (800) 827-5722. The *Directory of Microenterprise Programs*, published by the Aspen Institute in Washington, D.C., (202) 736-1071, contains information on more than 190 U.S. microlending programs.

Entrepreneurial Attitude

One of the major problems entrepreneurs will have to face up to and overcome is their own resentments toward the people in the financial world. Just think for a moment of what they can do to entrepreneurs.

First, nobody likes to beg. Entrepreneurs are likely to feel that they are begging for money from the financial people, and they don't like it. Well, they must forget that attitude. They are not begging; they are offering to let investors in on a business opportunity. The financial people make their money by servicing entrepreneurs. Entrepreneurs are their customers.

Second, the money people are blocking the entrepreneurs' way. They have what entrepreneurs need to go ahead. They hold the key to the golden door and won't give it up. This frustrates entrepreneurs and angers them. Entrepreneurs must conquer that attitude by understanding that the only way to get the key is to sell the deal to investors.

Third, the money people make entrepreneurs jump through hoops, which the entrepreneurs don't like to do. They don't like a lot of things—income taxes, sales taxes, paperwork—but they accept those things as necessary.

Finally, raising money can be insulting. The entrepreneur's character will be questioned. Money people may assume the entrepreneur is dishonest and tell him or her to prove them wrong. Well, entrepreneurs have been insulted before. If they aren't tough enough to take it, then the money people are probably right in not giving them the money.

Conclusion

Many entrepreneurs do not thoroughly understand when and how to use traditional money sources. To successfully design a creative financial strategy, it is critical for entrepreneurs to understand how each money source works, what types of loans each offers, what information they must provide to secure capital, and at which cycle in their ventures' growth to contact such sources. Most astute investors will ask for the same return of their investment that a venture capitalist demands. When the entrepreneur seeks a loan from a friend, most often the friend will ask for the same type of collateral that a banker does.

Entrepreneurs should study each potential source of money just as they would a market for a product. Know what it wants and what the entrepreneurs must do to sell it.

If entrepreneurs plan on going public, then they need to prepare for it right from the start. They should find interested investment bankers to bring along until they are ready for the market.

It is advisable to cultivate good banking connections. The entrepreneur must have a good bank that can support his or her operations. Entrepreneurs must plan ahead so they will know when they need money and won't have to go scrambling around at the last minute trying to find it.

Exercise 25a. Loan Application Evaluation

Scenario

You are the loan officer of a local bank that is very active in making loans to small businesses in the community. You closely evaluate each loan application according to the C's of banking: credit, character, collateral, capacity (to repay the loan), and conditions (of the economy). Recently you received the following loan applications. What would you do?

A. Allison Duncan

Allison has worked part-time in a flower shop all during college. As her employer has relied on her extensively over the last several years, Allison is very knowledgeable about both the product (flowers) and managing a flower shop. Allison dreams of opening her own shop and plans to do so next year. She has just recently completed her college education. Allison's research indicates a need for this type of store on the south side of town where the community is growing rapidly. Allison's parents have indicated that they will loan her $15,000 to get started, but Allison still needs another $50,000 to open her store. The only asset that Allison has is her 1999 Honda Civic, which is almost paid off. Unfortunately, while in college, Allison ran up two credit card bills in the amount of $10,000, which she has been slow to pay off. Allison has come to you with a well-written business plan for her flower shop, which she prepared in her entrepreneurship class in college. The marketing information and financial projections indicate that the flower shop may indeed be a viable business.

---

1. Will you loan Allison the money? Why or why not? If you choose not to approve the loan, how would you suggest Allison raise the capital for her business?

B. Pete Fisher

Pete has owned and operated a small print shop for the last three years. Over this period of time, the shop has gradually increased its sales. Pete's company has always paid its bills on time, and recently paid off the loan for the printing equipment he purchased when he opened his store. The growth of the print shop has put a strain on Pete's ability to continue to complete customers' jobs in a timely manner. Because of this, Pete has come to you for a new equipment loan of $40,000. Although the local economy has remained stable, the economy at the national level is experiencing much uncertainty in the area of company layoffs and lower sales and profits.

2. Will you loan Pete the money? Why or why not? If you choose not to approve the loan, how would you suggest Pete raise the capital for his business?

C. Mitch Henderson and Brooke English

Mitch and Brooke left their jobs in the information technology field three years ago to start a computer consulting business. Both have extensive experience in the field and were able to generate a profit the first year of business. The company has continued to be profitable and experienced a steady growth over the past two years. Mitch and Brooke are currently working on a project for a large local company that will not be billed for another 45 days. In the meantime, the company's cash reserves are becoming extremely low. Mitch and Brooke are at a point where they need to hire additional help if they plan to grow. They would like to hire another full-time consultant as well as an administrative assistant. They feel they need an additional $75,000 to finance their current working capital situation and to expand the company. The financial section of their business plan indicates the company will be able to support the loan payments. Mitch owns his own home and has $40,000 in equity in his home. Brooke also owns a home and has over $50,000 in home equity. Although Mitch's credit history shows one or two slow paying accounts, Brooke's credit history is impeccable.

3. Will you loan Mitch and Brooke the money? Why or why not? If you choose not to approve the loan, how would you suggest they raise the capital for their business?

The Entrepreneur and the Community

Learning Objectives

In this chapter, students will learn

- The extent to which the entrepreneur's interests should be in social and political affairs.
- The problems commonly encountered by entrepreneurs that can affect their reputations in their communities.

There is no need to look any further than the daily newspaper or the television news programs to become aware of the great involvement of entrepreneurs with the various communities in which they operate and the governments that regulate their doing business in those communities. Thus, some thought should be given to the problems inherent in community relationships. It is up to each entrepreneur to determine how he or she will be involved with the community.

Social and Political Franchise

America's entrepreneurs exist and are allowed the freedom to do business only by the people and their government. Many societies prevent entrepreneurial activity. Experience clearly shows that the entrepreneurial activity in a culture is directly related to the attitudes of the people and their governments toward it. Two key ingredients are the political license and the social contract.

Political license. In many cultures people are not allowed to have their own businesses. Many governments so stringently regulate and tax private enterprise that entrepreneurship is effectively stifled. Entrepreneurship requires a favorable political climate combined with stable, predictable judicial and financial systems to thrive. Few people care to start a business in a society that has unstable or unpredictable financial or political systems.

One only has to study recent legislative history to appreciate the impact of governmental attitudes and legislation upon entrepreneurial activity. Entrepreneurship began flourishing in the early 1980s partly because of favorable income tax regulations that stimulated private investment in a wide multitude of enterprises through various tax-credit programs and accelerated-depreciation provisions. That was suddenly changed in 1986, when Congress changed the tax laws in such ways as to greatly discourage investment in entrepreneurial ventures.

Consequently, entrepreneurs must appreciate that their continued opportunity to be in business for themselves depends on the political climate in which they live; thus, they should be doing everything possible to make that climate hospitable to entrepreneurial enterprises.

This should not be confused with private enterprise. It is quite possible to have a private-enterprise society made up of huge organizations with entrepreneurs left out.

Social contract. Underlying the relationship of business with society is an implicit contract between them in which society grants people the right to do business in exchange for their promise to satisfy society's demands for goods and services. When business fails to satisfy the demands of society, serious conflicts arise. Conversely, when a society unduly shackles business, the supply of needed goods and services is curtailed.

Social Responsibility

Socially responsible business practices will fail if they are just add-ons to established business practices.

Most entrepreneurs and corporations are passionately motivated to share their successes and wealth by giving back and supporting their communities and society as a whole. Most are socially responsible and don't operate their businesses in a vacuum. The rule of social responsibility stems from the value system of the founder and the corporate culture that he or she creates by recognizing the company's socially reflective role in the community.

Social responsibility blends business practices into a socially reflective and responsive business culture that thrives with the attention and support of the founder and top management. Most people try to create an ethically motivated workplace. They are committed to improving their workplace, employee productivity, and retention, thus increasing customer goodwill while strengthening their communities. They use their entrepreneurial creativity to fill market niches while addressing social needs and implementing socially responsible business practices.

Entrepreneur's Scope of Concern

Entrepreneurs should support and contribute time, talent, and leadership to the community.

The extent of the entrepreneur's interests in social and political affairs is quite broad and encompasses participation in local communities, political activism, economic well-being, ethics, and personal life.

Participation in local communities. Look around town. Who runs things? Who are the people involved in the multitude of community affairs: the United Fund, the school board, little leagues, scouting, churches? Typically, local businesspeople are the backbone of the town. Without their support, communities would have an entirely different character.

It is to the entrepreneur's distinct advantage to do business in a community that is thriving, healthy, and operating smoothly. Sick communities are not good places in which to do business. Several entrepreneurial magazines annually list the best communities for entrepreneurial activity.

Political activism. Previously, the importance of the political climate was stressed. It doesn't just happen. It is shaped by the people who actively participate in the process, and that means doing more than just voting or contributing money to some politician's coffers. It means spending some time in meetings that are often frustrating to the person who is used to making decisions and taking action.

If entrepreneurs don't get involved, the political system will be taken over by others who do, and those others may not always be friends of entrepreneurs.

Economic well-being. Economic prosperity depends in large part on what the entrepreneur does. The entrepreneur creates jobs, buys goods, and creates events that provide income to many people. A company's growth plans directly affect the economy. If it fails, the impact is widely shared. Thus, entrepreneurs are a vital cog in the economy. Without vigorous entrepreneurial activity, the economy lags.

Ethics. The entrepreneur's ethical code continually affects every aspect of the society and business community. Indeed, one of the major reasons our culture has been so economically successful is that, by and large, businesspeople do what they promise to do. They can be trusted. They pay their bills, they perform their contractual obligations, they obey the law, they treat people decently, and they try to behave in ways that result in a better life for everyone. It is difficult to do business in a society in which people do otherwise. Most business is done on trust. The person without credibility has a difficult time in business. Others don't believe that person and eventually won't do business with him or her.

Honor and credibility are reflected in business decisions. Entrepreneurs always need to be ethical and treat others as they want to be treated.

While cynics may snicker at what seems to be a goody-goody attitude, it has been noted after many years of observation and experience that the people who take the short cuts usually end up with disaster. They may look like winners for a short time, but sooner or later an ethical code in conflict with the mores of the culture will catch up with those individuals.

Personal life. There is much more to life than just business. People do have private lives. They have families. They have activities. The entrepreneur who ignores this reality will pay a price, often a high one, in terms of broken families, unsatisfactory personal relationships, and unhappiness. The old dictum, "All things in moderation!" comes to mind.

Balance business life, social life, personal life, and family commitments.

Impact of Cultural Attributes

Entrepreneurs are very much a part of the culture. In comparison to the rest of the world, the American culture is very entrepreneurial. America had to be. The country was founded by a variety of people who all had one thing in common. They were fleeing some large institution elsewhere, a displeased king, an oppressive government, an onerous church, prison, pauperism. One does not come to a wilderness from a relatively prosperous society without forceful reasons. So here they found themselves without any institutions to support them. They were on their own to survive.

Desperation has made countless entrepreneurs. Thus it is not surprising that America is the home of the entrepreneurial movement; it's the country's heritage.

In contrast, some cultures with strong caste systems greatly discourage entrepreneurship by removing an extremely important factor from the entrepreneurial equation: incentive. If people are not allowed to advance themselves socially through economic skills, then why bother trying?

The economic well being of a society is directly affected by its attributes: religion and philosophy, language, political stability, and personal values. People are what the culture allows them to be and what it encourages them to become.

Religion and philosophy. The role of religion in the economic success of western civilization has been well documented. The advent of Calvinism gave moral permission to people to prosper. Indeed, it was God's desire that they work hard and be fruitful. This philosophy is also found in Buddhism and is cited by the noted Japanese philosopher, Yamamoto Shichihei, in his book *The Spirit of Japanese Capitalism*. According to Yamamoto Shichihei, all occupations are Buddhist practice; through work one is able to attain Buddhahood; there is no calling that is not Buddhist; all is for the good of the world. Thus Calvinism is not the only religion that extolled the virtues of work. In contrast, many of the world's religions discourage business in general and entrepreneurship in particular.

Language. The role of a culture's language has been critical to its success. Many of the world's cultures have not had a written language. Thus, they could not record knowledge or pass it along other than by folklore. Many had difficulty even communicating among themselves. Moreover, many of the world's written languages suffer some severe limitations in their use for economic affairs. People think in their language, and if that language lacks certain concepts and is limited, so then do people's thinking skills.

Political stability. Economic development requires a stability of political institutions and economic systems if people are to be encouraged to invest both money and energy in economic ventures that will span decades. If people have no way of knowing what will likely happen in their society in the next few years, then why would they invest money in a new venture? Why would they commit their lives to building enterprises that would likely be wiped out in the near future by some political development?

Historically, the United States has enjoyed relatively stable political and economic systems. Entrepreneurs can plan for their ventures with some assurance that basic assumptions about the economy are correct. One problem with the economic development of many Third World countries is that their political systems are so unstable that entrepreneurship is discouraged.

Personal values. Personal values are closely related to ethics but encompass a broader scope of behavior. Of particular importance is one's attitudes toward materialistic matters in preference to more aesthetic areas. If people didn't seek the material things in life, then much of the incentive for success in business would be absent.

Company Culture

A strong entrepreneurial climate attracts and encourages entrepreneurial achievers and helps perpetuate the intensity and pace of successful ventures.

Much has been written about corporate cultures largely in reference to living and working in large organizations. However, organizational cultures exist everywhere, especially in entrepreneurial enterprises both large and small. Indeed, the cultures entrepreneurs create in their ventures greatly affect their attractiveness to employees. Many people prefer working for smaller companies, where they can have direct personal relationships with the boss.

They often like having to do many tasks and not having to be a small cog in a big machine. Thus, entrepreneurs should be aware that the working environments they create greatly affect employees' satisfaction.

Environmental Constraints

Certainly the environmental movement must rank as one of the top forces at work in society and the economy today. Indeed, the next decade may see more legislation regulating what firms can and cannot do in matters that affect the environment. Make no mistake, these regulations are expensive. They will drive many entrepreneurs out of business because they are unable to afford the changes demanded of them by the environmentalists.

Yet these same environmental concerns offer alert entrepreneurs opportunities for new ventures. Waste management is a big business and will become even more so. The firm that can solve a toxic-waste problem will likely reap big dividends.

More important, the alert entrepreneur does not wait until the environmental axe falls to alter operations but anticipates the developments. Many firms have already moved operations from certain areas that are known to be extra sensitive to environmental concerns. One manufacturer of wire shelves sold to retail stores anticipated the regulation of its painting operations and installed a dry-powder process that emits no vapors or toxins.

> Environmental constraints and regulations are expensive. Their costs must be factored into overhead expenses.

Economic Constraints

An obvious relationship exists between the strength of the overall economy and the performance of individual businesses within the economy. Yet the extent and nature of the relationship can vary significantly. Many enterprises prosper during times of economic distress and chaos. Nonetheless, the entrepreneur must understand the constraints that the economy places on the firm. If money is tight and costly, then the firm's financial planning must recognize that constraint. If costs are rising, entrepreneurs should keep a close watch on pricing and consider purchasing supplies in anticipation of higher prices.

Common Problems

Certain problems are so commonly encountered by entrepreneurs and are so serious that special mention of them needs to be made. These problems can destroy the entrepreneur if they are improperly handled or ignored.

Conflicts of interest. One of the most pervasive problems in business and government is conflict of interest. People have vested interests in many things: their careers, the fortunes of the firms for which they work, the welfare of their families, their personal lifestyles, their investments, and their communities. It would be nice if all these interests were in harmony, but they aren't. People are often asked to do things that are in conflict with some of their interests. They may be asked by some sales representative to buy something that would benefit their employers but would jeopardize their careers.

The business owner asks employees to work at night for the benefit of the firm. They need to be at home for whatever reason. There's conflict.

> **Common Problems**
> Conflicts of interest
> Desperation or survival
> Associates and peer pressure
> Legal roulette

It is in the interest of the community's environment that a business stop all painting in its plant. If it does so, many people will be out of a job, and costs will rise. Conflict.

The business owner wants to be paid more money as the firm's president. The directors want to receive more dividends. Conflict.

The point is that just about every decision in some way involves a conflict of interests. Although those interests can usually be easily resolved, sometimes they cannot be resolved at all. Often they cost money one way or another.

Inherent business conflicts must be recognized and each side of the issue weighed, and then creative solutions should be found.

The adept businessperson learns to recognize the conflicts of interest inherent in any situation and tries to allow for them in some way. Hidden conflicts usually cause the most trouble. A business owner hires an outstanding person as marketing manager, not knowing that the person is planning to start his or her own firm to compete with the employer's when ready.

Desperation or survival. Entrepreneurs have been known to do a lot of things they preferred not to do, just to survive. Desperation fathers many illegitimate offspring. People who would have never considered cheating a creditor out of money may do just that if it seems to be the only way to save their enterprise. It has been observed that one's ethics are unknown until tested. It is easy to be honest if one has no need to be crooked. Starve for a while, and then a person will know his ethical code.

There will likely be times in entrepreneurial careers when desperation will be the plight. The entrepreneur is hurting, owes money, and can't pay it. He or she may lose home, family, self-respect. This is when the entrepreneur's ethical code needs to be strong.

Associates and peer pressure. Entrepreneurs will be subject to many pressures to do things that either they don't want to do or shouldn't do. Associates want big bonuses; entrepreneurs know their firms need the cash for expansion. Who gets the money? The firm or the associates? All sorts of players are urging the entrepreneur to take the company public, sell stock, establish a market price for its paper. The lawyers think it's a good idea. There's an investment banker who is pushing it. The outside investors want it. Yet down deep the entrepreneur just doesn't want to operate as a public company. Real conflicts push and pull every which way.

Legal roulette. In most instances, there are grey areas in the law in which one can operate with impunity. Income tax compliance policies are perhaps the most common illustration of trying to walk a line that isn't clearly illegal. Such legal dilemmas, however, are far more prevalent than just taxes. How does the entrepreneur play it? Close or safe? Even when thinking they're safe, entrepreneurs may have some surprises coming. Many entrepreneurs don't want to play games with the law. Others seem to delight in pushing the law as far as they can, and some of them can push it mighty far.

It must be admitted, however, that many entrepreneurs worked long and hard running their businesses strictly according to the rules and still, for one reason or another, encountered serious legal difficulties not of their doing. This is mentioned only as a warning to entrepreneurs who feel secure, since they know they have not violated any laws, that they still should be vigilant of potential or looming legal difficulties. It may not be enough just to be passively safe, sitting in the office, knowing that the company is operating legally. Business owners may have to aggressively protect themselves from legal attacks by people with other agendas—competitors, for example.

One large water meter repair company that was operating within the law was set up by a competitor in collusion with a newspaper reporter on charges of bribing public officials. It caused no end of trouble and hurt the company severely. Sharp legal counterattacks were necessary.

Conclusion

The entrepreneur has far more to think about than how to make and sell his or her wares. There are many social, cultural, and legal relationships that require attention. One does not operate in a vacuum. All sorts of people and institutions in the environment require consideration.

Entrepreneurs should look for innovative ways to build their companies and communities to show they truly care. They should lead by example.

Exercise 26a. Socially Responsible Entrepreneurs

Identify examples of local entrepreneurs who are acting in socially responsible ways to help your community.

Company/Entrepreneur	Action

Appendix

Presentation Skills

Venture Presentation Checklist

Guidelines for Preparing Venture Presentations

How to sell the big picture, more than product, to possible investors

Putting together a winning presentation is an art. It takes preparation, design time, and lots of practice. Most venture teams feel they can present themselves in a professional and convincing manner, but that doesn't happen easily.

Talking to a room full of potential investors is much different than selling a venture to customers. Product or service features and benefits pitched to customers don't necessarily excite investors

Investors are more interested in seeing the big picture at the beginning of the venture presentation. They want an engaging story about the venture's profitability, profit margins, the management team, product development, size of market, competitive climate, and the market niches.

Briefly cover these 10 basic areas: company history and background, concise product or service description, proprietary rights, unique features, management team, market analysis, financial picture and cash needs and how the money will be spent, growth and spin-off opportunities, potential risks, and most important, the exit strategy for investors to capitalize on their investment.

Make sure the financial projections are error-free, and have well-founded assumptions that explain the projections. Typically, entrepreneurs spend too much time on the technical aspects of the product or service and fail to mention how the investor's money will be used.

Some entrepreneurs present their investment opportunities solo, while others have their key management members participate. Many investors prefer to meet and hear the management team. Whichever method is used, the presenter must be convincing and display leadership ability and passion—crucial to the success in raising investor money. Remember, investors bet on the person; the product or service is secondary.

If you have 20 minutes for the presentation, leave 10 minutes for questions and answers, the most important part of the presentation. This time allows the opportunity to build rapport and establish the management team's credibility. Anticipate questions, and prepare responses.

Repeat the questions asked before responding, allowing you time to formulate your response. If you can't answer the question, say so. Then explain that you will obtain the information requested and supply the answer later.

Many experts warn against giving a live demonstration during a venture presentation. Any difficulties with technical glitches could ruin the chances of attracting investor dollars. Other reasons that investors frequently turn down venture opportunities are blemishes on the key members of the management team, overly optimistic market projections, no clear explanation of how the investment dollars will be used, and having a number of historical problems to overcome.

How to Enhance the Presentation's Visual Appeal

Use visual aids whenever possible unless you are an experienced, accomplished, and charismatic public speaker. The visuals should highlight the presentation, stimulate interest, and accentuate key points rather than tell the whole story.

Whether the visuals are computer-generated or video-enhancements, include short sound bites of customer testimonials. Investors are much more attracted to deals that already have customers purchasing the product or service even if the venture is in the early developmental stage. Also include a picture of the product or service.

Regardless of the technology used, have a set of overheads to use as a backup if all else fails.

If the size of the room and audience permit, consider using hard copies of oversized color visuals in a presentation notebook that can be placed on a table and easily flip through while talking. Make sure the visual aids are readable from the back of the room.

Don't put too much information on visual aids and follow these guidelines: Use graphs, charts, and pictures of equipment to give the audience insights.

Start with a headline on each visual and present only one key idea per visual. Use seven lines per side with no more than seven words on each line. Limit the key points to no more than five per side.

Add color carefully with no more than three or four colors per visual. Colors should contrast to provide maximum visibility. Avoid "data dump" by crowding the presentation with too many visuals or too much information, which will reduce their effectiveness.

Use no more than two different type faces and a 30-point or larger font size. Add borders on slides or overheads to highlight key information.

Don't talk to the screen or to the overhead projector. If you are comfortable using a pointer, point to the overhead, not the screen. Hold the pointer in the hand closest to the screen. Place the overhead or screen at a 45-degree angle to one side of the center of the room so you occupy the center position.

Consistently focus your eyes on the audience. Don't focus on the back of the wall, a screen, or at notes. Pick out a few friendly smiling faces, make eye contact for a couple of seconds per person, then move on to another person. Involve and connect with the audience often.

Avoid repeating the information on the screen. The audience is already reading this information and you may insult them by repeating it. Use the information displayed to highlight key points you want to make while you tell the story. If you are speaking to more than 50 persons, you will probably need a microphone.

Venture Presentation Checklist

1. Introduction
- Introduce the venture team
- Briefly highlight the team's expertise
- Start by explaining what the venture is solving
- Identify potential risks

Tips
- Exhibit smooth transitions as team members present
- Display the venture team's leadership skills

2. Audio/visual
- Use PowerPoint® (or similar software)
- Incorporate video and sound if possible
- Use taped testimonials and sound bites
- Use music with the transitions
- Include any photos of the company, product, and the like
- Have sample brochures and business cards

Tips
- If using overheads, don't "talk" to the screen
- Have backup overheads/video (in case of equipment failure)
- Expand on key points, don't repeat what's written on the visuals

3. Presentation
- Demonstrate the team's understanding of launching this venture
- Use stories when talking about the venture
- Address how long before the venture is profitable
- Cover investor payback issues
- How long before investors recover their investment?
- Explain when the venture break-even hits
- Explain what the investors' money will be used for
- Focus on the venture's competitive advantage
- Prove that it has one
- How long is the advantage sustainable?
- Use potential customer testimonials and letters of intent

Tips
- Team members should interact with one another
- Display lots of enthusiasm
- Focus your eyes on the audience

4. Summary
- Be direct when answering questions
- Know who's the "leader" fielding questions, redirecting
- Show how the management team works together
- Close with a sizzle
- Thank the audience for the opportunity to present the venture

5. Key success factors
- Why will the venture succeed?
- Highlight the tested product
- Show success of the prototype
- Demonstrate the product's competitive advantage
- Prove the venture has customers
- Explain target market
- Identify competitors
- Explain pricing
- Outline legal structure
- Mention operational controls in place
- Forecast growth strategies

Key points
- Don't use notes if you are comfortable doing so
- Stay on time!